Everyday Morality

AN INTRODUCTION TO APPLIED ETHICS

Third Edition

Mike W. Martin

CHAPMAN UNIVERSITY

Wadsworth
Thomson Learning

Australia • Canada • Denmark • Japan • Mexico •
New Zealand • Philippines • Puerto Rico • Singapore •
South Africa • Spain • United Kingdom • United States

Dedicated to *Sonia Renée Martin* and *Nicole Marie Martin*

Philosophy Editor: Peter Adams
Assistant Editor: Kerri Abdinoor
Editorial Assistant: Mark Andrews
Marketing Manager: Dave Garrison
Print Buyer: April Reynolds
Permissions Editor: Bob Kauser

Production Services: Shepherd Incorporated
Cover Painting: Zifen Qian, SuperStock
Cover Designer: Bill Stanton
Compositor: Shepherd Incorporated
Printer: Webcom Limited

Printed in Canada
  2 3 4 5 6 7 04 03 02 01

For more information, contact
Wadsworth/Thomson Learning
10 Davis Drive
Belmont, CA 94002-3098
USA
http://www.wadsworth.com

International Headquarters
Thomson Learning
International Division
290 Harbor Drive, 2nd Floor
Stamford, CT 06902-7477
USA

UK/Europe/Middle East/South Africa
Thomson Learning
Berkshire House
168-173 High Holborn
London WC1V 7AA
United Kingdom

Asia
Thomson Learning
60 Albert Street, #15-01
Albert Complex
Singapore 189969

Canada
Nelson Thomson Learning
1120 Birchmount Road
Toronto, Ontario M1K 5G4
Canada

Library of Congress Cataloging-in-Publication Data

Brief Contents

Detailed Contents

Preface

*There is no such thing possible as an ethical philosophy
dogmatically made up in advance. We all help to determine the
content of ethical philosophy so far as we contribute to the
[human] race's moral life.*[1]

William James

This book is an introduction to applied ethics—that is, to the philosophy of
morality as it applies to practical moral needs. It focuses on the moral concerns
of everyday life more than on abstract ethical theories or general social issues, although many of these are discussed as well. Moral character is explored in all its
dimensions: virtues and vices, commitments and attitudes, and personal relationships and community involvement, in addition to right and wrong conduct.

Why study ethics with this emphasis on everyday issues and on the kinds of
persons we aspire to be in our daily relationships with others? Because the moral
aspects of day-to-day living are directly engaging, persistent, and urgent. Each
day, fundamental moral considerations affect our lives in commonplace ways. Perhaps today we told or laughed at a joke expressing sexist attitudes we would eagerly disavow. Or maybe we were sufficiently angry at a friend to harbor sweet
fantasies of revenge that, if implemented, would inflict extraordinarily cruel retri-
bution, not to mention destroy the friendship. Possibly we were envious of a co-
worker and expressed the envy in a way that undermined mutual respect. We may
have failed to respond to an act of kindness with the gratitude dictated by common decency. Perhaps we abused alcohol, drugs, or food with a compulsiveness
that made us wonder whether we respected ourselves anymore. These everyday
aspects of our lives provide an immediate stimulus for thinking about morality.

But why study morality at all in college courses? Can such studies contribute
to morally responsible lives, given that the core of character is largely fixed during much earlier years of development? Yes! Rather than being all or nothing,
moral responsibility is an ongoing process of development of skills, sensitivities,
and commitment. It requires many specific skills: the ability to identify moral
problems and reasons; sensitivity to alternative perspectives; creative vision in
discerning solutions; skill in reasonably weighing conflicting moral reasons;
adeptness in clarifying concepts that otherwise might be vague or ambiguous. It
also requires moral concern and responsible commitment. All these capacities
mature through studies in the liberal arts, of which ethics is central, that aim at
liberating us from parochial prejudices while deepening our understanding of
our own moral traditions and those of others.

A Socratic faith guides this book. "The unexamined life is not worth living,"
or rather, morally examined lives are far more worth living. Rather than a set of
alien rules imposed on humanity, morality is a natural expression of our lives as
autonomous agents and social creatures. Approaching ethics in that personal

spirit, I occasionally argue for my views, in addition to presenting an array of alternative views, in order to stimulate personal reflection and group dialogue. This book seeks to capture some of the enormous richness of contemporary philosophical thinking about ethics, while heeding Molière's injunction to "humanize your talk, and speak to be understood."[2]

Third Edition

Six new chapters are added. Four of them—Chapters 4, 5, 6, and 7—are on multicultural themes and greatly expand earlier discussions of feminism, race and ethnicity, religious ethics, tolerance and moral diversity. Chapter 21 explores responsibility within our increasingly therapeutic-oriented culture. It also serves as an entrance to the chapters on drugs and suicide that follow. Chapter 24 discusses practical money matters such as gambling and saving. It also provides an overview of theories of economic justice, thereby setting a fuller context for subsequent chapters on work and community service.

Other chapters have been reworked, and there are new or extended discussions of ethical egoism, ethical relativism, pragmatism, and Nietzsche. Taken together, the changes were sufficiently numerous to prompt a reorganization of the entire book into eight parts, thereby increasing thematic unity throughout. As in previous editions, ample discussion topics are provided for each chapter, along with suggestions for further reading.

Acknowledgments

Many of the improvements in this edition were stimulated by the insightful comments of four Wadsworth reviewers: Robert Hollinger, Iowa State University; David Ramsey Ohayon, Los Angeles Harbor College; Ronald Cox, San Antonio College; Eric Gampel, California State University, Chico.

I also wish to thank reviewers of earlier editions who helped to shape the best of what remains from previous editions. For the first edition these reviewers were Shane Andre, California State University, Long Beach; John Arthur, State University of New York at Binghamton; Joseph Des Jardins, College of St. Benedict; Ronald F. Duska, Rosemont College; Thomas K. Flint, North Idaho College; Ruth B. Heizer, Georgetown College; Craig Kei Ihara, California State University, Fullerton; Tom Moody, California State College, San Bernardino; Ellen K. Suckiel, University of California, Santa Cruz; and Joel Zimbelman, California State University, Chico.

For the second edition the reviewers were Judith A. Boss, University of Rhode Island; Roger Ebertz, University of Dubuque; Michael S. Pritchard, Western Michigan University; Stephen Schwarz, University of Rhode Island; Hilquias Cavalcanti, University of Richmond.

I was able to complete work on this edition because of a semester sabbatical from Chapman University. The first edition was made possible by an Arnold L. and Lois S. Graves Award from Pomona College, administered under the auspices of the American Council of Learned Societies.

I especially wish to thank my students, who led to me to write this book in the first place and shaped the topics that found their way into various editions.

Above all, I am grateful to my wife, Shannon, for her love and support.

PART ONE

Character and Conduct

Moral judgements . . . are, like other judgements, always accountable. We can reasonably be asked—sometimes by others and always by ourselves—to give reasons for them. We can then be expected to give those reasons from a system, however rough and incomplete, with which the rest of our lives coheres, and which is understandable both to outward and inward questioners.[1]

Mary Midgley

Everyday morality concerns the kinds of persons we aspire to be in our daily relationships with others. Are we grateful and generous, or envious and filled with spite? Are we trying to become more sensitive to the suffering of other people and animals, or weak of will and readily self-deceived about the good we can do? Do we strive to be honest and open, or to avoid hurting others' feelings, and which do we choose when we cannot do both? Do we genuinely respect ourselves and other people?

In grappling with these questions in everyday life, we usually apply a multitude of specific moral reasons, rather than invoking grand theories about morality. Nevertheless, as Mary Midgley reminds us, we also seek to maintain coherence among our attitudes and actions, our responsibilities and relationships, our motives and ideals. Ethical theories are attempts to identify the unity underlying moral reasoning, to discern its structure, and to render it more consistent.

Chapter 1 highlights the complexity of moral reasoning about character and conduct. Moral reasoning is contrasted with subjective and egoistic outlooks that make up two of many forms of moral skepticism. More positively, strong links between morality and self-interest (happiness, self-fulfillment) are identified. Chapter 2 introduces several major theories about right action, and Chapter 3 sketches theories about virtue and good character. These key concepts and theories will be used throughout the book.

CHAPTER 1

Morality and Self-Interest

At 3:20 A.M., Kitty Genovese was returning from her work as a bar manager to her home in a middle-class neighborhood in Kew Gardens, Queens (New York). After parking within a hundred feet of her apartment, she noticed a man hiding in the shadows of the parking lot. Alarmed, she turned in the direction of a police call box, but before she reached it the man caught up with her and stabbed her with a knife. She screamed, "Oh, my God, he stabbed me! Please help me! Please help me!"[1]

Her screams awoke thirty-eight people living in a ten-story apartment house overlooking the well-lit scene. One man yelled, "Let that girl alone!" No one else did anything. The attacker, who was a complete stranger to Kitty Genovese, was scared away by the lights that went on, the windows that opened, and the excited talk that ensued. He walked toward his car, but a few minutes later returned to find Kitty Genovese staggering toward her apartment. He then stabbed her again, and she again screamed, "I'm dying! I'm dying!" As before, no one did anything. The man went to his car and drove away, only to return yet a third time. Kitty Genovese was still alive. This time he killed her.

Over half an hour passed from the first to the third fatal stabbing. When the police were finally called, they arrived within two minutes. Any of the thirty-eight witnesses had plenty of time to prevent the murder by making a phone call. Each day newspapers, radio, and television report additional horrors that raise troubling questions about personal responsibility.

What Is Morality?

What are moral values, and what are the moral reasons for the conduct and character that they generate? Each of us can offer a list of examples. The Kitty Genovese tragedy reminds us that morality implies not being cruel and also helping others in desperate need, certainly when we can do so with no more inconvenience than making a phone call. We can also bring to mind familiar rules about honesty ("Don't lie"), fidelity ("Keep your promises"), fairness ("Do your share"), and respect for property ("Don't steal").

Providing a comprehensive definition of morality, however, turns out to be a complicated task. Morality concerns what we ought to become, how we ought to relate to others, and how we ought to act. These "oughts," however, are *moral* oughts; they differ from other kinds of "oughts," such as what ought to be done in order to start a car or achieve some other definite end. Hence, a definition of morality as what we ought to do is circular and somewhat empty, because we have essentially used a grammatical variation of the word we are trying to define.

The moment we invoke more focused concepts to characterize morality, we move toward theories that are controversial. Each of the following definitions, for example, suggests a particular theory that we discuss in later chapters and that may be open to challenge: Morality is a matter of respecting human rights; morality is fulfilling our duties to others; morality concerns the most important values, which should override all others (such as the values of art); morality is obeying God's commandments; morality centers around the happiness or self-fulfillment of all persons.

For now, let us say that morality concerns the recognition of the inherent value of people, both ourselves and others, a value that is not reducible to how others benefit us. The stranger who attacked Kitty Genovese represents an extreme failure to value persons, as do sociopaths in general, that is, individuals who can murder or steal without any sense of wrongdoing or guilt. Morality also involves sensitivity to the suffering of animals.

In addition to how we should act, moral reasons also apply to the kinds of persons we should become, the kinds of relationships we should have, and the kinds of communities and institutions we should promote. It calls for *sensitivity* to people as morally significant creatures who sometimes deserve esteem, compassion, and support and who sometimes experience guilt, shame, vulnerability, and despair. It involves *appreciating* those aspects of situations that are relevant to valuing persons (and animals). It requires *understanding* our emotions and commitments in a way that reveals their moral significance and that is *responsive* to the worth of others. Appreciation, sensitivity, understanding, and responsiveness are not mere means to "doing the right thing." Instead, they constitute our character—the moral substance of who we are.

Morality is complex, for several reasons: factual uncertainty, vagueness, conflicting reasons, and conflicting perspectives. *Factual uncertainty* means that we are often unsure of the facts relevant to applying moral values. Do the screams I hear indicate a serious assault which should concern me, or a family squabble with which it is none of my business to get involved? Have the police been called, or does someone's life depend on my calling for help? These factual matters are crucial in making everyday decisions, and they also engage social scientists who have much to offer in thinking about moral matters. In particular, the Kitty Genovese tragedy generated a substantial literature about bystander apathy. One primary discovery was that we tend to assume someone else has called for help in emergency situations, and hence we should learn to call for help whenever there is any doubt about whether help is on the way.

Vagueness surrounds many moral principles. Precisely what is cruelty? Exactly how much are we obligated to help others in desperate need? It is perfectly clear that we should not wantonly inflict suffering on others, as did the stranger who attacked Kitty Genovese. It is clear enough, too, that we ought to be willing to phone the police to protect someone from being murdered. But how much more is required of us by way of not hurting or of helping others? Did the thirty-eight witnesses have a responsibility to undertake any personal risk in order to save Kitty Genovese?

Conflicting reasons arise because morality involves many different reasons. These reasons often come into conflict, creating *moral dilemmas*. Moral dilemmas are situations in which two or more moral reasons point to different courses of action and it is not altogether obvious which reasons should take precedence. For example, should a student report a friend who cheats on an exam at a school with a strong honor code that requires reporting cheaters? Again, how should we balance our obligation to help others in desperate need against our responsibilities to our family and to ourselves? What if one of the thirty-eight witnesses had directly confronted the assailant and had been killed, leaving a spouse and children? Often it is impossible to rank moral rules in priority as a means of resolving moral dilemmas.

Conflicting perspectives arise in part because it is often permissible to emphasize specific moral reasons differently in our conduct. In large measure, moral values center on our relationships with other people, and yet people may have contrasting understandings of moral values. For example, once we move beyond our agreement about the wrongness of wanton killing, torture, and rape, we may have very different outlooks on family responsibilities, sexual conduct, and the responsibilities concerning animals and the environment. Let us acknowledge at the outset that morality leaves room for differences among reasonable persons who share overlapping, though not identical, ways of understanding moral reasons.

Applied Ethics

Ethics, as we shall use the term, is moral philosophy: the philosophical study of moral values. It embraces four main interests: (1) *clarification* of important moral ideas and issues; (2) *critical assessment* of moral claims by testing their truth, justification, and adequacy through argument; (3) development of a *comprehensive perspective* on moral ideas and principles by uncovering their interconnections and their roles in our lives; and (4) *moral guidance,* sometimes via simple principles, but more often through improved practical judgment about what we should aspire to be, what forms of relationships are desirable, and how we should seek those ends. Philosophical ethics is a *normative* study, a study of which values are morally warranted, which actions and features of character is morally desirable, which beliefs and attitudes are supported by sound reasons.

Philosophical ethics encompasses general and applied ethics. (See Figure 1.1.) *General ethics* deals with the more abstract theoretical issues, such as those touched on in the remainder of this chapter and in Chapters 2 and 3. *Applied ethics* or, as it is also called, *practical ethics,* focuses on more practical concerns of the sort emphasized throughout the rest of this book. This distinction is only rough, and general and applied ethics are interwoven. Wherever helpful, applied ethics integrates the comprehensive theories of general ethics, but its aim is practical clarity and guidance rather than the development and testing of general theories. Applied ethics is the activity of clarifying, organizing, and occasionally refining moral ideas with the goals of enriching moral experience and guiding moral judgment.

Some issues in applied ethics pertain to public policy and the professions. For example, in recent decades entirely new specializations in applied ethics have arisen in such diverse fields as medicine, business, law, engineering, environmental policies, and the media and journalism. Other issues focus on the more everyday needs of individuals in shaping their characters, maintaining desirable forms of relationships, and exercising responsible conduct in everyday life. These everyday issues are emphasized in this book, but their connections with social and political issues are often explored as well.

FIGURE 1.1 *Branches of Philosophical Ethics*

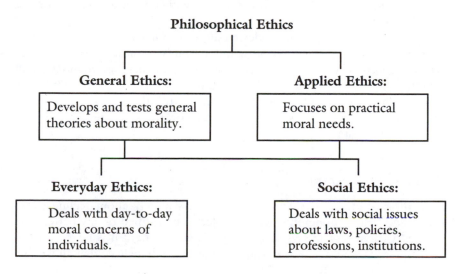

Before proceeding, we should take note of further meanings of the word *ethics*. We have defined ethics as: (1) *a normative study* of moral values, that is, a study aimed at discovering which beliefs, attitudes, principles, policies, and so on are justified or warranted in terms of sound moral reasons. Ethics can also refer to (2) *a scientific study* of moral values. When scientists study morality, they seek to describe the beliefs and conduct of individuals and cultures, and to explain why these beliefs and conduct arise. The tasks of describing and causally explaining are part of psychology, sociology, anthropology, and sociobiology (the study of genetic origins of social behavior and attitudes). Although we will distinguish between the philosophical and the scientific study of morality, note that these fields are interrelated and mutually enriching.

Sometimes the word *ethics* is used as (3) a synonym for *morality*. For example, we speak interchangeably of moral or ethical issues, experiences, judgments, and so on, as a category of human interest distinct from law, religion, art, science, economics, or sports. Thus, an ethical controversy is one involving moral reasons, and an ethical judgment is one using moral concepts or backed by moral reasons.

In another sense, ethics refers to (4) *moral beliefs*, that is, to what an individual or group actually believes about moral matters. Thus, we speak of the Protestant work ethic, the ethics of Albert Schweitzer, and the ethics of Victorian England. This usage relates to the Greek word *ethos*, which means customs or characteristic habits (just as the Latin root of the word "morals" is *mores*, meaning customs).

In yet another sense, *ethical* means (5) *morally desirable*. It has strongly positive connotations, pointing to admirable character traits and morally correct judgments and acts. This honorific or praising meaning applies when we say that a friend acted ethically or when we call Abraham Lincoln an ethical person. The intended contrast is with unethical conduct or immoral character.

We can now sharpen our understanding of moral values and moral reasons by responding to two views about morality: ethical subjectivism and ethical egoism. The adjective *ethical* connotes that these are theories about morality (not that they are morally sound). The theories are familiar in everyday life, and each contains an element of truth that can give it an initial attractiveness. Nevertheless, each denies or constricts our ordinary understanding of moral reasons.

Ethical Subjectivism

According to ethical subjectivism, morality is merely about feelings, attitudes, and beliefs, none of which are objectively justified or any better than others. A naive version says that a moral belief is true if it is held with sincerity and conviction. Thus, if some people sincerely believe that all women should remain in the traditional roles of wives and mothers, then this belief is "true for them." And if I believe women should have equal opportunities in all social roles, then this belief is "true for me." Neither view is objectively true; neither is true in a manner that makes its denial false.

This naive version makes nonsense of beliefs. A belief is something that is true or false, but not both. Hence, more sophisticated ethical subjectivists deny that morality is about beliefs, truth, or falsehood. Instead, morality is "noncognitive"; it is a matter of feelings and attitudes, much like one's tastes in music or sports. This version of ethical subjectivism is called *emotivism:* to say that an act is right, or a person is good, is merely to emote; it is to show or *express* emotions (as distinct from dryly *reporting* that one feels these emotions). No one's feelings are more justified than another's, assuming they are compatible with any relevant factual information.

David Hume (1711–1776) articulated a version of this view:

> Take any action allow'd to be vicious: Willful murder, for instance. Examine it in all lights, and see if you can find that matter of fact, or real existence, which you call *vice*. . . . The vice entirely escapes you, as long as you consider the object. You never can find it, till you turn your reflexion into your own breast, and find a sentiment of disapprobation, which arises in you, towards this action. Here is a matter of fact; but 'tis the object of feeling, not of reason. It lies in yourself, not in the object.[2]

Thus, when we call the murder of Kitty Genovese vicious we are merely expressing our feelings of horror and outrage. Hume attempted to identify an objective aspect of morality based in widely shared human sentiments of caring for people. Hume's successors, however, have been less optimistic about the extent of shared feelings.

Charles L. Stevenson (1908–1979) developed emotivism and helped make it an influential theory during the 1930s and 1940s. In his view, moral terms are used to express feelings and attitudes, but also to try to influence others to share our sentiments. Thus, my statement "This act is wrong" is used to express my negative attitude toward the act and tacitly to urge you to disapprove as well. Again, my assertion "This act is right" expresses my approval of the act and urges you to adopt a similar attitude. Indeed, Stevenson drew a sharp distinction between facts and values of all kinds: Facts are matters of truth, falsity, and scientific inquiry; values are matters of emotions and attitudes.

Emotivism contains an element of truth: Moral judgments do involve expressions of feelings and attitudes. Furthermore, emotions and attitudes are crucial in motivating us. If we lacked the capacity to feel, we might be unable to respond to moral values. But morality also involves reasons that focus on the well-being of people, on character, and on relationships. When we condemn the murder of Kitty Genovese, the focus is on her, rather than on our emotions. In addition to expressing our disapproval, we are saying there are sound moral *reasons* for not taking her life.

These reasons, which center on her value as a human being, prohibit taking her life. As we discuss more fully in the next chapter, this moral value is sometimes expressed in terms of human rights: Killing her violated her right to life. Or it is understood in terms of duties: Killing her violates duties to respect her as having inherent worth. And it is also expressed in terms of consequences: Killing her destroys the good that her life makes possible (for herself and others). In each case, the meaning of these moral reasons is not reducible to expressions of our feelings.

A further criticism of emotivism is that some feelings and attitudes are justified and others are not. Kitty Genovese's murderer may have had a strongly favorable attitude toward killing women, and found pleasure in doing so. We have different attitudes and feelings. Moral reasons are the basis for rationally determining which attitudes and emotions are morally appropriate. Once again, emotivism cannot adequately make sense of these moral reasons.

As this discussion suggests, to assert that an act is morally right is to assert that it is an act for which the most compelling moral reasons can be given. Does this clarification about the nature of moral assertions refute ethical subjectivism? Ethical subjectivists are unlikely to abandon their view so quickly. They will acknowledge that most people believe morality is about good reasons, just as they believe in moral truth. But subjectivists will reformulate their view this way: There are no objectively sound or binding moral reasons. This addendum clarifies why it so difficult to decisively refute ethical subjectivism. Presumably, to refute it would involve setting forth a moral argument, using sound moral reasons, aimed at establishing moral truths. But the possibility of moral reasoning is precisely what ethical subjectivists deny.

We have made progress, however, by coming to see clearly that ethical subjectivism easily becomes a form of *moral skepticism,* doubt about the cogency of moral reasons and moral reasoning. Like other forms of skepticism, it is difficult to refute it directly. One response to skepticism is to study ethics, in the hope that exploring the wider network of moral reasons will restore appreciation of moral reasons. Another response is to think through, with regard to specific events and areas of our lives, the implications of abandoning or affirming moral reasoning. We engage in such thinking on many occasions: not only in taking a course on ethics, but also in watching and discussing films, reading novels, talking with friends, being involved in a religion, participating in community activities, and encountering cruelty in everyday life.

All these occasions evoke the basic moral concern and decency that all moral reasoning presupposes. In this way, moral reasoning is as much a matter of the heart as the head, of emotions and attitudes. This emotional content is the element of truth that emotivism contains but exaggerates. Moral reasons are practical; they both justify and motivate. Thus, a sociopath who lacks even minimum moral caring (usually because of being severely abused as a child) is extremely unlikely to become responsive to moral reasoning by studying ethics. Fortunately, most ethical subjectivists and moral skeptics are not sociopaths!

Ethical Egoism

Unlike ethical subjectivists, ethical egoists agree that morality is about reasons, but they reduce all sound moral reasons to one dictum: Promote one's own good. Ethical egoism reduces all moral responsibilities to one: Look out for Number One—always and exclusively. According to ethical egoism, an act is right when it promotes one's own best interests, that is, what is good for oneself overall and in the long run. As the novelist–philosopher Ayn Rand (1905–1982) contends in *The Virtue of Selfishness,* a person's "*concern with his [or her] own interests* is the essence of a moral existence."[3]

By "selfishness" Rand means thoroughgoing concern for one's own interests, rather than the more common pejorative meaning in which selfishness is bad, by definition. Nevertheless, she clearly endorses a preoccupation with one's own interests that traditional morality condemns as excessive and opposed to what we owe to others. She is not merely saying that morality requires prudent attention to one's interests—that would be uncontroversial. Instead, she contends that altruism is immoral, where altruism is concern to promote the well-being of others for their sake (rather than solely for what one can gain from them). We should help others only when it benefits us, in particular through trades and exchanges in which we gain things we want for ourselves.

Are there any arguments in favor of ethical egoism? It will not do to argue that if everyone were exclusively self-interested then everyone would benefit through their own self-reliance. The main problem with this argument is not that it is false, although it is—all of us need help from others sometimes. Instead, the main problem is that ethical egoists cannot use the argument to defend their view. For, appealing the benefits to the wider society presupposes that we should care about other people for their sake. That is precisely what ethical egoists deny.

Rand has two primary arguments for her view. First, she attempts to derive ethical egoism from certain general facts about biology. Humans, like other living organisms, are natural organisms who must struggle to survive by using all their inherited talents, especially their reasoning: "Life can be kept in existence only by a constant process of self-sustaining action. The goal of that action, the ultimate *value* which, to be kept, must be gained through its every moment, is the organism's *life*."[4] Happiness comes as we meet the varied goals that contribute to our survival and flourishing. In this way, the moral mandate to pursue our interests and happiness are fixed by nature: "The fact that a living entity *is,* determines what it *ought* to do. So much for the issue of the relation between '*is*' and '*ought*'."[5]

In reply, it is true that humans are natural organisms who must struggle to survive and prosper through working, maintaining self-esteem, and exercising reason. But we have also evolved as social creatures whose friendships, loves, and community loyalties enable us to survive and flourish. We have evolved with natural dispositions to care about each other—imperfectly, to be sure, but dramatically, nonetheless. Attempts to ground ethics in our biological nature must take fuller account of these other-directed dispositions than Rand does.

Another difficulty with Rand's argument concerns her attempt to directly infer moral conclusions from biology or psychology. Can we derive an *ought* from an *is* without invoking additional moral premises? This question, asked first by David Hume, has generated a large is–ought debate in ethical theory, and here only a brief caution is offered.

We can agree that ethics must be *realistic* in its expectations by taking account of human biology, psychology, and other important human sciences.[6] That insistence on realism is behind the frequent linking of ethics and psychology throughout this book. But that does not imply we can derive moral values from scientific facts. As Rand herself emphasizes elsewhere, what is *morally desirable* is distinguishable from what is *desired;* what is *morally good* is distinct from what *feels good;* and what we *morally ought* to do or become is distinguishable from what we *are.* But this also implies that when Rand selects certain facts about human nature (our self-seeking tendencies) and ignores others (our social tendencies), she is already presupposing the moral outlook she claims to argue for.

Rand's second argument is that self-respect requires complete devotion to one's interests: "Altruism permits no concept of a self-respecting, self-supporting man."[7] Altruists hold degrading attitudes toward themselves as being servants to others, as existing for the sake of others rather than for one's own well-being. In addition, altruists are invariably filled with guilt for not helping as much as they think they should. Altruism is bad for receivers, as well as givers. Beneficiaries of help become servile and dependent. Altruism can be blamed for socialist agendas and for social welfare programs that are based on stealing from successful people, in the form of taxation, to give to people who have failed to earn their own livelihood.

The difficulty with this argument is that it presents us with a simplistic dichotomy: Either sacrifice oneself continually (in self-degrading ways) or be entirely self-seeking. This dichotomy blurs a large middle ground in which self-concern and concern for others are balanced and reasonably blended, so as to contribute to our own happiness as much as to others. What the proper balance is depends on specific contexts and circumstances, and there is considerable room for reasonable persons to disagree about how much we owe to ourselves and to others. But all major ethical theories, of the sort discussed in the following chapters, affirm the moral significance of oneself, as well as others, whether that worth is understood in terms of duties to ourselves, exercising human rights, or the good of individual happiness.

Rand is correct that some forms of altruism are misguided, unhealthy, and wasteful. Yet, that does not establish that all altruism tends to bring unhappiness to oneself. Again, she downplays the vulnerabilities we all share, our need for help and concern from others. What, for example, would she say about helping Kitty Genovese?

The answer can be found in her essay "The Ethics of Emergencies." There she strongly objects to the preoccupation that ethicists have with helping others in desperate need. Such an emphasis degrades us by suggesting we exist to help others; it also degrades others by suggesting they are helpless rather than capable of helping themselves. She goes on to admit, however, that in emergencies we should sometimes help others, when doing so does not risk our own lives. Why? Because in general a rational person will grant that others have some value as "a consequence, an extension, a secondary projection of the primary value which is himself."[8]

It is unclear what Rand means. The context suggests that she means that the stranger we help might turn out to be someone interesting, who will enrich our lives in some way. Hence, we should play it safe by assuming the person might turn out to have a (self-reliant, talented) character that enriches us: "A rational man regards strangers as innocent until proved guilty, and grants them that initial good will in the name of their human potential."[9] And when she speaks of "the value of human life" she seems to mean the value to us. This interpretation is consistent with her ethical egoism, but surely that is not the only or primary reason why bystanders should get on the phone to help Kitty Genovese! The primary reason is that she is a person with the same inherent moral worth that we have. That inherent moral worth is not reducible to benefits we might gain from subsequent interactions with her (which is not to dismiss those benefits as unimportant).

Again, Rand has much to say about the "rights of man," and that has led some readers to interpret her as a libertarian ethicist. As discussed in the next chapter, libertarian ethicists believe that all persons have rights to life, liberty, and property (although not rights to receive help beyond what is specified in contracts they make with others). Genuine libertarians ascribe human rights to all people as a way to express their inherent moral worth, a worth that morality requires us to respect and value—in addition to pursuing our self-interest. By contrast, consistent with her ethical egoism, Rand seems to think of rights in a very different way. She thinks of them as legal restrictions that individuals endorse because doing so furthers their own interests: "Individual rights are the means of subordinating society to moral law"—where the moral law is to maximize one's self-interest.[10]

These matters of interpretation are important, if only because they suggest ethical egoism is difficult to maintain consistently. Our primary question, however, is whether ethical egoism is true. Are there any other better arguments for ethical egoism than Rand provides? Some ethical egoists think the strongest support for ethical egoism comes from a doctrine called psychological egoism.

Psychological Egoism

Psychological egoism portrays all people as motivated solely by what they believe to be good for themselves in some respect. This view was embraced by Thomas Hobbes (1588–1679) and by many leading psychologists in this century, including the psychoanalyst Sigmund Freud (1856–1939) and the behaviorist B. F. Skinner (1904–1990). Psychological egoism is a theory about the facts concerning human motivation, rather than an ethical theory—hence its name, *psychological* egoism. Nevertheless, if true it would render ethical egoism more plausible. If we were able to care only about ourselves, then we should focus on our long-term good in order to avoid foolish and self-destructive conduct.

But is it true that we can only care about ourselves? Even Rand agreed that very often we fail to care about ourselves by engaging in self-hurtful actions, and we also engage in altruism. Why do psychological egoists think otherwise?[11] The arguments are surprisingly brief, thereby adding to their seductive appearance.

1   *People always act on their own desires; therefore they always and only seek what they believe is good for themselves in some respect, namely the satisfaction of their desires.* **Reply:** There are two kinds of desires, depending on the object of the desire (that is, the thing desired). Self-seeking desires are desires to get things for me, for my sake; altruistic desires are desires to promote the good of others, for the sake of others. Granted, we always act on our own desires, and in order to satisfy our desires. By definition, my acts are motivated by my desires! It does not follow that I desire only to get things for myself. Nor does it follow that I care only about the self-centered indulgence of my desires.

2   *People always and only seek pleasures for themselves; therefore, they seek only something good for themselves, namely their pleasures.* **Reply:** The premise of this argument is false. Sometimes we act selflessly to promote others' interests. Even if the premise were true, however, psychological egoism would not follow. There are two sources of pleasure: One source is in obtaining things we see as good for ourselves, but another source is in obtaining things we see as good for other people (whom we care about, at least in part, for their sake). It is true that in helping our friends and people we love we derive pleasure, but that pleasure is not all we seek. We also want to help them, for their sake, and the pleasure comes from seeing them happy. Indeed, we are unselfish insofar as we obtain pleasure from helping others.

3   *For any type of action, we can always imagine a self-serving motive; therefore, psychological egoism is true.* **Reply:** To imagine is one thing; to be correct is another. Letting my imagination run wild, I can imagine that soldiers who jump on enemy grenades to protect their comrades do it only to gain fame, or that Mother Teresa devoted her life to helping impoverished people in Calcutta, India, only to gain heavenly rewards. But only a cynic who held a thoroughly pessimistic view of human nature could conclude that these were in fact the only motives present in these cases.

4 *When we look closely we always find that an element of self-interest was a motive for helping others; therefore, psychological egoism is true.* **Reply:** This premise is controversial, but perhaps it is true. Notice, however, that it says that self-interest is *one* motive, not the only motive, or even the primary motive for helping others. Hence it does not show that psychological egoism is true. At most it suggests that helping is usually motivated by mixed motives: disinterested care for others plus some concern for ourselves (if only a concern for the pleasure we hope to receive in helping others).

Self-interest is a powerful human motive, even the strongest motive most of the time. To grant that it is the predominant motive, however, is not to grant that it is the only motive. As long as we acknowledge some capacity for caring for others for their sake, psychological egoism is false.

Self-Fulfillment

We have rejected psychological egoism and several other arguments for ethical egoism. Have we thereby refuted ethical egoism? No, for perhaps there are further arguments we overlooked. Here, and throughout this book, we need to appreciate that philosophy is a living enterprise in which striking new arguments and subtle new approaches emerge frequently. Our discussions are only beginnings that lead to conclusions open to challenge.

Let us conclude by emphasizing an important truth: Morality and self-interest are not identical, but they are interwoven in innumerable and important ways. We can appreciate these connections without becoming ethical egoists. For one thing, heeding the ordinary dictates of morality does tend to promote our good. If we keep our commitments, people will respect us. If we help others in need, they are more likely to reciprocate when we need help. Hence, there are self-interested reasons for being moral, in addition to moral reasons.

For another thing, some of the most important moral relationships blend self-interest and moral concern in ways that make it almost impossible to pry them apart. Love and friendship, in particular, involve tightly interlocking self-interest with the moral values (caring, trust, etc.) that structure them.

For yet another thing, morality does recognize the importance of our own good, as well as the good of others. Some ethicists express this point by saying that we have moral responsibilities to ourselves, such as to maintain our health and develop our talents. Others express the point by saying that prudence (in the sense of concern for one's well-being) and self-respect are moral virtues.

These connections can be summarized by saying that *self-fulfillment* is an especially important moral good. Today, some worry that the pursuit of self-fulfillment has become so excessive as to overshadow commitments to other individuals and to communities. Yet, what if self-fulfillment actually requires enduring relationships, moral commitments, and community ties? We can develop this idea by outlining a conception of self-fulfillment as a process of self-development, that, pursued authentically, leads to a meaningful and (with any luck) a happy life.

Self-development is a normative (value-guided) process in which many valuable capacities and talents unfold. Of course, not all valuable potentials can be developed. Each of us has more talents than could be realized in a lifetime. Developing our interests in one profession, for example, demands forgoing other careers that would develop our talents in other directions.

Meaningful lives are intelligible in terms of the values that make life worthwhile. Meaningful lives cohere around worthwhile commitments. Subjectively, they are enlivened by a sense of the importance of one's life. Objectively, they embody and express justified values. There are many such values, including physical excellence, appreciation of beauty, scientific knowledge, and humanistic study. Here we focus on moral values that affirm the worth of persons.

Happiness follows from a life rich in enjoyable activities and relationships, but it is not reducible to pleasures. It implies an overall satisfaction with one's life as a whole. We are happy to the degree that we can affirm the entire pattern of activities, relationships, and social practices in which we participate.[12]

According to an ancient paradox, happiness and self-fulfillment are achieved through caring for people and for valuable activities. The paradox takes several forms: In helping others we help ourselves; in giving we receive; self-sacrifice promotes self-development; freedom is won by surrendering it (in serving worthy causes); we find ourselves by losing ourselves (in caring for others); to get happiness, forget about it (while promoting the happiness of other people). This paradox is embedded in many religious outlooks, and it was also expressed by John Stuart Mill:

> Those only are happy. . . who have their minds fixed on some object other than their own happiness; on the happiness of others, on the improvement of mankind, even on some art or pursuit, followed not as a means, but as itself an ideal end. Aiming thus at something else, they find happiness by the way.[13]

The idea is that our lives are most satisfying when we participate in activities and relationships that we find inherently valuable, rather than constantly thinking about our narrow self-interest. Self-preoccupation undermines our capacities to care about people and communities.

More generally, self-fulfillment usually demands that we respond to values that are not merely subjective preferences. We have wide discretion in choosing our friendships, loves, work, and community involvements; but we need to respond to them as valuable in themselves, rather than merely as contributions to our good. If I try to pursue them solely with an attitude of "what's in it for me," I will fail to be enriched by them. First, I recognize their valid claims on me; then they can enrich my life.

Why is this? The answer concerns personal identity. We are what we care for. In particular, we are defined largely by the values and relationships to which we are committed. Who I am is a combination of my connections to my family, friends, work, and community. If I tried to justify my values solely by reference to obtaining things for myself, I would reduce my identity to a narrow and shallow set of self-seeking pleasures. By contrast, insofar as I understand myself in terms of ideals and relationships, my identity is enriched and my life becomes more meaningful.

This somewhat abstract sketch of self-fulfillment is not yet complete. Decisions about which specific activities and relationships to pursue is a highly personal matter. This is where *authenticity* enters. In a wide sense, authenticity is genuineness, or being oneself.[14] In the normative (that is, value-laden) sense used here, authenticity is being true to one's best self and to one's own distinctive way of thinking and experiencing the world. Authenticity emerges as we assume responsibility for governing our lives in accordance with our vision of a life worth living. Psychologically, it implies identifying with and affirming the main aspects of our lives and experiencing them as expressions of ourselves. Morally, it implies more specific values such as honesty, courage, and moral autonomy is exercising one's moral reasoning and sensitivities.

SUMMARY

In studying morality, philosophical ethics has four aims: clarity, comprehensive perspective, critical assessment, and guidance. Applying moral reasoning to everyday living becomes complex because moral reasons (1) are numerous; (2) are sometimes vague; (3) can conflict, thereby creating moral dilemmas; (4) often cannot be placed in a simple hierarchy of relative importance; (5) can be understood from conflicting perspectives; (6) involve a plurality of permissible conceptions of goodness; and (7) are difficult to apply when we are unclear about the facts.

Ethical subjectivism is the view that morality is merely a matter of feeling; emotivists, in particular, regard moral statements as expressions of emotions. Ethical egoism is the view that morality consists in pursuing our self-interest. Whereas ethical subjectivism leaves no room for moral reasons, ethical egoism reduces all moral reasons to self-interest. Both views fail to capture how moral reasons derive from the worth of people (and other conscious beings), which makes them worthy of respect and consideration. To assert that an act is morally right is to assert that it is an act for which the most compelling moral reasons can be given.

Moral reasons presuppose that we are capable of caring about the good of other people (and animals). Although self-interest is perhaps the predominant motive for our actions, it is not the only motive, contrary to psychological egoism—the view that we only care about what we believe to be good for ourselves in some respect. Arguments for psychological egoism lump all desires and pleasures into the same category, when in fact desires differ greatly according to their objects (what they are desires for), just as pleasures differ according to their sources.

Moral reasons and self-interest are interwoven and for the most part are mutually reinforcing, both in terms of motivation and in terms of identifying standards of right and wrong. Moral reasons take into account the importance of our self-interest, and any moral theory must take account of the facts about human motivation. Yet moral reasons also place restrictions on the pursuit of self-interest. They prohibit killing, raping, stealing, and so on, even when these acts might promote our narrow self-interest (assuming we could get away with them). More positively, self-fulfillment is an important moral good, the good of self-development that leads to happiness and a meaningful life.

DISCUSSION TOPICS

1 How do you define morality? Do you think your definition is objective, such that other reasonable people should agree with it?

2 How much was required, as a moral responsibility, of the bystanders in the Kitty Genovese case? What general principle would you use to defend your view?

3 Can moral reasons correctly be defined as those reasons that are always most important and that should override all other kinds of reasons, such as reasons concerning art, science, and self-interest? In particular, consider the artist who decides that his art is more important than his responsibilities to his family. Such is the popular (though perhaps not entirely accurate) image of the Post-Impressionist painter Paul Gauguin (1848–1903), who left his family in Paris to devote himself to the study of art. Could Gauguin's very important contributions to art outweigh his neglect of his family?[15]

4 In *The Republic*, Plato (428–348 B.C.) imagined a situation in which morality and self-interest seem opposed. According to the Legend of Gyges, Gyges was a shepherd who discovered a ring which, when he turned its bezel, made him invisible. Using his newly found powers, he entered the palace of the king, seduced the queen, murdered the king, took over the kingdom and gained great fame and fortune. What reasons can be given against doing what Gyges did? How would ethical egoists reason concerning this case? In general, why be moral if we can get away with immorality?

5 The self-fulfillment paradoxes are often used to encourage self-sacrificing conduct. How might they be abused in this regard? Think of an example in which the cause that one is urged to sacrifice for is unjust.

6 Ethical egoists like Ayn Rand tend to think of persons as separate individuals who contract with each other to obtain goods that are defined without reference to valuing other persons as having inherent moral value that places moral claims on us.[16] (a) Can self-interest be understood in terms of goods—such as money,

power, pleasure—that do not refer to caring relationships with others, such as friendship, love, and loyalty to communities? (b) Can the "self" be understood without reference to caring relationships with others? (c) If, contrary to Ayn Rand, we partly define persons in terms of caring relationships (as some psychologists do), such that caring for the good of others becomes part of caring for our self-interest, would we be modifying or rejecting ethical egoism?

7 The existentialist Jean-Paul Sartre rejected emotivism but, like ethical subjectivists, he denied there are objectively justified values: "Nothing, absolutely nothing, justifies me in adopting this or that particular value, this or that particular scale of values."[17] Moral values, in his view, are subjective and come into existence after we make choices, and hence they cannot guide our choices. In illustrating this view, Sartre describes one of his students, who was faced with the choice between volunteering to go to war to defend his country or staying with his aging mother, who depended completely on him for support. Sartre says the student must invent the moral reasons applicable to his situation. Is Sartre correct? And if there is an element of creativity involved in this decision, is any decision as good as another, or are there moral reasons to be weighed and balanced? What if the student simply decides to take an extended vacation in Southern California until the war ends and his mother dies?

8 We have all heard, "Let your conscience be your guide." In this maxim, presumably conscience refers to an accurate sense of right and wrong, rather than one's mere beliefs about morality (which may be mistaken). Joseph Butler (1692–1752), who was a major critic of ethical egoism, developed an ethical theory whose standard of right conduct was obedience to conscience.[18] Do you find such an approach promising? Could such a view avoid ethical subjectivism?

SUGGESTED READINGS

Becker, Lawrence C. (ed.). *Encyclopedia of Ethics.* 2 vols. New York: Garland Publishing, 1992. Second edition forthcoming.

Chadwick, Ruth (ed.). *Encyclopedia of Applied Ethics.* 4 vols. San Diego: Academic Press, 1998.

Frankena, William K. *Ethics.* 2nd ed. Englewood Cliffs, NJ: Prentice-Hall, 1973.

Gewirth, Alan. *Self-Fulfillment.* Princeton, NJ: Princeton University Press, 1998.

Gladstein, Mimi Reisel, and Chris Matthew Sciabarra (eds.). *Feminist Interpretations of Ayn Rand.* University Park: University of Pennsylvania State Press, 1999.

Hull, Gary, and Leonard Peikoff (eds.). *The Ayn Rand Reader.* New York: Plume, 1999.

Kavka, Gregory S. *Hobbesian Moral and Political Theory.* Princeton, NJ: Princeton University Press, 1986.

Kavka, Gregory S. "The Reconciliation Project," in Joel Feinberg (ed.), *Reason and Responsibility,* 9th ed. Belmont, CA: Wadsworth Publishing Co., 1996: 623–636.

Martin, Mike W. "Applied and General Ethics." In Michael Bradie, Thomas W. Attig, and Nicholas Rescher (eds.), *The Applied Turn in Contemporary Philosophy.* Bowling Green, OH: Bowling Green State University, Department of Philosophy, 1983.

Nielsen, Kai. *Why Be Moral?* Buffalo, NY: Prometheus Books, 1989.

Norton, David L. *Personal Destinies: A Philosophy of Ethical Individualism.* Princeton, NJ: Princeton University Press, 1976.

Olson, Robert G. *The Morality of Self-Interest.* New York: Harcourt Brace Jovanovich, 1965. (Defends ethical egoism.)

Paul, Ellen Frankel, Fred D. Miller, and Jeffrey Paul (eds.). *Self-Interest.* Cambridge: Cambridge University Press, 1997.

Rachels, James. *The Elements of Moral Philosophy.* 3d. ed. New York: McGraw-Hill, 1999.

Rogers, Kelly. (ed.). *Self-Interest: An Anthology of Philosophical Perspectives.* New York: Routledge, 1997.

Singer, Peter. (ed.). *A Companion to Ethics.* Cambridge, MA: Basil Blackwell, 1991.

Singer, Peter. *How Are We to Live?: Ethics in an Age of Self-Interest.* Amherst, NY: Prometheus Press, 1995.

Stevenson, Charles L. *Ethics and Language.* New Haven, CT: Yale University Press, 1944.

Stout, Jeffrey. *Ethics After Babel: The Languages of Morals and Their Discontents.* Boston: Beacon Press, 1988.

Taylor, Charles. *The Ethics of Authenticity.* Cambridge, MA: Harvard University Press, 1992.

Uyl, Douglas J. Den, and Douglas B. Rasmussen (eds). *The Philosophical Thought of Ayn Rand.* Urbana: University of Illinois Press, 1984.

Theories of Right Action

"I did not have sexual relations with that woman, Miss Lewinsky." When President Clinton made this statement in January 1998, he was lying. To lie is to state something we believe to be false with the intention of deceiving our listeners.[1] Whereas lies are attempts to deceive, deception itself implies successfully misleading someone. Deception takes forms other than lying, including pretense, withholding information, drawing legalistic distinctions inappropriately, and purposefully giving so much information that a hearer is overwhelmed and thereby misled. We will focus on lying, however, as a useful point for comparing and contrasting ethical theories about right action, although other examples will be used as well.

Three types of ethical theories have been especially influential since the eighteenth-century Enlightenment Era: utilitarianism, rights ethics, and duty ethics. All have many different versions, and with regard to each theory we will introduce two variations. We will conclude by discussing pragmatism as one additional alternative in ethics that is receiving increased attention.

Aims of Ethical Theories

Why do we need ethical theories? As noted in Chapter 1, morality is complex because of vagueness about moral reasons, conflicting reasons (that create moral dilemmas), conflicting views among individuals affected, and uncertainties about facts relevant to moral values in particular situations. Often we need guidance, and ethical theories attempt to provide such guidance at a general level.

Like applied ethics, though on a broader scale, ethical theories aspire to present moral ideas and issues clearly, consistently, in comprehensive frameworks that provide balance and perspective on all moral issues, and in ways compatible with relevant facts. Above all, theories attempt to fit together and build upon what we most confidently and firmly believe about fundamental moral matters, and thereafter, to extend our judgments into less-certain areas. If, for example, a theory implied that it is all right to torture babies or lie just to hurt others for fun, we would know something was wrong with the theory!

We assess the adequacy of ethical theories, then, using five criteria: The theory must genuinely provide (1) clarity about key ideas and issues, (2) logical consistency (no self-contradictions within the theory), (3) consistency with the relevant facts (including being realistic about human nature), (4) comprehensive perspective (applicable to all kinds of issues), and (5) compatibility with our most carefully considered moral convictions. We might call this the *5-C Test* for ethical theories.

Implicitly, we already employed this test in critiquing ethical egoism. Ethical egoism met the more formal criteria of clarity, logical consistency, and comprehensive applications. We raised questions, however, about some relevant facts: Does ethical egoism rely on a false theory of human motivation (psychological egoism), and would caring exclusively about ourselves genuinely promote our happiness? But most important, we challenged whether it was compatible with what we are most certain of: Morality involves caring about others, as well as about ourselves.

As we turn to more widely held ethical theories, we might keep in mind several questions that generate alternative emphases among the theories.

Moral bedrock. What is the most basic moral concept, the bedrock or moral bottom line in approaching moral issues? *Duty ethics* regards duty as the fundamental moral concept, *rights ethics* sees human rights as basic, and *utilitarianism* views overall good consequences as the ultimate moral standard. *Pragmatism* rejects the attempt to provide a moral system singling out one type of value concept as most basic.

Resolving dilemmas. How do we go about formulating and resolving moral dilemmas—that is, situations in which moral reasons come into conflict with each other? This concern is linked to the first one. On the one hand, in articulating what dilemma is being confronted, do we use the language of conflicting duties, rights, goods, and so on? On the other hand, how do we go about setting priorities—which duties, rights, goods, and so on are most important in the situation?

Rules and contexts. How important are moral rules or principles, and are details about context equally or more important than general rules?

Partiality versus impartiality. When does morality require complete impartiality? When is it permissible or even obligatory to give emphasis to ourselves and to our friends and family, and how much emphasis should we give?

Utilitarianism: Mill and Act-Utilitarianism

Utilitarians believe there is a single moral requirement—to produce the most good for the most people, giving equal consideration to everyone affected. Thus, the moral bedrock is good consequences. Right conduc~~t~~ termined entirely by reference to the goods and bads that follow fr~~om~~ actions.

Recall that ethical egoism, like utilitarianism, is a *consequentialist* theory; it also understands rightness solely in terms of good consequences. The dramatic difference is that utilitarians require us to consider—and to consider equally and impartially—the effects of our conduct on everyone affected. Our obligation at any moment and in any situation is to choose that option, among those open to us, that is likely to create the greatest total balance of good effects over bad effects.* "Utility" is the name for that balance, although that word is sometimes also used to refer solely to the good consequences.

Utilitarians disagree about how important rules are in comparison with individual situations and actions. *Act-utilitarianism* focuses on the consequences of individual actions: Examine the optional actions in each situation, and always choose the action that produces the most overall good. *Rule-utilitarianism* focuses instead on the consequences of rules: Examine possible sets of rules for a society to live by, and always follow the set of rules that produces the most overall good. We will begin with act-utilitarianism because that is the version that the classical (nineteenth-century) utilitarians like Jeremy Bentham (1748–1832) and John Stuart Mill (1806–1873) usually stated (although in some passages Mill may have been a rule-utilitarian).

Act-utilitarians, then, believe the right choice is the one that maximizes overall good. When we are inclined to tell a lie, we need to estimate the good and bad effects likely to follow from lying; likewise, we estimate the good and bad effects of not lying and instead doing other things (the consequences of which we estimate separately). Then we compare these estimates, selecting the action that maximizes overall good while minimizing overall bad. Hence, there is no absolute (exceptionless) rule against all lying. When the only way to save an innocent person is to lie to a kidnapper who is demanding a ransom, we should lie. And when there are no better options, we should sometimes lie to protect our families and ourselves from intrusive strangers.

Was President Clinton justified in lying to protect his personal privacy? No, because the overall consequences were worse than telling the truth. President Clinton's lies had devastating consequences for his presidency. One lie led to another, and eventually Clinton was telling not only "cover

---

*Usually utilitarians say *likely* to produce more good than bad, because in looking to the future we must always act in light of uncertainties. But some utilitarians say what is objectively right is what *actually* maximizes overall good consequences. Hence, the objective good is what we discern retrospectively (looking to past) as having actually maximized overall good, and when we look to the future we are attempting to judge which actions will have those results.

lies," designed to conceal other deceptions, but he also asked members of his Cabinet and staff to say things that he knew were untrue. When the lies were uncovered, trust was eroded among Americans (although most continued to support his general leadership in economic matters). When all these consequences are taken into account, it is clear his lies were unjustified using the act-utilitarian's standard. Indeed, his lies are something of a cautionary tale that bring to mind Sir Walter Scott's stanza

> O, what a tangled web we weave,
> When first we practise to deceive.[2]

Although act-utilitarians say we should look at situations rather than general rules, everyday rules like "Do not lie," "Keep your promises," and "Do not steal," do have some importance. According to Mill, they are helpful reminders of what is usually right. Usually, more bad than good results from lies, broken promises, and theft. Hence, in most situations we should not engage in lengthy deliberations about whether to lie; we should simply not lie. But, life being complex, there are exceptions,

> the chief of which is when the withholding of some fact (as of information from a malefactor, or of bad news from a person dangerously ill) would save an individual (especially an individual other than oneself) from great and unmerited evil, and when the withholding can only be effected by denial. . . . It is not the fault of any creed, but of the complicated nature of human affairs, that rules of conduct cannot be so framed as to require no exceptions, and that hardly any kind of action can safely be laid down as either always obligatory or always condemnable.[3]

There is another source of complexity. According to utilitarians, the standard of rightness is the balance of more overall good than bad, but what is good and bad? These things must be understood without bringing in other moral terms, like duties and rights, lest some other kind of ethical standard is smuggled in. But utilitarians must give some account of *intrinsic goods,* goods worth seeking and having for their own sake, in contrast with *instrumental goods* that bring about intrinsic goods. Without a clear theory of intrinsic goods, the utilitarian theory is utterly vague and incomplete, as if we are told to maximize some unknown thing.

At this point, the seemingly simple standard becomes more complex and controversial. Mill's predecessor and the first important utilitarian, Jeremy Bentham, said the only intrinsically good thing is pleasure, and the only intrinsically bad thing is pain. But is that true? It is repellent to say that the pleasures of rapists are good. Conversely, some mild pains seem to be part of an inherently good process, such as those of an athlete striving for excellence. (Similar objections can be raised against the view of some contemporary economists who, seeking a more public criterion of good than subjective feelings, say that satisfying preferences as shown by what people buy, is good.)

According to Mill's influential view, the only intrinsic good is happiness. But what is happiness? Sometimes Mill confused it with pleasure (as did Bentham). In his more careful moments, however, he distinguished between pleasures, which are short-term emotions, and happiness, which is a long-term state composed of many and varied pleasures, mixed with some inevitable pains. Moreover, Mill stated that the happy life is rich in "higher pleasures," which are better in quality than lower pleasures. The higher pleasures are those of the mind: pleasures of the intellect, of friendship, of love, of art and beauty. The lower pleasures are those of the body: pleasures of eating, drinking, sex, and napping on a sunny afternoon. The exact combination of happiness-producing pleasures is, of course, a highly individual matter. Going beyond Mill, we might say that happiness is that combination of pleasures (especially higher ones), activities, and relationships that we can affirm overall: That is the way I want my life to be.

The distinction between higher and lower pleasures greatly complicates matters. How can we make reliable judgments about quality with a precision needed to make the utilitarian theory practicable? G. E. Moore (1873–1958), an influential later utilitarian, attempted to resolve the difficulty by identifying some things we "intuit" as intrinsically good, such as the pleasures of friendship, love, and beauty.[4] That suggestion, however, seems like either a blind alley (intuitions differ!) or a presupposition that human relationships and other activities are morally valuable in ways that usher in a more complex standard than utilitarianism. In general, how can some pleasures be ranked as better or worse without assuming we already know what is right or wrong, or morally desirable or undesirable, independently of the utilitarian standard?

Mill addressed himself to this question, but his answer is unsatisfying. He suggested that we measure quality by taking a poll of qualified judges— that is, people who have experienced and appreciated both of the pleasures being compared. A large majority is decisive.

> Of two pleasures, if there be one to which all or almost all who have experience of both give a decided preference, irrespective of a feeling of moral obligation to prefer it, that is the more desirable pleasure. . . . Now it is an unquestionable fact that those who are equally acquainted with and equally capable of appreciating and enjoying both, do give a marked preference to the manner of existence which employs their higher faculties. Few human creatures would consent to be changed into any of the lower animals for a promise of the fullest allowance of a beast's pleasures.[5]

In a famous sentence he adds, "It is better to be a human being dissatisfied than a pig satisfied; better to be Socrates dissatisfied than a fool satisfied."[6]

Something puzzling occurs in the longer passage quoted. Mill begins by comparing the qualities of kinds of pleasures, but ends up talking about "manners of existence" or ways of life involving various kinds of pleasures. It is true that few humans would choose to change places with pigs, but how does that fact prove that physical pleasures are inferior in quality to mental pleasures? Even if philosophers and artists did the voting, would the pleasures of eating and sex (at their best) be voted inferior to those of philosophy and art? The happy life does not banish or minimize physical pleasures; it integrates both physical and mental pleasures.

At this point let us state several challenges to utilitarianism. The first challenge, on which we have dwelt, is how to state an adequate theory about intrinsic goodness that is both clear and practicable. A second difficulty concerns the impartiality requirement embedded in utilitarianism: take into account the effects of our actions on everyone, equally and impartially. That seems to go against common sense. Aren't we morally justified—both permitted and required—in giving some emphasis to our own happiness and to that of people we love or are friends with? Act-utilitarianism would have us constantly striving to be benevolent so that each of our actions would bring about maximum good. Such moral pressure is perhaps better suited to saints than to humans.

Third, act-utilitarianism does not capture what we believe about basic justice and decency. It is immoral to punish people for crimes they did not commit, but suppose in a particular instance the best way to remove a clever thief from society is to convict him of a crime he didn't commit?

Utilitarianism: Brandt and Rule-Utilitarianism

In the twentieth century, many utilitarians thought they could answer these objections to act-utilitarianism by shifting to rule-utilitarianism, together with refining their theories of intrinsic good. This shift was led by Richard B. Brandt (1910–1997), who both coined the expression *rule-utilitarianism* and introduced a sophisticated theory of good.

To begin with his theory of good, Brandt places restrictions on which pleasures are intrinsically good. He suggests that only rational desires, rational preferences based on those desires, and rational pleasures derived from satisfying those desires should be counted in calculating good and bad consequences. Intrinsic good thus becomes the satisfaction of rational desires.

Rational desires are those that survive after intensive and persistent scrutiny in light of all facts relevant to them and on the basis of clear and logical thinking. Desires to overeat, to smoke, to use harmful drugs, or to hurt ourselves in other ways would not survive this scrutiny. Nor, Brandt hopes, would cruel desires such as those of the rapist and the sadist. This process of making ourselves vividly aware of the full implications of our desires is "cognitive psychotherapy" in that it involves the same kind of dramatic transformations brought about by therapeutic psychology.

An act-utilitarian who accepted this view of intrinsic goodness would define right acts as those that maximize satisfaction of the rational desires of all people affected. Brandt, however, does not proceed in this direction.

Like all the ethicists discussed in this chapter except for Bentham and Mill, Brandt thinks that morality must give more weight to principles or rules than to individual actions. He suggests that calculation of the consequences of each act individually encourages biased reasoning rather than impartial concern for all people's interests. It also means we are less able to count on how others will behave. For example, it is more impartial, as well as more publicly reliable, to have all people obey the rule "Pay your taxes as required by law" than to encourage each person to calculate the good and bad effects of reporting all their taxable income. Similarly, it is better for people simply to obey the rule "Don't lie," except in certain exceptional instances (such as to protect innocent life), than to encourage people to calculate the good and bad effects of each contemplated lie.

For this and other reasons, Brandt affirms *rule-utilitarianism:* We should follow a set of rules that, were they adopted by the society in which one lives, would produce the most good for the most people. The set of rules is called a moral code. Individual acts are right, then, when they conform to the moral code that would produce more overall good than would alternative moral codes. To be workable, the rules must not become too complex, but to be sound they will usually build in some exceptions: for example, "Tell the truth except when great harm would result."

This emphasis on rules seems promising in dealing with the other two difficulties with act-utilitarianism. Recall that the second difficulty was that act-utilitarianism seems to require far too much of us by way of self-sacrifice. Rule-utilitarians deal with this problem by formulating rules about more reasonable requirements. A realistic morality would require only limited benevolence, such as helping other people who are in desperate need.

The shift to rules also seems fruitful regarding the third difficulty, matters of justice. Because rule-utilitarians have us focus on consequences of sets of rules, not individual actions, they can point out the overall benefits of following rules like "Only punish individuals for crimes they commit." Alternative rules like "Punish innocent individuals when doing so benefits the community" would lead to widespread fear and anxiety in the society that we might be the next innocent person sacrificed for the community; it would erode respect for individual life; and it would encourage sloppy administration of justice.

Rule-utilitarianism is not without problems of its own, however. One difficulty is that it seems to smuggle in other moral standards. Isn't the real reason it is unacceptable to punish an innocent person, or to violate any number of specific rules, is that morality requires respecting individuals' rights? This brings us to the next type of ethical theory.

Rights Ethics: Locke and Liberty Rights

Utilitarians focus entirely on good consequences of actions, whereas rights ethicists focus on the nature of actions: Do they respect people's rights?

Utilitarians leave some room for rights, but ultimately they reduce rights to utility. In their view, rights are simply areas of liberty that should be protected because they tend to have especially good consequences. By contrast, rights ethicists make rights the moral bedrock by introducing a conception of *human rights*. Human rights specify the moral significance and authority of each human being. As the name suggests, we have human rights simply because we are human beings.

We are familiar with this idea from the American Declaration of Independence: "We hold these truths to be self-evident; that all men are created equal, that they are endowed by their Creator with certain unalienable Rights, that among these are Life, Liberty, and the pursuit of Happiness." John Locke (1632–1704), who was a major influence on Thomas Jefferson as he drafted the Declaration of Independence, listed the three fundamental rights as life, liberty, and property. Other rights ethicists offer different lists, but the key idea remains constant: All people have rights, simply because they are people.

Human rights are "unalienable"; they cannot be given or taken away (made alien to us). We may, of course, decide not to exercise them on certain occasions or to allow someone else to exercise them on our behalf. For example, we may sign a living will and a durable power of attorney, documents that authorize our selected guardian to exercise our rights in deciding how we should be treated by physicians if our capacity to think is irreversibly damaged by accident or disease. Even in a coma, however, we retain rights; we merely transfer their exercise to our guardian.

The human rights mentioned in the Declaration of Independence are recognized but not created by that document. By recognizing these human rights, the document established them as *legal* (and political) rights, that is, rights upheld in the law. But as human rights, the rights were morally binding even before the legal document was written and affirmed them. The idea is that human rights ought to be affirmed and protected in the law, but the law does not create human rights. Citizens of China, for example, have human rights that their government violates. As another example, the human rights of women and minorities, especially black people and Indians, were widely violated in the United States long after they were officially endorsed in legal documents.

In addition to human rights, there are special moral rights that are created by commitments and within special relationships. Thus, children have a special right to care from their parents, and students have special rights to attend classes at the colleges and universities they enroll in. Again, when a promise is made, the recipient of the promise acquires a special right to have the promise kept. These are not human rights, because not all people have them. Nevertheless, rights ethicists usually trace their foundation to human rights. For example, it is because of rights of freedom, property, and security that special rights created by contracts ought to be kept.

Locke was especially interested in liberty rights, that is, the rights to be left alone by governments and by citizen majorities, which sometimes persecute individuals. Because liberty rights are rights not to be interfered with, they are also called *negative rights*. Today, ethicists (and political thinkers) who assert that human rights consist entirely of liberty (or negative) rights are called *libertarians*. In politics, libertarians emphasize the (liberty) rights to property and to privacy—that is, the general right to live as we choose without interference from others. They oppose all government welfare programs, such as aid to education, the elderly, and the disabled, although many support aid to these groups through voluntary giving. The only positive rights are special rights created through contracts: For example, I have the right to receive the goods for which I pay money. Libertarians affirm as legitimate only minimum government roles, such as national defense and a legal system to protect property and safety.

Rights Ethics: Melden and Welfare Rights

Although libertarians have recently exerted considerable influence in ethical theory and politics, most rights ethicists and most Americans believe that the libertarian view of rights is too narrow. In their view, moral community requires far more than recogizing liberty rights by leaving people alone. Communities are possible only if additional rights are recognized. Indeed, even liberty rights are at risk unless some support systems are affirmed. These additional human rights are called *welfare rights*—or *positive rights*— to receive certain goods, by contrast with liberty or negative rights to be free from interference.

A. I. Melden (1910–1991) is an example of someone who affirms both liberty and welfare rights. Going beyond Locke, Melden suggests that the basic right to pursue our interests entails rights to be helped in some situations. Melden argues that contemporary societies ought to institutionalize welfare systems (contrary to the libertarian political ideology) to support the disadvantaged—who, under certain circumstances, could be any of us.[7] The basic right to pursue our affairs entails a right to the minimal necessities for a decent existence within societies that can easily provide them. This right is limited, however, by the resources available within the community, and determining what is reasonable to make available is a matter of political controversy and compromise.

Just as duty ethicists try to identify a hierarchy of importance among the various duties, so rights ethicists try to distinguish between more and less fundamental rights. Unlike Locke and Jefferson, who singled out three rights as basic, Melden suggests there is just one ultimate right from which others can be derived and justified: the right to pursue one's legitimate interests. Legitimate interests are those interests that do not violate other people's similar and equal rights. In effect, Melden's most fundamental human

right is the same right to liberty affirmed by libertarians! The important difference, however, is that Melden is convinced that this basic right to liberty
implies some welfare rights. In his view, it is a mockery to say that people
have rights to freedom but no rights to the minimum prerequisites (such as
work or medical care) for exercising that freedom.

What are the precise limits of welfare rights to be helped and of liberty
rights to pursue our interests? At what point do others' rights restrict our
own? No answer is both general and specific enough to resolve all practical
disagreements. The extent of rights, and the reasonable exercise of rights,
must be understood within given communities of people who live together, make certain claims on one another, and are in a position to help
one another. Melden's view of the interplay of rights within communities
of shared moral concern is as complex as Ross's account of how duties are
interrelated.

How does rights ethics pertain to lying? Both Locke and Melden recognize the important role of privacy rights in everyday life. These rights justify
some lies (for example, lies to strangers who ask prying questions). Intrusive
callers have no right to know certain information, and if a lie is the only way
to protect our privacy, so be it. Parents may prudently exercise rights to security when they teach their children to tell certain lies to strangers who call
when the children are at home alone.

Nevertheless, most lies are unjustified because they subvert liberty. Lies
give misleading information that interferes with the pursuit of our interests
in large or small ways. Lying subverts, or at least shows a willingness to subvert, the agency (i.e., ability to act) of the person lied to, thereby infringing
on that person's right to pursue her or his interests. Justified lies involve situations in which more pressing considerations enter, such as the right to life
(as in the violent spouse example) or the rights to privacy and security (as in
the example of telephone lies).

In some special situations, people have an especially strong right to be
told the truth. For example, citizens within a democracy have a right to be
informed of important governmental actions (except when national security
requires secrecy—a much-abused exception). Consumers have the right to
be warned of the risks in using products and services, a right that derives
from the fundamental right to life. And spouses or close friends may have
the right to be told many things that a stranger has no right to know.

More generally, rights ethicists (and not only libertarians) tend to give
considerable emphasis to the rights of individuals connected to us by ties
of family, community, and nation. They also give emphasis to rights to
pursue self-interest. All people have rights that place duties on us, but
rights ethicists tend to move away from utilitarians' stricter requirements of
impartiality in distributing goods. The difference is one of emphasis, however, and much turns on the details worked out within rights ethics and
rule-utilitarianism.

Duty Ethics: Kant and Respect for Persons

Even if human rights are expanded beyond liberty rights to include some positive rights, some ethicists see the rights emphasis as inevitably too self-oriented: "My rights" is too much the resounding theme in American moral debates. Nevertheless they retain the rights–ethics idea that morality is not reducible to producing good consequences, and that the very nature of some actions carries moral significance. These ethicists embrace a new starting point and moral bedrock: duties to respect persons.

Most rights and duties are correlated: they imply each other. For example, if I have a duty to you to tell the truth, then you have a right to be told the truth; if I have a right not to be killed, then you have a duty not to kill me. So does it genuinely matter whether we begin with human rights or basic duties to respect persons? Perhaps not, but there does seem to be a noteworthy difference in emphasis. Imagine that Jefferson had phrased the Declaration of Independence this way: All persons have duties to respect each other because of each person's inherent moral dignity and worth. Would this emphasis have made Americans more likely to think in terms of community, rather than their individual well-being? In any case, the history of ethics has a strong tradition of duty ethics that is somewhat distinct from, though it overlaps with, rights ethics.

The most influential duty ethicist was Immanuel Kant (1724–1804). Kant endorsed a long list of duties, such as to be honest, to keep promises, to be fair, to help others, to show gratitude for favors, to develop our talents, and to refrain from hurting others or ourselves. For Kant, morality consisted of always trying to do our duty—because we see it is our duty. His importance as a moral philosopher rests in his account of what makes something our duty. He suggested that three abstract duties underlie all others: (1) act so as to respect persons, (2) act on universal principles, and (3) act autonomously. Let us consider each of these duties.

First, to respect persons is to recognize them as being rational or autonomous in ways that should restrict our own actions. Rationality or autonomy is the capacity to make decisions for oneself in the pursuit of reasonable purposes, such as seeking happiness, developing talents, and obeying universal principles of duty that apply to all rational beings. Kant expressed this idea of respect by saying that people are "ends-in-themselves," as opposed to mere means to be used for our own purposes or ends. To put it another way, people have their own rational purposes, which place moral constraints on how we may treat them. Their rationality or autonomy gives them a worth and dignity beyond any price.

For example, to murder, rape, or torture other people is to flagrantly treat them as objects to be used for our purposes, in disregard of their own rational desires not to be treated in these ways. Kant also thought that by lying to and deceiving other people we are using them as objects. To deceive is to manipulate people's beliefs, as well as their actions based on those beliefs, thus assaulting their rationality. Lying also represents a kind of coercion by which we seek to distort other people's minds.*

Second, all duties have in common that they are universal; that is, they apply to all rational beings, both human beings and supernatural beings (if they exist). To determine how we ought to act, we must formulate principles that we can envision and affirm everyone acting on. For example, we can easily imagine everyone acting on the principle "Do not lie," but we cannot imagine everyone acting on the principle "Lie when it suits your own purposes." If everyone followed the latter principle, communication would break down. People would no longer take one another's statements seriously, so both sincere and deceitful statements would become impossible to make. In trying to conceive of everyone acting on the principle "Lie when it suits your own purposes," a contradiction arises: Everyone does tell lies (which is the hypothesis we begin with) and no one can tell lies, in the sense that it would be impossible to attempt seriously to deceive anyone (which is the implication of the hypothesis).

In other cases we can conceive of everyone acting on a principle, but the principle conflicts with what we *will* (or choose) as rational beings. For example, we can imagine everyone acting on the rule, "Do not help others who are in desperate need." Yet, as rational agents—by Kant's definition of *rational*—we would want people to help us when we are in desperate need. The no-help rule conflicts with our own rational purposes. Thus, the attempt to will the no-help rule as a universal principle results in a conflict within our own will. By contrast, there is no conflict when we universalize a principle of mutual aid: "Help others in desperate need, at least when no great personal sacrifice is required."

Third, the duty to respect persons entails the duty to respect oneself. That duty involves appreciation of our own autonomy as we recognize and respond to specific duties. It is not enough to do only what is required by universal duties; we must also act out of a sense of duty. This is the good will: the good intentions to act on principles that respect all rational beings. This sense of duty is the only thing Kant praises as intrinsically good—good in and of itself, independent of its consequences.

Our nobility lies in this capacity to do what is right because we see it is right, and not solely from ulterior motives, such as to make our parents or peers or ourselves happy, advance our careers, or gain religious rewards. Because this good will is a personal expression of our own rational nature, we can be said to "give ourselves the moral law" we live by. And because the moral law consists of universal principles applicable to everyone, we can also regard our own rational nature as the source of moral principles.

---

*Kant also thought that in lying to ourselves we undermine our own purposes as rational beings. In Chapter 19 we will take up the topic of self-deception and self-directed lies.

To sum up, Kant thought there were three principles underlying all the more specific principles of duty or, as he called them, *maxims* and *moral laws*. In his words, these principles are as follows:

1 *Respect persons:* "Act so that you treat humanity, whether in your own person or in that of another, always as an end and never as a means only."[8]

2 *Universalize principles:* "Act only according to that maxim by which you can at the same time will that it should become a universal law."[9]

3 *Be autonomous:* "Act only so that the will through its maxims could regard itself at the same time as universally lawgiving."[10]

Kant spoke of his three fundamental duties as three versions of *the categorical imperative*. He also referred to specific duties like "Don't lie" as categorical imperatives. An imperative is simply a command, and a categorical command is one without conditions or qualifications attached. This is Kant's way of emphasizing that morality requires us to fulfill our duties simply because those duties make valid claims on us, and not solely because we have self-seeking desires. For example, a slogan such as "Honesty pays" says, in effect, that if (on the condition that) you want to be successful in business, then you ought to be honest. Such "iffy" commands are *hypothetical imperatives,* to which a condition or hypothesis is attached. Categorical moral commands, by contrast, prescribe such behavior as "Be honest" and "Don't lie"—period.

Despite his insights, Kant made two glaring (and related) mistakes. On the one hand, he thought that most everyday moral principles were absolute, in the sense of having no justified exceptions. In particular, he believed there is an absolute (exceptionless) duty never to lie. (His argument is left as a discussion topic later.) He was oblivious to how frequently moral rules come into conflict with each other, such that one rule has to have an exception in order to heed the other rule.

On the other hand, and connected with his absolutism, Kant did not take sufficiently full account of contingencies and context. It is difficult to think of any other ethicist of Kant's stature making the following claims: "I do not . . . need any penetrating acuteness in order to discern what I have to do in order that my volition may be morally good. Inexperienced in the course of the world, incapable of being prepared for all its contingencies, I ask myself only: Can I will that my maxim become a universal law?"[11] Although Kant's ideas of autonomy and respect for individuals have been enormously important in shaping the history of ethics, he failed to struggle with how to deal with moral dilemmas. Remedying that failure has been a key concern of other duty ethicists.

Duty Ethics: Ross and Prima Facie Duties

More recent ethicists who share Kant's basic orientation reject his belief that everyday principles such as "Don't lie" are absolute. To take an extreme case, suppose that the only way to protect a friend is to lie to her violent spouse who comes looking for her. Here two duties come into conflict: the duty to protect innocent life versus the duty not to lie. One duty has to give way in order that the other duty can be met. Virtually all duty ethicists agree that the duty to protect innocent life should have priority. In fact, even Kant's own fundamental principle to respect persons supports this judgment. Respecting the autonomy of the friend implies protecting her against her violent spouse.

David Ross (1877–1971) was a duty ethicist who was especially sensitive to conflicts among duties. To underscore the frequency of these conflicts, he introduced a technical term widely used today. He said that duties which have justified exceptions when they conflict with other more pressing duties are *prima facie duties*. Most familiar moral maxims, such as "Tell the truth" and "Keep your promises," express prima facie duties in that they all have the potential to conflict with and be overridden by other duties. Even the duty "Do not kill" may be overridden by the duty to defend innocent life, as in a war, or to defend oneself or others against a murderer. Our *actual duty* is what we should do in a specific situation, all things considered, and after we have weighed all applicable prima facie duties reasonably.

What is involved in weighing prima facie duties reasonably so as to determine our actual duty? How should we decide which duty has priority on a particular occasion? There is no infallible test. Kant's guidelines of respecting other persons, universalizing the principle we act on, and being autonomous are too general to resolve all practical dilemmas. Ross argues that we must simply think through all relevant aspects of the situation and exercise our most careful judgment.

> When I am in a situation, as perhaps I always am, in which more than one of these *prima facie* duties is incumbent on me, what I have to do is to study the situation as fully as I can until I form the considered opinion (it is never more) that in the circumstances one of them is more incumbent than any other.[12]

This context-bound reasoning, in addition to sensitivity to conflicting duties, is an important improvement over Kant.

When are we allowed to make exceptions, say, to the duty not to lie? Sometimes we may do so to conform to the duty of benevolence, as when we lie to protect the friend from a violent spouse. Should we lie, however, out of benevolence to a close relative who is dying from cancer and does not know it? It depends perhaps on whether the person would want to know the truth in order to make final decisions about his or her affairs or whether the person would want a few peaceful final hours. As Kant would say, the final touchstone is respect for the person's autonomy.

Unlike Kant, Ross saw no need to search beneath the numerous prima facie duties for underlying fundamental moral principles. He does, however, organize prima facie duties into clusters that highlight certain connections among them, yielding the following organizational scheme.[13]

1   Duties deriving from my previous acts
    a Duties of fidelity: those arising from my promises and commitments
    b Duties of reparation: those arising from my previous harm to others

2   Duties deriving from other people's acts
    a Duties of gratitude: duties to return favors or unearned services

3   Duties of justice: to support fair distribution, and oppose unfair distribution, of benefits and burdens in accord with merit

4   Duties of beneficence: duties to help other people

5   Duties of self-improvement: duties to improve our own virtue, intelligence, and talents

6   Duties of non-maleficence: duties not to injure others

Ross contended that it is intuitively obvious, at least to morally mature adults, that each of these is our (prima facie) duty, and they need not be based on more fundamental duties. This intuitive obviousness vanishes, however, when duties come into conflict with each other, creating moral dilemmas. Then we must simply exercise our best moral judgment, realizing, we might add, that others can sometimes aid our reflections.

Other duty ethicists have been unhappy with the excessive reliance on intuition in Ross's theory. They attempt to reduce the number of principles of duty and to identify priority principles—that is, principles that state which rules have precedence when rules conflict. William Frankena, who is cited in a discussion topic at the end of the chapter, is one ethicist who made such attempts, and John Rawls, who we discuss in Chapter 24, is another.

Which Theory Is Best?

Each of the theories we have examined has many defenders who think it best passes the 5-C Test, and philosophical debates over the theories as applied to specific cases are subtle and centuries-old. What does this controversy imply for applied ethics? Does it mean that we should disregard all theories until disputes about them are resolved? Or should the applied ethicist simply pick the one that seems most reasonable?

Should we just pick a theory, somewhat arbitrarily or on the basis of debatable intuitions? Or should we jettison all the theories while doing applied ethics? I suggest that we are free to employ all the theories. But in doing so, we are not willy-nilly opting for one over the others. The ethical theories are general frameworks for approaching moral issues, but what matters is how the details of the theories are worked out. This point was emphasized earlier, by citing two very different representatives in each of the three traditions or "styles" of moral theory.[14]

There are three reasons for allowing ourselves this freedom. First, for the most part the theories are compatible; they usually agree with each other in their practical implications (with the possible exception of act-utilitarianism).

For example, duty ethics, rights ethics, and rule-utilitarianism all condemn lies that wantonly hurt people. They all justify the principle "Do not lie except in special circumstances where a more pressing moral principle justifies the lie." With the exception of Kant's absolutistic versions of duty ethics, all the theories also agree that lies to protect innocent life—as in the case of the violent spouse—are justified.

Such a wide agreement in applications should not be surprising. All the theories are designed to express the common or overlapping moral experiences of people, and all are roughly consistent with it. These wide areas of overlap suffice for many purposes of the applied ethicist. Examined in this light, the theories are alternative ways of systematizing our view of morality, rather than competing foundational principles that attempt to provide more basic and certain principles. Indeed, do we need any more fundamental principles to establish our convictions that rape and torture are wrong?

Second, besides being largely compatible, the theories are also complementary. Each points to important moral considerations but highlights them in different ways. Suppose, for example, we ask whether it is permissible to lie to our parents to protect a friend whom the parents unfairly condemn because of her or his ethnic identity. The duty ethicist emphasizes the relationships of trust with both the parents and the friend, as well as the duties to maintain trust in those relationships. The rights ethicist emphasizes the rights of parents to know certain things about their children, and also the rights of children to lead their own lives. The utilitarian points to the effects of lying on both relationships. Although the three theories have different emphases, each appreciates the importance of the relationships involved, and each tries to balance conflicting moral reasons.

Third, relatively little turns solely on whether one is a duty ethicist, a rights ethicist, or a rule-utilitarian. What matters are the details about how the theory is developed. Theories are best viewed as general frameworks for organizing moral reflection and for developing moral arguments. The precise practical implications of those arguments depend on the specific version of the theory employed. Notice the remarkable differences between the two versions of each theory that we mentioned. Kant's absolute (exceptionless) duties are dramatically different from Ross's prima facie duties that must be weighed against one another on the basis of contextual judgments. Locke's emphasis on liberty rights has vastly different practical implications from Melden's acceptance of welfare rights. Mill's act-utilitarianism, which also stresses certain kinds of pleasures, is considerably different from Brandt's rule-utilitarianism, which stresses rules and rational desires.

In fact, for practical purposes it seems that Brandt's rule-utilitarianism has more in common with Ross's duty ethics than it does with Mill's act-utilitarianism. Act-utilitarianism might allow occasional cheating on taxes when good effects for oneself outweigh minimal good effects to others. Brandt is as stern as Ross, however, in urging obedience to rules that sustain social trust. Again, a libertarian who, like Locke, emphasizes liberty rights

(rights to be free from interference by others) would find many taxes immoral because they are used to support welfare systems. Hence, he or she may feel justified in not reporting some taxable income. In contrast, a rights ethicist who shares Melden's appreciation of welfare rights would stress the importance of paying taxes to benefit those in need.

In short, the applied ethicist should feel free to employ all three types of ethical theories insofar as they aid practical reflection. The concepts of duties, rights, and utility are all of practical use in doing applied ethics; it is unnecessary to decide which is most fundamental. Nevertheless, some applied ethicists have moved away from an emphasis on general theories, whether in the name of explicit opposition ("anti-theory") or in spirit of pragmatism—which is another ethical tradition whose origin was the early twentieth century.

Pragmatism

Pragmatism is a distinctively American approach to moral issues, both in its general tenor and given that it originated with the American philosophers Charles Sanders Peirce (1829–1914), William James (1842–1910), and John Dewey (1859–1952), on whom we focus here. At present, pragmatism is undergoing a resurgence, and a number of applied ethicists count themselves in the pragmatic tradition. In some ways, that resurgence is part of an anti-theory movement that has become wary of attempts to encapsulate morality in grand systems of the sort we have examined thus far.

Dewey's starting point was the conviction that abstract theories fail to capture the concrete texture of morality. He set himself against moral absolutes and formulas of all kinds. Instead, he insisted that moral decision making is always highly contextual and consists of an attempt to integrate into a reasonable unity a varied set of moral considerations—some of which are naturally formulated in the language or duties or responsibilities, others as rights or liberties, and still others as goods and bads. In any problematic situation calling for choices, morality requires "creative intelligence" to find a solution that "coordinates, organizes and functions each factor of the situation [or moral reason] which gave rise to conflict, suspense and deliberation."[15]

Moral principles are not like cooking recipes that tell us exactly what to do, especially when rules come into conflict with each other. Principles do play a role in making moral decisions, however, as important reminders about the kinds of moral reasons we should consider and weigh. Hence it is unfair to dismiss pragmatism as sheer expediency that abandons all moral principles.

> A moral principle, such as that of chastity, of justice, of the Golden Rule, gives the agent a basis for looking at and examining a particular question that comes up. It holds before him certain possible aspects of the act; it warns him against taking a short or partial view of the act. It economizes his thinking by supplying

him with the main heads by reference to which to consider the bearings of his desires and purposes; it guides him in his thinking by suggesting to him the important considerations for which he should be on the lookout.[16]

Interpreting and applying moral principles requires creative intelligence and sound judgment based on experience. This steady emphasis on experience and context makes Dewey closer in spirit to Ross and to utilitarians than to Kant, although he appreciated Kant's emphasis on the value of the individual.

To be sure, Dewey emphasized some values over others. He was fundamentally committed to democratic principles about social interactions as most important: fairness, equal opportunity, equal rights, freedom (both from unjust interference and as powers to act), and especially education for all. Along with these principles he esteemed the values of continual personal growth. By growth he included both creative experiences and developing more effective habits, an idea especially important for Dewey (as for Aristotle, who we discuss in the next chapter). "Character is the interpenetration of habits," where a *habit* is an acquired activity that orders aspects of our lives and acquires a power ("dynamic quality") of its own.[17] Often when we experience our lives as out of control, it is because we have developed habits that are handicapping ourselves, such as drug and alcohol abuse (addiction), patterns of negative thoughts (depression), and wasting our resources (gambling, etc.)—an idea relevant to topics taken up in subsequent chapters of this book. Forming and modifying habits should be informed by the results of ongoing scientific studies, and of all philosophers we have discussed Dewey gave greatest emphasis to the connections between morality and science.

Finally, Dewey was convinced that the search for complete agreement in contested moral issues is naive. In light of our different experiences and temperaments, each of us will tend to give different emphases in balancing moral reasons, sometimes dramatically different emphases. In tune with his emphasis on democratic values, Dewey emphasized the need for compromise and mutual conciliation within contexts of shared responsibility for decision making. Areas of agreement must be sought while respecting differences.

The possibility of uncovering agreement is testified to by Albert Jonsen and Stephen Toulmin who, in a pragmatic spirit, have recently emphasized the role of paradigm cases and models in refining ordinary intuitions. Jonsen and Toulmin participated in The National Commission for the Protection of Human Subjects of Biomedical and Behavioral Research, from 1975 to 1978, charged with developing guidelines for protecting research subjects in human experimentation. The commission's members included representatives from many different religious and political orientations, thereby precluding any hope for agreement at the level of general theory. Nevertheless, the group found themselves able to reach substantial agreement about specific cases:

So long as the debate stayed at the level of particular judgments, the eleven commissioners saw things in much the same way. The moment it soared to the level of 'principles,' they went their separate ways. Instead of securely established universal principles, in which they had unqualified confidence, giving them intellectual grounding for particular judgments about specific kinds of cases, it was the other way around.[18]

This result does ring true of many situations; however, the opposite may be true in other situations. For example, we may agree on the values of respect for life and for individual choice, but disagree about how to balance these values with respect to abortion decisions.

SUMMARY

Three main types of ethical theories about right (obligatory) action, each of which can be further subdivided based on the viewpoints of individual philosophers, have been influential during the past three centuries. Duty ethicists define right acts as those required by duties. Kant views duties as absolute (having no exceptions); however, Ross believes that duties are typically prima facie (i.e., they may have exceptions when they conflict with other duties). One's actual duty is determined by context-bound reasoning about which prima facie duty is most important on a specific occasion.

Rights ethicists define right acts as those that respect rights. Locke sees the basic human right as liberty, or the negative right not to be interfered with by others. Melden theorizes that the basic human right is to pursue one's legitimate interests, and he argues that we have welfare or positive rights to be helped by other members of a community.

Utilitarians reduce all obligations to one moral requirement: to produce the most good for the most people, giving equal consideration to each person affected. Mill defends act-utilitarianism, which requires each act to produce the most good, and he understands goodness to be happiness. Brandt favors rule-utilitarianism, which classifies right acts as those falling under a moral code (set of rules) that, if adopted in a specific society, would produce the most good. He construes goodness as the satisfaction of rational desires (those desires that survive scrutiny in light of all relevant facts).

Details matter. Differences within each ethical tradition are as or even more important than differences between traditions. For that reason, some applied ethicists pay little heed to abstract theory; others work within one or all of the traditions, paying attention to details; still others work in the tradition of pragmatism. Pragmatism accents the variety of values and the diversity of views that need to be integrated in practical contexts. Although it is a flexible moral approach, pragmatism leaves room for principles and ideals as focal points in moral reasoning.

DISCUSSION TOPICS

1 Was President Clinton justified in trying to conceal his sexual relationship with Monica Lewinsky by engaging in deception? Why or why not? What special circumstances, such as his family responsibilities and his being under investigation for what later became impeachment charges, bear on evaluating his lies?

2 In each of the instances a–e, decide whether it is permissible (all right), obligatory (required), or impermissible (wrong) to deceive. If you cannot answer, what other information do you need to know? Which moral considerations are relevant to each case according to duty ethics, rights ethics, act-utilitarianism, and rule-utilitarianism?

   a   You are invited to a party that you do not wish to attend. So as not to hurt the host's feelings, you lie, saying you have to go somewhere else that night.

   b   Persistent insomnia and nervousness send you to your doctor seeking tranquilizers. Your doctor discerns that the problem is psychosomatic, caused by temporary problems at home. When she cannot convince you of this, she says she will give you only one month's supply of tranquilizers. Unbeknownst to you, she writes a prescription for a placebo—a sugar pill—that actually calms you down because you believe it is a tranquilizer.

   c   You know your car needs major repairs, but you also need to sell it for more than it is worth in order to pay an overdue college tuition bill. When a potential buyer asks if anything is wrong with the car, you state emphatically that it is in great shape.

   d   Like 20 million other Americans, you have genital herpes, a viral disease, usually transmitted through sexual contact, whose symptoms range from painless blisters to extremely painful sores, shooting muscle pains, and fever. You have been celibate for fifteen months when the partner you are dating offers to change that. You very much desire to consent and do not think that the affair would be immoral. At the time, you have good reason to believe that the herpes is not contagious, because you have no open sores or incipient sores. In a half-joking tone your partner asks, "You don't have any medical problems, do you?" With similar playfulness you shake your head no.

   e   In a situation similar to the previous one, your potential partner this time lies to you to conceal the fact that he or she has AIDS, the deadly, sexually transmitted Acquired Immune Deficiency Syndrome.

3 In an essay titled "On a Supposed Right to Lie from Altruistic Motives," Kant argued that if we lie in an attempt to prevent a murder, we are legally and morally blameworthy for any ill effects of the lie:

> If by telling a lie you have prevented murder, you have made yourself legally responsible for all the consequences; but if you have held rigorously to the truth, public justice can lay no hand on you, whatever the unforeseen consequences may be. After you have honestly answered the murderer's question as to whether this intended victim is at home, it may be that he has slipped out so that he does not come in the way of the murderer, and thus that the murder may not be committed. But if you had lied and said he was not at home when he had really gone out without your knowing it, and if the murderer had then met him as he went away and murdered him, you might justly be accused as the cause of his death. For if you had told the

truth as far as you knew it, perhaps the murderer might have been apprehended by the neighbors while he searched the house and thus the deed might have been prevented. Therefore, whoever tells a lie, however well intentioned it might be, must answer for the consequences, however unforeseeable they were.[19]

Do you agree with Kant? In your answer, distinguish between the question of right and wrong conduct and the question of blameworthiness and guilt for wrongdoing.

Also, in commenting on Kant's view, consider a lie told in Jean-Paul Sartre's short story, "The Wall."[20] A soldier tries to deceive enemy interrogators by saying his compatriot is hidden at a cemetery. The soldier believes he is lying because he is confident that his compatriot is staying at a cousin's house, not at the cemetery. Unbeknownst to the soldier, the compatriot sneaks to the cemetery, where he is captured and shot by the enemy soldiers. Is the soldier guilty for the death of the compatriot?

4 List all the absolute moral principles you can think of; that is, all the moral principles for which you believe there are no permissible exceptions under any circumstances. Is it a long list?

5 The protagonist in Dostoevsky's novel *Crime and Punishment* plans and carries out the murder of a very wealthy pawnbroker. He does so with the intention of stealing her money and distributing it to poor people who desperately need it. The idea was inspired by the following remarks about the pawnbroker he overheard in a restaurant.

> On one side we have a stupid, senseless, worthless, spiteful, ailing, horrid old woman, not simply useless but doing actual mischief, who has not an idea what she is living for herself, and who will die in a day or two in any case. . . . On the other side, fresh young lives thrown away for want of help and by thousands, on every side! A hundred thousand good deeds could be done and helped, on that old woman's money. . . . Hundreds, thousands perhaps, might be set on the right path; dozens of families saved from destitution, from ruin, from vice. . . . Kill her, take her money and with the help of it devote oneself to the service of humanity and the good of all. What do you think, would not one tiny crime be wiped out by thousands of good deeds?[21]

How would a duty ethicist, a rights ethicist, an act-utilitarian, a rule-utilitarian, and a pragmatist respond to this question?

6 A person makes a promise to her or his dying parent; then the parent dies. Is the promise still binding? That is, is there any duty at all to keep it (assuming the promise is to do something that is not inherently immoral, such as kill someone)? How would utilitarians answer this question? How would duty and rights ethicists? Which provides the best answer?

7 William Frankena attempted to capture insights from both utilitarians and duty/rights ethics by setting forth two basic moral principles.[22] The principle of beneficence says the following four requirements should be met, in descending order of importance: Do not inflict harm; prevent harm; remove harm; promote good. The principle of justice says that in distributing goods and bads, treat people equally (unless very great good is produced by unequal treatment). Do you find such an approach promising?

SUGGESTED READINGS

Bok, Sissela. *Lying: Moral Choice in Public and Private Life*. New York: Vintage Books, 1979.

Brandt, Richard B. *A Theory of the Good and the Right*. Oxford: Clarendon Press, 1979.

Brandt, Richard B. *Facts, Values, and Morality*. Cambridge: Cambridge University Press, 1996

Dewey, John. *The Moral Writings of John Dewey*, ed. James Gouinlock. Amherst, NY: Prometheus Books, 1994.

Frankena, William K. *Ethics*. 2d ed. Englewood Cliffs, NJ: 1973.

Gert, Bernard. *Morality: Its Nature and Justification*. New York: Oxford University Press, 1998.

Gowans, Christopher W. (ed.). *Moral Dilemmas*. New York: Oxford University Press, 1987.

Griffin, James. *Value Judgement: Improving Our Ethical Beliefs*. Oxford: Clarendon Press, 1997.

Hill, Thomas E. *Dignity and Practical Reason in Kant's Moral Theory*. Ithaca, NY: Cornell University Press, 1992.

Kant, Immanuel. *Foundations of the Metaphysics of Morals*. Trans. L. W. Beck. New York: Liberal Arts Press, 1959.

Locke, John. *Two Treatises of Government*. Cambridge: Cambridge University Press, 1960.

Melden, A. I. (ed.). *Ethical Theories: A Book of Readings*. 2d ed. Englewood Cliffs, NJ: Prentice-Hall, 1967.

Melden, A. I. *Rights and Persons*. Berkeley, CA: University of California Press, 1977.

Mill, John Stuart. *Utilitarianism*. Indianapolis, IN: Hackett, 1979.

Narveson, Jan. *The Libertarian Idea*. Philadelphia, PA: Temple University Press, 1988.

Norman, Richard. *The Moral Philosophers: An Introduction to Ethics*. 2d ed. Oxford: Oxford University Press, 1998.

Nybert, David. *The Varnished Truth: Truth Telling and Deceiving in Ordinary Life*. Chicago: University of Chicago Press, 1993.

Pojman, Louis P. (ed.). *Ethical Theory: Classical and Contemporary Readings*. 3d ed. Belmont, CA: Wadsworth, 1997.

Rachels, James. *The Elements of Moral Philosophy*. 3d ed. New York: McGraw-Hill, 1999.

Rawls, John. *A Theory of Justice*. Cambridge, MA: Harvard University Press, 1971 (the most influential Kantian of the 20th century).

Ross, David. *The Right and the Good*. Oxford: Clarendon Press, 1930.

Singer, Peter (ed.). *Ethics*. New York: Oxford University Press, 1994.

Smart, J. J. C., and Bernard Williams. *Utilitarianism: For and Against*. Cambridge: Cambridge University Press, 1973.

Wallace, James D. *Moral Relevance and Moral Conflict*. Ithaca: Cornell University Press, 1988.

Theories of Virtue

Everyday patterns of living both manifest and mold character. This chapter introduces key ideas of some influential *virtue ethicists:* Plato, Aristotle, Aquinas, Hume, MacIntyre, and Pincoffs. According to these philosophers, the moral aim of life is to be a good person—to have a virtuous character and to relate to other people in desirable ways. Right conduct is important, but its role is to express and to support good character.

Virtues as Desirable Character Traits

What is a virtue? It is a trait of character that is desirable because it contributes to the good of humans (and sometimes of animals). Usually the human good includes both the good of the person who has the trait and the good effected by that person. In contrast, a vice is an undesirable trait of character that causes unjustified harm to people (or animals).

What is a trait of character? It is a general feature of a person that is manifested in patterns of actions, intentions, emotions, desires, attitudes, and reasoning. Virtues thus involve, but are not reducible to, actions. Virtues involve tendencies to act *in the right spirit*—that is, for the right reasons, with the right intentions, motivated by appropriate emotions, desires, and attitudes. Moreover, character traits can be revealed not only through actions, but also in feelings, wants, intentions, hopes, interests, attitudes, thoughts, reasoning, relationships, and speech—hence, in essentially every dimension of a human life.

As an illustration of how character traits involve more than acts, consider the difference between beneficent (helping) acts and the virtue of benevolence. Imagine a wealthy person making a very large donation to a charity that distributes food and shelter to the needy. Considered by itself, the act can be called a beneficent one. Does it necessarily follow that the person is benevolent (concerned for others), at least on this occasion? No, for suppose the government had just passed a law allowing large tax deductions for contributions to this charity. Suppose, also, that the sole reason the individual made the donation was to gain the deduction, based on the strong recommendation of a financial advisor. Perhaps the person even feels some regret about the donation and wishes that a better tax deduction had been available, yet takes some consolation from the public recognition he or she receives after making sure that others learn about the donation.

Benevolent people are kindhearted, generous, of good will. Their actions often spring from concern for the well-being of others. They experience satisfaction in seeing someone helped and in being the one who helps. It is their hope, wish, desire, and intention to benefit others, and they act with the aim of doing so.

In general, virtues require that we act with appropriate attitudes and commitments. They require our actions to be motivated by a perception of the moral good to be achieved rather than by ulterior self-seeking motives alone. Virtues involve our inner life, which defines us just as much as do our actions.

Human Nature and Virtue Theories

Traditional theories of virtue are grounded in theories about human nature, that is, theories about what it means to be a human being. Human nature is described in terms of the capacities, possibilities, limitations, and aspirations of people. Virtues are the character traits that enable people to achieve the good that is possible for them. Virtue theories also offer systematic frameworks revealing the connections among the various virtues and explaining which are most fundamental. Theories of virtue seek to do three things: (1) provide a theory of human nature that identifies morally relevant facts about human possibilities; (2) use that theory of human nature to define those character traits, or virtues, that enable people to achieve the good made possible by their nature; and (3) present a schema for understanding the relationships among the virtues.

Plato and Aristotle, the two great Greek ethicists inspired by Socrates, base their theories of human nature on a key assumption: that reasoning is the primary purpose or function that sets humans apart from other creatures. In their view, virtues are the excellences that enable humans to exercise their powers of reasoning and live accordingly. Hence, to be virtuous is to live effectively the distinctive form of life for humans.

Plato: Moral Health

According to Plato, the function of something is the task that it is best or uniquely suited to perform. As an example he noted that many objects can be used to trim vines: a carving knife, a chisel, fingernails, or a sharp rock.

Only a pruning knife, however, is perfectly suited to the task. Hence, pruning is the function of pruning knives but not of the other objects.

As another example Plato noted that parts of the body have functions to which they are especially well suited: eyes for seeing, ears for hearing, and lungs for breathing. And workers also have professional functions defined by their social roles: for physicians, promoting health; for soldiers, defending the country; for teachers, teaching. By analogy he concluded that humans have a distinctive function to which their lives as a whole are best suited: to exercise, and live by, reason.

Plato developed this thesis by distinguishing three main parts of the mind (or soul): Reason, the Spirited Element, and the Appetites. Each has a characteristic function to perform. Reason coordinates and directs the diverse activities of the individual. The Spirited Element, which we might call a sense of honor or pride, has the task of supporting reason in controlling the Appetites. Even though Reason has its own motives for self-control, the Spirited Element is needed to strengthen Reason's ability to maintain control and to avoid shameful conduct. The Appetites maintain the body by satisfying physical cravings for food, drink, exercise, and sex; but they also include undesirable urges.

Why did Plato divide the mind into three parts? These divisions seemed to him to explain psychological conflict. For example, a person has a desire to eat too much and also a directly opposed desire not to overeat. These conflicting desires suggest that one part of the person, Reason, is at war with another part, the Appetites.

Wrongdoing occurs when Reason and the Spirited Element are unable to control the Appetites. Immoral action is thus a symptom of a disordered personality whose proper functions are out of balance. In contrast, morally right action is a sign of inner harmony, in which each part of the mind performs its function well. Virtues make this harmony possible.

Each mental part has its own distinctive virtue that enables it to perform its function with excellence. (The Greek word for excellence, ARETE, also translates as "virtue.") *Wisdom* is the virtue that enables Reason to effectively guide both the Appetites and the Spirited Element. *Courage* makes it possible for the Spirited Element to support Reason in controlling troublesome Appetites. *Temperance,* or moderation, enables the Appetites to be satisfied to a healthy degree and without overindulgence. *Justice* is simply a summary label indicating the presence of the other three virtues: The just (or moral) person is someone whose Reason wisely supervises the Appetites in a temperate manner with the help of a courageous Spirited Element. The four classical Greek virtues, then, are wisdom, courage, temperance, and justice.*

---

*In the *Republic,* Plato develops an elaborate analogy between good character (inner harmony) in individuals and moral justice in countries (or city–states). He divides countries into three main parts—Rulers, Guardians (police and military), and Producers (farmers and businessperople)—each with a corresponding virtue: wisdom, courage, and temperance.

Just as Reason is the most important faculty of humans, wisdom is the most important virtue. In fact, wisdom makes possible all the other virtues. The insight it provides guides the Spirited Element and determines how far the Appetites should be restrained or indulged. Thus, genuine courage and temperance are expressions of wisdom. Plato also believed that complete wisdom would automatically lead to courage and temperance and hence to justice. This belief is called the Doctrine of the Unity of the Virtues: to fully have any one of the main virtues is to have them all.

Plato also applied the idea of virtue as inner harmony in defending another controversial doctrine: that the life of virtue is the happy life. Today we do not think of virtue and happiness as necessarily connected; a good person might be unhappy, and a very bad person might be happy. By happiness, however, Plato did not mean emotional contentment or satisfaction with life. Instead he meant self-fulfillment. He was convinced that the fulfilling life was guided by the virtues, which bring inner harmony. Moreover, he argued, because wisdom makes inner harmony possible and because people gain wisdom through philosophical reflection, the most happy life was that of the philosopher!

Aristotle: Rational Emotions and Desires

Even if there existed a supernatural Form of the Good inaccessible to the senses, Aristotle asserted, it would have no relevance to morality. Morality is concerned with practical understanding within this world of experience. Goodness is known through practical endeavors and relationships rather than through semimystical encounters with supernatural entities.

Nevertheless, Aristotle accepted virtually all of Plato's other main ethical doctrines. He agreed that the distinctive function of humans is to exercise reason. Good character entails reasoning in accord with wisdom. In turn, wisdom brings with it happiness, understood as well-being and self-fulfillment. And the highest form of happiness is a life based on philosophical reflection.

Aristotle developed these themes in rich detail, the intricacies of which defy brief summarization. Here we will focus on his central doctrine concerning the virtues: the Doctrine of the Mean, or the Doctrine of the Golden Mean, as it has since been called. The Doctrine of the Mean is intended to apply only to moral virtues such as courage, temperance, justice, and generosity, which Aristotle distinguished from intellectual virtues such as wisdom, intelligence, and prudence. The two groups of virtues are intimately connected in that intellectual virtues are necessary for complete moral virtue (just as Plato believed that wisdom makes the other virtues possible). However, the moral and intellectual virtues differ in two respects.

First, intellectual virtues represent excellences in reasoning skills that can be taught through inquiry and study. Moral virtues, by contrast, are products of habits that begin in childhood and are strengthened in adult life. For example, intellectual understanding of the virtues can be taught in an ethics course, but prudence and courage in confronting danger must evolve from habitual acts of facing risks with discipline and self-control.

Second, there are no limits on the skills and desires involved in exercising intellectual virtues; when it comes to insight and careful reasoning, more is indeed better. By contrast, the moral virtues are defined precisely by limits. That is, moral virtues are tendencies to seek and to identify an intermediate point, or mean, between two extreme desires, emotions, or actions. At one extreme is excess (too much), while at the other extreme is deficiency or defect (too little): "Moral virtue is . . . a mean between two vices, one of excess and the other of deficiency, and . . . it aims at hitting the mean point in feelings and actions."[1] That is, moral virtues involve our ability to regularly discern and act on the appropriate middle ground between extremes (of feeling and action), assuming we are not prevented by external obstacles. In this sense, moral virtues are dispositions or habits.

Each moral virtue is directed toward a specific range or spectrum of emotions, desires, and actions. For example, courage consists of excellence in responding to danger and in experiencing fear and confidence. Cowards feel fear on inappropriate occasions or respond to fear and danger without confidence and self-control (that is, they are deficient in self-confidence or self-control). At the other end of the spectrum are foolhardy or rash people, who increase their chances of harm by being excessively confident. Because courage involves *appropriate* confidence and self-control in confronting dangers—which serves to minimize the likelihood of harm—it represents the mean between too little daring and confidence (the defect of cowardice) and too much (the excess of foolhardiness).

Temperance, proper pride, and friendliness are other virtues that were especially important for Aristotle and classical Greek society. Temperance is the tendency to hit the mean between unrestrained indulgence of the appetites (the excess of gluttony) and too little enthusiasm for the pleasures of the appetites (the defect of lacking lively tastes and being inhibited). Proper pride is the mean between self-glorification (the excess of vanity) and insufficient self-confidence (the defect of "poor-spiritedness," which today we might call an inferiority complex). Friendliness is the mean between disingenuous flattery of others (the excess of obsequiousness) and aloofness or surliness (the defect of rudeness). Table 3.1 summarizes these and other virtues that Aristotle discussed (the terminology is updated in a few places).[2]

It may come as a surprise to see wittiness included in the table, since we do not generally think of wit and a sense of humor as moral virtues. For Aristotle, however, *all* desirable qualities of persons were virtues, either moral or intellectual; thus, wit, friendliness, good manners, and social decorum all counted as excellences.[3]

Aristotle intended his Doctrine of the Mean to apply to emotions and desires as well as to the actions they motivate. The Doctrine of the Mean is

TABLE 3.1 *Summary of the Virtues as Discussed by Aristotle*

Sphere of Action: Kind of Situation	Type of Emotion, Desire, Attitude	Vice of Too Much (Excess)	Virtue (Mean)	Vice of Too Little (Deficiency or Defect)
Responses to danger	Fear, confidence	Foolhardiness	Courage	Cowardice
Satisfaction of appetites	Physical pleasure	Overindulgence	Temperance	Inhibition
Giving gifts	Desire to help	Extravagance	Generosity	Miserliness
Pursuit of accomplishments	Desire to succeed	Vaulting ambition	Proper ambition	Unambitiousness
Appraisal of oneself	Self-confidence	Vanity	Proper pride	Sense of inferiority
Self-expression	Desire to be recognized	Boastfulness	Truthfulness	False modesty
Response to insults	Anger	Irascibility	Patience	Apathy
Social conduct	Attitudes to others	Obsequiousness	Friendliness	Rudeness
Awareness of one's flaws	Shame	Shyness	Modesty	Shamelessness
Conversation, humor	Amusement	Buffoonery	Wittiness	Boorishness

a theory about rational desires and morally desirable emotions. This may seem problematic: We tend to think of morality as concerned with what is under our immediate control, which appears to rule out emotions from a discussion of morality. Recall, however, that Aristotle regarded moral virtues as the product of years of training in proper habits and modes of response that shape emotions and desires.

Virtue consists in "hitting the mean" of emotions and desires as well as of the actions they motivate; but how is this mean determined? Is it simply moderation in the sense that our feelings and desires should always be "lukewarm," never very strong or very weak? Definitely not! Very strong emotions—even distressing emotions such as anger or very exciting emotions such as joy, love, and political enthusiasm—often are precisely the mean in the sense that they are morally reasonable. Hence, the maxim "moderation in all things" does not accurately express Aristotle's view. Furthermore, if mere emotional calm were the goal, virtue would be relatively easy to identify. As Aristotle emphasizes, this is not the case.

It is a difficult business to be good; because in any given case it is difficult to find the midpoint—for instance, not everyone can find the center of a circle; only the man who knows how. So too it is easy to get angry—anyone can do that—or to give and spend money; but to feel or act towards the right person to the right extent at the right time for the right reason in the right way—that is not easy, and it is not everyone that can do it. Hence to do these things well is a rare, laudable, and fine achievement.[4]

The mean, as Aristotle defines it, is not the lukewarm, but instead the morally reasonable. Reasonable emotions and desires are those directed toward the appropriate person or object, on the suitable occasion, for the correct reason, and with fitting intensity. Unfortunately, this is not very informative: Aristotle seems to move in a circle that does not advance understanding. Having explained morally reasonable conduct in terms of finding the mean, he then explains the mean in terms of morally reasonable conduct. Virtue may indeed be the mean between extremes, and the mean may indeed be the virtuous middle ground between two nonvirtuous extremes. But how is the virtuous middle ground determined?

Aristotle offers two ways out of the circle. First, for each virtue he analyzes in detail the many occasions and motives appropriate to it and its characteristic sphere of action, emotion, and desire. Many of these analyses remain helpful starting points for more precise contemporary discussions of the virtues. Second, Aristotle insists there is a limit to how far such analyses can go. Morality is too complex and too imprecise to be captured in simple rules. It requires the finely tuned sensitivity of wise and prudent individuals. Indeed, Aristotle completes his definition of virtue by alluding to such individuals: "So virtue is a purposive disposition, lying in a mean that is relative to us and determined by a rational principle, and by that which a prudent man would use to determine it."[5] By *rational principle* Aristotle does not mean an abstract rule, but instead the exercise of sound practical judgment.

Critics of Aristotle charge that this ultimate appeal to moral prudence is as much a dead end as Plato's fruitless appeal to the Form of the Good. Most of the rule-oriented ethicists discussed in Chapter 2 also criticize Aristotle for failing to look further for general rules about right action.

Yet perhaps Aristotle is simply being true to the moral facts! Even though rational emotions and desires are an essential aspect of the moral life, they defy precise formulation in abstract rules, which cannot express the intricacies of the actual circumstances. Moreover, the subtleties of moral insight and sensitivity that develop through years of experience, study, and habit formation cannot be reduced to simple generalizations.

Difficulties with Greek Ethics

Much of classical Greek ethics has contemporary relevance, such as Plato's idea of virtue as moral health (an idea we develop in Chapter 21) and Aristotle's

ts into practical reasoning. Yet Greek ethics rests on three questionable
: (1) Human beings have one distinctive function; (2) that function is
reasoning; and (3) because this function is distinctively human, it defines
human good (as life in accord with reason). Many contemporary ethicists
would reject all these claims.

To begin with the third questionable claim, is it obvious that the dis-
tinctiveness of a function should define goodness? How do we move from
"is distinctive of" to "is the basis of goodness"? (Recall a similar problem
raised in discussing Ayn Rand in Chapter 1: How do we move from "is" to
"ought"?) It is also distinctive of humans that they display more cruelty
than any other earthly creature, but obviously that capacity does not define
the good. Perhaps human good lies instead in developing capacities that are
shared with other mammals; for example, the capacity to care for members
of one's species, or even for members of other species. (Here we think of
Koko, the gorilla who lovingly raised a kitten.)

Concerning the second questionable claim, is it true that reasoning is
distinctive of human beings? Today we know that some mammals, such as
gorillas, chimpanzees, and dolphins, have remarkable reasoning capacities.
Admittedly there are great differences of degree between their reasoning capacities and ours. That is also true, however, of many other shared capacities, such as caring for others, forming social ties, or even enjoying
sophisticated physical pleasures—capacities that Plato and Aristotle refused
to regard as distinctively human.

Turning to the first questionable claim, is it true that humans have just
one distinctive function? Humans do many things better than members of
other species. Perhaps most of those things involve reasoning in the very
wide sense of making inferences and thinking cogently; however, this wide
sense of "reason" is too broad to define what is good for humans. Such reasoning is also used in pursuing ingenious forms of evil, as well as sophisticated forms of play, work, and inquiry. Moreover, what about capacities
that are not reducible to reason, such as living by religious faith or being
altruistic?

Aquinas: Religious Virtues

Emphasis on human capacities other than reason has formed the basis for
alternative theories about human nature and virtue. Let us briefly consider
two of these theories, one stressing religious faith and the other stressing
altruism.

Like other religious traditions, the Christian tradition defines human nature by reference to faith in God. Saint Thomas Aquinas (1224–1274) is of
special interest because he developed his virtue ethics as a synthesis of the
Greeks' four cardinal virtues—wisdom, courage, temperance, and justice—
and the key Christian virtues—faith, hope, and charity (love).

Aquinas agreed with Plato and Aristotle that the one purpose of human beings is to live by reason and that pursuing this purpose results in well-being or happiness. Aquinas, however, saw the primary role of reason was to prove that God exists and to discern the "natural law" that God built into our very nature. Hence, for Aquinas, the natural purpose in living by reason became a supernatural purpose: supreme happiness through communion with God, a happiness imperfectly realizable in this world and perfected only in life after death.

Aquinas thought that wisdom (the paramount Greek virtue) implies the theological virtues of faith, hope, and love. He also thought he could use wise reasoning to give several proofs that God exists. Then, from the premise that God is loving and commands that we love, Aquinas derived the virtue of love for God and for humanity. Faith became fidelity to God's commandments with the hope of salvation. The other Greek virtues were also reinterpreted along Christian lines. Courage became the virtue that enables us to endure the dangers of this world, in particular the temptations of sin on the journey toward salvation. Temperance was expanded to include patience and humility, fasting and chastity.

Aquinas's approach to the virtues differs greatly from Aristotle's. For example, Aristotle would view the Christian virtue of humility as more like the vice of failing to have proper pride. Christian discipline of the body through chastity and fasting hardly jibe with the Greek exuberance in the physical. And the idea of charity as the virtue of loving all humankind would be alien to Aristotle, who valued only those exceptional people who achieved high degrees of virtue.

Even more foreign to Aristotle and Plato would be the Christian idea of sin as betrayal of God. For Aquinas and other orthodox Christians, pride, in the sense of setting oneself above God by refusing to live by God's commandments, is the worst sin. By contrast, Aristotle did not view pride in this sense as a vice at all. Earlier than Aquinas, the monastic movement had stressed seven deadly sins: pride, envy (covetousness), anger, sloth, avarice, gluttony, and lust. Aristotle would not have regarded at least two of these—anger and lust—as vices; nor would he have singled out the others as the worst failures of virtue.

Hume: Benevolence and Sympathy

Now consider a very different kind of virtue ethics, the one offered by David Hume (1711–1776). Hume was a skeptic who incisively criticized Aquinas's attempts to offer proofs of God's existence. His view of human nature was based neither on religious faith nor on praise of reason, but rather on the psychology of his day combined with his own attempts to explain the origin of virtue. Yet there is an important overlap between Hume and Aquinas: Both view benevolence as a central virtue. Hume makes it the supreme virtue, and hence of all virtue ethicists Hume most deserves to be called the philosopher of benevolence.[6]

Hume divided the human mind into the domains of reason and sentiment. Unlike Plato, Aristotle, and Aquinas, Hume argued that reason does not provide the moral ends of human life. It merely identifies facts and logical relationships among ideas. Moral purposes in human life derive from sentiment—that is, from our emotional capacities and attitudes. One sentiment in particular is crucial: sympathy, which is the capacity and tendency to feel distress when we see others in distress, and to be pleased when we see them happy. Sympathy, for Hume, is not a virtue, but it enables us to identify and appreciate virtues. It makes us naturally inclined to approve of benevolence in all its forms.

> It may be esteemed, perhaps, a superfluous task to prove, that the benevolent or softer affections are estimable; and wherever they appear, engage the approbation and good-will of mankind. The epithets *sociable, good-natured, humane, merciful, grateful, friendly, generous, beneficent,* or their equivalents, are known in all languages, and universally express the highest merit, which *human nature* is capable of attaining.[7]

Accordingly, for Hume the worst vice is cruelty, not ignorance (as Plato and Aristotle thought) or pride (as Aquinas thought).

In Hume's view, reason does play an important role in morality by providing information about how to act virtuously and by enabling us to adopt an impartial point of view that counteracts bias and ensures consistency. Reason also aids in the development of useful social conventions about how best to distribute property. Because societies differ so greatly, Hume recognizes as legitimate variations in the social conventions that define justice. He also refers to justice as an "artificial virtue," that is, one defined by social conventions, in contrast with the "natural virtue" of benevolence, which recommends certain responses independently of laws and customs.

From Theory to Practice

Our four classical theories of virtue all attempt to identify distinctive human capacities and use them to show the direction of human good and self-fulfillment. Yet these theories are founded on ideas of human nature that differ greatly, some stressing reason, others faith, and still others sympathy. Which theory of human nature is correct or best?

Whereas theoretical ethics has the luxury of engaging in subtle disputes over these theories—as it has done for many centuries—applied ethics must proceed with the urgent task of addressing practical moral needs. Because applied ethicists cannot hope to resolve all theoretical disputes before proceeding, it may seem that the theories are irrelevant for our purposes. Alternatively, should each of us simply choose a theory we find personally appealing and apply it to practical issues?

The view advanced in this book is that the applied ethicists—you and I—are justified in bypassing abstract disputes about human nature and the ultimate theoretical foundations for the virtues. We are free to borrow from any and all theories that offer insights into practical concerns. Notice that we have begun to do that already by emphasizing Plato's notion of inner harmony, an idea of contemporary relevance. We have also focused on Aristotle's Doctrine of the Mean independently of his theoretical contentions about the function of humans. To continue in this eclectic way does not lead to methodological chaos. It simply indicates a desire to benefit from the practical wisdom of great thinkers, a wisdom that can be disentangled from their more debatable speculations.

MacIntyre: Self-Knowledge and Social Goods

This approach to the rich legacy of philosophical theory is in tune with the works of two recent virtue ethicists: Alasdair MacIntyre in *After Virtue* and Edmund L. Pincoffs in *Quandaries and Virtues*. Both MacIntyre and Pincoffs retrieve and develop central concepts from the tradition of virtue ethics while freeing them from any narrow view of human nature.

MacIntyre retains the hope of grounding the virtues in a theory of human nature, perhaps one emerging from contemporary social science. In this and other respects he can lay claim to an Aristotelian perspective. Yet, unlike Aristotle, he stresses that individuals find their good in an enormous variety of ways. He is sensitive to the great range of settings and legitimate emphases on particular virtues that individuals might reasonably embrace. Above all, he emphasizes that the good for an individual cannot be spelled out all at once in advance on the basis of abstract notions such as "reason." Instead, it must be uncovered piecemeal by each of us through a continuing search for self-knowledge.

MacIntyre views each human life as a "narrative quest": a search through time, with intricate threads connecting past, present, and hoped-for future. The quest is a search for self-fulfillment that also allows us to maintain unity among our activities and relationships. At every step there is uncertainty, unpredictability, conflict, and confusion. Hence, we have a recurring need to reexamine our purposes and our grasp of the good. In this sense a human life "is always an [ongoing] education both as to the character of that which is sought and in self-knowledge."[8]

Virtues in this view represent qualities that support us in this pursuit of our good; they do not represent a complete vision of what that good is. MacIntyre writes: "The good life for man is the life spent in seeking for the good life for man, and the virtues necessary for the seeking are those which will enable us to understand what more and what else the good life for man is."[9] This aspect of MacIntyre's theory reminds us more of Socrates' ongoing search for a meaningful life, with the virtues as aids in that search, than of Plato's and Aristotle's belief that the virtues fully define the good and happy life.

Yet the quest for our good and its supporting virtues is not conducted in a vacuum. Many of its key ingredients derive from *social practices*—complex forms of cooperative human activity, such as professions, academic disciplines in science and the humanities, the fine arts, political institutions, families, and even games like chess. Each such practice is directed toward its distinctive "internal goods," that is, toward desirable ends that partially define the practice itself. For example, the profession of medicine aims at health, law aims at social justice, and family life aims at intimate relationships. Achieving these internal goods is largely made possible by the practice itself. In contrast, "external goods" like money, power, and fame do not define the nature of a social practice; they can be achieved in many other ways besides engaging in a particular practice.

Virtues are traits that enable individuals effectively to pursue these internal goods and thereby to enrich their lives. As it pertains to practices, MacIntyre defines a virtue as "an acquired human quality the possession and exercise of which tends to enable us to achieve those goods which are internal to practices and the lack of which effectively prevents us from achieving any such goods."[10] For example, conscientiousness, trustworthiness, loyalty, benevolent concern for the public good, and respect for colleagues are virtues that contribute to the successful pursuit of the internal goods of most professions.

Virtues also help make social practices prosper. Without displays of virtue by many individuals, the practices could not survive or advance. For example, courage in undertaking risks and challenges makes possible the advancement of medicine. Honesty in being careful about facts is essential to all professional practices. And justice plays a role in the recognition of proper authority and respect for others' contributions to a profession.

Each of us participates in many practices, and those forms of participation can come into conflict. Familiar examples might include professional versus private life, college studies versus parental demands, one friendship versus another. The virtues, especially practical wisdom, enable us to integrate the numerous roles we play in various practices and keep them in proper perspective. MacIntyre's most complete characterization of the virtues as aids to our achievement of unity and self-fulfillment is in the following sentence:

> The virtues . . . are to be understood as those dispositions which will not only sustain practices and enable us to achieve the goods internal to practices, but which will also sustain us in the relevant kind of quest for the good, by enabling us to overcome the harms, dangers, temptations and situations which we encounter, and which will furnish us with increasing self-knowledge and increasing knowledge of the good.[11]

In addition to their role in relation to practices, the virtues are exercised within particular moral traditions that individuals inherit. The good for members of particular families, religions, nations, and cultures is not altogether the same as for others.[12] We are free to modify, but not altogether remove, the influence of the traditions within which we conduct our personal quest for the good. Sometimes, in fact, to deny their influence and relevance is immoral, as in the case of those Americans who deny any responsibility for dealing with contemporary racism on the grounds that they never owned slaves or killed Indians. In his most recent book, *Dependent Rational Animals,* MacIntyre accents our shared vulnerabilities to disabilities and our mutual dependencies that require virtues of mutual caring and support.

Pincoffs: Choices Among Persons

Edmund L. Pincoffs is another contemporary theorist who frees virtue ethics from any narrow theory of human nature. Pincoffs, however, criticizes MacIntyre for focusing so much on practices. In Pincoffs's view, the primary focus in understanding the virtues should be choices among persons rather than social practices: "The natural home of the language of virtue and vice is in that region of our lives in which we must choose between, not acts, lines of acting, or policies, but persons."[13] Choosing among persons has many dimensions: choosing to pursue personal relationships with individuals such as friends, lovers, or a spouse; deciding how to raise children; picking people for a job or public office; and choosing a lawyer, physician, or other professional for some service. It also includes making nuanced adjustments in relationships.

Although Pincoffs is critical of all attempts to confine the virtues within a theory of human nature, he sees it as a legitimate task to organize and clarify connections among the virtues. His classification scheme is depicted in Figure 3.1.[14] As the figure indicates, Pincoffs, like Aristotle, includes as virtues (which are special instances of personality traits) all excellences of the personality, not just moral excellences. Unlike Aristotle, however, he tries to distinguish between moral virtues and nonmoral good traits like wit, social decorum, and noble bearing. Let us briefly explain the terms he uses as headings in the figure.

Instrumental virtues are traits that enable people to pursue their goals effectively or to perform tasks well, whether as individuals (*agent instrumental virtues* such as persistence) or as part of a group (*group instrumental virtues* such as cooperativeness). *Noninstrumental virtues* are traits that are inherently desirable, whether or not they serve as means to further ends. Some noninstrumental virtues, such as nobility and charm, are aesthetic, that is, aspects of beauty. Others are *meliorating;* they make life with other people more tolerable. Meliorating virtues include those of tolerance, tact,

FIGURE 3.1 *Pincoffs's Classification of Virtues*

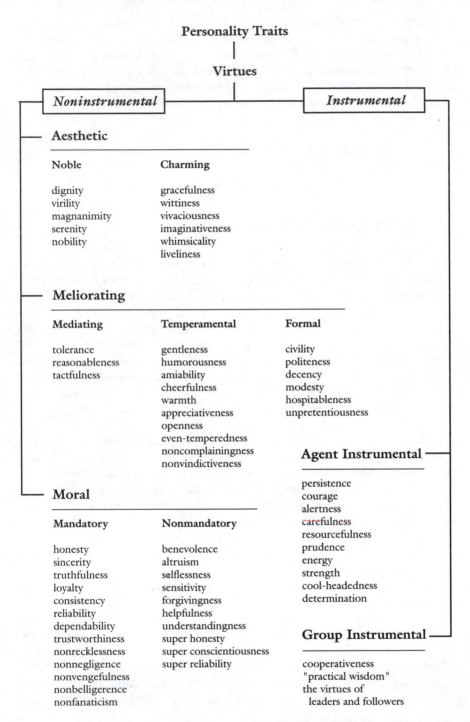

Personality Traits
|
Virtues

| Noninstrumental | Instrumental |

Aesthetic

Noble	Charming
dignity	gracefulness
virility	wittiness
magnanimity	vivaciousness
serenity	imaginativeness
nobility	whimsicality
	liveliness

Meliorating

Mediating	Temperamental	Formal
tolerance	gentleness	civility
reasonableness	humorousness	politeness
tactfulness	amiability	decency
	cheerfulness	modesty
	warmth	hospitableness
	appreciativeness	unpretentiousness
	openness	
	even-temperedness	
	noncomplainingness	
	nonvindictiveness	

Agent Instrumental

persistence
courage
alertness
carefulness
resourcefulness
prudence
energy
strength
cool-headedness
determination

Moral

Mandatory	Nonmandatory
honesty	benevolence
sincerity	altruism
truthfulness	selflessness
loyalty	sensitivity
consistency	forgivingness
reliability	helpfulness
dependability	understandingness
trustworthiness	super honesty
nonrecklessness	super conscientiousness
nonnegligence	super reliability
nonvengefulness	
nonbelligerence	
nonfanaticism	

Group Instrumental

cooperativeness
"practical wisdom"
the virtues of
   leaders and followers

Source: Edmund L. Pincoffs. *Quandaries and Virtues: Against Relativism in Ethics.* Lawrence, KS: University Press of Kansas, 1986. p 85. © 1986 University Press of Kansas. Reprinted by permission of the publisher.

and other qualities of peacemakers and negotiators (mediating virtues); virtues such as gentleness and cheerfulness, which make individuals more pleasant to live with (temperamental virtues); and traits such as politeness and decency, which make interactions more pleasant (formal virtues).

Finally we arrive at the specifically *moral virtues.* According to Pincoffs, moral

> virtues and vices have the common characteristic that they are forms of regard or lack of regard for the interests of others. They are, roughly, of two closely related classes: those that have to do with direct concern or lack of concern for the interests of other persons, on the one hand, and those that have to do with the unfair advantage that one accords to one's own interests over the interests of others.[15]

For Pincoffs, forgoing unfair advantages to ourselves is the minimal requirement of morality, and it is a firm requirement. The *mandatory virtues* pertain to this area of morality. Honesty, truthfulness, and nonrecklessness, for example, are always required. The *nonmandatory virtues,* by contrast, indicate desirable, though not obligatory, traits. Their presence in a person is good, but their absence need not indicate a vice. This is true of benevolence, altruism, forgivingness, and exceptional ("super") degrees of honesty and conscientiousness.

It is possible to accept Pincoffs's main distinctions while objecting to his classification of specific virtues. For example, some of the virtues he lists as nonmoral, such as tolerance, appreciativeness, and decency, might better be regarded as moral virtues, at least insofar as they are forms of direct regard for the interests of other people.

Another objection concerns his characterization of the "natural home" of the virtues as those matters in which we must choose among persons, which oddly centers virtue ethics on acts (acts of choosing among people). It might be closer to the truth to say that virtues guide our *evaluations of* and *attitudes toward* persons, as well as our *relationships with* them. Moreover, choosing among persons, even in Pincoffs's wide sense of choosing, represents only one dimension of evaluating them. Other dimensions include understanding, encouraging, being inspired by, pitying, and criticizing them.

To say that the virtues guide only our evaluations of other persons, however, is still too restrictive. The virtues are just as important in shaping and fulfilling our own lives and, as MacIntyre argued, in evaluating practices. Moreover, the virtues serve as guides for all our actions, not just those of choosing among persons. Very often moral reasoning and guidance arise from asking what is the honest, decent, considerate, or courageous thing to do. Admittedly, this guidance is rough, as Aristotle emphasized; but the point is that virtues play multiple "natural" roles in our lives, guiding actions, habits, participation in practices, and relationships, as well as guiding choices among persons.

Beyond noting these criticisms, we need not choose between MacIntyre's and Pincoffs's theories. Each offers enriching theoretical frameworks for doing applied ethics without entering into disputes over theories of human nature.

SUMMARY

Virtues are desirable character traits consisting of patterns of emotions, desires, attitudes, intentions, and reasoning as well as actions. Classical virtue theories sought to link the virtues to particular theories about human nature, that is, about the distinctive or most significant human capacities and possibilities. Virtues were then defined as excellences that enable people to achieve their good by fulfilling their human nature. Virtue theories also identified the virtues most important for self-fulfillment. Table 3.2 summarizes some key concepts discussed in four classical theories of virtue.

Applied ethics bypasses theoretical disputes over which aspects of human nature are most significant for understanding morality and which virtues are paramount. Applied ethicists are free to draw on insights from all virtue theories whenever they are helpful in dealing with practical concerns. MacIntyre and Pincoffs have provided theories of virtue that offer frameworks for doing applied ethics of this sort. MacIntyre defines the virtues as desirable traits that bring unity to the lives of people whose specific good is constantly being reshaped through participation in practices, moral traditions, and personal relationships. Pincoffs defines the virtues as excellences used in choosing among persons. For our purposes, the virtues are best viewed as desirable traits that guide our attitudes toward other people and provide ideals for shaping our own lives and relationships. Pincoffs also offers a classification of the virtues and distinguishes the moral virtues as forms of regard for others' interests.

TABLE 3.2 *Four Classical Theories of Virtue*

Theorist	View of Human Nature	Main Concepts	Paramount Virtues	Worst Vice
Plato	Exercise reason to achieve happiness	Moral health as inner harmony	Wisdom, courage, temperance, justice	Ignorance
Aristotle	Exercise reason to achieve happiness	Golden Mean	Wisdom, courage, temperance, justice	Ignorance
Aquinas	God's plan leading to happiness after death	Faith; sin	Faith, hope, charity	Pride
Hume	Sentiment vs. reason	Sympathy	Benevolence	Cruelty

DISCUSSION TOPICS

1   Discuss Plato's (and Aristotle's) Doctrine of the Unity of the Virtues, which says that to have any one of the main virtues is to have them all. This doctrine contradicts common sense, which tells us that people can be courageous but not benevolent, or honest but not temperate. Is Plato's doctrine plausible only as applied to the four main virtues he discusses, indeed, only if those virtues are perfectly achieved? In particular, do complete temperance and courage require wisdom?

2   Plato divided the mind into three parts in order to explain inner conflict and to understand mental health. Discuss whether his distinctions are plausible and helpful. Compare and contrast them with Hume's distinction between the sentiments and reason.

3   Plato described the relationship between good character and right conduct in the following passage.

> Justice [i.e., morality] . . . is not a matter of external behavior, but of the inward self and of attending to all that is, in the fullest sense, a man's proper concern. The just man does not allow the several elements in his soul to usurp one another's functions; he is indeed one who sets his house in order, by self-mastery and discipline coming to be at peace with himself. . . . When he speaks of just and honorable conduct, he will mean the behavior that helps to produce and to preserve this habit of mind; and by wisdom he will mean the knowledge which presides over such conduct. Any action which tends to break down this habit will be for him unjust; and the notions governing it he will call ignorance and folly.[16]

This passage seems to suggest that right conduct is determined by looking within our personalities and characters. Do you agree? What would Aristotle say about this, given his Doctrine of the Mean?

4   In this chapter we focused on virtues while alluding to vices. Based on what was said, compare and contrast the views of Plato, Aristotle, Aquinas, and Hume about which vices are worst. In doing so, explain their views by reference to their theories of human nature. Which view do you find most insightful?

5   On the basis of Pincoffs's definition of a moral virtue, is faith in God a moral virtue? How about faith in the prospects for sustaining human community and for avoiding nuclear holocaust?

6   Apply to education MacIntyre's distinction between the internal and the external goods of practices, from both a student's and a teacher's viewpoint.

7   Select four of the moral virtues listed in Figure 3.1, two mandatory ones and two nonmandatory ones. For each, try to identify what Aristotle would call their corresponding vices (excess and deficiency), their characteristic spheres of action, and their types of emotions and desires.

SUGGESTED READINGS

Annas, Julia. *The Morality of Happiness*. New York: Oxford University Press, 1993.

Aquinas, Saint Thomas. *Introduction to St. Thomas Aquinas*. Anton C. Pegis (ed.). New York: Modern Library, 1948.

Aristotle. *Ethics*. Trans. J. A. K. Thomson and Hugh Tredennick. New York: Penguin, 1976.

Crisp, Roger (ed.). *How Should One Live?: Essays on the Virtues*. Oxford: Clarendon Press, 1998.

Crisp, Roger, and Michael Slote (eds.). *Virtue Ethics*. New York: Oxford University Press, 1997.

Deigh, John (ed.). *Ethics and Personality: Essays in Moral Psychology*. Chicago: University of Chicago Press, 1992.

Foot, Philippa. *Virtues and Vices*. Berkeley: University of California Press, 1978.

French, Peter A., Theodore E. Uehling, Jr., and Howard K. Wettstein (eds.). *Midwest Studies in Philosophy*, Volume XIII. *Ethical Theory: Character and Virtue*. Notre Dame, IN: University of Notre Dame Press, 1988.

Hooke, Alexander E. (ed.). *Virtuous Persons, Vicious Deeds*. Mountain View, CA: Mayfield Publishing, 1999.

Hudson, Stephen D. *Human Character and Morality*. Boston: Routledge & Kegan Paul, 1986.

Hume, David. *Hume's Ethical Writings*. Alasdair MacIntyre (ed.). New York: Macmillan, 1965.

Kekes, John. *The Examined Life*. London: Associated University Presses, 1988.

Kruschwitz, Robert B., and Robert C. Roberts (eds.). *The Virtues: Contemporary Essays on Moral Character*. Belmont, CA: Wadsworth, 1987.

Kupperman, Joel. *Character*. New York: Oxford University Press, 1991.

MacIntyre, Alasdair. *After Virtue,* 2d ed. Notre Dame, IN: University of Notre Dame Press, 1984.

MacIntyre, Alasdair. *Dependent Rational Animals: Why Human Beings Need the Virtues*. Chicago: Open Court, 1999.

Meilaender, Gilbert C. *The Theory and Practice of Virtue*. Notre Dame, IN: University of Notre Dame Press, 1984.

Paul, Ellen Frankel, Fred D. Miller, and Jeffrey Paul (eds.). *Virtue and Vice*. Cambridge: Cambridge University Press, 1998.

Pincoffs, Edmund L. *Quandaries and Virtues*. Lawrence: University Press of Kansas, 1986.

Plato. *The Republic of Plato*. Trans. Francis MacDonald Cornford. New York: Oxford University Press, 1945.

Sherman, Nancy. *Making a Necessity of Virtue: Aristotle and Kant on Virtue*. Cambridge: Cambridge University Press, 1997.

Slote, Michael. *From Morality to Virtue*. New York: Oxford University Press, 1992.

Statman, Daniel (ed.). *Virtue Ethics: A Critical Reader*. Washington, DC: Georgetown University Press, 1997.

Thomas, Laurence. *Living Morally: A Psychology of Moral Character*. Philadelphia, PA: Temple University Press, 1989.

Wallace, James D. *Virtues and Vices*. Ithaca, NY: Cornell University Press, 1978.

PART TWO

Multicultural Ethics

Cultural diversity can and should be honored, but only within the context of respect for common values. Any claim to diversity that violates minimalist values—such as claims defending child prostitution or the mutilation of girls and women on 'cultural' or 'aesthetic' grounds or insisting that human sacrifice is religiously mandated—can be critiqued on cross-cultural grounds invoking the basic respect due all human beings.[1]

Sissela Bok

Multicultural ethics refers to the study of moral issues surrounding differences among cultures, including issues about race, ethnicity, nationalism, gender, disability, and economic class. It can also refer to the study of all moral issues with attention to their implications within different cultures. *Cultures* are any groups joined by customs (social practices) and beliefs, such as tribes, ethnic groupings, societies, nations, and religions.

In addition to exploring multicultural themes, Part Two extends the discussion of ethical theory begun in Part One. We will introduce and discuss new types of ethical theories: ethical relativism, religious ethics, and feminist ethics. We will ask whether these theories complement theories like utilitarianism and rights ethics, or whether they are entirely new alternatives.

CHAPTER 4

Diversity and Relativism

In April 1999, John Daniel Kingston pleaded no contest to charges that he severely beat his 16-year-old daughter for fleeing from an arranged polygamous marriage to his brother (her uncle).[1] From its founding in the mid-nineteenth century, the Mormon Church, more formally named The Church of Jesus Christ of Latter-Day Saints, had practiced polygamy in the form of polygyny—men allowed and encouraged to marry more than one woman (versus polyandry, in which women have more than one husband). But the Church abandoned the practice in 1890, paving the way for Utah to enter the United States.[2] Today the Mormon Church strongly distances itself from polygamy and excommunicates any of its members found to engage in the practice. Kingston, however, was a member of the Latter Day Church of Christ, one of the half-dozen renegade groups that continues to practice polygamy in Utah and other western states. Since the 1960s, state governments in Utah, Arizona, and Montana have tended to indulge the estimated 30,000 polygamists, prosecuting them only for related crimes such as child abuse and incest. Vastly larger numbers of people elsewhere in the world practice polygamy, including many Muslims and some African tribes.

Some people find polygamy an appalling and degrading practice; others see it as permissible when freely engaged in by consenting adults or even preferable to monogamy; Mormons held all these attitudes during different episodes in their history. Is the moral status of polygamy merely relative to particular groups at particular times? More generally, are all moral values simply relative to what various societies accept as binding for their members? For example, if state governments condone polygamy (prosecuting only when bigamy laws forbidding multiple official marriages are violated), should they also be more tolerant about how groups discipline their children, allowing Kingston to engage in more severe forms than the wider society currently employs? And is the moral status of incest merely relative to group customs?

The question of whether moral values are relative is actually three different questions, depending on what is meant by *relative*: relative to what, in what ways, and to what extent? First, are moral values *reducible* to the customs of groups? *Ethical conventionalism* says morality is indeed reducible to customs; there are no objective or justified moral values that can be applied in critiquing some customs and endorsing others. This is an alarming view, and I will argue that it should be rejected.

Second, without embracing ethical conventionalism, could there be more than one morally reasonable perspective? *Ethical pluralism* is the view there can be more than one reasonable moral outlook, although not all outlooks and customs are morally reasonable. It follows that moral judgments need to be sensitive to a wide range of permissible customs and take into account the historical, environmental, and religious contexts of cultures. Customs are morally *relevant* (pertinent), and moral judgments often must take them into account and be made in relation to them, but morality is not reducible to customs. I will argue in favor of that view.

Third, are moral values relative to conceptual perspectives that are distinct although overlapping? *Conceptual relativism* says that all beliefs, including moral beliefs, are shaped by the wider conceptual schemas or frameworks in which they are embedded. I will suggest that some versions of conceptual relativism are true, but that not all moral perspectives are equally valid.

Ethical Conventionalism

Ethical conventionalism reduces moral values to the conventions of groups—to their customs (mores), laws, and socially approved habits. What is right is simply what the group approves of, and what is wrong is what the group condemns. In the words of anthropologist Ruth Benedict: "We recognize that morality differs in every society, and is a convenient term for socially approved habits. Mankind has always preferred to say, 'It is morally good,' rather than 'It is habitual.' . . . But historically the two phrases are synonymous."[3] Notice that Benedict is not a moral skeptic who thinks there is no justified standards. On the contrary, her view is that the customs decisively set the standard for a given society.

Ethical conventionalism was defended by many anthropologists and other social scientists during the twentieth century. Their defense centered around four primary arguments that appeal to group-authority, sheer-diversity, human survival, and tolerance. Each argument contains an element of truth, but none provides a sound defense. Ironically and inconsistently, the arguments attempt to defend ethical conventionalism by appealing to cross-cultural values that are not reducible to customs.

Group-Authority Argument

Societies, as well as many sub-groups within societies, are structured by authority. One argument for ethical conventionalism is that the authority of the group expressed in its customs determines what is right. The sociologist William Graham Sumner expressed this idea in *Folkways,* whose title is a synonym for customs:

> The folkways are the 'right' ways to satisfy all interests, because they are traditional. . . . The tradition is its own warrant. . . . The notion of right is in the folkways. It is not outside of them, of independent origin, and brought to them to test them. In the folkways, whatever is, is right. This is because they are traditional, and therefore contain in themselves the authority of the ancestral ghosts.[4]

In outline, the argument is this: Customs of groups express the authority of groups; authority is what is legitimate within the group; therefore, the customs of a group authoritatively express what is right or justified for members of the group to do.

One difficulty with the group-authority argument is that it appeals to a wider value—authority—that is not itself reducible to customs. Authority is a form of power legitimated by the group, as an expression of the group's solidarity and sovereignty. Respect for that autonomy is a cross-cultural value that is not reducible to customs. Of course, group authority takes many forms, and some societies are substantially structured by authority relationships, and others more loosely.

Another difficulty with the group-authority argument is that legitimate (socially endorsed) authority—whether the authority of law, social regulations, or religion—is only *one* value, and it is a value limited by other values such as basic decency and justice. These limits and values refer to sound moral reasons that are not reducible to what a group happens to endorse at a given time. The reasons also enter into justifying hierarchies and domains of authority. Thus, in a constitutional democracy such as the United States, authority is set by the U.S. Constitution in areas of basic liberties, but there are additional domains of authority in terms of federal laws and state laws, such as those prohibiting polygamy.

Yet another difficulty is that if the group-authority argument were sound, we could justify virtually anything by simply finding and joining a society. For example, the Internet can quickly put us in touch with groups that advocate having sex with children. We join and presto: What was immoral child abuse becomes morally permissible for us. Ethical conventionalism seems to make a mockery of our fundamental conviction that some customs are justified by sound moral reasons and other customs are morally objectionable. Moral reasons can be used to critique moral customs; they are not reducible to customs.

Sumner and Benedict would reply that this last objection misses their point. Their intention is to defend the customs of societies that evolve naturally, not groups we can join. But this reply suggests several additional difficulties for ethical conventionalism. What exactly is meant by *groups* or *societies* in the definition of ethical conventionalism? Why privilege some groups (say, naturally evolved societies) over others (such as religions and other groups we can join)? And if we are members of several groups and societies that have different standards, which standards are overriding?

For example, state laws forbid polygamy, but various groups believe polygamy is morally permissible—which customs should have priority, and why? U.S. law permits abortion, but suppose we are Catholics who agree with the Pope's view that abortion is a serious sin? Bribery is officially illegal in some countries, but it is widely accepted as an informal custom by most businesspersons in some countries. Which customs ought to take precedence? These questions can be answered, but only by engaging in moral reasoning that extends beyond a mere appeal to custom. Indeed, the reasoning will be nuanced, sometimes showing the priority of federal law over religious practice and individual conscience and sometimes the opposite.

Benedict often celebrated the study of simpler "primitive cultures" as enabling us to see the role of custom more clearly, but the problem is that in simpler cultures there is far greater consistency throughout the formal laws, informal habits, and religious practices. Applied to contemporary societies, ethical relativism becomes internally incoherent because the customs of different groups of which we are members point in inconsistent directions.

Sheer-Diversity Argument

Early anthropologists were astonished by the extent of cultural differences they discovered, and many of us have had similar experiences, whether through reading or through personal experience. Dazzled by diversity, we easily lapse into thinking the sheer diversity is so great as to make implausible any search for common values—*common* in either the sense of (1) objectively justified values that ought to be accepted in all societies, as well as (2) values that as a matter of fact are shared cross-culturally. Thus, after discussing a long list of exotic practices, such as cannibalism, head-hunting, and polygamy, Benedict immediately infers that morality is mere custom.

That inference is mistaken; the mere fact of diversity of custom does not establish that customs are self-justifying. Thus, the following argument is invalid—its conclusion does not follow from its premise.

1 Different societies have vastly different moral beliefs.

2 Therefore, whatever a society believes to be right *is* right (for members of that society).

Notice that this argument moves from an uncontroversial statement of fact about different moral beliefs to an enormously controversial claim about values. It moves from an *is* (there is diversity of belief) to an *ought* (people ought to follow their customary beliefs). By itself that transition is problematic, as we noted in Chapter 1: How can a simple statement of fact, by itself, establish a very different kind of claim about values? It is a fact that Nazi Germany was brutal toward Jews, but in no way does it follow that the Holocaust was permissible.

Equally important, some recent anthropology has drawn attention to greater areas of shared basic values than first appeared.[5] That should not surprise us: All human societies have had to face some similar problems concerning survival and the limitations imposed by biology. This point will be expanded in discussing the next argument for ethical relativism.

Survival Argument

Let us now assume that customs are clear, uniform, and integrated throughout a single society. Why not simply flaunt the customs, if we so desire and if we can do so without getting punished by those in authority? Benedict's answer does not appeal to sheer self-interest. That is, she does not say that disobeying the custom is against one's self-interest because it usually lands one in trouble with the powerful authorities in the society. That appeal would be more like the view of the ethical egoist, who reduces morality to self-interest, not the ethical relativist who reduces it to social customs. Instead, Benedict appeals to group survival.

Each society faces special difficulties in dealing with its environment and with the tensions within the group. To survive, it must become integrated and cohesive. These integrated patterns bind together the group in ways that enable it to survive and prosper. Without uniformity of speech, a group cannot communicate; likewise, without some uniformity of customs, a group cannot form an economy, establish child-rearing practices, and resolve disputes. There are indefinitely many ways of forming customs by selecting among types of human behaviors and interest, but, once selected, customs carry moral force.

In fact, this argument does not support ethical conventionalism. For notice that it appeals to a value that is objective, in the sense of being justified and applying cross-culturally: human survival. This value can be used to criticize specific customs that thwart, rather than promote, human survival. Moreover, human survival implicitly refers to the moral value of persons as individuals, for why should the survival of groups matter unless the individuals composing the group have moral worth? These values of human survival and individual worth move us beyond a crude appeal to custom and provide a basis for a moral critique of some customs.

More specific values are implied as well. As Sissela Bok argues in *Common Values,* the survival of all societies depends on their embracing at least minimal understandings of three classes of values: (1) mutual support, loyalty, and reciprocity, (2) constraints on violence, deceit, and betrayal, and (3) fairness and procedural justice.[6] The precise interpretation and full expression of these values ("maximal ethics") varies considerably among cultures, but a rudimentary versions of the values ("minimal ethics") are essential to survival. Although Bok seems in places to rest her defense of common, cross-cultural values on the ground of group survival, she also appeals to respect for individuals as having inherent worth.

To develop Bok's point, let us consider whether a society could exist for long if its customs were systematic selfishness, cruelty, disregard of children's well-being, a complete lack of cooperation and reciprocity. One such society was studied by Colin Turnbull. In *The Mountain People* he describes the Ik (pronounced "eek"), a tribe in northeast Uganda.[7] Members of the tribe will steal the last cup of tea from a dying relative. They leave their children to roam free after only minimal attention to the very young. They will refuse to share even when it is clearly in their best interest to do so. But the Ik are hardly a counterexample to Bok's claims. They are a moribund society. Indeed, their current customs evolved when the they were forced by government policy to abandon their tradition hunter–gatherer lifestyle that was supported by earlier patterns of cooperation and mutual decency.

Tolerance Argument

On the surface, ethical conventionalism seems to express tolerance and respect for cultures. Respect for other cultures is vitally important in the increasingly multicultural, global environment in which we live today. It is important not only because our self-interest is promoted by being able to work, trade, and live with diversity within a global economy, but also because people deserve respect for their individuality, which includes their religious, family, and cultural traditions. It is to avoid *ethnocentrism:* the assumption that one's own culture is superior to all others. Indeed, we can gain from understanding cultures that are better than ours in some respects. For example, the so-called primitive society of the !Kung, in Botswana, southern Africa, manages far better than we do in caring for all members of its population and in maintaining ties of community and mutual respect.[8] No members of that community, including the most severely disabled and diseased, are left homeless and uncared for.

There are two difficulties with this tolerance argument, however. On the one hand, insofar as it appeals to respect for persons, it actually refutes ethical conventionalism. For again, ethical conventionalism states that morality is reducible to group customs, and hence there are no valid cross-cultural moral principles that can be used to criticize customs. But respect for persons is certainly a fundamental moral value, highlighted by Kant but also expressed in all the ethical theories discussed in Chapters 2 and 3.

On the other hand, ethical conventionalism is actually not a tolerant doctrine. There was nothing tolerant about the sanctioning of bigotry, racism, and genocide in Nazi Germany. Nor does tolerance require standing back—without even voicing criticism—of the Serbian atrocities against ethnic Albanians in

Kosovo, and also reciprocal cruelties inflicted on the Serbs. Indeed, by equating moral values with customs, the ethical relativist tacitly draws us into complicity with intolerance and cruelty by telling us to respect whatever customs a group adopts, no matter how contrary they are to common decency.

Customs are often morally relevant factors in deciding how we should act. Obviously, in England we ought to drive on the left side of the road in order not to kill people, and when entering a traditional Japanese home we should take off our shoes as a sign of respect. All plausible ethical theories acknowledge these truths, but if we need a label to remind us of them we might speak of *contextualism:* In making specific moral judgments, we need to take account of particular contexts and the customs, history, environment, and difficulties confronted by particular societies.

Ethical Pluralism

Ethical pluralism is the view that alternative and conflicting moral perspectives are sometimes morally justified, but it retains a conviction that many moral values are objectively defensible and that some customs and conduct are unacceptable morally. Ethical pluralism accepts and tolerates multiple conceptions of the good life—within limits—and it acknowledges that those views are morally relevant in deciding how we should act toward other people. The spirit of pluralism is captured in the phrase, "Let a thousand flowers bloom" (or at least several dozen!). It insists, however, that we can and should "kill the weeds," that is, reject grossly immoral practices.[9]

Like Bok, pluralists typically distinguish a minimal ethics of widely shared cross-cultural values, specified in general terms such as those Bok listed, and maximal ethics that provide detailed understandings of those values within particular societies, together with additional forms of good that lead societies and individuals to flourish.[10] Pluralism recognizes that moral judgments need to take into account the customs of groups and the commitments made by individuals, but it rejects ethical conventionalism that reduces moral values to customs. It acknowledges some objective values that we use in determining whether customs are good or meet the standards for justice.

For example, Stuart Hampshire was an ethical pluralist who argued that polygamy is at least sometimes morally permissible.

> Just as there is no ideally rational arrangement of a garden, and no ideally rational clothing, so there is no ideally rational way of ordering sexuality and there is no ideally rational way of ordering family and kinship relationships. The ordering is subject to rational control, specifically in respect of the comparative fairness or unfairness of the arrangements and of their tendency under particular conditions to promote happiness or harm.[11]

Thinking along these lines, imagine a society in which repeated wars make it impossible for many women to have sexual partners. Both men and women in the society decide voluntarily to engage in polygamy, as the best way for them to find mutually satisfying sexual and family experiences. The practice as a whole tends to promote happiness, and safeguards are instituted to promote fairness in how wives are treated. Perfect happiness and equality are never achieved, although that same objection can be raised against monogamous marriage in our society.

Of course, not all polygamy fits this description. Pluralists point out that some forms of polygamy can be criticized because they involve male dominance and denial of equal opportunities to women whose participation in the practice may be coerced rather than free. Child abuse may also be involved, and some forms lead to incestuous inbreeding, whether as a matter of associated doctrine or as a result of keeping the practice secretive to protect it against legal interventions. In the spirit of contextualism, ethical pluralists have us attend to specific situations and raise criticisms based on specific harms and injustices.

What arguments support ethical pluralism? We will consider two.

Multiple Goods and Emphases

There are many virtues, ideals, and principles that it is permissible to emphasize, either in a given culture or an individual life. In addition, there is no systematic way to rank these values and to establish that one of them should always take precedence, although in particular situations it may be clear which should have priority. To be sure, fundamental values like justice and benevolence (or at least nonmaleficence) are *universally applicable,* in the sense that they apply in all cultures and virtually all kinds of situations. But that does not mean they are *absolute* in the sense of never having justified exceptions when they conflict with other values. Moreover, moral values are somewhat value, and their content and implications are open to different interpretations among morally reasonable persons of good will. These interpretative differences are especially important in situations where important values come into conflict—as they do regarding most of the practical issues discussed throughout this book.

For example, some individuals and groups give greater emphasis to truthfulness, not just in speech, but in the vigorous pursuit of the truth. Others emphasize love and friendship. When these values conflict—for example, when maintaining friendship requires less than full candor about a friend's shortcomings—different individuals and cultures may emphasize one value or the other. As we saw in Chapter 2, the ethics of truth-telling and lying is complicated, and sometimes a particular situation allows room for reasonable persons to disagree about whether a particular lie is justified.

Self-Fulfillment Argument

Human nature is complex and varied. Individuals have different temperaments, interests, and capacities, and find their self-fulfillment and happiness through freedom to express them. All the major ethical theories take account of this. Rights ethics highlights the rights of individuals to pursue their views. Duty ethics makes central respect for individuals' rational autonomy in guiding their own lives. Virtue ethics is sensitive to many forms of human excellence, not all of which one individual could pursue. And utilitarianism highlights the contribution of variety and freedom to individual happiness and the wider public good.

To expand on utilitarianism as an example, John Stuart Mill in *On Liberty* urged that we should value "different experiments of living; that free scope should be given to varieties of character, short of injury to others; and the worth of different modes of life should be proved practically, when anyone thinks fit to try them."[12] Note that Mill says "short of injury to others." Our experiments of living must be conducted within the boundaries of moral responsibility.

Nevertheless, these boundaries provide wide scope for creativity and for developing the best in ourselves. They also allow greater scope for an array of personal relationships. One of Mill's provocative examples was polygamy. He expressed strong personal distaste for the practice, but he defended the right of nineteenth-century Mormons to practice it, as long as the participants chose to do so without coercion.

Mill warned that even in democratic societies there can be a "tyranny of the majority" that suppresses the development of individual tastes and talents. That warning may seem unnecessary in a post-1960s climate of personal freedom; yet today we face pressures toward uniformity arising from mass media and the dominance over our lives of large corporations and government bureaucracies. These forces sometimes narrow and flatten life, generating the kind of collective mediocrity that Mill warned against.

Closer to our own time, Isaiah Berlin has defended the value of pluralism. Pluralism is the acceptance of multiple conceptions of the good life. As such it is central to democratic societies. Pluralism is not the same as ethical relativism, which endorses the outlooks and customs of all groups as equally valid. Nor does it imply the subjectivism that reduces moral values to mere preferences unsupported by reasons. Instead, as Berlin wrote, pluralism is "the conception that there are many different ends that men [and women] may seek and still be fully rational, . . . capable of understanding each other and sympathising and deriving light from each other."[13] Pluralism adds to democratic freedoms the attitude that we all benefit from a society that tolerates diversity. Our outlook is enriched insofar as we learn to see the world through the eyes of people with strikingly different views.

Conceptual Relativism

Conceptual relativism is the view that moral values and all other beliefs are relative to conceptual schemas, which are the complexes of language, ideas, assumptions, and interests that structure worldviews. Conceptual relativism became a fundamental theme in many academic disciplines during the twentieth century, including the social sciences, linguistics, literary theory, philosophy, and reflections on science.[14]

Exactly what conceptual relativism means and implies is a subject of ongoing debate. Here our limited aim is to suggest two very different views of what conceptual relativism implies concerning morality. One version construes conceptual relativism as showing that morality is radically relative to the conceptual schemas of groups in ways that return us to ethical conventionalism. Alternatively, they are radically relative to individual cognitive schemas in ways that entail ethical subjectivism. Thus, polygamy as practiced by a group of Africans or early Mormons is so entwined with their entire way of life that we may be unable to fully understand its meaning to them, let alone evaluate it. Ultimately, conceptual schemas are incommensurable with each other: One cannot be used to critique another. A quite different version insists that conceptual relativism does not, or at least need not, draw us into subjectivism and skepticism about moral values.

These two versions are often blurred. Indeed, distinguishing them is difficult because key thinkers tend to blur them. The blurring occurs, for example, in the writings of Friedrich Nietzsche (1844–1900), whose influence has been enormous during the past century.

There are many passages where Nietzsche asserts a form of ethical subjectivism that he calls *perspectivism*. These passages suggest that no moral perspective is more justified than any other, and there is no privileged objective standpoint from which *the* truth can be discerned. Indeed, "there are no moral facts whatever."[15] All values are expressions of our "will to power," which is the instinct to assert ourselves: "Evaluation is creation: hear it, you creative men! Valuating is itself the value and jewel of all valued things. Only through evaluation is there value."[16]

Without objectively defensible values, moral criticism becomes at most what Nietzsche calls the *genealogy of morals:* the identification of origins of moral perspectives, so as to illuminate their functions in human life. In this connection he criticizes Judeo-Christian self-denial and humanitarian love as slavish values that express the fearful and secretively revengeful outlook of groups dominated by Roman emperors. He contrasts slave morality with noble morality, the perspectives of groups who have power and hence tend to be self-affirming, self-confident, and healthy.

As the terms *noble* and *slavish* suggest, however, Nietzsche clearly favors some values. He also advocates an aristocratic version of ethical egoism: exceptionally creative individuals give meaning to the entire human race, which is otherwise composed of the "herd" of mediocre individuals. Is he simply expressing his personal taste, or does he think some perspectives are more valuable than others, contrary to his perspectivism? I believe he regards some values are more valuable than others. Sometimes he singles out intellectual honesty (truthfulness) as a fundamental value: "Honesty, supposing that this is our virtue from which we cannot get away, we free spirits—well, let us work on it with all our malice and love and not weary of 'perfecting' ourselves in *our* virtue, the only one left us."[17] Other times he celebrates a wider set of "noble" values that includes courage and creativity, pride and self-reverence, love of wisdom and celebration of fate (*amor fati*). The key value Nietzsche celebrates and uses in assessing other value perspectives is health, which for him implies vitality, self-mastery, and self-love (as we discuss more fully in Chapter 21).

Probably Nietzsche's thought is too rich and fluid to be interpreted in any one way.[18] His many-faceted thinking, usually presented in the form of aphorisms rather than systematic argument, will probably always license the kinds of perspectivism on his writings that he insists humans bring to the world. Something like this conclusion applies to the contemporary movement called multiculturalism.

Multiculturalism

Multiculturalism (note the *ism*) refers to a cluster of outlooks and movements occurring during the 1980s and 1990s and continuing today. Two very different strands in these outlooks need to be distinguished, and they are reflected in the strikingly different definitions of multiculturalism.

According to one definition, multiculturalism refers to an outlook that endorses various forms of subjectivism and relativism: Moral perspectives are merely personal, and no perspective is more valid than another; moral judgments are no more than expressions of feelings, power, and status within groups; values are radically relative to groups; there are no universal values; no society should criticize other societies. In this vein, multiculturalism is frequently associated with Nietzsche-style perspectivism, albeit renamed as *postmodernism*. For example, the editors of an anthology on the topic define multiculturalism as

> a movement that radicalizes and Nietzscheanizes the liberal ideal of tolerance . . . by tending to deny the possibility of universal truth as well as of nonoppressive power and by seeking, through this very denial, a comprehensive redistribution, not so much of wealth as of self-esteem, and not so much to individuals as to various marginalized groups.[19]

These editors understand multiculturalism as a rejection of the possibility of objective truths. Rather than objective truth and justified views, about morality or any other topic, there are only perspectives motivated by power and special interests, especially those of economic class, race, and gender. As a sociopolitical movement, the goal of multiculturalism is to empower oppressed and impoverished (marginalized) groups.

On the other hand, multiculturalism is more often defined as a moral ideal, or set of ideals, about embracing diversity. To be sure, sometimes multiculturalism is little more than what literary critic Stanley Fish calls "boutique multiculturalism": the appreciation and enjoyment of ethnic restaurants, weekend festivals, musical innovations, and friendships across lines of race, ethnicity, and nationality.[20] As a distinctively moral ideal, however, multiculturalism specifically implies the objectively-justified values of tolerance, acceptance, respect, and good will across cultural lines. A definition along these lines is the following:

> Multiculturalism involves an understanding, appreciation and valuing of one's own culture, and an informed respect and curiosity about the ethnic culture of others. It involves a valuing of other cultures, not in the sense of approving of all aspects of those cultures, but of attempting to see how a given culture can express value to its own members.[21]

Defined in this way, multiculturalism is one of the most important moral movements of our time, whether in education, business, or everyday life.[22] It signals a concentrated effort to help us live together in peace, while increasing freedom for individuals to express themselves.

The American *culture wars* blur and blend both senses of multiculturalism. Whether the war is about abortion, euthanasia, gun control, or any number of practical issues discussed in this book, the battles are fought along confusing lines. There is a call for tolerance and pluralism in accepting differences over a wide range. There is also a worry that important values are being eroded as our society moves toward ethical relativism, subjectivism, and perspectivism. One of our aims in turning to these issues is to gain clarity about exactly what is at stake.

In my view, multiculturalism as Nietzsche-style perspectivism should be challenged, but multiculturalism in the second sense should be celebrated. Regarding the first sense, abandoning the search for truth and moral justification is both harmful and incoherent as a social agenda. If all values and perspectives are mere expressions of power or social position, what basis is there for the deep need to attend to social injustice? Justice loses its substance and function in justifying some perspectives and criticizing others. Even the rationale for the kinds of appreciation and respect for others cited in the second definition of multiculturalism are left without foundation. We slide into identity politics in a crass form: Assertions of power based on group identities, without any framework of justice and decency from which to assess those assertions.

Regarding the second sense, most of the major movements of our day involve, in one way or another, the importance of appreciating differences among individuals. As just one example, let us consider people with disabilities.

Disabilities and Diversity

According to the 1992 U.S. Census, there are about 50 million Americans—about one in six Americans—who have a disability that restricts their performance in some area of life.[23] About half of those—one in ten Americans—are severely disabled in being completely unable to see, hear, talk, walk, or perform some other major function. Obviously, statistics about disability depend on the definition of disability. For our purposes, a disability is any major impairment in cognition, perceiving, or physical activity. This definition needs to be sharpened for various specific purposes, such as legal protections of the disabled at the workplace or in education. The important point is that there is no one fixed class or culture of people with disabilities. Disabilities form a continuum—they are a matter of degree. And they are something to which all of us are vulnerable.

If ethical conventionalism were correct, it was once entirely permissible to shunt aside the disabled, as not fully equal members of society. Competition for education and jobs was for the "able," and the "disabled" were regarded as unlucky outsiders. To be sure, "benevolence" required offering special aid so that they could function within their own groups within institutions, special schools, private homes, and other segregated forums.

It took millenia for women and people of color to gain recognition as moral equals, and to see their historical status as the product of social bigotry rather than subhuman abilities. We are still only beginning to conceive of disabilities as largely socially constructed obstacles that deny equal opportunity. The turning point was The Americans with Disabilities Act (ADA), passed in 1990, that signaled a new understanding of disabilities as socially constructed obstacles to equal opportunity.

As Anita Silvers argues, the spirit of the ADA was not to create sameness of success in competitive situations, but to "equalize environments" so that people with disabilities have the opportunity to compete within mainstream society, instead of being isolated in protected roles. Rather than viewing disability rights merely as positive rights to receive special benefits, they are instead liberty (negative) rights to equality that have been denied to a minority group:

> Failure to provide instrumentally effective accommodation illegitimately impinges on the negative freedom of disabled program users and workers. To illustrate, absence of access to public transportation limits impaired people's freedom to be employed, be educated, be refreshed by recreation. The limitation is arbitrary; access to this social necessity is absent only because impaired people happen to be a disregarded minority rather than an influential majority. For were a majority rather than a minority of users disabled, the initial designs of public transportation would have had to accommodate them, or there would have been too few riders.[24]

Legal protection of equal rights is one thing; equal acceptance in everyday life is something else. With many variations, we tend to think of people with disabilities as oddities. Or perhaps we find ourselves uncomfortably reminded of our own vulnerabilities—for we are all subject to becoming impaired in a great many ways. Again, perhaps we are insecure about our own abilities to relate to people whom we perceive as different. Silvers quotes the following excerpt from the *New York Times* (August 1, 1996) as expressing the typical experience of people who become disabled:

> Faruk Sabanovic, 21, who was felled by a sniper on a street in central Sarajevo last year, must now use a wheelchair. "It's strange," said Mr. Sabanovic, a paraplegic

who slaloms along the rutted sidewalks or down the streets, going about his business in his Quickie, a state-of-the-art, lightweight wheelchair. "I was walking normally like anybody else. A few days after I was wounded, I was meeting the same people and they treated me differently. There's something in people's minds that makes them think because we are in wheelchairs we are weird.[25]

There are additional insensitivities in which we fail to be attuned to the needs of people different from us in some ways. Silvers reports that on the day she completed her work on a book manuscript, she and a faculty colleague were forced to sit in their wheelchairs outside a grocery store in the rain until a passerby became available to contact the manager. The manager had padlocked the only wheelchair-accessible door to the store in order to prevent customers from using it to take shopping carts out of the store. Later her colleague, who had recently been disabled when a reckless driver knocked him off his bicycle, wrote to her: "The aspect of these situations that pushes me over the edge is how someone else's problem (in this case, shopping cart migration) becomes my problem (cannot enter)."[26]

SUMMARY

Ethical conventionalism reduces morality to customs of groups. Yet, customs are not self-certifying. Although moral values are embedded in many customs, moral reasons can also be used to evaluate customs as desirable or undesirable. Attempts to defend ethical conventionalism by appealing to group authority, sheer diversity of customs, group survival, or tolerance all appeal to cross-cultural values that are justified for reasons other than being customary.

Ethical pluralism says there can be more than one justified moral perspective, certainly with regard to controversial issues like abortion, euthanasia, and lying. At least in its defensible versions, it avoids reducing morality to customs, while remaining sensitive to the contexts in which groups struggle to survive or unfold alternative visions of the good life. It can be defended by noting the variety of moral goods and alternative ways of emphasizing them, as well as by appealing to the importance of self-fulfillment that is pursued through varied lifestyles.

Conceptual relativism says that moral beliefs, indeed all beliefs, must be understood within conceptual schemas. In a radical version, conceptual relativism rejects the possibility of moral dialogue and critique across the boundaries of particular cognitive schemas, thereby leading us back to ethical subjectivism and ethical conventionalism. In a more moderate version, however, the emphasis is on the possibilities of overlap among conceptual schemas, thereby recognizing opportunities for dialogue and mutual moral criticism across conceptual schemas.

Multiculturalism is a movement and outlook comprised of many strands, some desirable and some not. As an assertion that morality is merely the expression of power and the special interests of individuals and groups—based on their economic class, race, gender, and so on—multiculturalism leads to ethical subjectivism that is inconsistent with the call for respect for individuals. By contrast, as a call for broad sensitivity and tolerance of differences, multiculturalism is an ideal having enormous importance in fostering respect for individuals within our increasingly diverse society.

One of many dimensions of diversity, but an especially neglected one, concerns people with and without disabilities relating to one another as moral equals. In the past, people with disabilities were at most seen as needing special help, and the tendency was to segregate them from mainstream society. Today the process is underway to fully integrate the disabled into mainstream social practices by creating equal environments that provide equal opportunities. Here, as elsewhere, affirming diversity is a moral opportunity in everyday life.

DISCUSSION TOPICS

1   Evaluate the following arguments:
    a   Beliefs about morality differ from culture to culture. Therefore, what is right in one culture is wrong in another culture where beliefs differ. (Be sure to distinguish "what is right/wrong" from "what is believed to be right/wrong.")
    b   Beliefs about morality differ from society to society. Therefore, what is right for one society may not be right for another society. (In your answer, distinguish between two senses of "right for a society, "defined alternatively as "morally justified in the society" or "believed to be justified in the society.")
    c   Some Eskimos and Native Americans once practiced the custom of leaving their elders to die when they could no longer travel with the tribe to fresh hunting grounds. Because this was the accepted custom, their conduct was morally permissible.
    d   Sometimes what is morally right (permissible or obligatory) in one society is wrong in another society. This is not merely because customs differ, but because the customs might be morally justified in one situation and not in another. For example, economic conditions are sometimes relevant in evaluating the customs of a society. When the Eskimos and American Indians lived under conditions of extreme scarcity, they may have been justified in leaving their elderly to die if they became unable to travel with the tribe to find new hunting territories, even though comparable neglect of our elderly would be immoral in contemporary Eskimo and Indian societies.

2   Ethical conventionalism was defended by the ancient sophists, who were teachers exposed to many different customs as they traveled from Greek city–state to city–state. Plato was only the first of many ethicists to attempt to refute the ethical conventionalism voiced by the sophists. In doing so, he went to the other extreme of arguing that valid moral ideals are written into the very structure of the universe, as part of the eternal Form of the Good, such that moral ideals are universal (applying to all societies) and absolute (no permissible exceptions). This began a tradition that continues today of opposing relativistic versus absolute views of morality, and also confusing the idea of universal applicability with the absence of permissible exceptions when values come into conflict. But these are not the only options. With regard to polygamy, discuss how the following values

might all be universal in their applications while still having permissible variations in how they are applied in different cultural settings: respect for autonomy; happiness and self-fulfillment; equality of opportunity.

3 Consider whether there might be any circumstances in which the following practices would be morally permissible, and where they would not be: (a) cross-dressing; (b) a strict ban on premarital sex; (c) incest. Insofar as these practices are condemned (as they currently are in much of our society), what reasons justify the condemnation?

4 Assess Nietzsche's view that Judeo-Christian values of love, as well as their secular legacy in ideals of equal moral worth, were products of weak groups trying to gain power by getting those in power to live by standards of justice. In doing so, comment on whether you agree with philosopher-sociologist Max Scheler that Nietzsche accurately portrayed only distorted forms of love, not "genuine love," which Scheler described this way:

> [Genuine love] is motivated by a powerful feeling of security, strength, and inner salvation, of the invincible fulness of one's own life and existence. All this unites into the clear awareness that one is *rich enough* to share one's being and possessions. Love, sacrifice, help, the descent to the small and the weak, here spring from a spontaneous overflow of force, accompanied by bliss and deep inner calm."[27]

5 Whether we are evaluating other societies or individuals, we need to distinguish between two types of moral judgments: (1) judgments about right and wrong, and (2) judgments about culpability and blame. We can condemn practices like head-hunting, cannibalism, and persecuting witches (who were usually nonconformist women). We can reasonably judge that engaging in these practices is typically immoral. That does not mean, however, we must always blame individuals in the past who engaged in such practices. They may have been "victims of their time," brought up in cultural beliefs that we now regard as discredited. With regard to current practices, however, this distinction between the two types of judgments might be more difficult to apply. For example, what should be said about the practice of female genital mutilation—the cutting of genitalia of young girls, usually at an early age—that continues to be practiced in many parts of the world?

6 Alasdair MacIntyre, among others, has pointed out that until recently philosophers only discussed people with disabilities as "possible subjects of benevolence by moral agents who are themselves presented as though they were continuously rational, healthy and untroubled. So we are invited, when we do think of disability, to think of 'the disabled' as 'them,' as other than 'us,' as a separate class, not as ourselves as we have been [as infants], sometimes are now and may well be in the future."[28] Have you encountered a similar attitude in everyday life? What is the source of the attitude, and how should it be changed?

SUGGESTED READINGS

Archard, David (ed.). *Philosophy and Pluralism*. Cambridge: Cambridge University Press, 1996.

Arthur, John, and Amy Shapiro (eds.). *Campus Wars: Multiculturalism and the Politics of Difference*. Boulder, CO: Westview Press, 1995.

Belliotti, Raymond A. *Seeking Identity: Individualism Versus Community in an Ethnic Context.* Lawrence: University Press of Kansas, 1995.

Berlin, Isaiah. *The Crooked Timber of Humanity.* New York: Vintage, 1992.

Bok, Sissela. *Common Values.* Columbia: University of Missouri Press, 1995.

Davis, Leonard (ed.). *The Disability Reader.* New York: Routledge, 1997.

Foster, Lawrence, and Patricia Herzog (eds.). *Defending Diversity: Contemporary Philosophical Perspectives on Pluralism and Multiculturalism.* Amherst: University of Massachusetts Press, 1994.

Goldberg, David Theo (ed.). *Multiculturalism: A Critical Reader.* Cambridge, MA: Blackwell, 1994.

Gutmann, Amy (ed.). *Multiculturalism: Examining the Politics of Recognition.* Princeton, NJ: Princeton University Press, 1994.

Harman, Gilbert. *Moral Relativism and Moral Objectivity.* Cambridge, MA: Blackwell, 1996.

Heyd, David (ed.). *Toleration: An Elusive Virtue.* Princeton, NJ: Princeton University Press, 1996.

Hinman, Lawrence M. *Ethics: A Pluralistic Approach to Moral Theory.* 2d ed. Fort Worth, TX: Harcourt Brace, 1998.

Kavka, Gregory. "Disability and Right to Work." *Social Philosophy and Policy,* 9 (1992): 262–290.

Kekes, John. *The Morality of Pluralism.* Princeton, NJ: Princeton University Press, 1993.

Krausz, Michael (ed.). *Relativism: Interpretation and Confrontation.* Notre Dame, IN: University of Notre Dame Press, 1989.

Ladd, John (ed.). *Ethical Relativism.* Belmont, CA: Wadsworth, 1973.

Larmore, Charles. *The Morals of Modernity.* Cambridge: Cambridge University Press, 1996.

Melzer, Arthur M., Jerry Weinberger, and M. Richard Zinman (eds.). *Multiculturalism and American Democracy.* Lawrence: University Press of Kansas, 1998.

Miller, Richard W. *Moral Differences: Truth, Justice and Conscience in a World of Conflict.* Princeton, NJ: Princeton University Press, 1992.

Nehamas, Alexander. *Nietzsche: Life as Literature.* Cambridge, MA: Harvard University Press, 1985.

Nietzsche, Friedrich. *Basic Writings of Nietzsche.* Ed. Walter Kaumann. New York: Modern Library, 1992.

Nietzsche, Friedrich. *Thus Spoke Zarathustra.* Trans. R. J. Hollingdale. New York: Penguin Books, 1969.

Outka, Gene, and John P. Reeder, Jr. (eds.). Prospects for a Common Morality. Princeton, NJ: Princeton University Press, 1993.

Paul, Ellen Frankel, Fred D. Miller, Jr., and Jeffrey Paul (eds.). *Cultural Pluralism and Moral Knowledge.* Cambridge: Cambridge University Press, 1994.

Rescher, Nicholas. *Pluralism: Against the Demand for Consensus.* Oxford: Clarendon Press, 1993.

Siegel, Harvey. *Relativism Refuted.* Dordrecht, The Netherlands: Reidel, 1987.

Silvers, Anita, David Wasserman, and Mary B. Mahowald. *Disability, Difference, Discrimination: Perspectives on Justice in Bioethics and Public Policy.* Lanham: Rowman & Littlefield, 1998.

Stocker, Michael. *Plural and Conflicting Values.* Oxford: Clarendon Press, 1990.

Stout, Jeffrey. *Ethics After Babel: The Languages of Morals and Their Discontents.* Boston: Beacon Press, 1988.

Wendell, Susan. *The Rejected Body: Feminist Philosophical Reflections on Disability.* London: Routledge, 1996.

Wong, David B. *Moral Relativity.* Berkeley: University of California Press, 1984.

Religious Ethics

Most people hold religious or spiritual beliefs that they link closely with their moral outlooks. How exactly are these beliefs, as well as organized religions, connected with morality? And what implications do these connections have concerning respect for persons' religious outlooks? For example, presumably respect for persons implies respect for their rights to exercise their religious faith, but does that mean we must respect religious beliefs that support violence against women?

Five specific connections are especially important in thinking about *religious ethics*, which is an ethics linked to religious beliefs, and *religion ethics*, which is the study of the ethics of organized religions.[1] First, many people's moral motivation is strengthened through religious faith and participation in religions. Second, religions offer guidance in the form of simplifying and unifying principles, as well as through moral exemplars (divinities, saints, sages), moral narratives (stories), and rituals. Third, religions often set higher moral standards than are customary in a given society. Fourth, religions make claims about justifying or grounding morality. Fifth, religions are open to moral criticism of specific practices and doctrines. In considering each of these connections, we will use examples of different world religions, but given their complexity, we will necessarily have to be brief.

Motivation: Surrender, Community, and Karma

What is a religion? Ludwig Wittgenstein (1889–1951) argued that most important ideas, including the idea of religion, cannot be defined by an "essence," that is, by a simple set of properties that (a) must be met ("necessary conditions") and that (b) suffice to specify what the idea refers to ("sufficient conditions"). Instead, there are "family resemblances," or overlapping similarities among religions. Earlier this idea was developed by William James in *The Varieties of Religious Experience.* According to James, when we closely examine religions, "we may very likely find no one essence, but many characters [that is, features] which may alternatively be equally important to religion."[2] For example, some religions make central the belief in one deity (Christianity, Judaism, Islam), others are polytheistic (Hinduism, ancient Greece religions), and still others are nontheistic (Zen Buddhism). In the following discussion, we will refer to typical features, but these features might not be necessary and sufficient features defining all religions.

Three typical features are important in connection with how religious belief contributes to moral motivation: worldview, community, and ritual. A religious *worldview* usually embodies basic beliefs about human destiny, the proper structure of societies, and the origin of the universe. The worldview is expressed in scripture or sacred literature, as well as religious commentaries that apply scripture to changing human conditions and challenges. A religious *community* is the unity among members of a religious faith. Insofar as religions transcend national boundaries, most religious communities embrace considerable diversity of practices and faith. Religious *ritual* refers to practices in which members of a religious community express their faith. Rituals range from prayer and ceremonial fasting to attendance at church, synagogue, or mosque. Each of these three features provides a vehicle for strengthening moral motivation and putting morality into practice.

Consider Islam. The Islamic worldview and central rituals are summarized as the Five Pillars (or obligations) stated in the Qur-an (Koran):

1   Believe that there is only one God (Allah) and that Muhammad is his prophet.

2   Pray five times daily.

3   Give alms (a religious tax, roughly an annual 2.5% of one's net financial worth).

4   Fast during the holy month of Ramadan (by abstaining from all food and drink from dawn to sunset).

5   If possible, make a pilgrimage to Mecca, the sacred birthplace of Muhammad.

Widely shared recognition of these obligations unites the billion members of the Muslim community (the *ummah*), but subcommunities within Islam are sometimes at odds with each other, especially the Shiites (a minority party who believe the descendents of Muhammad should rule the ummah) and the Sunnis (the majority party who do not vest religious authority along genetic lines of Muhammad). There is also a strong mystical tradition of Sufism, often criticized by more mainstream believers, which pursues a direct union with God rather than participation in the wider religious community under guidance by religious leaders.

Almsgiving is one obvious moral dimension of Islam, but more basic is the wider moral motivation linked to submitting to a just and generous deity (Allah). Since its inception, mainstream Islam has refused to separate the secular and the sacred. A practicing Muslim expresses devotion to a morally perfect deity in all areas of life, both through a sense of shared worship with others and a personal sense of surrender to a sustaining goodness. The very name *Islam* means surrender to the will of God. This surrender can strengthen personal moral commitment by unifying and guiding all aspects of one's life around what is believed to be a moral deity.

William James emphasized this element of surrender in all religions as liberating the self from its narrow preoccupation with self-seeking, while paradoxically bringing about self-fulfillment: "Let go your hold, resign the care of your destiny to higher powers, be genuinely indifferent as to what becomes of it all, and you will find not only that you gain a perfect inward relief, but often also, in addition, the particular goods you sincerely thought you were renouncing."[3] There are, of course, varied ways and motivations for surrendering. One motive is fear of an authority that punishes, but it would be unfair to stereotype Islam or any other major world religion as primarily fear oriented. For surrender can be motivated by love of moral goodness, a love that is then translated into moral aspects of life.

In addition to the morally reinforcing motives from community and surrender to a deity, religious faith offers an array of specific beliefs that contribute to moral motivation. Consider the Hindu (and subsequently the Buddhist) doctrine of *karma*. Hinduism is even more varied than Islam, which is not surprising, given its much earlier beginnings, but a recurring theme is deliverance or release (*moksha*) from this world of illusion (*maya*) through a series of transmigrations or reincarnations in different forms of life. Progress toward moksha or regression occurs through a kind of moral causation or karma: Each morally good action causes something good later, and each bad deed carries bad consequences for oneself later (in this incarnation or a later one).

The doctrine of karma asserts that morality is built into the universe, such that good character and conduct produce benefits to the individual, and bad produces bad. The doctrine is sometimes popularized, however, as saying that others will treat us as we treat them: "What goes around comes around." The doctrine is also popularized as a psychological doctrine: Guilt feelings or self-esteem accrue and shape us according to bad or good deeds. In any case, belief in karma provides a strengthening motivation for morality. If one firmly believes one's actions will rebound on oneself and on people one cares about, then a certain self-interested poignancy is added to moral reasons. One is motivated to practice various disciplinary practices (yoga) aimed at self-mastery.

Guidance: The Golden Rule

Like parents, religions teach moral values using an array of techniques: behavior modification through religious activities begun at an early age, conveying values through scripture and narratives, and moral dialogue about moral principles and ideals. These techniques are interrelated. Thus, general principles are taught through stories, and activities are structured around values. The golden rule is an especially interesting example because of its general scope and because it is embedded in nearly all world religions.

For example, the principle is important in Confucian ethics, as expressed in the *Analects*, with its strong emphasis on respectful conduct within communities and families. Confucius (551–479 B.C.E.) understood the moral path (*dao*) in terms of participating in social ritual (*li*) in a spirit of humanity (*ren*). What that meant requires understanding the detailed customs that bind communities and families together. Confucius was once asked whether these complex details could be conveyed by any unifying value. His reply was that reciprocal consideration for one another (*shu*) was such a unifying value and could be understood as what we now call the golden rule: "Tzu-kung asked, 'Is there a single word which can be a guide to conduct throughout one's life?' The Master said, 'It is perhaps the word '*shu*. Do not impose on others what you yourself do not desire.'"⁴

As a second illustration, Judaism also emphasizes the golden rule. Like Confucian ethics, Judaism takes seriously the importance of ritual and community, but it accents the Ten Commandments. Some of the commandments explicitly mention God: Believe in a single deity, do not take God's name in vain, and keep the Sabbath holy. Others, however, are moral rules requiring that we honor our parents, do not murder, do not commit adultery, do not steal, do not bear false witness, and do not covet others' possessions (which were then understood to include their wives). Is there any unifying idea running through these obligations? Justice (*tsedakah*) is sometimes seen as that idea, but so is the golden rule. When asked to encapsulate the basic message of the Hebrew scripture, Rabbi Hillel (30 B.C.E. to 10 C.E.) said, "What is hateful to you, do not do to your neighbor: that is the whole Torah, while the rest is commentary thereon; go and learn it."⁵

Confucius and Rabbi Hillel assert a negative version of the golden rule: Do *not* do to others what we do *not* want done to ourselves. The emphasis is on self-restraint, on not allowing expression of malicious and selfish desires. Defenders of the negative version praise it as expressing a strong minimum standard without enjoining unrealistically high requirements. They see in the negative version a spirit of leaving one's neighbors alone to pursue their own lives without criticism, until they harm others. Others, including later Confucian and Jewish thinkers as well as Jesus, see the negative version as setting the standard too low. They favor the stronger version that enjoins helping others: *Do* unto others as you would have them do unto you. The difference in emphasis reflects wider disagreements about minimal libertarian ethics and more extensive standards of beneficence. In either formulation, however, the golden rule simply and powerfully expresses values of reciprocity, fairness, and justice.

Nevertheless, the golden rule is not the comprehensive standard it is sometimes presented as being. Suppose we are masochists who desire to be hurt or killed? The golden rule then seems to enjoin harming others. Or suppose we desire a free car from others; then apparently the rule says we ought to give a car to others. In light of such examples, it might seem the golden rule has little moral content; it is only a formal principle that requires consistency among our desires for receiving and giving, without telling us what those desires should be. Yet, certainly the spirit of the rule calls for reshaping the content of our desires in the direction of fairness and justice.

Another interpretation is that the golden rule is addressed to individuals who have sufficient moral maturity to have appropriate or justified desires. In this regard, the golden rule functions as a facilitating technique that gets us to see our desires through the eyes of others. It enjoins moral imagination that transforms self-seeking by getting us to imagine how we would be affected by our desires if we were other people. As Jeffrey Wattles suggests, "The golden rule is a searchlight, not a map," that helps us discern right action by getting us to reason in the following way:

1   Treat others as you want others to treat you.

2   You want others to treat you with appropriate sympathy, respect, and so on.

3   Therefore, treat others with appropriate sympathy, respect, and so on.[6]

The word *appropriate* is crucial. The golden rule presupposes a framework of basic decent values, a conscience or sense of what is morally reasonable, and a substantial degree of moral maturity.

Once again, then, the golden rule illustrates how a principle central to most religions is connected with wider moral viewpoints. Not only does the golden rule express ideas of reciprocity and justice that are not essentially tied to belief in a deity, but the rule needs to be applied against the background of a wider understanding of moral reasons.

Ideals and Exemplars

Religions often aspire to a higher moral standard than the lowest common denominator in society. Sometimes they do so through specific beliefs and doctrines about ideals of character. For example, whereas public moralities tend to focus on conduct, religious ethics often require greater attention to the inner life of emotion and attitude. They set high ideals for emotional purity, as when Jesus said that avoiding cruelty includes rooting out hatred, and avoiding adultery includes removing lustful desires. Religions also set higher than usual standards for compassion and love manifested in helping others. Here their teachings are more often in the form of parables and injunctions to emulate moral models (deities, saints, sages).

Christianity takes many forms, including hundreds of American churches, but all of them focus on the figure of Jesus. According to many versions of Christianity, God became man in the person of Jesus, and underwent suffering in order to make possible the redemption of humanity. In understanding what love requires of us, the good Samaritan parable is central. Jesus was asked to explain the commandment to love one's neighbor as one loves oneself: Just who are one's neighbors, and what does it mean to act with love toward them? Rather than answering with more specific rules, he told the story of a man attacked by robbers who was left half-dead on the roadside. Others passed the man by, but a Samaritan stopped to help. After giving the man first aid, he carried him on his donkey into town, where he paid to have the man cared for at an inn. The injunction to "go and do likewise" enjoins a degree of helping well beyond the customary in that society or ours. It is a standard that was emulated by Mother Teresa (Catholic), Martin Luther King, Jr. (Baptist), and many others.

Buddhism also makes compassion—the morally caring response to suffering—central by rendering suffering central, although the focus shifts from suffering as redemptive (in the Christian tradition) to escape from suffering. The life of Gautama Buddha (563–483 B.C.E.), whose given name was Siddhartha, is a focus in Buddhism. Born a prince, Siddhartha married and had a son before renouncing the world at age twenty-nine. At age thirty-five he gained "enlightenment," after which he spent forty-five years as a monk. The enlightenment, or liberating experience, is a full realization that what we ordinarily think of as our "self," which is composed of a mass of desires attaching us to the world, is an illusion. Understanding of the "egolessness" of all sentient beings comes from a lived understanding of Four Noble Truths of Buddhism: (1) life is suffering, (2) the cause of suffering is desire (attachment to the world), which invariably leads to frustrations, (3) suffering ceases when desires cease, and (4) the way to remove desire is the eightfold path of right views, right intention, right speech, right action, right livelihood, right effort, right mindfulness, and right concentration. Nirvana, the highest good, is the release from all suffering and from the bondage of this world (*samsara*).

How Nirvana is to be achieved, and hence details about the eightfold path, take several forms in Buddhist traditions. Whereas Theravada Buddhism heavily accents the direct achievement of Nirvana, Tantra Buddhism accents magic, and Zen Buddhism the use of paradox. Mahayana Buddhism makes central the compassionate involvement with other people. Again, by contrast with Theravadas who emphasize an enlightenment leading directly to Nirvana, Mahayanas accent compassionate involvement in the world. In their view, buddhas-to-be (*bodhisattvas*) resolve to seek enlightenment for the sake of other sentient (and suffering) beings. They also postpone their own enlightenment motivated by compassionate concern for helping others.

As these examples illustrate, religious ethics often highlights particular virtues and ideals. The specific highlighting may be central to defining the religion as a whole, by contrast with other religions, or the specific version of the religion. In addition, religions involve shifting emphases over time in relation to particular social problems confronted by their membership. Even within the same religious tradition, the saints and moral exemplars vary considerably, some manifesting in exceptional degrees of love and compassion, others courage and perseverence, others serenity and peacefulness, and still others wise insight and humility.

Owen Flanagan draws attention to the other side of these observations.[7] In developing some virtues in exceptional degrees, saints and saint-like individuals often have other very human weaknesses, sometimes falling below even usual standards. This is true of some of the great moral exemplars of the twentieth century—for example, the extramarital affairs of the Holocaust rescuer Oskar Schindler and by Martin Luther King, Jr., or Gandhi's exploitive effort to test his chastity by having beautiful young women sleep in his bed. Moral exemplars are generally not morally perfect.

Justification: Divine Command Ethics

It is frequently claimed that religion is the foundation or justification of morality. Philosophers' name for that claim is *divine command ethics:* The meaning, content, and justification of moral values must be understood in terms of God and God's commandments. In particular, to say an act is morally obligatory means that God commands or approves of it. Stated negatively, if there is no God, then there cannot be meaningful and justified moral judgments. As Dostoevsky says in one of his novels, "If God is dead, anything goes." That is, if there were no God, then moral reasons could not be meaningful, cogent, and binding on us.

One way to think of divine command ethics is in terms of moral authority, distinguishing expert and executive authority.[8] In any area of life, *expert authority* is the skill and insight that enables excellence, and such expertise is typically a matter of degree. Just as physicians are experts in varying degrees in judging matters pertaining to health, God is a moral expert in discerning right and wrong. For theists (believers that God exists), God is morally perfect and as such a supreme moral authority.

Divine command ethics goes far beyond this claim by regarding God as an executive authority in establishing moral values. *Executive authority* is the legitimate power and right to make decisions and set standards. Thus, in a democracy the final authority for laws rests in the collective citizenry, and in a corporation the authority resides in stockholders (for-profit companies) or board of trustees (nonprofit corporations), as long as they act within the law. Divine command ethics says that God's commands create, with decisive executive authority, the content of moral rules. Moral values are valid only because God commands them.

Interestingly, most theologians agree with secular moral thinkers in rejecting divine command ethics, as having things backward. Assume that a morally perfect deity exists and issues commandments. *Why* does that deity issue certain commandments rather than others? Since God is morally perfect, presumably the commandments are the ones that are valid or justified in their own right; they are morally reasonable rather than whimsical. God chooses to command them precisely because they are morally justified. Divine command ethics denies this. According to it, moral reasons and rules come into existence only after (or with) God's commandments, and hence they cannot be a basis for those commandments.

This point was made by Socrates (470–399 B.C.E), as recorded by his student Plato (428–348 B.C.E).[9] Socrates posed the question, Is what is holy holy because the gods approve it, or do they approve it because it is holy? Let us rephrase the question, replacing the reference to many gods (polytheism) with a reference to one god (monotheism): What makes right acts right? Are they right simply because God commands them, and for no other reason? Or does God command them because God (as a morally perfect being) sees that they are morally right? For example, is rape immoral only because God forbids it, so that rape would be unobjectionable in a universe without God? Or does God forbid rape precisely because it is immoral (by inflicting cruelty, violating human rights, etc.)? If the latter is true, then moral reasons are not reducible to divine commands and religious beliefs.

Both religious and secular thinkers have also been concerned about Dostoevsky's statement that if there is no God then anything is permitted. Surely we can know that wanton murder, torture, and rape are immoral without knowing there is a deity. Indeed, the Catholic tradition emphasizes this point with the idea of a *natural law* that all humanity can be expected to discern, whether or not individuals have correct religious views.

Moral Critiques of Religion

The right to religious freedom is among the most basic moral and legal rights in Western democracies. But having a right does not automatically mean that what one does is morally all right (permissible). Just as a right to smoke does not entail that smoking is right or good, a right to practice religion does not mean that everything done in the name of religion is morally permissible, much less desirable. As human institutions, religions are subject to specific moral criticisms by both nonmembers and members of the religion. Three examples of moral critiques of religion concern treatment of children, violence, and attitudes toward women.

First, religious freedom implies a right to raise one's children in a religion, but how far does that right extend? Christian Scientists, among others, believe that physical health is primarily a product of religious faith.[10] Hence, the remedy for sickness lies in greater religious faith, and when young children are sick the faith is primarily needed by parents. To be sure, Christian Scientists allow that some "mechanical injuries" such as broken bones are properly treated by conventional medicine, but precisely what is mechanical is a matter of some debate. In a famous 1986 case, two-year-old Robyn Twitchell died after six days of intense pain and vomiting. During those days Christian Science practitioners ministered to the child and urged the family to prayer. As it turned out, Robyn had a simple bowel obstruction that could easily have been corrected. Was this a case of child neglect by the parents and religious authorities? The laws defining child abuse and neglect vary from state to state. The parents were charged under Massachusetts state law with involuntary manslaughter and they were convicted, although in 1993 the conviction was overturned.

Second, regarding violence, few beliefs have caused more cruelty than the conviction that God is on one's side as one engages in violent acts. Examples of religious fanaticism include the Christian crusades, Islamic holy wars, and Hindu violence against other Hindus. (The Hindu Mohatma Gandhi, who more than anyone in the twentieth century stood for nonviolence, was killed by a fervent and fanatical Hindu who opposed Gandhi's support for separating India and Pakistan). Some argue that the belief in exclusive truth lies beneath such terror, as opposed to an ecumenical spirit open to alternative faith. Yet, belief in exclusive truth need not be accompanied by violence. What matters are the moral attitudes with which religious views are held. Tolerance and respect for persons who disagree with us are crucial. In this way, moral values place constraints on religious motivation and actions done in God's name. Of course, religious believers will understand those values as what a morally perfect deity would condone or command.

Third, feminists argue that most world religions have institutionalized patriarchy, and sometimes misogyny, into their doctrines and practices. A glaring example is female genital mutilation. Most feminists also view the ascription of male identity to God, and the restriction of the priesthood or other religious authority to men, as examples of grounding religions in male-oriented attitudes that then filter into everyday religious practices such as prayer (to a male rather than a female) and heeding church authority (of males rather than females).

SUMMARY

Morality and religion are distinct but interconnected in ways that invite mutual dialogue. Moral and religious values overlap in terms of motivation, guidance, and higher ideals. Religions play a vital role in sustaining a sense that moral values matter and that they have objective warrant. Although religions play an enormously important role in supporting morality, moral values are not reducible to religious values, either in terms of their content or the justification of morality. But religious and secular morality are not inherently at odds. Indeed, religions themselves raise moral criticisms of other religions, and one branch of a particular religion raises moral (and religious) criticisms of other branches of the religion.

Religious motives for moral conduct should not be stereotyped as self-interested concerns for rewards from a deity. One of the most powerful religious motives is love of a deity, conceived as morally perfect, with whom one enters into a relationship of love and respect. Another example is the Hindu–Buddhist doctrine of karma that understands good and bad deeds as connected within a cosmic circle that reflects back on one's life (or next lives).

The golden rule is an example of a powerful, seemingly simple idea that is promulgated in most religions and that provides practical moral guidance. But the rule is not as simple as it seems, and it requires expansion in light of practical moral understanding. It takes a negative form that accents avoiding harm to others (Do not do unto others as you would not have them do unto you) and a positive form (Do unto others as you would have others do unto you) that seems to call for more helping of others, although the differences may be matters of degree.

Divine command ethics says that morality has meaning and justification only because God commands it. As such, it would leave no room for morality in a universe without God, and would also tie moral disputes directly to disagreements about religious doctrines. The main difficulty with it, however, is that it omits the central role of moral reasons as the basis for divine commandments.

DISCUSSION TOPICS

1 Return to Kitty Genovese, discussed in Chapter 1. What do (i) the golden rule and (ii) the good Samaritan story imply regarding what the bystanders ought to have done? Do you agree or disagree with what they imply? In this case, does religion set a higher standard, or instead reflect the standard embedded in ordinary moral beliefs?

2 Are the beliefs that God is male and that the highest religious authority is reserved for males morally objectionable?

3 According to the book of Genesis, Abraham was convinced that he heard God command him to kill his son Isaac as a sacrifice. Without asking any questions, Abraham proceeded to obey the command.

> God did tempt Abraham, and said unto him . . . Take now thy son, thine only son Isaac, whom thou lovest, and get thee into the land of Moriah; and offer him there for a burnt offering upon one of the mountains which I will tell thee of. . . . And they came to the place which God had told them of; and Abraham built an altar there, and laid the wood in order and bound Isaac his son, and laid him on the altar upon the wood. And Abraham stretched forth his hand, and took the knife to slay his son.[11]

Hitchcock never set a more chilling scene. Fortunately, the angel of the Lord intervenes, telling Abraham to replace Isaac with a sacrificial ram.

Jean-Paul Sartre (1905–1980) suggested that Abraham should have been more self-critical about interpreting the initial voice he believed was from God telling him to sacrifice Isaac.[12] Sartre was an atheist, but other liberal interpretors of this scripture suggest that Abraham was mistaken or deluded because a morally perfect being would not command such a thing, not even to test Abraham's faith. The philosopher Søren Kierkegaard (1813–1855) held a different view.[13] He thought that the Abraham–Isaac story illustrates how God sometimes overrides human morality for some higher, divine purpose. Kierkegaard called this the "teleological suspension of the ethical," that is, the subordination of morality to some higher *telos*, which in Greek means "purpose." Discuss these various responses as you present and defend your interpretation of the Abraham-Isaac story.

4 Hebrew and Christian scriptures make prominent the commandment to love one's neighbor as one loves oneself (Leviticus 19:18, and Romans 13:9). Whereas the golden rule begins with our desires to have others act toward us in certain ways and then enjoins comparable relations with others, this rule begins with love toward ourselves and then enjoins similar love toward others. Are there any limitations of this rule in discerning the content of morally justified desires and conduct?

5 Buddhism contends that ultimately the suffering self, with its desires attaching it to things and people in the world, are not real. Again, both Hinduism and Buddhism accept the doctrine of karma, extending through several incarnations in which a person might become another life form, such as a cow. Can these religious doctrines make sense of our ordinary concept of individual persons who are responsible for their desires and for achieving moral integrity?

6 India has traditionally been a caste system, each with very different social status, duties, and privileges. Priests, the highest class, have the duties of gaining and spreading wisdom; warriors the role of giving protection; farmers and merchants generating wealth and material goods. Paid workers are lower in the caste system, and the untouchables are the wretched "outcasts," the lowest. In the eyes of some, the doctrine of karma provides a perverse rationale for the caste system, insofar as social caste is thought to reflect moral status. Discuss this problem, linking it to analogous U.S. beliefs connected with the Protestant work ethic that wealth is a sign of moral achievement. Also, how would a human rights ethicist critique the caste system?

7 Some people believe in the existence of hell, in the sense of eternal damnation for sins committed in this life. Do you see anything morally objectionable about this belief? Also, compare and contrast belief in hell with the Hindu–Buddhist doctrine of karma.

8 In 1989, Iran's Ayatollah Khomeini issued a *fatwa*, or religious order, condemning writer Salman Rushdie to death for writing the novel *The Satanic Verses*. Until the order was countermanded in 1998, Rushdie was forced to live in hiding or with bodyguards and others associated with Rushdie were assaulted or killed in several countries. For example, Itoshi Igarashi, a scholar who translated the book into Japanese, was murdered in 1991. Comment on the requirements and limits of moral tolerance, whether by Muslims or nonMuslims, during and following the *fatwa*.

9 Observers of American culture wars are struck by new political alliances in debating issues like abortion, education, pornography, and the arts. In place of tradi-

tional oppositions among religions—for example, Catholic versus Protestant or Jewish versus Muslim—there are coalitions among conservative branches of various religions that oppose more liberal branches of religions.[14] In *Culture Wars,* sociologist James Hunter suggests that these new social alliances arise because of deeper moral differences within religions. In general terms, each major religion has an impulse toward orthodoxy of belief defined by emphasis on historical tradition and literal interpretations of scripture. They also have an impulse toward cultural progressivism that is more open to influence by social currents and hence to reinterpreting historic faith in light of current realities. Discuss what you see as the moral implications of these new political alignments regarding such issues as abortion and family structure.

SUGGESTED READINGS

Allen, Douglas (ed.). *Culture and Self: Philosophical and Religious Perspectives, East and West.* Boulder, CO: Westview Press, 1997.

Battin, Margaret P. *Ethics in the Sanctuary: Examining the Practices of Organized Religion.* New Haven, CT: Yale University Press, 1990.

Byrne, Peter. *The Moral Interpretation of Religion.* Grand Rapids, MI: William B. Eerdmans, 1999.

Carmody, Denise Lardner, and John Tully Carmody. *How to Live Well: Ethics in the World Religions.* Belmont, CA: Wadsworth, 1988.

Cooper, David E. *World Philosophies: An Historical Introduction.* Oxford: Blackwell, 1996.

Diener, Paul W. *Religion and Morality: An Introduction.* Westminster: John Knox Press, 1997.

Green, Ronald M. *Religion and Moral Reason.* New York: Oxford University, 1988.

Hunter, James Davison. *Culture Wars: The Struggle to Define America.* New York: Basic Books, 1991.

Kung, Hans. *Global Responsibility: In Search of a New World Ethic.* New York: Crossroad Publishing, 1991.

Lammers, Stephen E., and Allen Verhey (eds.). *On Moral Medicine: Theological Perspectives in Medical Ethics,* 2d ed. Grand Rapids, MI: William B. Eerdmans, 1998.

Markham, Ian. "Religion and Ethics," *Encyclopedia of Applied Ethics,* Vol. 3. San Diego: Academic Press, 1998. pp. 799–808.

Phillips, D.Z. (ed.), *Religion and Morality.* New York: St. Martins Press, 1996.

Schimmel, Solomon. *The Seven Deadly Sins Today.* New York: Oxford University Press, 1997.

Sharma, Arvind (ed.). *Our Religions.* New York: HarperCollins, 1993.

Sharma, Arvind, and Katherine K. Young (eds.). *Feminism and World Religions.* Albany: State University of New York, 1999.

Wattles, Jeffrey. *The Golden Rule.* New York: Oxford University, 1996.

CHAPTER 6

Feminism

As a social movement, feminism is grounded in a commitment to the empowerment and equal opportunities of women. As individuals and within social institutions, women have been subjected to *sexism* (prejudice or bigotry on the basis of sex), *misogyny* (hatred of women), *exploitation* (unfair usage), and *patriarchy* (socially sanctioned male dominance). (*Male chauvinism* is sometimes used as synonym for patriarchy. The term was coined during the late 1960s by women working in the civil rights and student movements to apply to male colleagues who relegated women to secondary roles in the fight against racism).

All these forms of bigotry take two forms. *Individual bigotry* is manifested in the attitudes, emotions, and conduct of individuals. *Institutional bigotry* is manifested in laws, institutions, and practices (including language). Both individual and institutional bigotry can be overt (easily discernible) or covert (more concealed and less obvious to all).

As an ethical orientation, *feminist ethics* seeks to (1) take women's interests, identities, and issues seriously; and (2) "recognize women's ways of being, thinking, and doing as valuable as those of men."[1] But feminist ethics is not one simple theory. It embraces a rich variety of ethical orientations, some of which are sharply at odds with others. These disagreements will be noted as we proceed, but the focus will be on five areas of shared feminist interest: equal social roles, care ethics, sexist language, rape and other violence, and sexual harassment. These are only sample interests; indeed, feminists have written on all the topics discussed in this book.

Gender Roles

Liberal feminism is the view that injustices against women are due primarily to beliefs that women are inferior to men, as well as to oppressive customs and laws that deny equal opportunities to women. Mainstream American feminism, as represented today by The National Organization for Women (NOW), is predominantly liberal, and historically the women's movement was rooted in the liberal commitment to extend to women the same rights that men have enjoyed. Thus, British writings by liberal feminists include Mary Wollstonecraft's (1759–1797) *A Vindication of the Rights of Woman* and John Stuart Mill's (1806–1873) *The Subjection of Women*. American writings include Elizabeth Cady Stanton's (1815–1902) co-authored "Declaration of Sentiments and Resolutions" and Betty Friedan's *The Feminine Mystique*, written in 1963.

Liberal feminists frequently employ human rights ethics as a basis for arguing that women have the same rights as men (although Mill was a utilitarian). In particular, the "Declaration of Sentiments and Resolutions," adopted at the first convention on women's rights in 1848 at Seneca Falls, New York, was closely modeled on the language of the Declaration of Independence:

> We hold these truths to be self-evident: that all men and women are created
> equal; that they are endowed by their Creator with certain inalienable rights;
> that among these are life, liberty, and the pursuit of happiness. . . . The
> history of mankind is a history of repeated injuries and usurpations on the part
> of man toward woman, having in direct object the establishment of an absolute
> tyranny over her.[2]

The document asserted that fundamental rights were being denied to women, including the right to vote, to own property (including their earned wages), to initiate divorce, to retain custody of their children when a husband initiated a divorce, to guide business activities without supervision by their husbands, and to attend college. (Except for Oberlin College, which had become coeducational, all American colleges and universities refused to admit women students.)

Defining these actions as rights, and demanding their exercise, was an explosive act. Even the right to vote was regarded by many convention members as too radical to assert at that time. Indeed, it was another seventy-two years before women's voting rights were recognized in the Nineteenth Amendment to the U.S. Constitution in 1920. Pursuing marriage and divorce rights was viewed as even more unrealistic and harmful. As for equal employment opportunities, the feminist movement had to struggle well into the 1960s before substantial progress was made, and progress continues today in securing complete equality of opportunity and pay.

Whereas liberal feminists focus on removing barriers of custom and law, more recent feminists have pointed to deeper obstacles. As Rosemarie Tong explores in *Feminist Thought*, radical feminists trace women's subordination to underlying forms of power and hierarchy within patriarchal systems; psychoanalytic feminists locate the primary problems in psychological development; existentialist feminists emphasize the need for women freely to define themselves (Simone de Beauvoir's *The Second Sex* influenced all twentieth century feminist thought); Marxist feminists see the problem as capitalism, which results in unfair class distributions of wealth; socialist feminism also emphasize the effects of economic class while integrating insights from other feminist traditions; and postmodern feminists highlight how the enormous differences among women—in terms of their class, race, and sexual orientation—preclude any one feminist perspective.

All these nonliberal traditions make salient the idea that women's desires and preferences are often distorted (by economic oppression, psychological development, social conditioning, etc.). This means that their current beliefs and values may not express their authentic outlooks, the outlooks they would have in the absence of patriarchal oppressions. This theme of authenticity generates great controversy, not only from critics of feminism but also within feminism itself.

For example, consider the traditional roles of homemaking, which include more specific roles as wife, mother, child caregiver, home manager, and volunteer. Insofar as women are not pressured into these roles, liberal feminists would see them as legitimate choices. Critics of liberal feminists, however, as well as critics of traditional roles, have often questioned whether women are genuinely free when they make such choices.[3] Haven't they been socially conditioned to desire such roles? If so, they are not genuinely free. Women who make traditional choices, however, object to this criticism as a patronizing failure to respect them as autonomous and intelligent.

Similar disagreements within feminism arise in many other areas. For example, when is femininity (in dress, speech, etc.) a free choice, and when is it socially forced? When is participation in making pornography a free choice, and when is it forced on women by males? And is it sexist or accurate and respectful to think of women as more caring than men? Regarding the last question, Stanton suggested that women are ensnared by society when they emphasize caring. She urged that "Self-development is a higher duty than self-sacrifice" should be woman's motto henceforward.[4] Let us turn to this question of whether women do or should have a distinctively female ethic.

Care Ethics

Do men and women, as groups, differ in the kinds of moral perspectives and virtues they emphasize? Carol Gilligan, in her book *In a Different Voice,* raised this issue in a manner that engendered considerable philosophical controversy.[5]

Gilligan distinguishes between two general outlooks on morality: a justice perspective and a care perspective. According to the results of her experiments, these views are roughly linked to gender. That is, men and women adopt both perspectives, but on average men emphasize justice and women emphasize care.

The justice perspective stresses abstract rules, which deal primarily with the right to be left alone, free from the interference of others. Within this perspective, moral dilemmas are questions of conflicting rights that are resolved by identifying which right has the highest priority in general. Morality, in short, is viewed as a set of rules about rights, ordered hierarchically by relative importance. The moral identity of people is defined primarily in terms of their rights: It is the assertion of the right to pursue their lives freely while respecting the freedom of others. The aim of autonomous moral reasoning is to determine how to balance rights fairly or justly.

"Heinz's Dilemma" illustrates the kind of reasoning used within the justice perspective. This story, which poses a moral dilemma, was written by Lawrence Kohlberg (1927–1987), but is used by Gilligan as well.

> In Europe, a woman was near death from a very bad disease, a special kind of cancer. There was one drug that the doctors thought might save her. It was a form of radium that a druggist in the same town had recently discovered. The drug was expensive to make, but the druggist was charging ten times what the drug cost him to make. He paid $200 for the radium and charged $2,000 for a small dose of the drug. The sick woman's husband, Heinz, went to everyone he knew to borrow the money, but he could get together only about $1,000, which was half of what it cost. He told the druggist that his wife was dying and asked him to sell it cheaper or let him pay later. But the druggist said, "No, I discovered the drug and I'm going to make money from it." Heinz got desperate and broke into the man's store to steal the drug for his wife.[6]

The question is, Was the husband's act justified (permissible, or obligatory)?

According to Kohlberg, morally mature individuals resolve this dilemma by contrasting the pharmacist's property rights with the wife's right to life and then deciding which right should have priority. Typically, they argue that the universally applicable principle of rights to life is more important than other universal principles about the right to property and the duty not to steal, and hence that the husband should steal the drug. They might also reason that the general principle of respect for life has priority over the principle of respect for property.

Less mature individuals, by contrast, reason in terms of what is good for themselves (preconventional level) or what society demands (conventional level). Thus, Kohlberg lists three levels of moral development, each with a characteristic view of right action:

1 *Preconventional level:* Right action is defined in terms of what brings pleasure or reward to oneself.

2 *Conventional level:* Right action is interpreted as loyalty to others and respect for law and custom.

3 *Postconventional level:* Right action is identified in terms of general principles discerned with one's autonomous judgment.

Each level is further divided into two stages, as summarized in Table 6.1.

TABLE 6.1 *Kohlberg's Schema of Moral Devlopement*

Level of Moral Development	Stage or Orientation	View of Right Action
1. Preconventional	1. Punishment and obedience	Avoid punishment and submit to power
	2. Egoistic	Satisfy one's own needs
2. Conventional	3. Good-boy, nice-girl	Please and help others
	4. Society-maintaining	Respect authority and social rules
3. Postconventional	5. Social contract or legalistic	Obey useful, albeit arbitrary, social rules
	6. Conscience and universal principles	Autonomously recognize universal rules such as the golden rule

Kohlberg claimed that these stages represent the appropriate steps of moral growth for all people in all cultures. People reach advanced stages only after progressing through earlier ones, and only a few rare individuals such as Socrates reach the highest stage. In addition, Kohlberg asserted that fewer women than men move beyond the conventional level to the post-conventional level.

Gilligan charges that these conclusions, and indeed Kohlberg's schema of moral development, are biased. She points out that Kohlberg studied only males in creating his schema and then simply assumed that it was equally valid for both sexes. Moreover, in structuring the stages of moral progression, Kohlberg also assumed that reasoning based on abstract rules reflects greater moral maturity. As a result, caring-based reasoning focused on specific circumstances is condemned in advance as conventional in a pejorative sense. Thus, Kohlberg's emphasis on general rules about justice and rights may express his own bias as a male.

Gilligan offers an alternative schema, based on several studies and summarized in Table 6.2, of the levels of development:

1 *Preconventional level:* Rightness is viewed exclusively as what is good for oneself.

2 *Conventional level:* Right action is viewed as self-sacrifice in always placing the interests of others before one's own—the socially favored view of how women in particular should behave.

3 *Postconventional level:* Both one's own interests and those of others are valued and balanced with the aim of maintaining attachments to all people involved in specific situations.

TABLE 6.2   *Kohlberg's and Gilligan's Schemes of Moral Development*

Levels of Moral Development	Kohlberg's Justice Perspective	Gilligan's Care Perspective
1. Preconventional	Self-centered, with concern for (1) avoiding punishment and (2) satisfying one's own needs	Self-centered: viewing one's own needs as all that matters
2. Conventional	Expectation-meeting, with concern for (3) pleasing others and (4) meeting society's expectations	Self-sacrificing: viewing others' needs as more important
3. Postconventional	Autonomous recognition of (5) social agreements and (6) universal rules	Mature care ethic: able to reason toward a balance of one's own and others' needs

Gilligan contrasts Kohlberg's justice-oriented approach with the care perspective in which priority is placed on kindness, giving, and caring about the needs of others. The aim is to avoid hurting others and to maintain relationships without hurting oneself. Moral dilemmas thus revolve around competing needs and incompatible ways of caring. They are resolved through communication and sensitivity to particular circumstances rather than through imposition of general rules and priorities among rules. Moral reasons are defined through a web of caring relationships rather than through the interplay of rights to be left alone. In this view, autonomous moral reasoning seeks a proper balance between the others' needs and one's own.

"Heinz's Dilemma" also illustrates the use of reasoning within the care perspective. Perhaps surprisingly, Kohlberg's studies suggested that fewer females than males endorsed Heinz's theft of the drug. (Those studies have since been found inconclusive.) Kohlberg interpreted this as a sign of moral immaturity, contending that women were bound by social conventions about respecting property and obeying laws. In applying the care perspective, however, Gilligan offered a very different interpretation. Gilligan suggests that the reluctance to steal the drug reveals sensitivity to the personal relationships at stake. Not only will Heinz probably end up in jail, where he can no longer help his wife, but also the relationship with the pharmacist will be severed altogether. In Gilligan's studies, women frequently recommended further discussions with the pharmacist in hopes of changing his mind, or proposed innovative ways of raising money to pay for the drug.

Gilligan's criticisms of Kohlberg led him to modify his claims about the universal applicability of the six stages of development. He came to acknowledge that they merely represent growth within a justice perspective and that a care-oriented perspective may be equally valid. For her part, Gilli-

FIGURE 6.1 *Duck-Rabbit*

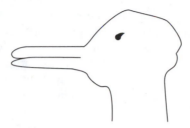

gan has emphasized that both the care and the justice perspectives express important aspects of most moral situations. As an analogy, she cites the alternative ways of perceiving visual data: Just as the image in Figure 6.1 can be seen as a duck or a rabbit, many moral situations can be viewed in terms of either rights or caring.

According to Gilligan, the richest and most acceptable moral outlook would combine both moral perspectives. Men can benefit from integrating elements of the care perspective more fully into their moral outlook, and women can benefit from appreciating the justice perspective. In fact, the justice perspective can aid women in advancing from the conventional self-sacrificing level to the postconventional level, which balances the needs of others and oneself. Women often need to pay greater attention to matters of justice. In this connection, Gilligan refers to Elizabeth Cady Stanton's appeal to rights as a way of raising women's awareness of their needs and their legitimate self-development. Gilligan might thus rephrase Stanton's slogan, "Self-development is a higher duty than self-sacrifice," to read, "Self-development is *as high* a duty as caring for others." At the same time, Gilligan is aware that on some occasions there are good reasons to emphasize one's own rights and needs. This is consistent with the sensitivity to context—rather than the reliance on abstract rules—that is integral to her ethic of caring.

Gilligan's work has influenced feminist ethics in three very different directions.[7] One group of ethicists has developed ethics centered on caring and related values of empathy and trust. A second group of ethicists has sharply criticized the idea of a women's ethics emphasizing caring. That group warns that such an emphasis reinforces traditional stereotypes of women as caregivers, and thereby tends to limit their choices to roles as homemakers and care-oriented professions like nursing and teaching. A third group argues that caring and justice are not separable. Caring is a virtue only insofar as it is *appropriate* (fair, just) caring, as opposed to pathological or exploitive, and justice itself implies caring. Both men and women have blended senses of caring and justice, although there may be different styles of caring and justice typical of many men and women.

Language

An area where feminists largely agree is that sexist (gender-biased) language should be abolished. Language is used to formulate and express thoughts, but it also shapes thoughts. Words and ways of speaking are to a large extent historical products that embody assumptions, attitudes, and emotional responses. As Ludwig Wittgenstein (1889–1951) argued, linguistic practices are intimately joined to "ways of life" defined by communal practices, beliefs, and attitudes. Wittgenstein's later philosophy emerged after he traced his early errors in doing philosophy to naiveté about how language influences thought. In reflecting on those errors, he remarked, "A picture held us captive. And we could not get outside it, for it lay in our language and language seemed to repeat it to us inexorably."[8] Earlier thinkers such as Francis Bacon (1561–1626) were also sensitive to this danger: "People believe that their reason governs words. But words turn and twist the understanding."[9]

One of the most important applications of how language embeds and sanctions misleading "pictures"—that is, perspectives and ways of thinking—has been made by feminists who uncovered sex biases built into language. This linguistic sexism still permeates everyday language use and raises moral questions about whether we should feel comfortable in allowing it to continue. Consider some of the ways in which linguistic practices reflect and reinforce sexist biases.[10]

1   Men are referred to as *Mr.* while women are identified by marital status: *Mrs.* or *Miss* (a problem now easily solved by the use of *Ms.*).

2   According to custom and continuing social pressure, after marriage only the woman is encouraged to change her last name, thereby symbolically expressing a new identity oriented toward the man.

3   Everyday locutions place the male first, as in *husband and wife* (not *wife and husband*), *men and women,* and *son and daughter.*

4   Until recently, names for occupations were male-oriented, as in *fireman* (versus *firefighter*), *mailman* (versus *mail carrier*), *congressman* (versus *member of Congress*), and *chairman* (versus *chair* or *chairperson*).

5   Adult women office workers are often referred to as *the girls in the office,* while male workers are called men. (Compare the racist use of *boy* to refer to adult black men.)

6   The same personality traits are labeled positively when found in males and negatively when found in females: Males are assertive but females are bitchy; men are blunt but women can't hold their tongues; men discuss but women gossip.

7   Far more than men, women are referred to with terms that tie them to their anatomy or to animals, often vulgarly so: *broad, chicks, piece.*

8   God is referred to as *He,* even in religions that officially find it blasphemous to ascribe human properties to God.

9 *Man* (versus *humans* or *persons*), its variants (*mankind, man*), and male pronouns (*he, his*) are used in contexts referring to both men and women, while the reverse would not convey the same universal meaning.

Despite the systematic and varied ways in which male biases enter into language, some people see no need to change our ways of speaking and they object to these changes as based in "politically correct" ideologies. They insist that language should be preserved as it is, and they deny that anyone's thoughts or attitudes are influenced by such trivial linguistic customs. There are two rejoinders to this linguistic conservatism. First, common-sense or naive beliefs about how language affects thought and attitude need to be examined in light of scientific studies. A classic sociological experiment challenges the naive view that using *man* to apply to both men and women has no effect on thought and action:

> Some three hundred college students were asked to select from magazines and newspapers a variety of pictures that would appropriately illustrate the different chapters of a sociology textbook being prepared for publication. Half the students were assigned chapter headings like "Social Man," "Industrial Man," and "Political Man." The other half were given different but corresponding headings like "Society," "Industrial Life," and "Political Behavior." Analysis of the pictures selected revealed that in the minds of students of both sexes use of the word *man* evoked, to a statistically significant degree, images of males only—filtering out recognition of women's participation in these major areas of life—whereas the corresponding headings without *man* evoked images of both males and females. In some instances the differences reached magnitudes of 30 to 40 percent. The authors concluded, "This is rather convincing evidence that when you use the word man generically, people do tend to think male, and tend not to think female."[11]

Second, even those who seek to honor custom must recognize that customs have already changed dramatically in this area, and presumably, once established, those emergent customs will warrant the same respect claimed for the older ones. Increasingly, publishers, writers, public speakers, and conversationalists are paying heed to ways to root out sexism in language. In such a climate of change, it is, at the least, rude to refuse even to try to adjust one's language, and such a refusal may indicate sexist attitudes.

Rape

Fear of violence enters into the daily life of many women, whether in the form of wife battering, incest, or rape, which is the focus here. Rape is a clear-cut paradigm of immorality, but precisely why is it immoral? Part of the answer concerns motives; in particular, rape is immoral if the rapist's motives are to enjoy illegitimate control over the victim, to degrade an innocent person, or to enjoy the victim's suffering. Most of the answer, however, pertains to the act of rape itself and its effects on the victim. In an insightful essay, Susan Griffin offered the following explanation of why rape is immoral:

> Rape is an act of aggression in which the victim is denied her self-determination. It is an act of violence which, if not actually followed by beatings or murder, nevertheless always carries with it the threat of death. And finally, rape is a form of mass terrorism, for the victims of rape are chosen indiscriminately, but the propagandists for male supremacy broadcast that it is women who cause rape by being unchaste or in the wrong place at the wrong time, by behaving as though they were free.[12]

Griffin suggests that rape is immoral because it causes at least three kinds of harm to women. First, the act is a violation of a woman's right to self-determination or personal autonomy, a view that follows logically from the definition of rape as sexual intercourse against or without a person's consent. Second, rape inflicts suffering of several kinds: terror, fear for one's life, immediate physical pain, and trauma that can endure years after the assault. Third, because rape is widespread, it creates warranted fear that restricts the range of women's activities, thereby again violating their right to autonomy.

There is yet another reason why rape is deeply immoral. In our culture sexuality is regarded as central to a person's identity. Sexuality is also an aspect of one's life in which freedom and self-determination are very highly valued. In violating this area of private life, the rapist directly assaults the self-respect of his victim. Usually he is well aware of this fact, and he intends to communicate utter disrespect and contempt for the victim as a woman.

Susan Griffin's essay, which appeared in 1971, focused on rapists who choose their victims indiscriminately. Since then it has been learned that most rapists are acquainted with their victims prior to the rape. This is especially true when the victim is a college student. Such "acquaintance rape" sometimes occurs on dates, as in the following examples of "date rape" taken from studies done by the sociologist William B. Sanders:

> [1] A blind date had been arranged between the victim and suspect. The couple went out to dinner together and then for drinks. At the apartment, the man began making overtures to the victim, and she declined. Then the suspect began slapping the victim and took her into the bedroom, where he raped her.

> [2] Victim picked up suspect in a bar and drove him in her car to a college parking lot. The suspect propositioned the victim, and the victim said she was "in the mood for some loving." At the parking lot, the victim changed her mind since the man's demeanor became ugly—he offered her money. The suspect then grabbed the victim and demanded she take her pants off, which she did after repeated demands and in fear for her safety, and he raped her.[13]

In the first case there is clearly no consent at any time. What should be said, however, about the second case, in which there is initial consent that is later withdrawn? Does the victim's initial agreement constitute a tacit consent to the man's subsequent conduct, especially if they had already voluntarily engaged in some sexual activity? Surely not. An agreement to play a game of tennis does not give one's partner consent to force one to finish the game against one's later wishes; the same is far more true regarding sexual activity. Both a woman and a man have the right to end a sexual encounter at any time, in particular when what is intended as a mutually pleasurable activity ceases to be so.

Gradually, the law has begun to accept what women have been saying for some time: No means no—at any time during a sexual encounter. In 1992, Mike Tyson, heavyweight champion boxer, was found guilty of rape and sentenced to six years in jail. He and the woman involved had been drinking and then went to his room in the early morning hours. Tyson took for granted that the woman was giving tacit consent, but the courts made it clear that a woman is free to refuse intercourse at any stage of flirting or sexual foreplay.

Is the woman nevertheless partially responsible and blameworthy for "precipitating" a rape when she engages in provocative behavior? Susan Brownmiller offers the following answer in *Against Our Will: Men, Women, and Rape,* a book that has drawn increased attention to rape:

> Some men might consider a housewife who lets a strange man into her house for a glass of water guilty of precipitant behavior, and more men would consider a female hitchhiker who accepts a ride from an unknown male guilty of precipitant behavior. Rape-minded men would consider both actions tantamount to an open invitation. I, on the other hand, consider the housewife and hitchhiker insufficiently wary, but in no way would I consider their actions provocative or even mildly precipitant. Similarly, most men seem to consider a woman who engages in sex play but stops short of intercourse guilty not only of precipitant behavior, but of cruel, provocative behavior with no excuse, yet I and my sister feminists would argue that her actions are perfectly allowable and quite within the bounds of human decency and rational decisions.[14]

Brownmiller here argues that women have the same right to control over their lives and sexual conduct that men take for granted over theirs. The right to self-determination is held equally by women and men, despite the unfair double standard by which our society conventionally affords men greater license in their sexual activities.

This double standard, we might add, has even entered into the traditional legal definition of rape. That definition explicitly excluded forcible and violent intercourse within marriage after a wife has refused her husband's sexual advances. The exclusion was based on the assumption that wives are the sexual property of their husbands, and it also presupposed that a consent to marriage entailed a sweeping consent to sexual intercourse at any time. Laws are changing, but it remains difficult to prove in court that a rape took place when a married or unmarried victim has consented on previous occasions to sexual intercourse with the rapist.

Sexual Harassment

In October 1991, Anita Hill testified at the confirmation hearings for Supreme Court nominee Clarence Thomas. Hill reported that, years earlier, when she worked for Thomas, he had sexually harassed her with lewd remarks and sexual provocations. Hill's credentials were impeccable, and at the time of the hearings she was a respected professor of law. Thomas insisted he was an innocent victim of a "high-tech lynching." The majority of Americans believed him, paving the way for his ratification as the only African-American Supreme Court justice (replacing the retired Thurgood Marshall, who had been the only other African-American Supreme Court justice). About one-third of Americans believed Anita Hill and were convinced that a person who had engaged in sexual harassment had been appointed to the Supreme Court.

Sexual harassment is any sexually oriented act or practice involving intimidation, coercion, or unfair sexual conduct. (This definition applies to sexual assault, although assault is sometimes treated as a distinct offense.) In everyday speech the word *harassment* suggests repeated aggravation or persistent annoyance. As part of the expression "sexual harassment," however, it carries the special connotation of misuse of power or authority, where authority consists of institutionally granted forms of power. This can occur in a single episode that is not repeated. The primary habitats of sexual harassment are authority relationships, in particular at work and school. Before focusing on these authority contexts, however, let us mention cases involving unequal power that do not involve authority.

When a man leers, jeers, or whistles at a woman in a public setting, he may be hassling her, that is, bothering or irritating her. Hassling becomes sexual harassment when similar acts occur in threatening situations (for instance when the man and woman are strangers alone on an isolated street at night). Another such situation occurs when the man is part of a group of men confronting and blocking the woman's path. Whatever the man's actual intentions may be, his conduct is reasonably interpreted in such situations as endangering or disrupting the woman's life, whether at the workplace or in academia.

The Workplace

Sexual harassment by an employer (usually, though not always, male) of an employee (usually female) involves abuse of institutional authority—that is, the abuse of power given to the employer by the institution. Recent legislation and Supreme Court rulings define sexual harassment in the workplace as essentially any sexually oriented practice that threatens jobs or work performance.

Obvious examples include threats to fire or demote an employee unless sexual favors are granted, deliberate touching in unwanted ways, and inappropriate comments on the clothing and physical appearance of an employee. A different kind of sexual harassment occurs when employers reveal details about their personal sex lives to their employees against the employees' wishes. The courts have also ruled that harassment occurs when a male supervisor or colleague posts *Playboy* centerfolds in an office to which women have access. All these forms of behavior are restricted by sex discrimination laws that prohibit differential treatment of women and men in unfair ways.

Academia

Academia, like the workplace, is structured according to authority relationships. This fact is downplayed on campuses where faculty members are encouraged to give personal attention to students, where there is trust between students and professors, and where eccentric behavior is tolerated. Nevertheless, professors do have considerable control over their students through grading practices and their institutional authority to guide the educational process. In addition, professors are granted an exceptionally high degree of personal autonomy in carrying out their functions.

As in the workplace, in academia there are three types of sexual harassment: (1) threats of penalties, (2) annoyance, and (3) offers of rewards. *Sexual threats* take the form of indicating that a student must accede to a professor's sexual wishes and do something unwanted or run the risk of receiving an undeserved grade. *Sexual annoyance* occurs when a professor's sexual overtures cause a student to feel uncomfortable or anxious, or when the overture in any other way creates a climate that distracts from the learning process. *Sexual offers* represent attempts to influence behavior by promising a benefit, such as a higher grade. All three types of harassment are unethical and unprofessional because they impede or threaten to impede the learning relationship between student and professor, are unfair to other students who are placed at a grade disadvantage, and show disrespect by focusing attention on one aspect of the student—the sexual one—in a context where that focus is understood to be inappropriate.

SUMMARY

As a social movement, feminism is grounded in a commitment to the empowerment and equal opportunities of women. It opposes patriarchy (socially sanctioned male dominance) and sexism (prejudice on the basis of sex), as well as misogyny (hatred of women) and exploitation (unfair usage). It opposes both individual bigotry (manifested in the attitudes, emotions, and conduct of individuals) and institutional bigotry (manifested in laws, institutions, and practices). Examples of institutionalized sexism include sexism in language, such as the use of male pronouns to refer to both women and men, and restrictions on equal opportunities for work and other social roles.

Psychologists who study moral development are exploring the possibility that there may be gender-linked differences in how virtues are emphasized. Lawrence Kohlberg identified patterns of moral development that he thought were universal, although he later accepted Carol Gilligan's criticisms that these patterns represented only the development of a sense of justice, not all important dimensions of morality. Kohlberg defined morally mature reasoning as the autonomous recognition of universal moral rules—especially rules about rights to be free from the interference of others—and their order of priority. Gilligan argued that this justice perspective is favored by males and that females often emphasize a care perspective based on sensitivity to needs and personal relationships within particular contexts.

Kohlberg and Gilligan agree that moral autonomy, in the sense of the ability to reason for oneself without passive adherence to social conventions, emerges from earlier stages of moral development. Both of them also distinguish three basic levels of moral development—preconventional, conventional, and postconventional—and agree that the preconventional level is characterized by a self-centered preoccupation with satisfying one's own needs. Kohlberg describes reasoning at the conventional level as primarily based on a concern to please others or to meet society's expectations, whereas the postconventional level reflects autonomous recognition of social conventions as morally justified or (at the highest stage) autonomous acceptance of universal moral rules. Gilligan, in contrast, describes the conventional level as reasoning that is based on the self-sacrificing attitude that other people's needs are more important than one's own, and the postconventional level as autonomous reasoning in balancing one's own needs with the needs of others.

In addition to being a form of gross cruelty in which suffering involves both immediate physical pain and terror and long-term trauma, rape violates personal autonomy by denying sexual choice, an area of self-determination central to personal identity and self-respect. This is true of individual acts of rape, which by definition involve the violation of consent. It is also true of rape as a widespread practice, because the very real threat of rape forces women to restrict their activities.

Although sexual harassment often involves cruelty, it is of special interest because of the ways it violates self-determination. It can be defined as any sexually oriented act or practice involving intimidation, coercion, or unfair sexual conduct. Most often it involves abuse of authority relationships at work and school. Sexual harassment is most commonly exhibited through sexual threats, sexual annoyance, and sexual offers, each of which creates conditions that disrupt work and learning.

DISCUSSION TOPICS

1 Is sexism involved in allowing sports teams to restrict members to one sex? In answering this question, consider each of the following contexts: junior and little league sports supported by communities; elementary school teams; high school teams; college teams; professional sports.

2 Elizabeth Wolgast contends that women should have special rights, such as the right to pregnancy leave with a guaranteed job upon return to work. Do you agree? Is her view compatible with the Equal Rights Amendment?

3 Since the following two dozen words were first formulated in 1923, opponents have continually blocked their addition to the Constitution as the Equal Rights Amendment (ERA): "Equality of rights under the law shall not be denied or abridged by the United States or by any State on account of sex." In 1982 this proposed amendment failed to gain the required ratification of three-fourths of the state legislatures, even though it was passed by the U.S. Senate and House of Representatives and had the approval of the majority of Americans. Why is the ERA so controversial? Should it be adopted?

4 Studies have shown that a large majority of American couples prefer to have boys for their first babies.

a Is this preference a form of sexism? Is the case different if a couple insists they like boys and girls equally but assert they need a boy in order to carry on the family name?

b Suppose that a couple learns the sex of the fetus several months into a pregnancy (as is possible using amniocentesis, the process by which cells from a sample of the fluid surrounding the fetus are analyzed to discover its chromosomes). Upon learning that the fetus is female, they plan to have an abortion because they want a boy and plan to have only one child. Is the abortion an act of sexism?

5 Gilligan suggests that most moral situations can be interpreted in terms of both the justice and care perspectives. Yet, is the justice perspective perhaps better suited to social and political contexts and the care perspective better suited to more personal relationships among people (and perhaps animals)? In answering this question, compare and contrast public debates over abortion laws with personal decisions about abortions. Are different moral concepts emphasized in these two contexts? Should they be?

6 Return to the biblical story of Abraham and Isaac cited as a discussion topic in Chapter 5. In her book *In a Different Voice* Gilligan links Abraham's willingness to sacrifice his son to a male, justice-oriented way of thinking. Do you agree? Is it less likely that a woman would do what Abraham did, as Gilligan also suggests?

7 Date rape sometimes occurs when the rapist is drunk or on drugs, and it also occurs when the victim is intoxicated. Explain what you see as the problems in determining whether there is consent when the victim is partially or completely intoxicated. Should it be assumed that when individuals are intoxicated, they cannot give voluntary consent to intercourse? Also, is an intoxicated rapist less blameworthy than a sober one?

In answering these questions, identify and discuss the moral issues involved in the following rape reported by Robin Warshaw in *I Never Called It Rape*. At the time of the rape the woman was in her first year attending a large university and living in coed dorms. She met an attractive football player at a dorm party.

> He wasn't drinking, but he was feeding me alcohol. He asked me to come back to his room—it was right down the hall from where all of us were [partying]. . . . I thought it was just like, "Let's get out of this party." When we got to his room and I saw there was nobody there, I didn't think I could do anything about it.
>
> We started kissing and then he started taking off my clothes. I kept telling him to stop and I was crying. I was scared of him and thought he was going to hurt me. . . . He had a hand over my face. I was five foot two and weighed 110 pounds. [He weighed 265 pounds.] I didn't have any choice.[15]

8 Men (and some women) sometimes consider that sexually provocative clothing and conduct justify or excuse sexual harassment and rape. Discuss why they might think this and whether it has any justification. Would the same conclusion apply to men who are sexually provocative?

9 If a woman does not actively resist sexual intercourse, does that entail that she is giving consent? If you think context is important in answering this question, describe several contexts that yield different answers.

10 If a woman does not actively protest another person's unwanted and annoying sexual advances at the workplace or in academic settings, does that mean that she finds the conduct acceptable and that no sexual harassment takes place? What would you say to critics who charge that Anita Hill is blameworthy if her accusations are true because she did not explicitly object to Clarence Thomas at the time when she alleges he sexually harassed her?

11 Should there be absolute (that is, exceptionless) prohibitions on sexual relationships between professors and (a) students currently registered for their classes, (b) students attending their school but not registered in their classes, (c) students who are their advisees?

SUGGESTED READINGS

Brownmiller, Susan. *Against Our Will: Men, Women, and Rape*. New York: Simon & Schuster, 1975.

Card, Claudia (ed.). *Feminist Ethics*. Lawrence: University Press of Kansas, 1991.

Card, Claudia. *The Unnatural Lottery: Character and Moral Luck*. Philadelphia: Temple University, 1996.

Cole, Eve Browning, and Susan Coultrap-McQuin (eds.). *Explorations in Feminist Ethics*. Bloomington: Indiana University Press, 1992.

Collins, Patricia Hill. *Black Feminist Thought: Knowledge, Consciousness, and the Politics of Empowerment*. New York: Routledge, 1991.

Collins, Patricia Hill. *Black Feminist Thought*. New York: Routledge, 1990.

Dziech, Billie Wright, and Linda Weiner. *The Lecherous Professor: Sexual Harassment on Campus*. 2d ed. Chicago: University of Illinois Press, 1990.

Gilligan, Carol. *In a Different Voice: Psychological Theory and Women's Development,* rev. ed. Cambridge, MA: Harvard University Press, 1993.

Griffin, Susan. *Rape: The Politics of Consciousness.* 3d ed. New York: Harper & Row, 1986.

Held, Virginia (ed.). *Justice and Care: Essential Readings in Feminist Ethics.* Boulder, Co: Westview Press, 1995.

Jaggar, Alison M., and Paula S. Rothenberg (eds.). *Feminist Frameworks: Alternative Theoretical Accounts of the Relations Between Women and Men.* 3d ed. New York: McGraw-Hill, 1993.

Kittay, Eva Feder, and Diana T. Meyers (eds.). *Women and Moral Theory.* Totowa, NJ: Rowman & Littlefield, 1987.

Koehn, Daryl. *Rethinking Feminist Ethics: Care, Trust, and Intimacy.* New York: Routledge, 1998.

Larrabee, Mary Jeanne (ed.). *An Ethic of Care: Feminist and Interdisciplinary Perspectives.* New York: Routledge, 1993.

MacKinnon, Catharine A. *Sexual Harassment of Working Women.* New Haven, CT: Yale University Press, 1979.

Minas, Anne (ed.). *Gender Basics: Feminist Perspectives on Women and Men.* Belmont, CA: Wadsworth, 1993.

Morrison, Toni (ed.). *Race-ing Justice, En-gendering Power: Essays on Anita Hill, Clarence Thomas, and the Construction of Social Reality.* New York: Pantheon Books, 1992.

Noddings, Nel. *Caring: A Feminine Approach to Ethics and Moral Education.* Berkeley: University of California Press, 1984.

Nussbaum, Martha C. *Sex and Social Justice.* New York: Oxford University Press, 1999.

Nussbaum, Martha C., and Jonathan Glover (eds.). *Women, Culture and Development: A Study of Human Capabilities.* Oxford: Clarendon Press, 1995.

O'Toole, Laura L., and Jessica R. Schiffman (eds.). *Gender Violence.* New York: New York University, 1997.

Sommers, Christina Hoff. *Who Stole Feminism: How Women Have Betrayed Women.* New York: Simon & Schuster, 1994.

Spelman, Elizabeth V. *Inessential Woman: Problems of Exclusion in Feminist Thought.* Boston: Beacon Press, 1988.

Tong, Rosemarie. *Feminine and Feminist Ethics.* Belmont, CA: Wadsworth, 1993.

Tong, Rosemarie. *Feminist Thought: A More Comprehensive Introduction.* Boulder, Co.: Westview Press, 1999.

Vetterling-Braggin, M. (ed.). *Sexist Language: A Modern Philosophical Analysis.* Totowa, NJ: Littlefield, Adams, 1981.

Wall, Edmund (ed.). *Sexual Harassment.* Buffalo, NY: Prometheus Books, 1992.

Warshaw, Robin. *I Never Called It Rape: The Ms. Report on Recognizing, Fighting, and Surviving Date and Acquaintance Rape.* New York: Harper & Row, 1988.

CHAPTER 7

Race and Ethnic Identity

The end of the cold war between Western democracies and Soviet communism brought new hopes of global peace, but it also unleashed a host of ethnic conflicts. About the same time, the United States became embroiled in its own "culture wars," as ideological conflicts transformed into *identity politics,* that is, politics based on conflicts among groups shaped by identities linked to such things as ethnicity, race, gender, and religion, as well as age, disability, and economic class. The challenge is for cultural groups to live together while seeking greater justice. Yet, steps designed to improve mutual understanding, such as multicultural curricula in schools and continuing use of affirmative action programs, often seem to intensify rather than lessen conflict.

In this chapter we begin with a discussion of racial bigotry and then widen the topic to ethnic prejudice and understanding. We then contrast two visions of the overarching goals: assimilation versus accommodation of diversity. We conclude by discussing two controversial attempts to oppose racism, as well as sexism: speech codes and affirmative action.

Racism, Race, and Ethnicity

Ralph Ellison's *Invisible Man* explores how stereotypes prevent white Americans from understanding black Americans, but its themes apply to all forms of bigotry. The central metaphor of the novel is set forth in the opening passage:

> I am an invisible man. No, I am not a spook like those who haunted Edgar Allan Poe. . . . I am invisible, understand, simply because people refuse to see me. Like the bodiless heads you see sometimes in circus sideshows, it is as though I have been surrounded by mirrors of hard, distorting glass. When they approach me they see only my surroundings, themselves, or figments of their

imagination—indeed, everything and anything except me. . . . That invisibility to which I refer occurs because of a peculiar disposition of the eyes of those with whom I come in contact. A matter of the construction of their inner eyes, those eyes with which they look through their physical eyes upon reality.[1]

These distorting inner mirrors are preconceived beliefs and attitudes about black people. They are the "prejudging" inherent in prejudice. In contemporary psychological terms, they represent biased "cognitive schemas" through which experiences are filtered. In ordinary language, they are negative stereotypes, that is, simplistic views based on false beliefs, incomplete information, or unjustified value judgments.

Later in the novel, the Invisible Man relates the incident that forced him to grasp how cognitively distorting mirrors had rendered him invisible. Walking alone at night, he accidentally bumped into a white man who called him "an insulting name." He exploded in rage, attacking the man and demanding an apology. During the ensuing fight the white man continued to shout racist obscenities even after the Invisible Man held a knife to his throat. Suddenly he realized that "the man had not seen me, actually; that he, as far as he knew, was in the midst of a walking nightmare" involving an insane assailant who had no reason (that the white man would grasp) for attacking him.[2] He also realized that the man's verbal assault resulted from a stereotypic view that operated outside the man's full awareness.

This is an example of prejudice that is individual, but prejudice can also be institutional and covert. As noted in Chapter 6, individual prejudice is bigotry manifested in attitudes, emotions, and conduct of individuals. Institutional prejudice is manifested in practices, laws, and institutions. We also noted that both individual and institutional prejudice can be overt or covert. Overt prejudice is easily discernible and involves consciously held prejudiced attitudes. For example, the racist bigot self-confidently asserts that Latino people are inferior, the anti-Semite passionately denounces Jews as dangerous, and segregation laws and institutions deny equal opportunity to African Americans. Covert prejudice, also called "visceral" bigotry, is hidden, especially to the prejudiced person, and hence it is often more difficult to remove. It is shown, for example, in ridicule through bigoted humor, as we discuss later.

Even more than the words *prejudice* or even *bigotry,* the term *racism* carries explicit connotations of immorality. As Naomi Zack reminds us, "the meaning or concept of racism for the majority of white Americans refers to hatred, hostility, contempt and harmful intentions in individuals' hearts and minds."[3] But Zack's definition does not capture the full condemning connotations surrounding the term. To call someone a racist is typically to make a serious moral criticism of them. In this way, the term is used to express strong disapproval of other persons because they hold the attitudes Zack lists. Racism is immoral hostility toward other groups. To be sure, bigots sometimes do say, "I am a racist and proud of it," thereby asserting that their hostility toward other groups is something good (a usage consistent with Zack's definition). Yet, this usage is secondary to the primary usage in which the term conveys criticism and fault.

Some have argued that the idea of race is itself a product of bigotry. Usually we think of race as a straightforwardly *biological* concept, that is, one defined by bodily features, especially skin color, based on the added assumption that bodily features have a genetic cause. But a moment's reflection casts this idea into doubt. Some African Americans have skin color that is as light in color as the skin of typical white persons, as well as hair texture and other features that makes them visually "white." What basis is there for insisting the person is really black rather than white?

Much of the answer resides in the legacy of slavery and racism, which insisted that even a "drop of black blood" made one black. The aim was to segregate and oppress people of African heritage, by contrast with those of European heritage. *Heritage* refers to history, to geography, to culture. In short, it refers to *ethnicity,* which is defined more by culture than biology. (Typically, though not always, ethnic cultures are defined by history and geography, together with historical family ties, rather than by religion and nationality). The insistence that any genetic link to African-American ancestry renders one black rather than white may therein be suspect.

These considerations led the powerful thinker W. E. B. DuBois to set forth this definition of race:

> It is a vast family of human beings, generally of common blood and language, always of common history, traditions and impulses, who are both voluntarily and involuntarily striving together for the accomplishment of certain more or less vividly conceived ideals of life.[4]

In this definition the biological or genetic element ("common blood") is present but greatly deemphasized. Others have gone further, however. For example, the repeated abuses of the idea of race led Kwame Anthony Appiah to suggest that we might do best to abandon the idea altogether, certainly as a biological notion. "The truth is that there are no races: there is nothing in the world that can do all we ask race to do for us."[5]

Concerns about meanings of race, of course, are not unique to African Americans. Why should it be assumed that a person whose heritage is half Scottish, one quarter French, and one quarter Hispanic is Latino? Why assume that a person whose mother was Chinese and whose father was German is Asian American? Concepts of race and ethnicity can be useful for limited purposes, but they are readily misused.

In any case, there are *self-identifications* that individuals adopt in matters of their ancestry, whether or not they understand that ancestry is in terms of race and ethnicity. The psychological affirmations shape individuals' sense of who they are, and thereby enter into how they value themselves (in terms of self-esteem). These group identifications have acquired considerable importance, due largely to appreciation of how power differences result in unfair advantages and disadvantages to various groups, and perhaps due as well to the fragmentation of communities. Today, identity issues are second only to economic concerns in shaping social debates. Is this a temporary transformation or something more permanent? How far *ought* race to be important?

Explaining Racism

Many perspectives have been developed by social scientists and philosophers to understand the causes and functions of bigotry. Today the most familiar starting point is the identity of individuals and groups, the theme central to Ellison's novel. Thus, when psychologist Raphael S. Ezekiel conducted a ten-year study of the militant white racist movement, his guiding framework centered around two questions.

> Who am I? How do I fit in the world?

> We ask this of ourselves, each of us, including the Klansman and the Nazi. For these people, the answer is race: 'I am a member of the white race. My people built this civilization, built this country. We have the intelligence and the initiative for the task. Our blood is different and special. Our heritage has been taken from us; inferior races have taken power through their cunning. My race is near destruction. Most of my people are numb and passive, seduced and tranquilized by the enemy. The enemy plans the full destruction of my race's genius—its blood— through racial mixture. Ultimately, we or our enemy will be destroyed.[6]

The elements of fear, anger, paranoia, hatred, and embrace of violence expressed in this passage reflect the militancy of the groups studied by Ezekiel, but they are elements present in other forms of racial bigotry. How should they be understood? Let us contrast three perpectives that attempt to answer this question: moral, psychological-social, and biological perspectives.

Moral Perspectives

Moral perspectives highlight the role of choice in bigotry. According to Jean-Paul Sartre's *Anti-Semite and Jew,* a book devoted to bigotry against Jews but that applies to other forms of prejudice as well, anti-Semitism is not an opinion but instead a "passion" chosen as the core of an entire personal identity. The passion is in part hatred, which constitutes a choice to be terrifying in ways that elevate oneself. At a deeper level, however, it is a choice to think and reason in irrational ways, a choice to devalue reasons that reveal the ignorance and fear manifested in hating entire groups of people based on their skin color or culture.

At a still deeper level, anti-Semites fear accepting personal identity for their lives, choosing instead to blame other groups as scapegoats for their problems. In short, the anti-Semite is "afraid. Not of the Jews, to be sure, but of himself, of his own consciousness, of his liberty, of his instincts, of his responsibilities, of solitariness, of change, of society, and of the world."[7] Thus, anti-Semitism is not one small part of a personality but a core part of the identity a person forms in response to a host of "existential" (fundamentally human) anxieties.

Psychological–Sociological Perspectives

Psychological–sociological perspectives avoid the use of moral language as they identify multiple rather than single causes of bigotry.[8] Scientific studies reveal at least four major types of factors supporting bigotry. First, economic competition for limited resources invites shutting out entire groups from desirable jobs. Thus, during economic downturns we might expect to see an increase of bigotry, and that is what happens. (Recent increases in hate crimes during favorable economies seems to go against this idea, but perhaps the economic frustrations are intensified by vast differences in wealth that the current economy has generated.) Second, individuals frustrated by their own economic situation, or indeed by any other deep-seated frustration and fear, tend to blame others, making them scapegoats. (This is Sartre's point rendered as a psychological generalization rather than a moral perspective.) Third, some prejudice is linked to personality traits, such as rigidity, suspiciousness, and punitiveness. Finally, much prejudice is simply a response learned from the family or other groups: It expresses simple conformity to social norms.

Biological Perspectives

Biological perspectives trace prejudice to biological roots. We have evolved as social creatures whose survival is linked to groups.[9] Prejudices that create "us versus them" serve to strengthen group survival by intensifying bonds of kinship. Prejudice based on ethnicity, race, and culture are extensions of these kinship ties. This view, together with psychological–sociological patterns of human behavior, lead some observers to think of prejudice as natural rather than as an abnormality or anomaly.

   Which of these perspectives is most insightful: Is bigotry an immorality for which we are responsible, a learned or socially conditioned response, or part of our biological inheritance? No doubt all three make a contribution to our understanding, but which perspective we emphasize will be important in our responses to the bigotry we encounter in others—and in ourselves.

Assimilationist and Pluralistic Ideals

What would an ideal society be like, or at least a society where there is as much justice as could realistically be hoped for, regarding matters of race and ethnicity? In a pioneering discussion of racial and gender differences, whose import seemingly extends to ethnic differences, Richard Wasserstrom contrasted two ideals: assimilationist and pluralist. According to the *assimilationist ideal,* things like skin color, racial and ethnic classification, and gender roles would have no particular connection with how individuals are treated. Thus, "a nonracist society would be one in which the race of an individual would be the functional equivalent of the eye color of individuals in our society today."[10] Eye color plays a relatively minor aesthetic role, but it has no bearing on moral or political rights, opportunities, duties, benefits, or burdens. Similarly, race, gender, and ethnicity would essentially become irrelevant morally, socially, and politically.

By contrast, the *pluralistic ideal* would continue to recognize racial, ethnic, and gender differences as socially significant. To be sure, in matters of basic political rights and duties they would be irrelevant. Legal justice would be blind to them. But in everyday social life they would be as important as religion is. Like religious differences, race and ethnicity would be the basis for special associations, such as educational and social groups. They would also be significant factors in selecting associates and friends.

Wasserstrom argues in favor of the assimilationist ideal, for several reasons. First, the assimilationist ideal is far more clear and simple: We readily understand what it means and we avoid all the complicated aspects of a pluralistic ideal. Second, the assimiliationist ideal removes the unfairness resulting from racial and ethnic stereotypes and restrictions based on them. Finally, the assimilitationist ideal maximizes individual autonomy by ensuring that all social roles and opportunities are open; that none of them are closed on the basis of morally irrelevant factors such as skin color.

Iris Marion Young rejects Wasserstrom's arguments. She defends the pluralistic ideal and calls for "a politic of difference" that is sensitive to groups based on race, ethnicity, gender, and disabilities. Her central contention is that such differences are genuine and that the attempt to treat them as morally irrelevant invariably results in oppression and neglect of legitimate claims: "The ideal of a universal humanity without social group differences allows privileged groups to ignore their own group specificity. Blindness to difference perpetuates cultural imperialism by allowing norms expressing the point of view and experience of privileged groups to appear neutral and universal."[11] Individuals *are* different. In addition to their given legacies of history and economic status, they choose to identify themselves—in varied and complex ways—with their racial and ethnic heritage, as well as with gender roles. Ignoring these differences weakens rather than strengthens their exercise of autonomy. Granted, the pluralist ideal is messier; it is also more just.

Young is sensitive to the concerns expressed by Wasserstrom about the continual threat that group differences will generate hurtful stereotypes: "The danger in affirming difference is that the implementation of group-conscious policies will reinstate stigma and exclusion."[12] To counter that threat, she insists that our sense of justice and difference must always be *contextualized,* so as to take account of special obstacles and needs: "For example, in the context of athletics, health care, social service support, and so on, wheelchair-bound people are different from others, but they are not different in many other respects."[13] Similarly, claims based on race, ethnicity, and gender must be tailored to particular situations. Thus, the special claims of American Indians to tribal governance are unique and must be understood in light of the specific oppression inflicted on them historically. In light of the singular history connected with American slavery, African Americans might also have unique moral claims along other lines.

It might seem that Wasserstrom and Young are talking at cross purposes. Wasserstrom discusses alternative ideal societies, whereas Young addresses procedures on the way to such ideals. In fact, part of Young's point is that the pursuit of unrealistic ideals, like the search for universal solutions, can be harmful. Any realistic and viable ideals of justice must be rooted in history and ongoing political tensions.

The disagreement between Wasserstrom and Young about general ideals of justice is reflected in differing social visions of the culture wars, but not necessarily along conventional lines of liberals versus conservatives. Although many political conservatives have been critical of multiculturalism, so have some liberals, e.g., the distinguished historian Arthur M. Schlesinger in his book *The Disuniting of America: Reflections on a Multicultural Society.* As the book's title suggests, Schlesinger is concerned that America is losing its unity amidst divisive wars along lines of ethnicity and race, as well as religion, gender, and economic class. Reminding us that the United States was founded on a vision of diverse people becoming one—*e pluribus unum* (one out of many)—he contrasts this "melting pot" vision with what he calls the current *cult of ethnicity:* "A cult of ethnicity has arisen both among non-Anglo whites and among nonwhite minorities to denounce the goal of assimilation, to challenge the concept of 'one people,' and to protect, promote, and perpetuate separate and racial communities."[14]

In reply to the criticism that he is being ethnocentric, that is, centered in an objectional way on his own ethnic tradition (Anglo-American), Schlesinger insists that Western democracies deserve to be defended for their sponsorship of values worthy of becoming common values across cultures: "Whatever the particular crimes of Europe, that continent is also the source—the *unique* source—of those liberating ideas of individual liberty, political democracy, equality before the law, freedom of worship, human rights, and cultural freedom that constitute our most precious legacy and to which most of the world today aspires. These are *European* ideas, not Asian, nor African, nor Middle Eastern ideas, except by adoption."[15] He concludes that diversity must be appreciated but within a context of common values: "Our task is to combine due appreciation of the splendid diversity of the nation with due emphasis on the great unifying Western ideas of individual freedom, political democracy, and human rights."[16]

These assertions sound abstract until we look closely at what specific trends Schlesinger find worrisome, as failing to give due emphasis to Western ideas. Perhaps his deepest concern is what he sees as using ethnicity to distort rigorous history, as well as rigorous academic work in schools. The cult of ethnicity seeks to elevate the self-esteem of minorities by highlighting the contributions of minority ethnic groups in shaping history. In particular, some African American writers argue that Egyptians were black people who, in turn, shaped Greek culture, and hence the Greek roots of Western democracies actually derive from African roots.[17] But history and other academic disciplines should be pursued and taught with a rigorous concern for truth, not a social agenda of elevating self-esteem. In any case, genuine self-esteem is created through personal accomplishment, not by artificial manipulations.

Another specific concern is with language. Schlesinger objects to the call for bilingual education, such as in using both English and Spanish in teaching Latino and Latina students. Language is the single most important means to maintaining a shared culture. Moreover, some studies reveal that minority students are placed at a great disadvantage, both in education and later in obtaining jobs, when they are not immersed in English language throughout their education.

Yet another concern is the *canon wars*—disagreements about which books will be emphasized in general education courses. Multiculturalists have strongly urged the integration of writings by minorities into college courses, and have largely succeeded in doing so. Their commitment, in part, has been to bring recognition to minorities and thereby strengthen their self-esteem, as well as bring social recognition by fostering in white students greater appreciation of minorities' contributions. But each book by a minority displaces more traditional books by Anglo-Americans.

What should we make of Schlesinger's concerns? No doubt he is correct that excesses have occurred, for example in introducing biases into historical studies. Nevertheless, historical studies have always had to grapple with biases from Anglo-American sources, and insofar as history is a science it contains the procedures to correct such distortions. As for language, compromises seem available as remedies, such as temporary use of bilingual education for one or two years, followed by immersion in English. The canon wars, too, admit of creative compromises. Not every minority group can or should be represented in every course, but a willingness to tailor curricula to local needs, together with some specialized courses, seems to be successfully working at most schools. In short, Schlesinger voices genuine concerns, but perhaps they are ones that can be dealt with creatively.

Let us turn to two further ways of opposing prejudice that do not seem to admit of compromise so readily, at least on the surface: speech codes and affirmative action.

Speech Codes

One attempt to oppose racism is to block its overt expressions in speech. The attempt includes banning the use of overtly racist epithets as well as more indirect expressions of racist attitudes. As an example of the latter, consider racist humor.

We might think of humor as enjoyment of incongruity as expressed through laughter, pleasant inclinations to laugh, and moments of cheerfulness.[18] To ridicule is to mock or arouse scorn by portraying someone (or something) in a negative way, and often this is done through malicious uses of humor. Ridicule through humor constitutes a seductive and camouflaged way to spitefully mock an individual or a group. It is seductive because it catches us by surprise, evoking spontaneous reactions of amusement. It also camouflages prejudice with apparently innocent pleasures: the physical pleasure of laughter, the social pleasure of sharing laughter with others, and the intellectual pleasure of wittiness. Because it seems good to bring people pleasure, ridicule through humor appears to have at least something good about it; but does it really?

In fact, jokes afford a virtual haven for the expression of covert prejudice. Consider these examples, bearing in mind that citing any examples here runs the risk of reinforcing stereotypes. Light-bulb jokes, which became popular in the United States during the late 1960s and 1970s, were used to portray Polish-Americans as stupid: "How many Polacks [to use the offensive slur] does it take to change a light bulb? Three: one to hold the bulb and two to turn the ladder." And anti-Semitic jokes frequently portray Jews as cheap while mocking their physiognomy: "Why do Jews have big noses? Air is free." Jokes are retold, often spreading with remarkable speed across the country, especially through the mass media. Even recounting these jokes as examples in this book risks that effect.

Telling these jokes in the presence of members of the groups being ridiculed will generally directly insult those persons and cause both hurt and resentment. If no members of the group are present, however, is any harm done? Whether we tell a bigoted joke or laugh at one, we are usually sharing the prejudiced attitudes expressed in the joke. In finding the joke enjoyable, we embrace, at least for that moment, the derogatory attitudes underlying the negative stereotype of a group of people. The fun comes through "making fun of" groups by affirming negative stereotypes and inviting hearers to do likewise. Bigoted humor endorses or condones bigoted attitudes and supports a social climate of disrespect for groups of people. Telling and laughing at bigoted jokes usually joins speaker and hearer in a conspiracy of social oppression.

We should, however, qualify this point with several observations. For one thing, in special circumstances it is possible to tell or enjoy some otherwise bigoted jokes without being prejudiced. Much depends on the context. For example, there is such a thing as having a right to laugh at a particular joke in a particular situation. Members of a minority group often have the right to tell and enjoy a joke about their group that outsiders do not have (unless they have been accepted by the group). That is because the motives and attitudes expressed in telling the joke are different. Instead of "putting down" and alienating people, intergroup humor can invite mutual understanding—"laughing with," in good will and shared identification, rather than "laughing at," with contempt and alienation.

These nuances are only one dimension of the complexity in the recent attempts to ban racist language on many college campuses. For example, The University of Michigan's speech code made the following behaviors subject to disciplinary action by university officials:

> Any behavior, verbal or physical, that stigmatizes or victimizes an individual on the basis of race, ethnicity, religion, sex, sexual orientation, creed, national origin, ancestry, age, marital status, handicap or Vietnam-era veteran status, and that
>
> a. Involves an express or implied threat to an individual's academic efforts, employment, participation in University sponsored extracurricular activities or personal safety;
>
> b. Has the purpose or reasonably foreseeable effect of interfering with an individuals' academic efforts, employment, participation in University sponsored extracurricular activities or personal safety; or
>
> c. Creates an intimidating, hostile, or demeaning environment for educational pursuits, employment or participation in University-sponsored extracurricular activities.[19]

Because of the broad scope and areas of vagueness in the code, the courts rejected it as violating constitutionally protected free speech.

In general, the courts have tended to overthrow most speech codes, although some very narrowly drawn codes, especially at private universities, have not been ruled unconstitutional. But what about the moral status of speech codes that do not attach official penalties and punishment? We have a strong moral and legal *right* to free speech, but it does not follow that everything we say is *all right* (morally permissible). Having a right implies protection against official punishment, but peer pressure against racism is both permissible and desirable. Speech codes are a type of peer pressure, assuming students are significantly involved in drafting them, and they also represent an official statement by entire university communities against bigotry. Shouldn't universities strongly condemn the kinds of assaults on individuals when they threaten their academic work and related activities? In fact, shouldn't something like the University of Michigan's code be endorsed as a powerful affirmation of individual dignity, assuming formal penalities were not involved? These questions will be left as a discussion topic.

Affirmative Action

Affirmative action is by far the most controversial social program aimed at countering racism and promoting equal opportunity in education and work. Narrowly defined, affirmative action is the pursuit of active measures in advertising, hiring, promotion, training, and education to ensure that prejudice does not deny minorities and women equal opportunities. For example, employers state in their advertisements that they are equal opportunity employers, thereby encouraging all qualified people to apply. Once applications are received, employers make sure that full and fair attention is given to each applicant, making special efforts to counter any possible prejudice that could affect decisions.

A very different meaning of affirmative action is *preferential treatment* (or *reverse* preferential treatment): the preference afforded to members of groups that in the past were discriminated against, in particular women and minorities. *Weak* preferential treatment gives an automatic advantage to a woman or minority who is equally qualified as a white male. *Strong* preferential treatment gives an advantage even when the woman or minority is less qualified than a white male, although still competent to succeed (in employment or education). Although affirmative action in the narrow sense is relatively uncontroversial, both forms of preferential treatment are highly controversial.

Defenders of preferential treatment programs have three main arguments. First, they appeal to *compensatory justice:* the obligation to compensate for past and present injustice in the forms of racism and sexism. As groups, women and minorities have suffered from the subtle forms of bigotry that permeate society. For example, on average they have received fewer educational resources and less encouragement to undertake challenging educational and career options. Preferential treatment balances out this effect. In terms of rights ethics, women and minorities have a right to compensation; in terms of duty ethics, they are owed a duty of compensation; in rule-utilitarian terms, the rule that gives them preference is justified by the overall good it promotes in counting women and minorities equally.

Second, defenders of preferential treatment argue that it is needed to ensure equal opportunity within a society that continues to be racist. This argument looks to the present, rather than the past. It is based on the body of empirical evidence that racist attitudes continue to permeate our society, sometimes in overt forms but other times in covert forms. In order to ensure equal opportunity overall, prejudice needs to be countered by equally strong social programs aimed at providing education and jobs for minorities.

Third, preferential treatment programs have valuable benefits for society as a whole. They bring women and minorities into positions of responsibility and authority, and thereby enrich the mixture of views and talents in the educational system and work force. New role models are created that encourage additional women and minorities to excel. Society as a whole is encouraged to move toward greater mutual respect and acceptance of cultural diversity. This argument is utilitarian in spirit, although rights ethicists and duty ethicists also emphasize the support for equal respect that derives from a fully integrated society, which preferential treatment promotes.

Opponents of preferential treatment regard it as compounding past injustice with a new form of prejudice—*reverse discrimination*—which is tantamount to an attempt to make two wrongs add up to a right. It is true that equal respect for persons is a demand at the heart of rights ethics, duty ethics, and rule-utilitarianism, and its requirement is straightforward: Give all people the same opportunities to compete according to their qualifications for work and educational opportunities. Where bigotry operates to deny equal opportunity, it should be countered directly, not by creating additional unfairness. Although it is also true that specific individuals who are denied equal opportunity are owed compensation, opponents of preferential treatment argue that such programs are not focused on specifically wronged individuals. Instead, they target all members of groups, some of whom are already privileged because of their wealthy parents.

In regard to good consequences, opponents contend that preferential treatment is a recipe for lowering excellence at the workplace and in all fields of human endeavor that demand advanced education. In admissions to college, as well as in acceptance for jobs and promotions, they argue that the standard must be excellence, not minimal competence plus extraneous factors such as race and gender. Moreover, they contend, preferential programs foster deep resentment among white males and their families regarding the denial of equal opportunities. They also create a stigma that women and minorities are incapable of making it on their own, without special breaks. This stigma furthers, rather than counters, prejudice. It also adds to self-doubts among minorities about the true extent of their talent, according to writers such as Richard Rodriguez in *Hunger of Memory* and Shelby Steele in *The Content of Our Character*.

SUMMARY

Prejudice, in the sense of unfair and unreasonable attitudes toward members of a group, can be overt (consciously held and easily discerned by others) or covert (less conscious and more concealed). At least in its central usage, racism is immoral hostility to entire groups based on racial criteria. Attempts to explain the source of ongoing racism and other forms of bigotry include moral explanations that refer to hatred and dishonest reasoning; psychological–sociological explanations that refer to economic downturns, personal frustrations, rigid personalities, and social conditioning; and biological factors that see prejudice as an extension of kinship ties.

Race is often understood to refer to biological and genetic features, such as skin color, but increasingly that idea has become controversial. Thinkers like W. E. B. DuBois suggest it is better to think of race as essentially referring to ethnicity, that is, cultural identity, while Appiah urges abandoning talk of race (other than one "human race") and replacing it with ethnic groupings.

Portraits of ideal societies can help focus values. Richard Wasserstrom defends an assimilationalist ideal in which race would essentially have no significance. By contrast, Iris Young argues for a pluralistic and diverse society in which ethnic and gender differences are highlighted. Historian Arthur Schlesinger reminds us that United States seeks unity amidst plurality, but cautions that the multiculturalism may be going too far in furthering ethnic tensions.

Language is one dramatic way of sustaining practices of racism, through using derogatory racial epithets and racist humor, for example. Speech codes that ban racist and other hate speech raise concerns about constitutional protection of free speech, as least when the codes are accompanied by official penalties. On the surface, humor seems innocent in that it is is based on our enjoyment of incongruity for its own sake, which is expressed through laughter or episodic cheerfulness. But humor can be morally objectionable when the enjoyment comes at the expense of others, and malicious when others are intentionally degraded. Determining when that occurs requires attention to context and motives.

In the strict sense, affirmative action programs are aimed at ensuring equal opportunity to all individuals. Reverse preferential treatment programs have the further aim of giving preference to women and minorities over equally qualified white males (weak preferential treatment) or more qualified white males (strong preferential treatment). Defenders of the programs emphasize society's responsibility to compensate for the effects of past and present prejudice; they also point to the benefits of a fully integrated society. Critics claim that the programs violate equal opportunity principles and cause additional bad consequences.

DISCUSSION TOPICS

1 How should "race" be defined? Is it a useful concept, or does it do more harm than good? Is there just one human race, manifested in an enormous variety of ethnic groups?

2 Based on your own experience, is bigotry best understood in terms of moral perspectives, psychological–sociological perspectives, or biological perspectives?

3 Describe a situation in which the following jokes would be morally objectionable and a situation (if there is one) in which they would not:

What's black and catches flies?

—Willie Mays (former centerfielder of the San Francisco Giants).[20]

What is the difference between a Jewish Mother and a vulture?

—A vulture waits until you are dead to eat your heart out.[21]

4 Are speech codes against bigotry morally desirable as an expression of a university community's way of opposing racism? Consider both codes backed by disciplinary penalties and codes that do not carry such penalties.

5 Wasserstrom believes that in an ideal society all racial differences would be irrelevant to how people responded to one another in such a society. Do you agree or disagree?

6 Prejudice consists of unfair and unreasonable attitudes toward members of a group. Is the African American or the Mexican American who is raised as a second-class citizen in a ghetto or barrio prejudiced if that person is hostile toward white people and chooses to associate with them as little as possible in his or her personal life?

7 Jimmy ("the Greek") Snyder commented during an interview that black athletes have special physical prowess because their ancestors were "bred" to have strong thighs during the days of slavery in the United States. In widely quoted remarks, Snyder said that "the slave owner would breed his big black [man] with his big woman so that he would have a big black kid." Snyder, a prominent sports broadcaster, was fired from his job because of these remarks. Some people defended Snyder on the grounds that he had portrayed black athletes as superior, praising them rather than intending to make a racial slur. Is Snyder's remark racist? Is it unfair that he was fired? (In your answer, take account of the fact that there is no evidence supporting his "pop" evolution theory.)

8 In recent years a number of incidents on college campuses created a concern that a "new racism"—that is, renewed racism—confronts black students. For example, a brawl between white and black students occurred at the University of Massachusetts at Amherst following the final game of the 1986 World Series; a fraternity at the New Jersey Institute of Technology held a party advertised with handbills glorifying violence against blacks; a fraternity at the University of Wisconsin at Madison placed a caricature of a black man with a bone through his nose on the fraternity's front lawn; vandals carved "KKK" in a black student's dormitory room at the University of California at Berkeley.[22] Related events occurred elsewhere, such as in the Queens section of New York City, where a black man was killed by a car while fleeing a group of white teenagers who believed they had a right to keep black people away; in Forsyth County, Georgia, where an all-white community insisted on keeping black people out of the neighborhood; in Texas where a black man was chained to a truck and dragged to death and dismemberment; in Illinois where a white supremacist went on a spree shooting minorities; and in Littleton, Colorado, where two students murdered as many of their fellow students as they could before killing themselves. How would you explain this renewal of overt racism in recent years, especially among students at schools that attract well-educated students? What should be done about it?

9 Present and defend your view as to whether reverse preferential treatment, in either its weak or strong form, is morally justified. In doing so, take into account several different contexts, including public universities, private universities, and for-profit corporations.

SUGGESTED READINGS

Appiah, Kwame Anthony. *In My Father's House.* New York: Oxford University Press, 1992.

Arthur, John, and Amy Shapiro (eds.). *Campus Wars: Multiculturalism and the Politics of Difference.* Boulder, CO: Westview Press, 1995.

Babbitt, Susan E., and Sue Campbell (eds.). *Racism and Philosophy.* Ithaca, NY: Cornell University Press, 1999.

Baird, Robert M., and Stuart E. Rosenbaum (eds.). *Bigotry, Prejudice, and Hatred: Definitions, Causes, and Solutions.* Buffalo, NY: Prometheus, 1992.

Bell, Linda A., and David Blumenfeld (eds.). *Overcoming Racism and Sexism.* Lanham, MD: Rowman & Littlefield, 1995.

Belliotti, Raymond A. *Seeking Identity: Individualism Versus Community in an Ethnic Context.* Lawrence, KS: University Press of Kansas, 1995.

Boxill, Bernard R. *Blacks and Social Justice* Rev. ed. Lanham, MD: Rowman & Littlefield, 1992.

Cohen, Marshall T., T. Nagel, and T. Scanlon (eds.). *Equality and Preferential Treatment.* Princeton, NJ: Princeton University Press, 1977.

Cudd, Ann E. "Psychological Explanations of Oppression," in Cynthia Willett (ed.), *Theorizing Multiculturalism* New York: Blackwell, 1998, pp. 187–215.

De Sousa, Ronald. "When Is It Wrong to Laugh?" In *The Rationality of Emotion.* Cambridge, MA: MIT Press, 1987.

DuBois, W.E.B. *The Souls of Black Folk.* New York: Penguin Books, 1989. First published 1903.

Dundes, Alan. *Cracking Jokes: Studies of Sick Humor Cycles and Stereotypes.* Berkeley, CA: Ten Speed Press, 1987.

Ezorsky, Gertrude. *Racism and Justice: The Case for Affirmative Action.* Ithaca, NY: Cornell University Press, 1991.

Goldberg, David Theo (ed.). *Anatomy of Racism.* Minneapolis: University of Minnesota Press, 1990.

Kymlicka, Will. *Multicultural Citizenship.* Oxford: Clarendon Press, 1995.

Martin, Mike W. "Invisible Man and the Indictment of Innocence." *College Language Association Journal,* 25 (1982): 288–302.

Morreall, John (ed.). *The Philosophy of Laughter and Humor.* Albany: State University of New York Press, 1987.

Philips, Michael. "Racist Acts and Racist Humor." *Canadian Journal of Philosophy,* 15 (1984).

Pittman, John P. (ed.). *African-American Perspectives and Philosophical Traditions.* New York: Routledge, 1996.

Rodriguez, Richard. *Hunger of Memory.* New York: Bantam, 1982.

Sartre, Jean-Paul. *Anti-Semite and Jew.* New York: Schocken, 1965.

Shelby, Steele. *The Content of Our Character.* New York: Harper Perennial, 1990.

Thalberg, Irving. "Visceral Racism." *Monist,* 56 (1972).

Thomas, Laurence Mordekhai. *Vessels of Evil: American Slavery and the Holocaust.* Philadelphia: Temple University Press, 1993.

Wachtel, Paul L. *Race in the Mind of America.* New York: Routledge, 1999.

Wasserstrom, Richard A. "On Racism and Sexism." In R. A. Wasserstrom (ed.), *Today's Moral Problems.* 3d ed. New York: Macmillan, 1985.

Young, Iris Marion. *Justice and the Politics of Difference.* Princeton, NJ: Princeton University Press, 1990.

Zack, Naomi (ed.). *RACE/SEX: Their Sameness, Difference and Interplay.* New York: Routledge, 1997.

Zack, Naomi. *Thinking About Race.* Belmont, CA: Wadsworth, 1998.

PART THREE

Moral Standing

Until now the great weakness in all ethical systems has been that they dealt only with the relations of [hu]man to [hu]man. In reality, however, the question is, What is our attitude toward the universe and all [life] that it supports?[1]

There is a development under way by which the circle of ethics always grows wider, and ethics becomes more profound.[2]

Albert Schweitzer

Who and what has moral standing or significance? That is, what kinds of things in the universe count morally, are members of the moral community, and should be taken into account, for their sake, in our moral reasoning? This is a particular kind of issue about moral relevance. Many things deserve consideration in our moral reasoning because they pertain to pursuing moral values. How abortions are performed is relevant to protecting the health and safety of women. But are human fetuses persons, or in some other way inherently significant morally, such that we have responsibilities to them? Again, animals and ecosystems indirectly contribute to human survival, but do they deserve any moral consideration in their own right?

When Albert Schweitzer spoke of the "circle of ethics" growing wider, a metaphor that Peter Singer later made familiar,[3] he referred to a historical progression in which appreciation of moral significance broadened gradually. At first people recognized as inherently valuable only members of their immediate families and tribes. Gradually they came to affirm the moral worth of members of wider communities or nations, or members of ethnic or racial or religious groups. The affirmation of all human beings as having inherent moral worth was a gradual evolution. It took far longer before higher mammals and other conscious creatures began to be granted moral significance, and today there is still no consensus about the moral status of the human fetus. Schweitzer urged that the circle of moral significance should be expanded even further to all living organisms, and others argue for the moral significance of even the inorganic natural world.

Chapter 8 takes up the difficult issues surrounding abortion, including the moral significance of the fetus and how its significance should be balanced against other moral factors. Chapter 9 explores moral responsibilities concerning conscious nonhuman animals. Chapter 10 discusses whether the scope of ethics needs to be expanded further, or whether traditional human-centered ethics can accommodate the increased need for protecting the environment.

CHAPTER 8

Abortion

Since 1973, when the Supreme Court issued its ruling in *Roe v. Wade,* abortion has become an increasingly divisive issue in the United States.[1] The Supreme Court ruled that women have the right to abortions until the fetus becomes viable, that is, until it can live outside the uterus. (The Court also upheld the right to an abortion after viability if the abortion is necessary for the health of the woman). As a rationale, the Court cited a woman's right to privacy—her right to make decisions without interference by the government. This ruling made unconstitutional most state laws prohibiting abortion.

In the abortion controversy, much is at stake concerning respect for persons. *Pro-life* ("conservative") groups, who favor prohibition of all or most abortions, claim that abortions kill babies—one million each year in the United States alone. *Pro-choice* ("liberal") groups, who favor permissive laws on abortion, regard attempts to restrict abortions as assaults on the fundamental freedoms of women. The confrontations between pro-life and pro-choice groups sometimes conceal the "in-between" or moderate positions. *Moderates* regard some abortions as morally permissible and other abortions as unjustified. Interestingly, more than half of all Americans define themselves (in opinion polls) as moderates, although most also believe that people should be allowed to make their own abortion decisions.[2]

The dichotomy between pro-choice and pro-life groups also conceals the fact that there are *three* important moral issues concerning abortion. First, is the fetus a person, with a right to live? If it is not fully a person, what is its moral status? Second, if we assume that the fetus is a person with a right to life or is otherwise morally valuable, how should that right or value be weighed against other moral reasons, in particular the rights of the woman? Third, what laws and government policies concerning abortion are morally justified?

With regard to each of these issues there are conservative, liberal, and moderate views. Indeed, one might be a conservative or moderate on some of the issues and a liberal on others. This adds to the complexity of the abortion question. In this chapter we can sketch only a few of the many arguments found in the extensive literature on this topic.

Issue 1: Are Fetuses Persons?

The first issues we consider concern whether the fetus is a person (and, if so, when it becomes one) or whether it has some other moral status. We will use the word *fetus* to refer to the prenatal (unborn) stage from conception until birth, rather than the narrower medical sense of "fetus," which refers to the unborn from the time when brain waves can be monitored at about eight weeks. We will use the word *person* to refer to beings who have a moral right to life or who are otherwise defined as full members of the moral community. Where, in the continuous development from conception to birth to infancy, do we "draw a line" and understand the fetus as a person?

We might note that in *Roe v. Wade*, the Supreme Court refused to rule on whether the viable fetus is a person with a right to life. The Court instead ruled that states could pass laws forbidding abortions after the stage of viability because of states' "legitimate interest in potential life" (*Note:* "potential life"). The Court said it lacked the knowledge to rule on when the fetus becomes an actual person. The Court also ruled that states could pass laws governing where and how a fetus of three months' development can be aborted, because at that time abortions become more hazardous and because states have a legitimate interest in protecting the health of women. Also, in 1973, the point of viability was about six months, but since then medical technology has made it possible for many fetuses to survive weeks earlier.

Conservatives

Conservatives draw the line that distinguishes the point where fetuses become persons at conception—at the moment when a sperm fertilizes an ovum to form a zygote, a single cell that contains forty-six chromosomes (unless genetic abnormalities occur). Often conservatives have religious beliefs that lead them to view the zygote as a person with a soul, but conservatives also set forth moral arguments for their view. The moral arguments are relevant here, since our concern is with arguments that carry force beyond particular religious faiths.

One argument focuses on the immediate properties of the zygote.[3] The zygote is the product of two humans and it has forty-six chromosomes; therefore it is a human being. Because all humans have a right to life, the fetus is a person with a right to life.

This argument assumes that a zygote is a human being because it is produced by humans and has forty-six chromosomes. Critics disagree and find it odd to think of a single cell as a human being. They point out that every cell in the body has forty-six chromosomes (except for sperm and ova, which have twenty-three chromosomes) and can be viewed as a "living thing" and a product of humans, but of course these cells are not human beings.

Liberals draw a sharp distinction between two senses of "human": (1) a biological or genetic sense, in which a fetus might be counted as a member of the species *Homo sapiens* simply because of its chromosomal count inherited from other humans, and (2) a moral sense in which a human is a person with a right to live or otherwise has full membership in the moral community. They charge conservatives with erroneously sliding from the first to the second sense. Liberals claim that the fact that it has forty-six chromosomes may make the fetus human in the biological or genetic sense, but it does not follow that it is therefore human in the moral sense.

A second conservative argument begins not with the zygote, but with the point at which everyone will agree there is a person. Most people (though not all) will agree that a healthy newborn baby is a person. If that fact is challenged, then we can choose a later stage at which everyone will agree that the infant is a person, and consider the process that led up to that stage. The process is one of continuous development of a single being, so continuous that, in reverse chronology, it would be arbitrary to draw a line at any point short of the zygote and say there is no longer a person at that point. Therefore, a zygote is a person.

Critics of this argument insist there are nonarbitrary lines that can be drawn at dramatic points along the way. Viability is one such dramatic point, at which the fetus becomes capable of existing outside the uterus. Another dramatic point is marked by the development of brain waves, which suggests the beginnings of or foundation for consciousness. Even if a precise line cannot be drawn, at least a blurry line, sufficient for moral purposes, might be drawn at such points.

A third conservative argument looks to the future of the zygote. In one version this is the potentiality argument: Because the zygote will develop into an infant (that is, a person in its infancy), it is already a person. That is a fallacy: A potential person is not yet a person. More generally, a merely potential anything is not yet that thing.

More recent versions of this look-to-the-future argument, however, are not so obviously fallacious. Don Marquis argues that the fetus is morally comparable to you and me in one key respect: It has a future that is valuable. It will have this future, given normal development, whether or not we conclude it is now a person. That is what matters morally, according to Marquis, because that explains why it is wrong to kill you or me: "When I am killed, I am deprived both of what I now value which would have been part of my future personal life, but also what I would come to value. . . . Inflicting this loss on me is ultimately what makes killing me wrong."[4] The same principle that forbids killing creatures that have a valuable future applies to fetuses:

The future of a standard fetus includes a set of experiences, projects, activities, and such which are identical with the futures of adult human beings and are identical with futures of young children. Since the reason that is sufficient to explain why it is wrong to kill human beings after the time of birth is a reason that also applies to fetuses, it follows that abortion is prima facie seriously morally wrong.[5]

Is this argument sound? (This question is left as a discussion topic.)

Liberals

Liberals draw the line defining persons at viability, birth, or even much later. Mary Anne Warren, for example, argues that a fetus is not a person because it lacks the five features characteristic of persons:

(1) *sentience*—the capacity to have conscious experiences, usually including the capacity to experience pain and pleasure;

(2) *emotionality*—the capacity to feel happy, sad, angry, loving, etc.;

(3) *reason*—the capacity to solve new and relatively complex problems;

(4) *the capacity to communicate,* by whatever means, messages of an indefinite variety of types; that is, not just with an indefinite number of possible contents, but on indefinitely many possible topics;

(5) *self-awareness*—having a concept of oneself, as an individual and/or as a member of a social group; and finally

(6) *moral agency*—the capacity to refulate one's own actions through moral principles or ideals.[6]

To qualify as a person, according to Warren, at least one of these conditions must be met; but the fetus, even at seven or eight months, does not meet any of these conditions, and therefore is not a person.

Is it true, as Warren contends, that a developed fetus meets none of these conditions? Studies of advanced-stage fetuses suggest they have a capacity for pain, and conservatives and moderates suggest that perhaps some of the other criteria are also met. Is it possible to give a more decisive criterion for being a person?

Michael Tooley thinks that self-awareness (Warren's fifth criterion) is both necessary and sufficient for being a person. He argues that "an organism possesses a serious right to life only if it possesses the concept of a self as a continuing subject of experiences and other mental states, and believes that it is itself such a continuing entity."[7] To have a right to something means that if we desire that thing then other people are obligated not to deprive us of it. In particular, to have a right to life means that if we desire to live, then others are obligated not to kill us. In turn, to desire life entails that we have a concept of our life, as well as a concept of ourselves as wanting to live (allowing that we have this concept even when asleep, in a coma, or depressed). To have any rights at all, then, one must have self-awareness. Since at no stage is the fetus self-aware, the fetus is not a person.

The obvious objection to Tooley is that newborn babies and even one-year-old infants also fail to meet his criterion, and hence are not persons according to his criterion. Tooley does not see this as an objection, however, for he believes that persons emerge only later in infancy as they develop a self-concept. Does this mean that infanticide—killing of infants—is justified, since the early infant is not a person? Yes, says Tooley, or rather he suggests that in some cases infanticide is justified, namely, those babies with severe birth defects. Healthy and moderately handicapped infants should not be killed, because of utilitarian reasons, such as the interests and concerns of other members of the moral community.

Tooley's view seems astonishing. If anything is clear to most of us, it is that infants are persons—persons in their early infancy. But then, what criterion establishes personhood? Is the criterion viability, the ability to live outside the woman? Or is it arbitrary to draw the line at that point, rather than, say, at a day or two (or week or so) earlier?

Moderates

Moderates adopt one of two approaches. One approach is to "draw a line" between nonpersons and persons at an earlier stage than liberals but at a later stage than conservatives. Some moderates, for example, are struck by the emergence of brain-wave activity during the second month of fetal development.[8] They interpret brain wave activity as indicating the beginning of consciousness, or at least the foundation for the conscious life that is characteristic of persons. This view draws some support from the contemporary legal definition of when a person is dead. According to the "brain dead" definition, a person is dead when an electroencephalogram detects no electrical activity in the brain, even though the heart and lungs may continue to function. Since the cessation of brain function signals the death of a person, is it not reasonable to understand the beginning of brain functioning as the beginning of personhood?

A very different approach adopted by moderates is to abandon the effort to draw a line between persons and nonpersons. As Jane English writes, "There is no single core of necessary and sufficient features which we can draw upon with the assurance that they constitute what really makes a person; there are only features that are more or less typical."[9] These typical features include the ones cited by Mary Anne Warren—sentience, emotionality, reason, communication capacities, self-awareness, and moral agency. However, they also include physical factors such as genetic makeup and physical appearance, social factors such as the ability to form relationships and interact within communities, and legal factors such as status before the law. There are innumerable distinctive characteristics of persons, but none of them constitutes the defining essence of persons. As a result, there is no reasonable way to draw a line at one point of development and proclaim that there, for the first time, a person exists.

Nevertheless, English suggests that the very early fetus, which is only a cell or clump of cells, is very unlike a person. The fetus gradually becomes more person-like as it develops. Hence the fetus, at least at some of its stages, has an intermediate moral status. It is not yet a person with a full-blown right to live, but neither is it a mere "tumor" that lacks all moral status. Moreover, the moral value of the fetus changes and increases during the course of its development. No precise quantification of that value is possible, but the more-advanced fetus has greater moral significance than the less-advanced fetus.

This second approach by moderates leaves us with ambiguity, uncertainty, and perhaps ambivalence, rather than clear guidelines for understanding the fetus. Does this result amount to being "wishy-washy," or does it capture the vagueness inherent in the concept of persons?

Issue 2: Balancing Moral Reasons

Where does this disagreement over the moral status of the fetus leave us? In disagreement! The previous arguments (and others) sometimes do lead individuals to change their attitudes about whether a fetus is a person, but no widespread consensus has emerged on this first issue. Is it possible to make progress by moving to the second issue, which concerns the attempt to balance the moral significance of the fetus against other moral reasons, in particular, against the rights of the woman?

Conflicting Rights: Liberals Versus Conservatives

For a moment, let us stipulate (for the sake of argument) that the fetus is a person with a right to life. With regard to abortion, what follows from this assumption? At first glance it may seem obvious that a person's right to life is momentous enough to outweigh whatever inconvenience a pregnancy might impose on a woman. Pregnancy involves more, however, than a minor inconvenience! This first glance also overlooks the importance of women's rights to autonomy (self-determination) and to decide what happens to their bodies.

Judith Jarvis Thomson argues that a right to life, by itself, does not give anyone a right to use another person's body for nine months. In general, our right to decide what happens to our bodies is not trivial compared with another person's right to life. She asks us to imagine this:

> You wake up in the morning and find yourself back to back in bed with an unconscious violinist. A famous unconscious violinist. He has been found to have a fatal kidney ailment, and the Society of Music Lovers has canvassed all the available medical records and found that you alone have the right blood type to help. They have therefore kidnapped you, and last night the violinist's circulatory system was plugged into yours, so that your kidneys can be used to extract poisons from his blood as well as your own.[10]

The Society of Music Lovers apologizes to you, but they emphasize the importance of the violinist's right to life, which is in fact of obviously greater importance than any inconvenience to you.

Most of us would be outraged if this happened to us, and we would reject the notion that another person's right to life gives that person a right to use another's body. To allow the violinist to remain hooked up to one's blood supply would be an act of generosity, but the violinist's right to life does not by itself confer an obligation. By analogy, the fetus's right to life does not by itself give it a right to a woman's body. In general, a right to life does not entail an unconditional right to any and all resources that society has available to keep us alive; nor does it give us an absolute right never to be killed (or allowed to die) under any circumstances. It gives only a right not to be killed unjustly, and we need further argument to show whether abortion constitutes an unjust killing of a fetus.

Indeed, conservatives do have a further argument. They argue that, in most instances, a woman tacitly gives the fetus a right to use her body. The violinist case is analogous only to pregnancies caused by rape (as Thomson is also aware). When a woman engages in sexual intercourse, she knows of the risk of getting pregnant, or at least she can be expected to know that risk. Hence, she can be held responsible for the pregnancy that results from her conduct, and she implicitly grants the fetus the right to the essential means for its survival until it becomes able to survive outside the uterus. The logical implication is that women unwilling to accept that responsibility—even with accidental pregnancy—should remain sexually abstinent.

Is sexual abstinence an unreasonable demand? Liberals insist it is. By taking every reasonable precaution in using birth control, a woman shows she is not granting a fetus (caused by an accidental pregnancy) the right to use her body. Thus, liberals argue that in these cases, at least, abortion is permissible. Liberals go even further, however. Suppose we could agree that responsible sexual conduct implies the use of birth control (both to prevent unwanted pregnancies and, by means of condoms, to prevent AIDS). We might recognize that a woman who has several abortions—essentially using abortion as a form of birth control—is not acting responsibly. Does it follow that she gives the fetus a right to use her body, and hence that the fetus's right obligates her to give birth to the fetus, as conservatives contend? Liberals argue that the woman's failure to engage in responsible sex does not imply that she has given the fetus the right to her body for nine months. A woman's right to decide what happens in and to her body overrides any right the fetus has.

We have returned to moral gridlock between liberals and conservatives. The assumption that the fetus is a person with a right to life does not bring conservatives and liberals closer together. Conservatives weigh the fetus's right to life more heavily than liberals, and liberals weigh the woman's right to decide what happens to her body more heavily than conservatives. What do moderates have to say at this point?

Moderates

Jane English, who argued that we cannot determine precisely when a fetus becomes a person, asks us to assume for the sake of argument that a fetus is not a person. What follows? It does not follow that we can treat the fetus in any way we like. Animals are not persons, but it is immoral to torture them for fun, and perhaps it is wrong to kill them without a good reason. Just because a living thing is not a person does not mean it has no moral significance at all. Advanced fetuses are at least person-like, and that gives them moral significance. Less-advanced fetuses, at least at intermediary stages of development, may also have some moral significance that demands we have good reasons before aborting them.

Even if we are unhappy with this talk about "some moral significance," we need to attend to certain psychological facts about our response to person-like fetuses. To maintain our moral sensitivity we must preserve a coherence among such moral attitudes as respect, sympathy, and guilt. A casual attitude about abortion can erode that coherence. English writes, "Thus, I think that anti-abortion forces are indeed giving their strongest arguments when they point to the similarities between a fetus and a baby, and when they try to evoke our emotional attachment to and sympathy for the fetus. An early horror story from New York about nurses who were expected to alternate between caring for six-week premature infants and disposing of viable 24-week aborted fetuses is just that—a horror story."[11]

English appeals to the bad consequences that can follow from a failure to recognize some moral significance to fetuses, even if they are not fully persons. In effect, this part of her argument is rule-utilitarian in that it attends to the consequences of adopting certain general attitudes and rules regarding fetuses. Other moderates think in more contextual terms, perhaps act-utilitarian terms. They recommend a case-by-case analysis of each abortion decision, asking: What are the consequences, good and bad, of abortion or childbirth in particular circumstances? This approach bypasses the abstract arguments over rights that characterize the disagreements between conservatives and liberals.

For example, suppose that giving birth would bring into the world an unwanted child whose mother is unable to give loving care to the child. Suppose that having a child would subvert a woman's education and career plans, as well as lead her peers to stigmatize her. Suppose a fetus has been diagnosed with a very serious genetic disease that calls into question whether it will have a meaningful life and adds great hardship to its caregivers. Suppose a woman is willing to give the child up for adoption, but for various reasons the child would be unlikely to be adopted and the government happens to provide inadequate resources to care for orphans. The possible situations are varied, and each example must be examined in its full complexity. As a result, moderates urge that women's rights sometimes, but not always, override the moral status of the fetus.

Issue 3: Laws and Government Policies

Disagreements over the first two issues—the status of the fetus and the balance of moral factors—are reflected in the differences over the third issue: What laws and government policies concerning abortion are morally justified? Liberals support *Roe v. Wade*. They also favor government-funded abortions for women who lack the financial resources for abortion. Conservatives seek to overturn *Roe v. Wade* and to pass laws preventing most abortions. Moderates want abortions to be legal at least up to two or three months, and are open to compromises that would modify *Roe v. Wade*.

The question of legality is a distinctive new issue that invokes new moral reasons. Justified laws must be sensitive to political settings—in particular, to the democratic setting in the United States—and to overall consequences of the laws. Thus, a conservative or moderate on the first two issues might consistently support *Roe v. Wade* on the grounds that in democracies adults should be allowed to make their personal choices, especially in situations where there is no moral consensus about the first two issues. This consistency is especially clear for those conservatives who understand their attitudes on abortion to be grounded in their religious beliefs, which they know cannot be the basis for laws in a democracy that separates church and state.

Again, there are consequences that need to be weighed in assessing which laws are morally justified. In particular, the illegality of abortion would not in itself end abortions, but only reduce them by making them more difficult to obtain, forcing women to travel to places where abortions remain legal. Restrictive laws would also result in death and injuries from illegally performed abortions by unqualified persons. These consequences need to be weighed by all parties in deciding which laws are feasible and desirable, although they do not by themselves settle the issue.

There are also consequences of the legal status of abortion, such as the continuing political turmoil and social disruption since *Roe v. Wade*. Since 1988, for example, the conservative group Operation Rescue has attempted (and often succeeded) in using civil disobedience to block entrance to or to close abortion clinics. Others have engaged in violent acts, including the bombing of abortion clinics. In March 1993, one pro-life activist murdered a Florida gynecologist who performed abortions. Conservatives regard this violence as minor compared with the scale of what they see as the widespread abortion-killings of babies.

Most laws are the products of compromises, and moderates urge that abortion laws clearly exemplify an instance where compromise is desirable. As Martin Benjamin points out, the abortion controversy meets all four conditions for circumstances calling for compromise:

1   The facts are uncertain (about world-views, about the long-term effects of new and traditional ways of life).

2   The moral issues are complex.

3 The disputing parties are in continuing and cooperative relationships as citizens of the same country.

4 The legal issues must be resolved to maintain community.[12]

What compromises concerning abortion laws are reasonable and possible?

Martin Benjamin supports the idea of a compromise that would reject *Roe v. Wade* by restricting abortions after three months or even ten weeks, except for unusual circumstances such as those presented by threats to the woman's health, severe genetic deformities, and cases of rape and incest (where the victim did not make an earlier decision for an abortion). In his view, this change in the law would embody genuine concessions on each side. Yet, the vast majority of abortions take place during the early months of pregnancy, and it seems doubtful that conservatives would endorse a compromise that left the number of abortions essentially unchanged.

Benjamin points out that compromise has proven extraordinarily difficult because abortion is at the center of wider controversies concerning the ethics of sex, love, and gender roles. Indeed, abortion is the lightning rod for disputes between religious conservatives and feminists—two groups which defend clashing ideals surrounding sexual conduct and gender roles.[13] The most vocal part of the pro-life movement sees abortion as violating its religious conviction that the proper role of sex is procreation within marriage. The most vocal part of the pro-choice movement sees the right to abortion as a symbol for diversity of outlook on sex in relation to love, and also as supporting the freedom of women to pursue careers previously closed to them.

One obvious hope for compromise is to find widely acceptable ways to prevent unwanted pregnancies. For example, most people agree that wider education may be helpful (though some conservatives oppose the funding of sex education programs, which in their view encourage sexual promiscuity). Another possible preventive measure would be to make birth control more effective, for instance, by making condoms easily available—a practice that is occurring anyway in order to prevent AIDS. Many conservatives have opposed this practice because it encourages premarital sex, which they find immoral. Another possibility is pregnancy counseling designed to inform women of their options, including adoption. Liberals have been opposed to this because they suspect it leads to coercion, rather than value-neutral counseling. Despite these difficulties confronting compromise, some legislators have managed to develop compromises on education and counseling programs in their states.[14]

Liberals might be open to the possibility of compromises that enable attention and resources to shift away from the preoccupation with abortion and toward other pressing social needs. For example, they might stop pushing for laws that allow public money to be used to fund abortions for women who cannot afford them, knowing that such laws require conservatives to pay taxes to fund acts that conservatives regard as killing.

Finally, there is always the hope for increased tolerance and understanding of opposing world views that often frame abortion debates. Is that hope realistic, and could it at least lessen the preoccupation with abortion that overshadows other issues that are also important for our society to confront?

SUMMARY

We distinguished three moral issues concerning abortion. First, is the fetus a person with a right to life (or who otherwise possesses full moral status in the community of persons)? Conservatives argue that the fetus is a person because it is genetically human, because the only nonarbitrary place to draw a line identifying personhood is at conception, and because fetuses are just like other humans in their prospects for a valuable future. Liberals argue that fetuses are not persons, because persons have features such as rationality and self-awareness that fetuses do not have. Moderates draw the line between persons and nonpersons at points in between conception and viability; alternatively they argue that no sharp lines can be drawn at all and that the fetus has a partial moral status (some moral worth, but not as much as persons).

The second issue arises when we assume the fetus is a person with a right to life (or otherwise has full moral status in the moral community). How is its right to life to be weighed against the woman's right to autonomy and her right to decide what happens in and to her body? Conservatives see the fetus's right as most important, while liberals regard the woman's right as most important. Moderates insist on examining particular cases and contexts, believing that some, but not all, abortions are morally justified.

The third issue concerns the moral justification of the laws and government policies governing abortion. This issue is closely related to the first two issues, but raises new questions about democratic rights to private decision making and the potentially adverse effects of all laws.

DISCUSSION TOPICS

1 Don Marquis argued that there is a strong moral presumption against abortion because fetuses have valuable futures, just as you and I have, and because it is prima facie immoral to kill creatures with valuable futures. Assess his argument, and in doing so consider the following questions.

   a Marquis does not think his argument applies to sperm and ova, since at the time of conception there are millions of sperm but no entity (sperm or ovum) that we can identify as having a valuable future like our future. Do you agree, or does this pose a problem for his view?

   b Does Marquis's argument assume that the fetus is the same creature as the adult person it may become, rather than just a precursor to that person? If so, does this pose a problem for his view?

   c Is the moral principle he cites justified, or is the justified principle something like: It is prima facie wrong to kill creatures that have a valuable future *and* are already valuable in some way?

2 According to the golden rule, we should do to others what we would have them do to us. Assuming that we value our lives, we are glad that our mothers did not abort us when we were fetuses. To universalize in the spirit of the golden rule, does it follow that we should not engage in abortions?[15]

3 Many (though not all) people believe abortion is permissible when a woman is made pregnant by a rapist, thereby recognizing the exceptional burden placed on women (and their husbands) who are victimized twice: once from the rape and again from bringing a rapist's child into the world. Yet, on the assumption that the zygote is a person, the rapist's child is completely innocent—as innocent as any other child. If the conservative allows an exception here, must a consistent perspective allow other exceptions when a woman may suffer great burdens in bringing a child to birth—burdens such as educational and career sacrifices? Or is the case of rape unique and not suitable to generalization?

4 Liberals sometimes point out that nearly everyone agrees that abortion is permissible in order to save the life of a woman, as when a pregnancy threatens a woman's life because of her poor health or because of other medical complications. They then extend the idea of self-defense to include the psychological defense of a woman who would suffer extreme emotional distress or damage to her career (and livelihood) by having an unwanted child.

    a If we assume (for the sake of argument) that a fetus is a person with a right to life, is it obvious that a woman's right to self-defense overrides the fetus's right to life?

    b What would you say about this argument: The woman has had an opportunity to live and hence, in fairness, the fetus should been given a similar opportunity?

5 Do you think a husband or lover who impregnates a woman should have the right to share in the abortion decision? If not, are we consistent when we demand that fathers assume full responsibility for their children? "Why should men share responsibility for child support or childrearing if they cannot share in what is asserted to be the woman's sole decision?"[16]

6 Amniocentesis and other prenatal diagnostic techniques provide detailed information about the genetic nature of developing fetuses at the stage when abortions are legal. This information sometimes influences abortion decisions. Are abortions for any of the following reasons morally acceptable? (a) The fetus has a severe genetic abnormality, such as spina bifida. (b) The fetus has a significant, but not life-threatening, genetic abnormality, such as Down's syndrome. (c) The fetus is a girl and a couple wants a boy instead (or vice versa).

7 Is abortion so important that it should continue to dominate American politics, especially in light of its current role as a focus for disagreements among religious conservatives and feminists? Or do you agree that, to minimize social turmoil, compromise is needed in the formulation of laws and social policies concerning abortion? If so, can you think of abortion laws that are promising compromises?

8 Anthony Weston views *Roe v. Wade* as already an acceptable compromise that reasonably balances conflicting reasons and views by forbidding some abortions (those after viability) while making others permissible. He also draws attention to what he sees as a "vital asymmetry" between the pro-life and pro-choice positions: " 'Pro-choice' is not 'anti-life'; the argument [for it] is only that other values also matter, that the appeal to 'life' does not close the question. 'Pro-life,' however, is anti-'choice'; the claim is that the value of one of the lives in question overrides all other values and all other lives, and precludes any other choice."[17] Is Weston correct in seeing a moral asymmetry in the pro-life and pro-choice positions? And does *Roe v. Wade* constitute a reasonable compromise on abortion?

9 One hope is that new medical technologies for birth control will quiet the abortion controversy. In recent years, liberals heralded RU 486, the newly developed French drug, as such a remedy. The drug induces abortions during the early weeks of a pregnancy and has a far lower rate of complication than other abortion techniques. Pressure from conservative groups led President Bush to prevent the Food and Drug Administration from testing the drug; President Clinton reversed that decision. If this or other drugs become available, abortion confrontations may be altered in some ways, if only because fewer abortion clinics—the visible target for anti-abortion groups—would be needed. Would this or other birth control techniques be likely to quell abortion controversies?

SUGGESTED READINGS

Baird, Robert M., and Stuart E. Rosenbaum (eds.). *The Ethics of Abortion*. Rev. ed. Buffalo, NY: Prometheus Books, 1993.

Brody, Baruch. *Abortion and the Sanctity of Human Life: A Philosophical View*. Cambridge, MA: MIT Press, 1975.

Callahan, Daniel. *Abortion: Law, Choice and Morality*. London: Collier-Macmillan, 1970.

Callahan, Sidney, and Daniel Callahan (eds.). *Abortion: Understanding Differences*. New York: Plenum, 1984.

Coward, Harold G., Julius J. Lipner, and Katherine F. Young. *Hindu Ethics: Purity, Abortion, and Euthanasia*. Albany: State University of New York Press, 1989.

Dwyer, Susan, and Joel Feinberg (eds.). *The Problem of Abortion*. 3d ed. Belmont, CA: Wadsworth, 1996.

Feinberg, Joel, and Barbara Baum Levenbook. "Abortion." In T. Regan (ed.), *Matters of Life and Death*. 3d ed. New York: Random House, 1993.

Garfield, Jay L., and Patricia Hennessey (eds.). *Abortion: Moral and Legal Perspectives*. Amherst: University of Massachusetts Press, 1984.

Kamm, F. M. *Creation and Abortion: A Study in Moral and Legal Philosophy*. New York: Oxford University Press, 1992.

Luker, Kristin. *Abortion and the Politics of Motherhood*. Berkeley: University of California Press, 1984.

Noonan, John T., Jr. *A Private Choice: Abortion in America in the Seventies*. New York: The Free Press, 1979.

Petchesky, Rosalind Pollack. *Abortion and Woman's Choice*. Boston, MA: Northeastern University Press, 1985.

Pojman, Louis P., and Francis J. Beckwith (eds.). *The Abortion Controversy: 25 Years After Roe v. Wade; A Reader*. Belmont, CA: Wadsworth, 1998.

Purdy, Laura. *Reproducing Persons: Issues in Feminist Bioethics*. Ithaca, NY: Cornell University Press, 1996.

Reiman, Jeffrey. *Abortion and the Ways We Value Human Life*. Lanham, MD: Rowman & Littlefield, 1999.

Schwarz, Stephen D. *The Moral Question of Abortion*. Chicago: Loyola University Press, 1990.

Sumner, Wayne. *Abortion and Moral Theory*. Princeton, NJ: Princeton University Press, 1981.

Tooley, Michael. *Abortion and Infanticide*. Oxford: Oxford University Press, 1983.

Weston, Anthony. *Toward Better Problems: New Perspectives on Abortion, Animal Rights, the Environment, and Justice*. Philadelphia, Temple University Press, 1992.

CHAPTER 9

Animals

About half of all Americans and Europeans have pets that they regard as companions. Generally, they devote large amounts of attention and significant financial resources to them, often more than they give to their neighbors. They are sensitive to their pets' needs and emotions and interact with them in caring ways that have moral significance, or so it will be argued here.

Our attitudes toward pets contrast sharply with our typical attitudes toward animals in general. Most people eat animals daily without a qualm and see no objections to the use of animals in experiments that help humans; yet the thought of eating their pets or allowing them to be used for experimentation may be as horrifying as the thought of eating or experimenting on a human stranger. Clearly, we attribute to our pets an importance that sets them apart from other animals. Do we perhaps exaggerate the importance of pets, or conversely, underestimate the value of animals we eat or use in medical experiments?

Animals as Companions

When John Steinbeck approached sixty, the age at which he would receive the Nobel Prize for literature, he felt the need to travel extensively in order to regain contact with the people he wrote about. He planned a trip around and through America in a camper truck, leaving his family during the months he traveled alone. His excitement about the planned trip, however, was dampened by "a very lonely, helpless feeling at first—a kind of desolate feeling."[1] The cure was to take along as a traveling companion his large French poodle, named Charles le Chien, or Charley for short. *Travels with Charley,* the literary offspring of the trip, is in part a record of Steinbeck's interactions with Charley.

Steinbeck already knew Charley well, but on the trip he came to know him better. He was previously aware, for example, that Charley was diplomatic rather than confrontational in dealing with other animals. In Yellowstone Park, however, Charley betrayed his usual good sense by trying to charge a bear: "Bears simply brought out the Hyde in my Jekyll-headed dog."[2]

The trip also led Steinbeck to a greater appreciation of Charley's superior intelligence in some matters. Charley lived in an entire world of smells to which Steinbeck and other humans were oblivious. More interestingly, Charley had an exceptional intuitive understanding of people. He would show contempt for incompetent veterinarians who mishandled him and spontaneous trust in skillful ones. He also avoided people who addressed him using baby talk, revealing, according to Steinbeck, a certain pride in not being a human infant. Yet he displayed a humanlike pride in being well groomed, a vanity Steinbeck shared concerning his own beard.

Charley had an equally subtle knowledge of Steinbeck. His understanding extended well beyond responses to verbal commands, for he could easily anticipate with excitement when he would be included in Steinbeck's plans or discern with chagrin that he would be left alone to guard the camper. His talents included several techniques for awakening Steinbeck in the morning: "He can shake himself and his collar loud enough to wake the dead. If that doesn't work he gets a sneezing fit. But perhaps his most irritating method is to sit quietly beside the bed and stare into my face with a sweet and forgiving look on his face."[3]

Like most people with pets, Steinbeck talked to Charley frequently and on a variety of occasions. He routinely spoke to him—greeting him, saying goodbye, comforting him when he was nervous, and relaxing both of them by chatting about a problem. Charley was also the object of conversations with strangers and served as an ambassador for Steinbeck in meeting people: "A dog, particularly an exotic like Charley, is a bond between strangers. Many conversations en route began with 'What degree [that is, pedigree] of a dog is that?' "[4]

Steinbeck and Charley were emotionally attuned to each other. On one occasion, for example, Steinbeck became depressed following a conversation with someone who had a special knack for sarcastically demolishing the simple pleasures of a sunny afternoon. Charley cheered him up by initiating puppylike games. On another occasion Charley was sick, and Steinbeck postponed the trip for an entire week while he recuperated. During this time Steinbeck reports feeling compassion for the suffering of his traveling companion as well as helplessness at being unable to alleviate the suffering.

The relationship with Charley that Steinbeck reports involves several elements that common sense recognizes as possible for human–animal interactions. Common sense suggests that animals are capable of beliefs and emotions, and also that animals of a given type are not alike—they have distinctive personalities. All these features enter into human–animal interactions in selective and personal ways akin to friendships among humans. It is

true that in a few places Steinbeck lapses into anthropomorphization of animals—that is, he ascribes human traits where they are inappropriate—as
when he speaks of Charley's pride in not being a human. Nevertheless,
Steinbeck's descriptions of his interactions with Charley, rather than striking
us as poetic fancies, for the most part ring true. Human relationships with
animal companions are far more akin to caring relationships among persons
than they are to children's relationships with dolls. Four points deserve emphasis in this connection.

First, companionship between humans and animals has moral importance. It affords humans comfort, security, and daily cheerfulness, and it obviously benefits specific animals. However, it also creates a bond or
relationship based on caring. The importance of this relationship is especially rich within families in which there is an interaction between several
humans and pets that exerts a unifying force. The pet becomes a focus of
shared concern, including shared activities (petting, feeding, exercising,
conversing, playing, and so on). Psychologists also emphasize that pets provide a sense of peace and security. (This is true for cats as well as for guard
dogs!) Pets serve as surrogate children for adults, fantasized babies for children, and real friends for all. Pets also generate problems, of course, but
even in that regard they are like people, reminding us that all valuable caring relationships require effort.

Second, relationships with animals enliven a sense of kinship with other
animals and nature. Living with animals adds to our delight in the simple
aspects of biological existence, including pleasure in a good meal or playing
a game. The relatively short life spans of pets remind us of the contingency
and fragility of our own lives.

Third, caring for animals can add to a capacity to care for people. This is
not always true, to be sure; occasionally, pets are used as a means to escape
from caring about people. We recognize such cases, however, as unhealthy
distortions rather than as typical products of relationships with animals. As
Mary Midgley emphasizes, it is a misconception to think that caring for animals somehow detracts from the care available for other people. Such an argument would imply that we should not aid a suffering dog hit by a car,
because our energies could in principle be used to help a human at that moment. Midgley writes, "The reason why this would be odd is that compassion does not need to be treated hydraulically in this way, as a rare and
irreplaceable fluid, usable only for exceptionally impressive cases. It is a
habit or power of the mind, which grows and develops with use."[5]

Fourth, reflection on our relationships with pets prompts us to reconsider
the capacities that bestow moral significance on creatures. The capacities for
feelings and social interactions take on greater importance than the traditionally emphasized capacities for rational thought and conduct. At this point,
however, we need to reflect more generally on the moral status of all sentient
(conscious) animals, not just those we choose to make our pets. Do such animals have any inherent moral worth, beyond what they contribute to us?

No Moral Worth

The attitude of most classical philosophers was that animals, including non-human higher mammals, have no intrinsic moral worth of any kind. They acquire value and moral relevance only insofar as humans choose to value them for human purposes. It follows that nothing is inherently wrong in hurting animals. For example, hunting becomes wrong only when the hunted animals are the property of other humans whose property rights would be infringed by hurting the animal; and the use of animals for food or in medical experiments that have human benefits raises no moral questions.

According to this attitude, attachment to animals may alleviate loneliness, induce calm, and provide delight—but so does television. Deep emotional attachment to or caring for animals is sentimental; that is, it reflects excessive and inappropriate emotional involvement. Pets are like pens or cars to which one might also become sentimentally attached, but they have value only insofar as humans give them value. They are household curios, not caring companions.

The philosophical basis for this attitude was uncompromisingly set forth by both René Descartes (1596–1650) and Benedict de Spinoza (1632–1677). Descartes viewed animals as "thoughtless brutes," sophisticated machines lacking consciousness.[6] Spinoza, by contrast, recognized that they could feel pain and pleasure, but he joined Descartes in banishing them from the realm of moral concern:

> The rational quest of what is useful to us further teaches us the necessity of associating ourselves with our fellow man, but not with beasts, or things, whose nature is different from our own. . . . Still, I do not deny that beasts feel; what I deny is, that we may not consult our own advantage and use them as we please, treating them in the way which best suits us; for their nature is not like ours, and their emotions are naturally different from human emotions.[7]

Surely the attitude of Descartes and Spinoza is wrong, tragically wrong. Many animals do feel emotions and have desires and beliefs similar to our own. Certainly, this is true of the higher mammals on which we will focus. Of course, we admit the conceptual danger in anthropomorphizing animals by ascribing unwarrantedly complex mental states to them; but the forms of behavior that warrant ascribing at least simple psychological states to people are also manifested by mammals. Moreover, numerous studies in comparative anatomy and neurophysiology also indicate similarities in the mental activities and functions of humans and higher mammals. Indeed, much of the ordinary rationale for using animals in scientific experiments is that their neurological structure, which makes possible conscious activities, resembles that of humans.

At the very least, it is wrong to torture animals for fun. Some philosophers have recognized that many animals feel pain and yet have refused to grant them any inherent moral worth. In particular, Immanuel Kant agreed that torture of animals was clearly immoral, but he also shared the view of Descartes and Spinoza that animals have no moral worth. According to Kant, only rational beings (humans, and possibly other beings such as angels and God) have inherent value. Rational beings are ends in themselves in the sense that they are autonomous beings who place moral limits on the actions of other rational beings. Everything else in the universe merely serves to gratify the reasoned purposes of rational beings. Animals in particular lack the capacity to reason about general principles of conduct that ought to guide rational living. Hence, we owe them no moral respect and have no moral duties to them.

Nevertheless, Kant believed there are duties to humanity and to ourselves that generate indirect duties to treat animals humanely. That is, we have duties concerning animals, but not to animals:

> So far as animals are concerned, we have no direct duties. Animals are not self-conscious and are there merely as a means to an end. That end is man. . . . Our duties towards animals are merely indirect duties towards humanity. . . . Thus, if a dog has served his master long and faithfully, his service, on the analogy of human service, deserves reward, and when the dog has grown too old to serve, his master ought to keep him until he dies. Such action helps to support us in our duties towards human beings. . . . Tender feelings towards dumb animals develop humane feelings towards mankind.[8]

Kant's idea is that tenderness with animals helps foster kindness toward humans, whereas cruelty to animals encourages cruelty to humans. Humane responses are a kind of practice exercise for kindness to people.

This is an interesting suggestion, but is it always true? Perhaps some individuals are actually kinder to people because they vent their hostilities on animals, which, in Kant's view, would justify their cruelty to animals. In any case, Kant mislocates the basis for condemning cruelty to animals. It is wrong to torture a dog or cat, not because such acts may indirectly influence one's subsequent behavior toward people, but because it harms the dog or cat! Furthermore, the act itself reveals cruelty in one's character, even if that cruelty is not also expressed toward people.

Full Moral Status

Without engaging in subtle debates about the precise degree to which various mammals are self-conscious or capable of rational endeavors and communication, we can recognize their capacity for social life and also their capacity for feeling. What follows from this acknowledgment? Some philosophers believe that these capacities give animals full moral status as valuable members of the moral community.

Jeremy Bentham (1748–1832) drew attention to the importance of the capacity to feel when he charged that the refusal of Descartes and Spinoza to grant any moral status to animals was akin to the sweeping blindness of racists. He drafted the following passage shortly after France prohibited slavery in French colonies:

> The French have already discovered that blackness of the skin is no reason why a human being should be abandoned without redress to the caprice of a tormentor. It may one day come to be recognized that the number of the legs, the villosity of the skin, or the termination of the os sacrum [i.e., the tail bone] are reasons equally insufficient for abandoning a sensitive being to the same fate. What else is it that should trace the insuperable line [between humans and animals]? Is it the faculty of reason, or perhaps the faculty of discourse? But a full-grown horse or dog is beyond comparison a more rational, as well as a more conversable animal, than an infant of a day or a week, or even a month, old. But suppose they were otherwise, what would it avail? The question is not, Can they reason? nor Can they talk? but Can they *suffer?*[9]

Mammals do indeed suffer, feel pleasure and delight, and have interests based on their desires and needs. They care for their young, interact with sensitivity to one another and sometimes to humans. Does it follow that this gives them full moral worth, in the sense of counting equally with humans in the moral community?

Let us turn to two contemporary philosophers who have drawn attention to the plight of animals in a human-centered world. Both are prominent members of the "animal rights movement" that has gained momentum in recent decades, and both sharply disagree with Kant's refusal to grant animals any direct moral status. Yet they offer very different defenses of the humane treatment of animals.

Peter Singer has been called the father of the modern animal rights movement, principally because of his influential book *Animal Liberation*. There is irony in this, however, because Singer denies that animals have rights! Even though in a few passages in *Animal Liberation* he speaks loosely about animal rights, he has since made it clear that, for him, talk of moral rights should be translated into talk about utility, whether one ascribes rights to animals or persons. Like Bentham, Singer is a utilitarian who believes that acts are right or wrong only insofar as they maximize or fail to maximize good consequences, evaluated with respect to all conscious beings affected by the acts. Rights are essentially those areas of freedom and benefit that should be protected in order to maximize utility. Mammals are conscious beings and as such should be taken into account in maximizing utility. Usually, it is wrong to cause suffering to animals because such suffering is rarely justified by some greater good produced for humans.

Animals who are conscious, and hence who are capable of feeling pain or pleasure, have preferences and interests just as humans do. In this respect, according to Singer, their interests should be considered equally with those of humans. To think otherwise is to be guilty of *speciesism*, which he defines as "a prejudice or attitude of bias toward the interests of members of one's own species and against those of members of other species."[10] Speciesism has caused harm as terrible as that of sexism and racism: "This tyranny has caused and today is still causing an amount of pain and suffering that can only be compared with that which resulted from the centuries of tyranny by white humans over black humans."[11] In Singer's view, animals are entitled to equal consideration, although not necessarily equal treatment. Our treatment of (behavior toward) particular animals should depend on their specific needs and capacities—as does our behavior toward humans. Nevertheless, sentient animals deserve to be considered equally in making utilitarian calculations.

Two major conclusions follow if Singer is right. First, just as we do not eat humans (except in extraordinary and tragic circumstances that might justify cannibalism), we should not eat sentient animals when there is any alternative. Since vegetarianism is a healthy alternative, it is immoral to eat animals. It is especially immoral to eat the majority of animals who are raised with mass meat-production techniques. Singer carefully shows how those techniques cause enormous suffering to animals who are raised in unnatural conditions that frustrate normal needs and desires.

Second, most contemporary medical experiments on sentient animals are immoral. In some instances we could use alternative modes of testing, such as computer simulation, that avoid the terrible suffering inflicted on animals. In other instances, the experiments cannot be justified in terms of educational purposes or the pursuit of new knowledge. Admittedly, some experiments are justified from a utilitarian point of view, but they are rare if we recognize animals' interests as worthy of equal consideration with human interests: "So whenever experimenters claim that their experiments are important enough to justify the use of animals, we should ask them whether they would be prepared to use a brain-damaged human being at a similar mental level to the animals they are planning to use."[12] Few (if any) experiments would pass this test.

Ethicists who regard moral rights, rather than utilitarian considerations, as the foundation of morality have developed a different argument for Singer's conclusions. Perhaps the most careful argument that animals have moral rights is presented by Tom Regan in *The Case for Animal Rights*. Regan begins with the premise that mammals (at least those of age one or older) have inherent value. They have this value not just because they are capable of feeling pain and pleasure, but also because they have beliefs, desires, memories, a sense of the future, preferences, the ability to act purposefully in pursuing their preferences, and a welfare (or set of interests) that goes beyond their potential uses for humans.

Regan contends that inherent value is not a matter of degree; one either has it or one does not. Hence, the value of mammals is equal to the value of humans. Moreover, this inherent value ought to be respected because it creates a valid claim on us. Because these valid claims are what is meant by moral rights, it follows that mammals have moral rights. Their inability to speak for their rights does not alter this fact; it merely makes animals dependent on surrogate agents for the defense of their rights. Their moral situation is in this respect exactly analogous to human babies, infants, and severely mentally handicapped people, who are also dependent on guardians to defend their rights.

For Regan, our goals should be to abolish completely experiments on animals that cause suffering or lead to their deaths, to bring an end to commercial animal agriculture, and also to end sport hunting and trapping (topics we shall consider in the next chapter). Above all, we must end the callous and cruel attitude that animals are mere things to be manipulated for human purposes.

Partial Moral Status

The philosophers we have considered up to this point share a common assumption: Either animals share full moral status with humans or, like rocks and other material objects, they lack any moral status. Kant, Descartes, and Spinoza reasoned that, because animals lack the rational capacities of humans, they are mere things undeserving of any respect. According to Singer, either animals' interests do not matter at all or else they matter equally with those of humans. Similarly, Regan asserts that either animals have no rights or else their rights are as important as those of humans.

Yet there is a middle ground to be considered. It affirms that, insofar as animals are conscious beings, they have some inherent worth, but human beings nevertheless have greater inherent worth. This position recognizes in human consciousness greater degrees of value and potential value, in the same way that John Stuart Mill distinguished degrees of quality among pleasures. This view might also grant that animals have important rights but deny that they have all the rights of human beings. Thus, although they have the right to be treated humanely and not to be tortured, they lack rights to social support through our welfare system. Moreover, even with respect to the same rights—say, a right to life—human rights are to be counted more heavily when they come into conflict with animal rights.

This view also distinguishes degrees of inherent worth among animals, depending on the extent of their capacities to feel pain and pleasure, to act purposefully, and to interact socially with one another and with humans. This would support the special status we have granted to higher mammals, who possess these capacities in greater degrees than do many other animals. It provides a rationale for developing laws to protect dolphins, whales, chimpanzees, and gorillas. Such laws are designed to protect individual animals, unlike other laws aimed at preserving an entire species (of fish, crab, and so on).

What does this "moderate" view imply concerning vegetarianism? The answer depends on the degree of moral importance conferred by "partial moral status." For some, the emphasis shifts to eating far less meat, rather than no meat, on the theory that even partial measures (on a wide scale) can substantially reduce the amount of suffering caused to animals. For others the emphasis shifts to eating only meat that is not mass-produced, since the conditions of animals raised on traditional farms does not involve anything comparable to the degree of suffering in the mainstream meat industry.

What does the moderate view imply concerning medical experimentation on animals? It makes the standards for acceptable experiments much more rigorous. For example, it prohibits experiments designed to confirm what is largely already known. It also requires that the promise of new knowledge be established by a greater burden of proof before experiments are permitted by Institutional Review Boards (IRBs: screening committees that are now required at all universities and that must follow federal and state guidelines for humane uses of animals).

Singer and Regan would reject this last approach as "speciesist" in that it explicitly shows unjustified favoritism for humans. Undoubtedly it constitutes favoritism, but is the favoritism unjustified or immoral? Mary Midgley, who explored this middle ground in *Animals and Why They Matter*, cautions us about the term *speciesism*. As typically used, the word is ambiguous, referring to either of two views: (1) Animals have no inherent moral significance, or (2) animals have inherent worth, although not as much as humans. Midgley rejects the former view while affirming the latter. It is not, she urges, a sheer prejudice akin to racism and sexism to give some preference to the interests of members of one's own species in situations where interests conflict. There are genuine moral differences between humans and nonhuman animals—not absolute differences of the sort Kant believed in, but differences in degree that justify us in regarding animals as partial (not fully equal) members of the moral community. Precisely when and in what degree preference is justified should be explored without the presumption either that animals lack all moral significance or that they have moral worth equal to that of humans.

Midgley also recognizes some special significance in the capacity of animals to interact with humans. Underlying this attitude is a clear acknowledgment of the special worth of humans, but also a sensitivity to genuine differences among animals that give them capacities we equally value among humans. Such a position helps make sense of our attitudes toward pets, as does the fact that a history of personal interactions with specific animals adds to the value of relationships with them.

SUMMARY

Most traditional ethical theories have been exclusively human-centered, regarding animals as mechanical playthings that were incapable of feelings (Descartes). Alternatively, they regarded animals' feelings as radically dissimilar to human emotions and insufficient to give them moral worth, which only "rational" beings have (Spinoza, Kant). Responses to animals, according to these theories, have moral relevance only as they affect responses to other humans. Thus, torture of animals is bad only because it encourages cruelty to humans, and gentleness to animals is good only insofar as it reinforces gentleness to humans.

Jeremy Bentham, however, stressed that the ability to reason and to experience complex emotions links humans and animals. In his view, it is morally significant that animals can suffer as well as feel pleasure. To torture an animal for fun is to do moral harm to it and to manifest a character that is cruel, no matter what further implications there are for one's treatment of humans. Contemporary philosophical advocates of humane treatment of animals differ over whether animals have rights, but they share Bentham's view that torture of an animal is a direct moral wrong—to the animal.

Bentham's view also lays a philosophical basis for the recognition of caring relationships between humans and animal companions. Insofar as animals have emotions and needs, it makes sense to care for them and to promote their interests, in the way people do with their pets or "animal companions." Moreover, caring relationships with animal companions take on increased worth insofar as animals are capable of reciprocal responses and interactions with humans.

Does a recognition of the value of animals require us to recognize their worth as equal with that of humans? According to some philosophers it does, and to treat them as moral inferiors is a form of prejudice that they call speciesism (Singer, Regan). Recognition that animals have inherent worth, however, is compatible with a position that allows that humans' moral worth is greater and that human interests may legitimately be given greater weight when they conflict with those of animals (Midgley).

DISCUSSION TOPICS

1 Evaluate the following argument: People treat their pets *as if* they were people. Much the same is true, however, of fictional characters in plays and movies: It is appropriate to respond with fear, affection, anger, and other emotions to characters whom we pretend are real people. In both cases, however, a game of pretense is involved. Neither pets nor fictional characters are real people, and we know this even at times when we pretend they are. Neither has any kind of inherent moral worth that makes them *deserve* to be treated as people.

2 Many pet owners spend more on their pets than they do on world hunger, even though their money for pet food and supplies could help save human lives. Discuss your view of whether this is morally permissible. If you think it is permissible to spend substantial amounts of money on pets, are there any limits to how much should be spent?

3 It is not uncommon for farmers to become emotionally attached to one animal of a species whose other members they are willing to eat. An example of this millennia-old practice is found in a story told in the Old Testament:

> The poor man had nothing, save one little ewe lamb, which he had bought and nourished up: and it grew up together with him, and with his children; it did eat of his own meat, and drank of his own cup, and lay in his bosom, and was unto him as a daughter.[13]

Is there anything morally inconsistent about having a caring relationship with this one sheep while being willing to eat other sheep?

4 Is it morally permissible to eat sentient animals? Jeremy Bentham thought it was, even though (as we saw) he affirmed the moral worth of animals that can feel pain and pleasure:

> There is very good reason why we should be suffered to eat such of them [i.e., animals] as we like to eat; we are the better for it, and they are never the worse. They have none of those long-protracted anticipations of future misery which we have. The death they suffer in our hands commonly is, and always may be, a speedier, and by that means a less painful one, than that which would await them in the inevitable course of nature.[14]

Contemporary mass production of meat, however, does involve considerable suffering for animals. One example that Peter Singer describes in *Animal Liberation* concerns the raising of calves for veal.[15] The calves are taken from their mothers at a very young age and placed in wooden stalls one foot, two inches wide. This prevents them from turning around during the thirteen to fifteen weeks before slaughter. During that time their diet is entirely liquid, which denies them their need for roughage. The lack of exercise and grass keeps their flesh tender. In addition, they are kept anemic to produce the pale pink flesh preferred by gourmets (even though the color does not affect taste). To reduce restlessness, some producers keep them in the dark at all times except for about two hours during feeding. Thus, the calves live in an environment without visual stimulation, physical activity, interaction with their mothers, or social interaction of any other kind. Is their suffering outweighed by the human pleasures in eating them? Would you agree with Bentham about other cases in which suffering to animals is far less extreme?

5 The Food and Drug Administration requires that many kinds of new substances be tested on animals before they are marketed for human use. For example, new cosmetics must be tested for possible eye or skin damage on humans. One test involves using unanesthetized rabbits whose heads are held firmly in place by a neck brace and whose eyes are kept open with metal clips. Concentrated solutions of the substance are dripped into the rabbits' eyes, often repeatedly for several days, and eye damage is measured. Peter Singer writes of such experiments that

> while it may be thought justifiable to require animal tests of potentially life-saving drugs, the same tests are done for products like cosmetics, food colorings, and floor polishes. Should hundreds of animals suffer so that a new kind of lipstick or mouthwash can be put on the market? Don't we already have enough of these products? Who benefits from their introduction, except the companies that hope to make a profit from their new gimmick?[16]

Do you agree or disagree with Singer? What general criteria would you endorse to morally justify experiments on animals?

6 Is bullfighting, which is still practiced in some parts of the world, morally permissible? In your answer, research the values by which other cultures justify the practice.

7 Some people object to our ordinary talk of "owning" pets, urging that instead we speak of being "animal guardians." Recalling from chapters 6 and 7 the dangers of language reinforcing prejudice, present and defend your view on this issue.

SUGGESTED READINGS

Adams, Carol J., and Josephine Donovan (eds.). *Animals and Women: Feminist Theoretical Explorations.* Durham: Duke University Press, 1995.

Baird, Robert M., and Stuart E. Rosenbaum (eds.). *Animal Experimentation: The Moral Issues.* Albany: Prometheus Press, 1991.

Bentham, Jeremy. *Introduction to the Principles of Morals and Legislation.* Chapter 17. New York: Hafner, 1948. First published 1789.

Carruthers, Peter. *The Animals Issue; Moral Theory in Practice.* New York: Cambridge University Press, 1993.

Clark, Stephen R. L. *The Nature of the Beast: Are Animals Moral?* New York: Oxford University Press, 1984.

Coetzee, J. M., and Amu Gutmann. *The Lives of Animals.* Princeton: Princeton University Press, 1999.

Donovan, Josephine, and Carol J. Adams (eds.) *Beyond Animal Rights: A Feminist Caring Ethic for the Treatment of Animals.* New York: Continuum Publishing, 1996.

Fox, Michael Allen. *The Case for Animal Experimentation.* Berkeley: University of California Press, 1986.

Frey, R. G. *Rights, Killing and Suffering: Moral Vegetarianism and Applied Ethics.* New York: Basil Blackwell, 1983.

Hearne, Vicki. *Adams' Task: Calling Animals by Name.* New York: Vintage, 1987.

Kant, Immanuel. "Duties Towards Animals and Spirits." In *Lectures on Ethics.* Trans. L. Infield. New York: Harper & Row, 1963.

Leahy, Michael P. T. *Against Liberation: Putting Animals in Perspective.* New York: Routledge, 1994.

Midgley, Mary. *Animals and Why They Matter.* Athens: University of Georgia Press, 1984. Reissued 1998.

Regan, Tom. *The Case for Animal Rights.* Berkeley: University of California Press, 1983.

Regan, Tom, and Peter Singer (eds.). *Animal Rights and Human Obligations.* 2d ed. Englewood Cliffs, NJ: Prentice-Hall, 1989.

Rollin, Bernard E. *Animal Rights and Human Morality.* Rev. ed. Buffalo, NY: Prometheus, 1992.

Rowls, Mark, and Mark Rowlands. *Animal Rights: A Philosophical Defense.* New York: St. Martin's Press, 2000.

Singer, Peter. *Animal Liberation.* Rev. ed. New York: Avon Books, 1990.

Singer, Peter (ed.). *In Defense of Animals.* New York: Basil Blackwell, 1986.

Environment

Environmental alarms are sounding on many fronts: polluted lakes and oceans, depleted natural resources, acid rain, endangered species, destruction of rain forests, pesticide poisoning, chemical dump sites, nuclear waste, global warming, and depletion of the ozone layer surrounding the earth. These alarms challenge us to expand our circle of moral concern to include the natural environment. Human survival, not just beautiful scenery, is at stake in the pursuit of a sustainable environment.

Each of us has the capacity to benefit or harm the environment through everyday choices made as consumers (for example, by buying energy-efficient appliances and cars); through habits such as recycling, ride sharing, and conserving electricity and water; through voting patterns; and through philanthropic giving to and voluntary service on behalf of effective environmental organizations. It is possible for us, as the environmental maxim enjoins, to "think globally, act locally." Is it also, however, a moral responsibility? If so, how strong is the responsibility, and what is its foundation?

During the 1970s, environmental ethics emerged as a new branch of applied ethics, signaled especially with the creation in 1979 of the journal *Environmental Ethics*. In this chapter we sketch several answers to an issue central to that field of thought: Should ethics be rethought in a fundamental way so as to abandon its traditional human-centered (*anthropocentric*) focus? That is, does the environment, or certain of its major aspects, have inherent moral significance of the sort that human beings have? In addition to these theoretical questions, there are numerous practical issues that must be addressed in balancing competing interests, human and nonhuman alike.

Human-Centered Ethics

Western civilizations have largely regarded the environment as a resource to satisfy human desires. In this view, the environment has no intrinsic or inherent moral worth. Rather, its worth is purely instrumental—the means for serving the interests of intrinsically valuable human beings. Some of those interests are *economic:* the management and conservation of resources essential for a productive economy. Other interests are *aesthetic:* the enjoyment of natural beauty and sublime vistas, waterfalls, and mountain ranges. Still others are *recreational:* for example, the enjoyments of backpacking or mountain climbing in wilderness areas. In addition, there are *scientific* interests: the ongoing study of the "natural laboratories" of wilderness areas. Increasingly important is the interest of sheer *survival*. Population has dramatically increased and resources have become scarcer, including resources essential to human life. Each of these interests provides a human-centered moral justification for restrictions on what individuals and corporations do to the environment.

From the perspective of rights ethics, humans have a right to life, liberty, and the pursuit of their happiness. That implies that other persons must not destroy the prerequisites for satisfaction of those rights—in particular, that they must not destroy the common resources of drinkable water, breathable air, and edible food. As William T. Blackstone argued, the basic rights to live and to pursue a fulfilling life imply a *right to a livable environment:*

> The answer then to the question, Is the right to a livable environment a human right? is yes. Each person has this right *qua* being human and because a livable environment is essential for one to fulfill his human capacities. And given the danger to our environment today and hence the danger to the very possibility of human existence, access to a livable environment must be conceived as a right which imposes upon everyone a correlative moral obligation to respect.[1]

A (prima facie) obligation not to damage the environment in ways that harm people can also be derived from duty ethics and utilitarianism. Duty ethics implies a duty not to erode the environment in ways that threaten the ability of people to lead autonomous and meaningful lives. Utilitarianism, with its goal of maximizing the well-being of all people, implies an obligation to avoid harming people and to promote the environmental conditions essential for human life.

Each of these theories of conduct takes into account not only people living today, but future generations as well. The same value that resides in our lives now will someday reside in the lives of others not yet born, and their welfare makes a claim on us now not to undermine their prospects for meaningful life.[2] To deny this by using up the world's resources for the benefit of our own generation would constitute a form of bigotry, a presumption that our lives have greater value than the lives of later generations. Such an attitude would also betray the special obligations of loyalty to the children and grandchildren of members of our current community.

What does virtue ethics, with its focus on the kinds of people we should become, have to say about responsibilities concerning the natural environment? Thomas E. Hill, Jr., begins his answer to this question with a story:

> A wealthy eccentric bought a house in a neighborhood I know. The house was surrounded by a beautiful display of grass, plants, and flowers, and it was shaded by a huge old avocado tree. But the grass required cutting, the flowers needed tending, and the man wanted more sun. So he cut the whole lot down and covered the yard with asphalt.[3]

Hill compared this action to strip mining and the destruction of redwood forests. He asks, "What sort of person . . . would cover his garden with asphalt, strip mine a wooded mountain, or level an irreplaceable redwood grove?"[4]

First, such a person lacks the virtue of moral humility. Humble individuals appreciate their place in nature, understood as a complex, interconnected network of plants and animals. They live with an attitude that they are part of a wider organic unity, and they value nature apart from considerations of how it affects themselves.

Second, such a person lacks a sense of aesthetic sensitivity to the beauty of natural objects. This aesthetic sensibility is not a moral virtue per se, but the capacities it reflects—sensitivity, wide emotional interest, and empathy—are also important elements of the moral virtue of sensitivity to persons. It is likely that the failure to respond to natural beauty is a sign of failures to appreciate human beings.

Third, such a person shows a failure of gratitude toward the natural world that makes life possible. This sense of gratitude may be understood in religious terms, as gratitude toward the creator of the natural world, or as a moral virtue, that is, an appreciation for the beauty and the life-support provided by the natural world. In addition, ingratitude regarding the natural world is likely to be reflected in ingratitude toward other persons.

Hill's focus is primarily human-centered in that it explores environmental responsibilities in terms of human ideals concerning human character. Nevertheless, Hill believes that those ideals imply an attitude of valuing nature for itself. We cannot manifest the virtues of humility, sensitivity, and gratitude unless we cherish nature, that is, care for natural things in themselves. This brings us to the question, central to the development of environmental ethics, of whether we should shift the locus of moral value to something wider than human beings.

Nature-Centered Ethics

Aristotle, Locke, Kant, Mill, and most other traditional ethicists took for granted that human beings were the exclusive focus of moral concern because they have an inherent worth missing from other natural creatures. Is that true? After all, humans are natural creatures. We are animals, and like all animals our survival and prospects for healthy lives depend entirely on numerous interdependencies with nonhuman animals, plants, and even the nonliving world.

Thinking along these lines, some environmentalists have reformulated moral philosophy by beginning with one of three proposals: (1) All conscious life has inherent moral value (consciousness-centered or sentientist ethics); (2) All life has inherent moral value (life-centered or biocentric ethics); (3) Ecosystems have inherent moral value (ecology-centered or ecocentric ethics).

Sentientist Ethics

The consciousness-centered perspective, which can be viewed as an extension of traditional moral theories, was broached in the last chapter. There we asked, Why is the torture of animals immoral? Is it (prima facie) wrong solely because it harms other people, either directly (e.g., by harming someone's pet) or indirectly (e.g., by harming our characters and thus influencing us toward cruelty to other people)? Or is it wrong because of the direct harm to the animal? If we believe torture is wrong because the animal is harmed, we are implying that conscious animals have inherent worth.

Conscious beings suffer, feel pleasure, and experience a range of other emotions. That gives them moral significance, whether we understand that significance within the framework of utilitarianism, rights ethics, or duty ethics. As a result, it is immoral to shoot animals solely for sport or to trap them to make fashionable fur coats (especially when the traps cause slow and painful deaths). Moreover, the well-being of sentient animals should be a serious consideration of commercial development that threatens the natural habitats of animals. Every effort should be made to minimize harm and to allow "green areas" where animals can flourish. According to sentientist ethics (as sketched in the discussion of Peter Singer and Tom Regan in the previous chapter), conscious animals should be killed only rarely, when there are no alternatives and only when basic human needs are at stake.

Biocentric Ethics

A life-centered perspective goes much further by affirming the intrinsic worth of all living things, including nonsentient animals and plants. This perspective is not an extension of traditional theories, but is instead a radical reconsideration of ethics.

Albert Schweitzer (1875–1965) encapsulated this view with his phrase "reverence for life." He contended that the most immediate intuition that each of us has is that "I am life which wills to live, in the midst of life which wills to live."[5] If I find goodness in acting on my will to live, consistency requires that I make a similar affirmation for all living things. The ethical person

> does not ask how far this or that life deserves one's sympathy as being valuable, nor, beyond that, whether and to what degree it is capable of feeling. Life as such is sacred to him. He tears no leaf from a tree, plucks no flower and takes

care to crush no insect. If in summer he is working by lamplight, he prefers to keep the window shut and breathe a stuffy atmosphere rather than see one insect after another fall with singed wings upon his table.[6]

Killing any living thing is permissible only when "unavoidable" or "necessary." (Schweitzer leaves these criteria somewhat vague, and, contrary to his intentions, they seem to suggest that human interests have priority over those of lower forms of life.)

Some biocentric philosophers reject Schweitzer's refusal to rank the value of various living things. For example, Kenneth Goodpaster allows that different life forms have different degrees of value, and in particular that human interests often outweigh the interests of plants. Nevertheless he shares Schweitzer's sense that all living things have intrinsic value and should be the object of moral concern. They all have "interests" in being alive and pursuing the kinds of life available to them: "The core of moral concern lies in respect for self-sustaining organization and integration in the face of pressures toward high entropy" (disintegration and loss of available energy).[7] A tree is an organism with biological needs, and to that extent it is akin to sentient beings. From an evolutionary perspective, consciousness is merely one of many biological functions (however important) that enable organisms to pursue their interests effectively.

Ecocentric Ethics

The ecocentric outlook sees intrinsic value even in nonliving aspects of nature, based on the theory that they are the evolutionary source of all life. This perspective sees inherent worth in ecosystems: systems of organisms as they interact with their environments.

Aldo Leopold, in his influential version of this view, calls ecosystems *biotic pyramids:* systems composed of layers, in which soil is the bottom layer and other layers are composed of the food chains of energy-absorbing plants, plant-eating insects, insect-eating birds, and (eventually) carnivorous mammals. To have an "ecological conscience" implies a respect for the health of biotic pyramids, and therefore a respect for their capacities for self-renewal. Leopold affirmed a "land ethic" that "enlarges the community [of moral concern] to include soils, waters, plants, and animals, or collectively: the land."[8] As an alternative to our domination of nature, Leopold urges that we learn to see ourselves as members of the "land-community" or "biotic community" by heeding the following standard of conduct: "A thing is right when it tends to preserve the integrity, stability, and beauty of the biotic community. It is wrong when it tends otherwise."[9]

Ecocentric ethics has a more holistic emphasis than sentientist and biocentric ethics, accenting entire systems and environments rather than individual creatures. For example, one of the primary concerns of ecocentric ethics is to preserve species (as a whole), especially more developed species, rather than to preserve each plant or animal. This holistic emphasis leads critics to charge ecocentrists with insensitivity to individual organisms because they are more preoccupied with the "whole" rather than its "parts." Critics fear that this bias results in insensitivity to individual persons and that efforts to protect the land may result in the sacrifice of basic needs of persons.

In reply, ecocentrists such as Holmes Rolston III and J. Baird Callicott have emphasized that priorities need not be abandoned in expanding the circle of moral concern—including priorities that sentientists sometimes overlook. Their writings affirm the paramount worth of human beings and recognize that responsibilities to humans are more stringent, while still extending to natural ecosystems a recognition of their inherent worth. Thus, Callicott writes:

> Nor does an ecocentric environmental ethic replace or cancel previous socially generated human-oriented duties—to family and family members, to neighbors and neighborhood, to all human beings and humanity. . . . The moral sphere, growing in circumference with each stage of social development . . . does not expand like a balloon—leaving no trace of its previous boundaries. . . . The discovery of the biotic community simply adds a new outer orbit of membership and attendant obligation. Our more intimate social bonds and their attendant obligations remain intact.[10]

Native American tribes provide a model for the sort of widened respect for nature that retains respect for persons. Native Americans learned to live in harmony with nature, using what was essential for their lives while maintaining attitudes of respect and even reverence for the environment. Members of traditional tribes lived with a sense that they were members rather than exploiters of a natural community, and they did so without losing a primary respect for one another.

Rules of Conduct

Even if we find meaning in the idea of intrinsic value in nonhuman animals, all life, or ecosystems, does a nature-centered ethics provide clear guidance in dealing with nature? Much turns on the specific version of nature-centered ethics, since different versions have different practical implications. For example, sentient-centered ethics advocates concern for each individual conscious animal, whereas biocentrism forbids the wanton killing of any living thing, and ecocentrism focuses more on protection of species (as a whole) within their environments.

Suppose that a herd of wild sheep is overgrazing an island so as to threaten several plant species and the ecosystem as a whole. Under the assumption that the sheep cannot be moved elsewhere, ecocentrism would imply selective killing of the sheep, sentientism would imply not killing them (since each animal has value, but the plants do not), and biocentrism seems on the surface to imply that nothing should be done (nature should take its course).

Even more pressing than conflicts within nonhuman nature are conflicts between humans and the natural environment, and here again the theories give different emphases. For example, ecocentrism would have us restrict construction and consumer products that threaten ecosystems, but sentientism would not place a priority on the ecosystems (except when the species therein affect the lives of conscious animals), and biocentrism would be concerned only with preservation of life rather than ecosystems per se. Clearly what is needed is a detailed elaboration of particular versions of nature-centered ethics.

As one example of the complexity to be found in new theories in environmental ethics, consider Paul W. Taylor's biocentric perspective set forth in his book *Respect for Nature*. Taylor locates inherent worth in each living organism, rather than in ecosystems, because each organism is "a teleological center of life, striving to preserve itself and realize its good in its own unique way."[11] The key idea is that each organism—plants, animals, and even one-celled creatures—has a good of its own, something that enables it to survive and flourish as the type of creature it is. Nonconscious (and even many conscious) creatures cannot envision that good, but we can. Our consciousness enables us imaginatively to see the world in terms of what helps the organism flourish, and to take into account what is good for it and weigh it against the good of humans. Our consciousness (and reason) does not, however, give our lives greater moral worth than other creatures. We are exactly like other living organisms in being members of a complex interdependent community of organisms, each of which has a good of its own to be pursued in its unique way.

The attitude of respect for nature consists of valuing all life and refusing to place ourselves above it. It implies four duties toward other life. (1) Nonmaleficence is the duty not to kill other living things. Nonmaleficence is the most important duty to organisms, and it forbids wanton killing of animals and plants, such as the killing of elephants to obtain decorative ivory, or fishing for sheer recreation (rather than for food). (2) Noninterference is the duty not to interfere with the freedom of organisms. This rules out, for example, the capture of tropical birds for sale as pets. (3) Fidelity is the duty not to violate the trust of wild animals (as occurs in deception used in hunting, trapping, and fishing). (4) Restitutive justice is the duty to make amends for violations of the other duties, if only by helping to promote the life of other organisms than those we have harmed.

All these duties are prima facie: They have some justified exceptions. In particular, they have some exceptions when they conflict with responsibilities to ourselves and to other human beings. How are these priorities to be set within Taylor's perspective, which refuses to place the inherent worth of humans above that of other animals and plants? Taylor formulates five additional principles of priority.

First, the principle of self-defense permits us to kill when we must in order to protect ourselves against dangerous organisms that threaten our lives. Second, the principle of proportionality asserts that priority is to be given to organisms the basic interests of which are most affected. Basic interests are survival needs, as well as the needs for living a life distinctive to a particular kind of organism. Third, the principle of minimum wrong asserts that we should minimize harm done to all organisms affected. Fourth, the principle of distributive justice asserts that the basic interests of all organisms should be treated as equally important. And fifth, the principle of restitutive justice asserts that, when any of the previous four principles have been violated, some compensation must be made to similar organisms.

What do these priority principles imply? Their implications must be unfolded contextually, but that is equally true of all moral principles applying to humans. They clearly imply, however, that the good of animals and plants must be weighed in decisions about whether to engage in new construction that would destroy indigenous plants and animals. These principles also demonstrate that a nature-centered ethics can provide some guidance in dealing with practical decisions.

Practical Conflicts and Consensus

The contrast between human-centered and nature-centered ethics is theoretically important and also has practical implications. Some environmental activists have used it as support for their sharp confrontations in the courts designed to block or slow commercial development, logging of redwood trees, strip mining, fishing (especially in forms that kill dolphins and whales), and destruction of natural habitats for recreational purposes. They have used it to justify civil disobedience, and even occasional violence, on behalf of their causes. In response, representatives of industry regard nature-centered ethics as the source of environmentalism gone mad, especially in the overwhelming number of new laws and regulations that threaten to strangle business. Not just profits, but thousands of jobs, are at stake.

There are no easy solutions to these political and practical confrontations. Much is at stake, and moral convictions are deep on both sides. Nevertheless, as these conflicts are pursued we need to appreciate that all informed and caring individuals should have concern for both the environment and for human communities. Balance and good judgment are required, with the object of finding the most reasonable accommodations possible among people of good will. It is important to get beneath slogans, stereotypes, and superficial characterizations of environmental disagreements. Often the fundamental differences cut across these disputes and concerns. In particular, clashes between environmentalists and business often reflect underlying differences between short- and long-term views of human good, differences that nature-centered ethicists can use in appealing to majorities who remain human-centered in their ethical perspectives. In this connection we make a few concluding comments.

The economist Adam Smith (1723–1790) argued that self-seeking within a free enterprise system created a self-correcting mechanism that benefited the entire community. He called this the "invisible hand" of free enterprise, but in outline there is nothing mysterious about it. In the pursuit of profits, entrepreneurs create businesses that attract employees, who are motivated by the wages offered. Consumers benefit because competition leads to lower-priced and higher-quality products and services.

In response to Smith's argument, the biologist Garrett Hardin argues that in the long run, individual self-seeking harms the entire community. Hardin describes the "tragedy of the commons."[12] The commons was literally a pasture at the center of town that farmers would use as a common grazing area. Ranchers were motivated to add additional cattle or sheep in order to maximize proceeds from their herds. Eventually, however, the commons was overgrazed and all ranchers were hurt as herds died off. Extending this image to current environmental concerns, the commons becomes usable air, water, forests, and other shared resources. If each person thinks only in terms of narrowly conceived self-interests, these commons will eventually be destroyed. Hence, there is a rationale in terms of long-term self-interest for each of us to agree to a reasonable degree of regulation, what Hardin calls mutually agreed-upon public coercion.

Consider the intense controversy between the logging industry in the Pacific Northwest and environmentalists who defended the endangered spotted owl. During this controversy, environmentalists were criticized for caring more for animals than for people. Yet their concern was not just to protect the appealing owl, but to protect the entire ecosystem in which the owl lived. The owl was scientifically determined to be an *indicator species,* that is, a species whose well-being accurately reflects the well-being of an entire ecosystem. Destruction of the owl's ecosystem can have numerous long-term effects on human well-being, if only in the loss of a renewable source of timber—a loss that would in the long run harm the logging industry and the people who conduct and benefit from that industry.

Concern for the owl, then, can be viewed as part of the concern for persons. The disagreement turned on long-term versus short-term harm to people, and hence was a conflict within a framework of human-centered ethics as well as nature-centered ethics. In fact, eventually it became clear that the salmon industry was threatened by the muddied waters caused by logging, thereby pitting industries against industries (a conflict within human-centered ethics).

Finally, just as we noted that nature-centered ethics takes many forms, we should note that human-centered ethics does, too. Even in rough terms we can contrast a strong and weak version of anthropocentrism (paralleling the distinction between two types of speciesism discussed in Chapter 9). The strong version asserts that only human satisfactions are relevant to decisions concerning the environment and that nonhuman creatures have no intrinsic value at all. The weak version allows that human beings have much greater value than nonhuman creatures, but it recognizes some inherent worth in nonhuman creatures, especially in higher mammals. This weaker version opens the door to a reconciliation with nature-centered perspectives, especially those that themselves give priority to basic human interests when they conflict with the interests of nonhumans.

SUMMARY

Human-centered ethics, which locates inherent moral worth only in rational creatures such as humans, tends to endow other living creatures with only instrumental value for humans. For example, rights ethics values the environment because humans have a right to a livable environment, and because nature has economic, aesthetic, recreational, and scientific uses. Virtue-centered ethics, however, while still human-centered, stresses the virtues of humility, gratitude, and sensitivity to the aspects of nature that have intrinsic value of their own; this view approaches the beginnings of a nature-centered ethics.

Nature-centered ethics, which locates inherent value beyond rational human beings, can take three forms: consciousness-centered ethics (sentientism, as defended by Peter Singer and Tom Regan), life-centered ethics (biocentrism, as defended by Albert Schweitzer, Kenneth Goodpaster, and Paul Taylor), and ecology-centered ethics (ecocentrism, as defended by Aldo Leopold, J. Baird Callicott, and Holmes Rolston III). Taylor's biocentrism, which illustrates how detailed such outlooks have become, formulates principles of duty to living organisms such as nonmaleficence, noninterference, fidelity, and restitution, as well as priority principles for balancing duties to humans and to nature, such as self-defense, proportionality, minimum wrong, distributive justice, and restitution.

Finally, the differences apparent in the practical implications of human- and nature-centered ethics reflect differences—possibly even more important—between long-term and short-term thinking about human good.

DISCUSSION TOPICS

1   Do you agree with Hill's assessment of his neighbor? Exactly what was objectionable in the neighbor's conduct? Was it the destruction of the avocado tree and the other extant plants, or their replacement with concrete? Would the neighbor be open to criticism if, after removing the greenery, he had replaced it with new plants, perhaps ones that required less maintenance? Similarly, are strip mining and the harvesting of redwood trees objectionable only when the land is not later restored?

2   Is there anything morally objectionable about hunting for sport (rather than for food)? In your answer, discuss the attitudes of the hunter who (in 1850) wrote the following description of shooting an elephant:

> The elephant stood broadside to me, at upwards of one hundred yards, and his attention at the moment was occupied with the dogs. . . . I fired at his shoulder, and secured him with a single shot. The ball caught him high on the shoulder-blade, rendering him instantly lame; and before the echo of the bullet could reach my ear, I plainly saw the elephant was mine. . . . I resolved to devote a short time to the contemplation of this noble elephant before laying him low; . . . I quickly kindled a fire and put on the kettle, and in a few minutes my coffee was prepared. There I sat in my forest home, coolly sipping my coffee, with one of the finest elephants in Africa awaiting my pleasure beside a neighbouring tree. . . .

> Having admired the elephant for a considerable time, I resolved to make experiments for vulnerable points. . . . [He bungles this again and again; eventually, after even he has become a little worried, he succeeds in wounding the elephant fatally.] Large tears now trickled from his eyes, which he slowly shut and opened, his colossal frame quivered convulsively, and falling on his side, he expired.[13]

3   Do you find anything morally objectionable in the following practice? If so, give your reasons and state whether they are human-centered, consciousness-centered, life-centered, or ecology-centered. "Certain rare species of butterflies occur in hummocks (slightly elevated forested ground) on the African grasslands. It was formerly the practice of . . . collectors to go in, collect a few hundred specimens and then burn out the hummock with the intention of destroying the species, thereby driving up the price of their collections."[14] Is the destruction of any species of organism objectionable (given that thousands of species disappear each year through natural causes), or only the destruction of certain types of species?

4   Human-centered environmental ethics relies heavily on the idea that we have an obligation to pass on a livable environment to future generations of human beings. Yet those human beings (by definition) do not yet exist. How could nonexistent persons make moral claims on us now? Do nonexistent persons have rights to the preservation (by us) of the environment? (In your answer, consider the analogy with parents' decisions to have children: The future children do not yet exist, and yet the parents have an obligation to prepare to give them meaningful lives before bringing them into existence. That responsibility includes the obligation not to use drugs or engage in other practices that might cause genetic deformities.)

5   What do you think Schweitzer means when he says that all living things have a "will to live"? Do the following organisms have a will to live in exactly the same sense: human beings, squirrels, mosquitoes, protozoans, grass, trees?

6   The tragedy of the commons results not just from the extraction of resources from a shared environment, but also (in reverse) from pollution of the environment. Identify an example from your local community of how the seemingly innocent (nonmalevolent) pursuit of self-interest by many individuals results in pollution that harms the community as a whole.

7 "Eco-feminists" have argued that there are important connections, both in theory and in historical practices, between the attitudes of male dominance involved in exploitation of women and exploitation of nature. Do you agree? In particular, respond to the following passage from Rosemary Ruether:

> Women must see that there can be no liberation for them and no solution to the ecological crisis within a society whose fundamental model of relationship continues to be one of domination. They must unite the demands of the women's movement with those of the ecological movement to envision a radical reshaping of the basic socioeconomic relations and the underlying values of this society.[15]

8 Some of the worst environmental problems have been caused in developed Western countries, but developing countries have begun to cause equally severe problems; examples include the destruction of Brazilian rain forests in order to clear land for farms and cattle, the widespread use of heavily polluting coal in China, the encroachment on wilderness areas in India, and expansion of populations in Third World countries. Given the increasingly global effects of environmental changes, Western countries have put increasing demands on Third World countries to conform to Western standards. Does fairness require that these demands be backed by economic support, which is likely to require higher taxes and self-sacrifice by Western populations? Should Americans be willing to offer what Al Gore calls (in his book *Earth in the Balance*) a Global Marshall Plan on behalf of the environment?

9 What would you say to someone who refused to conserve electricity, gasoline, or water on the grounds that such acts are so insignificant in scale that it makes no difference to the overall environmental problems? As part of your answer, consider (a) the virtues of authenticity and integrity, (b) utilitarianism, and (c) rights ethics.

SUGGESTED READINGS

Armstrong, Susan J., and Richard G. Botzler (eds.). *Environmental Ethics: Divergence and Convergence*. 2d ed. New York: McGraw-Hill, 1997.

Callicott, J. Baird. *Earth's Insights: A Multicultural Survey of Ecological Ethics from the Mediterranean Basin to the Australian Outback*. Berkeley: University of California Press, 1994.

Callicott, J. Baird. *In Defense of the Land Ethic: Essays in Environmental Philosophy*. Albany: State University of New York Press, 1988.

Cooper, David E., and Joy A. Palmer (eds.). *The Environment in Question: Ethics and Global Issues*. New York: Routledge, 1992.

DesJardins, Joseph R. *Environmental Ethics: An Introduction to Environmental Philosophy*. 2d ed. Belmont, CA: Wadsworth, 1996.

DesJardins, Joseph. *Environmental Ethics: Concepts, Policy and Theory*. New York: Mayfield Publishers, 1998.

Elliot, Robert (ed.). *Environmental Ethics*. New York: Oxford University Press, 1995.

Hargrove, Eugene C. *Foundations of Environmental Ethics*. Englewood Cliffs, NJ: Prentice-Hall, 1989.

Hargrove, Eugene E. (ed.). *The Animal Rights/Environmental Ethics Debate*. Albany: State University of New York Press, 1992.

Hill, Thomas E., Jr. "Ideals of Human Excellence and Preserving Natural Environments." In *Autonomy and Self-Respect*. Cambridge: Cambridge University Press, 1991: 104–117.

Johnson, Lawrence E. *A Morally Deep World: An Essay on Moral Significance and Environmental Ethics.* New York: Cambridge University Press, 1993.

Martin, Mike W. "Rethinking Reverence for Life," *Between the Species,* Vol. 9 (1993): 204–213.

Newton, Lisa H., and Catherine K. Dillingham. *Watersheds 2: Ten Cases in Environmental Ethics.* Belmont, CA: Wadsworth, 1996.

Passmore, John. *Man's Responsibility for Nature.* New York: Scribner, 1974.

Pojman, Louis P. (ed.). *Environmental Ethics: Readings in Theory and Application.* Boston: Jones and Bartlett Publishers, 1994.

Rolston, Holmes, III. *Environmental Ethics: Duties to and Values in the Natural World.* Philadelphia: Temple University Press, 1988.

Scherer, Donald. *Upstream/Downstream: Issues in Environmental Ethics.* Philadelphia: Temple University Press, 1990.

Sterba, James. (ed.). *Environmental Ethics, Animal Rights, and Practical Applications.* New York: MacMillan, 1995.

Taylor, Paul W. *Respect for Nature: A Theory of Environmental Ethics.* Princeton, NJ: Princeton University Press, 1986.

Tucker, Mary Evelyn, and Duncan Ryuken Williams (eds.). *Buddhism and Ecology.* Cambridge, MA: Harvard University Press, 1997.

VanDeVeer, Donald, and Christine Pierce (eds.) *People, Penguins, and Plastic Trees: Basic Issues in Environmental Ethics.* 2d ed. Belmont, CA: Wadsworth, 1995.

VanDeVeer, Donald, and Christine Pierce (eds.). *The Environmental Ethics and Public Policy Book.* 2d ed. Belmont, CA: Wadsworth, 1997.

Warren, Karen J. (ed.). *Ecological Feminist Philosophies.* Bloomington: Indiana University Press, 1996.

Westra, Laura. *An Environmental Proposal for Ethics: The Principle of Integrity.* Lanham, MD: Rowman & Littlefield, 1994.

PART FOUR

Sexual Morality

It is through sex . . . that each individual has to pass in order to have access to . . . [her or his] own identity. . . . Hence the importance we ascribe to it, the reverential fear with which we surround it, the care we take to know it. Hence the fact that over the centuries it has become more important than our soul, more important almost than our life.[1]

Michel Foucault

Sexual desire, according to traditional attitudes, is a valuable but dangerous force that needs control with a swarm of prohibitions. Its moral status centers on the biological purpose of producing children and is specified by five mandates: (1) to refrain from sexual activity until marriage, (2) to engage in marital sex without preventing the conception of children, (3) to refrain from sex with anyone but one's spouse, (4) to choose a spouse of the opposite sex, and (5) to love one's sexual partner, that is, one's spouse. A contemporary variation on this traditional view emphasizes that sex is morally significant in expressing and supporting love between married partners, in addition to its role in creating children.

The sexual revolution of the 1960s challenged these mandates by questioning the requirement that sex be joined with love, marriage, and children. New attitudes arose that accepted or advocated sex outside marriage, contraception, sex with more than one person, homosexuality, and sex without love. In the name of freedom (autonomy, self-determination) and respect for the freedom of others, proponents of the sexual revolution accepted virtually all forms of sexual expression by consenting participants.

Philosophical thinking about sex emerged largely in response to the sexual revolution. Before the 1960s, few philosophers regarded sex as a worthy topic.* Since 1970, however, philosophers have devoted increasing attention to the topics dealt with in the following four chapters: the moral relationships between sex and love, homosexuality and homophobia, pornography and fantasy, and marriage and adultery, respectively.

---

*A notable exception was Bertrand Russell (1872–1970), whose defense of sex outside marriage—"free love"—prompted universities to ban him from teaching for more than two decades.

Some have argued that the sexual revolution is over and that the horrifying epidemic of AIDS (Acquired Immune Deficiency Syndrome), as well as the increase in other, albeit less deadly, sexually transmitted diseases, is forcing a renewed interest in more traditional values. Others hope that sexual attitudes are undergoing a gradual evolution that will bring about a synthesis of the best ideas and attitudes of the sexual revolution and traditional perspectives. In any case, sexuality is a central topic for everyday ethics, especially regarding the attempt to understand our personal identities and the search for meaningful relationships.

CHAPTER 11

Sex and Love

What is the connection between sex, love, and moral values? In particular, is there an obligation to restrict sex to relationships involving love? Or, is the insistence that sex be accompanied by love based on a degrading view of sexuality—that sex is bad and in need of redemption by love? Is romantic (sexual, erotic) love a kind of illusion and trap, or at least so fraught with peril that it is best avoided?

In Marilyn French's novel *The Women's Room,* Val, a thirty-nine-year-old student, contends that sex ought to be separated from love. Val has come to believe that erotic love is a biological illusion and a trap for women:

> Love is insanity. . . . It is the taking over of a rational and lucid mind by delusion and self-destruction. You lose yourself, you have no power over yourself, you can't even think straight. That's the reason I hate it.[1]

By the time people recover from this insanity—and sooner or later they always do—they are often married and have children. According to Val, this works out well for men who wish to have wives at home with their children, but less well for women, who usually end up getting hurt.

Even though she rejects erotic love, Val is not cynical about sex, once it is freed from love. Indeed,

> for her, sex was almost a philosophy. She saw the whole world in terms of it. . . . Val slept with people the way other people go out for dinner with a friend. She liked them, she liked sex. She rarely expected anything from it beyond the pleasure of the moment. At the same time, she said it was overrated: it had been so tabooed, she claimed, that we had come to expect paradise from it. It was only fun, great fun, but not paradise.[2]

Definitions of Love

What does Val mean by "love"? Her interest, like ours in this chapter, is erotic, sexual, romantic love—that is, love involving sexual attraction. But Val also has in mind a particular conception of erotic love—the Romantic conception. When we speak of Romantic love (with a capital R), we will mean the view of romantic love (with a small r) that was dominant during the nineteenth century. It had as its precursor the courtly love tradition of the Middle Ages (as expressed in the legends of Lancelot and Guinevere, and Tristan and Isolde), and continues today in certain highly romanticized myths about being destined for one person whom one idealizes and with whom one can live happily ever after. Val seems to have in mind Romantic idealization: the process whereby two lovers each exaggerate the beauty and goodness of the other and become largely oblivious to the other's faults. We sometimes refer to such love as an infatuation that distorts one's normal degree of reasonableness. Is that true love?

Most of us distinguish "true" or "genuine" love—the "real thing"—from a variety of more superficial infatuations. We draw the distinction in different ways, however, reflecting differences in the values we hold. *True love* is a value-loaded expression: It refers to the kinds of responses and relationships (involving sexual attraction) that we consider desirable or ideal. Often we disagree with each other about what it is. Consider, for example, three different ideals of true love (and there are many more).

The Romantic ideal values passion above all else. Passion reflects an intense longing for someone, accompanied by an obsessive preoccupation with that person. In a passionate state one devotes frenzied attention to every aspect of the beloved and finds everything about the beloved glorious. It is the state most often referred to as "falling in love," although we might also call it the "in love" state. This is the conception of love that Val rejects.

A contrasting conception of true love stresses "loving" rather than being "in love." Loving consists of caring and commitment as opposed to passionate attention, although the caring on occasion may be expressed through passion. In *The Art of Loving* the humanistic psychologist Erich Fromm developed a strongly moralized view of love along these lines. Love, he suggests, is the attitude characterized by giving, caring, and acting responsibly and respectfully while also maintaining one's own integrity, self-respect, and individuality. "Falling in love," by contrast, is an immature and selfish preoccupation. In fact, Fromm continues, any form of intense preoccupation with one individual can be a distortion of true love, where true love is a general attitude toward all people:

> Love is not primarily a relationship to a specific person; it is an *attitude,* an *orientation of character* which determines the relatedness of a person to the world as a whole, not toward one "object" of love. . . . If I truly love one person I love all persons, I love the world, I love life.[3]

It is perhaps difficult, however, to see how Fromm's attempt to view all love as general humanitarian caring (or as he calls it, "brotherly love") can apply to erotic love. Humanitarian caring is inclusive: It is addressed to many people at the same time. Erotic love is exclusive: It focuses great concern and attention on one person (or at most a few persons), excluding most others. Fromm fears that this exclusivity leads to narcissistic distortions and *egoism a deux* (double and shared egotism) in which two people become unhealthily "addicted" to each other. Is that an inevitable result?

A third conception of love combines some elements from the Romantic and humanitarian views while discarding other elements. Erotic love involves preoccupation with one individual, but in a caring and committed way, not an unhealthy and selfish way. Thus, according to feminist Shulamith Firestone, in erotic love the personal identities of two equal partners are intermingled and reshaped. Each becomes "psychically wide-open" to the other, in terms of both complete emotional vulnerability and intellectual openness to the experience of the other. Commitment is crucial in order to create the trust and security needed to sustain this vulnerability. Yet the commitment is not entirely selfless; instead, it is based on a mixture of caring and self-interest:

> The self attempts to enrich itself through the absorption of another being. . . . Love between two equals would be an enrichment, each enlarging himself through the other: instead of being one, locked in a cell of himself with only his own experience and view, he could participate in the existence of another—an extra window on the world.[4]

In addition, Firestone insists that true love involves mutual understanding rather than illusion of the sort typical of romantic infatuation. In fact, love is a form of creative vision in which value is discerned (in the beloved) as well as affirmed and bestowed:

> Because of this fusion of egos, in which each sees and cares about the other as a new self, the beauty/character of the beloved, perhaps hidden to outsiders under layers of defenses, is revealed. . . . Increased sensitivity to the real, if hidden, values in the other . . . is not "blindness" or "idealization" but is, in fact, deeper vision.[5]

Yet Firestone would agree with Val that love is easily distorted in ways hurtful to women. She argues that, until women have economic status and power equal to that of men, true love will remain difficult to achieve. Unequal power tends to make women vulnerable to exploitation by men, who often have difficulty in giving the commitment and the emotional openness required by love.

These three conceptions of love—a Romantic, a humanitarian, and a feminist conception—are intended only as illustrations of how the expression "true love" is used to convey contrasting values. Love is not some simple "feeling," contrary to what contemporary popular music and romance novels often suggest. For the purposes of discussing the relationship between sex and love, however, it will be helpful to develop some minimal (if controversial) definitions.

By *erotic love* we will mean love expressed through sex, which includes sexual arousal, desire, and activity (ranging from a caress to intercourse). The adjective *sexual* thus refers to bodily states involving genital excitement and to thoughts, pleasures, and desires associated with that excitement. By *liking* we mean a positive attitude toward someone based on some attraction—one finds that person "to one's taste." *Affection* is an emotion of concern for another person's well-being, an emotion that may last for a shorter time than does the attitude of liking. *Love* refers to an attitude that involves caring, affection for, and commitment to the good of one's partner in a deeper degree than does liking. As deep caring and commitment are understood to involve further values that guide relationships—perhaps honesty, equality and fairness, responsibilities, and faithfulness—ideals of *true love* acquire further moral content.

With these distinctions in mind, let us consider an argument in favor of valuing sexual expressions without love and then an argument in favor of tightly linking sex and love.

Arguments for Sex without Love

In his book *Sex Without Love*, Russell Vannoy provides a philosophical defense of Val's attitudes. Vannoy focuses on people whom he calls "authentic" and "humanists." By *authentic* he refers to people who make decisions based on self-knowledge, under minimal influence from distorting external factors and in full awareness of relevant information. *Humanists* are individuals who value other people for their intrinsic worth and who display sensitivity, simple decency, and some generosity.

Vannoy believes that traditional views of sex are based on a simplistic dualism: Either sex is an expression of love or it is a degrading indulgence for selfish purposes. He argues that there is a large middle ground between these two extremes. For example, sex can express simple affection, liking, friendship, sheer delight in the beauty of another person, and physical recreation based on mutual consent and desire. In these ways, sex need not be degrading or exploitative, but neither must it involve anything as serious as love, which implies deep emotional ties and commitment. Traditionalists, Vannoy argues, have simply failed to acknowledge the full possibilities of nonloving sex:

> It can be an evening of sensuous eroticism that may continue for hours and include all the foreplay, afterplay, kisses and caresses that actual lovers enjoy, perhaps done simply out of deep mutual admiration for each other's sensuous qualities and out of gratitude for having been chosen by the other for such an evening. Yet the pair may go their separate ways in the morning and never see each other again, perhaps because they prefer their own independence and singlehood to permanent emotional involvement and marriage.[6]

Furthermore, Vannoy defends sex without love outside of romantic relationships. Masturbation and fetishes, for example, provide pleasurable experiences for people who prefer more private modes of sexual expression. In Vannoy's view, to deny that sex has many legitimate forms of expression outside romantic relationships is to embrace a degrading view of sex as something that by itself is bad and that stands in need of redemption through love, marriage, and procreation.

In addition to arguing that sex without love is morally permissible for authentic humanists, Vannoy defends two further theses. On the one hand, he contends that in many cases sex without love is better than sex with love in terms of pleasure and contribution to well-being. The practice of sex without love can yield higher degrees of excitement by allowing greater novelty, variety, and romantic adventure, whereas sex between married partners tends to become boringly routine. Inevitably, the initial romantic intensity fades, leaving at best lukewarm companionship and at worst mutual hostility due to the loss of other romantic options. Also, love burdens sex with demands that partners perform satisfactorily. It threatens the delights of sex by burying them within delicately balanced and emotionally complex love relationships. In this context, affectionate sex without the burdens of commitment is far preferable.

On the other hand, Vannoy attacks erotic love as an incoherent ideal riddled with inconsistent demands and illusions that inevitably cause frustration and unhappiness. For example, love seeks to endure forever ("until death do us part" or "for all eternity") and simultaneously to be ecstatically exciting, but it cannot be both: The initial intensity always fades. Again, lovers want their partners to be overwhelmed with emotions so intense as to blind them to their flaws, and yet simultaneously to choose rationally to love them from an understanding of their true natures. They also want partners who feel deeply dependent on them and who wish to serve their interests out of pure altruism, and yet who are secure and independent individuals with interests of their own that sometimes conflict with the demands of selfless giving.

In short, Vannoy argues for three theses: (1) All sex without love is morally permissible when engaged in by consenting adults who avoid cruelty and exploitation; (2) often sex without love is better than sex with love; and (3) traditional ideals about sexual love are irrational and incoherent. Can defenders of traditional views refute these theses?

Arguments for Sex with Love

Defenses of traditional views of sex often appeal to God's commandments as interpreted by particular religions. It is understandable that religious faith will influence one's views of sexual morality, but is it possible to defend traditional views without appealing to religious doctrines?

Roger Scruton attempts such a defense in his book *Sexual Desire*. His defense is based on the Aristotelian view that virtue and self-fulfillment go together, as well as on the claim that sex has a natural role in contributing to self-fulfillment.

Scruton first reminds us that sexual desire is not merely a desire to engage in intercourse with a body. Instead, it is a desire for another *person* who is, like oneself, an embodied consciousness, that is, a consciousness in a body. More specifically, sexual desire entails a longing to unite with a person, whether the longing is focused in a desire for intercourse or whether it is a less focused desire. It also implies a wish to have our partners enjoy being desired by us and to desire us in similar ways.

Sexual desires are satisfied through experiences of shared sexual excitement in which the consciousnesses of both partners are focused on the pleasures of both partners' bodies. Scruton eloquently describes this "mutual embodiment, the other's 'being in' his body and I in mine": "In our excitement we sense each other's animation, and become acquainted with the pulsing of the spirit in the flesh, which fills the body with a pervasive 'I', and transforms it into something strange, precious and possessible."[7]

What moral relevance does this experience have? When joined with love, this experience of embodiment provides a unique way for two people to affirm each other's value. In doing so, it teaches them to appreciate the basis of morality: the value of people as conscious beings with bodies. Without erotic love we would "appreciate less vividly the fundamental premise of morality: that the repository of infinite value which is the other self, exists not in some Platonic supersphere, but here in the flesh."[8] Thus, Scruton asserts, to give and receive this form of appreciation and affirmation is a crucial aspect of self-fulfillment:

> Erotic love involves an element of mutual self-enhancement; it generates a sense of the irreplaceable value, both of the other and of the self, and of the activities which bind them. To receive and to give this love is to achieve something of incomparable value in the process of self-fulfillment. It is to gain the most powerful of all interpersonal *guarantees;* in erotic love the subject becomes conscious of the full reality of his personal existence, not only in his own eyes, but in the eyes of another.[9]

Sex without love cannot yield this mutual affirmation of personal worth, which Scruton thinks is essential for self-fulfillment. Love affirms the interests of the beloved through a long-term commitment to promote them. Within love relationships sex becomes an expression and symbol of this enduring affirmation. In contrast, sex as a one-night stand, as a temporary recreation, or even as an act of affection is incapable of conveying the profound affirmation of the other person. Nor can masturbation or perversions (such as sex with animals and sex with dead people), which do not even involve two mutually excited conscious beings, convey any such affirmation. Moreover, according to Scruton's ideal of "sexual integrity," premarital sex is objectionable. Postponing sexual activity until long-term marital commitments are possible is a way to preserve the connection between sex and love. In short, there is an obligation to join sex and love because that conjunction allows individuals to affirm the other's moral worth in a singularly important way that contributes to self-fulfillment.

How, then, would Scruton respond to Vannoy's claims that sex without love is more exciting and that erotic love is an incoherent ideal? Recall that Vannoy viewed sex without love as often more exciting because it offers greater variety, novelty, and romance than does sex within long-term loving relationships. A traditionalist might admit there is a loss of newness and romance as partners become well acquainted with each other's bodies, but nevertheless insist that the loss is outweighed by the security and mutual affirmation offered by loving sex. Scruton, however, has a more positive rejoinder. He reminds us that erotic love offers unlimited variety, because sexual desire is focused on a conscious person, and consciousness is not something fixed: "Sexual curiosity . . . renews itself endlessly; for the object of curiosity is not the bodily region as such, but the region 'as inhabited by a pleased consciousness,' and pleasure is a dynamic thing, which has a constantly shifting significance in the experience of the person who feels it."[10] Sex within long-term relationships is as varied in what it expresses and affirms as are the two consciousnesses it joins together.

Is love an impossible ideal? Scruton might agree that it is when it involves the conflicting desires Vannoy lists: that love both last forever and provide constant ecstasy; that one's partner be overwhelmed by emotion and thereby blinded to one's flaws and yet rationally understand and appreciate one; that one's partner be perfectly altruistic and dependent on one and yet be an interesting and independent individual. Scruton, however, would probably view these desires, in contrast with the rational desires involved in the kinds of self-fulfilling love he describes, as unreasonable and immature.

Scruton might also point out that mature love relationships provide recurring moments of ecstasy interspersed with caring support for one's partner's endeavors, allow for honest recognition of faults, and admit to elements of both strong dependency and independence. Scruton does agree with Vannoy on one point: Love requires a thorough union of interests. Whereas Vannoy finds that union stifling, however, Scruton finds it liberating. This disagreement strikes at the heart of contemporary concerns to reconcile individuality and unity, or distinct and shared identities, in love relationships.

True Love: Obligations or Ideals?

We noted that the meaning of the expression *true love* is tied to one's value perspective on human relationships, and we have mentioned several such perspectives. Let us now ask whether the values that enter into conceptions of true love are universal obligations, as Scruton suggests, or moral ideals that individuals are free to embrace but that are not incumbent on everyone.

Scruton's defense of the traditional view of sex rests on the assumption that human sexuality has one "natural" aim in promoting self-fulfillment: to foster erotic love and its unique form of moral affirmation. Drawing on that assumption, he tries to demonstrate a general obligation to link sex and love. Is there, however, any one "natural" role of sex in contributing to human fulfillment? Cannot sex serve many legitimate roles in different lives, or in the same life at different stages?

There are alternative roads to self-fulfillment, and numerous ways to find affirmation of one's moral worth. The suppression or sublimation of sex is perhaps the best avenue for some people, such as priests and nuns, who take vows of chastity as part of a religious commitment. For other people (Vannoy, for example), who value variety and intensity of sexual passion, evasion of long-term commitments may contribute to self-fulfillment. For some, a variety of types of relationships, some long and some short, may be best. For those who value the constancy, support, and depth of long-term relationships, the lifetime commitments advocated by Scruton will be best.

According to this line of thought, there is no universal obligation to link sex and love in any one way. Instead, there are many permissible moral ideals concerning sex that individuals may choose among in seeking self-fulfillment. (The choice, we hope, would be made wisely, on the basis of self-understanding.) These are *moral* ideals in that they express visions of valuable forms of human relationships, ones that may in different ways combine affection, caring, mutual understanding, mutual respect, honesty, and mutual commitments. Moreover, once embraced, some of the ideals generate obligations. In particular, when two people accept Scruton's ideal of long-term commitments and make mutual commitments based on a shared acceptance of the ideal, they incur special obligations to conform to the ideal. There is, however, no single degree of commitment to these ideals that is obligatory for all individuals.

Recognition of a plurality of permissible sexual ideals should not be confused with acceptance of the attitude put forth in the 1960s that anything goes, at least as long as there is mutual consent. The difference arises from the fact that sexual ideals can be evaluated by reference to the self-fulfillment and personal well-being of individuals and couples. There are often very good reasons for certain individuals and couples (given their psychological natures and preferred lifestyles) to adopt one ideal rather than another in their pursuit of happiness and meaningful life.

This pluralistic model of sexual morality would certainly complicate sexual relationships, because individuals would bring to relationships different ideals about what is desirable for them; but people do so already to a large extent in our society. In any case, ideals are open to discussion and criticism by couples. They are also open to compromise, in the best sense of the term: reconciliation of differences by mutual concessions. As with all major aspects of loving relationships, the nature of love itself is mutually shaped by couples.

SUMMARY

True love is a term used to express value perspectives concerning what relationships are most desirable. The Romantic perspective focuses on passionate preoccupation with the beloved; Erich Fromm's humanitarian perspective stresses general caring for all people, even when expressed through a relationship with one person; and Shulamith Firestone's feminist perspective emphasizes emotional sharing between equals in a way that reshapes personal identity.

When is sex without love morally permissible? Russell Vannoy argues that it is permissible whenever the participants freely consent. He rejects the simple dichotomy between sex as an expression of love and sex as a selfish indulgence, drawing attention to ways in which sex can express affection, liking, and friendship. Roger Scruton argues that erotic love makes a unique contribution to self-fulfillment through a mutual affirmation of the moral worth of embodied conscious beings. Perhaps, however, sex can contribute in a variety of ways to the fulfillment of individuals and couples, and thus there may be several morally permissible ideals concerning sex.

Is sex without love more exciting because it allows greater variety and romance with different partners? No doubt it is for some individuals, but as Scruton points out, sexual desire is directed toward persons who have a consciousness as alive as one's own, and this enables long-term relationships to offer unlimited variety in what is enjoyed and expressed through sex.

Is sexual love an incoherent ideal, as Vannoy charges? Must it involve conflicting desires (such as those for constant ecstasy and permanence), overwhelming emotions and calm rationality, dependence and independence for both partners, unity and individuality? Although immature forms of love are characterized by incompatible demands, mature love need not be. As Shulamith Firestone suggests, love involves a profound reshaping of personal identity within a caring relationship with another person.

DISCUSSION TOPICS

1   Is there a universal moral obligation to refrain from sex except when it expresses deep affection and lasting commitment? Or are all forms of sexual expression morally permissible, so long as they are based on consent and respect for one's partner's consent?

2   In what ways is sex with love better (though not necessarily the only acceptable option) than sex without love, and vice versa?

3   Firestone believes that (genuine) erotic love is possible only between individuals who are equal in the kinds of power that mutual economic independence provides. Presumably, two people need not earn the same income, but both must have self-sufficient incomes; otherwise, harmful forms of dependency arise. In

contrast, Robert Solomon contends that love requires only equality of consent; that is, both partners agree to the roles they play in the relationship. Do you agree with what he says in the following passage?

> But what does "equality" mean in relations? It does not mean "being the same." It does not exclude all sorts of asymmetrical and uneven roles and relationships, including the absolute domination of one person by the other. It does not require, as such, the equal division of housework or "bread earning" tasks. . . . Equality in love essentially means a mutually-agreed upon indeterminacy [i.e., lack of fixedness or finality] . . . in which one's self-images and personal roles and identity are up for grabs, in negotiation with one other person, in which there are no preordained roles or predestined status relationships.[11]

4 Is it possible to love erotically more than one person at the same time? Before answering this question, first discuss what you understand it to mean. Are we asking whether one person could experience certain emotions at the same time toward more than one person? Are we asking a practical question about whether there is enough time and energy to pursue more than one relationship at a time? Or are we asking a value question concerning which kind of relationships have the highest value?

5 The French Romantic novelist Stendhal (1783–1842) argued that passionate romantic love is the highest form of love and that it always involves an element of illusion: "From the moment he falls in love even the wisest man no longer sees anything *as it really is.* He underrates his own qualities, and overrates the least favour bestowed by his beloved."[12] Love is a combination of illusion and esteem for the beloved and involves a process he called "crystallization." When a tree branch is thrown into the salt mines near Salzburg and remains there for a few months, it is transformed into a shimmeringly beautiful crystalline latticework. Analogously, the lover's imagination ascribes one perfection after another to the beloved. Does the process of falling in love always or usually involve illusions? Or can the intense preoccupation with the beloved be based primarily on insight into the special value the person has, as both Scruton and Firestone suggest?

If you think that love and illusion are often compatible, are there any limits you would draw concerning extreme illusions? For example, could we experience true love for someone whose gender we are mistaken about? In David Hwang's play *M. Butterfly,* a heterosexual man thinks he is deeply in love with a Chinese opera singer who he learns twenty years later is a man.[13] During the twenty years, the man believed he was deeply in love with the singer, but he later concludes that he loved only a fantasy, not a real person. Do you agree?

6 True love is a term used to express a value perspective on the most desirable forms of erotic relationships. Put into words your conception of true (erotic) love. In particular, discuss the moral values, if any, that enter into your conception of love. Include in your discussion a response to the following questions (which combine some of the preceding questions):

a Is true love something that has to last a lifetime, or can it exist for a few years (or a few days) and then end?

b Can a person love two people at the same time?

c To what extent does genuine love require that one share the interests of one's lover?

d Is true love purely altruistic, that is, completely selfless? Or does it involve a substantial element of self-concern or self-love mixed with elements of altruism?

e In what sense, if any, does true love require equality or fairness in relationships?

f Must true love be based on mutual understanding, or does it admit of large degrees of illusion and error about one's partner?

g Do we choose to love, or does love happen to us (as is suggested by such phrases as "falling in love" and "being hit by lightning")?

7 In *The Second Sex* Simone de Beauvoir writes, "The word *love* has by no means the same sense for both sexes, and this is one cause of the serious misunderstandings that divide them. Byron well said: 'Man's love is of man's life a thing apart;' 'Tis woman's whole existence.' "[14] De Beauvoir then goes on to say that women tend to think of love as unconditional and selfless devotion, whereas men typically do not think of love as requiring this consuming devotion for them, though they seek it from women.

In a variation of this theme, Robert Nozick writes:

> The individual self can be related to the *we* [i.e., a closely bonded couple in an intimate relationship] it identifies with in two different ways. It can see the *we* as a very important *aspect* of itself, or it can see itself as part of the *we*, as contained within it. It may be that men more often take the former view, women the latter. Although both see the *we* as extremely important for the self, most men might draw the circle of themselves containing the circle of the *we* as an aspect *within* it, while most women might draw the circle of themselves within the circle of the *we*.[15]

Do you agree with de Beauvoir and Nozick that, roughly speaking, most women tend to love in different ways than most men do? If so, what do you think might cause this to be? If not, why do you think de Beauvoir and Nozick were led to make their suggestions?

8 Today it is sometimes claimed that AIDS is "changing sexual morality." It is certainly altering many people's behavior patterns, but is this due to prudence about one's self-interest or to fundamental changes in moral beliefs and attitudes concerning sex?

SUGGESTED READINGS

Baker, Robert, Frederick A. Elliston, and Kathleen J. Wininger (eds.). *Philosophy and Sex*. 3d ed. Buffalo, NY: Prometheus, 1998.

Brown, Robert. *Analyzing Love*. New York: Cambridge University Press, 1987.

Firestone, Shulamith. *The Dialectic of Sex: The Case for Feminist Revolution*. New York: Morrow, 1970.

Fromm, Erich. *The Art of Loving*. New York: Harper & Row, 1956.

Gilbert, Paul. *Human Relationships: A Philosophical Introduction.* Oxford: Blackwell, 1991.

Hunter, J. F. M. *Thinking about Sex and Love: A Philosophical Inquiry*. New York: St. Martin's Press, 1980.

Lamb, Roger (ed.). *Love Analyzed*. Boulder, CO: Westview Press, 1997.

Lemoncheck, Linda. *Loose Women, Lecherous Men: A Feminist Philosophy of Sex*. New York: Oxford University Press, 1997.

Martin, Mike W. *Love's Virtues*. Lawrence: University Press of Kansas, 1996.

Minas, Anne (ed.). *Gender Basics: Feminist Perspectives on Women and Men*. Belmont, CA: Wadsworth, 1993.

Norton, David L., and Mary F. Kille (eds.). *Philosophies of Love*. Totowa, NJ: Rowman & Allanheld, 1983.

Nozick, Robert. "Love's Bond." In *The Examined Life*. New York: Simon & Schuster, 1989): pp. 68–86.

Nussbaum, Martha C. *Love's Knowledge: Essays on Philosophy and Literature*. New York: Oxford University Press, 1990.

Posner, Richard A. *Sex and Reason*. Cambridge, MA: Harvard University Press, 1992.

Santas, Gerasimos. *Plato and Freud: Two Theories of Love*. New York: Basil Blackwell, 1988.

Scruton, Roger. *Sexual Desire: A Moral Philosophy of The Erotic*. New York: Free Press, 1986.

Singer, Irving. *The Nature of Love*. 3 vols. Chicago: University of Chicago Press, 1984, 1987.

Sircello, Guy. *Love and Beauty*. Princeton, NJ: Princeton University Press, 1989.

Soble, Alan (ed.). *Eros, Agape and Philia: Readings in the Philosophy of Love*. New York: Paragon House, 1989.

Soble, Alan (ed.). *The Philosophy of Sex*. 3d. ed. Savage, MD: Rowman & Littlefield, 1997.

Soble, Alan. *The Philosophy of Sex and Love: An Introduction*. New York: Paragon House, 1998.

Solomon, Robert C. *About Love: Reinventing Romance for Our Times*. New York: Simon & Schuster, 1988.

Solomon, Robert C., and Kathleen M. Higgins (eds.). *The Philosophy of (Erotic) Love*. Lawrence: University Press of Kansas, 1991.

Sternberg, Robert J., and Michael L. Barnes (eds.). *The Psychology of Love*. New Haven, CT: Yale University Press, 1988.

Stewart, Robert M. (ed.). *Philosophical Perspectives on Sex and Love*. New York: Oxford University Press, 1995.

Vannoy, Russell. *Sex Without Love: A Philosophical Exploration*. Buffalo, NY: Prometheus, 1980.

Verene, D. P. (ed.). *Sexual Love and Western Morality*. Belmont, CA: Wadsworth, 1995.

Williams, Clifford (ed.). *On Love and Friendship: Philosophical Readings*. Boston: Jones and Bartlett, 1995.

Wilson, John. *Love, Sex, and Feminism*. New York: Praeger, 1980.

CHAPTER 12

Homosexuality and Homophobia

Homosexuality is the sexual orientation in which one's primary attraction is to members of one's own sex. Gays are men primarily attracted to men, and lesbians are women primarily attracted to women. In a wider usage increasingly accepted, *gay* refers to both gay men and lesbians. In heterosexuality the primary sexual attraction is to members of the opposite sex, and in bisexuality the attraction is to both men and women. Sexual orientation is defined by predominant patterns of sexual desires, emotions, fantasies, behavior, and the cues or stimuli that lead to sexual arousal. Sexual orientation differs from biological sex type (male versus female) and gender identity (one's conviction of being male or female and masculine or feminine).[1] It also differs from sex roles, that is, the social roles conventionally expected for men and women (as defined by physique, voice, clothing, personality, occupation, parenting styles, and so on).

Classical Greek culture accepted male homosexuality, but most Western societies have treated homosexuals with contempt and oppression. For a long while, homosexuality was viewed as a sickness, and today many people continue to condemn homosexual acts as deeply immoral. In this chapter we discuss whether those negative attitudes are justified or whether they are based on ignorance, prejudice, and fear, that is, homophobia. Homophobia is the excessive and unjustified fear and hatred of homosexuality, homosexual acts, and homosexuals. Often, homophobia leads to acts of prejudice and persecution: ridicule, discrimination, support of social policies that oppress homosexuals, and violence against gays and lesbians. Is homosexuality immoral, or is hatred of homosexuality an irrational prejudice (homophobic)? Is the moral problem homosexuality or homophobia? In this chapter we consider the arguments on each side of this issue.

Closets and Coming Out

Let us begin with two case studies illustrating the difficulties confronting gay and lesbian people. Negative social attitudes lead many homosexuals to live "closeted" lives of sexual isolation, loneliness, fear, and frustration. Not only does this compound the normal difficulties associated with finding sexual partners, it also encourages short-lived affairs rather than long-term relationships, which are publicly visible and hence dangerous in a climate of social oppression of homosexuality. Public affirmation of a homosexual identity— "coming out"—usually incurs the risk of reprisals: rejection, derisive laughter, physical assault, and violation of rights in gaining and retaining employment, in buying or renting homes, and in purchasing life insurance.

Social pressure also can make it difficult to "come out to oneself"—that is, to acknowledge and affirm to oneself one's sexual orientation. Whatever one's sexual identity, adolescence is a turbulent time in terms of awakening to, accepting, and expressing one's sexuality. For gays and lesbians, however, the obstacles are multiplied. The difficulties continue well into adulthood, as is illustrated in the autobiography of Malcolm Boyd, *Take Off the Masks.*

During the 1960s and 1970s, Boyd was well known as a nonviolent civil rights activist, Vietnam War protester, and religious thinker. As a prominent Episcopalian priest he crusaded for the rights of women to enter the priesthood, and he also sought to strengthen ties between Christians and Jews. Yet his acceptance of his own sexuality required a painful and gradual process.

At age ten he knew he was attracted to boys and men, but he suppressed the thoughts and impulses accompanying that attraction. During high school, he took a rare (and spontaneous) gamble in hinting to his closest friend that he was attracted to him. The friend never spoke to him again. In college and early adulthood he grew contemptuous of homosexuals and was willing to laugh derisively at them. Yet later he occasionally experimented with gay relationships, which led only to feelings of intense guilt and self-contempt.

Boyd was thirty-three when he began to accept his sexual orientation. He was able to do so through a love relationship with a man who reciprocated his feelings. The affair lasted eight months, until circumstances forced the two men apart. About the experience Boyd wrote:

> Could I not stand, alone before my God, and say, "This is who I am. I can be no other." Wasn't this the essence of Christianity—a direct and personal relationship between a human being and God? "Listen, for whatever reason you made me, I am part of your creation. I have found a capacity to love. I do not believe that that is sin."[2]

During the next decade Boyd fell in love twice more, but again it was impossible to pursue the affairs publicly in a way that would enable them to last. Gradually, he was able fully to accept his homosexuality and the form of love it made possible:

I cannot recall a sexual relationship that was ever simply casual for me. Always I felt an intensity, a yearning to belong and love, and an awesome sense of universal meaning in this act. Surely this has brought me sadness as well as joy.[3]

For lesbians, acceptance of homosexuality can be a process even more difficult, because of additional general social pressures against assertiveness in women in overcoming their expected social roles. Those individuals who achieve self-acceptance without major trauma tend to be unusually strong. One such woman is Martina Navratilova, the champion tennis player. Navratilova says she is bisexual (although she hates that "creepy sounding" label), but her primary adult sexual attachments have been with women.

During her early teenage years, Navratilova had crushes on both female and male teachers. Later, she felt strong attachments to a few women tennis players. Only when she turned eighteen, however, did she recognize and accept that these crushes involved a sexual interest. At that time she also had her first love relationship, one initiated by an older and more assertive woman:

When it finally happened, I said, this is easy and right. And the next morning— *voila*—I had an outright, head-over-heels case of infatuation with her. When will I see you again? What will we do with our time together? I was in love, just like in the story books, and everything felt great.[4]

Things were not so great when her parents learned about the affair. Her father immediately referred her to a book about "her sickness." There were vehement arguments. During one argument her father said he would rather see her become a prostitute than a lesbian (and he meant it). Navratilova also worried that her sexual orientation would disrupt her attempts to become an American citizen after defecting from her native country, Czechoslovakia (where, incidentally, gays were sent to insane asylums and lesbians never came out of the closet).

The Reproductive Purpose of Sex

Is there anything immoral about homosexual acts? One view, held by the Catholic church and some other major religions, is that homosexuality is *unnatural* in that it departs from (or "perverts") the proper role of sex in human life. Sex is properly viewed as the means of procreation—of having children. Because homosexual acts do not have the potential to generate children, they constitute a misuse of sex and are therefore immoral. According to Leviticus in the Old Testament, homosexual acts are an abomination warranting death by stoning.[5] And according to Romans in the New Testament, homosexuals are guilty of a "vile affection" that alters "the natural use [of sex] into that which is against nature"[6] (although it is noteworthy that Jesus never himself condemns or even mentions homosexuality).

If homosexual acts are immoral simply because they cannot lead to children, then it follows that all other kinds of sexual acts that cannot lead to children are also immoral. Masturbation and heterosexual intercourse using contraceptives, for example, would also have to be condemned. If we leave aside certain religious views, it is hard to see how such acts could be immoral; and if we accept that masturbation and sexual intercourse using effective contraception are not inherently immoral, the statement that all nonreproductive sex is immoral becomes false. Therefore, the mere fact that homosexual acts cannot generate children does not make them immoral.

This type of argument is known as *reductio ad absurdum* (reduction to absurdity), which is an attempt to refute a view by showing that it entails a falsehood, drawing on the logical point that true views do not entail falsehoods. The argument should be convincing for anyone who believes that masturbation and the use of birth control devices are not immoral per se. What could be said, however, to persuade someone who does not hold these beliefs?

For example, Saint Thomas Aquinas would not be convinced by the *reductio ad absurdum* argument. According to him, all use of sex except for procreation is immoral:

> The emission of semen ought to be so ordered that it will result in both the production of the proper offspring and in the upbringing of this offspring.

> It is evident from this that every emission of semen, in such a way that generation cannot follow, is contrary to the good for man. And if this be done deliberately, it must be a sin. . . . For which reason, sins of this type are called contrary to nature.[7]

In fact, Aquinas believed that masturbation and homosexuality constituted sins even worse than heterosexual rape, because rape could at least generate children. Today, the Catholic church does not share that view, nor does it agree with Aquinas that the *sole* legitimate use of sex is procreation: Sex also should express love. Nevertheless, the official Catholic view concurs with Aquinas that masturbation, use of contraceptives in heterosexual sex, and homosexual acts are all immoral for the same reason: They are not the type of acts that can lead to reproduction.

One way to proceed at this point is to argue that masturbation is surely morally permissible when it leads to pleasure and has no bad side effects; and that intercourse with contraceptives is morally permissible and often desirable when it supports loving relationships and yields no harmful side effects (as are other nonreproductive sex acts based on mutual consent, such as oral sex). Support for this view seems to be offered, at least on the surface, by utilitarianism (in emphasizing mutual pleasure and happiness), duty ethics (in emphasizing mutual respect and autonomous consent of adults), and rights ethics (in emphasizing freedom that does not harm others).

Let us shift the burden of proof, however, by asking whether there are any good reasons for believing that nonreproductive sex is bad. What could be morally objectionable about using sex solely to express affection and love, at least within long-term relationships of the sort that Boyd and

Navratilova sought to establish in their lives? Doesn't sex have several natural and legitimate uses in addition to procreation, enabling us, for instance, to obtain pleasure, relieve stress, strengthen self-esteem, show affection, and express love?

Notice that the question about moral reasons does not disappear if we appeal to God or stipulate that *natural* means "what God commands" and *unnatural* means "what God forbids." Even if we set aside religious disagreements about what God commands and whether God exists, recall the point raised in Chapter 4: It makes sense to ask why God commands certain things rather than others. Presumably, a morally perfect being would make commandments on the basis of good moral reasons rather than on whim or from prejudice. Are there any good reasons to believe that a morally perfect being would forbid all nonreproductive types of sex acts? This is essentially the same question as above: Are there any good reasons for believing that all nonreproductive sex acts are bad? This question will be left as a discussion topic.

Other Senses of "Unnatural"

If we set aside the senses of "unnatural sex" that mean "nonprocreative" and "contrary to God's commands," are there any other senses in which homosexuality is unnatural—senses that have some moral relevance? The words *natural* and *unnatural* do have other meanings, but it is doubtful that they have any moral significance or relevance for thinking about homosexuality.

First, one could define *natural* in terms of "the *primary* biological function." Thus, the natural function of the digestive system and of eating is to provide nutrition for the body; similarly, the natural function of genitals and sexual intercourse is procreation. If we adopt this definition, nonreproductive sex is unnatural (assuming the most important evolutionary role of sex is reproduction); but even though this may be true, critics argue that it is morally irrelevant to the topic of homosexuality. Just because the primary function of the digestive system and of eating is nutrition, it does not follow that it is immoral sometimes to eat just for pleasure or during an enjoyable luncheon with a friend or spouse, even though one is not hungry or in need of food. Similarly, even if the primary biological purpose of sex is procreation, it does not follow that it is bad to use sex solely for pleasure or for expressing love.

Second, *natural* might mean "healthy," both mentally and physically. Is homosexuality a mental illness? Here the expert testimony of health professionals is relevant (if not decisive). Before 1974, the American Psychiatric Association (APA) viewed homosexuality as a mental disorder and listed it as such in its *Diagnostic and Statistical Manual of Mental Disorders*. In 1974, however, the APA acknowledged that it had made a mistake and amended the *Manual*. Did the mistake arise because psychiatrists misinterpreted the anxieties they sometimes observed in homosexuals as symptoms of an illness rather than as largely the product of special societal pressures on homosexuals? Did the mistake perhaps express homophobia among health professionals of the time? Today, most health professionals—the vast majority—do not view homosexuality as unhealthy. Insofar as homosexuals suffer from any greater anxiety or depression, the cause is now understood to be society's rejection of homosexuality.

The physical health of many gays, of course, has been devastated by AIDS. Homosexuality is not, however, the cause of AIDS, and homosexual acts by themselves do not cause AIDS. AIDS is spread by the failure to use precautions (especially condoms) during homosexual or heterosexual intercourse (as well as by the shared use of needles by drug addicts and transfusions of contaminated blood).

Third, some people see a kind of naturalness in how genitals "fit together" during heterosexual intercourse. Here *natural* seems to mean "geometrically complementary." Is the notion of genital geometry, however, relevant to the debate over homosexuality as unnatural? Or does it express a heterosexual bias against homosexual experiences, especially in view of the fact that the alleged geometrical problem is never voiced by homosexuals?

Fourth, *natural* might mean "common" or "usual." Again, critics argue that this sense is also irrelevant morally. The fact that most people are heterosexual does not make it immoral to be in a sexual minority. If it did, then by analogy all left-handed people would be immoral too, because they represent a minority orientation to space and activities; likewise, windsurfing would constitute an immoral use of the sea.

Fifth, *natural* might be used to characterize something that "feels natural," in the sense that it is based on an inclination that one feels and with which one identifies. True, many heterosexuals do lack or are uncomfortable about homosexual impulses, which seem alien and repulsive, but isn't this only a statement about heterosexual tastes and orientation, a statement that lacks moral force? To illustrate, many people are repelled at the thought of eating snails, but it does not follow that a passion for escargot is immoral. Tastes in food, wine, books, and friends—and sex—involve deep feelings that can be as strong as moral emotions. For this reason, it is sometimes easy to confuse issues of taste and morality, but they are distinct.

Sixth, *natural* might be defined as that which conforms to the appropriate roles for men and women. Homosexuality, it is claimed, is morally objectionable because gays tend to be effeminate in gesture and voice, violating masculine role models; conversely, lesbians tend to be unfeminine. Critics point out that this argument falsely stereotypes the mannerisms of gays and lesbians, most of whom do not fit this profile. (For example, Rock Hudson was gay but not effeminate.) The argument also assumes that all males and all females have a moral obligation to fit a particular gender role, and it apparently misappropriates the word natural by applying it to what are primarily socially created (not naturally created) sex roles.

Promiscuity

Another stereotypic view of gays—that all gays are promiscuous due to something inherent in male homosexuality—merits a separate discussion. Whereas lesbians tend not to be promiscuous, there are in fact gay men who have many hundreds of sexual partners during a lifetime. Yet most gays have fewer partners than this stereotype suggests, and of course many heterosexual males are also promiscuous, and have sex as often as they can find a willing partner.

Nevertheless, Roger Scruton argues that male homosexuality *tends* to encourage promiscuity and thereby discourages long-term love relationships of the kind he values (see Chapter 11). According to Scruton, all males have a strong natural tendency to sexual predation, which means they will desire many sexual partners during a lifetime. This instinct is tamed through attraction to the "mystery" of the opposite sex. Because members of the opposite sex are radically unlike oneself (physically, mentally), in pursuing sexual relationships with them one knowingly undertakes great risks—the risks of the unknown. These risks encourage commitment and fidelity that form the basis for long-term relationships grounded in erotic love.

> The opening of the self to the mystery of another gender, thereby taking responsibility for an experience which one does not wholly understand, is a feature of sexual maturity, and one of the fundamental motives tending towards commitment. This exposure to something unknown can resolve itself, finally, only in a mutual vow. Only in a vow is the trust created which protects the participants from the threat of betrayal. Without the fundamental experience of the otherness of the sexual partner, an important component in erotic love is therefore put in jeopardy. For the homosexual, who knows intimately in himself the generality that he finds in the other, there may be a diminished sense of risk. The move out of the self may be less adventurous, the help of the other [within a long-term relationship] less required.[8]

In short, Scruton thinks that mystery heightens risk, and risk encourages the partners to make a mutual commitment that sustains them in taking the risk. Homosexual relationships offer less mystery because the participants are already familiar with the gender of their partners; therefore, the need for commitment is decreased, and promiscuity is encouraged.

Is this a sound argument? Scruton is sensitive to one difficulty: If the argument works for gays, why should it not also work for lesbians? Lesbian promiscuity is rare, and Scruton implies that the real problem lies in the sexual predatoriness of all males. But his "mystery of the opposite sex" argument seems to imply that lesbians would be less inclined to form commitments than other women, and no evidence supports that conclusion. A second difficulty is that the promiscuity of some gays can be explained in another way, which Scruton does not consider. As previously mentioned, the harsh social condemnations of homosexuality have made it very risky (often dangerous) for gays to be identified publicly, which discourages open, long-term relationships and encourages brief and secretive sexual encounters.

In assessing the "mystery and risk" argument, two further points need to be considered. There may be deep mysteries (and unknowns worth exploring) between any two lovers, whatever their sexual orientation. Were society to remove its taboo on homosexuality, couldn't the emotional and intellectual differences between two individuals suffice to encourage trust and commitment? Furthermore, shouldn't heterosexuals allow the possibility that homosexuality may contain its own domains of new and "mysterious" experience for those who choose to explore it? In this connection, consider the words of the poet and feminist Adrienne Rich concerning lesbian experience:

> Lesbian existence comprises both the breaking of a taboo and the rejection of a
> compulsory way of life. It is also a direct or indirect attack on male right of
> access to women. But it is more than these. . . . I perceive the lesbian
> experience as being, like motherhood, a profoundly *female* experience, with
> particular oppressions, meanings, and potentialities.[9]

Homophobia

At this point we leave for discussion whether there are any convincing moral reasons against homosexuality. Let us conclude with some comments about homophobia. Whatever one's considered views about homosexuality, it is one thing to believe that homosexual acts are bad; it is quite another to hate, detest, degrade, and condone repression of homosexual persons.

Not everyone who objects to homosexuality (perhaps because of religious beliefs) is homophobic. They might object to hatred of homosexuals as much as they object to homosexuality itself. Many people, however, feel justified in "putting down" gays and lesbians in a variety of ways, ranging from tasteless jokes and derisive laughter to indifference to their legal rights. Is this not a form of prejudice as bad as prejudice based on race, religion, or physique?

Imagine someone arguing that the hatred involved in homophobia is no more immoral than hatred involved in other phobias. According to this argument, it is not immoral to have and to act upon phobias about spiders or snakes, about open spaces or closed spaces, or about heights and airplane rides. Similarly, nothing is immoral about hating gays and lesbians (whatever the moral status of homosexual acts). In fact, this argument is based on a weak analogy. Homophobia is directed toward people, not animals, spaces, special locations, or modes of transportation. The argument is akin to the assertion that one is not a racist, rather one simply has a phobia about black or Jewish people.

Consider another argument that appeals to the right to pursue one's own tastes. Just as we have tastes in food, sex, and clothing, we all have tastes in the kinds of people with whom we interact. Some people, so the argument goes, are uncomfortable with gay people and have a right to dislike them, avoid them, and joke about them. We do, of course, have a right to pursue our tastes, including those concerning people; but there are limits to those rights, and they do not justify violating the rights of others.

An equally important point is this: The existence of a right to pursue a taste does not imply that the taste is "all right" (i.e., morally permissible). The right to pursue our tastes implies that others should not attempt to coerce us to act otherwise; our tastes and actions may nevertheless be objectionable because they are prejudiced. Hatred of all homosexuals is a form of dismissing and shutting out people on the basis of one of their attributes, their sexual orientation. In that respect, at least, it is similar to racism and sexism.

SUMMARY

Homosexuality is the sexual orientation in which one is primarily attracted to members of one's own biological sex. Homophobia is the irrational fear and hatred of homosexuality, homosexual acts, and homosexuals.

The primary traditional ethical argument against homosexual acts is that they are unnatural or perverted in that they cannot result in reproduction. Sexual intercourse and orgasm, it is contended, are morally permissible only when they involve the kinds of acts that could lead to children. If this view were true, masturbation and sexual intercourse with contraceptives must likewise be condemned as unnatural or perverted.

Various other arguments supporting the idea that homosexual acts are unnatural include the following: (1) The primary biological function of sex is reproduction; (2) homosexual acts are unhealthy; (3) only in heterosexual acts is there genital geometry; (4) heterosexual acts are usual or most common; (5) only heterosexual acts are based on an inclination with which most people identify; and (6) only heterosexual acts conform to gender roles. In each case we raised questions suggesting that these senses of unnatural lack moral relevance.

Roger Scruton argues that male homosexuality encourages promiscuity, which makes it objectionable in light of the traditional view that sex should be joined to long-term erotic love relationships. His argument is that homosexuals miss out on the mysteries involved in a relationship with a member of the opposite sex (with whom one is less familiar than with one's own sex type). Yet, the main mysteries of sex derive from an exploration into the unknown of another person, whatever that person's sexual orientation, and the stronger tendency to promiscuity in some gays may be due to social pressures against publicly visible, long-term gay relationships.

Homophobia is unlike most phobias in that it is directed toward people. There are limits to how far one can go in acting on one's tastes. Even when one has a right not to be interfered with by others in pursuing one's tastes, those tastes may involve prejudice based on religion, race, or sexual orientation.

DISCUSSION TOPICS

1 Are there good reasons for believing that the only morally permissible sex acts are procreative kinds, that is, acts of the general kind that could lead to children?

2 Sexual orientation is something that, unlike sexual activities, is usually not chosen. (If you are heterosexual, did you ever choose to be so?) The causes of heterosexuality and homosexuality are still uncertain, although scientists are exploring genetic and environmental causes and, more recently, hormone balances during early stages of (fetal and neonatal) development. Moreover, sexual orientation is usually impossible to change completely, because it involves fundamental patterns of desires, fantasies, and interests that are not easily altered. Do these facts have any moral relevance to the question of whether homosexual and heterosexual acts are morally permissible?

3 One objection raised against homosexuality is that, if everyone (or most people) became homosexual, there would not be enough children to sustain society. Is this a good argument?

4 Heterosexuals take for granted the legal right to marry in any state in the United States, but homosexuals are almost entirely denied this right. Is this unjust discrimination? In your answer, take note of the fact that even if homosexuality is believed to be immoral, that does not settle the question about the right of homosexuals to marry. (Consider as well the following analogous situation: Many people believe that the use of contraceptives is immoral but do not believe that laws should prohibit their use or prohibit people who use them from marrying.)

5 One of the earliest controversies in President Clinton's administration concerned whether acknowledged homosexuals should be allowed to serve in the armed forces. Are there any good reasons for prohibiting gay and lesbian soldiers from serving in the military, or has their past exclusion resulted from homophobia?

6 Some people say that, although they have nothing against homosexuals, they morally object to homosexuals "flaunting" their sexuality (for example, by holding hands or kissing in public). Often the same people do not object to heterosexuals engaging in similar conduct in public. What would you say to these people?

7 Homosexuals are often prevented from serving as scout leaders and camp counselors. Is this practice permissible, or is it a form of unjustified discrimination? In your answer, consider this: The practice is often defended by citing fears that homosexuals will molest young people, but it is now known that child abuse occurs at roughly the same rate among heterosexuals and homosexuals.

8 Assess the following claim: "Homosexuality is immoral because homosexuals caused the AIDS epidemic in the United States." In your assessment, take account of the fact that the existence of the AIDS virus was not even suspected (by homosexuals or by anyone) during the early years in which the epidemic spread. Also take account of the fact that, long after the gay community has taken decisive steps to control this epidemic, the drug culture and heterosexuals still are not taking adequate precautions.

SUGGESTED READINGS

Aquinas, St. Thomas. *On the Truth of the Catholic Faith.* Book 3: *Providence,* Part I, trans. V. J. Bourke. New York: Doubleday, 1956.

Baird, Robert M., and M. Katherine Baird (eds.). *Homosexuality: Debating the Issue.* Amherst, NY: Prometheus, 1995.

Batchelor, Edward (ed.). *Homosexuality and Ethics.* New York: Pilgrim Press, 1980.

Bentham, Jeremy. "An Essay on 'Paederasty.' " In Robert Baker, Frederick Elliston, and Kathleen J. Wininger (eds.), *Philosophy and Sex,* 3d ed. Buffalo, NY: Prometheus, 1998.

Boyd, Malcolm. *Take Off the Masks.* Philadelphia: New Society, 1984.

Card, Claudia. "Why Homophobia?" *Hypatia,* vol. 5 (Fall 1990): 110–117.

Corvino, John (ed.) *Same Sex: Debating the Ethics, Science, and Culture of Homosexuality.* Lanham, MD: Rowman and Littlefield, 1997.

Elliston, Frederick. "Gay Marriage." In Robert Baker, Frederick Elliston, and Kathleen J. Wininger (eds.), *Philosophy and Sex,* 3d ed. Buffalo, NY: Prometheus, 1998.

Engelhardt, H. Tristram. "The Disease of Masturbation: Values and the Concept of Disease." In T. L. Beauchamp and L. Walters (eds.), *Contemporary Issues in Bioethics.* 2nd ed. Belmont, CA: Wadsworth, 1982.

Hoagland, Sarah. *Lesbian Ethics: Toward New Values.* Palo Alto, CA: Institute of Lesbian Studies, 1989.

Koertge, Noretta (ed.). *Philosophy and Homosexuality.* New York: Harrington Park Press, 1985.

Levin, Michael. "Why Homosexuality Is Abnormal." *The Monist,* vol. 67 (1984).

Levin, Michael, Harold Brod, Harry Brod, and Laurence Thomas. *Sexual Preference and Human Rights.* Lanham, MD: Rowman and Littlefield, 1999.

Mohr, Richard D. *Gays/Justice: A Study of Ethics, Society, and Law.* New York: Columbia University Press, 1990.

Mohr, Richard D. *Gay Ideas: Outing and Other Controversies.* Boston: Beacon Press, 1994.

Murphy, Timothy F. (ed.). *Gay Ethics: Controversies in Outing, Civil Rights, and Sexual Science.* New York: Haworth Press, 1995.

Rich, Adrienne. "Compulsory Heterosexuality and Lesbian Existence." *SIGNS: Journal of Women in Culture and Society,* vol. 5 (1980). Reprinted in C. R. Stimpson and E. Spector (eds.), *Women: Sex and Sexuality.* Chicago: University of Chicago Press, 1980.

Rosario, Vernon A. (ed.) *Science and Homosexuality.* New York: Routledge, 1997.

Ruse, Michael. *Homosexuality.* Oxford: Basil Blackwell, 1988.

Scruton, Roger. *Sexual Desire: A Moral Philosophy of The Erotic.* New York: Free Press, 1986.

Stein, Edward. *Uncovering Desire: The Science, Theory and Ethics of Sexual Orientation.* New York: Oxford University Press, 1999.

Sullivan, Andrew. *Virtually Normal: An Argument About Homosexuality.* New York: Vintage Books, 1996.

Swidler, Arlene (ed.). *Homosexuality and World Religions.* Trinity Press International, 1993.

Thurston, Thomas. *Homosexuality and Roman Catholic Ethics.* International Scholars Press, 1995.

CHAPTER 13

Pornography and Fantasy

Sexually explicit magazines, books, and movies pervade our society. During the sexual revolution of the 1960s, supporters argued that such materials liberated sexual repressions and affirmed sex as good. In 1970, the President's Commission on Obscenity and Pornography concluded that pornography is not harmful but instead is a positive influence in releasing inhibitions, helping married couples with sexual difficulties, and encouraging frank discussions between parents and children about sex. Critics of this attitude were regarded as puritanical reactionaries who would have us retreat into the sexual hypocrisy and repression of the 1950s.

A decade later, however, these comfortable generalizations were subject to serious challenge (for different reasons) by two groups that had little else in common. Conservatives and some liberal feminists were both alarmed by the sheer magnitude of the multibillion-dollar pornography industry that was churning out obscenity on an alarming scale. Of greatest concern were two dramatic trends: the combination of sexual and violent images and the use of children in pornography. Hundreds of Web sites on the Internet have raised the saturation level of pornography to an unprecedented level. Liberation, it seems to many, has turned into degradation of women and exploitation of children.

During the past decade, attempts have been made to control pornography through legislation against its makers, civil suits against its distributors, and by support for economic boycotts and demonstrations against its merchandisers. Debates over such attempts address important and complex issues; yet they should not deflect attention from everyday questions we all face concerning the use of pornography. Whether or not censorship of pornography violates rights to expression and privacy, we still need to examine the moral effects of pornography on our lives. Even if legal and moral rights forbid others from interfering with the use of pornography, we still need to ask whether that use is sometimes morally harmful. A right to use something does not automatically imply that it is all right to use it.

We begin with a question of definition: Just what is pornography? We then ask several specific questions concerning use of pornography. Because many anxieties about pornography pertain to wider issues about fantasy pleasures, we next raise those concerns. The chapter concludes with a categorization of pornography to enable readers to pinpoint which kinds they find morally objectionable.

A Definition of Pornography

Disputes over pornography, whether between friends or among legislators, are often hamstrung by lack of clarity about the meaning of the term. It would be unreasonable to expect a definition to resolve all uncertainties about what material is pornographic: There will always be difficult cases, whatever definition we adopt. Yet, in order to avoid verbal disputes—disputes based on misunderstandings about the meaning of a term—it is crucial to begin with some shared definition. At the same time, we should bear in mind that in public debates substantive issues are often blurred by the use of different definitions by different parties to the debate. When participating in those debates, we should be prepared to deal with contrasting definitions.

Conservative thinkers and many lawyers and judges use "pornography" as a close synonym for *obscenity* in the sense of something disgustingly offensive to decency. In this usage, to label something as pornography is to condemn it or to express a negative attitude toward it as "lacking a redeeming social value." For example, in 1986, Attorney General Meese's Commission on Pornography wrote a letter to the owners of 7–Eleven stores suggesting that, by selling *Playboy* and *Penthouse* magazines, they were distributing pornography. It was understood that this was intended as a criticism of the magazines as obscene, and for a while it caused the stores to stop selling them.

Some feminists (not all) have also built negative attitudes into their definitions of pornography, usually defining it as any sexual material that degrades women and exploits children. They invoke the term *erotica* to refer to morally acceptable sexually arousing material—including some material that the conservative Meese Commission might label obscene. One definition of pornography along these lines is given by Helen Longino:

> I define pornography as verbal or pictorial explicit representations of sexual behavior that . . . have as a distinguishing characteristic the degrading and demeaning portrayal of the role and status of the human female . . . as a mere sexual object to be exploited and manipulated sexually. In pornographic books, magazines, and films, women are represented as passive and as slavishly dependent upon men. The role of female characters is limited to the provision of sexual services to men.[1]

Other feminist definitions are even narrower and specifically single out images of sexual violence against women. Robin Morgan implied such a definition in an essay with a title that quickly became a feminist slogan: "Theory and Practice: Pornography and Rape."[2]

These conservative and feminist definitions are "persuasive definitions" in that they define "pornography" in a way intended to persuade us to view pornography with a negative attitude. In the discussion that follows, however, we do not presuppose negative attitudes toward pornography. In fact, a more neutral definition is employed by most philosophers, literary critics, social scientists, and other feminists (who disagree with attempts to censor pornography). According to this neutral sense, pornography refers to sexually explicit material that is intended primarily to be sexually arousing, rather than, say, to serve some literary or educational purpose. Nudity shown in medical textbooks would not count as pornography, because its intended use is educational. Similarly, explicit depictions of highly erotic scenes in serious works of fiction, such as James Joyce's *Ulysses* or Philip Roth's *Portnoy's Complaint,* would not be considered pornographic, because the intended role of these depictions has a serious aesthetic purpose (beyond sexual arousal). As used here, *pornography* refers to any writing or image (in pictures, film, sculpture, music, and so on) that is sexually explicit and created with the primary intention of sexually arousing the reader, viewer, or audience. We will also speak of a *pornographic use* of nonpornography to refer to the use of any sexually explicit nonpornography (such as a photograph in a medical textbook, a scene in a serious novel, or an ad for lingerie) for purposes of sexual arousal.

These definitions are somewhat vague. They do not, for example, spell out what *sexually explicit* means. In any case, however, there will always be some uncertain or borderline instances of pornography, and this definition will at least enable us to proceed with some shared understanding.

Examples of Pornography

When is the use of pornography, or the pornographic use of sexual material, morally permissible, and when is it morally objectionable? Let us replace this general question with a few more specific questions, using several examples.

First, consider a married couple watching an X-rated video about another couple, who in real life happen to be married. The movie follows them from their first meeting through their honeymoon. The last half of the movie is devoted to graphic depictions of honeymoon lovemaking scenes. The lovemaking is lively, involves a remarkable variety of physical positions and locations, is visually explicit and somewhat exaggerated in terms of the moaning and exclamations of pleasure, and depicts mutual assertiveness and equal ecstasy for the two participants. The viewers struggle to contain themselves until the movie is over, at which time they jump into bed to engage in a considerably shorter version of what they have just seen.

This example is atypical. Very few X-rated movies depict men and women as sexual equals, or focus on sex between married people, or use actors who are married in real life. The example, however, provides a useful starting point for reflection. Is it at all morally objectionable for the couple to view the movie, or for the actors to perform in the movie? Assuming that both partners wanted to watch the film and did so in order to enhance their relationship, is there anything problematic about watching another couple make love on film? Would your answer change if the actors in the example were not a married couple?

Here is another situation. A high school student buys photographic art magazines containing nude pictures that art critics would consider to be in good taste. The student appreciates the beauty of the models and has a strong interest in imagining what the women are like in real life. In his own mind, at least, the pictures depict people with whom he feels some sense of personal connection. He is especially attracted to those models who convey in their facial expressions and bodily postures a sense of warmth, love, and ease with their bodies. Nevertheless, his use of the magazines is pornographic in that he buys them primarily because they are sexually exciting and he uses the pictures as the basis for his fantasies about making love and for masturbation.

Examples of this sort are part of the personal histories of most people. If the student is criticized for treating the models as "mere sex objects," then some account must be given of the role of the personal dimension of the fantasies. No doubt some individuals come to rely on fantasies to such an extent that they lose touch with reality, or else they allow the fantasies to foster distorted expectations of or attitudes toward women or men. When that does not occur, however, is there anything morally objectionable about this pornographic use of material, or is it instead a healthy form of sexual expression and a normal aspect of developing a gender identity? Would your answer change if, instead of art magazines, the young man were viewing the pictures in *Playboy*?

Suppose about once a week a young woman reads a romance novel which contains some sexually explicit scenes. She takes some interest in the plot and character development, but she regards such elements primarily as a prelude to the more sexually arousing scenes involving explicit sexual depictions. Her main use of the novels is pornographic. Occasionally, the scenes form the basis for sexual fantasies, but for the most part they heighten her sexual life with her husband. Is there anything morally problematic about the fact that married partners may enjoy fantasies about having love affairs with people other than their spouses? If so, are the objections mitigated when the overall effects on the relationship are beneficial?

Next consider a single, middle-aged man who subscribes regularly to several hard-core pornography magazines because they feature close-ups of female genitals. His sex life consists of occasional affairs and regular masturbation sparked by fantasy images of the sort depicted in the magazines. He may or may not wish he had a richer sex life, but he has found a satisfactory compromise for the time being. Is it immoral to have a fantasy about one part of the body? Is it immoral to become preoccupied with such fantasies to the point where they become the center of one's sexual life?

Finally, let us consider a man who takes intense pleasure in watching snuff films, that is, films in which actresses play characters who are murdered ("snuffed out"). His all-time favorite is the 1976 film *Snuff*, which was advertised as showing the actual murder of a woman, although its distributors denied a real murder was filmed (and let us assume they were right). The film is about a man named Satan who leads a South American cult of young women who are allowed to enter the group only after an initiation involving torture. The cult plans a slaughter of a mother and her near-birth fetus. Following the graphic and violent scene in which the mother and baby are stabbed, the camera pulls back to show the production crew. A young production assistant tells the film director that she was greatly aroused by the scene, and the director responds by asking her to bed to play out her fantasies about the stabbing scene. Here is what follows, in the words of Beverly LaBelle, who saw the film:

> They start fumbling around in bed until she realizes that the crew is still filming. She protests and tries to get up. The director picks up a dagger that is lying on the bed and says, "Bitch, now you're going to get what you want." What happens next goes beyond the realm of language. He butchers her slowly, deeply, and thoroughly. The observer's gut revulsion is overwhelming at the amount of blood, chopped-up fingers, flying arms, sawed-off legs, and yet more blood oozing like a river out of her mouth before she dies. But the climax is still at hand. In a moment of undiluted evil, he cuts open her abdomen and brandishes her very insides high above his head in a scream of orgasmic conquest.[3]

Beverly LaBelle felt revulsion, but the male film director in our example felt intense sexual arousal. Is our horror of this man due to a belief that he is likely to harm women? Or is there not something inherently immoral about someone's delight in such movies and fantasies, and about the attitudes toward women that underlie such fantasy pleasures?

Fantasy

Is pornography immoral insofar as it stimulates pleasurable fantasies about immorality, especially of the sort found in the last example? To answer this question we must first ask a more basic question: Is a fantasy immoral when (and because) it consists of pleasurable thoughts about immorality (whether or not pornography is involved)? Does the immorality of what is fantasized transfer in some way to the fantasy itself?

Fantasy as Morally Neutral

We do sometimes feel guilty or ashamed for enjoying thoughts about doing something we believe is wrong, but it does not follow that we actually are guilty of wrongdoing. Feelings, after all, can be inappropriate, excessive, and irrational. According to one view, familiar in popular psychology books, fantasies are harmless passing thoughts about which people should not feel guilt and for which they should not be criticized. Insofar as fantasies produce pleasure, they are good, and by themselves they cannot cause harm.

Furthermore, according to this view, fantasies are involuntary—they happen to us—and in this respect they are unlike voluntary actions with which morality is concerned. To be anxious about fantasies reflects a superstitious attitude. It is akin to the unreasonable anxieties of children who believe their nightmares or daydreams can magically cause events without further actions of their own. Indeed, criticism of fantasies on moral grounds is actually harmful, for it encourages repression of thoughts that should be freely brought to consciousness as aids to self-awareness.

This view is expressed by Nancy Friday in *My Secret Garden: Women's Sexual Fantasies*. According to Friday, fear of one's enjoyment of sexual fantasies is a sign of inhibitions that have been forced on women. Some sexual fantasies provide a healthy outlet (*catharsis*) for unrealized sexual desires, for desires for greater variety of partners and experiences or greater intensity of pleasure, for desires to control sexual encounters, and for the need for sexual approval and esteem.

Other sexual fantasies, according to Friday, do not express serious desires to do what is imagined:

> Fantasy need have nothing to do with reality, in terms of suppressed wish-fulfillment. Women . . . whose fantasy life is focused on the rape theme, invariably insist that they have no real desire to be raped, and would, in fact, run a mile from anyone who raised a finger against them, and I believe them.[4]

Women who have such fantasies are expressing only a desire for a ravishing sexual experience, while maintaining in their imaginations full control over what happens (unlike what happens in rape).

Fantasy as Sometimes Immoral

A sharply opposed religious view, however, does not accept all sexual fantasies as morally neutral. In a familiar passage in the New Testament we read:

> Ye have heard that it was said by them of old time, Thou shalt not commit adultery: But I say unto you, That whosoever looketh on a woman to lust after her hath committed adultery with her already in his heart.[5]

Whatever the intent of the author of these lines, many Christians have held that they condemn as immoral, pleasurable fantasies about certain sexual activities.

Is this religious view excessively moralistic? In his essay "Real Guilt and Neurotic Guilt," Herbert Fingarette finds some basis for it. Fingarette points out that, according to both Freudian psychoanalysis and common sense, fantasies express and are caused by wishes and desires. These wishes and desires, rather than fantasies per se, are subject to moral appraisal:

> Moral guilt accrues by virtue of our wishes, not merely our acts. . . . The question of moral guilt does not wait for acts; it is in profound degree a question of what one harbors in one's heart. . . . One only need wish evil in order to be genuinely guilty.[6]

Fingarette adds some important qualifications, however, that bring him somewhat closer to Friday's view. First, he is sensitive to the complexities involved in interpreting fantasies in order to uncover the wish or desire they express. As Freud emphasized, wishes are often distorted and disguised before they reach consciousness as fantasies and daydreams. Hence, the wish expressed in the fantasy may not be a wish actually to do what is fantasized; this notion is compatible with Friday's view that women's rape fantasies do not express a desire to be raped.

Second, Fingarette develops his thesis primarily with respect to neurotics who deceive themselves about their wishes. He emphasizes that, in order to confront these wishes, individuals must be willing to bring them to consciousness and reflect on them honestly. Here again he would agree with Friday about the importance of exploring rather than repressing dreams, daydreams, and fantasies of all sorts. He would also agree that an excessively harsh judgmental attitude toward fantasies can prevent honest self-exploration.

Third, the degree of guilt entailed in the act of wishing is obviously far less than that entailed in the actual commission of an immoral act. Common sense alone tells us that to murder someone is infinitely worse than to wish to murder them: The murder harms another person, whereas the wish need not affect others at all. Moreover, the murderer, by acting, has accepted and endorsed the wish to kill, which makes him or her far worse in character than the fantasizer.

This last comment suggests that guilt should be measured in part by the extent to which a person endorses and identifies with wishes to do immoral things, as shown, for example, by willingly indulging in fantasies about them. Although Fingarette might agree with this point concerning healthy people, he draws attention to a complication: Neurotics refuse to acknowledge and identify with troublesome wishes and instead deceive themselves about them. In this connection Fingarette notes that the disavowed wishes can wreak havoc in the neurotic's life, as well as harm others through actions that express those wishes. Hence, Fingarette suggests that the degree of guilt for wishes depends not just on how far one identifies with one's wishes, but also on the degree to which the wishes have harmful effects. We should take into account the actual effect the wish has on individuals and their relationships.

A Synthesis of Opposing Views

Which is correct: Friday's complete demoralization of fantasies or Fingarette's guarded moralization of them? However we answer this question, three points seem clear.

First, the crux of the matter, as both Friday and Fingarette agree, lies in the extent to which fantasies influence lives; in particular, how they influence actions, attitudes, emotions, and relationships. Fantasies vary considerably in how they function within individuals' personalities, characters, and relationships. Perhaps Friday is too optimistic in her effort to make us more accepting of sexual fantasies, and Fingarette unduly somber, perhaps as a result of focusing on neurotics.

Second, Friday and Fingarette also agree that we must take care in interpreting exactly what wish is being expressed in fantasies. Consider, for example, adultery fantasies. Some of them involve desires to hurt one's spouse, and therefore raise moral concerns. Others, perhaps most, involve no desire to hurt. They merely express a wish for an exciting experience, and they need have no adverse effects on relationships. Many adultery fantasies do not express a serious desire for an affair, but merely represent a wish to enjoy a pleasurable thought. These fantasies generate moral concern only when they become obsessive and strengthen strong desires that add to temptations to have affairs in which a spouse is betrayed.

Third, we have varying degrees of control over our fantasies. Some fantasies arise involuntarily and then drift out of consciousness, never to reappear. A censorious attitude toward them is surely inappropriate, not only because they come uninvited and have no further implications in our lives, but also because preoccupation with judging them deflects attention from matters of greater importance.

Other fantasies are intentionally brought to mind or reveled in once they enter consciousness. Occasionally, this provides an effective release for an impulse that would otherwise boil within and eventually cause outward harm. To deliberately feed the imagination with images of violence, however, is more likely to have the opposite effect of strengthening impulses. It is not prudishness, but common sense, to believe that at least some men who eagerly and repeatedly seek out violent sexual pornography are fostering desires and attitudes that they should instead work to overcome.

In sum, the moral status of sexual fantasies about immoral acts is complex. These fantasies are not automatically immoral; neither are they always immune from moral criticism. Similarly, the moral status of the use of pornography to stimulate fantasy is equally complex. We must assess our fantasies and the fantasies of others in light of overall patterns of behavior and attitude, avoiding the extremes of viewing fantasies either as always harmless or always subject to moral criticism. In making these assessments, we need to bear in mind that the pleasure we derive from fantasies can serve as a motive for self-deception about the subtle ways in which indulgence in certain fantasies can shape our attitudes, which, in turn, are expressed in conduct.

Obscenity

Private fantasies represent only one dimension of pornography use. There is another: the public reality of massive amounts of pornographic material. Pornography entails explicit *depiction* of sex through words or images intended to arouse sexually. Depiction requires the use of a medium or representational form—books, magazines, pictures, movies, taped telephone recordings, computer programs, and so forth. The extensive purchase, rental, and use of pornography contributes to this social practice. It would seem that repeated use of violent and degrading forms of pornography for pleasure constitutes a tacit endorsement of the objectionable attitudes underlying immoral forms of pornography.

Most of us do not object to all pornography, but we do regard some pornography as obscene. Obscenity is not defined solely in terms of the emotions it provokes, such as disgust, nausea, and abhorrence; after all, we can recognize obscenity even after becoming desensitized and jaded toward it. Obscenity refers to that which goes beyond decency, and hence refers to standards of decency and beliefs about those standards.

Obscenity is a wider concept than pornography. An action or a remark as well as a depiction may be regarded as obscene. Also, obscenity may take nonsexual forms. There are obscene ways of eating (gluttonously), and obscene depictions of excretion and defecation. Although *obscene* can be used as an aesthetic term alluding to nonmoral standards of beauty and taste, in discussions of pornography it has moral connotations. Obscene kinds of pornography violate standards of moral decency.

When is pornography obscene—that is, morally objectionable? And when does the use of pornography constitute participation in a morally objectionable practice?

These questions will be left as discussion topics, but before we conclude this chapter, a few additional comments should be made. First, it is important to distinguish between the depiction of something indecent and the depiction of something in an indecent way. Obscene things can be depicted in nonobscene ways. For example, depictions of rape and other forms of extreme sexual violence can be decent if they reveal the horror of the act, and good literature and art does just that. Conversely, nonobscene things can be depicted in obscene ways. Human nudity is not obscene, but in much pornography it is depicted obscenely. Furthermore, our discussion suggests that pornography comes in many forms. Four general categories—loveless sex, child pornography, nonviolent sexist pornography, and violent sexual imagery—deserve separate consideration.

First, much pornography is intended to convey the message that sex without love, affection, or commitment is permissible and desirable. It sympathetically portrays and tacitly endorses sex solely for pleasure, sex outside marriage, casual and anonymous sex, group sex, or public sex. Conservatives' objections to pornography have tended to center on this category, alleging that all such pornography is obscene. Is it?

Second, pornography that uses children as sex objects and that involves child nudity is immoral. It exploits the children used as models, and it condones and encourages child abuse. This is the one area in which conservatives and liberals can agree on the need for strict censorship laws. Yet many forms of advertising and modeling use sexually provocative pictures of children. Is the use of twelve- and thirteen-year-old models in sexually suggestive poses morally objectionable? Is it so for fifteen-or sixteen-year-olds? Is it objectionable to use adult models who look as if they were children?

Third, much pornography falls into the category of nonviolent but potentially sexist. The difficult question here is, What is sexist? Is it always sexist to portray a nude woman with a snake wrapped sensuously around her or with bunny ears (or with other animal suggestions)? Is every picture that emphasizes or exclusively shows women's sex organs sexist and degrading? Should we regard as sexist the nude photos in *Playboy* that show a complete figure in poses suggesting that women are primarily sexual playmates for men?

Finally, much pornography features the use of violent sexual images. In recent years this form of pornography has proliferated, and mostly involves obscene and violent images of women. With good reason, feminists have directed most criticism against it and have struggled to define it with sufficient precision to pass laws against it. One influential definition of obscene pornography (or what the authors call simply pornography) was developed by Andrea Dworkin and Catharine MacKinnon. It was presented as part of a model civil rights statute authorizing civil suits against makers and distributors of obscenity. A version of the model statute was adopted in Indianapolis, Indiana, but in 1984 the U.S. Supreme Court declared it an unconstitutional restriction of free speech. Nevertheless, the definition remains morally valuable, and it reminds us of the kinds of violent pornography that are mass-produced today:

1   *Pornography* is the graphic sexually explicit subordination of women through pictures and/or words that also includes one or more of the following: (i) women are presented dehumanized as sexual objects, things, or commodities; or (ii) women are presented as sexual objects who enjoy pain or humiliation; or (iii) women are presented as sexual objects who experience sexual pleasure in being raped; or (iv) women are presented as sexual objects tied up or cut up or mutilated or bruised or physically hurt; or (v) women are presented in postures or positions of sexual submission, servility, or display; or (vi) women's body parts—including but not limited to vaginas, breasts, or buttocks—are exhibited such that women are reduced to those parts; or (vii) women are presented as whores by nature; or

(viii) women are presented being penetrated by objects or animals; or (ix) women are presented in scenarios of degradation, injury, torture, shown as filthy or inferior, bleeding, bruised, or hurt in a context that makes these conditions sexual.

2   The use of men, children, or transsexuals in the place of women in (1) above is pornography for purposes of this law.[7]

Defenders of the violent forms of pornography contend that it provides a healthy release or catharsis, rather than encouraging violence. Although the full scientific evidence necessary to address such viewpoints has not yet been gathered, this generalization has been seriously challenged by recent experiments. For example, there is now solid evidence that long-term exposure to images of gross violence does strengthen negative attitudes toward women. Men are affected by repeated exposure to the myth that women want to be raped, a familiar theme in violent pornography. Anyone who reviews studies such as those in *Pornography and Sexual Aggression,* edited by Neil Malamuth and Edward Donnerstein, cannot be altogether complacent about the influence of violent pornography. At the same time, other studies reveal that most males are not aroused by violent pornography and instead find it revolting.

Finally, whatever the general experiments show about overall tendencies, it remains true that the use of pornography is a personal matter in the following sense: Its effect on individuals varies. Each of us must achieve a self-understanding of its sometimes beneficial and sometimes harmful effects on our lives.

SUMMARY

The word *pornography* has several different meanings. In a pejorative sense, pornography is obscene (immoral) smut. In a neutral sense, pornography is sexually explicit material intended primarily to be sexually arousing. We have used the second sense. Nonpornographic materials (such as nude pictures in medical books) also can be used pornographically in the sense of being used primarily for sexual arousal.

Is the use of pornography morally objectionable? No simple answer is possible, because the uses of pornography are too varied. This general question is best replaced by a series of more focused questions about specific uses of pornography. Such types of uses include: (1) married couples' use of pornography for enrichment of their sexual relationship; (2) use of nude photos for sexual arousal by someone who regards them (through imagination) as representing people for whom the viewer feels affection; (3) a spouse's use of romance novels to stimulate adultery fantasies; (4) preoccupation with "hard-core" pornography centered on genital pictures of members of the opposite sex; and (5) repeated use of violent pornography that portrays women as objects to be abused.

One way to evaluate these and other uses of pornography is to explore the role of the fantasies they produce in individuals. Nancy Friday argues that sexual fantasies are, in general, a healthy sexual expression, while Herbert Fingarette defends the New Testament view that fantasies about immoral acts frequently express immoral wishes. Both agree, however, on several points: Sexual fantasies should be evaluated in light of how they affect an individual's life and relationships; care must be taken in interpreting the wish expressed in a fantasy (because unconscious wishes are often disguised before they are manifested in a conscious fantasy); and the degree to which fantasies are voluntary may vary (ranging from a spontaneous, nonvoluntary fantasy to deliberate, repeated recourse to a fantasy).

The second way to evaluate pornography is as mass-produced and mass-consumed public objects that, by permeating our society, influence attitudes, especially about women. Obscene pornography is sexually explicit material that violates standards of moral decency. Four categories of pornography are often regarded as obscene: (1) material that conveys a message that sex without love is desirable, (2) material that portrays children as sex objects, (3) nonviolent sexist pornography, and (4) violent sexual imagery.

DISCUSSION TOPICS

1 We assumed that it is "prudish" (that is, excessively proper or modest about sexuality) to object to all uses of sexually explicit material for sexual arousal. Is this assumption perhaps unjustified? In defending your view, explain how this question (about moral justification) might be approached within each of the main types of ethical theory: utilitarianism, duty ethics, rights ethics, and virtue ethics.

2 A frequent criticism of pornography is that it treats women (and sometimes men) as "mere sex objects." What do you think is meant by this expression, and is it a valid complaint? Relate your answer to Kant's proscription against treating other people merely as a means to our own ends.

3 Are some fantasies, sexual or otherwise, inherently immoral, even though they do not lead to immoral actions? In giving your answer, comment on the view set forth in the New Testament and the views of Nancy Friday and Herbert Fingarette.

4 Discuss whether there is anything immoral about each of the following:
   a A rape fantasy spontaneously enters a man's mind and is quickly dismissed from attention.
   b A man deliberately and frequently brings to mind rape fantasies, even though he never has any strong urge to rape (and never does so).
   c Occasionally (about once every few months), a woman has the fantasy of being raped.
   d A woman has and enjoys recurring fantasies of being raped, even though she sincerely denies any desire to be raped.

5 Five different examples of pornography (or pornographic uses of nonpornography) were presented early in this chapter. Present and defend your answer to the questions raised at the end of each example.

6   Four general categories of pornography are most often criticized as obscene and immoral: (1) that which recommends sex without love or affection, (2) that which portrays children as sex objects, (3) nonviolent sexist pornography, and (4) violent sexual images, usually of women. Present and defend your view concerning whether each of these types of pornography is obscene.

7   Although feminists are united in condemning any pornography that contributes to violence against women, they are sharply divided over the issue of whether pornography should be censored. One major concern of feminists opposed to censorship is that if governments (which are often patriarchal) are allowed to regulate pornography, they could use that power to repress nontraditional forms of sexual expression that the majority of citizens may object to, such as homosexual pornography and pornography in which women are portrayed as assertive, eager, and equal sexual partners. Present your view on whether any pornography involving adults should be banned by law, and defend it by appeal to an ethical theory. If you think some pornography should be banned, can you formulate a law that would not be so inclusive as to ban morally permissible types of pornography?

SUGGESTED READINGS

Attorney General's Commission on Pornography: Final Report. 2 Vols. Washington, DC: U.S. Department of Justice, 1986.

Baird, Robert M., and Stuart E. Rosenbaum (eds.). *Pornography: Private Right or Public Menace?* Buffalo, NY: Prometheus, 1991.

Burstyn, Varda (ed.). *Women Against Censorship.* Vancouver, British Columbia: Douglas & McIntyre, 1985.

Copp, David, and Susan Wendell (eds.). *Pornography and Censorship.* Buffalo, NY: Prometheus, 1983.

Davis, Murray S. *Smut: Erotic Reality/Obscene Ideology.* Chicago: University of Chicago Press, 1983.

Fingarette, Herbert. "Real Guilt and Neurotic Guilt." In *On Responsibility.* New York: Basic Books, 1967.

Friday, Nancy. *Men in Love: Men's Sexual Fantasies, The Triumph of Love over Rage.* New York: Dell, 1980.

Friday, Nancy. *My Secret Garden: Women's Sexual Fantasies.* New York: Pocket Books, 1973.

Garry, Ann. "Pornography and Respect for Women." *Social Theory and Practice,* vol. 4 (1978).

Hill, Judith M. "Pornography and Degradation." *Hypatia,* vol. 2 (1987): 39–54.

Kimmel, Michael S. (ed.). *Men Confront Pornography.* New York: Meridian, 1991.

Lederer, Laura (ed.). *Take Back the Night: Women on Pornography.* New York: Morrow, 1980.

MacKinnon, Catharine A. *Feminism Unmodified.* Cambridge, MA: Harvard University Press, 1987.

Morgan, Robin. "Theory and Practice: Pornography and Rape." In L. Lederer (ed.), *Take Back the Night: Women on Pornography.* New York: Morrow, 1980.

Segal, Lynne, and Marry McIntosh (eds.). *Sex Exposed: Sexuality and the Pornography Debate.* New Brunswick, NJ: Rutgers University Press, 1993.

Singer, Jerome L., and Ellen Switzer. *Mind-Play: The Creative Uses of Fantasy.* Englewood Cliffs, NJ: Prentice-Hall, 1980.

Soble, Alan. *Pornography: Marxism, Feminism, and the Future of Sexuality.* New Haven, CT: Yale University Press, 1986.

Talese, Gay. *Thy Neighbor's Wife.* New York: Dell, 1980.

Tong, Rosemarie. *Women, Sex, and the Law.* Totowa, NJ: Rowman & Allanheld, 1984.

Wekesser, Carol (ed.). *Pornography: Opposing Viewpoints,* St. Paul, MN: Greenhaven Press, 1997.

Zillman, D., and J. Bryant (eds.). *Pornography Research: Advances and Policy Implications.* Hillsdale, NJ: Lawrence Erlbaum Associates, 1989.

PART FIVE

Caring Relationships

For what is love itself, for the one we love best?—an enfolding of immeasurable cares which yet are better than any joys outside our love.[1]

George Eliot

Caring for others entails that we desire their well-being and, when appropriate, seek disinterestedly to promote their good. Caring consists of more than respect for them and their rights; we want those we care for to prosper, and we enjoy helping them prosper.

To care for someone need not be "purely" or "solely" altruistic in the sense that we are concerned only with another's good, and not ours. Nor must it be entirely "selfless" in the sense of involving self-sacrifice. On the contrary, people who are most caring tend to see their own good as intimately tied to the good of those for whom they care. In caring for others, they see their own good promoted as well.

In this way, caring and self-interest can be compatible and reinforce each other. When we sustain relationships based on care, we promote both the good of others and of ourselves. That does not, of course, make caring "selfish." Selfishness is excessive concern for oneself at the expense of others. Caring is the opposite of selfishness, but it can also differ from self-sacrificial forms of 'selflessness.'

Caring relationships involve two or more conscious beings, at least one of whom cares about the other. They take many forms beyond the relationships of sexual love discussed in Part Four. In Part Five, we discuss caring relationships between spouses, parents and children, and friends.

CHAPTER 14

Marriage and Adultery

Despite sharp criticism, marriage continues to be a prevalent form of sexual relationship. Ninety percent of Americans marry. Half of all marriages end in divorce, but 80 percent of divorced people remarry, usually within five years. Perhaps no form of social relationship, however, has greater demands placed on it and, as a result, is burdened with so many difficulties. One difficulty is adultery, which occurs in more than half of all marriages.

Yet sexual exclusivity in marriage—that is, restriction of sex only to one's spouse—is only one aspect of traditional marriages. Even more central is the lifetime commitment to join one's life intensively and intimately to one other person. As traditionally conceived in Western culture, marriage combines several elements: (1) mutual commitments to lifelong companionship and (2) mutual commitments to sexual exclusivity (3) expressed publicly in formal legal or religious ceremonies and (4) made between one male and one female. We will focus on the first three conditions, especially the first two. The question of homosexual marriages was touched on in Chapter 12. Our primary interest is the moral significance of a formal commitment by two people to lifelong companionship and sexual exclusivity.

Is Marriage a Moral Issue?

Some religions regard marriage as a *religious* obligation (assuming the opportunity for it arises). It seems clear, however, that there is no general *moral* obligation to marry. Marriage is an option, not an obligation. Does that mean marriage is primarily a matter of personal preference rather than morality?

In our society, of course, decisions about marriage are based in large part on personal preferences (in contrast to societies favoring arranged marriages). Some people choose to marry because they believe it is the best avenue for finding love, emotional support, sexual satisfaction, an enriched sense of self-worth, and economic security. For example, in *Women and Love,* Shere Hite quotes one woman as reporting, "I didn't like being single. No emotional security, no stability, no financial security, no companionship, no closeness, no love or sharing."[1] For other people, however, marriage is followed by frustration and abuse that bring an end to happiness. Many of the women Hite interviewed reported a preference for being single:

> Life is much better for me as a single woman. I can choose my friends, plan my social life, plan my private life, do and say what I please at home, make my home MINE (reflective of me), and I don't have to answer to anyone or explain my actions to anyone. Isn't it funny how long it takes to find out that freedom feels so good? Why do we rush into marriage like we do?[2]

Marriage decisions, however, are not solely expressions of personal preference and self-interest. They are also moral decisions. Even though there is no obligation to marry, marriage embodies moral ideals and also moral commitments that generate responsibilities. Moreover, there may be an obligation for some people in some circumstances not to marry: Unless one is willing in good faith to undertake the commitments involved, one may be guilty of deceit, promise breaking, and betrayal. Perhaps most fundamentally, there is an obligation to make marital decisions wisely, because the good of one's partner, oneself, and often others (especially children) is at stake.

Potential Drawbacks to Marriage

Conventional thought asserts that marriage is worth the sacrifices it requires, because it offers the best hope for most people to find love, emotional richness, satisfying sex, and support and self-esteem. Critics of this view, however, urge that most marriages are bad overall and would not exist if people thought more clearly and honestly. In particular, John McMurtry in "Monogamy: A Critique" argues that marriage is bound to affect adversely most people's chances of finding love and happiness, for three main reasons.

Outside Control

McMurtry's first criticism concerns state and religious control of marriages: "Centralized official control of marriage . . . necessarily alienates the partners from [taking] full responsibility for and freedom in their relationship."[3] During the Roman Empire, marriage was a matter of personal agreement between the partners, and it automatically dissolved by similar mutual agreement. In contrast, under our tradition, which allows government and churches to control marriage ceremonies and relationships, freedom is restricted and individuals are encouraged to think of their relationship as partly the responsibility of larger social institutions, and are also influenced by peer pressure deriving from those institutions.

Certainly, such external forces do come into play. Social controls over marriages may generate coercive pressures and a sense that marital commitments are not entirely one's own responsibility. Moreover, there continue to be social pressures, especially on women, to marry and to stay married, even in extremely destructive relationships that ought to be dissolved. Yet much has changed since 1972 when McMurtry wrote his essay. There is greater social tolerance for people who live together before marriage (nearly half of recently married couples). Also, changes in divorce laws have made it easier to end a marriage. And when couples do marry, it is usually by choice and with the aim of expressing their commitments through a public ceremony.

Some couples regard public ceremonies and legal ties as superfluous or hurtful in the way McMurtry suggests. They may redefine marriage in purely moral terms as a relationship based on commitments to live together, without the need for legal or religious sanction. For others, however, the symbolism of public ceremonies provides a significant way to solemnize their commitments in the eyes of society and also in their own eyes; it is, or can be, a highly personal mutual expression between partners.

At this point, let us set aside this question about ceremonies in order to focus on a purely moral concept of marriage defined by lifelong commitments, whether or not legal and religious rites are involved. McMurtry's other criticisms are directed toward these commitments and their consequences.

Psychological Constriction

In the marriage vows of the sixteenth-century *Book of Common Prayer* of the Church of England, the man is asked: "Wilt thou love her, comfort her, honor and keep her, in sickness and in health; and, forsaking all others, keep thee only unto her, so long as ye both shall live?" In addition to making these same vows, the woman is also asked to obey and serve—an inequality usually avoided in contemporary vows! No doubt some couples speaking these words understand them as a kind of pleasant poetical expression rather than a literal commitment. Most couples, however, fully intend to make the commitment to lifelong companionship. Is such a commitment wise? Not according to McMurtry:

> The restriction of marriage union to two partners necessarily prevents the strengths of larger groupings. Such advantages as the following are thereby usually ruled out: (a) the security, range, and power of larger socioeconomic units; (b) the epistemological [i.e., mental] and emotional substance, variety, and scope of more pluralist interactions.[4]

More recently, feminist critics of marriage emphasize that these losses hurt women more than men. All too often in marriage, even when both partners have jobs, women's identities are based only on their roles as wives (and mothers), whereas men find greater enrichment through their work. For most wives, the result of one-sided dependency is that marriage involves more sacrifice than self-fulfillment. Marriage also provides a veil of privacy that conceals injustices and cruelties, including wife battering, child abuse, and gross imbalances in the benefits and burdens for women.

As Susan Moller Okin writes in a book-long critique of marriage,

> I argue that marriage and family, as currently practiced in our society, are unjust institutions. They constitute the pivot of a societal system of gender that renders women vulnerable to dependency, exploitation, and abuse. When we look seriously at the distribution between husbands and wives of such critical social goods as work (paid and unpaid), power, prestige, self-esteem, opportunities for self-development, and both physical and economic security, we find socially constructed inequalities between them, right down the list.[5]

In particular, Okin documents how husbands receive a far larger share of opportunities for recognition through careers and education. Women are given the bulk of housekeeping chores and child-raising responsibilities, even when they do paid work outside the home. Men exercise more control within relationships because they have greater economic power and because women reasonably fear that divorce would drastically lower their standard of living.

Okin is offering rough generalizations, of course. She is aware that there are exceptions to her claims. Marriage is changing and offers increasing variety and flexibility. If we take such things into consideration, what can we say in defense of (many) marriages, especially concerning the question of freedom? To begin with, while marriage takes away some freedom in the sense that it reduces some options, it need not reduce overall options; instead, it changes options—dramatically. Marriage does close some options. Single (and childless), one can come and go as one chooses without having to notify or negotiate with anyone. That changes with marriage, but marriage creates new options, such as the opportunity for steady companionship and the sharing of daily activities (including sex). Of course, only good marriages offer this; but then, only some forms of being single offer happy options, too.

McMurtry and Okin, of course, are concerned more with the quality of options within marriages than with the quantity of options. In their view, marital options are psychologically constrictive: Dependency on just one partner restricts the intellectual and emotional stimulation offered by a wider network of relationships, and also reduces the economic freedom of women in particular. We have all seen marriages in which this constriction occurs; but *must* it occur, or is marriage a sufficiently flexible practice such that couples can avoid this constriction?

Contemporary marriages are extremely diverse and include at least three general types, as distinguished by sociologist Francesca M. Cancian. Cancian suggests that two models have been overemphasized: "(1) the traditional family, based on restricting individual freedom, especially for women, and (2) the contemporary pattern of limited commitments between independent individuals, each focused on his or her own self-development."[6] Yet a third model, which is increasingly popular, views long-term love and self-development as equally important and mutually reinforcing: "(3) Love and self-development both grow from the mutual interdependence of two people, not from extreme independence nor from the one-way dependency of a woman on a man encouraged by traditional marriage."[7] This model of interdependence stresses growth through intimate caring relationships with as much equal sharing as possible. According to Cancian, such relationships tend to break down role differentiation based on gender stereotypes of women as submissive, gentle, sensitive, and supportive, and of men as assertive, dominant, emotionally reserved (except perhaps in showing anger), and economically and intellectually independent. On this model, both marital roles and love itself are *androgynous*.

Interdependent relationships require mutuality of effort, sensitivity, and adjustment, as well as a sense of fairness and commitment to mutuality as an ongoing process. The philosopher S. I. Benn earlier described this process, which is found among friends as well as spouses:

> It is the essence of this relation that it is fully participatory. Each respects and values every other as a full partner, and exerts his own effort in the expectation and trust that the other will do likewise. . . . [The relation is one of] mutuality, the extent to which each is sensitive to the others' response to his own effort, is prepared to monitor his own attitudes to his partners and to the partnership, and to adjust to changes in the interests, tastes, values and personalities of the others. . . . [The goal of] the enterprise is to keep the partnership moving, to make it a vehicle through which the personalities of the partners can develop autonomously, without destroying it.[8]

This kind of relationship need not foster isolation from other enriching relationships. Rather, it allows marriages to function as emotional anchors that strengthen capacities for friendships and community involvement. A sense of permanence makes partners feel confident that the relationship will not be destroyed by change and disagreements, but rather, that they will eventually enter into a sense of shared history together.

Having emphasized that marriage for many people is enriching, not constricting, we can agree that marriage is not good for everyone. Many marriages are harmful, especially to women—much depends on one's partner! Marriages demand an ability and a willingness to join one's activities continuously and intensively with those of another person. Usually, it requires a personal decision to value that relationship over attractive career options and other forms of relationships, and for some individuals that can be constrictive.

Sexual Confinement

Far from supporting erotic love, McMurtry maintains, marriage frustrates it: "Formal exclusion of all others from erotic contact with the marriage partner systematically promotes conjugal insecurity, jealousy, and alienation."[9] It does this by creating "a literally totalitarian expectation of sexual confinement" of one's spouse that is bound to create anxiety about potential violations of the commitment to sexual exclusivity by either spouse. Spouses become fearful of losing their counterparts, jealous about attention paid to others, and emotionally distanced from each other. In any case, the confinement is impractical: Affairs occur, accompanied by deception and antagonism between partners.

Even apart from consequences, McMurtry states, marriage is based on degrading attitudes that spouses "own" the sexual activities of their partners: "The ground of our marriage institution . . . is this: the maintenance by one man or woman of the effective right to exclude indefinitely all others from erotic access to the conjugal partner."[10] Marriage is a state of "indefinite, and exclusive ownership by two individuals of one another's sexual powers" and as such is "a form of private property" that treats people as if they were things to be possessed.[11]

Once again, McMurtry raises a valid criticism of some marriages. Some husbands do treat their wives as chattel. Yet it is entirely possible for spouses to view themselves as the beneficiaries of mutual gifts of free commitments rather than as possessors of ownership rights. If there is a right, it is the right created by freely given promises and commitments, not by ownership. There is also an awareness and appreciation that each spouse is dependent on the other for ongoing renewal of those commitments.

In regard to the charge that marriage promotes insecurity, jealousy, and alienation, no doubt these effects do sometimes occur. Are they, however, the result primarily of the commitment to sexual exclusivity, or are they instead due to the particular characters of the individuals involved? For many couples, commitments provide a stable context that promotes sexual satisfaction by creating both opportunities for regular sex and an atmosphere in which trusting sexual expression can take place. Commitments made in good faith also can dramatically lessen jealousy by allowing partners to feel confident that outside affairs will not occur. The ill effects that McMurtry emphasizes are due primarily to the personalities and characters of individuals, rather than to the nature of marital commitments per se.

Perhaps this reply is too hasty, however, since two related topics deserve further discussion: Even if we find value in marriage, we need to consider whether traditional marriages should be rethought so as to (1) permit extramarital love affairs and (2) minimize sexual jealousies that result when partners look beyond their spouses for sex, affection, or other attention.

Extramarital Affairs: Two Cases

Extramarital affairs, or acts of adultery, have always raised moral concern, and they continue to do so in both personal and public life. In 1998 the world learned the details about President Clinton's affair with Monica Lewinsky. In 1992, equally detailed information was disseminated about the extramarital affairs involved in the unraveling of the storybook romance of Prince Charles and Lady Diana. And in 1987, the press exposed the adulteries of Jim Bakker and Gary Hart. The differences between the cases of Bakker and Hart remind us that extramarital affairs take many forms, making it difficult to generalize about their moral status.

Jim Bakker was a successful television evangelist who created and directed the PTL (for "Praise the Lord" and "People That Love") Club. His affair had been a one-night stand six years earlier with Jessica Hahn, a twenty-one-year-old former church secretary. Bakker followers portrayed Hahn as a temptress who seduced Bakker during a troubled time in his marriage to Tammy Faye Bakker. Hahn's version, as recounted in *Newsweek* magazine, differed sharply:

> She was flown to Florida to meet Bakker by another evangelist, John Wesley Fletcher; she had baby-sat with Fletcher's children, and he knew she idolized Bakker. But at a hotel, so the story went, she was given drugged wine. Bakker appeared, dressed only in a white terry-cloth swimsuit, and she was told to give him a back rub. Dazed and sick, she resisted, but was unable to fight off Bakker's advances.[12]

Whichever version is true, the story is sordid—even setting aside the $265,000 in hush money that Bakker paid to Hahn a few years later and the subsequent legal conviction of Bakker for fraud and abuse of ministry funds. The Bakkers' marriage was based on traditional vows of sexual exclusivity, vows that were violated in a sexual episode that involved no love and apparent abuse of religious authority.

In 1987, Gary Hart was the leading Democratic candidate for president. Early in May he challenged reporters to scrutinize his private life by following him around. In mid-May he was seen entering and leaving his townhouse on Capitol Hill with model Donna Rice. The next day it was reported that in March he had gone on an overnight trip to Bimini (aboard a boat named Monkey Business) with a male friend and two women, one of whom was Rice. Hart and Rice insisted their relationship was platonic. Yet Hart's friends had worried for years that he was destroying his political career by "womanizing": "It's no secret among Hart staffers that Hart has had these romances," said one campaign official. "But we felt it wasn't anybody's business except his and [his wife] Lee's.' "[13]

Hart's political sense is open to challenge, but is the same true of his sexual ethics? If we assume that Gary and Lee Hart, unlike Jim and Tammy Bakker, did not have a traditional commitment to sexual exclusivity, is there anything immoral about Hart's extramarital sexual romances? In general, are not extramarital affairs immoral when and only when they involve a violation of commitments or promises?

Taylor's Defense of Extramarital Affairs

In *Having Love Affairs,* Richard Taylor provides a spirited defense of many extramarital affairs. His basic argument is simple: Love is the highest good, and hence extramarital affairs based on love are intrinsically good, although admittedly their good might occasionally be outweighed by bad effects. Unlike McMurtry, Taylor sees great value in marriages (based on love), but he vigorously defends McMurtry's favorable view of affairs as offering enriching human relationships, even for couples who began their marriages with traditional vows:

> The joys of illicit and passionate love, which include but go far beyond the mere joys of sex, are incomparably good. And it is undeniable that those who never experience love affairs, and who perhaps even boast of their faultless monogamy year in and year out, have really missed something.[14]

Just as marital love offers the special goods deriving from close companionship, extramarital affairs offer a unique combination of excitement, affection, recognition, and strengthened self-esteem. Few things are more flattering and exhilarating than being loved by someone willing to take risks in surmounting conventional pressures against extramarital affairs.

Of course, affairs do sometimes hurt spouses. Jealousy is natural, even though Taylor views it as always bad and destructive. Affairs need not hurt marriages, however: "No good marriage relationship can be threatened by a love affair so long as others keep out of it."[15] Good marriages are based on mutual love, which presumably is strong enough to survive affairs. Taylor admits that love affairs are not for everyone, and certainly not for those who prefer orderliness and security over the excitement and risk offered by affairs. He insists, however, that the risk of harm from affairs can be minimized if spouses and lovers follow some basic rules.

Specifically, spouses who suspect their partners are engaged in affairs should heed the following guidelines: (1) "Do not spy or pry," because to do so both degrades oneself and shows a lack of trust in the spouse's exercise of autonomy. (2) "Do not confront or entrap," because these actions are based on a cruel impulse to humiliate the spouse. (3) "Stay out of it," and cultivate instead an attitude of confidence that the love involved in the marriage will sustain it after the affair has run its course. (4) "Stop being jealous," for jealousy is an inherently ugly and self-torturing emotion.

Spouses engaged in love affairs should, in turn, heed the following rules, among others: (1) "Stop feeling guilty"; such feelings are irrational products of centuries of prejudice against affairs. (2) "Be aware of the needs of the other" (that is, of one's lover), because that is central to love. (3) "Be honest" (with one's lover), because absolute honesty is required by the special intimacy involved in affairs. (It is especially wrong to lie about one's marital status.) (4) "Do not exhibit and boast," but rather restrain the natural tendency to broadcast the joy the affair has brought.

Taylor's view of extramarital affairs turns traditional morality on its head! What should we say, however, about the deception involved in most affairs? Should we not object to infidelity, betrayal, and violation of marital commitments? Doesn't Taylor's view neglect the virtues of truthfulness and fidelity? Taylor, in fact, defends concealment of the truth from one's spouse: "Candor is not the first obligation of husbands and wives. The first obligation is to love, and a direct consequence of that love is the desire not to injure."[16] When the truth, if revealed, is likely to injure one's spouse and one's marital relationship, love justifies concealment—by means of lies, if necessary. On the issue of fidelity to one's spouse, Taylor is adamant that it has nothing to do with sexual exclusivity: "The real and literal meaning of fidelity is faithfulness; and what thinking person could imagine that there is only one way in which someone can fail to keep faith with another? Faithfulness is a state of one's heart and mind," rather than a matter of rules.[17] Infidelity represents a betrayal of love and the commitment to love. It takes many forms, such as when one neglects the sexual needs of one's spouse, is uncaring, or unappreciative of the spouse's talents, or diverts shared money into a secret savings account for one's selfish use. According to Taylor, however, love for one's spouse is not betrayed by extramarital love affairs.

Many extramarital affairs are entered into without serious thought. Taylor is the first major philosopher to view them as so important as to warrant a book-length examination. Whether his defense of affairs is adequate, or whether it is a one-sided and morally subversive argument, will be left as discussion topics.

Jealousy

Jealousy is different from envy. For one thing, whereas envy centers on hatred, jealousy centers on a sense of injury and loss. We are jealous when we believe we have lost or are threatened with losing the affection, love, or esteem within a relationship we value. Although jealousy may involve hatred, it need not. Frequently, we express a sense of injury or loss through the emotions of anger, sadness, depression, or an aroused desire to assert ourselves in order to regain lost affection.

Furthermore, whereas envy requires only two people, jealousy normally requires three—a triangle. For example, a sister or brother is jealous of a sibling because only one receives what both need: attention and recognition from their parents. A worker is jealous of a co-worker because the latter received an award or bonus from the employer. A lover is jealous because the beloved favors a rival suitor.

Finally, whereas envy is tied to feelings of inferiority, jealousy derives from feelings of insecurity. It entails a fear that one will lose something dear, or it brings a painful collapse after the loss of a hoped-for relationship. The vulnerability caused by love exposes even the most secure person to the insecurities of jealousy. For example, in Shakespeare's tragedy *Othello,* the title character, a socially secure and successful military leader, becomes intensely jealous when he (mistakenly) suspects his wife Desdemona of having an affair with his lieutenant, Cassio. (Note that Iago, who plots to make Othello feel this way, is motivated by envy, not jealousy.) Othello's jealousy and doubts about Desdemona's faithfulness become an obsession. He cannot work, love, or think rationally, and in a final rage he kills Desdemona.

Under this definition, is jealousy, like envy, always bad? It certainly has a bad reputation. Othello reminds us of its potential to foster destructive anger and hate. More recently, the 1960s free-love movement attempted to portray jealousy as based on an ugly attitude of possessiveness. The jealous person was viewed as treating his or her lover as a commodity that can be owned. Love, the free-love movement insisted, must be freely given and received as a gift, never claimed as a property right. Taylor defended this assessment of jealousy:

> Jealousy is the most wrenching and destructive of human passions. Not only is it painful, but the pain is self-inflicted; and unlike most other emotions, no good ever comes from it. . . . Jealousy always has its source in something almost as ugly as itself; namely, in the attitude of possessiveness towards another person.[18]

Taylor viewed jealousy as destructive of love, or at least of erotic love (which was his main concern):

> Possessive love, as it might be called, is no real expression of love at all, but its perversion. Loving an *object* is not really loving it at all; instead, it is an expression of self-love. A person who takes pride in his possessions, who glories in them, quite clearly does not love them for their own sake, but for his. They are just ornaments.[19]

Is this entirely negative evaluation of jealousy warranted? Granted, jealousy can become pathological, involving immoral possessive attitudes toward other people and their affection, but it need not. In fact, jealousy is very often a sign of love! Consider the traditional "love game" designed to test whether someone really cares about us. We contrive a situation in which the person being tested sees us with some attractive rival. Our goal is that the person will show displeasure, thereby confirming our hope that the person desires our affection, and that the person will become more ardent in pursuing us.

Of course, this is a *game*, most often a childish game of the sort encountered in soap operas. It can even cause harm when it backfires, by causing the beloved to feel betrayed or abandoned. Nevertheless, it provides a clue to a deeper truth: Feelings of jealousy show we care about the attention and affection of another, and this is frequently a sign of love. Imagine a married couple who are utterly incapable of feeling jealous of each other. No matter how much time, affection, and sexual attention each partner devotes to others, neither ever feels a twinge of jealousy. Either they are exceptionally confident they will never lose whatever it is they need from each other, or they do not care very deeply about each other.

Jerome Neu puts the point this way: "Behind jealousy lies love. . . . [For] 'jealousy' includes a positive evaluation of, or attachment to, the person (or thing or property) one is jealous over or about. One can be jealous only of something that it highly valued."[20] As Neu also emphasizes, jealousy may be an inevitable aspect of some personal relationships. Intimate love relationships usually demand large amounts of time and energy, and time and energy are limited quantities. It is understandable that jealousy will play a role when these quantities are too much diverted from the relationship.

Even if we grant that jealousy is frequently a sign of love, and perhaps an inescapable aspect of intimate relationships, does any real good ever come from it? Would anything be lost if all jealousy suddenly disappeared from human experience?

Something might indeed be lost. Two good things can be said about at least some jealousy, if it does not become obsessive and cruel. First, jealousy provides a helpful vehicle for self-discovery: Honest reflection on jealousy can yield insights about whom we love and how deeply we love (as the previous comments imply). Second, jealousy sometimes helps to protect and preserve love and friendship. It functions as an emotional alarm, warning us that caring relationships may be at risk from outsiders. As with the emotion of fear, jealousy can provide a painful but prompt warning before we can even articulate our concern for a relationship. Moreover, jealousy can strengthen, albeit temporarily, the ardor with which love is expressed, because we put more attention into valuable things when we believe they are at risk. In this role it serves on occasion to help sustain intimate and caring relationships.

SUMMARY

The traditional form of marriage in Western culture is based on mutual commitments between a man and a woman to lifelong companionship and sexual exclusivity (restriction of sexual relations to one's spouse). Although there is no moral obligation to marry, marriage nevertheless raises moral questions. Some questions center on happiness and self-fulfillment and concern decisions whether to marry and whether to stay married. Other questions, especially those concerning extramarital affairs and adultery, center around moral ideals embraced and commitments undertaken by couples who enter into traditional marriages.

Critics argue that traditional marital commitments are inherently harmful in several respects. First, they allow government or churches to exercise regulatory control over marriages, which lessens the spouses' sense of full responsibility for their relationship. Second, the commitments are psychologically constrictive and prevent enriching relationships with people other than one's spouse. Some feminists emphasize especially the economic and psychological damage done to women in particular. Third, the commitment to sexual exclusivity leads to sexual confinement, which causes insecurity and jealousy and betrays a degrading attitude of ownership of the spouse's sexual activities.

Richard Taylor defends extramarital affairs insofar as they are based on passionate love. He argues that such affairs are singularly exciting, supportive of self-esteem, and valuable for the affection and love they provide. They need not involve either infidelity or immoral deception. Infidelity is a betrayal of love, but one can love a partner in an affair while continuing to love one's spouse. Moreover, one's love for a spouse entails a desire not to hurt her or his feelings, and so one may be justified in concealing the affair with secrecy and deception. These provocative claims, however, are open to challenge, as the following discussion topics suggest.

Jealousy is the feeling that we have lost or may lose something dear to us, in particular the affection of someone we value. Jealousy is sometimes very bad, as when it becomes obsessive and destroys loving relationships. Sometimes, however, it has good effects: It can aid self-understanding, warn of dangers to relationships, and evoke increased attention to a relationship.

DISCUSSION TOPICS

1 An "open marriage" is one in which spouses mutually agree to permit each other to have extramarital affairs. In some open marriages there is an agreement to tell each other about the affairs; in others, disclosure is left to the discretion of the spouse having the affair; and in still others, there is an agreement not to tell each other about the affairs. Without appealing to religious beliefs (about divine commandments), can you find anything immoral about any of these forms of open marriage?

2 One objection to traditional marriages is that they are based on unrealistic commitments. No matter how intense one's feelings may be at the time of the marriage, no one can know for sure whether one will still love one's spouse twenty or fifty years, or even one year, later, because feelings are not entirely under one's control. Therefore, such commitments are either foolish or dishonest (based on pretense). Do you agree? In presenting your answer, clarify what you mean by *love*. Also, compare and contrast marriage vows to other lifetime promises, such as a promise made to a parent that one will become (and stay) a doctor, or a promise made to God to undertake a lifetime of humanitarian service.

3 Comment on sayings like "True love will last," "Love is all we need" (to make our relationship work), and "Love will keep us together." Distinguish different things that might be meant by *love* (some of which perhaps make the cliche false, and some true). In particular, does your conception of love incorporate the effort to cultivate such virtues as patience, persistence, flexibility, willingness to compromise, sensitivity, honesty, courtesy, and even a sense of humor? Does it include the willingness to "fight fair" during disagreements by not attacking one's partner in emotionally vulnerable areas, as well as the skill not to allow daily problems to escalate out of all proportion? How is the virtue of wisdom—which enables us to know when a marriage has become hopeless and is best dissolved—related to love?

4 Taylor argues compellingly that marital infidelity can take forms having nothing to do with sexual exclusivity. That does not prove, however, that violation of marriage vows of sexual exclusivity is not also infidelity. Isn't it a form of infidelity to have a sexual affair after one has promised (to one's spouse) not to have such affairs? If it is, can the obligation of fidelity sometimes be overridden by other considerations that justify sexual affairs?

5   Taylor contends that affairs do not threaten good marriages based on love. If by
    love he includes the willingness to indulge a spouse's affairs, the claim is true by
    definition; but Taylor seems to be making an empirical claim (one based on ex-
    perience) about the effects of affairs on marriages characterized by a deep sense
    of caring. He bases the claim on his own experience, together with more than
    sixty questionnaires filled out by people who answered an ad he placed in three
    newspapers. (The ad stated that a professor of philosophy was researching extra-
    marital love affairs and called for people willing to answer a questionnaire.) Do
    you agree with Taylor's claim that extramarital affairs do not threaten good mar-
    riages? What kind of scientific studies of marriages are needed to determine
    whether Taylor is correct?

6   Many people are currently experimenting with various forms of "marriage con-
    tracts." For example, before marrying, a couple might sign a legal document
    specifying the distribution of money and property in the event of divorce. (See
    Lenore Weitzman's book *The Marriage Contract* . . . for details.) Critics of
    these contracts contend that they convey doubts about whether the relationship
    will survive, and thereby weaken the hope for a permanent relationship based on
    trust. (Such contracts might even constitute a kind of self-fulfilling prophecy.)
    Defenders believe that the contracts are based on an attitude of realism (in fac-
    ing the fact that one in two marriages ends in divorce) and that such an attitude
    may actually benefit the relationship. What is your view, and why?

7   Does the fact that traditional marriages involve commitments to lifelong com-
    panionship imply that divorce automatically represents a kind of moral failure?
    Isn't it possible to be morally justified in withdrawing a lifetime commitment in
    light of major changes in one's life and the relationship with one's spouse? Is di-
    vorce sometimes a very good thing, even when children are involved?

8   Present and defend your view about whether sexual jealousy is good or bad.
    Bring to mind several examples from your experience and experiences of your
    friends. If jealousy is natural, how is it best dealt with?

SUGGESTED READINGS

Bernard, Jessie. *The Future of Marriage*. New York: Bantam, 1973.

Cancian, Francesca M. *Love in America: Gender and Self-Development*. New York: Cambridge
    University Press, 1987.

Clanton, Gordon, and Lynn G. Smith (eds.). *Jealousy*. Lanham, PA: University Press of Amer-
    ica, 1986.

Friday, Nancy. *Jealousy*. New York: Morrow, 1985.

Friedman, Marilyn. "The Social Self and the Partiality Debates." In C. Card (ed.), *Feminist
    Ethics*. Lawrence: University Press of Kansas, 1991.

Graham, Gordon. "Commitment and the Value of Marriage." In G. Graham and
    H. LaFollette (eds.), *Person to Person*. Philadelphia: Temple University Press, 1989:
    pp. 199–212.

Gregory, Paul. "Against Couples." *Journal of Applied Philosophy,* vol. 1 (1984).

Hite, Shere. *Women and Love: A Cultural Revolution in Progress*. New York: Knopf, 1987.

Houlgate, Laurence D. (ed.) *Morals, Marriage, and Parenthood: An Introduction to Family
    Ethics*. Belmont, CA: Wadsworth, 1999.

Hunter, J. F. M. *Thinking About Sex and Love*. Toronto, Ontario: Macmillan of Canada, 1980.

Lawson, Annette. *Adultery: An Analysis of Love and Betrayal*. New York: Basic Books, 1988.

Martin, Mike W. *Love's Virtues*. Lawrence: University Press of Kansas, 1996.

McMurtry, John. "Monogamy: A Critique." *The Monist*, vol. 56 (1972). Reprinted in R. Baker and F. Elliston (eds.), *Philosophy and Sex* Rev. ed. Buffalo, NY: Prometheus, 1984.

Neu, Jerome. "Jealous Thoughts." In A. O. Rorty (ed.), *Explaining Emotions*. Berkeley: University of California Press, 1980.

O'Driscoll, Lyla H. "On the Nature and Value of Marriage." In M. Vetterling-Braggin, F. A. Elliston, and J. English (eds.), *Feminism and Philosophy*. Totowa, NJ: Rowman & Allanheld, 1977.

Okin, Susan Moller. *Justice, Gender, and the Family*. New York: Basic Books, 1989.

Palmer, David. "The Consolation of the Wedded." In R. Baker and F. Elliston (eds.), *Philosophy and Sex*. Rev. ed. Buffalo, NY: Prometheus, 1984.

Russell, Bertrand. *Marriage and Morals*. New York: Liveright, 1929.

Sommers, Christina Hoff. "Philosophers Against the Family." In G. Graham and H. LaFollette (eds.), *Person to Person*. Philadelphia: Temple University Press, 1989, pp. 82–105.

Steinbock, Bonnie. "Adultery." In A. Soble (ed.), *The Philosophy of Sex*. Rev. ed. Savage, MD: Rowman & Littlefield, 1991, pp. 187–192.

Taylor, Richard. *Having Love Affairs*. Buffalo, NY: Prometheus, 1982.

Tov-Ruach, Leila. "Jealousy, Attention, and Loss." In A. O. Rorty (ed.), *Explaining Emotions*. Berkeley, CA: University of California Press, 1980.

Wasserstrom, Richard A. "Is Adultery Immoral?" In R. A. Wasserstrom (ed.), *Today's Moral Problems*. 3d ed. New York: Macmillan, 1985.

Weitzman, Lenore J. *The Divorce Revolution: The Unexpected Social and Economic Consequences for Women and Children in America*. New York: Free Press, 1985.

CHAPTER 15

Parents and Children

Relationships between parents and children are as morally perilous as they are momentous. They are the source of much suffering and even cruelty, yet they can also be full of caring and love. At least, we think they *ought* to be paradigms of relationships based on care and love. This "ought" raises interesting questions. Does it mean there is a "duty to love" one's children and, reciprocally, a duty for children to love their parents? Can there, in fact, be a duty to love? Isn't love something that must emerge spontaneously or not at all, rather than something that can be cultivated as a matter of duty? Does the "ought" perhaps express a moral ideal that is better understood in terms other than duties?

Surely parents have some duties to children, but what is the basis of those duties, and which duties are most important? Do all grown children have obligations to their parents? In thinking about children, should we emphasize their rights rather than their duties, as the recent children's rights movement insists?

Although it is impossible to generalize about family structures, especially with respect to contemporary society, it will help focus our discussion of these issues if we begin with two examples.

Two Examples: Franz Kafka and Maya Angelou

When he was thirty-six, the writer Franz Kafka (1883–1924) composed a forty-five-page letter to his father in which he sought to understand and to heal the emotional chasm between them. The letter is a vivid reminder of how relationships with parents have an influence well into adulthood. It begins: "You asked me recently why I maintain that I am afraid of you. As usual, I was unable to think of any answer to your question, partly for the very reason I am afraid of you."[1]

The fear arose from the father's thorough domination in raising his son: "From your armchair you ruled the world. Your opinion was correct, every other was mad."[2] The father defined the rules of the household, the children's behavior away from home, the family business, and the acceptable attitudes toward the world outside the family. His views were the final authority in determining everything important. They were also frequently self-contradictory or even preposterous, and this generated in Kafka the painful awareness of irrational authority that permeates his writings, for example in "The Metamorphosis" and *The Trial.*

His father's edicts were backed by threats, shouts, rage, and spiteful laughter at any sign of disobedience. Young Franz viewed such behavior as more than sheer bluster, as indeed a recurring condemnation of himself. When the rage was not followed by the threatened punishment, his feelings of guilt and failure were only compounded.

Even worse was his father's difficulty in showing simple affection and providing emotional support. On his return from school, Franz's excitement over his ideas or achievements would be disparaged by the father as childish and petty. He received encouragement only when he conformed to his father's image of manliness—a business-oriented, soldiery, beer-drinking tough guy. Franz's gradual development as a sensitive artist and writer was met with contempt or disregard.

Not surprisingly, Kafka developed a personality grounded in self-doubt and a sense of worthlessness: "Ever since I could think I have had such profound anxieties about asserting my spiritual existence that I was indifferent to everything else."[3] Even as an adult he continued to judge himself in the harsh terms set by his father. Marriage, for example, which he accepted as the sign of full maturity in his society, became impossible for him. Shortly before writing the letter, he could still be deflated by his father's critical view of his fiancée as a mediocre girl who seduced his son by wearing a fancy blouse.

After writing the letter to his father, Franz asked his mother to deliver it. This messenger role was in keeping with her subservient status within the family as go-between for the father and the children. She was a paragon of kindness, but always within the limits of her husband's dominance. This kindness served the cruel function, Kafka realized in retrospect, of the beater during a hunt. By constantly seeking to reconcile Franz with his father, his mother drove him back under the father's domination.

The Kafkas were typical of the nineteenth-century family, in which the father's authority was both unlimited and unquestioned by wives and children, a situation much rarer today. The authority of contemporary parents is now limited by the powerful influences of peers, teachers, and mass media, and is also undermined by greatly increased freedom for children. In fact, according to the Carnegie Council on Children, modern parents are like corporate executives responsible for loosely coordinating the activities of others who shape their children's lives. Confronted with an array of professionals who claim to understand their children better than they do, parents are also each like "a maestro trying to conduct an orchestra of players who have never met and who play from a multitude of different scores, each in a notation the conductor cannot read."[4]

Nevertheless, the fundamental parental role in providing early guidance and emotional support for children remains the same as in previous centuries. In fact, as the Carnegie Council also noted, this role has become even more important. In a world where work is increasingly impersonal, where ties with neighbors are weak, and where religions have lost their grip, the family can be a haven for emotional and moral nurturing of all family members.

Tragically, too often that does not occur. Political conservatives discern a breakdown of traditional parental responsibility, and political liberals point to a barrage of increasing pressures on parents. Both trends are illustrated in the parents of Maya Angelou, the distinguished African-American writer. Angelou's parents separated when she was three and sent her and her brother to be raised by their grandmother in Stamps, Arkansas.

The grandmother was exceptionally effective as a parent. With limited resources and within a society that was both racist and parochial, she gave Angelou a loving upbringing: "Her world was bordered on all sides with work, duty, religion and 'her place.' I don't think she ever knew that a deep-brooding love hung over everything she touched."[5] The grandmother reminds us that a family is defined as a circle of deep caring rather than any particular configuration of relatives.

When Angelou was eight she was sent to visit her mother in St. Louis. Because she suffered from nightmares, she was allowed to sleep in the bed with her mother—and her mother's boyfriend. One morning, after her mother left early for an errand, she was awakened by the boyfriend, who sexually abused her by touching her between the legs. At the time, Angelou did not understand this episode (and a later one) as sexual abuse because the boyfriend was gentle and seemingly affectionate. That changed when the boyfriend raped her. He warned her that if she told anyone he would kill her brother (whom she adored).

Angelou's mother sensed something was wrong and, while confronting the boyfriend, learned what had occurred. She kicked the boyfriend out and had him prosecuted for rape. Before the man could serve a one-year jail term, members of the local community killed him. Angelou, who was then eight years old, felt responsible for the man's death and punished herself by refusing to speak for years. Various relatives construed her silence as impudent sullenness and thrashed her. She was sent back to live with her grandmother until she turned thirteen, at which time she was sent again to stay with her mother.

With these examples in mind, we can turn to the question: What are the primary responsibilities of parents toward their children?

Parental Responsibility: Respect Versus Abuse

By *parents* we mean individuals who have primary responsibility and authority in raising a child. They may be biological parents, foster parents, or "significant others" who replace legal guardians as primary providers and protectors. Parents are those people who, by assuming responsibility for a child's development, serve as primary caretakers.

Parents' fundamental duty to their children is to respect them as persons—persons undergoing various stages of development. This may sound odd at first, because we expect so much more from parents than the respect that all people owe to children. Yet, just as parents are in a unique position to nurture and support their children, so too are they uniquely well placed to harm them by failing to show them even minimal respect, as we saw in the cases of Kafka and Angelou. Furthermore, precisely because parents do contribute so much to their children's development, it is easy for them to rationalize away the harm they do under the guise of exercising parental responsibility. Such rationalization frequently characterizes parents' actions in the areas of discipline, affection, and encouragement.

First, child abuse is sometimes rationalized as discipline or excused as an attempt to teach a lesson. Thus, a spanking turns into a beating without the parent's awareness of the transition. Kafka reported a related example in recalling his only direct memory from infancy. He had been whimpering for water, and ignoring several warnings to be quiet, when suddenly his father carried him outside and locked him out for a while on a cool evening when he was wearing only a nightshirt. This was devastating to Kafka, who remembered the episode as ultimate proof that he was worthless in his father's eyes.

Second, even gross abuse can occur in the guise of affection. Father–daughter incest and other forms of sexual abuse, which are estimated to occur to one of every six girls, rarely result from the use of overt force. Typically, at first there is enticement: kind words ("Daddy loves you") and gentle touching, as in the case of Angelou. Threats aimed at keeping the child quiet usually come after the sexual abuse. Sexual abuse, which so clearly exploits the vulnerability and trust of children, is sometimes rationalized by alleged paternal rights to the sexual satisfaction that the wife "fails" to give, combined with the self-serving belief that no real harm is done. Such beliefs have even been publicly defended: The Rene Guyon Society is a lobby of incest advocates that publicly espouses parent–child sex in the name of the sexual liberation of children.

Third, a great deal of psychological manipulation takes place under the guise of guidance and encouragement. Parents do have the right and responsibility to convey their own sense of moral decency to their children—within limits. That sense of decency may be prejudiced and narrow, and in some respects it almost always is. Nevertheless, it provides the essential foundation of values that children can subsequently modify. What is objectionable—obviously so, in the case of Kafka's father—is the use of tactics that crush a child's attempts to assess those values and to modify them as the child develops capacities for autonomous reasoning. Furthermore, overzealous parental concern can mask an attempt to live vicariously through children, to derive esteem and vent frustrations by pressuring children in harmful ways.

Definitions of Child Abuse

Child abuse takes many subtle forms, which prompts us to define it carefully in regard to parental duties to children. Traditional definitions of child abuse were developed in the legal context, because courts needed a criterion for justifiable forced removal of children from homes. Studies showed that forced removal of children does more harm than good, except when abuse is very severe. This fact, coupled with a concern for preserving family unity, led courts to define child abuse very narrowly as a pattern of either severe battery or deprivation of necessities such as food, shelter, clothing, affection, and education. Hence, the legal definition does not apply to an array of moral harms that are less severe or unsolvable through legal remedies.

At the opposite extreme is a definition of child abuse as any failure to promote the child's best interests. This definition, however, is much too wide. For one thing, there is always some alternative home where the interests of a given child might be better promoted. This would make most parents abusers because they lack ideal resources for maximizing their child's interests! Another objection is that, according to this definition, parents would be abusers each time they failed to place a given child's interests above all others; yet those interests must always be balanced against the needs and interests of other family members, including parents.

If the definition of child abuse as extreme deprivation is too narrow, and the definition of child abuse as a failure to maximize the child's interests is too wide, then perhaps child abuse should be defined as a failure to meet the child's basic needs that handicaps the child's basic development. This definition would have to be linked to a theory about needs, development, and growth toward maturity. Because these are all value concepts, such a theory would draw on both psychological and value assumptions about mature and responsible conduct, which is the goal of healthy psychological development.

Although this definition is an improvement over the others, Natalie Abrams suggests it is still too limited. Abrams points out that abuse of people in general consists of more than simply harm to their development. In a legal context, for example, the term *battery* refers to an infringement on the liberty of another against that person's will or choice. This is wrong, because battery also constitutes an assault on the person's dignity, even if it does not actually handicap development. Similarly, Abrams suggests, abuse of children is best conceived as an assault on their dignity as persons:

It is this concept of an affront to dignity that is totally omitted in the definitions of child abuse or neglect, which focus solely on actual or risked harmful consequences. It is not enough simply to say that the harmful consequences constitute assaults on one's dignity and, therefore, that the child's dignity is indirectly being protected. Although harmful consequences must be prohibited in order to ensure the possibility of the child's development, the prevention of these harms does not amount to respect for the child's dignity, any more than it would amount to respect for adult dignity.[6]

This definition, which is plainly inspired by Kantian rather than utilitarian thought, coheres with our earlier emphasis on respect for children as persons. Yet there is a problem with the definition, Abrams acknowledges. The dignity of adults is defined by reference to their consent. Violation of their rights without their consent, that is, without their voluntary and informed agreement, constitutes an assault on their dignity. How can this standard be applied to young children, who lack the capacity to give consent?

Abrams offers the following suggestions. The concept of consent is indeed inapplicable to very young children, and a minimum standard for the decent treatment of children should be established. Even young children can express their wishes, verbally or nonverbally. These wishes should be respected as far as possible, except when to do so would be detrimental to the child's development or prohibited by the needs of other family members. Thus, this standard does not require that maximum amounts of money be spent on the child, as the best-interests standard might imply. It requires only that a fair share of family resources be spent in the direction indicated by the child's wishes, except when that would harm the child's development.

It follows from this standard that there are limits on how far parents can justifiably manipulate their children to adopt particular interests, values, careers, religious beliefs, and tastes. The appeal to their best interests, for example, does not automatically justify coercion of older children to adopt particular religious practices. Nor are parents warranted in coercing children to pursue careers that, in the parents' judgment, are in the children's best interests. Instead, parents should help provide the conditions that will enable children to make their own career choices.

Beyond their basic physical needs, the essential ingredients for children's well-being are the skills and enthusiasm for independent thought and action. Note that this is also at the heart of personal and moral autonomy: the active capacity to create and pursue a rational and moral plan of life. Hence, one of the primary duties of parents is to provide conditions that foster the growth of autonomy.

Before turning to the reciprocal duties that children owe to parents, let us briefly consider two further objections to Abrams's emphasis on consent as a moral limit on how children can be treated. The first objection is that the emphasis is hollow because it allows exceptions whenever harm to the child is involved, and parents will inevitably apply their own views of what this harm is. Thus, for example, parents will continue to force their religious beliefs on their children in the name of the children's interests, even when the children clearly refuse consent.

This objection highlights a practical difficulty in applying Abrams's standard, although the objection should be qualified. The standard Abrams has in mind is not parents' views of the proper development of the child, but instead the actual healthy development of the child. Parents are required to become informed and intelligent about what that development is! Moreover, the consent requirement clearly does imply increased respect for the child's own views about proper development as the child matures. Eventually, at the morally vague stage of "maturity," the parent should recognize the consent of the son or daughter as final. Between early infancy and maturity, however, children have a gradually developing capacity for consent that should be respected in such matters as religion.

The second objection to an emphasis on consent concerns incest. Suppose there are rare instances when incest does not harm a child's development and when an older child of fifteen years or more gives consent. Does it follow that the incest is permissible and is not an assault on the child's dignity? If so, this might imply that we should no longer regard incest as taboo, that is, as absolutely prohibited.

In response to this objection we should emphasize that the chances of psychological and developmental harm from incest are so high, and the degree of possible harm so enormous, that it makes sense to retain an absolute ban on it. (This is a rule-utilitarian argument that recognizes the need for all to adhere to a general rule because of the important good consequences that follow from doing so.) Furthermore, there is the question of whether even a fifteen-year-old child (or young adult) is capable of giving consent freely in a situation that combines sexual inexperience on the child's part and psychological authority on the part of a parent or older relative. Finally, there remains the ideal that parents ought to love their children as parents, not as sexual partners. Incest threatens the kind of love that for children is both inherently valuable and the basis of self-respect in adult life.

Filial Duties and Gratitude

Let us now shift the moral focus from parental responsibilities to children's duties. What is the appropriate moral attitude of children, especially grown sons and daughters, toward their parents? Recent social thought has stressed that the relationship is largely one of rights. Reacting to the horrors of child abuse and neglect, members of the children's rights movement, such as Abrams, have emphasized children's rights to be given what is necessary for proper development ("positive rights") and their rights to have as much freedom as possible without interference from others ("negative rights"). These human rights are viewed as one justification for claiming that parents have duties toward children—that is, duties to respect their children's rights.

Duties

Young children, of course, also have duties to obey and cooperate with parents once they grow beyond infancy. The duties are limited, because there is no duty to do everything—however immoral or inappropriate—a parent commands. Nevertheless, children's duties are important because other members of the family have needs that must be recognized and balanced. Young children are not able to balance these other needs, and hence should generally defer to their parents' judgment. As they grow older, however, they should be allowed an increasing voice in family decisions in order to aid development of their autonomy. Furthermore, children's own sense of autonomy can arise only on a foundation of early development guided by their parents.

The traditional Judeo–Christian view of what is owed to parents goes far beyond this, however. Children and adults alike are enjoined, according to one of the Ten Commandments, to "Honor thy father and thy mother." This is usually interpreted as a requirement to respect them and be grateful to them, and is a prescription for a lifetime, not just during childhood. Failure to be grateful reflects the vice of extreme ingratitude. Thus, Franz Kafka was accused by his father of ingratitude for becoming estranged from him.

This traditional view has been challenged on several counts. First, gratitude is an emotion, and emotions are not under our direct control. Therefore, we cannot have a duty to feel gratitude, because we do not have duties to do things beyond our control. One possible reply to this challenge is that the duty of gratitude refers more to *showing* gratitude than to *feeling* grateful. To show gratitude is to perform acts that manifest or express gratitude, and these are under our control.

Perhaps, however, this preliminary reply is superficial. The duty of gratitude is a duty to show genuine or sincere gratitude, which entails that one actually feel grateful rather than merely pretend to be. Can there, then, be a duty to be grateful if such a duty entails a duty to have certain emotions?

Gratitude

In order to answer this question, we need to know what the emotion of gratitude is. If it is an inner sensation or feeling (for instance, a warm glow inside) over which we have no control, then it would seem absurd to speak of a duty of gratitude. Fortunately, it is not! Like other important and complex emotions, gratitude is not a set of inner twitches and tingles, but instead a structure involving beliefs, attitudes, and desires.

Gratitude has the following ingredients: (1) a belief that one or more people voluntarily did something good for us, or at least intended it to be good for us, (2) a positive attitude of goodwill toward those benefactors (such as a hope for their well-being), and (3) a desire to show them appreciation (in an appropriate way, whether with a reciprocal gift, a simple thank you, or any number of other signs of appreciation). In addition, when we have received a gift that is actually good for us, gratitude also requires us (4) to appreciate and properly use the gift. With "white elephant" gifts, however, which we cannot be expected to appreciate, this last condition does not apply. We are free to dispose of the gift with discretion, that is, without hurting the feelings of the giver.

Understood in this way, gratitude is somewhat under our control; to some extent we can influence our beliefs, attitudes, and desires. We can often allow (or refuse to allow) gratitude to develop within us by attending to the benevolent motives of the giver, dwelling on the value or intended value of the gift, and reminding ourselves of the importance of sustaining our relationship with the person by acknowledging his or her kindness.

Admittedly, there are some occasions when one either cannot or should not foster gratitude in this way. Perhaps, for example, to do so would add to an already harmful sense of dependence on a parent whose motives in giving were as much an attempt to manipulate as to help. The following statement illustrates this point: "If you do not complete medical school and stay active in our church, then you are an ingrate for all we have given you!" Gratitude, even for benefits received, is sometimes inappropriate and misplaced.[7]

A second challenge to the traditional view that children owe gratitude to their parents is the assertion that parents, in giving their children the necessities for development, are merely doing their duty. Gratitude, it is implied, is owed only when people do something good that is not required by duty. This argument is unsound. Sometimes, we owe gratitude for acts on our behalf that were required by duty. It would, for example, be callous for someone who was saved by a lifeguard or police officer to dismiss that act as undeserving of gratitude on the ground that the rescuer had a duty as a professional. When we benefit from a great good, we should be grateful. For most of us, the greatest goods we receive include those from our parents. Moreover, parents are usually motivated far more by love than by a sense of duty. Raising children requires sacrifices, and parents usually make those sacrifices voluntarily and lovingly. To fail to respond with gratitude as the beneficiary of this love and these sacrifices is a moral failure as well as a betrayal.

A third and more forceful challenge to the view that parents are owed honor and gratitude was given by Jane English, who found it objectionable to talk about *owing* parents for their sacrifices. The notion of owing is appropriate in regard to repaying debts, meeting contracts, and returning favors; adult children, however, ought not to think of their relationship with their parents in such ways:

> Parents' voluntary sacrifices, rather than creating "debts" to be "repaid," tend to create love or "friendship." The duties of grown children are those of friends and result from love between them and their parents, rather than being things owed in repayment for the parents' earlier sacrifices.[8]

English makes an important point: The adult son or daughter does not owe parents in the same way he or she might owe an unpaid debt or owe a favor in return for having received one. This legalistic way of thinking actually threatens the kind of mutual caring about one another's needs that under-lies loving relationships.

Moreover, when parents sever an ongoing loving friendship with their children, they should not expect gratitude for the earlier sacrifices they made. As English notes, if biological parents who are fully able to raise their child decide instead to give it up for adoption, they should not expect grati-tude for any sacrifices they made in having the child. Again, if parents dis-avow their children because they refuse to marry within a preferred religion or to pursue careers favored by their parents, and the parents thereafter have nothing to do with them, the children have no obligation years later to pay their medical bills in old age. For similar reasons, Franz Kafka's father had no right to expect gratitude from him.

Perhaps, however, we may hesitate to embrace English's emphasis on friendship in the relationship between parents and grown children. Notice that a consequence of her view is that, once friendship ceases on the part of either party, duties of friendship also cease. Is there not, however, a stronger obligation to try to sustain a loving relationship with one's parents than there is to sustain friendships? More basically, isn't it inappropriate to construe the relationship with parents either as primarily friendship or as primarily a matter of rights and duties? What about love?

Love

As we saw in Chapter 11, love is as complex conceptually and morally as it is complicated in real life. Here we will mention an aspect of love that war-rants further discussion. The issue is whether most of what has been said thus far in this chapter is inappropriate because the relationship between parents and children ought to be one of love, rather than duties and rights. Parents, ideally, have children out of love and out of a desire to create an in-timate loving relationship. Moreover, to be a successful parent one must raise children with love, and in such a way that children know they are deeply loved and singularly important to the parents.

The failure of Kafka's father was a failure to love, as well as a failure of duty (and perhaps the same is somewhat true of Franz Kafka with respect to his father). On the same principle, the idea of a child's duty of gratitude is in-sulting to many parents precisely because they seek love, not dutiful respect and gratitude, from their children. For a similar reason, mere friendship is not sufficient to capture the hoped-for relationship between parents and children.

Perhaps to a large extent this emphasis on love need not undermine the relevance of the preceding discussion of duties, rights, and responsibilities. The kind of parent–child love that is most important and worth promoting encompasses and transcends, without replacing, the duties of mutual respect and caring. Love is the aim and ideal of parent–child relationships. It is itself an ideal, not a duty.

The important question at this point is: What kind of love represents the ideal? Is mutual caring for one another's interests sufficient? Is self-sacrifice implicit in the ideal? Is the desire for love a desire for an unconditional love that does not depend on any particular achievements or traits of character in the family members? These questions will be left as discussion topics.

Surrogate Motherhood

Medical technology has added a new dimension to traditional concerns about parenting: surrogate motherhood. In one case, a woman is artificially inseminated with sperm of a man who contracts with the woman—the surrogate mother—to bring the child to term and give it up to the man (and usually his wife) for adoption. In another case, a man's sperm inseminates his wife's ovum and the fertilized ovum is then implanted in the uterus of a second woman, who carries the child to term and transfers its custody to the couple whose genetic material was used to create it. In both cases, a contract is signed by all parties whereby the adoptive parents pay the surrogate mother about $10,000 (in addition to paying medical costs and costs of agencies which arrange the contract, often another $30,000).

Surrogate motherhood generates disturbing moral questions, several of which we will raise and leave for discussion. First, does surrogate motherhood constitute a form of baby selling (and buying)? Baby selling is illegal, and for good reason: It degrades a human child by treating the child as an object to be transferred on the market like other objects. In surrogate motherhood, at least one genetic parent receives the child, and to that extent it is unlike traditional baby selling.

Nevertheless, it also involves payment of money to receive from another woman a baby that is not generated in traditional ways. Supporters of surrogate motherhood view the $10,000 as a compensation for inconvenience, of the sort that a Peace Corps volunteer receives for voluntary service. Opponents, however, see the exchange of money for babies as simply a variation of baby selling, and they point out that the money is a strong incentive for many women to make money through surrogacy (just as traditional forms of baby selling posed incentives for lower-class women to make money by giving up their babies for adoption).

Second, supporters of surrogate motherhood view it as a straightforward extension of normal parental practices that takes advantage of new medical technology. Opponents object that the surrogate mother is essentially deciding to have children without assuming responsibility for the child (and instead is carrying the child simply for the purposes of transferring it to others). They point to the importance of sustaining the traditional tie between having a child and assuming personal responsibility for its care.

Third, supporters of surrogate motherhood (including some feminists) emphasize the autonomy of women to make their own decisions about engaging in this practice, whatever their motives, without government interference. To prohibit the practice would constitute objectionable paternalism, that is, an interference with the autonomy of adults in order to promote their good (as the government sees that good). Opponents (including other feminists) view the practice as a new form of exploitation of women. The practice is essentially a form of "renting a uterus" (usually that of a lower-class woman who needs the money), and thus treats women as objects to be used.

Fourth, what are the effects of surrogate motherhood on children? Supporters argue that there is not yet good scientific data about any harmful side-effects to children. They predict that there will no doubt be some psychological problems, but no more than in other cases of adopted children. Opponents argue that the risk is too great and point to cases that have already gone seriously wrong. For example, in the famous "Baby M" case, Mary Beth Whitehead, the surrogate mother, changed her mind and decided she wanted to keep the child, thereby provoking a lengthy court battle for custody of the child. (The New Jersey Supreme Court eventually awarded custody to the genetic father, while entitling Mary Beth Whitehead to visitation rights; the court's reasoning centered on which party would best be able to give parental care to the child. The decision also voided legal contracts that did not leave the surrogate mother ample time to change her mind about whether to keep the child.) In other cases, the child may have genetic deformities or for other reasons may be rejected both by the individuals contracting for the child and by the surrogate mother, thereby making the child a ward of the taxpayers. Additionally, when a surrogate mother has other children of her own, those children may feel great anxiety that they too are vulnerable to being given away.

SUMMARY

Parents are any persons who assume responsibility for the primary caretaking of a child. Their most fundamental duty to the child is respect, which includes a duty to provide the basic necessities of life during the time when the child is completely dependent on the parents. In regard to discipline, affection, and encouragement, this duty requires parents to avoid abuse and forms of manipulation that restrict the child's potential for subsequent autonomous growth.

Child abuse is an assault on the dignity of children, in the form of actions that either disregard their needs, undermine their autonomy as they move toward adulthood, or in other ways unjustifiably harm them. Respect for children requires parents to refrain from imposing their own convictions on them, but instead to provide conditions that enable children to develop a capacity for creating and pursuing their own rational plans of life.

Children have obligations of gratitude for the benefits and the benevolence received from parents. Gratitude has the following ingredients: belief that someone voluntarily did something intended to be good for us, usually motivated by a concern for our good; a consequent feeling of goodwill toward the benefactor; a desire to show appreciation; and appreciation and proper use of the gift. Gratitude is under our control and is appropriate even though parents have an obligation to promote their children's good.

Although there are mutual obligations involved in parent–child relationships, the ideal form of the relationship is centered on mutual love and mutual caring about one another's good.

A surrogate mother is a woman who carries a fetus to birth and then transfers it to other individuals who have made a contract with her to adopt the child and who pay her about $10,000, plus medical expenses. Does the practice of surrogate motherhood treat babies as objects and thereby amount to a high-tech form of baby selling? Does surrogate motherhood erode the connection between having children and responsibly caring for them? Does it exploit women? Are its effects on children morally objectionable?

DISCUSSION TOPICS

1 What kind of love between parents and adult children do you see as most desirable? Is it a form of friendship (as Jane English suggests) or is it more like the identity-shaping aspects involved in romantic love?

2 Do adult children have an obligation to feel and show gratitude to parents who have greatly contributed to their good? Or is sincere gratitude to one's parents a moral virtue that is highly desirable but not obligatory?

3 Is there an obligation to give financial support to one's parents in their old age, should they need it? Does the obligation depend on whether one's parents were caring and loving? Is there an obligation of parents not to become a financial burden on their children?

4 Evaluate the following argument: Parents should not raise their children in any particular religion, because that brainwashes them in a matter of great importance. Instead, parents should take them to several churches in order to lay a foundation for children to make up their own minds about religion later. Is your view on this issue the same with respect to early moral training?

5 Given the enormous potential for parents to cause harm, should the government require that parents take courses on parenthood before they are permitted to have children? Should the state be allowed to decide who can be a parent (as is currently the case with respect to adoption of children)?

6 Two parents who believe that homosexuality is immoral learn that their son or daughter is homosexual. In a rage they sever all ties with their child—those of emotion, finance, communication, and so on. The last time they talk with their child, they disavow their identity as parents, exclaiming, "You are no longer our child." Have the parents done anything immoral? If so, which ethical theory best captures what is wrong: utilitarianism, duty ethics, rights ethics, or virtue ethics?

7 During 1986 and 1987, there were several widely publicized cases of children (teenage and preteenage) who reported their parents to the police for using illegal drugs. Some of the children were given recognition awards by police departments. Identify and discuss the moral issues you see raised by these cases. Are the issues the same or different with respect to parents who turn in their adult children for drug use?

8 Decisions about whether to have children include decisions to beget, to bear, to keep, and to adopt a child. We speak of such decisions as "deciding to have a baby," which reflects our preoccupation with cuddly, dependent infants (rather than merely reflecting the biological fact that babies are children in the early stages of development). Yet the decision to have a child is or should be a decision to enter into a long-term, complex, changing, and largely unpredictable intimate relationship with another person. Discuss the main moral considerations that should be weighed by prospective parents in deciding whether to have a child. At the time when the decision is made to beget a child, are there obligations to the future child (who does not yet exist)?

9 Ideally, parent–child relationships are based on mutual trust. Does that make it worse to lie to one's parents than to lie to a stranger? Consider several examples, and also review the discussion of lying in Chapter 2.

10 Present and defend your view concerning surrogate motherhood. (a) Is the practice morally acceptable, or should it be discouraged or even prohibited by law? (b) Should the government regulate the practice in any way, or should it permit all contracts among adults, thereby permitting the cost of surrogate motherhood to be set by whatever the market will pay (so as to entitle women to earn whatever they can through surrogate motherhood)?

SUGGESTED READINGS

Abrams, Natalie. "Problems in Defining Child Abuse and Neglect." In O. O'Neill and W. Ruddick (eds.), *Having Children: Philosophical and Legal Reflections on Parenthood*. New York: Oxford University Press, 1979.

Aiken, William, and Hugh LaFollette (eds.). *Whose Child?: Children's Rights, Parental Authority, and State Power*. Totowa, NJ: Littlefield, Adams, 1980.

Archard, David. *Children: Rights and Childhood*. London: Routledge, 1993.

Becker, Lawrence C. *Reciprocity*. New York: Routledge and Kegan Paul, 1986.

Berger, Fred R. "Gratitude." *Ethics*, vol. 85 (1975): 298–309.

Blustein, Jeffrey. *Parents and Children: The Ethics of the Family*. New York: Oxford University Press, 1982.

Camenisch, Paul F. "Gift and Gratitude in Ethics," *The Journal of Religious Ethics*, vol. 9 (1981): 1–34.

Card, Claudia. "Gratitude and Obligation." *American Philosophical Quarterly*, vol. 25 (1988): 115–127.

Daniels, Norman. *Am I My Parents' Keeper?: An Essay on Justice Between the Young and the Old*. New York: Oxford University Press, 1988.

English, Jane. "What Do Grown Children Owe Their Parents?" In O. O'Neill and W. Ruddick (eds.), *Having Children: Philosophical and Legal Reflections on Parenthood*. New York: Oxford University Press, 1979.

Feinberg, Joel. "The Child's Right to an Open Future." In W. Aiken and H. LaFollette (eds.), *Whose Child?: Children's Rights, Parental Authority, and State Power*. Totowa, NJ: Littlefield, Adams, 1980, pp. 124–153.

Gostin, Larry (ed.). *Surrogate Motherhood: Politics and Privacy*. Bloomington: Indiana University Press, 1990.

Janeway, Elizabeth. "Incest: A Rational Look at the Oldest Taboo." In *Cross Sections from a Decade of Change*. New York: Harcourt Brace Jovanovich, 1977.

Jecker, Nancy. "Are Filial Duties Unfounded?" *American Philosophical Quarterly,* vol. 26 (1989): 73–80.

Keniston, Kenneth, and The Carnegie Council on Children. *All Our Children: The American Family Under Pressure*. New York: Harcourt Brace Jovanovich, 1977.

Ladd, R. E. (ed.). *Children's Rights Re-Visioned*. Belmont, CA: Wadsworth, 1996.

McConnell, Terrance. *Gratitude*. Philadelphia: Temple University Press, 1993.

Neu, Jerome. "What Is Wrong With Incest?" *Inquiry,* vol. 19 (1976).

O'Barr, Jean F., Deborah Pope, and Mary Wyer (eds.). *Ties That Bind: Essays on Mothering and Patriarchy*. Chicago: University of Chicago Press, 1990.

O'Neill, Onora, and William Ruddick (eds.). *Having Children: Philosophical and Legal Reflections on Parenthood*. New York: Oxford University Press, 1979.

Pagelow, Mildred Daley. *Family Violence*. New York: Praeger, 1984.

Purdy, L. M. *In Their Best Interest?: The Case Against Equal Rights for Children*. Ithaca, NY: Cornell University Press, 1992.

Purdy, Laura. "Surrogate Mothering: Exploitation or Empowerment?" *Bioethics,* vol. 3 (1989): 18–34.

Ruddick, Sara. *Maternal Thinking: Toward a Politics of Peace*. Boston: Beacon Press, 1989.

Scarre, G. (ed.). *Children, Parents, and Politics*. Cambridge: Cambridge University Press, 1989.

Schoeman, Ferdinand. "Rights of Children, Rights of Parents, and the Moral Basis of the Family." *Ethics,* vol. 91 (1980).

Stainton Rogers, W., D. Hevey, J. Roche, and E. Ash (eds.). *Child Abuse and Neglect: Facing the Challenge*. London: Open University Press, 1992.

Trebilcot, Joyce (ed.). *Mothering: Essays in Feminist Theory*. Totowa, NJ: Rowman & Allanheld, 1983.

Wringe, C. A. *Children's Rights: A Philosophical Study*. Boston: Routledge & Kegan Paul, 1982.

CHAPTER 16

Friendship

Ethics books emphasizing theories about right conduct rarely give friendship more than passing mention. At best, they treat it as one of many sources of obligation or as a context in which moral dilemmas might arise. At worst, they dismiss it as a source of private pleasure that poses a threat to justice in that it involves a kind of favoritism seemingly incompatible with the demands of impartiality and fairness.

A shift in emphasis to character and personal relationships, however, invites a different perspective that is closer to common sense. We do, after all, ordinarily think of the caring involved in friendship as having special significance morally; moreover, we are uneasy about people who strike us as incapable of friendship. These considerations led Aristotle to devote two of the ten books of his *Nicomachean Ethics* to friendship. In this chapter we examine the moral value of friendship, the responsibilities accompanying friendships, and the moral limits on friendship.

An Example of Friendship

Each of us will have in mind personal examples of friendship, but it may be helpful to cite one example here. In her memoirs, titled *Pentimento,* the American playwright Lillian Hellman describes her friendship with a person she calls Julia. Hellman and Julia were close friends from the time they were twelve until Julia's death almost twenty years later. Their friendship began with mutual interests and enjoyment of each other's company and deepened through shared activities and experiences. Hellman recalls, for example, the first time she was allowed to sleep overnight at her friend's house on a New Year's Eve in New York when they were both twelve:

> Each New Year's Eve of my life has brought back the memory of that night.
> Julia and I lay in twin beds and she recited odds and ends of poetry . . . Dante

in Italian, Heine in German, and even though I could not understand either language, the sounds were so lovely that I felt a sweet sadness as if much was ahead in the world, much that was going to be fine and fulfilling if I could ever find my way.[1]

Hellman and Julia spent many hours together, often seeing each other daily. Although their conversations were permeated by their shared love of literature, they "also talked like all young people, of possible beaux and husbands and babies, and heredity versus environment, and can romantic love last, mixing stuff like that in speeches made only for the pleasure of girls on the edge of growing up."[2] They went on several camping trips, including a particularly memorable one when they were sixteen. On that trip Julia captured a rabbit that the two young women skinned, cooked, and ate for dinner. The experience left a permanent mark on Hellman: "Even now, seeing any island, I am busy with that rabbit and fantasies of how I would make do alone, without shelter or tools."[3]

As with most friendships, there were disagreements and frictions that periodically strained their closeness, but these were relatively mild. By the time they turned eighteen, however, circumstances separated them: Julia moved to Oxford for undergraduate studies and later to Vienna for medical school, while Hellman attended college in New York, where she began writing plays. Yet their feelings for one another never diminished, and they continued to write and occasionally to see each other. During the 1930s, Julia had become a socialist and had moved to Berlin to join the anti-Hitler underground and fight fascism. Her socialist principles led her to distribute her considerable wealth to the poor she met in Berlin. Contrary to those principles, she sent frequent and extravagant gifts to Hellman whenever she saw anything she might like.

In 1937, while visiting Paris, Hellman accepted an invitation to attend a theatre festival in Moscow and called Julia to arrange a brief meeting on the way. To her surprise, Julia asked her to stay in Paris a few days longer, until she could send a messenger with a special request. Despite the mystery, Hellman immediately agreed to wait: "It would not have occurred to me to ignore what Julia told me to do because that's the way it had always been between us."[4] When the messenger arrived, he requested that Hellman carry to Berlin $50,000 of Julia's money from her Paris bank, to be used to buy the freedom of Jews and other victims of Nazi persecution. The messenger also said that, even though every precaution was to be taken, there would be some danger, and Julia would completely understand if Hellman was unable to grant her request.

Hellman agreed to the request and, not without intrigue, smuggled the money into Berlin. For safety's sake, she was allowed to meet with Julia only briefly in a restaurant. There she burst into tears when she saw that one of Julia's legs had been amputated following an injury sustained in a Nazi attack. Less than a year later she was informed by telegram that the Nazis had murdered Julia. It was twenty-five years before Hellman was able to write about the incident, and then, out of respect, she withheld Julia's true name in order to protect her family and friends who were still alive.

Definition of Friendship

The example of Hellman and Julia illustrates many features typical of friendship. Yet friendship comes in many forms, and it would be futile to try to define it with a simple set of conditions that sharply distinguish it from other relationships based on caring. The best we can do here is to indicate several criteria that characterize central (or "paradigm") examples of friendship.

First, friendship entails mutual liking, where liking is understood as a special affection for and delight in a person. Friends each enjoy the other's company, enjoy hearing news about the other, accept the other's imperfections, and delight in the other's particular characteristics. In some of the deepest friendships the affection is an instance of love (usually, though not always, nonerotic love). As with other forms of love, even the deepest friendships permit times of emotional distance, irritation, or anger. Hence, the relevant sense of *liking* implies a general attitude and a disposition to affection, rather than a continuous feeling.

Second, friendship involves sharing: mutual activities, shared experiences, reciprocal interests in each other, and intimate communication. This was notable in the early years of the Hellman–Julia friendship, and it continued during the years when an exchange of letters was the main shared activity.

Third, friendship involves reciprocal giving. Hellman and Julia gave freely of their time, attention, and energy, in addition to their exchanges of material gifts. The reciprocal nature of the giving was not diminished by Julia's ability to give far more materially because of her inherited wealth.

Fourth, the motive for sharing and giving is mutual caring, which consists of both friends' desire for the well-being of the other, as well as an especially deep affirmation of the other person's importance. It is true that Julia made a request that placed Hellman at risk, but the request derived from a matter of extraordinary moral importance, and Julia took every possible precaution to protect her.

Fifth, friendship is built on a sense of mutual understanding, based on direct acquaintance with each other and shared personal knowledge. In part this understanding arises from the time spent together, and in part from personal conversation and correspondence. The relationship is "intimate" not only in the sense that it involves close emotional ties, but also in the willingness of friends to disclose more about themselves than they would to most other people.

Sixth, there is trust on the part of both friends. The trust is based on mutual commitments to care about the other's well-being, together with mutual understanding that friends can count on each other in difficult circumstances.

Seventh, friends share mutual respect, especially respect for the other's needs for freedom and self-respect. The friendship is entered into and sustained voluntarily. It is not based primarily on a desire to dominate and manipulate, nor on a desire to be submissive.

Eighth, friendships are (in part) chosen. To be sure, they begin and are sustained on a foundation of feelings of affection that are not wholly under our immediate control: As with erotic love, we cannot simply choose by fiat to be friends with just anyone. Nevertheless, for a friendship to be developed and sustained, friends must make a series of voluntary decisions. Because of this element of volition, friendships reflect important aspects of our personalities that may not be developed through family relationships (which often result from choices made by others rather than by ourselves, such as the decision to have or adopt children).

Ninth, in friendship there is mutual acknowledgment and affirmation of the relationship (as characterized by the preceding features). Each friend is aware of the ties joining them, hopes that the ties will be maintained, and is committed to making an effort to preserve the friendship. In fact, to some extent the high degree of caring involved depends on an anticipation that the friendship will continue.

The Value of Friendship

Why, and when, is friendship valuable, in particular morally valuable? Aristotle stated that friendship is most valuable when based on the friend's admiration for the good traits of character in each other, rather than on mutual usefulness or mutual pleasure, because friendship reinforces and develops good character through mutual inspiration and edification. The same value might accrue when the shared activities joining the friends are altruistic causes, such as helping the poor, promoting world peace, or working to preserve human rights. However, let us set aside these special cases for a moment and require only that the shared activities be morally permissible (not necessarily admirable) and that the mutual liking not be centered on immoral traits.

In moral terms, the most significant aspect of friendship is the mutual caring based on mutual respect and understanding. Each friend is especially concerned about the other's well-being, and each willingly expresses that concern without losing either self-respect or respect for the freedom of the other person. This is morally desirable and admirable in and of itself—as virtue ethicists would emphasize, as well as those utilitarians who count friendship as an especially important intrinsic good. Moreover, the degree of moral goodness involved in friendship depends on the degree of caring.

This view contrasts with Kant's narrow claim that the only thing morally good in and of itself is the desire to act for the sake of duty. It also differs sharply from all theories based on Kant's definition of the "moral point of view" as impartial regard for all people equally. The caring involved in friendship is morally valuable precisely because it is grounded in especially deep concern based on an appreciation of what is unique in the friend. It constitutes a singularly important recognition of the worth of individuals, and fulfills the human need to feel liked on the basis of another's intimate knowledge about oneself.

Friendship is also morally valuable because of its consequences, as utilitarians emphasize. Friendship offers primary support for self-respect and self-esteem: Our sense of self-worth is more vulnerable than we like to think, and nothing can help it more than supportive friendships (with the possible exception of erotic love). In times of difficulty, friends provide emotional support, sometimes more effectively than immediate family.

Friendship contributes in further ways to happiness and personal well-being. It affords friends delight in each other's company, in working and playing together on the basis of mutual concern. To be sure, friendship (like other forms of love) puts us at risk to suffer. The agonies of friendship include grief at the harm that befalls a friend, sadness at the inability to help when circumstances prevent us, and anguish at our failure to help because we are apathetic or selfishly preoccupied. Even when friendship is painful, however, it usually adds to the sense of worth of our lives. It also evokes our interests and enlivens our activities to know that they matter to our friends.

Moreover, friendship often increases our capacities for understanding and appreciating people who are not our friends, but who are either friends of our friends or people they otherwise care about. It can provide a quickened sense of why people have moral worth and thereby augment our sensitivity to the needs of strangers.

Marilyn Friedman has drawn attention to an especially important contribution of friendship to moral growth. Moral development is a lifelong process in which we come to see the world in new ways. Friendship, because it involves trust and intimacy, facilitates this awakening to new perspectives. This happens in both directions: We learn directly from our friends about their responses and attitudes, and we learn about ourselves as we are able to explore our own responses and values through conversations and shared activities.

Friendship makes possible special ways of learning, often unlike learning in more formal contexts such as the classroom or reading. In part this is due to what friends reveal, due especially to the detailed richness with which friends express their experiences and attitudes to each other. In part it is due to how they reveal it: "In friendship, there is a substantial measure of trust in the ability of our friends to bear what I call reliable 'moral witness' to their own experiences."[5] That is, because of the framework of mutual trust, we are able to appreciate our friends' values internally, from within their frame of reference: "[F]riendship, that is, a relationship of some degree of mutual intimacy, benevolence, interest, and concern, constitutes a context of trust and shared perspectives which fosters *vicarious participation in the very experience of moral alternatives.*"[6] Not only do we gain detailed knowledge about our friends' perspectives, thereby widening the range of our own experience, we also enter sympathetically into alternative conceptual and value perspectives that widen our appreciation of human reality. We take seriously our friends' outlooks because we deeply value them as individuals.

Of course, if we were to choose only friends who shared our values in detail, friendship could not open our eyes to new perspectives. In fact, however, friends rarely (if ever) share precisely the same tastes, attitudes, and principles. Even if friendships are formed during periods when individuals have much in common, friendships that endure through time must inevitably accommodate changes in friends. Indeed, often the friendship helps the friends to adjust in the course of changes in education, jobs, and marriages. A close friend helps us understand parts of our life that may be very different from the friend's.

Our acknowledgment of these good consequences of friendship does not imply that we should be preoccupied with them. Although they may serve as reminders of the value of friendship, they cannot provide the primary reasons for having friends. To repeat, friendship is based on care and concern, and its origins lie in spontaneous liking. Motivation that derives primarily from an attitude of self-interest only inhibits or erodes friendship.

Responsibilities

A similar remark applies to the idea of duties, obligations, and responsibilities to friends: A primary motivation of duty is for the most part consistent with friendship. A sense of duty motivates us to pay our taxes and not to cheat; by contrast, affection motivates us to give presents to our friends. Nevertheless, there are responsibilities that accompany friendship.

Consider this illustration from David B. Annis:

> For example, if you have an important job interview, but when you start to leave for it, your car won't start, you might legitimately expect your friend, who can easily drive you, to help. If your friend refuses, you would justifiably feel hurt and betrayed, and not understand how your friend could treat you this way. . . . Not helping seems inconsistent with the friendship, and if it happens often, the friendship has been abandoned. Notice that we wouldn't in general expect a stranger to drive us.[7]

One response to this example is that, at most, there is what Kant called a *hypothetical* duty: "If you want to maintain the friendship, then you ought to help the friend." This is not a moral *(categorical)* duty, however, but is instead only a counsel of prudence concerning how to satisfy a desire to keep a friend. This response will not do, however: Unless one has a good excuse, failure to help the friend violates the understanding and trust involved in the friendship (we are assuming there is a genuine friendship at the time). In some situations, where much is at stake, we speak of *betraying* the friend—not just of letting the friend down—and also of violating one's own integrity.

How can friendships generate special responsibilities, obligations owed to the friend in particular, but not to just any stranger? Utilitarians will attempt to trace these obligations to the good consequences accruing from friendships. Act-utilitarians encounter difficulty here, since it is not clear that one's aid to a friend will generate the best overall consequences in every situation. Act-utilitarians can still argue, however, that in general it is morally obligatory to help a friend, and in other cases one would have an excuse for not helping. Rule-utilitarians have a more promising approach in emphasizing the general benefits of maintaining the trust so essential to valuable friendships.

Annis, however, suggests that a still more promising approach to understanding the basis of duties of friendship is to emphasize the elements of voluntary choice and commitment typical in friendships: "Friendship involves various voluntary and consented to interactions and shared activities. As the friendship develops, an intricate web of reciprocal and mutual dispositions, beliefs, understandings, feelings, etc., develops."[8] This web of understandings generates trust, including trust that the friend cares and can be relied on to help in some situations. Usually there is no explicit promise to give help (or to maintain a friendship); but there are tacit commitments that arise as a friendship develops, and those tacit commitments generate obligations.

Moral Limits on Friendship

Praise for friendship has sometimes been excessive. Writing in the sixteenth century, for example, Montaigne asserted that "a single dominant friendship dissolves all other obligations" and that in an ideal friendship "each one gives himself so wholly to his friend that he has nothing left to distribute elsewhere."[9] This suggests that deep friendships generate paramount or absolute obligations that can never be overridden by other moral responsibilities. Responsibilities to a friend, however, like virtually all responsibilities, are prima facie; they sometimes have justified exceptions when other pressing obligations conflict with them, including obligations to other friends.

Montaigne's assertion represents harmful hyperbole in view of the numerous moral obligations limiting the claims of friendship. Earlier we assumed that the shared activities in friendships were of a morally permissible nature; now consider situations in which they are immoral. For example, there is friendship among criminals and in the "brotherhood" of organized crime. Insofar as these relationships involve genuine mutual caring, they have moral worth. That worth may be overshadowed, however, by the harm to which the friendship contributes.

It would be moral idolatry to elevate friendship to moral supremacy. No simple general ranking system dictates when the loyalties of a friendship should outweigh or temper loyalties to other friends, to family, or to one's community. Julia provides an interesting illustration of this. In her gifts for Hellman, she allowed personal affection to override her socialist principles of egalitarianism, which prohibit exorbitant gifts to financially secure friends. In response to the possibility of saving innocent human lives, however, she was willing, on the basis of higher principle, to request that Hellman make the personal sacrifice of putting herself at risk.

Strict egalitarians sometimes object that friendship preferentially bestows what they believe is owed equally to all other human beings, or at least to those having the greatest need. For them, the designation of a few individuals for special attention conflicts with the ideal of universal love for all. As our earlier discussion of the value of friendship might imply, we strongly disagree with that position. Nevertheless, there are special contexts in which the claims of justice for all people—the imperatives of impartiality and fairness—ought to restrict the exercise of generosity to friends. When a public official is responsible for appointing the best person for a job that requires the utmost competence (for example, police chief or chief surgeon), a selection influenced by friendship represents a violation of public trust.

At the same time, even in public life—in politics, business, and the professions—we place a high value on friendship and its special loyalties. It is often desirable to work with colleagues who are also friends, and we may give some preference to friends when we are not strictly prohibited by professional responsibilities. Even the competitive world of profit-making business recognizes the importance of "mentor relationships" involving friendship, whereby an established member of a company helps a younger one to advance in the company. Is this aid unjustified? Not insofar as friendships serve to humanize work situations that would otherwise be impersonal and even degrading.

In a famous passage, the novelist E. M. Forster expressed a sentiment related to Montaigne's view of friendship:

> I hate the idea of causes, and if I had to choose between betraying my country and betraying my friend, I hope I should have the guts to betray my country. Such a choice may scandalize the modern reader, and he may stretch out his patriotic hand to the telephone at once and ring up the police. It would not have shocked Dante, though. Dante places Brutus and Cassius in the lowest circle of Hell because they had chosen to betray their friend Julius Caesar rather than their country Rome.[10]

It is impossible to assess Forster's remark without first knowing about the particular context: the kind of country, the kind of friendship, the kinds of betrayal at issue and their probable consequences. If the country, for example, were a totalitarian state of the sort George Orwell described in *1984* (in which the government suppressed personal relationships as a threat to its absolute power), then Forster's remark is an admirable call for heroism. If, however, one's friend belonged to a terrorist group bent on destroying a democratic society, then Forster's remark is morally grotesque.

In *A Passage to India,* Forster portrays an example that supports his emphasis on the responsibilities of friendship. The example concerns a situation in which one's country is at fault, but one is placed under extreme pressure to support the country rather than a friend. Mr. Fielding, principal of an English college in India, had become a friend of Dr. Aziz, an Indian. As colonialists trying to maintain their dominance over India, the English were discouraged from forming such friendships, and the friendship emerged through natural affection despite differences, such as Aziz's Muslim faith and Fielding's atheism. When Aziz is falsely accused of assaulting an English woman while taking her on a tour of the Marabar Cave, the entire English community unifies to prosecute him, based on flimsy evidence (and confusion) of the English woman. Fielding, however, maintains a firm faith in his friend's innocence and takes his side in the social upheaval that ensues. When Fielding is asked, "You actually are on our side against your own people?" he answers "Yes. Definitely."[11] Despite pressures from many directions, including threats to his career, Fielding vigorously helps Aziz prove his innocence. We admire him for that, and we might doubt his integrity had he acted otherwise. Subsequently, the friendship is suspended when Aziz comes to believe that Fielding has stopped caring about the injustice done to him, but, after nearly two years, shared understanding is restored.

In addition to illustrating the strength of the responsibilities involved in friendship, the example reinforces Friedman's earlier point about how friendships widen our understanding and appreciation of the world. Fielding comes to understand India and Indians far more than most of the other English characters in the novel because of his capacity for friendship across cultural boundaries. There is an important lesson here for those who live in a world where multicultural understanding becomes increasingly important.

SUMMARY

Friendship has several characteristic features: mutual liking (i.e., the fact that each has affection for and finds enjoyment in the other); sharing and reciprocal giving motivated by caring (i.e., the desire of each to promote the well-being of the other); mutual understanding, trust, and respect; and mutual choice, recognition, and affirmation of the friendship.

Because it involves mutual caring, friendship has moral worth. Not only does it represent an important way to appreciate and affirm the worth of other individuals, it also frequently results in good consequences: It contributes to happiness, increases our capacity to understand people in general, and affords us new insights based on a friend's enriching perspective. Friendship entails special responsibilities, although it can be harmful when it leads to the violation of other important obligations.

DISCUSSION TOPICS

1   Philosophers influenced by Kant argue that morality, by definition, requires impartiality in our treatment of other people. Consider, for example, the following comment:

> Morality is, at the very least, the effort to guide one's conduct by reason—that is, to do what there are the best reasons for doing—while giving equal weight to the interests of each individual who will be affected by one's conduct.[12]

Present and defend your view of whether friendship has a moral importance that justifies (indeed, requires) a lack of complete impartiality in some contexts. Also, identify several contexts in which morality does require strict impartiality and forbids us to allow friendships to bias decisions.

2   Just as we speak of *true love,* we sometimes speak of *true friendship.* Presumably, true or genuine friendships meet some criteria that distinguish them from less valuable relationships. In your view, what are these criteria? That is, what features of some friendships make them especially valuable?

3   Lillian Hellman was willing, out of friendship, to undertake a course of action that involved some danger. What does this willingness indicate about the nature of the friendship she had with Julia? Also, in requesting that Hellman undertake the action, did Julia act disloyally toward Hellman or violate their friendship in any way?

4   Friendship requires mutual caring. Does that mean it requires "pure altruism" in the sense of a desire for the friend's well-being for its own sake, without any ulterior motives of self-interest? Or is friendship ultimately a matter of promoting someone's good in order to get something good for oneself in return? In your answer, take account of Lawrence Blum's view in the following passage, and give examples of what you think he means:

> Caring and the acts of beneficence in friendship are not separate from my own interests, from what is personally a good to me; it is not, in that sense, "disinterested." In fact, friendship is a context in which the division between self-interest and other-interest is often not applicable. The friendship itself defines what is of importance to me, and in that sense what is in my interest. In that sense I do not generally sacrifice my own interest in acting for the good of my friend. I act with a sense of the friendship's importance to me, even though it is the friend whose benefit I directly aim at (i.e., which is my motive for acting), and not my own.[13]

5   We can be friendly toward a great many people, but we can be close friends with far fewer people at any given time. Explain why this is, and in doing so, clarify the distinction between friendliness and friendship. At the same time, discuss whether the idea of having many friends simultaneously is less problematic than having many simultaneous erotic love relationships.

6   Express in your own words Aristotle's argument in the following passage:

> Whatever existence means for each class of men, whatever it is for whose sake they value life, in that they wish to occupy themselves with their friends;

and so some drink together, others dice together, others join in athletic exercises and hunting, or in the study of philosophy, each class spending their days together in whatever they love most in life; for since they wish to live with their friends, they do and share in those things which give them the sense of living together. Thus the friendship of bad men turns out an evil thing (for because of their instability they unite in bad pursuits, and besides they become evil by becoming like each other), while the friendship of good men is good, being augmented by their companionship.[14]

Is Aristotle's argument a good one?

7 When is it permissible or even obligatory to express to a friend your view about the friend's faults, especially those that threaten the friend's well-being (for example, the friend's drug problem, overeating, surliness to others, or dishonesty at school or work)? And when, if ever—and in particular if you believe that the friend will benefit in the long run—is it permissible to report a friend's wrongdoing to the relevant authorities? If you find these questions difficult to answer (in the abstract), discuss whether you think the answer turns (in part) on differences among friendships, including differences in what friends want or require from each other.

8 Is friendship gender-linked? Do men and women tend to display different patterns of friendships? Does your experience support or oppose the following observation by Lillian B. Rubin? "At every life stage between twenty-five and fifty-five, women have more friendships, as distinct from collegial relationships or work-mates, than men. . . . Generally, women's friendships with each other rest on shared intimacies, self-revelation, nurturance and emotional support. . . . In contrast, men's relationships are marked by shared activities."[15]

9 What do you make of Harry's comment, in the movie *When Harry Met Sally,* that it is impossible for men and women to be friends with each other because sexual interests always get in the way?

SUGGESTED READINGS

Annis, David B. "The Meaning, Value, and Duties of Friendship." *American Philosophical Quarterly,* vol. 24 (1987): 349–356.

Aristotle. *Nicomachean Ethics.* Trans. W. D. Ross. In R. McKeon (ed.), *The Basic Works of Aristotle,* Books 8 and 9. New York: Random House, 1941.

Badhwar, Neera Kapur (ed.). *Friendship: A Philosophical Reader.* Ithaca, NY: Cornell University Press, 1993.

Bernikow, Louise. "Friends." In *Among Women.* New York: Harper & Row, 1981.

Blum, Lawrence A. *Friendship, Altruism and Morality.* Boston: Routledge & Kegan Paul, 1980.

Cooper, John M. "Aristotle on Friendship." In A. O. Rorty (ed.), *Essays on Aristotle's Ethics.* Berkeley: University of California Press, 1980.

Forster, E. M. "What I Believe." In *Two Cheers for Democracy.* New York: Harcourt, Brace & World, 1951.

Friedman, Marilyn. *What Are Friends For?: Feminist Perspectives on Personal Relationships and Moral Theory.* Ithaca, NY: Cornell University Press, 1993.

Kant, Immanuel. "Friendship." In *Lectures on Ethics.* Trans. L. Infield. New York: Harper & Row, 1963.

Meilander, Gilbert C. *Friendship: A Study in Theological Ethics.* Notre Dame, IN: University of Notre Dame Press, 1981.

Montaigne. "Of Friendship." In *The Complete Essays of Montaigne*. D. M. Frame (trans.). Stanford, CA: Stanford University Press, 1971.

Pakaluk, Michael (ed.). *Other Selves: Philosophers on Friendship*. Indianapolis, IN: Hackett, 1991.

Pogrebin, Letty Cottin. *Among Friends*. New York: McGraw-Hill, 1987.

Porter, Roy, and Sylvana Tomaselli (eds.). *The Dialectics of Friendship*. New York: Routledge, 1989.

Raymond, Janice G. *A Passion for Friends: Toward a Philosophy of Female Affection*. Boston, MA: Beacon Press, 1986.

Sharp, Ronald A. *Friendship and Literature*. Durham, NC: Duke University Press, 1986.

Sherman, Nancy. *The Fabric of Character: Aristotle's Theory of Virtue*. Oxford: Clarendon Press, 1989, pp. 118–156.

Telfer, Elizabeth. "Friendship." *Proceedings of the Aristotelian Society*, vol. 71 (1970–1971).

Thomas, Laurence. *Living Morally: A Psychology of Moral Character*. Philadelphia: Temple University Press, 1989, pp. 97–158.

Welty, Eudora, and Ronald A. Sharp (eds.). *The Norton Book of Friendship*. New York: W. W. Norton, 1991.

Williams, Clifford (ed.). *On Love and Friendship: Philosophical Readings*. Boston: Jones and Bartlett, 1995.

Interpersonal Conflicts

Conflicts between individuals or groups are ubiquitous in everyday life. Here we are interested in conflicts that generate hostilities and threaten mutual respect, especially within what should be caring relationships. We begin by distinguishing several forms of hostility: anger, envy, *ressentiment,* and other forms of hatred. Then we discuss several creative responses to hostile confrontations: forgiveness, compromise, and other forms of conflict resolution.

Anger

Anger is easily confused with hatred, but they are defined by different beliefs and desires. Hatred is based on the belief that someone or something is bad, together with the desire to hurt, destroy, or at least remove it from our presence. Anger is based on the belief that an offense has occurred, together with the desire to punish or in other ways have the offense set right.

The intensity of anger varies from mild annoyance (being peeved or piqued) to rage (being outraged or furious). The complexity of anger also varies according to the perceived offense. *Simple anger* is the reflex of getting mad when something frustrates our plans, as when we kick a flat tire in a frustrated furor. *Indignation* is anger over a (perceived) violation of a principle or value that we cherish, as in the case of someone's outrage over the government's treatment of AIDS victims during the 1980s. *Resentment* is an angry response to an insult or injustice to us or to people we identify with, such as our family or friends. Indignation and resentment are moral emotions in that they are based on a response to (perceived) moral violations and injuries. They, rather than simple anger, will be the focus in what follows.

Anger—including the occurrence, continuance, and expression of anger—can be justified or unjustified. The initial experience of anger is justified or not, depending on the reasons for it. Indignation is justified if a genuine value has been violated by someone who should be held responsible for the violation. Resentment is appropriate when one has been wronged and someone is blameworthy for the wrong. I might understandably experience simple anger at some teenagers who play their radio too loud when I am trying to read, but (depending on the location) it might be inappropriate to react with indignation or resentment.

Justified anger is sometimes desirable, as well as permissible, in that it manifests moral concern and self-respect. The failure to feel indignation at gross injustice can be a fault, and a failure to feel resentment can be a sign that we lack self-respect. For example, persons who are sexually harassed should feel resentment. If they do not, we suspect they do not properly value themselves.

There is also a pragmatic justification for sustaining these emotions and acting on them. If we act on the anger (in a certain way), are we likely to correct an injustice, or will it make things worse for everyone involved? If an acquaintance insults us, perhaps an immediate and direct confrontation is appropriate. If a friend in an "off" moment insults us, perhaps we should let things cool down, and then forgive and forget. If an employer insults us, a controlled expression of resentment might damage the employee–employer relationship. The circumstances, as well as our personalities, determine whether anger is creative or harmful to relationships.

Envy

If anger is often fully justified, envy is not. Envy, in the special sense intended here, is *malicious envy:* hatred of others because of their possessions, achievements, or virtues. Suppose that someone wins an award. If we reasonably believe the award should have gone to us, we might feel justified resentment, but we would feel envy if we hated the person simply for winning an award he or she deserved. Envy is based on either a perception that one is inferior to someone else or a feeling that one's self-esteem is threatened by someone else's well-being. Envy is a form of unjustified hatred; as such, it is immoral, even when it is not expressed in outward attacks on others. Not surprisingly, medieval Christians included envy among the seven deadly sins.

Malicious envy differs from other kinds of envy not at issue here. *Admiration envy* is the admiration for and desire to emulate someone. When a person we respect wins a contest or receives an award, we might compliment them by saying, "I envy you." This remark conveys our admiration and makes the compliment more personal, as if we were saying, "What you have done is so superb I wish I had been able to do it." In contrast, envy in the more traditional sense used here is something we would be unlikely to acknowledge openly. Malicious envy is unjustified hatred of others because of their good fortune, as well as a desire to see that good fortune reversed because it makes us feel inferior.

Envy—by which we will now mean malicious envy—should also be distinguished from jealousy. When we feel envy, we perceive ourselves as inferior to others and want them brought down to our level or lower. When we feel jealousy, however, we feel hurt and afraid of losing something (or someone) dear to us. Unlike envy, jealousy is not always unjustified and bad, as we suggested in Chapter 14.

Envy takes two forms, particular and general.[1] General envy entails the hatred of entire classes of people because they have some good thing that we want for ourselves, or at least do not want them to have. For example, we might hate all rich people or detest people with better athletic skills than ours. Particular envy, by contrast, is directed toward specific individuals with whom we compare ourselves or against whom we compete.

A vivid example of particular envy is found in Salieri, a character in Peter Shaffer's play and movie *Amadeus*. The character is based on a composer who was a contemporary of Wolfgang Amadeus Mozart during the late eighteenth century. Salieri rose to prominence and became the official court composer for Austria's emperor. From his youth he burned with the ambition to become the greatest composer of his day, but that ambition was shattered when he encountered Mozart, whose talents were vastly superior to his own.

It was a tribute to Salieri's genuine abilities that he, unlike most of his peers, could fully appreciate the majesty of Mozart's music. His appreciation was tainted, however, with intense bitterness. Not only did Mozart's arrival make him feel inferior, empty, and worthless; it also generated rage against Mozart and a desire to see Mozart's superiority overthrown. The rage was accompanied by a sense of powerlessness to do anything about his inferiority. These, then, are the primary ingredients of particular envy: feelings of inferiority, hatred, and impotence.

In Shaffer's play, Salieri, tortured by envy, sets out to destroy Mozart. In conversations with influential people he downplays Mozart's talents. Using his influence as court composer, he prevents Mozart from obtaining the work and public recognition he deserved. When he learns later that Mozart is suffering from guilt and hallucinations following the death of his father, he proceeds to push him over the edge of sanity. Discovering that Mozart's hallucinations contain a father figure wearing a black mask and cape, he mimics the figure and appears at Mozart's apartment to commission a "death mass." Then he forces Mozart to complete the work at a frantic pace, periodically appearing outside the window of the apartment. A combination of alcoholism, overwork, poverty, and tortured guilt causes Mozart to die at the young age of thirty-five, but even Mozart's death does not end Salieri's self-imposed suffering. Rather, his envy continues as Mozart's reputation grows following his death.

Amadeus, we might add, explores envy within a religious context. When Salieri devoted his life to music at age sixteen, he promised God he would be morally conscientious if only God would grant him sufficient fame to enjoy his work as a composer. When he realized that Mozart's accomplishments would undermine his fame, he swore vengeance against God. God, he reasoned, had chosen to make Mozart rather than himself his musical agent; hence, God could be attacked by destroying Mozart. Recast in secular terms, the play suggests that, in envy, we feel we are outraged over a fate that made us inferior. In retaliation we assault the person who received the superiority we want for ourselves.

Envy can be overcome if we eliminate our feelings of hate and inferiority. Occasionally, rational reflection by itself enables us to purge these feelings by allowing us to see their unreasonableness. Usually, however, deeper emotional adjustments are required. Hating other people for their good fortune is best tackled with a combination of efforts to (1) increase one's own self-confidence, (2) strengthen the basis of one's self-esteem so it becomes more durable and less prone to collapse when confronted by others' well-being, and (3) increase one's capacity to appreciate, rather than hate, the achievements of others. These avenues for dissipating envy can be blocked when we avoid admitting our envy—admitting it to others or to ourselves.

Ressentiment

To acknowledge envy forces us to confront several unflattering truths: that we hate without justification, that we feel painfully inferior, and that our self-esteem is so flimsy as to depend on the misfortune of others. In avoiding these painful truths, we tend to deceive ourselves about envy, and when we do, the envy often finds devious ways of expressing itself. Nietzsche used the French word *ressentiment* to refer to unconscious envy, as well as to other forms of repressed hatred.

In one of his applications of this concept, as noted in Chapter 4, Nietzsche viewed strict egalitarianism as a moral distortion that expresses the self-interest of mediocre people who feel impotent to strive for greatness. Those who constantly downgrade and criticize as unjust anyone better off than themselves are probably expressing envy:

> You preachers of equality, the tyrannomania of impotence clamors thus out of you for equality: your most secret ambitions to be tyrants thus shroud themselves in words of virtue. Aggrieved conceit, repressed envy . . . erupt from you as a flame and as the frenzy of revenge.[2]

Nietzsche was alarmed by how societies were becoming increasingly uniform and morally bland. Democratic ideals, in his view, were being misused to justify the attitude that everyone is equally virtuous and no one is more noble or heroic than anyone else.

Nietzsche's insights were clarified, criticized, and developed by the philosopher–sociologist Max Scheler (1874–1928) in a book titled *Ressentiment*. According to Scheler, *ressentiment* arises not only when we feel inferior, hostile, and impotent to better our situation, but also when we feel unable to confront or express these feelings:

> Revenge, envy, the impulse to detract, spite, *Schadenfreude* [i.e., enjoyment of someone's misfortune], and malice lead to *ressentiment* only if there occurs neither a moral self-conquest . . . nor an act or some other adequate expression of emotion (such as verbal abuse or shaking one's fist), and if this restraint is caused by a pronounced awareness of impotence. . . . *Ressentiment* can only arise if these emotions are particularly powerful and yet must be suppressed because they are coupled with the feeling that one is unable to act them out.[3]

Self-deception results in a loss of conscious supervision over our envy and other forms of hatred, but the hate does not go away. It is merely released through avenues more subtle than Salieri's open campaign of vengeance; for example through snide remarks or by rechanneling hatred toward other objects—we kick the dog or yell at a friend. Its most devastating effect, according to Scheler, is its distortion of our values: Value standards are lowered or corrupted so as to make us look good in our own eyes. One approach is to bring everyone down to the same low level: No one has a better character than anyone else. Another approach is to claim that values are merely subjective, so that one person's values are as good as anyone's. On a more restricted scale, someone might attack the practice of grading on the grounds that it unfairly tries to distinguish and rate work that is essentially all the same, and because professors are all biased anyway.

Hatred

Not all hatred is inherently unjustified in the way that envy and *ressentiment* are. To begin with, there is *simple hatred:* strong aversion toward certain foods, discomforts, types of weather, or disappointing grades. Simple hatreds, like simple loves, are manifestations of strong tastes. In contrast, consider hatred toward persons whom we see as bad: Is such hatred justified when the person really *is* bad in the way we believe? Some world religions, especially Christianity, have condemned hatred (of persons, rather than of immoral actions) as always unjustified (unlike indignation, which Jesus and the Hebrew prophets sometimes manifested). Should hatred of persons be universally condemned?

Jean Hampton distinguishes three types of hatred (beyond envy and simple hatred), each of which is based on the belief that the hated person is morally bad, perhaps because she or he has personally injured us. *Malice* is the desire to get even with others in such a way that we win over them and are thereby elevated (at least in our eyes). *Spite* is the desire to bring others down to our level. *Moral hatred* is aversion toward persons who identify themselves with immoral causes. All these emotions are unjustified when based on false beliefs about another person, but let us consider cases where the other person really is at fault in the way we believe.

Hampton argues that malice and spite are inherently irrational, although moral hatred is not. Malice and spite embody efforts to assert our self-respect and self-esteem in ways that are self-defeating. Consider a case of malice:

Someone has insulted me, and rather than just feeling resentment about the insult, I maliciously hate the person. I set out to vindicate (vindictively!) my damaged or threatened self-esteem by attacking the self-esteem of the other person: "I'll show him!" If, however, I succeed in "putting down" the other person and elevating myself over my enemy, what do I gain? To win in competition with a bad person is to triumph over nothing. This is a theme in Western movies:

> An avenger uses the threat of death to master a hated wrongdoer in order to diminish him. Frequently this involves "making him crawl" before the avenger. . . . But as he looks upon the wretched and pathetic figure of the wrongdoer, the avenger invariably finds that he is getting no pleasure from his victory. He has shown that the wrongdoer is nothing, so that now he is the lord of nothing.[4]

Spite is even more clearly self-defeating, and in that way both imprudent and unhealthy. Spiteful haters seek to pull others down to the same low level with themselves (whereas malicious haters want to achieve superiority over them). Hampton's analysis brings to mind those persons who knowingly infect others with the AIDS virus in order to inflict on them the same fate as themselves. These spiteful haters irrationally believe that their own well-being is somehow improved by imposing undeserved suffering of the same kind they have undergone, and that belief is irrational.

Moral hatred is not so obviously bad, however. Hampton calls it "moral" because it is admirably motivated both by indignation toward persons who have identified themselves with immoral causes or practices, and by a desire to triumph over those persons and their immoral outlooks by acting on behalf of a morally good cause, such as justice. In this way, we might hate Hitler, Stalin, and terrorists. There need be nothing self-defeating about hatred in such cases. Our hate may motivate us to admirable conduct and lead to deserved self-respect for fighting on behalf of good causes and sometimes enjoying victory over evil. Nevertheless, Hampton asks whether it is better to act on indignation and resentment, rather than hatred, while striving to overcome our hatred through love. Here she is speaking on behalf of the injunction to love and forgive our enemies, even as we justifiably oppose their immorality. Is that injunction a religious principle that transcends our ordinary moral understanding, or is there some basis for it in ordinary morality?

Forgiveness

Forgiveness is the act of relinquishing or avoiding negative attitudes toward someone for a wrong they have committed. Distinct from the outward act of telling others they are forgiven, forgiveness is an inner act or activity; it is a change of heart from ill will (hatred, anger, or contempt) to good will. It need not imply a complete reacceptance of a person, nor a return to the same good relationship we may have had with someone. It does, however, open the door to a renewal or restoration of relationships with acquaintances, friends, or loved ones. That is one reason why it is so important in maintaining personal relationships. We all make mistakes and harm others in ways that threaten relationships. Forgiveness makes it possible for us to restore relationships based on mutual respect or caring. But is forgiveness always required? Is it always desirable? Apparently not.

Victims of rape, wife battering, murder of a family member, major theft, or arson may be fully justified in the bitter resentment (and hate?) they experience. Whether they decide to forgive is their choice, but if they too easily forgive we might wonder whether they lack self-respect and self-esteem. They have been wronged, seriously wronged; to forswear their resentment and hostility without good reasons is not admirable.

What are the reasons that justify forgiveness? Most of the reasons center on the wrongdoer. First, are there mitigating circumstances surrounding the wrongdoing? For example, did the person who interfered with our freedom at least have good intentions? Second, have the wrongdoers felt remorse and made amends, or are they simply enjoying the benefits they received in wronging us? Thieves who enjoy stolen goods and even mock the stupidity of their victims are typically not appropriate objects of forgiveness.

Other reasons for forgiveness concern our special relationship with the wrongdoer. We are more ready to forgive parents, friends, and lovers because of how much they have contributed to our lives in the past and because of the importance of our ongoing relationship with them.

Finally, some reasons for forgiving center on the person who has been wronged. Sometimes the bitterness we experience from a wrong causes us more suffering than the wrong itself. The ordeal of a divorce, for example, can leave lasting wounds of rage and hate. For the sake of our own happiness we may need to forgive, or partly forgive, the former spouse or lover. Again, in this case as in others, we may realize that we are also partly to blame, and hence may be in need of forgiveness ourselves. We may be in no (moral) position to blame, since we have committed similar wrongs (and not repented of them).

We have been discussing the forgiveness of specific wrongs, but there is also the question of general dispositions to forgive. Wholesale, unconditional forgiveness that is oblivious to reasons is objectionable, but the general unwillingness to forgive is equally objectionable. It may reveal a lack of generosity (especially regarding minor offenses), a lack of compassion (toward people who genuinely repent and make amends), or a lack of humility (in failing to recognize our equal faults).

Conflict Resolution and Peacemaking

Mutual respect is especially threatened when anger and hatred enter into conflicts involving clashing interests and values. The peaceful resolution of conflicts is perhaps the greatest moral challenge today, as individuals and groups find it increasingly difficult to maintain ties of community and mutual respect. Violence is a desperate last resort in conflicts, but so is the expulsion of people from the moral community.

Peacemaking, then, becomes an essential activity. Sometimes we think of peace as the absence of all conflict, but perhaps that is an unrealistic or even undesirable goal. Martin Luther King, Jr., was one of the greatest peacemakers of the twentieth century, but he understood the need for conflicts in order to arouse attention to important values. To silence conflicts in order to maintain a racist society yields the kind of peace that is not worth seeking. King used nonviolent civil disobedience as a way to generate creative conflicts that brought concealed injustices to the surface and enabled them to be overcome without violence.

If conflicts are inherent in life, perhaps we should think of peace as a creative way of dealing with conflicts, rather than as a state of nonconflict. We might define peace as the procedural framework in which conflicts are dealt with constructively. Or, following Gray Cox, we might define peace as "a process in which people freely and responsibly cultivate shared commitments to common expressions, projects and practices."[5] Just how this process unfolds depends largely on contexts in which conflicts arise.

Cox offers three examples. First, the context might be collective decision making within groups that have a dominant shared value perspective concerning the good ends in life, as is the case with many religious groups. The Quakers, for example, developed a five-stage procedure for resolving conflicts: (1) pacify impulses by diverting attention from disrupting desires and emotions; (2) address concerns, both by articulating them and through quiet contemplation; (3) gather consensus through dialogue and listen sympathetically to other perspectives; (4) find clarity, in the sense of forming a resolve to improve the problem being addressed; and (5) bear witness to the discovered truth by living rightly.

Second, the context might be the pursuit of justice in situations where one party to a dispute is heavily armed and capable of maintaining unjust policies through the use of force. Gandhi and Martin Luther King, Jr., are examples of how civil disobedience can be used to appeal to the basic decency of the wider community. Protesters engaged in civil disobedience break laws openly and nonviolently and are willing to go to jail to indicate their loyalty to their cause and also to show respect for the law. Their commitment in the face of great opposition draws media attention that sparks sympathetic attention from the community.

Third, most often the opposition is between individuals or groups that have some shared interests (although not as thoroughgoing as in the first context) and some clashing interests (although not on such a scale that civil disobedience is a genuine option). Most conflicts arise in this context. If we assume that the conflicting parties are willing to communicate with each other, principled negotiation makes sense.

As explained by Roger Fisher and William Ury, principled negotiation has four components: (1) tackle the problem rather than attacking the person with whom one disagrees; (2) concentrate on interests (of others and of oneself) rather than on stated positions—the game of adopting a negotiating position, then changing positions in response to the opponent, fails to get at the real goods at stake; (3) creatively generate a range of possible solutions, and discuss them, before settling on any one option; and (4) as early as possible, seek to find objective criteria that are acceptable as guidelines for acceptable solutions; especially important are principles of fair procedures in how agreements are pursued.

As an illustration, Fisher and Ury cite the 1978 Camp David Accord between Egypt and Israel. The Accord resolved the long-running hostilities concerning the Egyptian Sinai Peninsula, which Israel had occupied since the 1967 war between the countries. After accepting President Carter's invitation to talk, the leaders of both countries came to Camp David insisting on full sovereignty over the disputed area. During the talks, however, Egypt's President Sadat and Israel's Prime Minister Begin were able to come to understand the deeper interests that lay beneath their official positions. Egypt needed its own territory returned; Israel needed its security protected against Egyptian tanks that could quickly move into Israel. Exploring a range of possible solutions, the leaders were able to reconcile their interests by returning the land to Egypt, with the stipulation that the land would be demilitarized so as to keep Egyptian tanks at a safe distance from the borders of Israel.

Compromise

Conflict resolution often requires compromises, but there are two types of compromises, or even two senses of the word *compromise*. In the negative sense, *immoral compromises* involve a betrayal of one's integrity—"selling out." In the positive sense, *reasonable compromises* are rational accommodations based on making mutual concessions. The willingness to engage in reasonable compromises is a virtue; the tendency to engage in immoral compromises is a vice. What is the difference?

Immoral compromises occur when moral principles and ideals are violated, usually in the pursuit of private gain. Reasonable compromises, by contrast, are those in which we act on moral principles and ideals. The difference becomes somewhat blurred, however, when we consider that reasonable compromises do sometimes require us to limit the overzealous ("uncompromising") pursuit of a valid ideal. The *fanatic* is a person who is unwilling to make adjustments by scaling back or placing limits on the means employed in pursuing an ideal. For example, Palestinian terrorists may be justified in pursuing freedom for their homeland, but not to the point of using terrorism to draw attention to their cause.

To further clarify the difference in the two types of compromise, note that reasonable compromises tend to arise in particular circumstances. According to Martin Benjamin, the circumstances usually involve (1) disagreement about some of the facts relevant to making decisions, (2) moral complexity, involving moral reasons that point in different directions, (3) the need for decisions to be made promptly, rather than postponed indefinitely, and (4) the desirability for the parties involved to maintain an ongoing relationship with each other.[6] The last feature is especially important in understanding what Benjamin calls *integrity-preserving compromises.* Some of the ideals we most value in relationships are mutual respect and mutual caring. In making reasonable compromises we act on these ideals about relationships in placing limits on our pursuit of other important ideals. Reasonable compromises balance, rather than "sell out," our ideals; they also preserve our integrity as persons committed to the ideals.

Reasonable compromisers have good judgment. By contrast, fanatics lack good judgment. They suffer from "tunnel vision," seeing one moral imperative as having unlimited importance while remaining insensitive to the claims of other equally valid moral principles. As a result, their one commitment reveals excess: It is pursued with misguided and intolerant zeal.

SUMMARY

Resentment (in response to an injury) and indignation (in response to a violation of a moral principle) imply a desire to right a wrong. Hatred of persons, by contrast, involves ill will and aversion and implies a desire to hurt. In the form of malicious envy, hatred implies a desire that another's good be destroyed or taken away. *Ressentiment* is self-deceiving envy and hate expressed through unconscious spite or malice. More generally, malicious hatred implies a desire to elevate oneself by bringing down the person one hates, and spiteful hatred implies a desire to bring the other person down to one's low level. By contrast, moral hatred is admirably motivated by the desire to conquer over immoral people and causes.

Envy is overcome or weakened when one of its three aspects is removed or lessened. We can overcome feelings of hate, inferiority, and impotence by strengthening our self-confidence and self-esteem, and also by developing a capacity to appreciate the talents and achievements of other people. Forgiveness is sometimes the best or only way to restore mutual respect after injuries have been suffered, but forgiveness is sometimes inappropriate.

Rational approaches to conflict resolution vary according to contextual features, such as extensively shared values within a group, the potential for violence, and whether opposing parties are willing to build on areas of shared interest despite their conflicting conceptions of the good. Reasonable compromise is an integrity-preserving accommodation in circumstances where cooperation must be preserved amidst factual uncertainty, moral complexity, and urgent decision making. Immoral compromise, by contrast, betrays moral ideals and integrity. To distinguish between reasonable and immoral compromises demands good judgment in balancing moral ideals, including the ideal of maintaining mutual respect.

DISCUSSION TOPICS

1 To covet is to desire another's possessions in some objectionable way. How is covetousness related to envy? How do you interpret the proverb "Envy destroys the good it covets"?

2 This chapter emphasized the bad aspects of envy. Based on your own experience, is this emphasis unjustified? Can you see some possible good effects of envy (such as stimulating us to compete more fiercely)?

3 In *Moralities of Everyday Life,* John Sabini and Maury Silver write:

> Consider a relationship stricken by envy. A friend joyfully shares the news of her fine achievement. The less successful friend wishes to, wants to, intends to, and indeed tries to create a sincere congratulation fitting with the excellence of her accomplishment and the warmth of their friendship. But he botches it. The congratulations come out forced, choked, diminished, and cool.[7]

Describe two possible aftermaths, one in which the envy destroys the friendship and one in which the envy is overcome and the relationship stays intact. What might lead things to develop in the one way rather than the other?

4 Apply the following passage, written by Henry Fairlie, to Salieri:

> The envious man does not love himself, although he begins with self-love. He is not grateful for, or happy in, what he is or what he has. The sin is deadly, less because it destroys him, than because it will not let him live. It will not let him live as himself, grateful for his qualities and talents, such as they are, and making the best and most rewarding use of them. His disparagement of others is a reflection of his disparagement of himself; he regards himself with as much malice as he regards them.[8]

5 Kant wrote that "the three vices which are the essence of vileness and wickedness are ingratitude, envy, and malice. When these reach their full degree they are devilish."[9] What connections do you see among these three vices? Do they perhaps share a common core? In this connection, discuss the motivations of Eric Harris and Dylan Klebold, two privileged teenagers who massacred their fellow students at Denver's Columbine High School in 1999, in part because they resented how they were snubbed by the athletes at their school whom they saw as getting unfair attention and advantages from the community.

6 Discuss the ideal, usually associated with Christianity, that we should always forgive. Should it perhaps be interpreted to mean that we should be prepared to forgive if a person repents or there are other reasons for forgiving? Or is the ideal a religious goal that transcends ordinary morality in requiring people to forgive out of love, for the sake of helping the wrongdoer? Does forgiveness sometimes hurt, rather than help, the wrongdoer?

In discussing the last question, consider how, in Eugene O'Neill's play *The Iceman Cometh,* a man finds himself hating his wife for forgiving his drunken binges with prostitutes. Her constant forgiveness made him hate himself all the more. The man remarks, "I even caught myself hating her for making me hate myself so much. There's a limit to the guilt you can feel and the forgiveness and the pity you can take! You have to begin blaming someone else, too."[10]

7 If forgiveness consists of forgoing hostile feelings, mercy consists of forgoing or reducing the punishment that is normally warranted for wrongdoing. With this distinction, can you make sense of the idea of forgiving a drunk driver, but insisting that the driver should receive no mercy in being punished?

8 Apply the Fisher–Ury approach to principled negotiation to each of the following issues that on occasion generate conflict at most campuses. In each case identify at least two opposing positions and how they might be reconciled.

   a What should be the policies—both as written and enforced—on alcohol use in campus dorms?

   b What policies should apply to inviting controversial speakers to campus and paying their fees from student tuition?

   c Should nudity be allowed in college plays?

9 Sometimes we think of compromise as a sign of weakness of will and cowardice, but that is because we forget the importance of reasonable compromises. John F. Kennedy had in mind reasonable compromises when he wrote, in *Profiles in Courage,* that "compromise need not mean cowardice. Indeed it is frequently the compromisers and conciliators who are faced with the severest tests of political courage as they oppose the extremist views of their constituents."[11] Read a recent newspaper to identify a political issue in which compromise was involved. Do you suspect the compromise was a courageous act, a cowardly "sellout," or perhaps some of both?

SUGGESTED READINGS

Benjamin, Martin. *Splitting the Difference: Compromise and Integrity in Ethics and Politics.* Lawrence: University Press of Kansas, 1990.

Cox, Gray. *The Ways of Peace.* New York: Paulist Press, 1986.

Enright, Robert D., and Joanna North (eds.). *Exploring Forgiveness.* Madison: University of Wisconsin Press, 1998.

Fairlie, Henry. *The Seven Deadly Sins Today.* Notre Dame, IN: University of Notre Dame Press, 1979.

Fisher, Roger, and William Ury. *Getting to Yes: Negotiating Agreement Without Giving In.* New York: Penguin, 1981.

Haber, Joram Graf. *Forgiveness: A Philosophical Study.* Lanham, MD: Rowman & Littlefield, 1991.

Jacoby, Susan. *Wild Justice: The Evolution of Revenge.* New York: Harper & Row, 1983.

Kant, Immanuel. "Jealousy and Its Offspring—Envy and Grudge." In L. W. Beck (ed. and trans.), *Lectures on Ethics.* New York: Harper & Row, 1963.

McFall, Lynne. "What's Wrong with Bitterness?" In Claudia Card (ed.), *Feminist Ethics.* Lawrence: University Press of Kansas, 1991.

Murphy, Jeffrie G., and Jean Hampton. *Forgiveness and Mercy.* Cambridge: Cambridge University Press, 1988.

Newman, Jay. *Fanatics and Hypocrites.* New York: Prometheus, 1986.

Nietzsche, Friedrich. *On the Genealogy of Morality.* Maudemarie Clark and Alan J. Swensen (trans.). Indianapolis, IN: Hackett Publishing, 1998.

Nozick, Robert. "Self-Esteem and Envy." In *Anarchy, State, and Utopia.* New York: Basic Books, 1974, pp. 239–246.

Rawls, John. "The Problem of Envy" and "Envy and Equality." In *A Theory of Justice.* Cambridge, MA: Harvard University Press, 1971, pp. 530–541.

Richards, Norvin, "Forgiveness." In J. Deigh (ed.), *Ethics and Personality: Essays in Moral Psychology.* Chicago: University of Chicago Press, 1992, pp. 223–243.

Sabini, John, and Maury Silver. "Envy." In *Moralities of Everyday Life.* Oxford: Oxford University Press, 1982, pp. 15–33.

Schacht, Richard (ed.). *Nietzsche, Genealogy, Morality: Essays on Nietzsche's Genealogy of Morals.* Berkeley: University of California Press, 1994.

Scheler, Max. *Ressentiment.* W. W. Holdheim (trans.). L. A. Coser (ed.). New York: Schocken, 1972.

Schoeck, Helmut. *Envy: A Theory of Social Behavior.* M. Glenny and B. Ross (trans.). London: Secker & Warburg, 1969.

Shaffer, Peter. *Amadeus.* New York: New American Library, 1984.

Shakespeare, William. *Othello.* New York: New American Library, 1963.

Solomon, Robert C. *A Passion for Justice: Emotions and the Origins of the Social Contract.* Reading, MA: Addison-Wesley, 1990.

Taylor, Gabriele. "Envy and Jealousy: Emotions and Vices." *Midwest Studies in Philosophy, Ethical Theory: Character and Virtue,* vol. 13. Notre Dame, IN: University of Notre Dame Press, 1988, pp. 233–249.

Moral Autonomy and Integrity

Self-reverence, self-knowledge, self-control,
These three alone lead life to sovereign power.[1]
Alfred Tennyson

Part six explores some of the ways in which moral integrity is undermined and supported. Moral autonomy consists in guiding our lives in light of our moral understanding and with a commitment to maintain moral integrity.

Chapter 18 pursues Kant's suggestion that the core of moral autonomy and integrity is treating ourselves with respect. That requires caring about ourselves, valuing our talents and aspirations, and seeking self-fulfillment. It also requires avoiding self-destructiveness.

Self-understanding is needed in order to appreciate our moral worth and to assess our character in light of moral standards. We can become aware of our character flaws and wrongdoing only by being honest with ourselves, which requires that we avoid self-deception about immorality, as Chapter 19 discusses.

Chapter 20 discusses self-control and its opposite—moral weakness that undermines integrity and erodes self-respect. It also discusses courage in confronting risks and dangers so as to meet our moral and personal aspirations—the kinds of moral effort and courage that enable us to maintain integrity.

CHAPTER 18

Self-Respect

Self-respect is valuing oneself in morally desirable ways. As such, it concerns the ethics of attitudes as well as the ethics of conduct. Recalling Aristotle's Doctrine of the Mean, we can understand the virtue of self-respect as the appropriate middle ground between the undervaluation of oneself and inflated self-evaluation. We will discuss masochism, self-deprecation, and irrational forms of guilt and shame as examples of undervaluing oneself. We will discuss snobbery as an example of inflated self-evaluation. First, however, we will consider the idea of responsibilities (to ourselves) to respect ourselves.

Responsibilities to Oneself

Those philosophers who draw a sharp distinction between morality and prudence have denied that there are responsibilities to oneself. Prudence, they assert, involves promoting one's own good (self-interest), whereas morality is concerned with promoting the good of others. The only moral duties concerning self-interest are negative duties—duties *not* to pursue self-interest when it hurts other people.

This separation of morality and prudence seems tempting if we are preoccupied with the human tendency toward selfishness—that is, toward excessive pursuit of self-interest at the expense of other people. Thinking along these lines, it is easy to assume that people are naturally inclined to seek their own good and that morality essentially represents a set of restrictions on that pursuit. Yet, as the examples in this chapter remind us, we do not always pursue our own good; sometimes we unjustifiably harm ourselves.

Another source of the separation between morality and prudence is a narrow conception of rights. If morality is regarded essentially as respect for others' rights, then harming oneself does not seem immoral. If we choose to harm ourselves, that is our business—and our right—as long as we do not infringe on other people's rights. Some human rights ethicists, however, have rejected this line of thought, and for good reason. They emphasize that we ought to appreciate our own moral rights and assert them responsibly so that we do not allow other people to enslave or degrade us. Implicit in this argument is the idea that we ought to have a sense of dignity because we possess human rights.

Other ethical theories embrace the idea of responsibilities to ourselves even more directly. Utilitarians stress that we ought to produce the most good for the most people, counting each person equally—including ourselves. To inflict harm on ourselves without justification is as wrong as wantonly harming other people, and for exactly the same reason. Moreover, utilitarians emphasize that many of our actions primarily affect ourselves. Because we have direct control over our own actions, we have more chances to affect our own good.

Virtue ethicists stress that good character traits are often as beneficial to ourselves as to others. This is certainly true of the virtues of courage and self-discipline, which enable us to pursue both our own good and the good of other people. Similarly, vices harm not only others but also ourselves. For example, cruelty is bad whether it is directed toward other people or toward oneself, and weakness of will damages our interests as well as those of other people.

Of all the ethicists, Kant placed the greatest emphasis on self-respect, which he understood as a blend of moral humility and a certain pride or dignity:

> Humility, on the one hand, and true, noble pride on the other, are elements of proper self-respect. . . . In the light of the law of morality, which is holy and perfect, our defects stand out with glaring distinctness, and on comparing ourselves with this standard of perfection we have sufficient cause to feel humble. But if we compare ourselves with others, there is no reason to have a low opinion of ourselves; we have a right to consider ourselves as valuable as another. This self-respect in comparison with others constitutes noble pride.[1]

By "proper self-respect" Kant meant an appreciation of our own moral worth. We demonstrate this appreciation by acting in ways appropriate to our dignity. To treat ourselves with respect requires acting in ways that express our self-worth as moral agents, that is, as persons having moral capacities and concerns. In turn, to act so as to express our moral self-worth requires striving to be moral by treating ourselves and other people as having moral worth.

This connection between self-respect and moral striving makes sense of the Kant quotation: Self-respect entails moral humility, which is the awareness of our moral flaws; yet self-respect also entails having a sense of our moral worth and dignity—"noble pride"—as beings who strive to be moral. Because it has its basis in moral striving, self-respect is closely tied to moral integrity—the coherence of a life based on moral concern. In Kant's terms, integrity requires that we (1) commit ourselves to live by correct moral principles and (2) struggle to live up to those commitments in our actions and relationships. This effort to live a morally unified life is the basis for proper self-respect.

Kant suggested that self-respect implies duties to ourselves. Consider his fundamental principle to "act so that you treat humanity, whether in your own person or in that of another, always as an end and never as a means only."[2] The basic duty to treat ourselves with respect is not a mere "hypothetical imperative" that states, "*If* you want to be happy, then don't harm yourself." Instead, it is a categorical imperative that commands without conditions attached: "Respect yourself!"

Indeed, Kant thought that duties to ourselves were even more fundamental than duties to other people:

> Far from ranking lowest in the scale of precedence, our duties towards ourselves are of primary importance and should have pride of place. . . . The prior condition of our duty to others is our duty to ourselves; we can fulfill the former only in so far as we first fulfill the latter.[3]

In particular, failure to meet our duties to ourselves to maintain our rational capacities erodes our ability to meet our duties to other people. Some glaring examples, which are discussed in other chapters, are unjustified suicide and abuse of drugs and alcohol. In this chapter we will discuss instances of harming oneself through distorted emotional attitudes toward oneself.

Valuing oneself, then, is no less morally obligatory than valuing other people. We have a responsibility to respect ourselves, just as we have responsibilities to respect other people. Let us next clarify self-respect by distinguishing it from self-esteem.

Self-Respect Versus Self-Esteem

Self-respect is often confused with self-esteem. *Self-esteem* refers to self-affirmation—feeling good about oneself, approving of and liking oneself. It is a subjective matter, and the self-affirmation might be excessive and unwarranted. Self-respect, by contrast, consists of valuing oneself for the right reasons and in morally appropriate ways, on the basis of moral integrity. It is a justified attitude. It is a virtue.

In the following passage, John Rawls, an enormously influential Kantian philosopher, equates self-respect and self-esteem:

> We may define self-respect (or self-esteem) as having two aspects. First of all . . . it includes a person's sense of his own value, his secure conviction that his conception of his good, his plan of life, is worth carrying out. And second, self-respect implies a confidence in one's ability, so far as it is within one's power, to fulfill one's intentions.[4]

In equating self-respect and self-esteem, Rawls defines them interchange-ably in terms of two positive attitudes about oneself: (1) self-affirmation, the attitude that one's life is worthwhile, and (2) self-confidence, the attitude that one has the ability to meet one's goals if given the opportunity. Note that these attitudes could be held by sadists or entirely selfish people. Such people might value their lives and be self-confident. They would then have self-esteem but not self-respect, in Kant's sense, for they would lack moral integrity, which requires one to strive to unify one's life around moral com-mitments. Our *description* of them as having self-esteem would not entail an *evaluation* of them as having the virtue of self-respect. Self-esteem is a purely psychological idea; self-respect is a moral concept.

Despite this difference, Kant might agree with Rawls's insight into the psychological importance of self-esteem and extend it to emphasize the im-portance of proper self-respect.

> When we feel that our plans are of little value, we cannot pursue them with pleasure or take delight in their execution. Nor plagued by failure and self-doubt can we continue in our endeavors. It is clear then why self-respect is a primary good [i.e., a good that every rational person desires]. Without it nothing may seem worth doing, or if some things have value for us, we lack the will to strive for them. All desire and activity becomes empty and vain, and we sink into apathy and cynicism.[5]

Thus, in Kant's view, both self-esteem and self-respect are essential in pur-suing a life of moral integrity. Both bring a sense of significance to our en-deavors and lead us to pursue them with vigor. Without them we easily become cynical about the moral contribution we have to offer, and cyni-cism can damage our relationships with other people. In this and other ways, self-respect and self-esteem are prerequisites for respecting other people. At the same time, the primary importance of self-respect remains centered on oneself: Self-respect is the recognition of one's moral worth and the accompanying disposition to act in morally appropriate ways with regard to oneself.

We can distinguish between two types of self-respect that differ accord-ing to the reasons for valuing oneself.[6] *Recognition self-respect* is valuing oneself because one has inherent moral worth, just as each and every person does. This was Kant's notion. *Appraisal self-respect* is accurately evaluating oneself according to how well one sets and meets moral standards. It con-cerns assessments of one's specific character. Hence, it can be possessed in varying degrees, depending on how fully one meets one's standards, as well as on how high one sets those standards. By contrast, recognition self-respect is not a matter of degree, but instead a simple recognition of our moral worth. This distinction parallels two types of moral attitudes toward other people: recognition of their value as persons versus evaluation of their character as better or worse.

Recognition self-respect consists of valuing oneself as having inherent moral worth, but what is that? Each of the traditional ethical theories implies an answer. Kant's duty ethics locates the worth of persons in their capacities for rational action, and in particular in their capacities (or potentials) for responding to universal principles of conduct. Plato and Aristotle's virtue ethics also link the worth of persons to their rational capacities, but stress the role those capacities play in promoting self-fulfillment (rather than in discerning universal principles of conduct). Locke's rights ethics understands the worth of persons in terms of their possession of human rights. Mill's utilitarianism implies that persons have special worth because of their capacity for happiness, which is linked to friendship, love, and other caring relationships.

In the eyes of some philosophers, these traditional accounts of the basis for self-respect seem too narrow. Each attempts to pinpoint the inherent worth of persons in one abstract feature, whether rationality, the capacity for happiness, or the possession of rights. Alternatively, Robin Dillon suggests that an adequate conception of recognition self-respect would accent the individuality of persons and our responses to persons as individuals.[7] Writing from a feminist viewpoint and influenced by Carol Gilligan, Dillon seeks to enrich the idea of recognition self-respect with the idea of caring for oneself. Traditional conceptions of self-respect, especially Kant's, seem to her emotionally impoverished. Self-respect implies caring about and for oneself in an emotionally rich way. Thus, it implies paying attention to one's needs as they are perceived on the basis of self-understanding. It also implies valuing oneself as a specific individual, in awareness of one's particular features, as well as one's general human capacities. Because we view ourselves as individuals largely in terms of our social relationships, self-respect consists of valuing oneself in relation with other persons, rather than in the abstract.

Some philosophers would go further and expand the idea of self-caring to include self-love.[8] Just as parents should love their children unconditionally, or at least unconditionally within wide limits, so we should love ourselves. Self-love does not mean mushy sentimentality and self-indulgence. It means self-affirmation based on realistic self-understanding and self-control. It is unconditional in that it remains constant and does not waver according to our merits or faults at any given time.

Whether or not we expand traditional accounts of self-respect by introducing the emotionally rich ideas of self-caring and self-love, we can agree that self-respect requires certain minimum conditions. It requires due attention to our self-fulfillment and happiness and appreciation of our inherent moral worth as persons. Even more fundamentally, just as the most blatant way to undervalue other people is to inflict undeserved harm on them, the most obvious way to undervalue oneself is to inflict undeserved harm on oneself. Here we shall consider three examples of unjustified self-harm:

masochism, self-deprecation, and excessive shame and guilt. These examples provide an interesting range: suffering intentionally inflicted on oneself, passive submission to degradation, and irrational emotional responses.

Masochism

Let us begin with a clear-cut example of self-destructiveness. Lise, in *The Brothers Karamazov*, breaks her engagement to Alyosha. She explains to him that he is too gentle and forgiving for her taste:

> I was just thinking for the thirtieth time what a good thing it is that I broke off our engagement and decided not to become your wife. You wouldn't be much of a husband, you know. . . . I want someone to marry me, tear me to pieces, betray me, and then desert me. I don't want to be happy.[9]

After Alyosha leaves, Lise

> unlocked the door, opened it a little, put her finger in the crack, and slammed the door as hard as she could. Ten seconds later she released her hand, went slowly to her chair, sat down, and looked intently at her blackened, swollen finger and the blood that was oozing out from under the nail. Her lips quivered.
>
> "I'm a vile, vile, vile, despicable creature," she whispered.[10]

As this example suggests, we should distinguish between pain and emotional responses to pain, and between suffering and the attitudes adopted toward suffering. Pain cannot be defined as something inherently unenjoyable, or suffering as something that a person dislikes. Lise both seeks and causes her pain and suffering. To that extent she enjoys it and has an affirmative attitude toward it. This partially explains why she inflicts it on herself; the deeper explanation no doubt lies in her upbringing and social conditioning, which instilled in her low self-esteem and self-respect.

Lise is a masochist. She causes and enjoys her own pain, without justification. Many a saint and marathon runner have inflicted worse harm to their bodies and found value in doing so. And whereas many of us may have enjoyed "toying" with a loose and slightly irritating tooth, this pain, although lacking justification, is very mild. In contrast, people are masochists when, like Lise, they enjoy or seek severe pain, subjugation, or degradation because of irrational motives. As with Lise, the suffering of masochists is not redeemed by some reasonable goal for which the masochistic act is the necessary means.

Why, however, cannot the enjoyment of suffering for its own sake be morally permissible, or at least not irrational? There are many acceptable diversions that need not serve some overarching reasonable goal. Why is enjoyed pain not just an entertaining, albeit bizarre, form of diversion? Occasionally it is (as with the toothache example), depending on what motivates it and what role it plays in one's life. Most often, however, self-inflicted pain constitutes an attempt to damage oneself, if not to hurt others as well. The causes of masochism are a matter for psychology to explore, but whatever the explanation, masochists usually undermine their own capacities for enriching relationships as equals among other equals. They cut themselves off from the enjoyment of more fulfilling activities. And they are typically in conflict with themselves in ways that prevent a more meaningful life.

Lise's actions, for example, are compulsive, anxiety-ridden, and damaging to her relationships with other people. Many of us, however, perhaps even most of us on occasion, display masochistic tendencies that are not related to neuroses. In addition, we frequently fail to perceive (or deceive ourselves about) our self-destructive tendencies, which may be more vague and ambiguous than Lise's clear-cut self-hatred. Some of those self-hurtful tendencies involve self-deprecation.

Self-Deprecation

Self-criticism is sometimes justified, and mild self-effacement can be an endearing quality. *Self-deprecation* refers to more systematic and destructive ways of "putting oneself down." Servility, inferiority complexes, and excessive self-sacrifice are three (of many) varieties of self-deprecation.

Servility is the attitude that one lacks moral worth, or at least lacks moral worth equal to that of others. It is the failure to endorse oneself as being worthy of the same recognition respect due to every person. One form of servility is the excessively deferential or submissive attitude known as *obsequiousness*. Obsequiousness is illustrated by the sycophant who practices excessive flattery. Another example is the fawning attempt always to please others. Still another is the willingness to do whatever one is told by people in power, no matter what the circumstances.

What repels us in these examples is not just the groveling behavior itself, but the frame of mind the behavior expresses. Often it is the motive that is distressing, as in someone's attempt to gain money or power at the expense of his or her dignity, or in the attempt to create a basis for self-worth in the prestige of others. Yet we are also disturbed by the failure of the servile person to appreciate and honor his or her own worth.

A second form of self-deprecation is an anxiety-ridden sense of inferiority, or what Alfred Adler (1870–1937) called an *inferiority complex*. This consists of more than the occasional feelings of inadequacy we all experience; it involves experiencing these feelings in excess and on inappropriate occasions, typically accompanied by crippling anxiety and depression. The person with an inferiority complex is overwhelmed by these feelings and by being unable to cope with them. Sometimes the person develops irrational coping devices, such as the tendency toward self-deprecation and expectations of mistreatment, as if these help to maintain a stable self-identity as a failure.

A third form of self-deprecation is more ambiguous morally. This is the self-deprecation of the excessive altruist. Consider a woman who, pressured by cultural stereotypes, zealously devotes herself to her husband and children to the point where she betrays her own talents and interests. The psychiatrist Theodore Isaac Rubin captures the ambivalence we feel about such a person. Reflecting on his mother, who was overflowing with "love, esteem of me, devotion and care," he remarks:

> She was never exploitative and despite deep concern for me had never been manipulative, overprotective, or in any way stifling. So I describe the perfect mother? NO: she was exasperating in her compliance to my father. . . . I suppose she exasperated him, too, in her complete abandonment of herself in favor of him. This was certainly a form of glorious martyrdom for her.[11]

There is a fine line between sacrifice for the good of others, which is admirable and leads to one's own fulfillment, and destructive forms of self-deprecation. Rubin suggests that his mother displayed both, sometimes in inextricable combinations. And although he deeply admires her and is grateful for her sacrifices, he also sees her as falling into society's trap of glorifying the altruistic wife–mother, even when it leads to self-harm. Where we draw the line between admirable altruism and degrading self-deprecation might depend primarily on the motives of the person in question. Consider the difference between a genuine care for others versus an ulterior desire for gain (such as social approval); or the need to protect oneself and one's children from a violent husband versus the fear of asserting oneself and taking risks in order to develop one's talents. Rubin saw an element of timidity in his mother's relationship with her husband. Yet the line between altruism and self-depreciation can also be crossed when one habitually underappreciates one's worth.

In addition, there is a fine line between self-deprecation and genuine humility. Humility is the virtue of not being arrogant or, more positively, of maintaining perspective on one's accomplishments and possibilities. Truly humble people avoid the excess of arrogance (conceit or excessive self-regard) without falling into the defect of undervaluing themselves or failing to appreciate their achievements. Genuinely humble individuals do not "put themselves down"; instead, they put their lives into appropriate perspective, typically on the basis of a value perspective deeper than that which conventional society, with its preoccupation with prestige and reputation, has to offer. Their concern is for truth and accurate evaluation, not with self-disparagement and devaluation. Humility can be an honest recognition of one's lesser abilities and talents, and the moral virtue of humility reflects genuine acknowledgment of one's moral imperfections. Self-depreciation, by contrast, reflects an attitude of undervaluing the worth of one's genuine achievements, of one's worthwhile interests and activities, and of one's highest aspirations and capacities. Above all, it reflects the undervaluation of one's inherent dignity as the equal in moral worth of others.

Irrational Shame and Guilt

Shame and guilt are painful, self-critical emotions that are responses to what we believe are our failures to live by our values.* As such, they are inevitable aspects of being committed to values. Often they are fully appropriate and warranted aspects of maintaining appraisal self-respect. To never feel shame would imply a brazen—a "shameless"—apathy toward ideals and standards. To never feel guilt would imply that one holds a very low set of moral standards, or that one (psychotically?) believes oneself to be morally perfect, or even that one is a callous sociopath who, by definition, has no sense of moral right and wrong. We *ought* to experience shame and guilt insofar as we are blameworthy—"ought" in the sense that these emotions are appropriate reactions to many of our failures. Yet, as we know from personal experience, shame and guilt can be self-destructive when they are excessive or when we respond to them irrationally.

Shame and guilt can be felt simultaneously toward the same object, and even have similar physiological manifestations (such as tightened muscles, constricted breathing, and lowered energy level). Yet they are distinguishable. Whereas shame is focused on personal shortcomings and failures to meet standards, guilt is focused on harm done to people. Shame is the experience of feeling lowered self-esteem and self-respect because we believe we have betrayed our ideals, standards, or sense of propriety. *Nonmoral shame* pertains to nonmoral standards, as in feeling ashamed of one's social awkwardness, poor athletic ability, bowed legs, or crooked teeth. *Moral shame* is the feeling of lowered self-respect arising from failure to meet our moral ideals. By contrast, *moral guilt* is the pain we feel because we think we have morally wronged someone, whether by insulting them, physically hurting them, violating their rights to privacy, or breaking a promise to them. (In addition to moral guilt, there is *religious* guilt, in which a theist feels guilt for violating what are believed to be God's standards. The theist presumably harms himself or herself, not God.)

Irrational shame and guilt are usually based on unreasonable beliefs about one's wrongdoing or vices, beliefs that are false or unsupported by evidence. Such beliefs reflect unwarranted evaluations of our conduct or character traits. Shame and guilt can also be irrational because of their excessive intensity or because of our unreasonable reactions to them.

A vivid example of irrational shame is given by Virginia Woolf in her short story "The New Dress." Her main character, Mabel Waring, is a

---

*The words *shame* and *guilt* are ambiguous. In the sense intended here they refer to emotions, to *feeling* guilty or ashamed. They can also refer, however, to the moral status of persons: *being* guilty for wrongdoing or *acting* in shameful ways. *Feeling* guilty or ashamed does not imply that we actually *are* guilty or shameful, because we may be entirely mistaken in believing we are at fault or have failed. Conversely, we are frequently guilty or deserving of shame for faults to which we are blind or indifferent and concerning which we do not feel guilt or shame.

forty-year-old woman who displays the emotional flip-flops characteristic of adolescence. She has spent hours with her dressmaker helping to fashion a new yellow dress that will be perfect for a party, but upon arriving at the party she collapses in self-doubt:

> Mabel had her first serious suspicion that something was wrong as she took her cloak off. . . . No! It was not right. And at once the misery which she always tried to hide, the profound dissatisfaction—the sense she had had, ever since she was a child, of being inferior to other people—set upon her, relentlessly, remorselessly, with an intensity which she could not beat off . . . for oh these men, oh these women, all were thinking—"What's Mabel wearing? What a fright she looks! What a hideous new dress!"[12]

Mabel's spiraling shame quickly extends to include her own cowardice in being so ashamed about such a trivial matter and her pettiness in devoting so much time to the dress in the first place. Her shame revives a long-standing sense of failure for having chosen a safe, dull marriage, for being a mediocre mother and wife, and for leading a "creeping, crawling life" in which she feels like a fly struggling to escape a saucer while its wings are stuck together by milk. The story ends with her fantasies about becoming a nun to escape worries about clothes and about discovering an astonishing book at the library that will radically transform her life.

As this example suggests, intense experiences of inappropriate shame (as well as guilt) provide clues to understanding what most matters to us. Shame and guilt, like most emotions, are largely involuntary and spontaneous responses. As such, they have singular importance in revealing our values, because by definition they are painful experiences of having failed to live by those values.

Thus, for example, when parents and children catch themselves being ashamed of each other's appearance or clothing, they may be shocked into awareness of how self-centered their concern for each other has become. Similarly, writers who feel deep shame over negative reviews of their work may be forced to admit how dependent they have grown on praise from critics. And the guilt that some young adults continue to feel about their sexual desires may help them to see that they are not free from the inhibitions of a puritanical upbringing.

Irrational guilt can be as self-destructive as irrational shame, but with added complications arising from the sense of having wronged another person. When feelings of guilt are warranted, it is appropriate to make amends (where possible) for the wrong done. Perhaps all that is required is a sincere apology; other times one must try to compensate for the damage done. When guilt is irrational, however, matters can become painfully complex.

Let us consider an example of guilt that initially represents a rational or warranted emotion and later moves in an irrational direction. In *The Scarlet Letter,* Nathaniel Hawthorne tells the story of the adultery of Reverend Dimmesdale and Hester Prynne that leads to Hester's pregnancy. From their perspective, a serious moral wrong has occurred, and, given that perspective, their feelings of guilt are fully warranted. Although from our perspective their judgments may seem unduly harsh, we nevertheless see a deep moral wrong in Dimmesdale's cowardly refusal to assume responsibility for his adultery. He does not marry Hester, but instead conceals his role and allows her to bear the public shame by herself.

After Dimmesdale fails in his responsibility to make amends for his wrongdoing, his guilt quickly takes an irrational turn. He tortures himself with self-loathing and self-flagellation. By the end of his life he is left without self-respect or even a clear sense of his own identity. Hawthorne, summarizing the self-destructive effect of Dimmesdale's guilt and hypocrisy, writes that

> it is the unspeakable misery of a life so false as his, that it steals the pith and substance out of whatever realities there are around us, and which were meant by Heaven to be the spirit's joy and nutriment. To the untrue man, the whole universe is false—it is impalpable—it shrinks to nothing within his grasp. And he himself, in so far as he shows himself in a false light, becomes a shadow, or, indeed ceases to exist.[13]

Only near death does Dimmesdale attain a moment of peace when he seeks Hester's forgiveness.

Hester's guilt and responses to her guilt stand in sharp contrast with Dimmesdale's. In caring for their daughter under the cruel gaze of a Puritan society, she finds a way to make amends for any wrongdoing and thereby release her feelings of guilt. Whereas Dimmesdale's suffering is pathetic and tragic, Hester's is noble. Dimmesdale cowardly refuses to admit his guilt openly; Hester courageously refuses to betray her love by revealing Dimmesdale as her lover. Dimmesdale spurns responsibility for his daughter; Hester lovingly raises her. Dimmesdale shows how the self-condemnation inherent in guilt becomes unhealthy when indulged in masochistically; Hester reminds us of the creative growth that comes with acting responsibly concerning our feelings of guilt.

Snobbery

So far we have discussed undervaluing the self, but self-evaluations can also go astray in the direction of overvaluation. Snobbery is a notable illustration. Snobbery is the attitude that one is superior in worth to people who are not members of a select group to which one belongs. One can, of course, truthfully and humbly recognize that one is superior in certain talents or achievements without being a snob. Snobbery results when one withholds recognition respect from others, when one refuses to treat them with the dignity they deserve as persons. The snob regards others as inferiors to be treated with contempt and disdain, or at best with pity and condescension. In addition, often the snob wants others to suffer—to feel inferior—on the basis of one's alleged superiority.

The grounds for snobbery can be almost anything: wealth, intellectual capacity, skill in sports or chess, or taste in clothing or fine china. Sometimes it has nothing to do with abilities or achievements but instead is based on inherited name, social standing, or club membership. Whatever its basis, snobbery is usually accompanied by arrogance. Arrogance can take one of two forms: (1) making unwarranted claims to superiority or (2) flaunting one's genuine superiority in offensive ways. The first form is objectionable because it claims an unfair basis for social esteem, the second because it threatens the self-esteem of others.

Snobbery is also frequently accompanied by hypocrisy, as when one pretends to be better than one is. Snobs thus make ready-made targets for satire aimed at ridiculing and deflating their pomposity. Even when their accomplishments are genuine, snobs exaggerate them beyond any reasonable perspective, making themselves vulnerable to the satirist's way of providing perspective. In his *Book of Snobs,* William Thackeray satirizes most major varieties of snobbism, including academic varieties. Here, for example, is his portrayal of college president Crump:

> Crump thinks Saint Boniface [College] the centre of the world, and his position as President, the highest in England. He expects the fellows and tutors to pay him the same sort of service that Cardinals pay to the Pope. I am sure Crawley would have no objection to carry his trencher [i.e., academic cap], or Page to hold up the skirts of his gown as he stalks into chapel.[14]

Allegations of snobbery can themselves be expressions of snobbery and hypocrisy! Vice President Spiro Agnew became something of a professional debunker of snobs. With bitter wit he defended President Nixon's Vietnam policies against liberal journalists, whom he derided as pretentious and hypocritical snobs. Of all his targets, however, student radicals were dealt with most viciously. The leaders of the student protest movement were, according to his famous phrase, "an effete corps of impudent snobs who characterize themselves as intellectuals."[15] As he explained, "I call them snobs for most of them disdain to mingle with the masses who work for a living. They mock the common man's pride in his work, his family and his country."[16] In retrospect, however, Agnew can be seen as a snob who set himself above honest critics of the war. Beneath his eagerness to debunk anyone who disagreed with him was hypocrisy about his own pettiness. On October 10, 1973, he was forced to resign as vice president because of charges of bribery and tax evasion during his earlier career as county executive of Baltimore County in Maryland. In that role he had awarded county engineering contracts on the basis of lucrative kickbacks. As the example of Agnew suggests, both snobs and people who are eager to call others snobs can be hypocrites.

Snobbery can involve other vices in addition to cruelty, arrogance, and hypocrisy. It may be accompanied by cowardice and disloyalty; for example, one may fear to be seen in the company of certain relatives and friends lest they lower one's social status among the "in-group" to which one belongs. It can express a lack of collegiality, as when one snubs colleagues and co-workers in order to be accepted by a small group of "superior" people. It can lead one to ignore the needs of entire groups of people from whom one turns away as part of a preoccupation with a selected social group.

SUMMARY

Morality has to do with our relationship to ourselves as well as to others. As morally concerned persons, we have the same moral worth as other people, and we owe ourselves self-respect. Recognition self-respect consists of valuing ourselves for our inherent moral worth and caring about ourselves as unique individuals. Appraisal self-respect consists of accurately valuing one's character because one sets and meets high moral standards. Both forms of self-respect differ from self-esteem: Self-esteem simply entails feeling good about oneself (for whatever reason), whereas self-respect entails appreciating one's moral worth. This appreciation is shown by one's attempts to live up to duties to oneself, such as the duty not to harm oneself without justification.

Masochism, self-deprecation, and irrational guilt and shame are examples of harm to oneself that arises from inappropriate attitudes toward oneself. Masochism involves infliction of suffering on oneself for irrational motives. Self-deprecation is the attitude that one lacks full moral worth. The attitude is manifested in many ways, such as through servility (subservience to others at the expense of one's own rights and talents), inferiority complexes, or excessive altruism. Irrational guilt is the feeling that one has wronged another person when one has not done so, and irrational shame is the unjustified feeling that one has failed to live up to appropriate standards of personal excellence.

Snobs value themselves in inappropriate ways. They feel superior to people outside their select group, whether that group is defined by intellect, tastes, wealth, social status, or any number of other things. Often, snobs are cruel in making others feel inferior. Usually, they are arrogant hypocrites who fail to have a reasonable perspective on their own achievements. Frequently, they betray relatives and former friends as they aspire to be seen only with their "in-group."

DISCUSSION TOPICS

1   Masochism is not simply a matter of causing or enjoying one's pain; there must also be an irrational motive in doing so. Often, however, there are disagreements about which motives are irrational. Decide whether any of the following may reflect—at least in some cases—examples of masochistic behavior: (1) enjoyment of pain during sex; (2) injuries to oneself sustained in dangerous sports such as hang-gliding or auto racing; (3) risks to one's health incurred through excessive amounts of work.

2 Review the examples of Lise (in *The Brothers Karamazov*), Mabel Waring (in "The New Dress"), and Theodore Isaac Rubin's mother. These examples were used to illustrate the absence of the virtue of self-respect. Do the authors' remarks about these women amount to "blaming the victims" for their lack of self-respect, especially in light of traditional society's pressure on women to be self-sacrificing? In your answer, distinguish between the assertion that a virtue is absent and assignment of blame (where blame is a negative attitude).

3 What responses to our feelings of guilt are morally appropriate? Discuss this general question in connection with the following examples and more focused questions.

 a In *The Scarlet Letter*, Dimmesdale was able to find peace from the guilt that tortured him only when he sought Hester's forgiveness. Seeking forgiveness is an act of humbling oneself by placing oneself at the mercy of another person. Why is seeking forgiveness, as in Dimmesdale's case, often a morally appropriate response to guilt? Why is a resolution not to commit similar wrongs in the future insufficient? How does guilt differ in this respect from shame, and why?

 b We saw that, before seeking Hester's forgiveness, Dimmesdale punished himself in ways that were masochistic. Is self-punishment always an unhealthy response to guilt, or can you think of instances in which some kinds of self-punishment are appropriate?

 c Sometimes we seek to relieve guilt for hurting one person by engaging in a project to help other people, perhaps at some sacrifice to ourselves. Describe situations in which this compensation is not an appropriate response to guilt. (Examples might include Dimmesdale, who ministers to others while disregarding Hester, or a thief, who tries to make amends by giving a token donation to charity but does not return the rest of the money to its owner.) Describe other situations in which helping others is an appropriate response to guilt (as might be the case for a drunk driver who killed someone and cannot seek forgiveness from the victim). What is the moral difference between the two cases?

4 Is snobbery often inevitable, as the following passage from Judith N. Shklar suggests?

> Our most genuine experiences of equality, of intimacy, and of fraternity occur only within a "clique"—that is, in an excluding group of like-minded people, modeled on that most irreducible and necessary of all societies, the family. Many groups do not have exclusion as their main object, and some are hardly aware of it; but whatever their real ends may be, they exclude by including selectively. Snobbery is the by-product of this multiplicity, and it is a personal price that must occasionally be paid for the sake of freedom. Not all doors are or can be open.[17]

5 Thomas E. Hill suggests that "snobs, in a sense, undervalue themselves as well as others" by basing their "self-respect on an unstable ground."[18] By "unstable ground" he refers to things that may not be lasting, such as achievements, talents, reputation, or social class, rather than what we have called recognition self-respect. Is he right? Can inflated self-esteem be a sign of too little self-respect?

6 Moral snobbery—that is, snobbery in moral matters—is the devaluation of others because they are not as morally admirable as oneself. It is shown in the arrogant self-righteousness of persons who are excessively preoccupied with their own characters. Do you see a special danger of moral snobbery in the adoption of a virtue ethics perspective? Or is moral snobbery a potential risk in all moral self-appraisal? In your answer, discuss the difference between (a) concern to do a virtuous (honest, kind, generous) act, (b) concern to become a virtuous person, and (c) preoccupation with embellishing one's character so as to gain praise.

7 To betray another person is to violate a trust that is based on one's commitments or responsibilities to that person. What does it mean to betray oneself? Connect this idea with the idea of responsibilities to oneself to maintain one's integrity and self-respect.

8 In *Hamlet* (act 1, scene 3), Polonius gives the following advice to his son Laertes. What do you think Polonius meant, and is he right?

> This above all: to thine own self be true; And it must follow, as the night the day, Thou canst not then be false to any man.

9 Depression has been called one of the worst afflictions of the twentieth century. It is the emotional state in which we experience a sweeping loss of our responsiveness to values, and also a loss of self-confidence, self-esteem, and self-respect, so that our lives seem dull, boring, and hopeless. Is depression an emotional form of masochism? Consider both the tendency to frequent depression and individual episodes of depression. In doing so, respond to Robert Solomon's apparently positive view of (at least some) episodes of depression as expressed in the following passage:

> Our depression is our way of wrenching ourselves from the established values of our world, the tasks in which we have been unquestioningly immersed, the opinions we have uncritically nursed, the relationships we have accepted without challenge and often without meaning. A depression is a self-imposed purge. It is the beginning of self-realization, unless it is simply ignored, or drugged away, or allows itself to give in to the demands for its own avoidance—the most extreme of which is suicide.[19]

SUGGESTED READINGS

Bailey, F. G. *The Kingdom of Individuals: An Essay on Self-Respect and Social Obligation.* Ithaca, NY: Cornell University Press, 1993.

Benson, Jann, and Dan Lyons. *Strutting and Fretting: Standards for Self-Esteem.* Niwot: University Press of Colorado, 1991.

Darwall, Stephen L. "Two Kinds of Respect." *Ethics,* vol. 88 (1977).

Deigh, John. "Shame and Self-Esteem: A Critique." In John Deigh (ed.), *Ethics and Personality: Essays in Moral Psychology.* Chicago: University of Chicago Press, 1992.

Dillon, Robin S. (ed.). *Dignity, Character, and Self-Respect.* New York: Routledge, 1995.

Dillon, Robin S. "How To Lose Your Self-Respect." *American Philosophical Quarterly,* vol. 29 (1992).

Gilbert, Paul, and Bernice Andrews (eds.). *Shame: Interpersonal Behavior, Psychopathology, and Culture.* New York: Oxford University Press, 1998.

Goldstein, Irwin. "Pain and Masochism." *Journal of Value Inquiry,* vol. 17 (1983).

Greenspan, P. S. *Practical Guilt: Moral Dilemmas, Emotions, and Social Norms.* New York: Oxford University Press, 1995.

Hill, Thomas. "Servility and Self-Respect," "Self-Respect Reconsidered," and "Social Snobbery and Human Dignity." In *Autonomy and Self-Respect*. New York: Cambridge University Press, 1991.

Jones, Hardy. "Treating Oneself Wrongly." *Journal of Value Inquiry*, vol. 17 (1983).

Kant, Immanuel. "Proper Self-Respect" and "Duties to Oneself." In *Lectures on Ethics*. Trans. Louis Infield. New York: Harper & Row, 1963.

Lynd, Helen Merrill. *On Shame and the Search for Identity*. New York: Harcourt, Brace & World, 1958.

Martin, Mike W. "Depression: Illness, Insight, and Identity," *Philosophy, Psychiatry, and Psychology*, forthcoming.

Morris, Herbert (ed.). *Guilt and Shame*. Belmont, CA: Wadsworth Publishing Co., 1971.

Morris, Herbert. *On Guilt and Innocence: Essays in Legal Philosophy and Moral Psychology*. Berkeley: University of California Press, 1976.

Rawls, John. *A Theory of Justice*. Cambridge, MA: Harvard University Press, 1971.

Shklar, Judith N. "What Is Wrong with Snobbery?" In *Ordinary Vices*. Cambridge, MA: Harvard University Press, 1984, pp. 87–137.

Solomon, Robert. *The Passions*. Notre Dame, IN: University of Notre Dame Press, 1983.

Stocker, Michael, with Elizabeth Hegeman. *Valuing Emotions*. New York: Cambridge University Press, 1996.

Swann, William B. *Self-Traps: The Elusive Quest for Higher Self-Esteem*. New York: W. H. Freeman, 1996.

Taylor, Gabriele. *Pride, Shame, and Guilt: Emotions of Self-Assessment*. Oxford: Clarendon Press, 1985.

Taylor, Richard. "The Virtue of Pride." In *Ethics, Faith, and Reason*. Englewood Cliffs, NJ: Prentice-Hall, 1985, pp. 98–106.

Thackeray, William M. *The Book of Snobs*. In W. P. Trent and J. B. Henneman (eds.), *The Complete Works of William M. Thackeray*. Vol. XIV. New York: Thomas Y. Crowell [undated], pp. 1–240.

Warren, Virginia. "Explaining Masochism." *Journal for the Theory of Social Behaviour*. (1985).

Williams, Bernard. *Shame and Necessity*. Berkeley: University of California Press, 1993.

CHAPTER 19

Self-Knowledge
and Self-Deception

The virtue of self-respect consists of valuing oneself as a moral self, that is, as someone who has inherent moral worth and as someone who is responsive to moral reasons and ideals. Recall that self-respect is not reducible to self-esteem (in the sense of feeling good about oneself), because that feeling can be based on illusions about oneself. Self-respect demands of us a high degree of honesty with ourselves, which, in turn, requires that we avoid or overcome self-deception about our wrongdoing and character faults.

Self-deception about wrongdoing can undermine the basis for our self-respect by corrupting our integrity. At the same time, an interest in preserving self-esteem sometimes motivates self-deception: The desire for a high estimate of ourselves can prompt us to deceive ourselves. These connections among self-respect, self-esteem, and self-deception about immorality will be explored in this chapter.

Self-Knowledge

"Know Thyself!" This injunction, which was inscribed in stone at the Temple of Apollo at Delphi, was central to Socrates' quest for self-understanding. Socrates viewed self-understanding as the core of wisdom—the highest virtue, which makes possible the other cardinal virtues of courage, temperance, and justice. What is self-knowledge?

Self-knowledge involves both specific information about ourselves as individuals and more general information about human nature. Let us say that having this information consists of *knowing that* certain facts are true. But which facts? Surely we do not need to know the number of hairs on our heads or the latest predictions for our lives from the newspaper's astrology column. The kind of knowledge sought by Socrates had vital significance for living a good life. That means that the knowledge must be relevant and important to how we live; it also means that the knowledge must be active in motivating our conduct. Let us say this practical knowledge consists of *knowing how* to live in a manner that both leads to self-fulfillment and enables us to meet our responsibilities and contribute to the lives of others.

What does this practical knowledge involve? To begin with, it implies that we know what we want. What are our strongest desires, how can they fit together so as to be expressed coherently, and what is the relative importance of each? As the last question suggests, self-knowledge is not a mere grasp of fact; it requires interpretation of facts in light of values that specify the relative importance of our desires. Self-knowledge, then, requires knowledge of the values and ideals that give life meaning. Self-knowledge is value-laden: It is permeated by the values we use to interpret our lives.

Self-knowledge involves value-laden understanding of many other aspects of our lives besides our desires. It implies an understanding of our emotions, habits, personal relationships, and the wider ties to communities that add meaning to our lives. It implies an imaginative grasp of the possibilities that are open to us, as well as a realistic sense of our limitations. And it implies an understanding of our strengths, weaknesses, and faults. Self-deception arises in all these areas, but especially in connection with our faults.

Self-Deceiving Tactics

To deceive others is to purposefully mislead them, usually by concealing some truth from them. This can be accomplished by keeping them ignorant about a topic, leading them to believe something false, diverting their attention from an important matter, or distorting their attitudes and emotions. Similarly, to *deceive oneself* is purposefully to mislead oneself, usually by avoiding an unpleasant truth or a painful topic. It can be accomplished by keeping oneself ignorant about a topic, persuading oneself to believe something false, refusing to pay attention to an important matter, or distorting one's attitudes and emotions.

An example will help clarify what self-deception is and how we engage in it. In *The Death of Ivan Illych,* Leo Tolstoy describes a man who is forced to become aware that he has a terminal illness. In the days before his death, Ivan Ilych reflects honestly for the first time on the meaning of his life. He concludes that he had been living a lie. His life had been pleasant enough, but it was based entirely on a desire for his own comfort, social acceptance, and power. This selfishness had corrupted his relationships with his family and colleagues, and, as he painfully admits to himself, it was accompanied by self-deception concerning the deeper values of love, friendship, and community that should have guided him. He now feels alienated from his past—as if he had lived someone else's life, not his own authentic life.

How did he deceive himself? Consider these familiar psychological tactics. He *refused to reflect* on his deeper responsibilities, often stifling his impulses to stand up for values that were being trampled on at his job. No doubt he also *rationalized*—that is, reasoned in a biased way—that, since most people were comfortable with their failures to pursue higher values, it was acceptable for him to do so as well. He succeeded in *compartmentalizing* his life into separate channels, ignoring the moral implications that each of these aspects of his life had for the others. Thus, he managed to neglect his family in the midst of his preoccupation with social climbing. He also managed to keep himself ignorant—*willfully ignorant*—of much detailed information about his family's needs that might provoke him into doing something he would rather not do, such as pay greater attention to them.

Equally important in self-deception is our manipulation of our attention and emotions concerning what we already do know. For example, Ilych knew he would someday die, just like everyone else, but he refused to think about death and what it meant for how a life should be lived. He *selectively ignored* unpleasant facts and engaged in *emotional detachment* from unpleasant realities, such as occasional doubts, depression, and guilt feelings, that signaled something was amiss. Finally, in addition to all these tactics he undoubtedly *accepted social reinforcement* from his circle of friends and acquaintances, who were doing the same thing. A peer group in which most others act like oneself serves as a hall of distorting mirrors that reinforce self-deception.

These self-deceiving tactics are quite familiar. All of us have sometimes avoided acknowledging information that we suspected would be unpleasant to confront head-on. We are all aware of the various evasion tactics: We willfully ignore, selectively attend, become detached emotionally, manipulate our emotions so as to avoid acting, compartmentalize our lives, allow our biases to shape rationalized belief and attitudes, and acquiesce to peers who mold our opinions and self-images in comforting ways. No one of these tactics by itself constitutes self-deception, but they often serve as ways to evade painful realities.

Paradoxes

Even though these ways of deceiving ourselves are familiar, the idea of deceiving oneself has proven puzzling to some philosophers. They have argued that the idea is paradoxical—not just in the literary sense of paradoxes as mere seeming absurdities (which upon deeper understanding are perfectly coherent), but in the sense of paradoxes as contradictions. To actually deceive oneself, they argue, is an impossibility, especially in the sense of telling oneself a lie and coming to believe it.

In a situation in which one person deceives another, there is a deceiver, who is aware of a truth, and a deceived, who is not aware of it (and who is prevented from becoming aware of it by the lie). For example, consider an employee who lies to his employer about his alcoholism, and suppose that the employer is, in fact, deceived by the lie. The employee is fully aware that he is an alcoholic: He believes it, he knows it, and he is fully conscious of it (that is, he can and does attend to the fact that he is an alcoholic). The employer, by contrast, is not aware that the employee is an alcoholic: She does not believe it, she does not know it, and she is not conscious of it.

When we try to imagine the alcoholic lying to himself, we must, it seems, imagine him functioning simultaneously as the deceiver and as the victim of the deception. That seems impossible for three reasons. First, the person would have to believe and not believe the same thing at the same time. Second, the person would have to know and not know the truth at the same time. Third—and most puzzling—the person would have to use awareness of the truth as part of the process of hiding the truth from another person. In lying to the employer, both the content of the lie ("I am not abusing alcohol") and the way the lie is told (with apparent conviction) are guided by awareness of the truth. How, by contrast, could the alcoholic use awareness of the truth in pursuing his intention to deceive himself? It seems the alcoholic would have to maintain an awareness of the truth even while trying to block that awareness, thereby making the attempted deception self-defeating.

These three paradoxes all stem from the attempt to interpret self-deception on the model of a lie; but why should that model be accepted? After all, "deceiving" and "lying" are not synonymous terms, as we noted in Chapter 2. A lie is a false statement told with the intention to deceive. If, however, the lie is not believed, no deception occurs. Hence, there can be lies without deception. Conversely, there can be deception without lies. To deceive is to intentionally mislead someone into holding a false belief or into being ignorant. Such deception can be achieved without lying, perhaps by saying nothing in a situation in which the truth should be spoken or by engaging in pretense (using "body language").

The expression "lying to oneself" is a metaphor that, if taken too literally, leads to the three paradoxes. The concept of "deceiving oneself," however, is meaningful and nonparadoxical even when taken literally to mean purposefully misleading oneself. It need not involve full awareness of the truth at any time. Most often, the self-deceiver has only a suspicion that something might be true, or perhaps an intimation that an entire topic might prove deeply troubling if examined closely. This is illustrated by Ivan Ilych, who refused to reflect about death because he suspected it might lead him to make unwanted changes in how he was living. Similarly, alcoholics might deceive themselves by refusing to reflect fully and honestly (without bias) about a pattern of drinking and its effects on their lives.

These suspicions may involve fleeting moments of consciousness of the truth or just a vague, peripheral awareness that something may be amiss in certain areas of our lives. Moreover, if we engaged in honest reflection, we could in many cases obtain a clearer and fuller awareness. As self-deceivers, we avoid precisely this kind of honest self-scrutiny, for it threatens to reveal disturbing truths or topics that we are deliberately avoiding.

If Sigmund Freud was correct, there are additional forms of self-deception in which self-scrutiny by itself may be insufficient to bring truths to consciousness.[1] He postulated that there are psychological "defense mechanisms" that block truths from our awareness and that themselves operate (in the unconscious part of the ego) without our consciousness of them. We cannot become conscious of the mechanisms or the truths they conceal without (in most cases) the special help of psychoanalysts or other types of psychotherapists. One such defense mechanism, for example, is *repression,* the process by which ideas are blocked from being accessible to our attention. Repression operates unconsciously, unlike the act of *suppression,* in which we consciously avoid attending to something ("I must stop worrying about that exam and get my mind back on my work"). Another example is *projection,* in which people unconsciously ascribe their problems, hostility, or other attitudes to other people (often in modified forms). Thus, paranoid people who irrationally think everyone is out to get them are unconsciously ascribing both their own fears and their feelings of aggression to other people with whom they come in contact. Other defense mechanisms include *denial* (refusing to recognize an unpleasant reality by engaging in wish-fulfilling fantasies or conduct), *regression* (reverting to an infantile mode of behavior), and *reaction formations* (transforming an attitude into an excessive version of its opposite; for example, transforming hatred into effusive affection or resentment into servility).

Responsibility

Self-deception proceeds without our full awareness of either what we are deceived about or the act of deceiving ourselves. We ignore things, for example, without attending to the fact that we are ignoring them, or rationalize without admitting that we are rationalizing. Self-deception may also involve the unconscious process Freud described. Does this absence of full awareness mean that we are not responsible for any harm that may be attributable to our deception? Is self-deception an excuse, or partial excuse, for immorality?

Herbert Fingarette, in his book *Self-Deception,* suggests that self-deceivers' moral responsibilities are, at best, ambiguous. Usually, people are deemed responsible for their conduct on the basis of two conditions: First, they were aware or able to become aware of what they were doing; second, they acted voluntarily—that is, without coercion and without uncontrollable inner compulsions. Self-deceivers, by contrast, because they lose full awareness of what they are doing, are less able to fully control their actions.

Fingarette writes:

> There is thus in self-deception a genuine subversion of personal agency and, for this reason in turn, a subversion of moral capacity. The sensitive and thoughtful observer, when viewing the matter this way, is inclined not to hold the self-deceiver responsible but to view him as a "victim."[2]

In Fingarette's view, self-deception is a morally puzzling state about which it is impossible to make our usual moral judgments. Self-deceivers are not clearly acting voluntarily, because they are not fully aware of what they are doing. Nor are they clearly acting involuntarily—they are, after all, the source of their own deception. Should we accept Fingarette's view?

Fingarette was especially interested in neurotic forms of self-deception in which mental illness is involved. Neurotic persons are often handicapped in the attempt to gain full awareness of their self-deception and then to use their self-understanding to help control their actions. They may need the help of a psychotherapist, or sometimes just a supportive friend, in order to confront the truths they are avoiding. Fingarette's perspective on self-deception is not convincing, however, with respect to the many individuals who are able to become conscious of their self-deceiving activities and the truths they are evading. Certainly mere ignorance and lack of consciousness · are not automatically excuses for immorality. We are each responsible for knowing what our obligations are and for obtaining information relevant to meeting them. Our blindness to those obligations and facts does not automatically cancel or diminish moral accountability.

In fact, when the obligations involved are especially important, self-deception in the sense of willful ignorance about those obligations is itself immoral. In such cases, persons may be at fault for two reasons: (1) because of the wrongdoing they engage in and (2) because they deceive themselves about the wrongdoing in order to proceed without a troubled conscience. Joseph Butler (1692–1752) made this point. Self-deception about wrongdoing and character faults, he wrote,

> is essentially in its own nature vicious [that is, a vice] and immoral. It is unfairness; it is dishonesty; it is falseness of heart: and is therefore so far from extenuating guilt, that it is itself the greatest of all guilt in proportion to the degree it prevails; for it is a corruption of the whole moral character in its principle.[3]

Butler's expression "moral character in its principle" refers to conscience, to our sense of right and wrong. Self-deception about immorality corrupts conscience by preventing it from properly guiding conduct and character development.

Furthermore, Butler said that self-deception about immorality represents unfairness and hypocrisy. It is unfairness in that it involves cheating on our own moral standards. We gain undeserved advantages through wrongdoing and through an unwarranted view of our own character. Self-deception about immorality is "inner hypocrisy"—hypocrisy before ourselves—in that we appear better in our own eyes than we really are. Our unjustified self-esteem is bolstered by false beliefs about our conduct and character.

Self-Respect, Self-Esteem, and Immorality

Now that we have clarified the nature of and responsibility for self-deception, let us draw together the connections between self-respect, self-esteem, and self-deception about immorality. First, self-respect is based on self-understanding and on an appreciation of our true character and moral worth. Whereas mere self-esteem (a favorable view of ourselves) is often based on illusions or self-deceptions, self-respect requires that we value ourselves as morally concerned persons whose characters are based on moral commitments. Accordingly, self-respect is eroded when self-deception grossly distorts our understanding of our character. Thus, whatever positive feelings of self-esteem may accrue from self-deception about our wrongdoing, that self-esteem is not the same as genuine self-respect based on moral self-understanding.

Second, the desire to retain a sense of self-respect and self-esteem is a major motive for self-deception. We deceive ourselves about our wrongdoing and character flaws in order to avoid the pain that results from acknowledging those faults to ourselves, as well as to avoid the burden of having to alter them. We would have little reason to deceive ourselves if we were sociopaths who lacked all moral concern.

Third, a desire to maintain a sense of self-respect also motivates us to avoid acknowledging our own self-deceptions. We like to think of ourselves as having the courage to willingly face the truth, not as having the cowardice and hypocrisy implied in evading it. Of course, many other motives generate or support self-deception, including fear, laziness, envy, a desire for self-esteem, and so on. Perhaps no motive is stronger or more common, however, than the desire to sustain an attitude of self-respect. Thus, in everyday life we employ an array of devices for bolstering an unjustifiably high estimate of our own characters and the sense of self-respect based on it. Two centuries ago Samuel Johnson (1709–1784) identified several of these devices:

1   We selectively emphasize our occasional good deeds, eagerly treating one isolated act as if it were a habit constituting a virtuous character trait: "A miser who once relieved a friend from the danger of a prison, suffers his imagination to dwell for ever upon his own heroic generosity; he yields his heart up to indignation at those who are blind to merit, or insensible to misery . . . and though his whole life is a course of rapacity and avarice, he concludes himself to be tender and liberal, because he has once performed an act of liberality and tenderness."[4]

2   We dismiss our wrongdoing as uncharacteristic lapses or else as flaws belonging to everyone. Nights of debauchery, Johnson notes, are easily excused by noting that even great people have similar lapses. Such lapses, we tell ourselves, do not detract from our essential goodness.

3 We confuse "lip service" to virtue with the real thing: "There are men who always confound the praise of goodness with the practice, and who believe themselves mild and moderate, charitable and faithful, because they have exerted their eloquence in commendation of mildness, fidelity, and other virtues."[5]

4 We tend to focus our attention on the worst deeds of other people as a way to downplay our faults. To dwell on the worst faults of our acquaintances, or attend to the vicious deeds of criminals reported in the daily newspaper, brings a comforting sense of our superior virtue.

5 We choose friends who share our vices, and we eagerly listen to the words of flatterers. This reinforces our vices and enables us to avoid that serious self-reflection that Johnson calls "communion with our own hearts."

A fourth connection between self-respect and self-deception concerns overcoming self-deception about our faults. We must honestly acknowledge our lack of moral commitment before we can reclaim our self-respect. Initially, this acknowledgment diminishes our feelings of self-respect, assuming we are morally concerned. Within limits, this is as it should be, for at such times we feel guilt both for the wrongdoing concealed by the self-deception and for having deceived ourselves about it. There may sometimes be a sense of self-disillusionment, as with Ivan Ilych, who eventually sees through his own lies. Yet remorse and diminished feelings of self-respect can prepare the way for a renewed and stronger basis for self-respect. Genuine remorse should prompt a resolve to try to make some form of amends and to avoid similar self-deceptions in the future.

Fifth, even if we persist in self-deception about our faults, we may still experience diminished self-respect because of a haunting sense of our "inner dishonesty." Just as we can have a suspicion of the truths we are evading, we can have a sense that we are evading the truth—that we are not being fully honest with ourselves in acknowledging truths important to our lives. In severe cases of habitual self-deception, the consequences can be worse than mere anxiety, as Fyodor Dostoevsky (1821–1881) suggested in his novel *The Brothers Karamazov:*

> Above all, don't lie to yourself. The man who lies to himself and listens to his own lie comes to such a point that he cannot distinguish the truth within him, or around him, and so loses all respect for himself and for others. And having no respect he ceases to love. And in order to distract himself without love he gives way to passions and coarse pleasures and sinks to bestiality in his vices—all this from continual lying to other men and to himself.[6]

Sixth, some self-deception is damaging to our own talents, happiness, and self-development in ways that undermine self-esteem and sometimes self-respect. For example, self-deception can be used to conceal the motives and significance of tendencies to belittle ourselves—to "put ourselves down" with irrational condemnations. Painful feelings of inferiority can be generated in part by applying self-deceivingly unrealistic standards to ourselves. Many of the examples of masochism and servility discussed in the previous chapter involved self-deception of this sort. In such cases, self-deception conceals our capacities for goodness.

Here is a further example of how, through self-deception, we can hurt ourselves more than anyone else by weakening our appreciation of our own talents and possibilities. In her autobiography *From Housewife to Heretic*, Sonia Johnson describes her struggle to escape submissiveness to a male-dominated culture and servility toward a patriarchal religion. She writes, "I was a person who had unconsciously known for a very long time that something was wrong with patriarchy, but because my entire culture, to say nothing of my church, was based upon it almost as given, I hadn't had the courage to face what I knew."[7]

For the most part, she made innumerable accommodations and sacrifices that undermined her own opportunities and talents. These included the familiar one-sided burden of household chores and responsibility for her four children; the assumption that she was responsible for caring for her husband without comparable reciprocity; an automatic and largely uncritical dependence on the views of her husband and the male leadership of her church; indulgence not only of her husband's childish habit of emotional withdrawal when problems arose, but also of his frequent absences from home for work-related reasons (especially when he had the option *not* to go on business trips); and a blind trust in her husband of twenty years to the point where she was an easy dupe when he connived a plot to divorce her in a way that minimized his legal responsibilities—the act that finally shocked her into sustained self-reflection.

In retrospect, Johnson was able to see that her primary tactic of evading the truth about her submissiveness was a systematic suppression of her emotions:

> I was living a sort of half life, in half light, a grayish, half-awake limbo of neither clouds nor sunlight, a gray same numbness. . . . I accomplished this great reductionist feat by lowering the threshold of my awareness, allowing very little stimuli into my consciousness for fear of inadvertently letting in the scary things. At the same time, I unconsciously dulled my perception of the stimuli I did choose so that I would not see clearly what I did not want to see, would not feel what I did not want to feel, would not have to face what I feared to face.[8]

Suppression of so many of her own emotions, ideas, attitudes, and needs prevented her from emerging as fully authentic through fidelity to her own talents and aspirations.

Seventh, and finally, it should be pointed out that self-deception may in some situations be beneficial and supportive of self-esteem and self-respect. It sometimes can actually aid our personal growth and the development of our talents without harmful side effects. A familiar example is overcoming the fear of public speaking. Even without self-deception, if one ignores such stage fright by pretending not to be afraid, one can cultivate self-confidence and thereby strengthen one's speaking ability. Deceiving oneself into believing one is a better speaker than in fact one is may yield similar results. Likewise, an athlete might "psych up" for a race by engaging in a bit of innocent self-deception about her or his abilities to win.

Indeed, we frequently approach difficult tasks by self-deceivingly magnifying our abilities to succeed or minimizing the difficulties ahead. Such self-deception enables us at least to try things we otherwise might turn away from in discouragement. Undoubtedly, some distinctively moral commitments can be strengthened in this way as well. Many parents engage in some useful self-deception to help sustain their efforts in caring for their children—self-deception about the difficulties involved in raising children, for example.

Perhaps such forms of self-deception are not entirely rational in the sense of showing a full devotion to truth. Perhaps it would be more rational to proceed on the basis of hope and faith that did not involve self-deception. Certainly, habitual self-deception threatens to undermine the standards of rationality that are essential to living up to moral and other values—standards such as respect for evidence, concern for consistency, impartiality, clarity of thought, rigor of argument, and so on. Nevertheless, when isolated instances of self-deception do not contribute to general habits of irrationality, and when they are beneficial rather than harmful, it seems the element of irrationality (evasion of the truth) might be outweighed by other values.

SUMMARY

Self-deception is the evasion of painful truths or topics, whether specific or general. It is typically a refusal to acknowledge truths to ourselves, whether through ignoring something we suspect is true, avoiding inquiry into disturbing topics, engaging in rationalization (biased reasoning), emotionally detaching ourselves from difficult situations, conveniently acquiescing to social pressures, or using other tactics. These tactics are employed without attending to them with full consciousness. Understood in this way, self-deception does not involve paradox or self-contradiction.

Some self-deception may be beneficial, as it may contribute to personal development without having bad side effects. Self-deception is immoral, as Joseph Butler suggested, when it conceals wrongdoing, character faults, or facts we need to meet our obligations. In that context, our self-deception prohibits us from honestly confronting the morally harmful aspects of our lives. As such, the self-deception is a kind of derivative wrong; its badness derives from its support of other wrongdoing. In addition, apart from being a form of dishonesty about the truth, it reflects an "inner hypocrisy," that is, a propensity to think better of ourselves than is warranted by our character.

Insofar as we can refrain from or overcome self-deception about immorality, we are responsible for both the immorality of our actions and the self-deception. The extent to which we are blameworthy depends on the answers to several questions: How serious is the immorality about which we deceive ourselves? Are we aware of being in a situation where self-deception threatens to do harm? How much control do we have over the self-deception, and are we capable of facing the truth? Is there mental illness involved that weakens our capacity to confront the truth, and if so, is there help available that we can be expected to take advantage of? As these questions suggest, responsibility for self-deception mirrors the complexity of morality in general.

Self-deception is related to self-respect (proper appreciation of our moral worth) and self-esteem (a favorable view of ourselves) in a number of ways. First, because self-respect consists of an accurate appreciation of our moral worth, based on self-understanding, self-deception about our faults undermines self-respect. Second, one major motive for self-deception is the desire to maintain a high opinion of our own characters. Third, the desire to sustain self-esteem and a sense of self-respect motivates us to avoid acknowledging that we are self-deceivers, because the recognition of our cowardly evasions of truth is not flattering. Fourth, overcoming self-deception can bring a temporary deflation of self-esteem and self-respect, even as subsequent remorse and efforts to make amends can strengthen them. Fifth, habitual self-respect sometimes creates a nagging sense that we are not being honest with ourselves—a sense that weakens self-respect. Sixth, some self-deception damages self-development and the basis for self-esteem. Finally, some self-deception (as in the public speaking example) can contribute to self-development and can strengthen self-esteem.

DISCUSSION TOPICS

1   Suppose someone argued that the idea of "teaching oneself" is confused and self-contradictory because a person would have to know (as teacher) what he or she does not know (as learner). Respond to this argument, and in doing so compare and contrast what is involved in teaching oneself and in deceiving oneself.

2   Discuss the role played by self-deception in avoiding complete honesty regarding plagiarism and cheating in tests. In addition to rationalization, discuss the possible roles of other self-deceiving tactics such as refusal to reflect, selective attention, compartmentalization, willful ignorance (about the harm to other students), emotional detachment, acquiescence to social pressure, and so on.

3   Kant believed that all self-deceptions, or what he called "inner lies," are immoral because they violate our duty to be truthful with ourselves: "By a lie a man makes himself contemptible—by an outer lie, in the eyes of others; by an inner lie, in his own eyes, which is still worse—and violates the dignity of humanity in his own person."[9] In addition to finding it inherently objectionable, Kant be-

lieved that "the evil of deceitfulness spreads into man's relations with other men, when once the principle of truthfulness has been violated." How might an act-utilitarian and a rule-utilitarian reply to Kant's unqualified condemnation of self-deception?

Focus your answer by discussing whether you think self-deception is wrong or morally permissible in the following cases. If you are unsure, what further information would you need in order to make a decision about the case?

Case 1. A friend of yours is having trouble with her courses. It is clear to you that the reason is a deep lack of interest in the major selected by the student, and that, indeed, the "selection" was made primarily by the student's parents. The student has deceived herself into thinking that the problem is with the poor professors who fail to make the subject matter exciting.

Case 2. A player on the varsity basketball team is good, but not sufficiently talented to become a professional player after college. The player has deceived himself into thinking otherwise: that a lucrative profession is ahead if only he does his personal best. In fact, the self-deception actually improves the student's performance on the court, evoking the student's best efforts, and serving as a (partially) self-fulfilling prophesy that he will succeed. The deception also leads the student to focus his energies on his basketball practice and to minimize the time spent on classwork.

Case 3. A parent is diagnosed with a form of cancer for which physicians can offer little hope for a cure. The parent and the rest of the family deceive themselves into thinking the chances of a cure are high.

4 We suggested that self-deception can be permissible, benign, and even beneficial; but could it ever be morally obligatory? Jack Meiland offers the following two examples of when he thinks self-deception is obligatory. Do you agree with his view?

Case 1. "Suppose that Jones and Smith have been business partners and exceptionally close friends for more than thirty-five years. One day Jones discovers a discrepancy in the business's accounts. Upon investigation, he comes into the possession of sufficient evidence to justify the belief that Smith has been secretly siphoning off money from the business. Now Jones is in the following predicament. He is, and knows he is, the type of person who is unable to conceal his feelings and beliefs from others. He thus knows that if he decides that Smith has indeed been stealing money from the firm, it will definitely affect his behavior toward Smith. Even if Jones tries to conceal his belief, he knows that he will inevitably act in a remote, cold, censorious, and captious manner toward Smith, and that eventually both the friendship and the business partnership will break up. Jones decides that this price is too high and therefore decides not to believe that Smith stole money from the firm. In fact, he goes farther: he decides that Smith did not steal money from the firm."

Case 2. "Take the classical case in which a wife finds a blonde hair on her husband's coat, a handkerchief with lipstick on it in his pocket, a scrap of paper with a phone number scrawled on it, and so on, until everyone would agree that the evidence is sufficient that the husband has been seeing another woman. However, the wife believes that their marriage is basically sound and can weather this storm. Like Jones, she knows that she cannot conceal her suspicions and hence decides to believe that her husband is not being unfaithful to her."[10]

In defending your agreement or disagreement with Meiland, consider two possibilities: (1) Things turn out as hoped for—that is, Smith stops stealing and the friendship remains intact; and the husband stops having affairs and the marriage grows stronger than ever. (This is the situation Meiland had in mind.) (2) It is not known what consequences are likely to result from the self-deception.

5 When we accuse someone of self-deception, we usually mean they (1) hold a false belief or are ignorant of something they should have known (given the evidence available) and (2) purposefully avoid the truth. What should be said about the use of the concept of self-deception to criticize people's religious beliefs, which are based on faith?

In *The Future of an Illusion,* for example, Freud criticized theists (people who believe in God) for engaging in self-deceptive forms of wishful thinking (that is, believing what makes them happy). Jean-Paul Sartre made similar sweeping criticisms of theists, as did Karl Marx when he portrayed religion as "the opiate of the people."

Many theologians and ministers have made the opposite charge: Atheists are guilty of evading the recognition of God's existence. For example, the Protestant theologian Reinhold Niebuhr stated that rejection of belief in God is a sin of pride that bases human concerns above God. He traced this "sin" to willful dishonesty and self-deception: "Man loves himself inordinately. Since his determinate existence does not deserve the devotion lavished upon it, it is obviously necessary to practice some deception in order to justify such excessive devotion."[11]

In such charges and counter-charges, is the concept of self-deception being properly used or misused?

SUGGESTED READINGS

Ames, Roger T., and Wimal Dissanayake (eds.). *Self and Deception: A Cross-Cultural Philosophical Enquiry.* Albany: State University of New York Press, 1996.

Barnes, Annette. *Seeing Through Self-Deception.* New York: Cambridge University Press, 1997.

Butler, Bishop Joseph. "Upon Self-Deceit." In W. E. Gladstone (ed.), *The Works of Joseph Butler.* Oxford: Clarendon Press, 1896.

Dilman, Ilham, and D. Z. Phillips. *Sense and Delusion.* New York: Humanities Press, 1971.

Elster, John (ed.). *The Multiple Self.* Cambridge: Cambridge University Press, 1986.

Fingarette, Herbert. *Self-Deception.* Atlantic Highlands, NJ: Humanities Press, 1969.

Freud, Sigmund. *The Future of an Illusion.* New York: Norton, 1960.

Goleman, Daniel. *Vital Lies, Simple Truths: The Psychology of Self-Deception.* New York: Simon & Schuster, 1985.

Haight, M. R. *A Study of Self-Deception.* Atlantic Highlands, NJ: Humanities Press, 1980.

Kekes, John. "Self-Knowledge." In *The Examined Life.* Lewisburg, PA: Bucknell University Press, 1988.

King-Farlow, John, and Sean O'Connell. *Self-Conflict and Self-Healing.* Lanham, MD: University Press of America, 1988.

Lockard, Joan S., and Delroy L. Paulhus (eds.). *Self-Deception: An Adaptive Mechanism?* Englewood Cliffs, NJ: Prentice-Hall, 1988.

Martin, Mike W. *Self-Deception and Morality.* Lawrence: University Press of Kansas, 1986.

Martin, Mike W. (ed.). *Self-Deception and Self-Understanding: New Essays in Philosophy and Psychology.* Lawrence: University Press of Kansas, 1985.

McLaughlin, Brian P., and Amelie Rorty (eds.). *Perspectives on Self-Deception.* Berkeley: University of California Press, 1988.

Mele, Alfred R. *Irrationality: An Essay on Akrasia, Self-Deception and Self-Control*. New York: Oxford University Press, 1987.

Mele, Alfred R. "Real Self-Deception" (with replies). *Behavioral and Brain Sciences*, vol. 20 (1997): 91–136.

Santoni, Ronald E. *Bad Faith, Good Faith, and Authenticity in Sartre's Early Philosophy*. Philadelphia: Temple University Press, 1995.

Sartre, Jean-Paul. "Bad Faith." In *Being and Nothingness*. New York: Washington Square Press, 1966.

Sloan, Tod S. *Deciding: Self-Deception in Life Choices*. New York: Methuen, 1987.

Steffen, Lloyd H. *Self-Deception and the Common Life*. New York: Peter Lang, 1986.

Taylor, Shelley E. *Positive Illusions: Creative Self-Deception and the Healthy Mind*. New York: Basic Books, 1989.

Self-Control and Courage

Knowing what is right is one thing. Doing it is something else. No aspect of morality is more poignant than the struggle to live up to our moral convictions. Judging that we should perform some act or engage in some activity, all things considered, we may nevertheless fail to do so, even though we have the power to do so. This is *weakness of will*, and when the judgment is specifically moral it is *moral weakness*.

By contrast, *self-control* is the virtue of living according to one's values and standards of rationality insofar as one has the capacity to do so. In this chapter we discuss two important aspects of self-control that enable us to surmount weakness of will: moral effort and courage. We also discuss the related topics of inner conflict and the way we use excuses to protect self-esteem and self-respect.

Loss of Self-Control

Weakness of will can be occasional or habitual. Occasional weakness of will is one or a few periodic acts (or omitted acts). Habitual weakness of will involves a longer-term pattern of actions. As the following example suggests, habitual weakness of will takes various forms.[1]

A student begins the year with the firm resolve to study as hard as possible. Within a few weeks, however, the student *backslides*, forgetting on many nights to keep the resolution to study. The initially firm resolutions to do homework are transformed into *weak resolves, wavering commitments,* and increasingly *vague commitments* that lack clear implications for how many hours are to be spent studying. *Half-hearted* efforts are made in which only a small part of the requisite time and effort is invested. On some days a greater struggle is made to attend class and do homework, but too quickly the student surrenders the struggle, giving in to temptations to watch television or go to parties. On other days the student succumbs to strong emotions, perhaps anger or love, in ways that distort judgment about how time should be spent. When essays are assigned, days pass in procrastinating until the last moment.

Weakness of will, as it is usually understood, involves four elements: (1) judging that an act or pattern of activity ought to be avoided; (2) desiring to perform the act or engage in the activity anyway; (3) intentionally acting on that desire (that is, knowingly and purposefully acting to satisfy the desire, although usually not specifically intending to be weak of will); (4) doing so voluntarily, without external coercion or irresistible inner compulsions. (Sometimes the last condition is omitted, thereby widening the idea of weakness of will to include irresistible compulsions.)

Most of us are familiar with instances in our own lives when we could have exercised self-control but failed to do so because we did not try hard enough. Familiar examples include neglecting to write thank-you letters for gifts received, failing to keep promises, overeating, abusing alcohol, and missing important deadlines.

Paradoxes

Despite the familiarity of these examples of acting against our better judgment, some philosophers find weakness of will paradoxical. They question whether one can sincerely judge an act as right and then voluntarily fail to do it. This skepticism about weakness of will takes several forms, depending on whether judgments are understood as (1) knowledge or beliefs, (2) commitments, or (3) decisions that entail wants. We consider each of these grounds for skepticism in turn.

Socrates and Aristotle were skeptical about weakness of will because of their view that genuine moral knowledge must produce good conduct. Socrates held that "knowledge *is* virtue": To know what is morally right is to do it, when the opportunity arises, and unless outside forces prevent one.[2] As he also stated, "Knowledge is a fine thing quite capable of ruling a man, and . . . if he can distinguish good from evil, nothing will force him to act otherwise than as knowledge dictates, since wisdom is all the reinforcement he needs."[3]

Aristotle's view was more complex, but he agreed with Socrates that knowledge about how we ought to act, together with awareness of relevant information about our situation, leads us to act accordingly unless external obstacles interfere. He suggested that "incontinent [i.e., weak-willed] people must be said to be in a similar condition to men asleep, mad, or drunk."[4] Either they are momentarily blinded to the reality of what they are doing or they temporarily lose awareness of its wrongness.

Socrates and Aristotle remind us of how an intense pleasure close at hand can momentarily distort judgment or deflect attention from what we otherwise know is right. Yet their perspective obscures the important distinction between (a) knowing, believing, or judging something to be right and (b) being motivated to do it. Sometimes we are insufficiently motivated to do what we know is right, perhaps because we do not try hard enough or care deeply enough about our responsibilities.

In *Freedom and Reason*, R. M. Hare regards value judgments—in contrast to Socrates and Aristotle—as more closely resembling commitments than beliefs or knowledge. In Hare's view, to judge an act obligatory is to commit oneself to doing it when the occasion arises. Moreover, this commitment entails that one will perform the act unless prevented by external forces, by an absence of any opportunity to act, or by a psychological inability to so act (perhaps due to a powerful addiction). The idea of weakness of will, which requires that one could have acted differently but failed to do so because of a lack of effort, is a self-contradictory notion.

Hare's view has more plausibility than Socrates' and Aristotle's view when applied to simple cases such as failing to write letters to one's parents. Hare forces us to ask, "Are persons sincerely committed to writing the letters if they repeatedly fail to write them when the opportunity arises?" The familiar adage, "Actions speak louder than words," is relevant here in determining where a person's commitments really lie.

Yet is Hare correct in equating moral judgments with fully sincere commitments? A judgment that something is wrong is not the same as a full commitment to avoid it. Moreover, even when we are fully committed, we may have momentary lapses of effort and caring. Guilt feelings and efforts to make amends following the failures may confirm the sincerity of our commitments.

The third type of skepticism about weakness of will holds that value judgments entail wants or desires (rather than commitments). According to this view, our judgment that an act is right entails that we will most want to do it, which, in turn, entails that we will act when the opportunity arises. Thus, if we judge that it is right to keep a promise, all things considered, then we will most want to keep it. Since we always do what we most want to do, how could we fail to keep the promise (assuming we are able to do so)? In general, it seems impossible to act contrary to our evaluations about what ought to be done.

This view is based on the confusion of two senses of "wants most." In one sense this phrase means "values most highly." This concerns evaluations, and the relative value of things. Although we may value promise keeping more than promise breaking, it does not necessarily follow that we always make the effort to keep our promises.

In a second sense, "wants most" means "is most strongly motivated by." This is a psychological notion pertaining to the strength of a want or desire. (It should not be confused with a want "feeling strongest," or having the most psychological agitation accompanying it—that is, an emotional tone that might not translate into the most strongly motivating desire.) In this sense people do indeed—by definition—always do what they want most to do (when they are able). They may nevertheless, however, be subject to weakness of will. We judge that we ought to keep a promise, but our strongest motivating desire may be to do something else. Again, people may want most (in the sense of judging it most desirable, all things considered) to preserve their marriages by avoiding adultery. In a moment of weakness of will, however, they may want most (in the sense of being most strongly motivated) to have an affair.

Inner Conflict and Self-Respect

The most perplexing aspect of weakness of will is inner conflict, or the self divided against itself. By definition, weakness of will involves a split between our judgments and the desire that most strongly motivates us to act. Typically, it also entails conflicts among our desires. Usually we have at least some desire to do what we judge is right, a desire that conflicts with a second desire to act otherwise.

These inner conflicts are distressing. Unless they are successfully resolved, we suffer feelings of shame for being unable or unwilling to live up to our own standards, as well as feelings of guilt when our failures harm other people. If continued long enough, habitual weakness of will can cause self-alienation—a sense of being out of touch with who we are—because our sense of identity depends largely on our central commitments. Habitual weakness of will can erode our confidence in the genuineness of those commitments.

There are several ways to avoid these negative responses to weakness of will, which we now discuss. We can (1) try harder in the future, (2) honestly rethink our values, (3) accept our flaws, or (4) make excuses.

First, we can try harder in the future to live up to our moral convictions and other standards of conduct. "Trying harder" implies forming habits that minimize the temptations we feel. To overcome habitual weakness of will we must make long-term adjustments of conduct and attitudes, as anyone knows who has successfully gone on a diet. Certain kinds of food can no longer be brought home, and other foods must be available in abundance; hunger can be deflated by drinking water before meals; eating in front of a television, which invites casual munching, should be avoided; taking smaller bites and chewing longer helps; emotionally based attitudes, inherited from childhood, about food as a reward need to be rethought; and so on.

When we are faced with temptations, "trying harder" means making greater efforts of the sort summarized by Alfred Mele:

> An agent can, for example, keep clearly in mind, at the time of action, the reasons for doing the action that he judged best; he can refuse to focus his

attention on the attractiveness of what might be achieved by performing a competing action, and concentrate instead on what is to be accomplished by acting as he judges best; he can refuse to entertain second thoughts concerning matters about which he has just very carefully made up his mind; he can seek to add to his motivation for performing the action judged best by promising himself a reward . . . for successfully resisting temptation. Such exercises of self-control can have a desirable effect upon the balance of his motivation at the time of action.[5]

Mele refers to these tactics as *skilled resistance* to impulses that threaten to prevent us from doing what we judge best. They constitute rational attempts to strengthen our motives, in addition to the sheer *brute resistance* of exerting willpower so as not to give in to a temptation. Most weakness of will results from failures to exercise a combination of skilled and brute resistance to impulses contrary to our best judgment.

The second way we might contend with weakness of will is to reflect on and modify our value judgments and attitudes. Perhaps the struggling student is embarked on a self-defeating course of study in which she or he has little genuine interest. A change of major or career plans may be the best way to surmount the weakness of will.

Third, on some occasions and with respect to some habits, it may not be worth the effort necessary to avoid weakness of will altogether; or it may be worth only a moderate effort that only partially succeeds. At these times, an informal cost–benefit analysis of effort may be warranted. When the degree of effort required to achieve complete self-control would use up energies needed for more important endeavors, the best compromise might be to accept a particular shortcoming in order to channel effort where it can do the most good. Ironically, there can be strength in accepting some weakness of will, as Friedrich Nietzsche (1844–1900) suggested:

> To "give style" to one's character—a great and rare art! It is practiced by those who survey all the strengths and weaknesses of their nature and then fit them into an artistic plan until every one of them appears as art and reason and even weaknesses delight the eye. . . . For one thing is needful: that a human being should *attain* satisfaction with himself. . . .[6]

Each of these first three responses—rethinking our values, trying harder, and accepting ourselves—is subject to abuse. They can be made dishonestly, in self-deception rather than with genuine moral concern. The belief that we are trying hard may be only self-deception masking idle handwringing and token gestures. Again, rethinking our values may amount to little more than rationalization. As in Aesop's fable of the fox and the grapes, when we cannot reach the grapes (the good to which we aspire), we may persuade ourselves that the grapes are too sour to be worth seeking. Similarly, self-acceptance may be sheer complacency rather than creative resignation based on a reasonable apportionment of energies.

Excuses

Our tendency to make excuses, which is the fourth response to weakness of will, deserves a fuller discussion because of its importance in protecting our self-esteem and self-respect.[7] An excuse is a convenient explanation of a failure (or seeming failure) to live up to our standards. Some excuses are made primarily to protect us from criticisms by other people. Most are designed to maintain our own self-image, our own sense of self-esteem and self-respect. They may represent reasonable explanations, or may be the dishonest product of hypocrisy or self-deception.

Justification strategies arise when the excuse is intended to justify the act. For example, recall (from Chapter 1) that any of the thirty-eight witnesses to the murder of Kitty Genovese had plenty of time to prevent the murder by making a telephone call. Most of the witnesses, when interviewed later, attempted to justify their inaction with excuses to the effect that "It wasn't my responsibility to get involved" or "I thought someone else would call." One witness went further, saying that he had thought it was a lovers' quarrel with which it would be wrong to interfere.

By contrast, *blame-lessening strategies* occur when one admits one's wrongdoing but tries to lessen the resulting blame by appealing to extenuating circumstances. In the Kitty Genovese case, a few witnesses admitted that they should have called the police; but their excuses for failing to do so reflected blame-lessening strategies such as, "Frankly, we were afraid." Some also indicated that it had been the middle of the night and they had been too tired and upset to think clearly.

Blame-lessening strategies take two forms. *Consensus-raising* strategies appeal to the notion that most people act similarly in similar situations. The idea is to lessen blame by arguing that one's actions conform with what can be expected from others. This would be illustrated by witnesses who comforted themselves by saying, "Everyone else did what I did, too." Many everyday excuses fall into this category: "I know the joke was racist, but everyone else laughed at it, too." "Sure, adultery is wrong, but the majority of married people do it sometimes, so don't come down hard on me."

In contrast, *consistency-lowering* strategies portray one's failure as a rare lapse that is inconsistent with one's general good character (in light of which one should be judged). This strategy is illustrated by the witnesses who claimed that fear or fatigue prevented them from acting with their normal degree of involvement and concern. This appeal to one's overall integrity and good character is also common in everyday excuses: "I know I didn't try very hard to resist the temptation to have the affair, but I've never done it before and I'll never do it again."

Excuses, understood as explanations of failures or apparent failures, sometimes succeed and are justified: Our act was in fact *not* bad, contrary to appearances, or we are in fact *not* as blameworthy as it first seemed. These are *valid excuses*. Other excuses, however, are not justified. How do we know which are valid and which are not? We draw upon our understanding of what we can reasonably require of people—both people in general and the individual in question—in the given circumstances. Hence, our assessment of excuses is as complex as our moral sensitivity itself.

To complicate matters further, we assess excuses by using pragmatic criteria, as well as criteria of validity. The struggle to maintain self-esteem is often difficult and sometimes demands any kind of excuse—valid or not—especially in light of the increasing complexity of contemporary life. Without excuses we would take fewer risks, knowing they might result in inexcusable errors. Preservation of self-esteem would become impossible without drastically lowering our value standards. Thus, giving and accepting excuses is a necessary way of coping with our imperfections.

In addition, our encouragement of excuse making helps us to maintain personal ties and support each other in matters of self-esteem. Consider a teenager who tells his parents he failed to show up for an exam because he did not feel like taking it and because he hates the class. Not only is he defying his parents, he may be threatening to drop out of the educational system. Friends or parents might ease tensions, however, by offering excuses as a kind of social lubricant that will help bring the student back into the school community ("I know it's tough staying with that class given all your other worries right now . . . "). In short, without excuses life might be unbearable. Within limits, excuse making is justifiable as a part of self-acceptance and tolerance of others' weakness of will.

Forms of Courage

Thus far, our discussion has centered around weakness rather than strength. Let us turn to a form of strength that is crucial in avoiding weakness of will in confronting dangers: courage. Courage comes in many forms, depending in part on the type of danger in question. *Physical courage* is a response to dangers to life or limb; *social courage* is a response to social dangers; and *intellectual courage* (or courage of one's convictions) is a response to threats to one's commitments. All these types of courage were exemplified by Elizabeth and Paul Glaser in their struggle against AIDS (Acquired Immune Deficiency Syndrome).

When the Glasers were married in 1980, they had every hope of a happy life together. Paul Glaser was quickly becoming a television star in his role as Starsky in the detective show *Starsky and Hutch*. Elizabeth had their first child Ariel a year later. Complications in the caesarean delivery required transfusions with blood, which, as the Glasers learned five years later, was contaminated with the AIDS virus. The virus was passed to Ariel during breastfeeding, and later to their second child Jake while he was in utero.

Ariel was diagnosed with AIDS in 1986 when she was five. This was the height of public panic over AIDS, and the Glasers immediately found themselves socially and emotionally isolated. Friends turned away, afraid to have their children play with Ariel, and schools blocked her admission. Family members drew strength from the courage of each other, especially from the courage of Ariel in undergoing repeated medical procedures. Ariel's courage continued to the end, according to Elizabeth's account of her death.

> Doctors were in and out, in and out, but we paid no attention to them.
>
> She [Ariel] looked at me. Paul was on the other side of her.
>
> I said, "You know it's going to be okay. Are you scared?"
>
> She said, "No."
>
> And then very quietly, but very quickly, she died as Paul and I lay beside her in her bed.[8]

The tragedy almost wrecked the Glasers' marriage, but somehow they coped. They continued with a campaign they had begun while Ariel was alive to gain funding for pediatric AIDS research. They met with President Reagan, who, while sympathetic, did not help them, because of conservative political pressures. Next they established a private foundation that raised research money from the Hollywood community and nationally. They pursued their activities despite knowing that if the press learned of their involvement, Paul's career could be ended (even though Paul had not himself contracted AIDS) because of the AIDS hysteria at the time. Eventually, intrusive reporters from the *National Enquirer* forced them to make their situation public, but that merely intensified their efforts, leading them to testify in congressional hearings about the need for increased AIDS research and therapy. Elizabeth spoke for both of them when she said, "I identify with the oppressed, but not as a victim. . . . Becoming active in the fight against AIDS made me realize I'm not a victim. I have power and I can work for change."[9]

Elizabeth Glaser died of AIDS in 1994, but throughout their ordeal, she and Paul manifested long-term patterns of physical, social, and intellectual courage in their actions. Courage can also be shown on a single occasion, however, as in the next example of physical courage.

In a wilderness area near the city where I live, a woman was hiking with her five-year-old daughter. A mountain lion attacked the girl and dragged her into some bushes. The mother's frantic screams were heard by Gregory Ysais, a thirty-six-year-old electronics technician who happened to be hiking in the same area. Without any hesitation Ysais ran to the scene to find the cougar gripping the bloody and squirming child by the back of her neck. Ysais grabbed a branch and repeatedly swung it over the cougar's head. The full-grown cougar responded with threatening roars and quick strikes with his huge paws. After a few minutes the cougar dropped the child long enough for her to be pulled away.

Ysais later reported that he had never been in a life-and-death situation before and had never thought of himself as a hero: "I didn't give it much thought. I just heard people crying for help, and I just ran as fast as I could. I was just doing what I had to do. I couldn't think of anything else."[10]

Courage, Cowardice, and Fear

Aristotle defined courage as the tendency to do good in situations where fear is involved. The courageous person tends to "hit the mean," that is, to find the reasonable middle ground between excess (too much) and deficiency (too little). Aristotle writes: "In the field of Fear and Confidence the mean is Courage; . . . the one who exceeds [the mean] in confidence [i.e., risk-taking] is called Rash, and the one who shows an excess of fear and a deficiency of confidence is called Cowardly."[11]

Aristotle's definition differs somewhat from the courage outlined in our examples, for two reasons. First, we called Ysais courageous even though he performed only one good deed in the face of danger, without knowing whether he had a habit or tendency of acting courageously. If in a later situation he acted cowardly, we would describe him, more cautiously, as a person who sometimes acts courageously and sometimes does not. As long as he is not a coward later, however, we are perfectly justified in calling him a courageous person because of his one extraordinary act. Thus, people are courageous if they either (1) show a tendency to do admirable acts in situations they see as dangerous or (2) act admirably to an extraordinary degree on one occasion, without acting cowardly on other occasions.

Second, Aristotle defines courage in terms of fear, but we have not done so. We have referred instead to behavior in situations regarded as dangerous, whether or not one actually feels fear in response to the danger. Ysais was courageous because he acted effectively in an emergency involving danger, whether or not he felt a fear that he had to overcome.

Cowardice, by contrast, is logically connected with fear. By definition, cowardice is a moral failing due to fear—fear that motivates one to flee, causes one's responses to freeze, or otherwise prevents one from confronting the danger in a responsible manner. People who fail to meet their obligations in dangerous situations because of sheer laziness are not cowards—they are just lazy. Cowardice arises when fear is the specific motive for the failure.

A Definition of Courageous Actions

We have defined courageous people as those who perform courageous acts (either as a pattern of behavior or as an extraordinary instance in the absence of later cowardice); but what is a courageous act? In *Virtues and Vices,* James Wallace offers the following defining criteria for courageous acts. Each criterion is set forth as a necessary condition (that is, one that must be met for an act to be courageous), and taken together the six criteria are intended to be sufficient (that is, enough to distinguish an act as courageous).

(a) *A* [a person] believes that it is dangerous for him to do *Y* [an action].

(b) *A* believes that his doing *Y* is worth the risks it involves.

(c) A believes that it is possible for him not to do Y.

(d) The danger A sees in doing Y must be sufficiently formidable that most people would find it difficult in the circumstances to do Y.

(e) A is not coerced into doing Y by threats of punishment, which he fears more than he fears the dangers of doing Y.

(f) A is under self-control, at least in the sense of not being in a frenzy, stupor, or intoxication.[12]

Focus on condition (b), which requires only that the person *believe* the act to be worth doing despite the risks, not that the act actually be good. Aristotle would require that courageous acts actually be good. Who is correct?

Wallace's definition seems preferable when we think of soldiers who fight with valor on an immoral side during a war. For example, Field Marshal Rommel was a highly distinguished and intrepid soldier for Hitler's side during World War II. Rommel repeatedly won battles by using daring tactics, frequently risking his own life. The Allied officers both feared and respected him. Because Rommel's acts were for an immoral cause, Aristotle's definition would not allow us to call him courageous, whereas Wallace's definition more plausibly does allow this conclusion.

Consider alternatively, however, someone who plays deadly games of "chicken." In a movie role made famous by James Dean, a teenager races at breakneck speed toward a high cliff, competing with a teenager in another car to see who "chickens out" first. Such acts are foolhardy, tragically stupid, or cruel. Here Aristotle's definition of courage seems preferable because it sees nothing courageous in such acts of daring, whereas Wallace's definition requires us to call such acts courageous when the individuals believe their acts are worth the risks involved.

Our hesitation or refusal to ascribe courage in the case of the chicken games reflects an important linguistic fact: The word *courage* carries strongly positive connotations. To ascribe courage to a person expresses some approval—at least with respect to the risk taking involved. There is, however, nothing worth approving in, say, the game of chicken. One way to refine our definition of courageous acts at this point would be to add a further condition to Wallace's list of criteria:

(g) We admire [person] A for [act] Y, at least for the risk taking involved in Y.

This would allow us to ascribe courage to Field Marshal Rommel (if we admire his risk taking) but not to the players of chicken games.

A complementary approach would be to insist that, to qualify as courageous, a person must have good reasons for his or her actions. Following a suggestion of Douglas Walton in his book *Courage,* we could modify Wallace's condition (b) as follows:

(b') A believes that doing Y is worth the risks it involves and A has at least one good reason for believing Y is worthwhile. Acting on these intentions, he intends Y to be good.

Field Marshal Rommel was mistaken in believing his acts were good, but no doubt he believed that it was his duty as a soldier to act as he did. If we see any value in this conscientiousness, we will see his conduct as courageous, unlike the conduct of the players in the chicken games.

The Good of Courage

Based on our revised version of Wallace's definition, courage always involves some good, for it entails an *intention* to do something good or right. Risk taking on behalf of such intentions is good, even though the act may be bad in other respects.

Courage is especially good when it contributes to the good of other people, as in the Glasers' campaign for AIDS research and in Ysais's rescue of the child. Walton makes some insightful comments about how risk taking on behalf of altruistic aims is especially admirable. He asks us to consider two men who perform acts with equally good intentions and consequences. In one case, all that is required is for the man to pull a child from a shallow pond into which the child has fallen. In the second case, the man saves a small child trapped in a burning auto following a crash. When he arrives at the scene of the accident, he sees a group of people shouting and waiting for a rescue team. Fearing that the gas tank is about to explode, he rushes into the flames and, at considerable risk to himself, pries the child free from the burning wreckage. In doing so, he is seriously burned and cut. Commenting on why we admire the second man even more than the first one, Walton writes:

> What is of moral import in evaluating actions over and above the goodness of an intention in itself is the commitment of the agent to carrying out that intention. The depth of that commitment is indicated by the time, effort, ingenuity, and sacrifice the agent is willing to put into the carrying out of his good intention. . . . The greater the sacrifice, risk, and danger of carrying out a good objective, the more meritorious is the course of action directed to that end.[13]

Courage, however, does not always involve altruism, that is, a desire to promote the good of other people out of concern for their welfare. It is also courageous to take risks in fulfilling our duties to ourselves and in pursuing self-fulfillment, rather than always taking the prudent course. As W. D. Falk pointed out,

> Prudence is only one way of looking after oneself. To act prudently is to play safe, for near-certain gains at small risks. But some good things one cannot get in this way. To get them at all one has to gamble, taking the risk of not getting them even so, or of coming to harm in the process. If one values them enough, one will do better by oneself to throw prudence to the winds, to play for high stakes, knowing full well the risk and the price of failure. Explorers, artists, scientists, mountaineers are types who may serve themselves better by this course. So will most people at some juncture.[14]

SUMMARY

Weakness of will is a failure to live up to our value standards and has four elements: (1) judging that an act or pattern of activity ought to be avoided; (2) desiring to engage in it anyway; (3) intentionally acting on that desire; and (4) doing so voluntarily, without external coercion or irresistible inner compulsions.

By definition, weakness of will involves a loss of self-control in the sense that we fail to guide our acts in light of our values; but it does not entail a loss of self-control in the sense that we are unable to act otherwise. Perhaps most weakness of will can be avoided if we make a greater effort to resist impulses contrary to our value standards, whether by exerting our energies (brute resistance) or by strengthening our motivation by concentrating our attention on what we ought to do and on why it is important (skilled resistance).

Weakness of will and the inner conflict it involves threatens self-esteem and self-respect. Its harmful effects can be lessened in four ways: We can (1) try harder in the future, (2) honestly rethink our values, (3) accept our flaws, or (4) make excuses.

Justification excuses portray an act as not really wrong, contrary to first appearances. Blame-lessening excuses are appeals to extenuating circumstances, made with the hope of reducing the blame incurred. They include consensus-raising strategies, which portray one's failure as comparable to similar failures by most other people, and consistency-lowering strategies, which portray the failure as a rare lapse in one's otherwise admirable character.

Courageous acts are performed in the face of danger in pursuit of what one believes, with some good reason, to be a good end. When the reason is insufficient to justify the act, the courage is misguided and not entirely good (as with Field Marshal Rommel). Courageous people either show a tendency to perform courageous acts or perform one extraordinary act of heroism not followed by cowardly acts. Courage is especially valuable when it promotes the good of other people or one's moral integrity and self-fulfillment, and also when it is prompted by good intentions and motives, or reveals skill and judgment in the face of great danger.

DISCUSSION TOPICS

1   Suppose half of the students in a class are cheating on an exam. How might they attempt to excuse their cheating using each of the following excuse strategies: (1) justification strategies and (2) blame-lessening strategies, including (a) consensus-raising strategies and (b) consistency-lowering strategies. Are any of the excuses valid?

2   Are the following people courageous? Explain, using your definition of courage. (1) A man who invests all his family's earnings in high-risk stocks with the aim of

making his family wealthy. (2) A mountain climber who risks her life for the sake of the joys and challenges of the hike. (3) A man who commits suicide by igniting his gasoline-soaked clothes to protest his government's immoral policies.

3 Is it more admirable to display courage without feeling any fear ("fearlessness") or to feel fear and act courageously despite it? Or is there no moral difference between the two? Consider, for example, two variations on the Ysais example: Ysais felt terror and struggled to overcome it before rushing to the aid of the child; or Ysais felt no fear whatsoever.

4 The first of Wallace's six criteria for courageous acts was that "A [a person] believes that it is dangerous for him to do Y [an action]." Consider situations in which this belief is irrational, as in the case of acts motivated by phobias. For example, a person with a spider phobia irrationally believes it is dangerous to be within yards of a perfectly harmless garden spider. Is the person showing courage by approaching the spider despite the fear? Or should we modify Wallace's criterion to require that the belief about the danger must be reasonable?

5 We noted that it is best to rethink one's moral views when one's conscience is mistaken, and not to exert an effort in obeying conscience. When a person's conscience is seriously distorted, is it perhaps obligatory not to live up to it? Would it be positively immoral to obey one's conscience?

Consider Huck Finn's decision not to return his friend, the slave Jim, to his master. As Huck was helping Jim escape on a raft down the Mississippi River, his conscience began to disturb him:

> Jim said it made him all over trembly and feverish to be so close to freedom. Well I can tell you it made me all over trembly and feverish, too, to hear him, because I begun to get it through my head that he was most free—and who was to blame for it? Why, me. I couldn't get that out of my conscience, no how nor no way. . . . I tried to make out to myself that I warn't to blame, because I didn't run Jim off from his rightful owner; but it warn't no use, conscience up an says, every time: "But you knowed he was running for his freedom, and you coulda paddled ashore and told somebody."[15]

Huck's conscience tells him that he ought to return Jim—that is what he takes to be morally obligatory. Nevertheless, he refuses to live up to his conscience, instead accepting himself as a sinner. Should we say that he was weak of will but his weakness is virtuous? Would he have displayed a vice by exercising greater strength of will in following his conscience?

6 Are self-control, self-discipline, perseverance, and strength of will always virtues? Clearly, deeply immoral people sometimes have great self-control and strength of will: witness Hitler, Stalin, and the Ayatollah Khomeini. The strength of will of these people gave them the power to accomplish their horrors. If we condemn their conduct, should we not also condemn the traits that enabled them to succeed?

The same question arises with respect to other words commonly used to refer to virtues, because many of them allude to self-control and strength of will. Courage, for example, entails the exercise of self-control in situations involving danger; temperance is the exercise of self-control when the appetites urge otherwise; and prudence involves self-control over one's thoughts and conduct in situations where one might "lose one's head." Villains can show self-control in pursuing evil ends; when they do so, are they displaying virtues, and are they in that respect admirable?

There are several options in answering this question. (1) We might admit that evil people can be virtuous in the limited respects these traits identify; thus, embracing the irony that virtues (admirable traits) can promote vice. (2) We might refuse to call something a virtue when it directly serves evil ends, and interpret the traits as good only when they serve good ends. In a sense they are "dependent virtues": Their qualification as virtues depends on their connection with a restricted range of goals and intentions.[16] (3) We might refuse to call them virtues at all, even dependent ones, and think of them instead as "powers" that, like all power, can serve either virtuous or immoral ends.

Which of these options is preferable? Is there a still better option?

SUGGESTED READINGS

Baumeister, Roy (ed.). *Losing Control: How and Why People Fail at Self-Regulation*. San Diego: Academic Press, 1994.

Davidson, Donald. "How Is Weakness of the Will Possible?" In Joel Feinberg (ed.), *Moral Concepts*. New York: Oxford University Press, 1970. Reprinted in Donald Davidson, *Essays on Actions and Events*. Oxford: Clarendon Press, 1980.

Dworkin, Gerald. *The Theory and Practice of Autonomy*. New York: Cambridge University Press, 1988.

Foot, Phillipa. *Virtues and Vices and Other Essays in Moral Philosophy*. Berkeley: University of California Press, 1978.

Hare, R. M. *Freedom and Reason*. New York: Oxford University Press, 1970, pp. 67–85.

Hill, Thomas E., Jr. "Weakness of Will and Character." In Thomas Hill(ed.), *Autonomy and Self-Respect*. Cambridge: Cambridge University Press, 1991.

Mele, Alfred R. *Autonomous Agents: From Self-Control to Autonomy*. New York: Oxford University Press, 1995.

Mele, Alfred R. *Irrationality: An Essay on Akrasia, Self-Deception, and Self-Control*. New York: Oxford University Press, 1987.

Meyers, Diana T. *Self, Society, and Personal Choice*. New York: Columbia University Press, 1989.

Milo, Ronald D. *Immorality*. Princeton, NJ: Princeton University Press, 1984. pp. 115–139.

Mortimer, G. W. (ed.). *Weakness of Will*. New York: St. Martin's Press, 1971.

Snyder, C. R., Raymond L. Higgins, and Rita J. Stucky. *Excuses*. New York: Wiley, 1983.

Tillich, Paul. *The Courage To Be*. New Haven, CT: Yale University Press, 1952.

Wallace, James D. "Courage, Cowardice, and Self-Indulgence." In *Virtues and Vices*. Ithaca, NY: Cornell University Press, 1978.

Walton, Douglas N. *Courage: A Philosophical Investigation*. Berkeley: University of California Press, 1986.

Watson, Gary. "Skepticism about Weakness of Will." *Philosophical Review*, vol. 86 (1977).

PART SEVEN

Moral Health

It appears, then, that virtue is as it were the health and comeliness and well-being of the soul, as wickedness is disease, deformity, and weakness.[1]

Plato

We readily call people sick when the harm they inflict on themselves and others becomes extensive, entrenched, or extreme. Upon hearing the details about a grisly murder we are likely to express our horror and disgust by exclaiming, "Sick!" Again, people who repeatedly abuse alcohol are now viewed as suffering from the "disease" of alcoholism and hence in need of therapy, whether from professionals or from self-help groups like Alcoholics Anonymous. And whereas suicide was once traditionally viewed as a choice, and condemned as immoral, now it is more often approached as a symptom of pathological depression.

The *therapeutic trend*—that is, the tendency to apply therapeutic approaches to what were previously viewed as moral matters—now permeates our culture. Bookstores contain large sections for self-help books and videos on topics such as love, anger, and forgiveness. Television talk shows invite a steady stream of psychologists, psychiatrists, and social scientists to discuss a host of moral issues. One of their familiar themes is that we should attend to how people are victims of their upbringing, environment, and genetics. Even religious sermons now routinely blend psychology with scripture, and counseling techniques have became a standard part of the training of ministers, priests, rabbis, and clerics.

Chapter 21 examines the therapeutic trend, suggesting that it is best interpreted as interweaving moral and therapeutic ideas, rather than as replacing morality with therapy. The concept of mental health embodies some moral values, and morality includes a responsibility to take care of our health. Because therapy raises special concerns about freedom, that chapter also discusses theories about freedom and determinism. Chapter 22 deals with alcohol dependency and other forms of drug abuse, and Chapter 23 discusses suicide and related issues about physician-assisted suicide. Those topics are used as illustrations of how problems can have moral and health dimensions.

CHAPTER 21

Responsibility and Therapy

When we discussed President Clinton's deceptions concerning Monica Lewinsky (in Chapter 2), we took for granted that he was responsible for the harm he caused. But what if instead we view him as sick, as suffering from a sexual addiction, such that his lying was only one of the pathological symptoms of his addiction? If we view him as sick, does it follow that he is not morally responsible for his actions?

The idea that pathology was involved is not farfetched. Before and during the impeachment proceedings against him, journalists and legislators frequently characterized his behavior as sick, compulsive, and recklessly self-destructive. Therapists did so as well. For example, Jerome D. Levin, a psychiatrist specializing in addictions, wrote a book titled *The Clinton Syndrome* that portrayed him as manifesting "the irrationally compulsive behavior of an addict seeking affirmation and reassurance," and as someone who "has undoubtedly lost control—to be specific, he has become powerless over his sexual impulses."[1]

Levin traced the roots of Clinton's sexual addiction and his "virtually suicidal relationship with Monica Lewinsky" to his childhood: "His legacy as an adult child of an alcoholic (ACOA) compelled him to fill the emptiness of his childhood and to repeat the addictive pattern of both his biological and his adoptive parents; his relationship with Lewinsky revived a longstanding behavioral pattern; she fulfilled a complex nexus of unconscious needs."[2] Like other addictions, Clinton's sexual addiction was "about insecurity, low self-esteem, and the need for affirmation and reassurance. The sex addict feels unloved and unlovable and therefore looks obsessively for proof that this is not so."[3]

Should we be alarmed by this tendency to use clinical terms such as *compulsions, unconscious needs,* and *low self-esteem* to an increasingly wide array of morally objectionable behaviors? Let us attempt to understand exactly what this tendency implies.

310

The Therapeutic Trend

The *therapeutic trend* is the tendency to apply therapeutic perspectives to problems that were previously approached with moral perspectives. *Moral perspectives* are networks of beliefs and attitudes that use concepts such as good and bad character, integrity and dishonesty, right and wrong conduct, guilt and shame, blame and punishment, moral responsibility and irresponsibility. By contrast, *therapeutic perspectives* use concepts such as good and bad health, disease and symptoms, fitness and unfitness, feeling well and suffering, treatment and therapy. Like moral perspectives, therapeutic perspectives take many different forms that are themselves often at odds, such as sociological versus psychiatric views. Here we will use illustrations drawn from psychiatry, the area of health care that continues to exert the greatest influence.

Even a quick glance at the American Psychiatric Association's *Diagnostic and Statistical Manual of Mental Disorders* (DSM-IV) reveals how extensive this "medicalization" of moral matters has become. Thus, when involvement with alcohol or other drugs becomes extensive and harmful it is a *substance abuse disorder*. When gamblers reach the point of causing great harm they suffer from pathological gambling, which is only one of many instances of *impulse-control disorders*. In place of traditional talk about lack of self-discipline, there are various *eating disorders* such as anorexia nervosa and bulimia. Flagrant law-breaking and socially harmful behavior falls under such headings as *kleptomania, pyromania,* and *anti-social personality disorder* (what was previously called sociopathy). An array of difficulties with sex fall under *sexual disorders,* including exhibitionism, pedophilia, and hypoactive sexual desire disorder (deficient sexual desire). In addition to hundreds of specific categories, there are open-ended categories, such as *impulse-control disorder not otherwise specified* and *sexual disorder not otherwise specified,* that leave open many additional clinical diagnoses. These are only a few of hundreds of examples taken from the 886 pages of the DSM-IV, and each new edition of that book expands the list of disorders.

Critics of the therapeutic trend warn that what they call *medicalizing morality* is dangerous. It gives far too much power to health professionals who are elevated to the status of moral experts. Worse, the trend threatens to undermine moral responsibility by encouraging people to think of themselves as victims rather than agents. Journalist Charles Sykes contends that we have become a "nation of victims" in which we excuse virtually any wrongdoing by seeing sickness everywhere:

> we have multiplied the number of diseases exponentially. In place of evil, therapeutic society has substituted "illness"; in place of consequence [that is, holding people responsible for the consequences of their actions], it urges therapy and understanding; in place of responsibility, it argues for a personality driven by impulses. The illness excuse has become almost routine in cases of public misconduct.[4]

Sykes offers many examples. Robert Alton Harris, who viciously murdered two teenagers, argued in court that he suffered from fetal alcohol syndrome. Richard Berendzen, while president of American University, made obscene phone calls, and then traced his behavior to having been abused as a child. Marion Barry, who while mayor of Washington, D.C., was caught on videotape smoking crack cocaine, saw himself as a victim of drug addiction and quickly checked himself into a hospital. And Dan White, who murdered San Francisco's mayor and a City Supervisor, argued that junk food had caused his violence—what the press labeled the "Twinkie Defense."

Sykes is correct that there have been abuses, but his own examples suggest that our society is far from abandoning moral perspectives in favor of therapeutic perspectives. Robert Harris's attempted defense failed, and he was executed for his crimes. Richard Berendzen's career as a president abruptly ended when he was caught. The jury rejected Dan White's Twinkie Defense. Although Marion Barry retained some popularity, his political career was greatly damaged. And when Hillary Clinton referred to her husband's troubled childhood an interview after the Lewinsky scandal was resolved and she prepared to campaign for the Senate, a political flap forced her to make clear that she did not regard that childhood as an excuse for his infidelities. These examples do not establish that our society is abandoning moral perspectives altogether in favor of therapeutic perspectives.

On the surface, therapeutic and moral perspectives seem quite different, but are they fundamentally opposed? As already noted, there are many different therapeutic and moral viewpoints, and what we say about some of them will not apply to all. Even in general terms, however, it is crucial to distinguish two interpretations of the therapeutic trend.

Most often the therapeutic trend is construed as a *replacement project*—the enterprise of replacing moral perspectives on human behavior with therapeutic perspectives. The replacement project interprets moral and therapeutic projects as not only different but opposed, and seeks to overthrow moral perspectives in favor of therapeutic perspectives. According to it, people are sick and therefore *not* wrongdoers. This is how Sykes construed the therapeutic trend, and that is why he is alarmed that it will subvert moral responsibility.

A quite different interpretation of the therapeutic trend, however, construes it as an *integrative project*—the enterprise of seeing human conduct as having both moral and health dimensions. According to the integrative project, morality and health-oriented perspectives are not opposed. Being sick does not automatically excuse wrongdoing. Like a great variety of factors, sickness must be weighed contextually to see how great an obstacle it places on individuals: Does it render their behavior entirely beyond their control, or simply add an additional obstacle that they are responsible for dealing with?

Historically, the rationale for the replacement project, and more generally for opposing therapeutic and moral perspectives, was the use of therapeutic perspectives to criticize conventional morality. Critics argued that morality—at least certain aspects of conventional morality—is harmful to our health. In particular, Sigmund Freud (1856–1939) and Friedrich Nietzsche (1844–1900) argued that Western morality, historically shaped by Judaism and Christianity, sets forth excessively high ideals that require more self-sacrifice and repression of biological instincts than is healthy. A closer look, however, raises doubts about whether the therapeutic values they applied were in fact morally neutral.

Nietzsche's Therapeutic Critique of Morality

Although Nietzsche often spoke of himself as an *immoralist,* his views are sometimes understood as highlighting some moral values—especially honesty, self-mastery, and self-respect—in critiquing others. At the same time, he develops these virtues within the context of an egoistic theory that highlights the highly creative individual. He was not an ethical egoist, as defined in Chapter 1, who says that everyone should always and only pursue their own interests. For Nietzsche cared little about most people, whom he dismissed as the "herd." His view, as expressed in *Thus Spoke Zarathustra* and many other writings, might be expressed this way: Great creativity has inherent value, and creative individuals ought to pursue their creative activities.

Throughout his writings, but especially in *On the Genealogy of Morality,* Nietzsche locates the source of moral values in the suppression of animal instincts. The most powerful and important instinct, in his view, is the *will to power*—a drive to exercise our personal influence and increase our abilities and influence. Morality, by which Nietzsche especially meant the Judeo–Christian ethics of altruism and its humanitarian variants such as utilitarianism and Kant's duty-ethics, represents a hidden social pressure to suppress the instincts in order to make social life possible. The result is pathology, manifested in guilt feelings or "bad conscience": "I take bad conscience to be the deep sickness into which man had to fall under the pressure of that most fundamental of all changes he ever experienced—the change of finding himself enclosed once and for all within the sway of society and peace."[5]

Are Nietzsche's ideas of health and sickness devoid of moral values or do they perhaps surreptitiously invoke certain moral values in criticizing others? Certainly Nietzsche rejects anything that smacks of conventional morality. His conception of health includes three key elements: vitality, self-mastery, and self-reverence.[6] Each of these ideas is presented in terms of asserting oneself, what he calls the *will to power,* and each is developed in the direction of egoistic concern for oneself.

Vitality is energy in pursuing one's aims, energy generated primarily from the will to power. It is shown in joyous activity and striving, and especially in creative activities that brings about valuable new things. It is also manifested in courageous risk taking as part of what he calls "self-overcoming." *Self-mastery* is discipline of one's instincts, but only in order to further their expression, not to suppress them as in the conventional idea of self-control. *Self-love* is affirming oneself as having singular value. In some ways it is a variation of the traditional virtue of self-respect, but it demands far more of us by way of striving for excellence. At the same time, it is shown in a deep affirmation of our lives in all their details—a love of fate *(amor fati)*.

Sickness, then, takes the forms of weakness and lethargy, lack of self-mastery, and above all, the failure to properly value oneself. Guilt arises when instincts are not expressed in ways that manifest energy and bring self-affirmation. In one of many passages anticipating Freud, he writes:

> All instincts that do not discharge themselves outwardly *turn themselves inwards,* and when aggression turned inward becomes guilt and self-hatred, the greatest and most uncanny of sicknesses was introduced . . . the suffering of man *from man,* from *himself*—as the consequence of a forceful separation from his animal past, . . . of a declaraton of war against the old instincts on which his energy, desire, and terribleness had thus far rested.[7]

Morality, with its emphasis on caring about others and selflessness, as well as guilt, blaming, and punishment for failures to be caring, is a poisonous and self-destructive stance of turning against life and our own will to power.

In addition to guilt, blame, and punishment, Nietzsche attacks other key ideas in ordinary moral views. For example, he rejects the call for equality, found in nearly all modern ethical theories, as a dishonest expression of weakness. The ideal of equality is part of *slave morality* that expresses the weakness of groups who lacked social power. Weak groups, such as the early Jews and Christians who were dominated by Romans and others, felt anger, hatred, and envy toward dominant groups. Impotent to express these powerful emotions, the emotions grew to smoldering and repressed resentment or *ressentiment* (mentioned in Chapter 17). Gradually *ressentiment* generates a slavish moral outlook with equality as its centerpiece. In a passage we quoted in Chapter 17, he wrote:

> You preachers of equality, the tyrannomania of impotence clamors thus out of you for equality: your most secret ambitions to be tyrants thus shroud themselves in words of virtue. Aggrieved conceit, repressed envy . . . erupt from you as a flame and as the frenzy of revenge.[8]

As even these few quotations make clear, Nietzsche's attack on morality is both provocative and sweeping. What shall we say in response? His psychological insights powerfully help us to understand various forms of pathology. There are individuals who seek to pull down others in the name of equality as a compensation for their own failings. Certainly guilt and blaming can become irrationally excessive. And concern for others can take distorted forms in which individuals fail to give due attention to their own needs. Nevertheless, Nietzsche provides no convincing support for his allegations that all forms of altruism, equality, and guilt are irrational. All his arguments rely on his assumptions that we are all primarily driven by a self-seeking will to power (self-assertion to gain personal benefits), that this drive deserves to be affirmed, and that the health of this drive is measured entirely in self-referential terms (vitality, self-mastery, self-love). That is, his arguments are based on assuming psychological and ethical egoism, as discussed in Chapter 1.

The important point here, however, is that he obviously draws on some values beyond the ordinary notion of health in offering his therapeutic critique. The ordinary notion of health, roughly, is the idea of being able to function effectively in one's environment. Nietzsche's emphasis on honesty and self-reverence, his rejection of envy and *ressentiment,* and even his call for creativity all add to the concept of health values that either have moral dimensions or assume egoism. In general, when we closely examine therapeutic critiques of morality we discover that the critiques invoke some sound moral values in rejecting other aspects of conventional morality.

Freud's Therapeutic Critique

In *Civilization and Its Discontents,* Freud suggested that civilization is made possible by the systematic and widespread control and suppression of basic human instincts. Two instincts in particular, sex and aggression, had to be controlled in order for complex cooperative human endeavors to become possible. Control mechanisms include laws and legal punishment, but they also include ethics. Ethics is a cultural conscience—what Freud calls a *cultural super-ego*—whose rules and ideals are essential but also liable to excess. Insofar as those excesses cause needless human suffering, they should be criticized from a therapeutic perspective: "We are very often obliged, for therapeutic purposes, to oppose the super-ego, and we endeavour to lower its demands. Exactly the same objections can be made against the ethical demands of the cultural super-ego."[9]

Many of Freud's key terms became part of everyday language, but related ideas were anticipated by Plato 2,400 years earlier.[10] Like Plato, Freud divided the mind into three main parts: the ego, the id, and the superego, each having distinctive function. The *ego,* which corresponds roughly with Plato's Reason, integrates activities and deals with problems. It plays the executive role in guiding our lives by reconciling the multitude of pressures on us. The *id* is something like the unconscious parts of what Plato called the Appetites, especially the sexual and aggressive desires. The *superego* is composed of the values instilled by parents and society. Although the superego involves more than the Spirited Element (the sense of honor), both can be viewed as aspects of conscience (the sense of right and wrong). To carry the analogy one step further, note that the superego pressures the ego to control the id, much as the Spirited Element helps Reason control the Appetites.

Furthermore, both Freud and Plato hypothesized that this three-part framework could be used to explain mental conflicts and to understand mental health. Freud regarded human life as best when the ego is in full control in dealing with the pressures from the id, the superego, and every-day reality. Neuroses and other forms of mental illness arise when the ego is overwhelmed by an out-of-control id, an overdemanding superego, or a traumatic experience. The ego's psychological defense mechanisms (mentioned in Chapter 19) become overwhelmed, including such mechanisms as repression (keeping impulses and ideas unconscious), projection (ascribing features of oneself to others), and reaction formation (going to opposite extremes, for example becoming excessively tidy as a defense against sexual fears). Mental health involves inner harmony, or at least a healthy balance of tensions, which we achieve when we are able to confront internal and external dangers courageously as a result of self-understanding. According to Freud, self-understanding makes a meaningful life possible through socially acceptable forms of pleasure (especially love) and work, even though it does not guarantee self-fulfillment, as Plato thought.

There are major differences, however, between Plato and Freud. One difference is that Plato believed that moral values are objectively justified, indeed written into the universe as the Form of the Good, whereas Freud largely equated moral values with human conventions. Another major difference, of more immediate interest, is that Plato equated morality with mental health, whereas Freud used mental health ideas to critique morality. But perhaps this second difference is not as great as first appears. Plato has in mind *justified* morality, or what he calls virtue. By contrast, Freud is criticizing some *conventional* moral beliefs as causing harm by being psychologically unrealistic in their demands on us. He is not rejecting all moral values. Nor does he suggest abandoning the need for considerable restraint of sexual and aggressive instincts; to do so would threaten civilized society that requires that restraint.

Far from abandoning moral values, Freud is using a morally resonant therapeutic perspective to criticize selected aspects of conventional morality. These conventional aspects—excessive blaming, excessive guilt feelings, psychologically unrealistic demands—are objectionable for both moral and therapeutic reasons. Again, Freud's conception of health incorporates moral values. The healthy person, in his view, is someone who works responsibly, engages in mature love relationships, and in general accepts responsibility for conduct. As we noted in Chapter 11, love is an idea that embodies moral values, and we will explore in Chapter 25 that work does too. Indeed, therapy itself is based on the conviction that the well-being of humans has moral significance, and that unnecessary suffering is morally undesirable.

In addition, Freud also endorsed various values as part of the procedures of therapy. In particular, the cardinal rule of psychoanalysis is to be completely candid in revealing one's experiences to the therapist. Patients are also expected to be conscientious in showing up for therapy on time and in paying their bills! Underlying these more specific procedural values is a key therapeutic value: accepting responsibility for one's health, where health includes physical, mental, and social dimensions. This responsibility is moral in nature, as well as therapeutic.

Integrating Morality and Therapy

The therapeutic trend may better be understood as a movement toward integrating moral and therapeutic approaches. The discussions also suggest several important bridges between (justified) moral perspectives and therapeutic understandings.

The first and most important bridge is *responsibility for one's health*. This idea is not the absurdity that our health is entirely under our control. Instead, it is the obligation to take prudent steps to develop and maintain healthy habits, both with regard to our physical and mental well-being.

A second bridge is that moral values shape the goals and procedures of therapy. The central goal is to help enable clients to gain more responsible control over their lives, and the procedures include respecting client's autonomy and providing supportive care. Even the very definition of *mental disorders* in the DSM-IV indirectly alludes to moral values by taking for granted that such things as suffering and impairment are undesirable:

> [a mental disorder is a] behavioral or psychological syndrome or pattern that occurs in an individual and that is associated with present distress (e.g., a painful symptom) or disability (i.e., impairment in one of more important areas of functioning) or with a significantly increased risk of suffering death, pain, disability, or an important loss of freedom.[11]

Third, justified moral perspectives can agree with therapeutic perspectives that *blaming* is suspect when it becomes excessive. To blame others without limit is cruel, as well as unhealthy. To blame oneself excessively, whether in the form of pathological guilt or depression, is equally cruel.

Finally, moral perspectives, as well as therapeutic perpectives, take many forms, and the two can be shaped so as to capture what is important in each. With this in mind, let us take note of a few integrative projects.

Within twentieth-century psychology, integrative projects were pursued by humanistic psychologists such as Abraham Maslow (1908–1970), Carl Rogers (1902–1987), and Erich Fromm (1900–1980). These psychologists sought to overthrow the pretense that psychology is entirely neutral morally. For example, Fromm explicitly linked moral responsibility and psychological maturity: "The character structure of the mature and integrated personality, the productive character, constitutes the source and the basis of 'virtue' and . . . 'vice,' in the last analysis, is indifference to one's own self and self-mutilation."[12] He also argued that the deepest human need is to overcome isolation by engaging in morally resonant relationships of love with other people. Far from being the exclusively self-oriented creatures that Freud and

Nietzsche portrayed, and contrary to Nietzsche's characterization of altruism and equality as expressions of weakness, we need to enter into mature love relationships based on caring, responsibility, and mutual respect.

Words like *maturity* and *needs* are Janus-faced: They face toward both psychology and morality. Fromm understood maturity as a "productive orientation" to all aspects of life, whereby persons express their abilities and powers actively in the world, in contrast with being alienated. As for needs, they include not only physical needs but also psychological needs for creativity, a sense of individuality, and social relatedness, rootedness in human communities and the world as a whole, as well as the need to find meaning.[13] These ideas implicitly invoke moral ideas.

Turning to philosophy, we already noted that Plato set the historical backdrop for philosophical versions of the integrative project: "It appears, then, that virtue is as it were the health and comeliness and well-being of the soul, as wickedness is disease, deformity, and weakness."[14] More recently, philosopher Lawrence Becker outlined a conception of moral agency as interwoven with psychological maturity.

Becker suggests that moral–psychological health "will include effective powers of deliberation and choice, and the disposition to use them. It will include curiosity, abundant agent energy, a developed self-concept, and a disposition to regularize, to seek consistency and integration within and among one's endeavors."[15] Psychological health will *ex*clude

> "the basic personality tenors [or tendencies] (phobias, distrust, pessimism, depression) that paralyze agency or render agents unable to feel or express empathy, or unable to take a benevolent interest in others"; "the extremely asocial (autistic or introverted) dispositions that prevent the development of cooperation, reciprocity, conviviality, and benevolent initiatives"; "the extremely antisocial dispositions that generate acting out unprovoked malice, hostility, and deliberatively injurious attacks on others"; . . . "the sort of ungovernable impulsiveness and emotionality that make the self-protective exercise of agency impossible"; and "extreme anhedonia [that is, inability to enjoy life] and detachment."[16]

The integrative projects outlined by Becker, Plato, and Fromm invite us to speak of *moral health* as the active exercise of capacities for responsible conduct, where those capacities are simultaneously moral and psychological. *Moral sickness* is the impairment of those capacities in ways that we are in some part responsible for. Thus, to call vicious murderers sick does not automatically excuse them as lacking all moral accountability for their actions and for the disordered character expressed in those actions.

Yet, this interweaving of mental and moral health stands in need of several qualifications. There are at least four reasons why we should not *completely* equate moral with therapeutic perspectives. First, from the direction of mental illness, severe mental disorders like schizophrenia and Alzheimer's disease can completely undermine moral capacities, so that talk of immorality is entirely out of place. Second, very minor psychological problems, such

as a mild spider phobia or anxiety disorder, might have no particular connection with moral values. Third, from the direction of morality, it would
be patronizing and belittling to say that heroic acts of courage and compassion are merely signs of good mental health. And fourth, most isolated acts
of wrongdoing due to weakness of will, negligence, carelessness, and lapse
of judgment are not connected with mental illness. A single act of driving
drunk is irresponsible, but only when alcohol abuse is repeated often would
we say a person is sick.

Determinism and Responsibility

An additional obstacle to integrating moral and therapeutic perspectives
concerns freedom. Morality is based on the assumption that we are free,
within limits, to make choices: We are accountable for our actions because
we chose them. Therapy is based on the assumption that we are victims of
biology and environment—genetics and early childhood development. The
underlying assumptions are wholly opposed, and hence ultimately the two
perspectives cannot be reconciled.

The debate over free will versus determinism is enormously complex.[17]
Here we will only enter into the debate enough to challenge the linkage between therapeutic perspectives and determinism in the specific version that
threatens moral responsibility. That version is called *hard determinism:*
Every human action is caused by forces outside the realm of conscious
agency. Hard determinism rejects the idea that people ever choose freely, in
a manner that justifies holding them morally accountable for their actions.

The therapeutic view is sometimes thought to be based on hard determinism, and therein opposed to moral perspectives. Indeed, both Freud and
Nietzsche were hard determinists who sought to uncover the hidden "inner
forces" that have as much power over us as a gunman's threat, whether the
inner forces are traceable to biology (genetics and physiology), psychology
(unconscious ideas, compulsions), or environmental factors (early childhood
development, peer pressure, etc.). But a moment's reflection shows that
therapeutic perspectives themselves deny hard determinism. Therapy calls
for people to accept responsible for their health, and both Nietzsche and
Freud made that same appeal. That acceptance is a choice!

Hard determinism is only one form of *determinism,* which is the view
that every event, including every human action, is caused. Determinism is
incompatible with holding people responsible—as long as we leave room for
the idea that *people cause actions!* We are causal agents who, within limits,
are able to shape our lives autonomously, as we discussed in Part Six. To be
sure, our actions are influenced by many factors, but we are not puppets.
We are able to choose how we respond to those influences—again, within
limits. In situations where our actions are entirely or largely shaped by
forces (outer or inner) beyond our control, we are not responsible, or have,
at most, limited responsibility.

Do psychiatrists portray us as mere puppets? Some disorders, such as Alzheimer's disease, are caused by organic factors over which we lack control. But the DSM-IV does not classify most mental disorders according to their causes. As quoted earlier, the definition of "mental disorders" refers to distress and impairments—to patterns of disordered behavior, thought, and emotion—but not complete incapacitation by causes over which people have no control whatsoever. The degree of causation by outside forces is left open for investigation with regard to specific disorders and particular individuals.

Science does search for causes. When it succeeds in establishing that a particular disorder is completely caused by factors entirely beyond our control, then it does and should lead us to limit moral responsibility. In this way, science is directly relevant to morality (which is another reason we have often linked them throughout this book). But no such claim of thoroughgoing fatalism is made for most of the disorders classified in the DSM-IV. In fact, the scientific literature usually uncovers influences—causal factors—but not complete causal determinants.

Many influences contribute to shaping our *motives,* which, in turn, lead to our actions. Our actions are the product of our desires and our beliefs about how to satisfy those desires—that is true by definition of the very words *actions, desires,* and *beliefs.* Together, our desires and beliefs constitute our motives. We have some degree of autonomy in influencing our own desires and beliefs—through self-valuing, self-reflection, and self-control (as discussed in Part Six).

Interestingly, motives can also refer to *reasons* that justify actions or purport to do so. The reason that we go to work is to earn money, and hopefully to engage in a meaningful activity. That reason is spelled out in terms of my beliefs and desires, which also motivate my going to work. Nevertheless, citing motives to *explain* actions is different from citing them to *justify* actions. When we look at ourselves from outside, the way we often look at other people, it may seem we are determined by influences beyond our control. But the moment we return to our awareness of how we routinely engage in autonomous self-direction by engaging in reasoning, our appreciation of our capacity for choice returns. The difficulty in unraveling disputes about determinism center on whether we can fully understand how causal and reason explanations are compatible.

SUMMARY

The therapeutic trend is the tendency to apply health-oriented perspectives to issues that were once exclusively regarded as moral matters. The trend is open to two interpretations, both of which can be found in our society. Interpreted as a replacement project, the therapeutic trend is the enterprise of rejecting moral perspectives and replacing them with therapy-oriented perspectives. Interpreted as an integrative project, the therapeutic trend is the enterprise of interweaving moral and therapeutic ideas. The replacement project does threaten our ordinary practices of holding individuals responsible for their conduct, but the integrative project does not.

Nietzsche and Freud both raise therapeutically oriented critiques of morality. A close look at their critiques reveals that they are also relying on some moral values to criticize the unjustified elements in conventional moral beliefs. What first appears as replacement projects turns out to move us toward integrative projects. Key integrative ideas that bridge moral and therapeutic perspectives include responsibility for one's health, the moral goals and guidelines of therapy, and how excessive blaming is open to both moral and therapeutic objections.

Determinism is the view that all human actions, like all other events, have causes. As such, determinism may be compatible with free choice if we grant that humans are themselves causal agents. Hard determinism denies free choice, asserting that human actions are caused by biological and environmental forces beyond our control. The debate over hard determinism is complex, but it is not obvious that therapeutic perspectives imply hard determinism, especially since therapeutic perspectives also make use of moral ideas such as responsibility for one's health.

DISCUSSION TOPICS

1 Neal O. Weiner celebrates the interweaving of moral and therapeutic perspectives: "A semi-moral/semi-medical way of thinking about what the self ought to be has become dominant in many circles, and might well be said to constitute an original American contribution to popular ethics, the moral equivalent of jazz."[18] The opposing attitude of critics such as Charles Sykes is that our therapeutic culture, in which virtually all moral issues are recast in therapeutic terms, is leading to irresponsibility and selfishness. Which attitude is closest to the truth regarding how we treat criminals in our society?

2 Ethical relativists, like Ruth Benedict, reduce both moral values and standards of mental health to social customs. By contrast, Freud, Nietzsche, and Fromm are quite willing to critique customs as unhealthy, such that they produce "social neuroses" or "pathology of cultural communities."[19] Customs are subject to clinical evaluation; entire societies can be sick, at least in certain respects. Are there aspects of our society that you would be willing to call sick, or do you find this clinical assessment of customs itself objectionable?

3 Influenced by Freud, psychoanalyst James Gilligan rejects "morality as a force antagonistic to life and to love, a force causing illness and death—neurosis and psychosis, homicide and suicide."[20] His argument is that morality is an outlook based on contrasting egoism and altruism, and then establishing obligations that become the locus for attitudes of guilt and shame, and blaming others and ourselves. The upshot is inner conflict, anxiety, depression, and compulsions. He

recommends replacing morality with a "psychotherapeutic approach": "If mental and emotional health and maturity mean anything, they seem to me to mean the ability to structure one's relationships with others in such a way that it is through meeting one's own needs that one meets others' needs as well. And this can be acccomplished only through love, not through morality." For, in love relationships "the conflict between egoism and altruism has been transcended, because through meeting one's own needs one meets another's, and vice versa."[21]

a   Assess this argument, drawing on your view of how love and morality are related (see Chapter 11).

b   As it happens, James Gilligan is married to Carol Gilligan, discussed in Chapter 6. Compare and contrast their approaches to morality.

4   Like Nietzsche, Freud was a psychological egoist who reduced all motives to self-oriented and ultimately instinctual drives. For example, he says that secular ethics "has nothing to offer here [as a compensation for society's demands] except the narcissistic satisfaction of being able to think oneself better than others," and religious ethics promises additional rewards in the after-life.[22] With regard to both Freud and Nietzsche, discuss how the tendency to reduce complex human motives to a few instinctual drives influences the particular direction of therapeutic critiques of unhealthy aspects of conventional morality.

5   We suggested that a key link between moral and therapeutic perspectives is the idea of responsibility for one's health. Politically conservative politicians sometimes draw on this idea to justify removing expensive government health programs and shifting health care burdens more fully to individuals. Liberals object, however, that this approach *blames the victim* who, because of poverty and absence of adequate health care, is unfairly punished for lacking access to proper health care: "initiatives to promote health by placing responsibility exclusively on the shoulders of the individual have the effect of blaming the victim of poor health and social conditions."[23] Discuss this criticism, and in doing so outline what the obligation to care for one's health should and should not imply.

6   One of Charles Sykes's examples was Robert Harris, who was convicted of murdering two sixteen-year-olds. Harris was especially vicious in that he laughed as he killed the boys and, feeling no remorse whatsoever, then casually ate the hamburger one of the teenagers had just bought at a San Diego, California, McDonalds, where Harris and his brothers had kidnapped the youths. Harris was severely battered and emotionally abused by both his parents as a child, in ways that undoubtedly exerted a strong influence on his vicious conduct as an adult. Gary Watson argues that we should respond to Harris with ambivalence and confusion in ways that render us unable to make clear assignments of moral responsibility. Evaluate Watson's claims in the following passage:

> The sympathy [we should feel] toward the boy he was is at odds with our outrage toward the man he is. These responses conflict not in the way that fear dispels anger, but in the way that sympathy is opposed to antipathy. In fact, each of these responses is appropriate, but taken together they do not enable us to respond overall in a coherent way.[24]

7   John Hospers was one of the first philosophers to argue that the discoveries made by psychoanalysts like Freud should lead us to embrace hard determinism. Evaluate his argument in the following passage:

An act is free when it is determined by the man's character, say moralists; but what if the most decisive aspects of his character were already irrevocably acquired before he could do anything to mould them? What if even the degree of will power available to him in shaping his habits and disciplining himself now to overcome the influence of his early environment is a factor over which he has no control? What are we to say of this kind of 'freedom'? Is it not rather like the freedom of the machine to stamp labels on cans when it has been devised for just that purpose?[25]

SUGGESTED READINGS

American Psychiatric Association. *Diagnostic and Statistical Manual of Mental Disorders: DSM-IV*, 4th ed. Washington, DC: American Psychiatric Association, 1994.

Becker, Lawrence C. *A New Stoicism*. Princeton, NJ: Princeton University Press, 1998.

Bok, Hilary. *Freedom and Responsibility*. Princeton, NJ: Princeton University Press, 1998.

Dilman, Ilham. *Free Will: An Historical and Philosophical Introduction*. New York: Routledge, 1999.

Edwards, Rem B. (ed.). *Ethics of Psychiatry*. Amherst, NY: Prometheus Press, 1997.

Fischer, John Martin, and Mark Ravizza (eds.). *Perspectives on Moral Responsibility*. Ithaca, NY: Cornell University Press, 1993.

Graham, George, and G. Lynn Stephens (eds.). *Philosophical Psychopathology*. Cambridge, MA: MIT Press, 1994.

Kane, Robert. *The Significance of Free Will*. New York: Oxford University Press, 1998.

Kenny, Anthony. "Mental Health in Plato's Republic," in *The Anatomy of the Soul: Historical Essays in the Philosophy of Mind*. London: Basil Blackwell, 1973.

Martin, Mike W. "Moral Health: Responsibility in Therapeutic Culture," *The Journal of Value Inquiry*, forthcoming.

Nietzsche, Friedrich. *On the Genealogy of Morality*. Trans. Maudemarie Clark and Alan J. Swensen. Indianapolis: Hackett Publishing, 1998.

Pestana, Mark. *Moral Virtue or Mental Health?* New York: Peter Lang, 1998.

Sadler, John Z., Osborne P. Wiggins, and Michael A. Schwartz (eds.). *Philosophical Perspectives on Psychiatric Diagnostic Classification*. Baltimore, MD: Johns Hopkins University Press, 1994.

Schacht, Richard (ed.). *Nietzsche, Genealogy, Morality: Essays on Nietzsche's Genealogy of Morals*. Berkeley: University of California Press, 1994.

Scheler, Max. *Ressentiment*. Trans. W. W. Holdheim. L. A. Coser (ed.). New York: Schocken, 1972.

Schoeman, Ferdinand (ed.). *Responsibility, Character, and the Emotions*. New York: Cambridge University Press, 1987.

Sleinis, E. E. *Nietzsche's Revaluation of Values: A Study in Strategies*. Urbana: University of Illinois Press, 1994.

Wallace, R. Jay. *Responsibility and the Moral Sentiments*. Cambridge, MA: Harvard University Press, 1996.

Watson, Gary (ed.). *Free Will*. New York: Oxford University Press, 1982.

Weiner, Neal O. *The Harmony of the Soul: Mental Health and Moral Virtue Reconsidered*. Albany: State University of New York Press, 1993.

CHAPTER 22

Drug Abuse

Responsibility for one's health interweaves with responsibilities to others. Nowhere is this clearer than in regard to responsibilities concerning drug abuse. Driving under the influence of drugs risks both one's own life and the lives of others, and becoming addicted to a dangerous drug threatens our well-being and the well-being of people who care about us.

What attitudes should we adopt concerning our own and others' use of drugs for nonmedical purposes? What responsibilities do we have in responding to the drug problems that afflict our society? These are troubling and difficult questions about which there is little consensus. Hardliners condemn all nonmedical uses of drugs. Softliners point to the positive aspects of some drugs and the rights of individuals to make their own decisions. Moderates offer complex assessments of drug use that are often morally ambiguous.

Problem Drugs

We speak of *the* drug problem, but of course different problems are associated with different drugs. *Drug abuse* refers to any nonmedical use of a drug that causes or has a substantial risk of causing harm, whether to oneself or to others. The expression is pejorative; it is a label for drug uses that are objectionable in some way. Thus, if we consider it objectionable to break the law, we will view all illegal uses of drugs—as well as morally objectionable though legal uses—as drug abuse.

For our purposes, a *drug* can be defined as any psychoactive chemical, that is, any chemical that directly and significantly influences consciousness.[1] Drugs are classified according to what kind of influence they have on the central nervous system. Since a given drug can have a variety of effects, classification schemas vary. The following is only one possible schema, illustrated with a small sampling of frequently abused drugs.

Stimulants ("uppers") arouse the central nervous system, producing alertness or excitation. They include amphetamines such as Benzedrine and Dexedrine, which operate much like natural bodily substances that prepare us to deal with stress. They also include nonamphetamines such as cocaine, crack (a crystalline form of cocaine), nicotine, and caffeine. *Depressants* ("downers") slow down the impulses transmitted within the central nervous system. Some depressants are analgesics (pain killers), in particular narcotics such as opium and its derivatives (morphine, heroin, codeine)—all of which are addictive. *General depressants,* which have a wider effect than killing pain, include alcohol, sedatives such as barbiturates and Quaalude, tranquilizers such as Valium and Librium, and many inhalants such as aerosols, benzene, and glue. *Hallucinogens,* such as LSD, mescaline, and many "designer drugs" (synthetically manufactured chemicals) alter the mind so as to produce visual, auditory, or other kinds of perceptual illusions. PCP ("angel dust") is a depressant capable of producing extreme violence, bizarre hallucinations, and permanent alterations in the personality, making it one of the most dangerous illicit drugs. Marijuana is usually placed in a category by itself because it produces a combination of sedation, mood change, and mild hallucination.

Why Use Drugs?

Drugs serve many purposes. *Medical* purposes include pain relief and healing. *Recreational* use has as its object an enjoyable experience sought for its own sake. *Creative* uses are intended to produce an interesting imaginative experience, perhaps affording insights (as celebrated by Aldous Huxley in *The Doors of Perception*). *Instrumental* purposes consist of the enhancement of work performance or some other practical activity. An example is the use of caffeine (in coffee, tea, or colas) while studying for an exam. *Religious* purposes include not only personal quests but also ceremonial uses. For example, some groups have believed that peyote, which contains the hallucinogen mescaline, is a messenger from the gods. Such groups have used peyote in religious ceremonies for centuries. The ceremonies began with the Aztecs and are continued today by members of the Native American Church.

Whatever their intended purpose, drugs produce experiences that go beyond the chemical effects of the drug. A particular drug experience is shaped by the mind-set of the user (including mood, expectations, and imagination), the user's physiological and psychological tolerance for the drug, the immediate social setting in which the drug is taken, and the wider social and cultural setting that attaches meanings to specific drugs. Similarly, the amount of use depends on the dynamics between social setting and personal choice. For example, more than 70 percent of the U.S. soldiers who became dependent on heroin in Vietnam, where heroin was plentiful and inexpensive, voluntarily gave up its use when they returned to the United States.

Peer pressure, a desire for social interaction, curiosity, and a desire to experiment are frequent motives for nonmedical drug use. In addition, many drugs are charged with symbolic meanings that enhance their attraction. For example, marijuana may convey a sense of rebellion against parents and conventional society. Cigarettes are for some teenagers a sign of growing up. Cocaine seems to add glamour to life, if not a charming element of danger. And alcohol is widely touted as a social lubricant and vehicle of holiday cheer.

Not everyone gets hurt by using dangerous drugs. Most people do not, and it is impossible to know exactly who will. We are familiar with how all forms of drug abuse can have devastating effects: ruined health, destroyed education, loss of job, child abuse, and fatal car crashes. Yet none of these consequences usually occur, which makes it easy for risk-takers to believe they will be exempt from harm in using drugs.

Much of the appeal of drugs has to do with control over our lives. We have a curious double-mindedness here. On the one hand, drugs promise greater control over our immediate consciousness and hence over our lives. They charm us with a sense of power by stimulating our energies, reducing stress, or inducing euphoria. On the other hand, if they do not satisfy our expectations, they offer ready-made excuses for the problems they cause. Irresponsible conduct is readily dismissed as the fault of the drug, rather than the person using the drug. Drugs, then, have a double allure. They promise greater self-control and simultaneously offer excuses for our failures to exercise control when we are under their influence.

This double-mindedness about the power of drugs is reflected in two general perspectives about drug abuse. From a medical perspective, drug abusers are regarded as sick and unfortunate victims who need medical attention. Witness the proliferation of "rehabilitation programs" at drug "clinics" for "treating" drug abuse. Also, the medical profession has taught us to speak of the "disease of alcoholism." From moral and legal perspectives, by contrast, drug abusers are chastised as immoral lawbreakers who ought to be punished.

These two perspectives are often mixed and conflated in confusing ways, but in fact they can be appropriate with respect to different aspects of drug use. Perhaps someone's initial decision to use a dangerous drug was fully voluntary, but subsequent addiction removed or seriously impaired control, turning the drug use into a sickness. Conversely, perhaps the original use was partially excusable as a product of intense peer pressure, but at present it is within the user's power to stop abusing the drug. Even when full-blown addiction has developed, individuals have the power to ask for help. We respect and admire people who seek help, and this presupposes that we do not view them as completely helpless invalids, although their immediate and direct control over the drug may be seriously impaired in dependency and addiction.

Dependency and Addiction

Drug abuse takes many forms. *Periodic abuse* is the occasional misuse of a drug in a manner that generates problems, such as disrupting a party or driving a car while intoxicated. *Drug dependency* occurs when drug use becomes more frequent and is relied upon more heavily. Health professionals have yet to agree on a more precise definition of dependency. One often-cited defining criterion is the physiological withdrawal syndrome—that is, bodily changes that occur when the drug is withdrawn, such as chills, sweating, nausea, aches and pains. Another criterion is drug tolerance, in which an increasingly higher quantity of the drug must be taken to achieve the same effect. *Physical dependence* occurs when either of these criteria is met.

A different criterion for drug dependency is *psychological dependence,* which is shown by strong cravings for the drug when it is withdrawn or by behavioral patterns of compulsive drug use. Cravings may or may not be resistible without help from others, but (by definition) they entail a strong desire that can be resisted only with great effort. Compulsive drug use is indicated by the extent to which a person's life is oriented toward obtaining and using the drug and by how much a person is willing to sacrifice to use the drug.

Addiction is an overwhelming involvement with a drug—the kinds of preoccupation with a drug produced by high degrees of physical or psychological dependence. It is manifested in one's extreme difficulty in giving up drugs. Addictions may seem utterly irrational, but they serve various psychological purposes. For example, all the anxiety-producing complexity of life may become focused on obtaining and using a substance.

> A heroin addict may be trying to reduce all the problems of life to a single one, so that it will no longer be necessary to make fundamental choices or be subject to ordinary emotional vicissitudes. A life is given structure of repetitive acts that produce an artificial stability. Addicts can be devoted as much to hustling—the daily routine of getting the next fix—as they are to the drug itself. It becomes a way of life.[2]

Addictions usually produce only an illusion of control over one's life, not genuine control. Even setting aside the damage done to one's health, to relationships with others, and to innocent bystanders, there are moral objections to becoming addicted that are linked to the virtues. Addictions diminish rational self-control and threaten self-respect. Often they dramatically restrict our capacity to choose from the full range of human goods in pursuing a fulfilling life.

In extreme cases, addicts lose not only self-respect, but even the sense of who they are. Eugene O'Neill explores this loss of identity in *Long Day's Journey Into Night,* an autobiographical play about his mother, who was addicted to morphine, and about himself, his father, and his brother, each of whom was an alcoholic. O'Neill viewed the addictions as interwoven with self-deception about the addiction and about underlying problems that led to the addiction. The fictional version of his mother says at one point, "I've become such a liar. I never lied about anything once upon a time. Now I have to lie, especially to myself. . . . I've never understood anything about it, except that one day long ago I found I could no longer call my soul my own."[3]

Problem Drinkers

Alcohol is the most widely used drug that causes problems; more than 100 million Americans drink. Alcohol may cause more harm than all illegal drugs put together. One in ten drinkers—some 10 million Americans—becomes an alcoholic. (By contrast, there are fewer than 500,000 heroin addicts.) In addition, about half of all fatal car collisions, accidental drownings, violent crimes (including rapes, spouse abuse, and child abuse) are alcohol-related. One of the most common severe birth defects, fetal alcohol syndrome, is caused by women who drink while pregnant. And alcohol costs our economy $120 billion yearly in work, property, and medical costs.

We would not legalize any currently illegal drug that caused even a fraction of these problems, yet we tolerate alcohol. Perhaps we do so with the misimpression that the attempt at prohibition during 1920–1933 was a ludicrous mistake. In fact, prohibition succeeded in dramatically lowering the use of alcohol and its attendant problems. More startling, adjusting for the relative scale of drug problems, "alcohol prohibition probably worked just about as well (or badly) as present drug prohibition laws work. Repeal came not because prohibition was totally ineffective, but because we decided—although we seldom express it this way—that we wanted the pleasure of convenient, legal alcohol more than we feared an increase in drunkenness and alcoholism."[4]

Laws can discourage abusive drinking in ways short of outright prohibition. For example, high taxes on alcohol are an effective way to lower usage. Again, thousands of lives have been saved as a result of campaigns by MADD (Mothers Against Drunk Driving) and SADD (Students Against Drunk Driving) that helped raise the legal drinking age to 21 and toughened laws against drunk drivers. Nevertheless, it is clear that America's alcohol problem will need to be addressed in additional ways that encourage responsible ways of drinking.

Earlier we emphasized that drug experiences are largely the result of the user's social setting and mental state rather than simply the chemical effects on the body. Nowhere is this more important than in regard to alcohol. It comes as a surprise to learn that many societies have few problems with alcohol. For example, Americans in the seventeenth and eighteenth centuries (including Puritans!) drank much more than Americans today, with relatively minor problems. Their drinking was integrated into structured social activities and controlled by strong social attitudes against abuses.

The fact that some societies have no major problems with alcohol is one reason why some researchers are uneasy with the idea that alcoholism is a disease that removes all ability to control drinking. "It's not your fault" has been the message. Scientific studies are confirming that alcohol abuse probably has some loose connection with genetic, physiological, and family influences; but these are merely influences, to which we can respond in a variety of ways, including seeking help.

Herbert Fingarette argues that problem drinkers are far more able to control their conduct than the disease model allows. In his view, heavy drinkers have made drinking a "central activity" or a deeply entrenched way of life adopted to deal with anxiety and problems. The way of life acquires a momentum: "When we speak of the momentum of a way of life, we are using a convenient label to refer to the cumulative impact of many long-cultivated and interrelated habits of mind, heart, soul, and body."[5] Changing this way of life can be enormously difficult, but not impossible when help is available. Most heavy drinkers need help that matches the drinker's particular personality to one of the many different types of supportive programs.

Fingarette's criticism of the dominant disease model is controversial. Nevertheless, it draws attention to the mixture of responsible conduct and supportive help from others that is usually required in order to break addictions. Consider Alcoholics Anonymous (AA), which embraces the ideology that alcoholism is a disease. Heavy drinkers are told they must admit their utter helplessness to solve their problem and seek the help of others, including other members of AA and a "Higher Power" whose precise identity is left for each drinker to decide. Simultaneously, they are told they must solve their problems through personal effort and by accepting help! Fingarette views this as a paradox: Drinkers who seek treatment "are told that they are the unwilling victims of a disease that destroys their ability to manage their drinking and yet that they must strive to exert absolute self-control, that only total abstinence can save them."[6] Alcoholics Anonymous does not work for everyone—indeed most of its participants drop out—so why does it work for some? Fingarette argues that it helps those individuals who find it an appealing alternative central activity—a new way of life—replete with numerous reinforcement meetings, social activities, and a new network of emotional bonds.

Of course, major problems can arise from periodic, rather than habitual, heavy drinking. Here we can note the same kind of double-mindedness mentioned earlier. One widespread attitude is that drinking relaxes moral requirements or even provides a moral "time-out." Thus the familiar excuse for misbehavior at a party: "I'm sorry, but I just wasn't myself last night after that second drink." Yet, most adults quickly learn their personal "limit," the point beyond which drinking threatens to lower their responsible conduct. They also learn the wisdom of finding ways to control drinking situations, such as the appointment of "designated drivers" when attending parties.

The Right to Smoke

Whereas moderate drinking can be harmless, the same is not true of smoking. Cigarettes lead all drugs in death statistics, killing five times the number of people killed by alcohol. Each year, 350,000 people die from smoking-related causes that include an array of cancers (of the lungs, mouth, larynx, and esophagus), emphysema, and heart diseases. About one in four people who smoke a pack of cigarettes a day will die from that addiction.

So what? Do we not have a moral right to smoke if we freely choose to do so? Isn't smoking just a high-risk behavior, like hang-gliding, scaling mountains, and having sex with strangers? Whether these activities are foolish depends on one's risk-taking attitudes, and these attitudes are no one's business but one's own!

In reply, note first that smoking can cause serious harm to others, in four ways. (1) Smoking adds greatly to the social costs of medical care. Although insurance companies now penalize smokers, all of us pay the government costs for smoking-related diseases. (2) Smoking during pregnancy harms the fetus, contributing to premature births, low birth weight, and higher infant mortality. (3) A quarter of all fire-related deaths in the United States—some 2,300 people (including nonsmokers)—are caused by smoldering cigarettes. (4) Most important, secondary or "passive" smoke causes several thousand deaths each year and adds to a variety of other health problems. This fact has led to increasingly restrictive laws against smoking on airplanes, in restaurants, and in government buildings. In addition, employers have had to ban smoking because of successful lawsuits by non-smoking employees. The smoker's right to smoke is trumped by the nonsmoker's right to breathe clean air, a right implied by the right to life.

Furthermore, is the choice to smoke always completely voluntary? Consider the initial decision to smoke. The great majority of smokers are "hooked" before they reach adulthood, and about 60 percent of smokers began smoking by age fourteen. Granted, each pack of cigarettes is now labeled with a brief warning about the health hazards, but during adolescence such warnings have little effect. Again, while cigarette ads must carry the same warning, the message is easily lost amidst the sex appeal and glamour of the person shown smoking. Few smokers completely avoid knowing that cigarettes are dangerous, but do they genuinely understand, emotionally appreciate, and appropriately attend to the full risks?

Next consider people who have become addicted. Nicotine is as addictive as heroin or cocaine. To stop smoking usually causes strong withdrawal symptoms such as anxiety, headaches, irritability, dizziness, and sweating. In addition, there are innumerable symbolic connections that must be broken, as in the case of the emotionally resonant after-dinner or after-sex cigarette. Arguing in a vein opposed to Fingarette's approach to alcoholism, Robert E. Goodin argues that addicted smokers have impaired voluntary control and are not fully responsible for their habit. He contends that government action should aim at abolishing smoking: "People may bear responsibility for their own bad habits and for whatever follows from them. They bear responsibility for having become addicted to drugs. Once addicted, though, they ought no longer be considered responsible for their addiction-driven actions."[7]

Is Goodin's claim justified? Granted, nicotine addiction makes quitting very difficult, but does it make quitting impossible? Smoking is what Fingarette called a central activity, one that is intermingled with many other central activities. That psychological dependence, combined with physiological dependence, makes change difficult but usually not impossible. Many people manage to quit smoking through great effort and with the support of a caring community, as annual "smoke outs" have shown.

Illegal Drugs

Society has dealt with dangerous drugs other than alcohol and cigarettes primarily by making them illegal. Laws provide two additional reasons against the use of dangerous drugs. One reason is prudential: Avoid illicit drugs in order to avoid legal penalties. The other reason is moral: Avoid illicit drugs in order to heed the *prima facie* obligation to respect the legal system that makes civilized life possible.

At least 26 million Americans use illegal drugs. Marijuana, which is the most widely used illegal drug, has been tried by 60 million Americans, and 20 million use it regularly. For years the government has blamed international drug dealers and waged "a war" against suppliers of drugs. At a cost of $100 billion during the last decade, the war has been lost, at least if its goal was to end the easy availability of low-cost drugs. The enormous profits to be made in illicit drug trafficking continue to attract an ample number of people willing to run the risks of being caught.

Some critics of the government have abandoned all hope of reducing the supply of illegal drugs. They include conservatives such as the journalist William F. Buckley, Jr., and libertarians such as the Nobel-laureate economist Milton Friedman, who have recommended legalizing most abused drugs.[8] They acknowledge that to do so will dramatically increase drug use, at least doubling the number of addicts, but they point to overriding benefits. Legal drugs will be far less expensive, which would lower the incentive to commit crimes to support drug habits. This benefit is substantial: One study showed that an average heroin addict in Miami, Florida, commits 375 crimes each year![9] In addition, the huge amount of money required for law enforcement could be put to better use, as could taxes imposed on the newly legalized drugs.

Nevertheless, most drug experts reject wholesale legalization. They point to the success of laws in containing the scale of problems by discouraging millions of citizens from experimenting with drugs. Increasingly, however, they recommend a shift in priorities away from stopping international traffickers and toward addressing the ultimate problem that lies with users.

Some of these experts are pessimistic about seriously reducing usage but more hopeful about managing problems. Erich Goode, a sociologist, concludes that drug problems, like automobile and environmental problems, are here to stay for the foreseeable future: "To be plain about it, there will always be certain forms of behavior that will produce, or will be associated with, the use of drugs. The use of mind-altering drugs is linked to broader social forces and influences that are not going to change very much, at least during this century."[10] Although Goode is opposed to legalization of all drugs, he recommends reduction or removal of the penalties for the use of marijuana. He also recommends making free therapeutic (and methadone) programs available to heroin addicts.

Other researchers are more optimistic about programs currently being tested. They draw attention to the fact that greater health awareness and social attitudes against drug use have succeeded in lowering drug abuse since the end of the 1960s. Mathea Falco, who spent four years as assistant secretary of state for international narcotics matters, calls for massive support for programs designed to prevent drug use through education, advertising campaigns to change attitudes, and wide community involvement.[11] Educational programs, Falco emphasizes, must be realistic. By contrast with the bumper-sticker approach ("Just Say No"), programs must be tailored to the needs of each age group. For example, programs for early adolescents must provide detailed suggestions about how to refuse offered drugs without inviting rejection by peers. Other programs dealing with high-risk children must involve entire families and communities where drugs are widely used.

SUMMARY

Drugs are used for many purposes, including medical, recreational, instrumental, and religious purposes. "Drug abuse" refers to illegal or morally objectionable uses of drugs. Drug dependency is substantial reliance on drugs, whether manifested in physiological withdrawal symptoms, drug tolerance, or psychological difficulty in abandoning drug use. Addiction is the special case of overwhelming involvement with a drug.

Drugs are doubly seductive because they promise increased control over our lives and also provide ready-made excuses when that control is not achieved. Heavy dependency and addiction constitute an immediate loss of rational self-control, but researchers disagree over how many addicts can, by themselves, effect long-term change. Herbert Fingarette views alcoholism and other addictions as central activities that, like any strong habits, require great effort to alter. Robert Goodin, by contrast, emphasizes that smoking addiction decreases voluntary control and hence must be prevented from occurring in the first place.

Several questions are pertinent in assessing responsibility for particular drug uses. What direct or indirect harm to others might be caused? What is the threat to our own health, and what are the legal implications? Is it worth the risks, given the likely benefits? Are we becoming so preoccupied with the drug that our attention, energy, money, and time are diverted from worthwhile activities? Is the drug causing a dependency that lessens our sense of self-control, autonomy, and self-respect? Does the drug threaten to distort our capacity to process information rationally and to conduct a meaningful life?

DISCUSSION TOPICS

1 Sketch how a rule-utilitarian and an act-utilitarian might approach the question of whether to use illegal drugs. How might each respond to what Kant says in this passage: "A drunkard [sometimes] does no harm to another, and if he has a strong constitution he does no harm to himself, yet he is an object of contempt. We are not indifferent to cringing servility [to drugs]; man should not cringe and fawn; by so doing he degrades his person."[12]

2 Emotions and moods usually have strong correlation with our beliefs about events; indeed, beliefs partly define what emotions are. For example, when we are cheerful, it is usually because our lives seem to us to be going well, and when we are sad, it is because of a loss of something or someone we value. What would you say about a repeated use of drugs to alter the emotions appropriate to various situations—for example, in order to feel cheerful at the funeral of a friend, or to feel exhilarated after failing exams?

3 Does peer pressure constitute coercion to use drugs, such that people are not able to make voluntary decisions based on their own wishes? Are "Just Say No" clubs and other peer groups that influence people not to use drugs also coercive in a way that undermines the ability of people to make their own decisions, or do they support autonomy?

4 Compare two groups of drivers who cause serious accidents: (a) sober but reckless drivers, and (b) drivers who are so intoxicated that they are unable to prevent an accident. Are the second drivers less blameworthy for their actions and thus deserving of lighter penalties?

5 Many corporations have adopted random drug-testing programs as a condition of employment. These programs are relatively uncontroversial where safety is a major part of the job, as in the case of soldiers, police officers, pilots, and public transportation drivers. Some companies, however, such as Texas Instruments, require random drug-testing of all employees, including engineers and top management. Critics charge that this violates privacy rights.[13] They argue that drug use either harms work performance or it does not. If it does, then an employer can penalize an employee because of the bad performance itself; if it does not, then drug use is not the employer's business. Defenders of the programs argue that the widespread drug use in our society inevitably lowers overall work productivity. How would you balance employee and employer rights on this issue?

6 Attempts are being made to ban all drugs, including muscle-building and performance-enhancing drugs such as steroids, in both amateur and professional sports. Critics of these attempts argue that people have a right to make their own decisions about drug use and to undergo any risks the drugs involve. They point out that participation in sports is itself inherently risky. Defenders argue that drugs unjustifiably add to the risks incurred by athletes and pressure competitors into using steroids to compensate for their opponents' use of steroids. They also suggest that drugs change the nature of sports so that they are no longer expressions of natural talent combined with effort. Formulate and defend your view on this issue.

7 Several general responses to weakness of will were described in Chapter 20: One can revise one's values, try harder in the future, accept one's flaws, or make excuses. Illustrate how a chain-smoker might use each of these responses in (a) an honest way and (b) a self-deceiving and dishonest way.

8 Executives and professionals (including physicians) who work for tobacco companies often argue that they are not engaged in a harmful enterprise, since consumers are free to choose whether to use their product. Do you agree? What tactics (such as those discussed in Chapter 19) might employees of tobacco companies use to deceive themselves about their work?

9 David A. J. Richards advocates the legalization of most currently illegal drugs, using the following argument.

> It is initially important to distinguish two kinds of paternalism: interference on the basis of facts unknown to the agent, in order to save the agent from harms that he would wish to avoid, and interferences on the basis of values that the agent does not himself share. Paternalism of the first kind, as applied in such laws as those securing the purity of drugs, is unobjectionable. Paternalism of the second kind, which underlies many laws currently criminalizing drug use, is not only objectionable, it is a violation of human rights."[14]

Assess Richards's view, focusing your discussion on the issue of whether marijuana should be legalized.

SUGGESTED READINGS

Bakalar, James B., and Lester Grinspoon. *Drug Control in a Free Society*. New York: Cambridge University Press, 1988.

Douglas, Mary (ed.). *Constructive Drinking: Perspective on Drink from Anthropology*. New York: Cambridge University Press, 1987.

Dworkin, Gerald. *The Theory and Practice of Autonomy*. New York: Cambridge University Press, 1988.

Falco, Mathea. *The Making of a Drug-Free America: Programs that Work*. New York: Times Books, 1992.

Feinberg, Joel. *Harm to Self*. Vol. 3 of *The Moral Limits of the Criminal Law*. New York: Oxford University Press, 1986.

Fingarette, Herbert. *Heavy Drinking: The Myth of Alcoholism as a Disease*. Berkeley: University of California Press, 1988.

Goode, Erich. *Drugs in American Society*. 5th ed. New York: McGraw-Hill, 1998.

Goodin, Robert E. *No Smoking: The Ethical Issues.* Chicago: University of Chicago Press, 1989.

Husak, Douglas N. *Drugs and Rights.* New York: Cambridge University Press, 1992.

Huxley, Aldous. *The Doors of Perception and Heaven and Hell.* New York: Harper, 1963.

Krogh, David. *Smoking: The Artificial Passion.* New York: W. H. Freeman, 1991.

Levinson, Peter K. *Substance Abuse, Habitual Behavior, and Self-Control.* Boulder, CO: Westview Press, 1984.

Liska, Ken. *Drugs and the Human Body, With Implications for Society.* 5th ed. New York: Macmillan, 1996.

Luper-Foy, Steven, and Curtis Brown (eds.). *Drugs, Morality, and the Law.* Hamden, CT: Garland Pulbishing, 1994.

Martin, Mike W. "Alcoholism as Sickness and Wrongdoing," *Journal for the Theory of Social Behaviour,* vol. 29 (1999): 109–131.

Nakken, Craig. *The Addictive Personality.* 2d ed. Centre City, MN: Hazelden, 1996.

Orford, Jim. *Excessive Appetites: A Psychological View of Addictions.* New York: Wiley, 1985.

Peele, Stanton. *The Meaning of Addiction: Compulsive Experience and Its Interpretation.* Lexington, MA: Lexington Books, 1985.

Richards, David A. J. *Sex, Drugs, Death, and the Law: An Essay on Human Rights and Overcriminalization.* Totowa, NJ: Rowman & Littlefield, 1982.

Seeburger, Francis *Addiction and Responsibility.* New York: Crossroad, 1995.

Torr, James D., Karin Swisher, and Schott Varbour (eds.) *Drug Abuse: Opposing Viewpoints.* St. Paul, MN: Greenhaven, 1999.

Vaillant, George E. *The Natural History of Alcoholism Revisited.* Cambridge, MA: Harvard University Press, 1995.

CHAPTER 23

Suicide and Euthanasia

Albert Camus (1913–1960) remarked, "There is but one truly serious philosophical problem, and that is suicide. Judging whether life is or is not worth living amounts to answering the fundamental question of philosophy."[1] Notwithstanding his literary use of hyperbole, Camus insightfully draws attention to how suicide raises fundamental issues about morality, the meaning of life, and the responsibilities of communities. Suicide is an issue for old and young alike, and it is especially alarming with regard to teenagers, for whom suicide is the second leading cause of death (next to car accidents).

Euthanasia—*mercy killing*—also raises basic issues about the conditions under which life is worth living. It has emerged as a pressing issue as medicine extends life beyond the point that many people find desirable. After discussing suicide we will turn to the question of whether euthanasia is justified.

What Is Suicide?

Defining suicide seems easy enough. Unlike accidental death or being killed by someone else, suicide is the act of killing oneself voluntarily (without extreme coercion) and intentionally (acting knowingly with the purpose of killing oneself). Our actions can be voluntary, however, to greater or lesser degrees, and some degrees of coercion may be compatible with suicide. Also, suicide often occurs when persons are severely depressed, which raises questions about whether they are acting freely. Finally, can it be considered suicide if one's ultimate intention is to defend someone else or to preserve one's integrity, rather than to secure death per se?

Consider first the situation in which a suicide occurs during severe depression or emotional distress. In such cases, do individuals genuinely choose to kill themselves, or are their acts symptoms of a psychological (if not physiological) illness beyond their control? For centuries coroners

tended to view self-killing as strong evidence of insanity, and hence techni-
cally not suicide, unless there was explicit evidence to the contrary, such as a
carefully written suicide note.[2] This trend reversed with the development of
insurance policies that refuse benefits in cases of self-killing. Perhaps for the
purposes of business and law, a wider definition of suicide is needed, but
should severe depression lead us to question whether persons are acting voluntarily in killing themselves?

Furthermore, what should be concluded when persons kill themselves
because of duress or coercion (from outside) rather than compulsions (from
within)? Did Socrates, for example, commit suicide?[3] On the basis of
trumped-up charges, he was found guilty of corrupting the young and in-
venting false gods and was given the choice between exile from Athens or
death by drinking hemlock. He "chose" to drink the hemlock—did he
commit suicide?

Finally, consider heroic persons whose intentions are to serve a worthy
cause and at the same time preserve their own integrity as someone committed to that cause. A soldier, for example, might take a cyanide pill rather
than be subjected to torture that could force revelation of secrets to the
enemy. During the Vietnam War, Buddhist monks burned themselves to
death to protest the war. During the 1910–1912 expedition to the South
Pole Captain Oates, who was too sick to continue with the group being led
by Captain Scott, left camp to walk into a blizzard so that the group could
continue unhampered by him. In all these cases, the primary intention was
not to die, but instead to achieve some larger noble purpose. Were these
people martyrs, suicides, or both?

For the purposes of moral inquiry, it seems preferable to adopt a wide
interpretation of suicide, and then inquire into the reasons for and against
suicide in a particular case. Unless there is clear evidence of insanity beyond
the act of self-killing, we will count depression-motivated self-killing as suicide. We will count Socrates' death as suicide because he had at least one
option, exile. And we will also count as suicide cases where the self-killing
has a strategic intent to serve some additional noble purpose.[4] The following discussion, however, will focus on clear-cut instances of suicide.

Is Suicide Ever Justified?

Saint Thomas Aquinas argued that all suicide is immoral. Most of his reasons were religious. In his view, suicide violates the natural laws created by
God, usurps God's power over life and death, and destroys bodies that are
the property of the God who created them. Not all theists share Aquinas's
interpretation of scripture, but it is clear that one's religious views will influence one's understanding of whether suicide is ever justified.

Without invoking religious beliefs, can we find distinct moral reasons
against suicide? Aquinas mentioned one moral reason that provides a useful

starting point: Suicide is contrary "to charity whereby every man should love himself."[5] Let us develop the idea that the virtue of self-respect (or self-love) poses a strong presumption against suicide. Then we will ask whether that presumption can ever be overridden by other moral considerations.

Thomas E. Hill, Jr., distinguishes four cases of suicide that reveal conduct that is less than morally ideal or virtuous:

1 *Impulsive suicide:* A person commits suicide as a result of a brief but intense emotion, such as grief in losing a spouse or lover, despair in losing one's job, or fear upon learning one has a serious illness.

2 *Apathetic suicide:* A person commits suicide because of a temporary or ongoing depression in which life seems empty and meaningless.

3 *Self-abasing suicide:* A person is filled with self-hatred and commits suicide as a form of self-contempt and self-punishment.

4 *Hedonistic calculated suicide:* A person commits suicide because he or she calculates that the future will probably bring more pain than pleasure.

In each case, the individuals fail to value themselves in appropriate ways and degrees. Self-respect requires us to resist suicide in these cases. Blame is not at issue here; often we should respond with compassion for individuals who were tragic victims of situations beyond their control. Even then, however, we can reasonably believe that no one who commits suicide for any of Hill's reasons has met our ideal of a morally good life. Inspired by Kant, Hill states the ideal this way: "A morally ideal person will value life as a rational, autonomous agent for its own sake, at least provided that the life does not fall below a certain threshold of gross, irremediable, and uncompensated pain and suffering."[6] (We might further attribute to this ideal person the virtues of faith, hope, courage, and caring, displayed in the search for meaningful life through personal relationships and through community.)

Hill acknowledges that sometimes suicide is justified in the following circumstances:

1 *Suicide to prevent subhuman life:* A person has good reason to believe that he or she will survive an illness physically alive but mentally destroyed with life reduced to the level of a lower animal or vegetable.

2 *Suicide to end severe irremediable suffering:* A person is in intense pain that can no longer be controlled by medication, short of constant unconsciousness.

3 *Morally principled suicide:* A person acts on justified commitments central to her or his moral integrity in order to help others and preserve that integrity.

In each of these three cases, self-respect is no longer an argument against suicide. Indeed, self-respect provides a reason for favoring suicide as a way to secure death with dignity.

So far, we have focused on self-respect, primarily within the framework of virtue ethics. How do the other ethical theories apply to suicide?

A human-rights ethics that emphasizes the right to liberty would recognize a right to make decisions about taking one's life. Nevertheless, a rights ethicist might add two qualifications. First, rights ethics implies that we should have a respect for ourselves as persons who have rights. That respect is lost in throwing away our lives without a compelling justification. Second, rights ethics requires us to take into account the rights of others. Although other persons do not have a right to demand that I live, people close to me do have rights not to be harmed wantonly. When suicide causes enormous suffering to family and friends, as it often does, there is a presumption against it.

Duty ethics balances duties to oneself and to others. Duties to others, especially duties not to inflict suffering on them, often provide strong reasons against suicide. In addition, Kant believed there is an absolute (exceptionless) duty to oneself not to take one's life. That belief seems too strong, however, since it disregards the equally significant responsibility to maintain one's integrity and a minimally decent human life—considerations that may justify some suicides.

Utilitarianism, which focuses exclusively on good consequences, justifies suicides that are reasonably intended to prevent irremediable suffering or the loss of humanly significant life or to heroically promote the good of others. At the same time, utilitarianism forbids many suicides by which meaningful life is prematurely cut short or needless suffering is inflicted on others.

Preventing Suicide

What are our responsibilities when we can prevent other persons from committing suicide? At first glance it seems the answer depends entirely on whether the suicide is justified: If the suicide is not justified then we should intervene to prevent it (when we can do so without great risk or cost), and if the suicide is justified we should refrain from intervening. Matters are not that simple, however; often we cannot tell whether an attempted suicide is justified, at least at the time the attempt is made.

Rights ethics, duty ethics, and rule-utilitarianism all justify a strong principle of autonomy (self-determination): People should be left alone to make their own decisions as long as those decisions do not harm others. John Stuart Mill (1806–1873) articulated this principle in *On Liberty:* "[T]he only purpose for which power can be rightfully exercised over any member of a civilized community, against his will, is to prevent harm to others. His own good, either physical or moral, is not a sufficient warrant."[7]

This principle may seem to suggest that we should leave alone those adults who decide to commit suicide; but in fact the principle of autonomy justifies suicide interventions when we have reasons to think the person is not acting autonomously or when we can reasonably presume they are not. Suicide is irreversible; it permanently ends the ability to exercise further autonomy. Thus, in order to support others' autonomy, we are often justified in intervening, especially with positive support intended to preserve their future agency.

The principle of autonomy, however, justifies only temporary intervention, as Glanville Williams argued:

> If one suddenly comes upon another person attempting suicide, the natural and humane thing to do is to try to stop him, for the purpose of ascertaining the cause of his distress and attempting to remedy it, or else of attempting moral dissuasion if it seems that the act of suicide shows lack of consideration for others, or else again from the purpose of trying to persuade him to accept psychiatric help if this seems to be called for. . . . But nothing longer than a temporary restraint could be defended.[8]

Those who oppose Mill's heavy emphasis on autonomy embrace *paternalism*. According to a strong version of paternalism, we are sometimes justified in promoting the positive well-being of others against their will, indeed forcing them to seek their own good. According to a weaker (but still potent) version of paternalism, we are sometimes justified in forcing people not to harm themselves or in preventing themselves from voluntarily harming themselves. Paternalists favor more insistent and thoroughgoing interventions to prevent suicide, including forced hospitalization if necessary. They tend to interpret suicide attempts as cries for help, and they also stress the value of human life.

Whether we agree with Mill or with paternalists, we can agree that a caring society will make positive resources available for suicidal individuals. For example, suicide hot lines, staffed primarily by volunteers, provide immediate support for individuals who need to talk with someone.

Assisting Suicide

Are we ever justified in actually helping someone commit suicide? In particular, suppose that a person who is mentally competent voluntarily chooses to commit suicide in circumstances where death is a reasonable option and where the person needs or requests help in committing suicide. Does respect for the person's autonomy permit (or even require) us to assist a suicide?

For several years, beginning in 1990, Dr. Jack Kevorkian assisted about 130 patients in committing suicide. In most cases he provided them with a simple "suicide machine" that they could operate by pushing a lever with one finger, so as to inject a lethal dose of potassium chloride through an intravenous needle he attached to them. Other times he made available a mask through which they breathed carbon monoxide. The people he assisted were not terminally ill, but they suffered from severe disabilities that in their view warranted suicide. For example, his first three patients in

Michigan suffered from one of the following conditions: Alzheimer's disease, multiple sclerosis, and a painful pelvic disease. At the time, there was no law in Michigan forbidding physician-assisted suicide, although by 1993 Michigan had passed such a law. Were Kevorkian's acts permissible? The courts and many members of the medical community were outraged and revoked his medical license. Members of the public were uneasy, but far from unanimously hostile to Kevorkian. Only when Dr. Kevorkian went beyond assisting suicide to actually performing euthanasia (allowing it to be filmed and broadcast on *60 Minutes*) was Kevorkian convicted of a crime (second-degree murder) in March 1999 and sent to jail.

Dr. Kevorkian acted in part to help particular individuals and in part to draw national attention to what he believed was a justified case for legalizing physician-assisted suicide. He was not alone in this belief. During these years several states placed on ballots proposals to legalize physician-assisted suicide in cases where a person is diagnosed with a terminal illness and has less than six months to live. In 1992, for example, a California ballot proposal won 43 percent of the general vote. In fact, before the election the polls showed a majority of Californians would vote for the proposal, but during the debate many voters became concerned about possible abuses if the law passed. Oregon has since then legalized physician-assisted suicide, with safeguards to ensure informed and voluntary consent.

Dr. Kevorkian's cases are not the only nationally debated examples of persons who, although they do not have terminal illnesses, have disabilities that they believe make their lives not worth living. Consider Elizabeth Bouvia, who in 1983 entered a hospital in Riverside, California, complaining of depression. After being admitted, she asked to be allowed to starve herself to death while receiving pain medication and sanitary care. At the time Ms. Bouvia was twenty-six years old. As a quadriplegic who was almost completely paralyzed, she was physically unable to kill herself without help. She also suffered palsy and severe arthritic pain that could not be entirely controlled by medication. Yet she could speak, was highly intelligent, and had earned a college degree. In defending her decision to die, she appealed to self-respect and personal dignity: "I hate to have someone care for every personal need . . . it's humiliating. It's disgusting, and I choose to no longer do that, no longer to be dependent on someone to take care of me in that manner."[9] Despite her initial complaint about depression, she was evaluated as fully competent to make her own decisions.

Almost no one would argue that her nurses and physicians were morally *required* to help her commit suicide, since that might violate their personal moral convictions, but were they morally *permitted* to assist Ms. Bouvia if they chose to do so?

Here is what actually happened. Ms. Bouvia's lawyer sought a court order forbidding the hospital from either force-feeding her or discharging her from the hospital against her will. The court refused to grant such an order. Ms. Bouvia soon checked out of the hospital, but in 1986 entered another hospital to try again. This time she won court approval not to be fed against her will, but then she changed her mind. A year later, however, she tried yet again to starve to death with the assistance of hospital personnel. The constant vomiting from pain-killing medication (taken on an empty stomach) was too exhausting an ordeal, and she abandoned her attempt. Since that time she has lived in a small hospital room in Los Angeles County.

As this example illustrates, the medical community, courts, and even patients like Ms. Bouvia are not altogether clear about the desirability of suicide when issues about quality of life are at stake. Nevertheless, the courts have increasingly come to recognize the legal and moral rights of mentally competent individuals to decide what happens to their bodies. Long ago the Supreme Court ruled that adult Jehovah's Witnesses have the right to refuse life-essential blood transfusions, not only because of their religious freedom to act on their belief that such transfusions were prohibited by the Bible, but because of their right to privacy—their right to autonomy or self-determination. More recently, the Supreme Court has ruled that a competent person has the right to refuse even food and water.[10]

Euthanasia

Death by starvation takes many days and can be unpleasant. Would it not be far more humane and merciful, once a mentally competent person voluntarily chooses to die, to end life instantaneously, perhaps with a simple injection of morphine? The taking of someone's life for humane reasons is called *euthanasia* or mercy killing. Is it morally permissible? Currently it is illegal, but let us consider the moral issues independently of that important fact. These moral issues will decide whether the law should remain the same or be changed in the future.

Precisely what is euthanasia? It implies an intention to bring about the death of someone and to do so from beneficent motives (concern for the person). Usually it is also understood to pertain to situations in which a person has a terminal illness or suffers from extreme disabilities such as those of Elizabeth Bouvia. *Passive euthanasia* is the omission of actions that would prolong life; examples include the withholding of medicine, medical technology, or food and water with the intention of letting a person die. Active euthanasia is the performance of actions that bring about death, such as the administration of lethal injections of morphine. The distinction between passive and active euthanasia is not crystal clear. For example, "pulling the plug" is the act of turning off a patient's respirator or removing a feeding tube, but it is usually viewed as passive euthanasia because it is the withholding of a technology that prolongs life.

We can also distinguish between voluntary, involuntary, and nonvoluntary euthanasia. *Nonvoluntary* euthanasia occurs without a person's consent, usually when the person is in a coma or otherwise mentally incapacitated. *Involuntary* euthanasia would be the special case of euthanasia that is performed against a person's wishes. *Voluntary* euthanasia occurs when a mentally competent individual requests euthanasia on the basis of free and informed consent—that is, without coercion and in possession of relevant information that a reasonable person would want to know. That consent may be given (as a precaution against the possibility one might enter a coma or lose mental capacities) by a *living will* or an *advanced directive* to physicians and courts. It can also be given by a surrogate, such as a close relative or someone one appoints (in a Durable Power of Attorney document) to make such decisions should one become incapacitated.

We will focus on voluntary active euthanasia, since it is the only type of legalization currently being debated. It has been permitted in the Netherlands for more than two decades under the following conditions: (a) A competent patient (b) who is suffering intolerably and without possible relief (whether or not a terminal illness is involved) (c) requests euthanasia voluntarily and consistently over a reasonable time and (d) secures the approval of both the attending physician and a second physician not involved in the case.[11] Despite polls that show the majority of Americans favor legalization of active euthanasia if adequate safeguards can be secured, the American Medical Association (AMA) continues to oppose active euthanasia while condoning passive euthanasia (in cases where a person is terminally ill and continued therapy holds no promise). Is this firm dichotomy between passive and active euthanasia justified?

James Rachels criticized the AMA's position. Contrary to the AMA, he argued that letting someone die is not in principle more acceptable than actively killing the person. He offers several arguments. First, compare Smith and Jones, each of whom will inherit a large amount of money if his six-year-old cousin dies. Smith drowns his cousin while the child is bathing and carefully makes the death look accidental. Jones is about to do the same thing when by chance he sees the child slip, strike his head, and fall unconscious into the water. He watches to make sure the child dies before sneaking away. Smith killed his cousin; Jones let his cousin die. Both, however, are equally blameworthy. Therefore, "the bare difference between killing and letting die does not, in itself, make a moral difference. If a doctor lets a patient die, for humane reasons, he is in the same moral position as if he had given the patient a lethal injection for humane reasons."[12]

No doubt the law would distinguish between the cases of Smith and Jones: Smith is guilty of first-degree murder, while Jones is not (and perhaps could not be convicted unless he had been in charge of the child's care at the time of the accident). Morally, however, the cases are equally immoral and horrifying. Rachels's example, then, does establish that *sometimes* the mere difference between killing and letting someone die is morally insignificant; but does the example show that the difference is always insignificant? Rachels's example involves malicious motives and the intention to kill. In medicine the motives and intentions are typically quite different. The intention is usually to respect a patient's right to refuse further medical treatment, or to acknowledge the desirability of withholding therapy in some cases where there is no reasonable hope of improving the patient's condition.[13]

Is it inconsistent to respect the right to refuse treatment and yet not condone active killing? Apparently not. The right of autonomy (self-determination) gives us a right to prevent health professionals from performing unwanted procedures on our bodies, but it does not imply a right to be killed. Thus, the intuitive distinction between killing and letting someone die does sometimes have moral significance, contrary to Rachels. However, there are other arguments favoring active euthanasia.

Active Euthanasia, Mercy, and Autonomy

Rachels's main argument appeals to mercy. To allow a person to die slowly rather than quickly seems patently cruel. In Rachels's view, once a decision has been made not to prolong life—indeed, to bring it to a rapid close by withholding life-essential medicine or food—the compassionate thing is to bring about that result quickly and without suffering, if a person so requests. (Notice that this argument actually distinguishes between the moral status of killing and letting someone die, and favors the former as more humane in this case.)

It might seem that the argument for mercy is not so important, given the techniques of modern medicine that enable physicians to control pain. In fact, however, there are instances in which pain cannot be controlled without simply making a person unconscious. As Margaret Pabst Battin, another defender of active euthanasia, points out, "Some people still die in unspeakable agony . . . [and] complete, universal, fully reliable pain control is a myth."[14] Indeed, suffering includes more than physical pain. It also involves the great discomfort of lying helplessly in bed in an utterly dependent state that one regards with abhorrence, or would so regard if one's consciousness were not blurred by medication.

Rachels's and Battin's appeal to mercy is compelling, but is it decisive? According to the AMA, mercy matters greatly but it cannot override the fundamental duty not to kill (innocent) persons. Mercy justifies administration of whatever medication is necessary to control pain, even if the medication might well lead to death, but it does not warrant intentional killing.

The AMA's position is supported by the principle of double effect, which was developed over hundreds of years in the Catholic church. A potentially lethal dose of morphine may have two possible effects: control of pain and death. According to the principle of double effect, the moral act is to intend only the control of pain while knowing, but not intending, that death will occur. More generally, the principle of double effect says that it is morally permissible to perform an act that will have an unintended bad side-effect when one's motive and intention are to achieve the good result only, when the side-effect does not directly produce the intended result, and when the good effect is at least as valuable as the bad effect. Since administering active euthanasia involves intentional killing (a bad effect) as a means to the good effect, the principle of double effect does not allow it.

It is understandable that the Catholic church and the AMA might emphasize not killing over other moral considerations regarding euthanasia; but what about the wider public (including many Catholics and physicians who disagree with their religious and professional organizations)? Should not individuals be free to make their own decisions in this matter? This returns us to the issue of autonomy and self-respect. It also returns us to the issue of assisted suicide, insofar as assisted suicide is sometimes preferable to active euthanasia.

Earlier we noted that the right to autonomy does not imply a right to be killed. Advocates of euthanasia, however, argue that it does sometimes imply a (positive) right to assistance in dying. Margaret Pabst Battin writes, "Although we usually recognize only that the principle of autonomy generates rights to noninterference, in some circumstances a right of self-determination does generate [justified] claims to assistance or to the provision of goods. We typically acknowledge this in cases of handicap or disability."[15] Is it not reasonable to extend this right to aid to a person who has become physically unable to carry out her or his intention to die? Or would doing so cross a taboo of active killing that is inherently unacceptable (because it devalues life) and possibly open to abuses?

SUMMARY

Suicide is intentional and voluntary self-killing, but questions arise about whether suicide occurs in cases of severe depression and coercion (where voluntariness is questioned) and altruism (where the primary intention is a noble goal rather than death per se). Thomas Hill argued for a strong presumption against suicide, especially in cases where it reveals a lack of self-respect. Whereas Aquinas and Kant viewed all suicide as immoral, however, Hill thinks suicide is justifiable to prevent conditions of subhuman life and severe irremediable suffering, and in some instances to achieve morally principled goals (such as helping others or preserving one's dignity).

Intervention to prevent suicide can be justified if one accepts the principle of paternalism: It is permissible to interfere with the freedom of others in order to promote their great good (strong paternalism) or to prevent great harms to them (weak paternalism). For Mill, by contrast, only temporary interventions are permissible in order to make sure persons are acting voluntarily; otherwise we fail to respect individual autonomy (self-determination). Assisted suicide is defended by Dr. Jack Kevorkian and much of the public on the grounds of one's autonomy to decide the kinds of suffering one wishes to prevent. Critics fear that legalization of physician-assisted suicide will generate too many abuses and mistakes.

Euthanasia can be active (killing someone) or passive (letting someone die), and voluntary (informed consent is obtained) or nonvoluntary. Passive, voluntary euthanasia is legal, including the withholding of food and water in some circumstances, but active euthanasia is illegal. Arguments for legalizing active euthanasia include appeals to mercy and patient autonomy. Arguments against legalization emphasize respect for life and concern over possible abuses. Opponents of active euthanasia sometimes invoke the principle of double effect to justify some acts that bring about death although death is unintended. That principle says that it is morally permissible to perform an act that will have an unintended bad side-effect when one's motive and intention are to achieve the good result only, when the side-effect does not directly produce the intended result, and when the good effect is at least as valuable as the bad effect.

DISCUSSION TOPICS

1 Do the following examples qualify as cases of suicide?
   a A soldier goes on a "suicide mission," as did Japanese kamikaze pilots who flew their airplanes into enemy ships.
   b A pilot dies because she decided not to parachute, in order to crash her plane away from a populated area.
   c A man jumps out of a lifeboat after losing in a lottery to see who would die in order that the others could survive with the limited supply of food and water.[16]

2 Is suicide ever morally justified? In which cases? Comment on why you agree or disagree with Thomas Hill's analysis of the examples he provides. In particular, do you agree with Hill that hedonistic calculated suicide is objectionable because it reveals a lack of self-respect?

3 Present and defend your view concerning the circumstances under which we are permitted and required to intervene to prevent someone from committing suicide. Would you emphasize the principle of autonomy or the principle of paternalism?

4 In 1975, twenty-one-year-old Karen Quinlan was brought to the hospital unconscious and seriously brain-damaged from an unknown cause (although it was known that she had been drinking some alcohol at a birthday party and had some traces of aspirin and Valium in her blood). Over several months her condition deteriorated. Her weight went from 120 to 70 pounds, and she shriveled into a rigid fetal position. She retained some brain function and hence was not "legally dead" (the state in which no electrical activity takes place in the brain), but she was in a permanent and irreversible vegetative state. Her parents went to court and, by proving to the court that Karen would not wish to continue life in a vegetative state, won the right to have a respirator removed. When the respirator was removed, however, Karen's anticipated death did not occur. At the time, laws required that she be given food and water. She remained alive in a comatose state for ten years before she died in 1985. Would active euthanasia have been justified in her case? More generally, is active voluntary euthanasia ever morally permissible? Defend your view by reference to one or more ethical theories.

5 Explain whether you agree with the principle of double effect. In particular, consider this: The principle of double effect is often used to justify giving a terminal-cancer patient a dose of morphine that the physician knows might be lethal but

that is intended only to alleviate pain. Is there any genuine moral difference in such cases between acting on the principle of double effect and acting with the intention to bring about a quick and painless death to a patient (thereby engaging in active euthanasia)?

6 Some people believe that particular acts of voluntary active euthanasia are morally justified, but they join with groups opposed to euthanasia to fight laws legalizing its practice. They are concerned about the possible abuses and mistakes that might occur if active euthanasia became widely practiced. They cite the following facts:[17] (a) Physicians sometimes make mistakes when they diagnose an illness as terminal or beyond hope. (b) There is always the possibility that medical research will discover new cures if persons just stay alive to wait for them. (c) Greedy relatives might pressure parents into requesting euthanasia. (d) To allow physicians to engage in euthanasia might cause them inner turmoil in their primary role as healers and undermine their patients' trust in them. (e) Laws permitting active euthanasia might make the public more callous about killing and might open the door (of Pandora's Box) to legalization of euthanasia in further contexts. Do these facts constitute decisive reasons against legalizing euthanasia?

7 In the past, questions about money were often dismissed as irrelevant to debates over euthanasia and assisted suicide, because human life is precious and beyond any dollar figure. Due to skyrocketing costs of medical care, however, paid for largely by the public through government programs, the question of money increasingly enters into the euthanasia debate. A huge percentage of medical costs goes to the care of terminal patients who require high-tech medical attention. In a time of dwindling resources for medical care, that means that fewer resources are available for preventative medical care, including prenatal and early child care. This raises questions about justice and fairness in the distribution of medical resources. Present and defend your view concerning whether and how questions about money should influence decisions about legalizing physician-assisted suicide and active euthanasia.

8 This chapter focused on voluntary euthanasia, but consider instances of nonvoluntary euthanasia. Do you think euthanasia (either passive or active) is justified in either of the following two cases?

a A bedridden and irreversibly senile eighty-year-old man, who can no longer communicate or be socially involved, never indicated his views on suicide.

b A child is born with a severe case of spina bifida, a genetic disability that greatly restricts possibilities of movement, so that many operations would be required to make possible a life of even very limited social interaction.

SUGGESTED READINGS

Battin, M. Pabst (ed.). *Ethical Issues in Suicide*. Englewood Cliffs, NJ: Prentice Hall, 1995.

Battin, Margaret Pabst. *The Least Worst Death: Essays in Bioethics on the End of Life*. New York: Oxford University Press, 1994.

Battin, Margaret Pabst, David Mayo, and Susan M. Wolf. *Physician-Assisted Suicide: Pro and Con*. Lanham, MD: Rowman & Littlefield, 1999.

Battin, Margaret Pabst, Rosamond Rhodes, and Anita Silvers (eds.) *Physician-Assisted Suicide: Expanding the Debate*. London: Routledge, 1998.

Beauchamp, Tom L. (ed.). *Intending Death: The Ethics of Assisted Suicide and Euthanasia.* Upper Saddle River, NJ: Prentice-Hall, 1996.

Beauchamp, Tom L., and Robert M. Veatch. *Ethical Issues in Death and Dying,* 2d ed. Upper Saddle River, NJ: Prentice-Hall, 1996.

Becker, Ernest. *The Denial of Death.* New York: The Free Press, 1997. First published 1973.

Byock, Ira. *Dying Well: The Prospect for Growth at the End of Life.* New York: Riverhead Books, 1997.

Donnelly, John (ed.). *Suicide: Right or Wrong?* 2d ed. Buffalo, NY: Prometheus Books, 1998.

Dworkin, Ronald. *Life's Dominion: An Argument about Abortion, Euthanasia, and Individual Freedom.* New York: Alfred A. Knopf, 1993.

Feldman, Fred. *Confrontations with the Reaper: A Philosophical Study of the Nature and Value of Death.* New York: Oxford University Press, 1992.

Fingarette, Herbert. *Death: Philosophical Soundings.* Chicago: Open Court, 1996.

Glover, Jonathan. *Causing Death and Saving Lives.* New York: Penguin Books, 1977.

Hill, Thomas E., Jr. "Self-Regarding Suicide: A Modified Kantian View." In *Autonomy and Self-Respect.* Cambridge: Cambridge University Press, 1991: pp. 85–103.

Kamm, F. M. *Morality, Mortality.* 2 vols. New York: Oxford University Press, 1993–1996.

Malpas, Jeff, and Robert C. Solomon (eds.). *Death and Philosophy.* New York: Routledge, 1998.

Moller, David Wendell. *Confronting Death.* New York: Oxford University Press, 1996.

Rachels, James. *The End of Life: Euthanasia and Morality.* Oxford: Oxford University Press, 1986.

Regan, Tom (ed.). *Matters of Life and Death,* 3d ed. New York: Random House, 1993.

Sartorius, Rolf (ed.). *Paternalism.* Minneapolis: University of Minnesota Press, 1983.

Weir, Robert (ed.). *Ethical Issues in Death and Dying,* 2d ed. New York: Columbia University Press, 1986.

PART EIGHT

Community and Wealth

*How rich this community is in meaning, in value, in
membership, in significant organization, will depend upon the
selves that enter into the community, and upon the ideals in terms
of which they define themselves, their past, and their future.*[1]
—*Josiah Royce*

Community and wealth are interwoven. A community's possibilities and prospects are significantly shaped by the wealth of its members, together with the values that guide how the wealth is used. In turn, wealth emerges from the traditions and resources that shape a community's economy. The very definition of money is community-defined; it is a socially standardized scale for measuring wealth and exchanging property. More generally, property is defined by a web of laws within a community. To own a car is to be able to do certain things with it, including to drive on public streets at posted speeds and with a valid driver's license, but not to drive it through our neighbor's front door.

Chapter 24 begins by noting that money has moral relevance to virtually all moral issues, including those discussed in this book. It then focuses on four topics: happiness (and self-fulfillment), gambling, consumerism, and economic justice. Chapter 25 discusses work and the values that shape it. And Chapter 26 explores community service, both in the form of making monetary contributions and in volunteering time and expertise.

CHAPTER 24

Money

As Woody Allen tells us, "money is better than poverty, if only for financial reasons."[1] Financial reasons have moral implications, such that morality pertains to all aspects of acquiring, possessing, and using money. Conversely, nearly all aspects of the moral life have an economic dimension. Think, for example, of the responsibilities of parents to their children, the economic trade-offs in order to preserve the environment, the economic hardship of the poor in obtaining abortions, and the multibillion-dollar pornography industry. Money is a primary domain of moral responsibility—of prudence and wisdom, caring and generosity, courage and cowardice, guilt and greed, envy and shame.

We begin by emphasizing the connections between money and happiness. Then we focus on a few topics where money matters are especially central: gambling, compulsive spending, and economic justice in wealth distribution.

Money and Happiness

Today we often talk more freely about sex than about the personal meaning of money. This secrecy is partly understandable, given fears about theft, malicious lawsuits, and relatives asking for loans. But our secrecy also reflects insecurities and perhaps ambivalence about how far we should and should not be concerned about money.

Our insecurities and ambivalence derive in part from powerful religious traditions. Churches, temples, and mosques rely on tithing and almsgiving bolstered by donations from the wealthy, hence presupposing the legitimacy of wealth. Yet some scriptures praise poverty and criticize wealth as a threat to higher ideals. Christian literature, for example, warns that the rich have a harder time entering heaven than a camel maneuvering through the eye of a needle, and also that "the love of money is the root of all evil."[2] Usually this passage is interpreted as condemning avarice or greed (one of the seven deadly sins)—that is, excessive preoccupation with money and property. Similarly, Jewish and Muslim scriptures call for finding a middle ground between excess wealth and poverty, so that money preoccupations do not eclipse more important values. Finding that golden mean is not easy.

Balance in money matters must take into account historical settings, but historical trends often compound uncertainty. During the 1980s, a strong cultural message was that "greed is good"—that is, it is admirable to aggressively compete for wealth without concern for who gets hurt. In addition, an era of inflation encouraged heavy spending rather than saving. This excess was not new in American history, which has always had cycles of "conspicuous spending" that served to establish social status, and it came partly as a backlash against President Jimmy Carter's call at the end of the 1970s for personal discipline within what some condemned as a "culture of narcissism."[3] The 1990s blurred the cultural landscape further with huge layoffs that for the first time cut deeply into the ranks of middle-class professionals, combined with accelerated global competition. By the end of 1990s, the U.S. economy had responded with historic success, but individuals were more insecure psychologically.

With these trends in mind, consider a couple of familiar clichés: Money can't buy love, and the best things in life are free—friendship, health, enjoyment of beauty, happiness, and joy. In part, the clichés imply a moral claim, and in part they make empirical claims that psychologists can study. To begin with psychologists' studies, they offer a partial affirmation of the clichés, although only partial. People do tend to be happier as they move beyond the poverty level, but once beyond that level, increasing income and overall wealth do not increase happiness—until the level of the very wealthy is reached, at which point there is (only) a slight increase. For the vast majority of the middle-class, money and happiness are not correlated at all. Moreover, studies show that lottery winners enjoy a period of increased happiness, typically a year, but then return to their previous level of happiness. The same is true of getting a pay raise, and in general, there is little correlation between levels of salary and happiness in the upper-half range of salaries.

These somewhat surprising facts have been explained by psychologists in four ways:

Adaptation: Although everybody feels happier after a pay rise, windfall, or pool win, one soon adapts to this and the effect very rapidly disppears.

Comparison: People define themselves as rich/wealthy by comparing themselves with others. However, with increased wealth, people usually move in more "upmarket" circles where there is always someone wealthier than themselves.

Alternatives: As economists say, the declining marginal utility of money means that as one has more of the stuff, other things such as freedom and true friendship seem much more valuable.

> *Worry:* An increased income is associated with a shifting of concern from money issues to the more uncontrollable elements of life (e.g., self-development), perhaps because money is associated with a sense of control over one's fate.[4]

Regarding worry, wealth also can create anxieties about losing money, whether by having it stolen or by being sued, although these worries are counterbalanced by pre-wealth worries about survival.

Although there is no general correlation between money and happiness, it is at most a half-truth that the best things in life are free. Enjoyment of the arts costs money. So does travel, recreation, housing in a safe area, and medical care. Although money cannot purchase love and friendship, there is some truth in the belief that money enhances sexual attractiveness, especially men's attractiveness to women. We can also purchase an array of goods—from cosmetics and clothing to cars—that enhance our attractiveness and our confidence in love pursuits. Attractiveness of jobs is obviously connected with the money they pay, and insofar as we find fulfillment through work, the risks of frustrating jobs that do not pay sufficiently are as great as the risks of "selling out" for an unfulfilling job that pays well. Perhaps most important of all, money buys freedom and time to do things we enjoy and need—not just entertainment, but such things as continuing education and rejuvinating vacations. In reply to Benjamin Franklin's maxim, "time is money," the novelist George Gissing said more profoundly that "money is time."[5]

As one final example of how money and happiness are related, the success of love relationships turns on shared and reciprocal responsibility concerning money, as well as fair negotiations and reasonable compromises. The most common source of friction and outright battles between couples is not sex, but how to use money. In part that is because money is a means to providing sustaining resources for the relationship. In part it is because money becomes a symbol of power in the relationship (as elsewhere in society). And in part it is because individuals have different money styles, (e.g., savers versus spenders, and compulsive versus conscientious consumers). Different money styles reflect different orientations to life, many of which are morally permissible, although some of which—like compulsive shopping and gambling—are morally problematic.

Money Madness and Financial Responsibility

If money can't buy happiness and love, according to advertisers it can at least purchase pleasure and sex. Ads tell (or show) us that if we purchase this car or that cologne, we will win an alluring sexual partner, and if we buy this diet pill or that exercise machine we will gain health and pleasure. We are often seduced by the ads, even though we know their exaggerations are silly. Or do we know this?

We have astonishingly many desires to buy things that we hardly need to survive. Advertisers are well-attuned to this, and seek to create an endless variety of desires to purchase new things. According to traditional economic theory, business simply responds to consumer desires, but, as economist John Kenneth Galbraith pointed out, business creates the desires for particular products that it then satisfies. He called this the *Dependence Effect:* "Wants depend on the process [of business and advertising] by which they are satisfied."[6]

Theodore Levitt, a former editor of the *Harvard Business Review,* celebrated this function of advertising in creating new desires, and he defended it in terms of consumers' freedom. We live in worlds of symbols, he reminded us, in which the things we purchase carry meanings beyond their instrumental (practical) value. Thus, the cars we drive affirm our power and taste, and the sneakers we wear identify us with famous athletes. Advertisers use and create symbols in order to answer to our needs for symbolic meanings. The deepest needs are existential projects in which each of us attempts to solve the problem of rising above our "own negligibility, of escaping from nature's confining, hostile, and unpredictable reality, of finding significance, security, and comfort in the things he [or she] must do to survive. . . . Without distortion, embellishment, and elaboration [by advertisers], life would be drab, dull, anguished, and at its existential worst."[7] Allowing for its hyperbole, this remark prompts us to reflect on the many ways we use commercial goods to bolster our sense of personal worth. It also, however, helps explain why intelligent middle-class individuals spend beyond their means in ways that render their lives anything but secure economically, or even psychologically.

Psychologists tend to approach money excesses as being compulsions or addictions that have unconscious motives.[8] Frequently the compulsions center around responses to money as a symbol for security, power, love, or freedom. Most attention is paid to money as a symbol of security. Thus, compulsive shoppers are obsessed with accumulating possessions in order to keep up with and feel superior to neighbors; compulsive bargain hunters spend excessive amounts of time looking for the perfect bargain, spurred by motives of outsmarting others; self-deniers enjoy self-imposed poverty, often masking motives of hostility and envy; and compulsive savers carry money owning to the point where they are unable to use it to grow or to help others. When the dominant symbolism is money as power, money becomes a way to manipulate and dominate others. When love is the main symbolic value, money is used unconsciously to attempt buying love, affection, and respect. And when freedom is the main symbolism, money is used in the irrational search for radical independence, perhaps even from death. There is nothing wrong with these symbolisms per se, but "wealth addictions" occur from the excessive and irrational pursuits centered around them.

What do these psychological matters have to do with morality? Although some cases of "money madness" or "affluence addictions" are genuine pathologies requiring therapeutic intervention, most of them are moral matters. As we noted in Chapter 21, the therapeutic trend often recasts moral matters in therapeutic language, such that the morally unreasonable is redescribed as unhealthy behavior. This moral link is expressed in the key words used in psychologists' descriptions of compulsions and addictions, such as *excessive, irrational,* or *disordered.* We do well to avoid a strong morality–therapeutic dichotomy, however, by understanding moral and therapeutic concepts as integrated rather than entirely separate and opposed. Apart from the extremes of pathology, many everyday consumer excesses are both morally unreasonable and unhealthy.

It will be objected that the notions of money madness and consumer compulsions are disguised forms of anti-capitalism. Within the bounds of law, people have rights to indulge in money in any way they choose, and the free market relies on exuberant playfulness in shopping. In reply, it is true that capitalism relies on consumer spending, but it also depends on capital! Capital is money invested in corporations, and the money that comes from building wealth rather than exhausting our income in consuming.

Income is money earned as a salary or from investments and gifts, but *wealth* is our overall financial worth. The distinction was driven home in a study published as the bestseller *The Millionaire Next Door.*[9] The authors of that book discovered that many of the stereotypes about millionaires are false. In 1996 there were about 3.5 million U.S. households having a net worth of a million dollars or more. (That number has risen dramatically since then). Eighty percent of those households were self-made millionaires, rather than wealthy because of inheritance. The typical millionaire did not live in exceptionally glamorous houses, drive expensive cars, or spend lavishly. Just the opposite. A crucial feature of most of millionaires is living frugally, well below their means, so as to be able to regularly invest at least 15 percent of their income.

Should the responsible use of money, then, be defined as frugality? This may seem odd, because we often think of frugality as a matter of personal taste, not morality. Granted, personal preferences do legitimately shape how extensively we allow ourselves to become caught up in "getting and spending." Attempts to mandate any one detailed vision of the moral worth of money is not only futile but harmful, given the variety of human temperaments and the manifold ways wealth contributes to communities. Nevertheless, we are responsible for living within our means, and that implies at least some degree of frugality. In addition, the morality of money involves more than duties incumbent on everyone. It also involves alternative moral ideals that guide how we use money, and these ideals shape our lives as dramatically as any other values.

The moral (and spiritual) ideal of *voluntary simplicity* has special interest. More accurately, this is not one ideal at all, but instead a varied collection of ideals. Historian David E. Shi, who has explored these ideals in the American tradition, concluded that "the simple life is not simple—either to define or to live." He concludes that the only unity in the idea of simple living is "the conscious desire to purge life of some of its complexities and superfluities in order to pursue 'higher' values,' " but what those values *are* varies considerably. Historically, the expression "the simple life" has been applied to all of the following:

> a concern for family nurture and community cohesion; a hostility toward luxury and a suspicion of riches; a belief that the primary reward of work should be well-being rather than money; a desire for maximum personal self-reliance and creative leisure; a nostalgia for the supposed simplicities of the past and an anxiety about the technological and bureaucratic complexities of the present and future; a taste for the plain and functional, especially in the home environment; a reverence for nature and a preference for country living; and a sense of both religious and ecological responsibility for the proper use of the world's resources.[10]

Thus, Henry David Thoreau's life at Walden Pond illustrates rustic simplicity, but the frugality of many entrepreneurs who become self-made millionaires constitutes another form. Each can be inspired by ideals of independence and of giving back to communities, although in different ways. For example, Thoreau was an important voice for ideals of respecting the natural environment, although he perhaps failed to appreciate the importance of the philanthropic giving that wealth helps make possible. Although there may be no basis for saying that everyone should aspire to such ideals of voluntary simplicity, nevertheless they illustrate how personal commitments to ideals reflect morally important attitudes about work, time, and activities, and also free up resources to help others.

Gambling

Gambling is any activity of risking money or other property in order to gain more money or assets from events that participants know or should know are random. Traditionally viewed with the same suspicion as prostitution and illegal drugs, gambling is today having something of a cultural heyday. Estimates are that more than three out of four Americans gamble in some form. Since the late 1980s, all but a few states have established and actively promote lotteries, and they have also loosened restrictions on private gambling. The impact has been dramatic: "The number of American households visiting casinos between 1990 and 1993 doubled, from 46 million to 92 million."[11] Gambling is a huge industry, running to several hundreds of billions of dollars each year, not counting illegal betting. State lotteries alone bring in nearly $100 million each day. The Internet and interactive-television gambling are making it even easier to gamble.

So are there any serious moral objections to gambling? We will consider five objections. None by itself provides a decisive reason to renounce gambling, but taken together they seem to make a strong case against heavy involvement in gambling.

First, gambling uses resources that might go to other purposes that are more productive. Religions traditionally condemned gambling as wasteful of resources God entrusts to humanity, and Lisa Newton defended a secular version of this argument. According to Newton, gambling is an "egregious violation" of the *duty of stewardship:*

> [T]here is a strong social interest in the care and conservation of all property in the commonwealth, that gives the public a justified and lively concern with the way people dispose of wealth that by law is private property. . . . Our duty of "stewardship" of the nation's property in general, then, can entail that putting that property at risk at the gaming tables is seriously wrong.[12]

This argument may seem like overkill. It seems to presuppose that gambling is inherently bad or wasteful. But is it? Most gambling is a recreational and even social activity that, when it uses only highly restricted amounts of resources, is not wasteful. In fact, it may be more socially useful than many other harmless entertainments, for example, when modest amounts are used on state lotteries that use half the money to support education. Perhaps if economic resources were in drastically short supply, the argument might have more teeth, but at present there are ample resources to support much gambling without undermining other important goals. Nevertheless, Newton sets forth her argument in an exploratory spirit, and it does sound an important theme about wastefulness. Rather than appealing to an abstract duty of stewardship, perhaps the argument is more engaging when recast in terms of using one's resources wisely in order to meet more specific responsibilities— such as to oneself, family, and society. Such an argument would apply against much, but not all, gambling.

Second, massive support for gambling, especially by government in the form of state-supported lotteries that advertise aggressively, fosters undesirable attitudes and character traits.[13] Getting something for nothing is not inherently objectionable. If it were, we would have to condemn gifts, inheritance, and many other forms of good fortune in investing. Nevertheless, the aggressive promotion of gambling by both government and the gambling industry replaces traditional cultural messages about the value of work and saving with endorsements of hopes for quick and easy luck. It sends messages of "Spend now for entertainment and for a chance at miraculous good fortune," rather than "Save and invest."

Third, gambling exploits the poor who are more desperate for a quick fix to their problems. Lower-income people, who can least afford to gamble, spend a much higher proportion of their income on gambling than do the wealthy. That fact has been confirmed repeatedly in studies of state lotteries, leading many to regard government-sponsored lotteries as a "regressive tax." That is, by contrast with "progressive" systems that tax the rich at a higher rate, states are in effect taking in gambling money (to use for schools or other community services) at a higher rate from the poor. Furthermore, the casino industry sometimes denies that the poor are heavy users of their facilities, encouraging the myth that the wealthy are the ones who gamble for entertainment. A study of Las Vegas and Atlantic City, however, found that "people earning less than $10,000 per year spent nearly two and a half times more on gambling as a percentage of their income than people earning $30–40,000."[14]

Fourth, gambling has wider negative effects on communities. It is true that real estate and business can benefit in the immediate areas that become tourist attractions because of casinos. Certainly Nevada's economy has benefited enormously from gambling. But in most states the particular areas that benefit are localized, and surrounding neighborhoods are actually harmed. In addition, it is no myth that gambling tends to bring with it prostitution, alcohol abuse, and crime. In addition, the public indirectly bears the burden for bankruptcies, broken families, and theft that results from problem gamblers—which brings us to the next concern.

Fifth, problem gamblers cause enormous damage to themselves and their families. Depending on the state, the number of problem gamblers ranges from 1.5 to 6.5 percent of adults.[15] These figures may seem small, but given the huge number of gamblers they represent a huge amount of suffering in bankruptcies, crimes, suicides, and much plain misery. About half of the problem gamblers are considered *pathological gamblers*—about 10 million Americans, roughly the same as the number of alcoholics.

Who are pathological gamblers? Psychiatrists define them as individuals who have "impulse control disorders" characterized by at least five of the following criteria: preoccupation (in thinking, imagination) with gambling; tendency to increase the amounts of money used in gambling; unsuccessful efforts to cut back or stop gambling; irritability when attempting to cut back; using gambling to escape from anxiety and other problems; gambling more after losing ("chasing one's losses); lying to family and others about gambling; engaging in illegal acts to finance gambling; risking relationships or work to gamble; relying on others to bail one out after losses.[16] Each of these criteria is also useful in understanding the kinds of problems gambling can generate.

These five arguments raise genuine concerns, but there are arguments on the other side as well. Michael Scriven develops opposing arguments in "The Philosophical Foundations of Las Vegas." As the title of his essay intimates, Scriven seems to defend not only keeping gambling legal but also gambling itself—gambling as a major human type of human activity. His main point is this: "The primary case *for* gambling, as for swimming, is that many people enjoy it; the secondary case is that it generates jobs, income for stores and hotels—and tax revenue for community services and education."[17] Given the very important enjoyment factor, the burden of proof is then placed on those who object to gambling to make their case. Admittedly, gambling causes some major problems, but so does swimming (drowning deaths), television (reduced time spent reading), and many other forms of entertainment and recreation. Moreover, attempts to suppress gambling also can be bad, not only by increasing illegal gambling, but losing the secondary benefits from the gambling industry.

Scriven discusses most of the five objections just cited, although not exactly in the form I stated them. He finds them insufficient.

1   Insofar as gambling brings genuine enjoyment, it is not wastefulness.

2   Most people who gamble work hard for their money, and the claim that gambling is undermining the work ethic is dubious.

3   Individuals in lower-income groups who gamble are not being exploited against their will, and it would be paternalistic to prevent them from using their money as they choose. Nevertheless, this area of concern is genuine and needs to be addressed creatively so as to help minimize damage.

4   The negative social side-effects can be minimized or remedied, for example, by increasing police protection in areas where crime becomes a problem.

5   Problem gamblers, like other addicts, need help, and society should make help available, perhaps by requiring the gambling industry to fund that help. We do not forbid alcohol, even though it creates as many or more addicts than gambling does, and it is unfair to deny people who enjoy gambling their source of enjoyment while allowing drinkers theirs.

Whether these lines of argument are persuasive will be left as a discussion topic.

Economic Justice

So far we have focused on the morality of acquiring and using money within the bounds set by law, but what about the law itself? What should it be in order to provide a morally fair economic system? These are questions in social and political philosophy that apply to the foundation of economic and political systems. As such, the questions can only be dealt with briefly here, but they deserve attention because they bear so centrally on how wealth is produced and distributed.

Utilitarians, rights ethicists, duty ethicists, and virtue ethicists have all developed theories of economic justice. As we noted in Chapter 2, all these theories have numerous variations, and we sample only a few of them, by way of review and further application.[18]

Capitalism or free enterprise is now the world's dominant economic system. The failures of the communist system of top-down economic management became clear to the world with the dissolving of the Soviet Union, and even China has moved a long ways toward integrating free trade. To that extent, Adam Smith in *The Wealth of Nations* (published in 1776) was prescient in his analysis of the benefits of free enterprise. Left alone without excessive government intervention in the forms of regulatory laws and taxation, the free market allows and encourages individuals to pursue profit in ways that unintentionally benefit all.

In a famous passage, Smith writes, "It is not from the benevolence of the butcher, the brewer, or the baker, that we expect our dinner, but from their regard to their own interest."[19] In seeking to maximize their profits, businesspersons and corporations must respond to consumers' preferences, which are generally to buy safe and useful products at reasonable prices. Competition leads to these results, as well as to creation of jobs. Businesspersons do not aim at the public good, but it is as if they were "led by an invisible hand [i.e., the hand of God] to promote an end which was no part of his intention."[20]

Smith defended capitalism primarily from a utilitarian standpoint: It maximizes the general good. Impressed by the wealth generated by emerging markets, nineteenth-century utilitarians like Jeremy Bentham and John Stuart Mill largely agreed with Smith. But by the late nineteenth and early twentieth century, a number of harmful side-effects of "laissez-faire" capitalism (that is, minimum government involvement in free enterprise) were beginning to become clear. For example, the lives of workers were impoverished as wealth accumulated in the hands of a few rich individuals; the environment was ravaged as business disregarded long-term effects in the pursuit of short-term profits; and a spirit of self-seeking replaced traditional professional ideals of concern for clients.

Today, utilitarians tend to favor more government involvement insofar as it helps disadvantaged members of society. Yet utilitarians also remain concerned not to strangle the marketplace with overregulation. Because the current issue concerns which rules should govern societies, the most straightforward utilitarian theories of economic justice are *rule-utilitarian*. Recall, from Chapter 2, that rule-utilitarians favor whatever system of economic–political rules most contributes to the overall good. Utilitarian theories about what is (intrinsically) good differ considerably, but in connection with the current issue utilitarians often seek simplicity and public usefulness by relying on a preference theory: The good is whatever satisfies preferences, where preferences are shown in how people spend their money.

Utilitarians debate over whether to maximize (a) the overall quantity of good or (b) the spread of good. Suppose that maintaining a lower economic class (or even, in some societies, a slave class) promotes the total mass of good. Then some utilitarians favor that system. But the spirit of utilitarianism has usually been to count the good of all individuals, and this moves us toward more equitable distributions (especially if the theory of good is modified so as to count equality itself as a good). In practice, according to Richard Brandt, utilitarianism favors more equal distributions rather than radical divisions between rich and poor—divisions that have grown dramatically in recent years.[21] That is because preferences for basic goods like food, shelter, and education are far more deeply preferred and bring far greater satisfactions than desires for luxury items. Thus, utilitarians favor tax rules that yield more equal after-tax income distributions.

Contemporary defenders of Adam Smith's anti-government stance are usually libertarians. Libertarians believe only in liberty (or negative) rights to leave people alone to pursue their interests, and as a matter of principle oppose any government involvement beyond the bare minimum. As Robert Nozick argued in *Anarchy, State, and Utopia,* "The minimal state is the most extensive state that can be justified."[22] By minimal state he means one limited to such functions as enforcing contracts, protecting public safety, and discouraging prople from violating each other's liberty. All taxation aimed at redistribution of income is unjustified. Nozick's "entitlement theory" is simple: People are entitled to keep what they earn (without theft), to transfer or trade it (without fraud), and to obtain restitution when their property or freedom is violated.

The vast majority of Americans have never embraced the libertarian outlook, largely because most middle- and lower-class Americans continue to benefit from education scholarships, social security programs, Medicare and Medicaid, unemployment compensation, and numerous other government programs. Most rights ethicists affirm that there are at least some positive rights to receive essential services from the community when one cannot earn them and when the community can afford to provide them. Even Nozick later expressed doubts about his earlier views, alarmed by their implications for diminished community and "human solidarity" shown in shared commitments through government activities.

> The libertarian position I once propounded now seems to me seriously inadequate, in part because it did not fully knit the humane considerations and joint cooperative activities it left room for more closely into its fabric. It neglected the symbolic importance of an official political concern with issues or problems, as a way of marking their importance or urgency, and hence of expressing, intensifying, channeling, encouraging, and validating our private actions and concerns toward them.[23]

Nevertheless, libertarian views have been influential in supporting a recent trend away from relying on government—for example, in the marked move toward lower taxes and dismantling many welfare programs, and toward relying on the prosperity created through the marketplace.

John Rawls's *A Theory of Justice* is the single most influential philosophical work on economic justice of the twentieth century. We might think of Rawls as exploring a middle ground between libertarian and utilitarian viewpoints, a middle ground he interprets as in the duty-ethics tradition of Kant and also as a revival of what is called *social contract theory.* Rawls defends two principles of justice that should govern the basic institutions and practices of society:

First: Each person is to have an equal right to the most extensive basic liberty compatible with a similar liberty for others.

Second: Social and economic inequalities are to be arranged so that they are both (a) reasonably expected to be to everyone's advantage, and (b) attached to positions and offices open to all.[24]

The first principle, which takes priority over the second, ensures that all members of the society are recognized as having the same basic political liberties—to speech, voting, practice of religion, personal property, freedom from arbitrary arrest, and so on. Taken by itself, this principle is in tune with libertarianism. The second principle, however, is in the spirit of utilitarianism. It says that differences in power and wealth are justified only insofar as they benefit everyone, especially (Rawls adds) the most disadvantaged members of society.

Rawls's argument for the principles is complex, but in outline proceeds this way. Justified principles of justice are those that would be chosen by rational persons who were entirely fair. As a way to ensure fairness, we can imagine ourselves behind a "veil of ignorance" in which we do not know any particular information that could bias our choice of principles. For example, we do not know if we are rich or poor, black or white, male or female, or born into a prosperous or disadvantaged country—because all such information might bias our reflections. We do, however, have general knowledge, especially concerning human sciences such as psychology, sociology, and economics. We also imagine ourselves concerned about our interests* and those of our family, and we imagine ourselves caring about "primary goods" such as liberty, wealth, and self-respect—the goods that "rational beings would desire." Because we must live together with one another, we need to form a consensus—a social contract—about the principles that will govern us. Which principles would we choose?

We would choose the first principle because it would ensure basic political and social liberties to us, no matter what situation we found ourselves in. Why is that so important, indeed paramount over matters about wealth and power? Because basic liberties ensure the opportunity to participate and to influence change. We would choose the second principle because, for all we know, we may end up at the most disadvantaged rung of wealth and power. Even then we would know the society's basic structures are working to benefit us.

Rawls's two principles need to be tailored to particular social settings, but in outline they seem to capture the heart of most democratic societies—another reason for Rawls's influence. Critics have raised many objections to

---

*This does *not* mean Rawls assumes psychological or ethical egoism, for he assumes we care about justice enough to imagine ourselves behind the veil of ignorance in a search for principles of justice.

Rawls, however. Can we genuinely imagine ourselves behind his veil of ignorance, not knowing anything about the specific things we enjoy or even knowing our gender? Again, is Rawls too conservative about risk taking? Libertarians might be more willing than him to risk ending up at the bottom economic rung of society in return for being allowed to keep more of the wealth they earn. Or, as some utilitarians have argued, isn't Rawls insufficiently concerned about spreading economic resources more equitably? Many liberals believe that only a minimum safety net is needed for the disadvantaged, rather than Rawls's insistence on always trying to improve their economic status. And a new social movement called communitarianism seeks a more pragmatic balance of individual rights and the needs of community, often guided by virtue-ethics ideals such as loyalty, gratitude, and reciprocity of citizens whose very identity is tied to the communities in which they live.[25]

SUMMARY

Just as most financial matters have moral dimensions, nearly all moral matters have financial dimensions. Certainly that is true of happiness and self-fulfillment, contrary to the half-truth that the best things in life are free. Although money cannot purchase many of the most meaning-giving relationships and values, it can build opportunities for fulfilling interactions with others.

If we should avoid romanticizing poverty, we should also be wary of unbridled consumerism in which primary hopes, anxieties, and power are expressed through an endless cycle of getting and spending. The simple life is a moral ideal of finding balance and restraint in living below one's means, so as to accumulate sufficient resources to achieve financial security without undue self-denial. But the simple life takes innumerable forms, and what is simplicity to one person strikes another as self-sacrifice and still another as undue complexity.

Gambling raising moral concerns. It can waste resources, encourage undesirable attitudes that erode a work ethic, exploit the poor who can least afford to gamble but tend to spend a higher percentage of their resources on it, downgrade local communites, and lead to pathological excesses that destroy lives and families. Most Americans enjoy some gambling as a pleasurable entertainment, however, and Michael Scriven argues that on balance gambling is a legitimate human activity.

Each of the major ethical theories sets forth its own perspective on economic justice, that is, morally justified systems of wealth production and distribution. Libertarians favor minimal government intervention, allowing the free market to create winners and losers without any redistribution of wealth through taxation. Rule-utilitarians favor tax rules and government regulation that contribute to the overall good. Most discussed in recent decades, John Rawls's Kantian-inspired contract ethics favors two principles: maximum equal political liberties together with allowing only those systems of wealth differences that benefit all people, especially the most disadvantaged members of a society.

DISCUSSION TOPICS

1 What ideals of voluntary simplicity, if any, do you find morally valuable? In your answer comment on the list of ideals cited from David E. Shi. As you state them, are these values morally mandatory for everyone, nonobligatory ideals of good, or a combination of both?

2 Is Michael Scriven correct that enjoyment of gambling creates a strong case for it, as a type of human activity, or are the five arguments presented against gambling more compelling than Scriven thinks?

3 Fyodor Dostoevsky's novel *The Gambler* is a powerful portrayal of a compulsive gambler, based on Dostoevsky's own gambling addiction. Alexei, the protagonist in the novel, defends his gambling as a noble act of taking risks. He also argues that whether or not we admire his 'courage' or self-confidence in taking risks, his actual luck would alter how we morally assess his activities of extravagant spending at the roulette tables: "The real point is that one single turn of the wheel could change everything, and then I'm sure the sternest moralist would turn to friendly banter and come to congratulate me."[26] Is Alexei correct that the consequences of his gambling determine its moral status, so that luck (or unluckiness) in gambling becomes a kind of moral luck (or unluckiness), or is something beyond consequences crucial here? What would utilitarians say?

4 Does the following television commercial by a Connecticut Lottery raise any moral concerns?

> Reflecting on his youth, a man says:
>
> "I suppose I could have done more to plan my future, but I didn't. I guess I could have put some money aside. . . . Or I could have made some smart investments. But I didn't. . . . Heck, I could have bought a one-dollar Connecticut Lottery ticket, won a jackpot worth millions, and gotten a nice big check in the mail every year for twenty years. . . ." A huge smile breaks over his fact. "And I did! . . . I won millions—me!"[27]

5 What would a libertarian, a liberal democrat, and a cultural conservative be likely to say about the trend toward heavy government involvement in fostering gambling? What is your view on this involvement? In your answer take into account this fact: An increase in taxes of one-half to one percent would suffice to provide the income from state lotteries; yet we live in a strong anti-tax climate. Is government sponsorship an acceptable compromise in gaining revenues?

6 Write a list of the kinds of things that it would be morally wrong to buy and sell. As a start, consider these possibilities: (a) human beings (as in various forms of slavery or in baby-selling); (b) body organs, such as kidneys and hearts, of basically healthy individuals; (c) illegal acts such as murder-for-hire, (d) basic political liberties and legal rights, such as rights to vote and also votes on specific

issues. Does your list include selling acts of sexual intercourse (prostitution), exemptions from military service, prizes for achievement in professions or the arts, religious benefits such as the promise of salvation and simony (the selling of religious offices)? How large is your list, and what (if anything) ties it together? How would you defend it against arguments that the free market should be allowed to go its own way, turning virtually anything into a commodity to be bought and sold?

7 Form and defend a list of things it is impossible to buy and sell (e.g., love). How long is the list, and does anything tie it together?

8 Outline your ideas on economic justice. In doing so, present and defend your view about the adequacy of Rawls's two principles of justice.

SUGGESTED READINGS

Daly, Markate (ed.). *Communitarianism: A New Public Ethics*. Belmont, CA: Wadsworth, 1994.

Dostoevsky, Fyodor. *The Gambler*. New York: Bantam, 1964. (A novel that continues to influence psychological studies.)

Furnham, Adrian, and Michael Argyle. *The Psychology of Money*. New York: Routledge, 1998.

Goodman, Robert. *The Luck Business*. New York: Simon & Schuster, 1995.

Jackson, Devin (ed.). *The Oxford Book of Money*. New York: Oxford University, 1996.

Lippke, Richard L. "Should States Be In the Gambling Business?" *Public Affairs Quarterly*, vol. 11 (1997): 57–73.

Murray, Patrick (ed.). *Reflections on Commercial Life: Anthology of Classic Texts from Plato to the Present*. New York: Routledge, 1997.

Needleman, Jacob. *Money and the Meaning of Life*. New York: Doubleday, 1991.

Newton, Lisa. "Gambling: A Preliminary Inquiry," *Business Ethics Quarterly*, vol. 3 (1993): 405–418.

Nozick, Robert. *Anarchy, State, and Utopia*. New York: Basic Books, 1974.

Rawls, John. *A Theory of Justice*. Cambridge, MA: Harvard University Press, 1971.

Rosenblatt, Roger (ed.). *Consuming Desires: Consumption, Culture, and the Pursuit of Happiness*. Washington, D.C.: Island Press, 1999.

Rowe, Dorothy. *The Real Meaning of Money*. New York: HarperCollins, 1997.

Scriven, Michael. "The Philosophical Foundations of Las Vegas," *Journal of Gambling Studies*, vol. 11 (1995): 61–75.

Shi, David E. *The Simple Life: Plain Living and High Thinking in American Culture*. New York: Oxford University Press, 1985.

Simmel, George. *The Philosophy of Money*. Trans. Tom Bottomore and David Frisby. New York: Routledge, 1992.

Smith, Adam. *An Inquiry Into the Nature and Causes of the Wealth of Nations*. 2 Vols. New York: Oxford University, 1976. First published in 1776.

Stewart, Robert M. (ed.) *Readings in Social and Political Philosophy*. 2d ed. New York: Oxford University Press, 1996.

Walzer, Michael. "Money and Commodities." In *Spheres of Justice*. New York: Basic Books, 1983: pp. 95–128.

Westra, Laura, and Patricia H. Werhane (eds.). *The Business of Consumption: Environmental Ethics and the Global Economy*. Lanham, MD: Rowman & Littlefield, 1998.

Yablonsky, Lewis. *The Emotional Meaning of Money*. New York: Gardner Press, 1991.

Meaningful Work

In a wide sense, work is any activity that yields products or services that have value, whether or not one is paid for it. In this sense, the unpaid homemaker who spends more than eighty hours a week tending children, cleaning, cooking, ironing, and running errands certainly works. In the narrower sense used here, however, work is an activity for which one receives financial compensation.

Because most people work out of the necessity to earn a living, we tend to think of the morality of work as simply the responsible performance of a job in return for money. Yet work is equally important as a context for caring relationships with colleagues, clients, and members of the public. Although a few types of work are conducted largely in isolation, most work requires shared activities, cooperation, and mutual respect. Collegiality is a virtue essential for both successful and enjoyable work. Moreover, most work situations involve caring relationships with people for whom one performs a service (clients and the public), and these require a range of virtues, from conscientiousness (in performing one's job) to loyalty. Caring relationships provide much of the meaning of work, as the following examples illustrate.

Examples of Two Workers

In his book *Working,* Studs Terkel records more than a hundred interviews with workers from many occupations. The first interview is with a thirty-seven-year-old steelworker named Mike Lefevre, who describes his job as "strictly muscle work . . . pick it up, put it down, pick it up, put it down."[1] His steel mill handles from forty thousand to fifty thousand pounds of steel each day, steel that has a final destination unknown to him. Lefevre takes no pride in his work, he explains, because "it's hard to take pride in a bridge you're never gonna cross, in a door you're never gonna open. You're mass-producing things and you never see the end result of it."[2] He is also nagged by a fear that he is replaceable at any time by a machine that can do his work more efficiently.

From his supervisor he receives neither respect nor recognition for his endeavors. Instead, the boss "spies" on him, thereby compounding the monotony of the work with anxiety. Nor is there recognition from co-workers or the public: "It's the nonrecognition by other people. To say a woman is *just* a housewife is degrading, right? Okay. *Just* a housewife. It's also degrading to say *just* a laborer."[3]

For Lefevre, work lacks intrinsic value: there is nothing in it worth doing for its own sake, nor are there any personal relationships to give it some meaning. Indeed, from his point of view, the work is inherently bad. He sees nothing in it that evokes his talents and interests: "My attitude is that I don't get excited about my job. I do my work but I don't say whoopee-doo. The day I get excited about my job is the day I go to a head shrinker. How are you gonna get excited about pullin' steel?"[4] Work for him represents a long series of daily humiliations, frustrations, and resentments that periodically erupt into after-work barroom brawls. He works solely for a livelihood and for the sake of his family, especially in order to send his children to college.

Matters are very different, however, with other workers Terkel interviewed. They do not find their jobs demoralizing, even though their work is seemingly as repetitive and difficult as that of the steelworker. Consider Dolores Dante, a waitress in the same restaurant for twenty-three years, working from 5 P.M. to 2 A.M., six days a week. She suffers from arthritis and on many days goes home physically and emotionally exhausted. Nevertheless, she enjoys her work and takes great pride in serving people.

To outside observers, many aspects of her work seem boringly routine, in particular waiting on an endless stream of customers. But Dante takes great interest in her work: "I have to be a waitress. How else can I learn about people? How else does the world come to me?"[5] She creates variety in her work through conversations with customers, and she takes pride in the considerable talents she has developed as a conversationalist.

She also introduces pleasing variations on routine work, for example, by developing a repertoire of ways to ask for a customer's order. She also values her skills in dealing diplomatically with temperamental cooks. At times she even creates an imaginative personal drama in her work: "To be a waitress, it's an art. I feel like a ballerina, too. I have to go between those tables, between those chairs. . . . I do it with an air."[6]

Like Lefevre, Dante is annoyed by people who reduce her to her work-role by treating her with the attitude that she is *just* a waitress. She takes the view, however, that those individuals fail to see the genuine value in the service she has to offer. She too has to contend with "spying" supervisors and the fear that she is replaceable by others who want her job. Yet she deals with these problems as she does with other difficult aspects of the work, without submitting to a sense of being superfluous or unimportant.

Unlike Lefevre, Dante finds her work inherently valuable, in addition to being instrumentally valuable (that is, valuable as a means to other good things, such as an income for herself and her children). A large part of the inherent value derives from the personal relationships she has with co-workers and members of the public she serves. These relationships bring recognition and a sense of cooperative endeavor and are, for the most part, based on mutual respect. She works with a clear sense of the connection between her work and the good of the people she serves and works with.

Alienation and Work Ethics

We can state that Lefevre *feels* and *is* alienated from his work, the things he produces, and the people with whom he works. He does not *identify with* his work, nor can he affirm its worth. This subverts the possibility for caring relationships in the workplace; conversely, the absence of those relationships also contributes to worker alienation, as do some attitudes toward one's work.

Karl Marx (1818–1883), who introduced the concept of worker alienation, describes alienation from work activities in terms that fit Lefevre perfectly:

> What constitutes the alienation of labor? First, that the work is *external* to the worker, that it is not part of his nature; and that, consequently, he does not fulfill himself in his work but denies himself, has a feeling of misery rather than well being, does not develop freely his mental and physical energies but is physically exhausted and mentally debased. The worker therefore feels himself at home only during his leisure time, whereas at work he feels homeless. . . . [Work] is not the satisfaction of a need, but only a *means* for satisfying other needs.[7]

In addition to this characterization of alienation from the activity of working, Marx also analyzes alienation from the product of one's labor (as exemplified by Lefevre's inability to experience the steel products as a personal self-expression), alienation from co-workers (the feeling that one is disconnected from colleagues), and alienation from other human beings in general. All these forms of alienation involve a lack of connection with and personal affirmation of the thing from which one is alienated. In Marx's view, work should be central to our self-esteem, self-respect, and sense of identity—that is, our sense of who we are. Hence, alienation from work is ultimately alienation from ourselves.

Marx argued that worker alienation was an inevitable product of capitalism, whereby workers sell their labor to someone else for money, which is then used to purchase things that satisfy the workers' desires. As the case of Dolores Dante suggests, however, the causes of worker alienation are more complicated. In subsequent sections we will focus on one such cause: the nature of the personal relationships at work.

Before continuing, however, we should note a few other moral attitudes toward work—other *work ethics*—than those of Lefevre (work as a necessary evil), Dante (work as a source of enjoyment through personal relationships), and Marx (work as the primary avenue to self-fulfillment). One is the *Protestant work ethic,* which the sociologist Max Weber saw as underlying the historical development of capitalism. According to this ethic, people are obligated to refrain from pleasures by engaging in work, however onerous and distasteful it may be. This enables us to serve the community, to avoid becoming a social burden, and to accumulate wealth in the service of God. Weber quotes an influential Protestant minister:

> If God shows you a way in which you may lawfully get more than in another way (without wrong to your soul or to any other), if you refuse this, and choose the less gainful way, you cross one of the ends of your calling, and you refuse to be God's steward, and to accept His gifts and use them for Him when He requireth it: you may labour to be rich for God, though not for the flesh and sin.[8]

As this ethic later became secularized, it tended to encourage the pursuit of wealth for its own sake. Perhaps it also formed a rationale for *workaholics* who devote themselves to work beyond reasonable bounds. Both the Protestant work ethic and compulsive attitudes elevate work over personal relationships (whether at work or in personal life).

An opposing work ethic is suggested by Gilbert Meilaender, who rejects the idea that we should "live in order to work" and favors instead "working in order to live." Whether work is inherently pleasant or unpleasant, its primary role in human life is to be an instrumental good. Work provides the leisure time necessary to sustain personal relationships with family and friends:

> When work as we know it emerges as the dominant idea in our lives—when we identify ourselves to others in terms of what we do for a living, work for which we are paid—and when we glorify such work in terms of self-fulfillment, it is time for Christian ethics to speak a good word for working simply in order to live. Perhaps we need to suggest today that it is quite permissible, even appropriate, simply to work in order to live and to seek one's fulfillment elsewhere—in personal bonds like friendship.[9]

Probably there is no single work ethic that is obligatory for all people; rather, various attitudes toward work seem morally permissible and warranted (depending on the worker's situation). Nevertheless, three features of work improve its moral worth whenever they are present: collegiality, loyalty, and caring for members of the public who benefit from one's work.

Collegiality

Collegiality requires that one do more than refrain from unjustly defaming, insulting, harassing, or degrading colleagues. It is a more positive ideal and virtue. Craig Ihara defines it this way:

> The conclusion I have reached is that collegiality is a kind of connectedness grounded in respect for professional expertise and in a commitment to the goals and values of the profession, and that, as such, collegiality includes a disposition to support and cooperate with one's colleagues.[10]

According to this definition, the key ingredients of collegiality are mutual respect, connectedness, and cooperation. These ingredients, and hence collegiality, can be present in all forms of work, not just professions such as law, medicine, and teaching, which require advanced education.

Respect for one's colleagues is an attitude, not simply a pattern of conduct. One who respects one's co-workers values them for their expertise and their devotion to serving some public good. As with friendship, Ihara claims that respect must be reciprocal; however, it seems possible for one person to display collegiality toward a colleague who does not reciprocate with the same attitude.

Connectedness consists of an awareness of being part of a social structure and a community of people who together pursue some shared good. It is a sense that the involvement of others makes one's endeavors possible. There must be at least a minimal sense of shared values concerning the goal that is collectively pursued.

Cooperation is the willingness to work together and to support one another in pursuit of the common goal. Although cooperation is compatible with moderate degrees of competitiveness in which co-workers help stimulate each other in their endeavors, it is undermined when competition with co-workers becomes cutthroat.

Collegiality, which thus encompasses the three elements of mutual respect, connectedness, and cooperation, is a moral virtue for two reasons, according to Ihara. One concerns the benefits to the public and the other concerns a benefit to workers. First, collegiality enables professionals (and, we would add, workers in general) to serve the public good because it strengthens their motivation at work. It does this by creating an environment that supports mutual endeavors, enlivens shared commitments, and encourages responsible work. Second, collegiality contributes to making work inherently worthwhile for those who engage in it. Dolores Dante found significance in her work in part because of the attitudes of goodwill and shared endeavor of co-workers. Mike Lefevre found work hateful in part because he lacked a sense of collegiality with co-workers.

Loyalty

Collegiality is one expression of the wider virtue of loyalty. Loyalty in the workplace has several dimensions: loyalty to colleagues, to one's employer, to one's corporation, and to the clients and public one serves. Many of the difficulties of professional life arise because of conflicts among two or more of these loyalties and the obligations they engender.

Loyalties involve obligations or role-defined duties, but they have other elements as well. To be loyal is to wish to meet one's obligations because of a concern for a person or group. One is motivated by something more personal than Kant's "acting for the sake of duty." There must be caring and concern for the person, group, or cause to which one is loyal.

Josiah Royce (1855–1916) proposed the following definition of loyalty: "Loyalty is the willing and practical and thoroughgoing devotion of a person to a cause."[11] As such, according to Royce, loyalty is inherently good. He recognizes that loyalty as practiced by fanatical devotees to evil causes can have very bad consequences, which make it "instrumentally bad" (i.e., bad as a means to bad effects). Nevertheless, it is always inherently good in relation to a person's character:

> Whoever is loyal whatever be his cause, is devoted, is active, surrenders his private self-will, controls himself, is in love with his cause, and believes in it. The loyal man is thus in a certain state of mind which has its own value for himself. To live a loyal life, whatever be one's cause, is to live in a way which is certainly free from many well-known sources of inner dissatisfaction. Thus hesitancy is often correct by loyalty; for the cause plainly tells the loyal man what to do. Loyalty, again, tends to unify life, to give it centre, fixity, stability.[12]

It is true, of course, that devotion to either moral or immoral causes can have some good effects on the personalities of particular individuals. That does not, however, make it inherently (always) good, as Royce goes on to suggest. In fact, when unity and stability that loyalty brings to a personality strengthen an individual's commitment to immoral causes, they are not desirable.

After raising similar criticisms against Royce, John Ladd suggests that we redefine loyalty. His definition makes loyalty a virtue, and hence inherently good, without implying there is anything good about immoral fanatics. His definition builds moral duties into the concept of loyalty:

> Loyalty, strictly speaking, demands what is morally due the object of loyalty. . . . Loyalty includes fidelity in carrying out one's duties to the person or group of persons who are the object of loyalty; but it embraces more than that, for it implies an attitude, perhaps an affection or sentiment, toward such persons. Furthermore, at the very least, loyalty requires the complete subordination of one's own private interest in favor of giving what is due.[13]

Because there are no moral duties to pursue immoral ends, the immoral fanatic cannot be called loyal. For example, there cannot be "loyal Ku Klux Klan members." The KKK cause is immoral, and there are no (moral) duties to serve it; hence, the crucial idea of fidelity to one's duties is missing. Loyalty presupposes that the group, individual, or cause to which one is loyal is morally good or permissible.

With the awareness that different writers develop different persuasive (value-loaded) definitions of the word *loyalty,* let us distinguish two general senses of the word. As an attitude and disposition, loyalty is the strong identification with and dedicated caring for a cause, institution, or person. As a virtue, loyalty is a desirable trait of character—desirable in some important respect, though not necessarily in all respects. In relation to work, the primary good of the virtue of loyalty is in shaping character— inducing us to be conscientious, responsible, and caring with regard to both the work itself and relationships at work. At this point, however, we must consider an objection: Is loyalty obsolete and even harmful in today's work environment?

Modern corporations, it might be argued, are abstract and impersonal entities. Employers have little or no loyalty toward employees: They fire them whenever they deem it necessary for the corporation. This makes it seem unfair to expect loyalty from employees. All that should be required is that employees do a responsible job in return for fair wages. (Such corporations contrast sharply with others—for example, many nonprofit American corporations foster close employer–employee relationships.)

Furthermore, loyalty can have bad consequences. When combined with employees' self-interest in keeping their jobs, it can lead workers to do whatever the boss orders, often at the expense of the public good. For example, many employees engage in or know about unethical practices at work about which they remain silent, motivated by a combination of self-interest and loyalty to the corporation. Only rarely do individuals, at great personal risk, "blow the whistle" by informing someone outside the corporation of dangers to the public.[14]

To develop this criticism, there are innumerable instances when whistle-blowing would serve the public good. One example concerns the first crash of a fully loaded jumbo jet, which occurred in 1974 when a cargo door blew open in midair. The open cargo door depressurized the cargo area, collapsing the floor of the passenger area, along which ran the pilot's steering mechanism. All 346 people on board were killed. Two years before the crash it was known that the door was unsafely designed. The senior engineer in charge of the design wrote a memo to his boss stating, "It seems to me inevitable that, in the twenty years ahead of us, DC-10 cargo doors will come open, and I would expect this to usually result in the loss of the airplane."[15] Without disagreeing with the engineer's judgment, top management decided on financial grounds that nothing would be done. The engineer did not whistle-blow to the government or to a journalist, and neither did any other engineers or managers who knew about the safety defect.

Do such tragedies suggest that loyalty to companies, colleagues, and employers is harmful? Perhaps not. Recall that Ladd's definition of loyalty places moral limits on what is required by loyalty. In his view, loyalty consists of the faithful and caring fulfillment of one's (prima facie) duties to one's corporation and to the people with whom one works. However, there are also (prima facie) duties not to harm innocent members of the public. In the airplane case, the duties to the public seem to override those to the employer.

There is, however, some truth in the objection that it is unfair to expect loyalty from employees when employers show little or no loyalty. Insofar as corporations encourage an entirely impersonal contract relationship with employees, the conditions for reciprocal loyalty and care are subverted, resulting in the depersonalized and alienated work relationships illustrated in the case of Mike Lefevre. Corporations do, in fact, vary greatly in the extent to which this occurs.

Career Choice and Community

Most careers, and all professions, have some effect on the public good. To become a professional is to acquire duties to the public. These duties place limits on duties to the corporation for which one works, as we saw in the case of the airplane disaster. Is there, however, a duty to embark on any particular kind of career? More generally, should any moral considerations enter into decisions about careers?

Two points are obvious. First, there is an obligation not to pick careers that are likely to cause more harm than good. This rules out "careers" in crime, and it also rules out careers that violate one's conscience. If one believes that the tobacco industry or the nuclear armaments industry is harmful, then one should not work in those industries. The argument that "if I don't take this job, someone else will" is not an excuse for doing something one views as harmful.

Second, individuals have a moral right to select their own careers, at least within a democratic society that values individual liberty. We have a human right to pursue our career interests given the available options, and we are also most qualified to judge what those interests are.

Nevertheless, the right to select a (morally permissible) career does not entail that one will select the morally best career available. Should we think in terms of the moral good we can achieve through a career, or is career choice entirely a matter of self-interest (as is commonly thought)?

Norman Care contends that the good of the community should enter into career decisions; that is, careers should be selected in light of our membership in a community. Each of us, he urges, is responsible for other people who share this world with us. Obviously, we live in a world where millions of people are destitute, where gross inequities exist, and where not nearly enough is done to help people in need. Caring for the public good should enter heavily into career decisions.

In developing this view, Care contrasts three approaches to career choice. A purely *self-realization ethics* would regard personal fulfillment as the sole principle guiding career choice. A purely *service ethics*, by contrast, suggests that careers should be selected on the basis of the maximum good we can do for people. Service to others should have a higher priority than self-realization. A *mixed ethics* states that self-realization has priority in career selection but that, once careers are chosen, they should be pursued in ways that serve the public good as much as possible.

Care argues that service ethics is the correct view. A purely self-realization ethics reflects and encourages callousness. It is based on the false assumption that we are in the world for ourselves rather than as participants in a community of people of equal worth and importance. The mixed-ethics view errs in making caring relationships with other people secondary to self-interest, when in fact they ought to have priority, at least as long as we live in a world where "relatively few are able to realize themselves, relatively many suffer destitution in some or many of its desperate forms, and no effective general ameliorating scheme is in place at all."[16]

A problem with this view, however, was voiced much earlier by Hastings Rashdall (1858–1924). Rashdall was a utilitarian who thought we are obligated to select careers that promote the most good for the most people. This would seem to commit him to a service ethics, but in fact Rashdall defended what Care calls a mixed ethics. He reminded us that careers extend over many years and make great demands. These demands can generate frustration and harm unless they fit our talents and interests. Thus, people who wish to succeed in a service career must have a "calling" for it, because to select a service career out of a sense of duty is probably harmful:

> Certain social functions require for their adequate fulfillment that they should be done in a certain spirit. Such functions demand the possession of certain qualities of mind or heart or character which cannot be summoned up at the command of the will, and cannot be satisfactorily performed merely as a matter of duty. . . . It is for the general good that every man should do the work for which he is most fitted; and as a general rule, a natural liking for the work or kind of life adopted is one of the most important qualifications for it.[17]

Using this line of reasoning, Rashdall concluded that it is morally permissible, in selecting careers, to place greater emphasis on self-realization than on service. Nevertheless, once a career is selected, caring relationships should be sought and sustained as much as possible in order to promote as much good as possible.

Whether Care or Rashdall is correct will be left as a discussion question, but we might conclude by noting that most careers provide opportunities for service, both during the routine course of the work and through periodic redirection of work. Consider Dr. David Hilfiker, who midway in his career formed a commitment to provide medical care to the poor. When he left a comfortable job in Minnesota to live and work for a decade in an impoverished ghetto in Washington, D.C., he took a two-thirds pay cut. He also lived with everyday dangers unlike any he had previously encountered. The needs of the community he served were at times overwhelming, as he had to confront large numbers of patients with inadequate housing and food, as well as medical services, and many of whom were drug addicts or mentally ill. His service was inspired by a "conscious desire to move into a closer relationship with God," and he reports that he derived joy in helping homeless persons return to a "community of hope."[18]

Dr. Hilfiker is an extreme example, but he highlights the opportunities for service that engage wider moral commitments. Professional ethics does require significant adjustments of our personal values in the workplace in order to maintain "professional distance." But it does not require a complete divorce between personal ideals and cooperative endeavors. Drawing the line between "compromise" in the sense of reasonable accommodations and "compromise" in the sense of betrayal of our moral commitments is occasionally difficult, and perhaps in some jobs impossible. For the most part, however, personal ideals add meaning to work, both for workers and for communities.

SUMMARY

There are various work ethics, that is, attitudes concerning the meaning of work. They include the attitudes that work is a necessary evil (Lefevre); work is (in part) inherently enjoyable (Dante); work is an opportunity to help others (Hilfiker); work is a primary avenue to self-fulfillment (Marx); maximization of personal wealth through disciplined work is socially desirable (the Protestant work ethic); and the main purpose of work is to support an independent life in which meaning comes primarily from relationships outside work (Meilaender).

Most work involves caring relationships, at least potentially, and these relationships add to the meaning derived from work. The meaning of work is subverted when workers become alienated from their work activities, the products of their work, or the people with whom they work. Alienation, as Karl Marx analyzed it, involves the inability to identify with something, that is, to see it as a personal involvement or self-expression, and to value it. The absence of caring relationships in the workplace is a major cause of alienation.

Collegiality as a virtue has three aspects: respect for one's co-workers and reciprocation of that respect, an attitude or sense of being connected with colleagues in a shared enterprise serving some public good, and cooperativeness in the sense of willingness to work together with colleagues. Collegiality is inherently good as one form of a caring relationship, and also as a means to whatever public good is served by work.

Loyalty can refer either to strong and caring identifications with persons, causes, or institutions, or to the virtue involved when these identifications are morally valuable in some way—especially when the identifications engender faithful devotion to the fulfillment of one's moral duties. Loyalty to colleagues, employers, and companies is appropriate if there is reciprocal loyalty and if genuine duties and goods are served by that loyalty. Loyalties frequently come into conflict in the workplace, however, and balanced reflection is needed to identify the primary duty in a given situation.

How far should moral reasons enter into the selection of a career? Self-realization ethics states that, unless the work is inherently immoral, one's self-interest is the only consideration. Service ethics states that careers should be selected on the basis of the maximum good we can do for people. Mixed ethics states that self-realization is most important but that, once a career is chosen, it should be pursued so as to maximize the public good.

DISCUSSION TOPICS

1 What moral considerations should be taken into account in choosing a career? On this issue, do you agree with Norman Care, with Hastings Rashdall, or with neither of them?

2 You are working with a colleague who confesses to you that he has been charging personal long-distance phone calls to the company for several years, against company regulations, but that he recently stopped doing so. Does collegiality obligate you to say nothing about the infraction to your employer? Does loyalty to the company obligate you to report the infraction? What should you do?

3 With respect to the case of the airplane crash in 1974, we stated that the obligation to warn the public of dangers should override the duty to the company to obey one's employer. However, it is likely that if the engineer had gone outside the company to inform the public of the dangerous cargo door ("blown the whistle"), he would have been fired. Most whistle-blowers are fired or demoted, and frequently they are "blacklisted"; that is, they are prevented from obtaining a comparable job because they are given negative evaluations when prospective employers call to check on the fired individual's references. Do these facts excuse the engineer from warning the public in view of the extreme self-sacrifice that would be required?

4 In a similar connection, consider the tragic explosion of the space shuttle *Challenger* on January 29, 1986. The disaster was due largely to unsafe seals joining segments of a booster rocket. A number of engineers for Morton Thiokol, the designer and builder of the rocket, argued against making the launch. One engineer, Allan McDonald, had been a critic of the seals long before the disaster. He urged both Thiokol and NASA officials to postpone the launch because the seals had not been tested under temperatures comparable to those at the launch site. Unfortunately, his protests were rejected by the Thiokol management, which had authority for making the final launch recommendation to NASA. Identify the obligations and loyalties relevant to McDonald's situation. Which should have priority? In vigorously protesting the launch, did McDonald do everything morally required?

5 Professions are occupations requiring advanced education, sophisticated skills, and service to some important public good. Usually, they involve special caring relationships with clients. Moral dilemmas arise for professionals when two or more professional duties or loyalties come into conflict, or when a professional obligation conflicts with personal conscience. Defend your view about what ought to be done in each of the following cases, basing your answers on an ethical theory about right action. Also, what virtues are at stake in each case?

a Judges are responsible for upholding the laws. Suppose, however, that a judge views a particular law as grossly immoral, such as a law requiring excessive punishment for people convicted of using marijuana. Is the judge obligated to enforce laws that violate his or her personal conscience? Can a judge's concern for a particular individual justify a departure from the law?

b Physicians have obligations to alleviate suffering and promote life. American physicians also work within a legal tradition that forbids euthanasia (that is, the intentional infliction, motivated by benevolence, of death on a hopelessly ill or injured patient). Consider a physician who disagrees with this tradition and who has a patient suffering from terminal cancer. Safe dosages of morphine are no longer sufficient to stop the pain, and the patient begs for increased dosages, knowing they will hasten death. If the physician's motivation is concern for the patient's good, is the physician justified in granting the patient's request?

c Politicians sometimes are asked to lie in order to protect national security. One example occurred in 1980 during the U.S. attempt to save fifty-three Americans held hostage in Iran.[19] President Carter believed that if the rescue attempt was to have a chance of success, the Iranians had to believe that no military action was being planned. As a decoy, he sent Secretary of State Cyrus Vance to assure U.S. allies publicly that the United States would not engage in military action if the allies would participate in enforcing economic sanctions against Iran. Vance made these deceitful assurances to people with whom he had previous relationships of trust. Before doing so, he submitted a confidential letter of resignation to President Carter, effective after the rescue attempt. Was his resignation inappropriate? Do you think he should have refused President Carter's order?

6 We suggested that the attitude "If I don't do it (this work) then someone else will" does not excuse participation in morally objectionable work. Is this suggestion perhaps mistaken? Consider this example from Bernard Williams:

> George, who has just taken his Ph.D. in chemistry, finds it extremely difficult to get a job. . . . His wife has to go out to work to keep them, which itself causes a great deal of strain, since they have small children and there are severe problems about looking after them. The results of all this, especially on the children, are damaging. An older chemist, who knows about this situation, says that he can get George a decently paid job in a certain laboratory, which pursues research into chemical and biological warfare. George says that he cannot accept this, since he is opposed to chemical and biological warfare.[20]

Suppose an act-utilitarian tells George that it is all right to accept the job because someone else will take the job if he does not. Is that an adequate excuse (or even justification) for taking the job? Are there other adequate justifications for taking the job in George's situation?

SUGGESTED READINGS

Applebaum, Arthur Isak. *Ethics for Adversaries: The Morality of Roles in Public and Professional Life.* Princeton, NJ: Princeton University Press, 1999.

Baron, Marica. *The Moral Status of Loyalty.* Dubuque, IA: Kendall-Hunt, 1984.

Bolles, Richard Nelson. *What Color Is Your Parachute?: A Practical Manual for Job Hunters and Career Changers.* Berkeley, CA: Ten Speed Press. New edition each year.

Callahan, Joan C. (ed.). *Ethical Issues in Professional Life.* New York: Oxford University Press, 1988.

Care, Norman S. "Career Choice." In *On Sharing Fate.* Philadelphia, PA: Temple University Press, 1987.

De George, Richard T. *Business Ethics,* 4th ed. New York: Macmillan, 1995.

De Grazia, Sebastian. *Of Time, Work and Leisure.* New York: Vintage, 1994. First published 1962.

Desjardins, Joseph R., and John J. McCall (ed.). *Contemporary Issues in Business Ethics,* 3d ed. Belmont, CA: Wadsworth, 1996.

Ezorsky, Gertrude (ed.). *Moral Rights in the Workplace.* Albany: State University Press of New York, 1987.

Flores, Albert (ed.). *Professional Ideals.* Belmont, CA: Wadsworth, 1988.

Fletcher, George P. *Loyalty: An Essay on the Morality of Relationships.* New York: Oxford University Press, 1993.

Frankena, William K. "The Philosophy of Vocation." *Thought,* vol. 51 (1976): 393–408.

Glover, Jonathan. "Work." In *What Sort of People Should There Be?* New York: Penguin, 1984.

Goldman, Alan H. *The Moral Foundations of Professional Ethics.* Totowa, NJ: Rowman & Littlefield, 1980.

Koehn, Daryl. *The Ground of Professional Ethics.* New York: Routledge, 1994.

Kultgen, John. *Ethics and Professionalism.* Philadelphia: University of Pennsylvania, 1988.

Martin, Mike W. *Meaningful Work: Rethinking Professional Ethics.* New York: Oxford University Press, 2000.

Marx, Karl. *Economic and Philosophical Manuscripts.* In E. Fromm, *Marx's Concept of Man.* Trans. T. B. Bottomore. New York: Ungar, 1966.

Novak, Michael. *Business as a Calling: Work and the Examined Life.* New York: Free Press, 1996.

Rashdall, Hastings. "Vocation." In *The Theory of Good and Evil,* Vol. 2. Oxford: Clarendon Press, 1907.

Sessions, Robert, and Jack Wortman (eds.). *Working in America: A Humanities Reader.* Notre Dame, IN: University of Notre Dame Press, 1992.

Solomon, Robert C. *Ethics and Excellence: Cooperation and Integrity in Business.* New York: Oxford University Press, 1992.

Sullivan, William M. *Work and Integrity: The Crisis and Promise of Professionalism in America.* New York: HarperBusiness, 1995.

Terkel, Studs. *Working.* New York: Avon Books, 1975.

Thomas, Keith (ed.). *The Oxford Book of Work.* New York: Oxford University Press, 1999.

CHAPTER 26

Community Service

Community service can refer to paid or unpaid service, as well as to the national service program in which community work provides a way to repay student loans. Here we will focus on unpaid service and giving, often referred to as philanthropy or voluntary service.

The word *philanthropy* often brings to mind large gifts made by very rich donors, but in fact the word now applies to all giving for community or public purposes. The expression *voluntary service* has a similar wide meaning, although it often connotes contributions of time rather than money. At least among professional fundraisers, both terms have largely replaced the word charity, which has several more limited meanings: (1) the legal sense of tax-deductible gifts, (2) the biblical sense of love, and (3) the pejorative sense of condescending gifts that suggest pity (rather than compassion), whereby the donor feels superior rather than equal to the beneficiary.

Here we will use the terms *philanthropy* and *voluntary service* interchangeably to refer to voluntary giving for community purposes, whether the gifts are large or small, or consist of money, time, talent, used clothing, blood, or take some other form. By *community purposes* we will include virtually all giving beyond one's circle of family and friends—for example, gifts to the arts, humanities, sciences, world hunger organizations, environmental and animal causes, political causes, churches and synagogues, hospitals, museums, libraries, and colleges. We will not assume that either the motives or the purpose of the gift is admirable; those are topics left open for inquiry in specific cases. We will also include giving to communities that are local, regional, national, and international in scope.

Voluntary service to communities occurs on a massive scale in the United States. It is not, however, the exclusive domain of a few rich people and wealthy foundations—they account for only 10 percent of private donations. The remaining 90 percent comes from individuals, half of them in families whose income is under $39,000. Moreover, about half of

Americans over age thirteen volunteer an average of 3.5 hours of their time each week.[1]

This aspect of everyday morality—voluntary contribution to communities—deserves more attention in ethics. When philosophers discuss moral community, they often have in mind an abstraction. The most famous such abstraction is Kant's "kingdom of ends": an imaginary situation in which all rational beings respect the autonomy and dignity of others. Here, by contrast, moral community refers to the moral ties that should be sustained by groups of people identified by their place of residence, shared traditions and culture, or common way of life within a neighborhood, state, country, religion, profession, or institution.

Consider, for example, a college. As a moral community, it is defined by the moral relationships that do or should exist among students, professors, staff, trustees, local citizens, and alumni (living and dead). These relationships involve special ties of loyalty, shared value, and meaning—*special* in that they center on the aims of the college rather than on the general connections among all rational beings to which Kant referred. These ties, in turn, provide a context for moral activity and virtue for members of that community. In fact, with respect to morally concerned individuals—those having a reasonable degree of moral caring—it is plausible to argue that self-fulfillment requires some voluntary service and giving to the community. A dramatic illustration is the life of Jane Addams.

An Example of Community Service

Jane Addams (1860–1935) was a pioneer in modern social work, a profession that did not exist in 1889 when she founded Hull-House. Hull-House was a "settlement house," that is, a community center created to serve the immigrant population in Chicago. In 1889, Addams and her friends renovated an old tenement building in an impoverished part of Chicago, moved in, and began to offer a variety of services in response to the needs of the local community. Initial services included first aid, a public kitchen for people lacking income, and a day-care service for children of working parents (most of whom worked twelve to fourteen hours a day). Later, many new buildings were built, including an art museum, a theater, and a gymnasium. They recruited hundreds of college students and professors (including John Dewey, the leading American philosopher at the time) to help serve and teach more than two thousand people each day.

It became clear to Addams that the immigrants had greater needs than even this monumental enterprise could fulfill. She initiated and supported a variety of legal reforms to reduce working hours, prohibit child labor, fund school playgrounds, improve sanitation, support women's voting rights, and create the first juvenile court in the country. Later, as World War I approached, she devoted her energies to peace activism, the role for which she was the first woman to receive the Nobel Peace Prize.

What motivated Addams and her colleagues at Hull-House? According to her own account, three motives were primary. First, they shared a conviction that democracy is more than a matter of political rights; it is the ideal of universal participation in the community. This ideal is based on the awareness that in a democracy the good of individuals is interwoven with the good of the masses: "The good we secure for ourselves is precarious and uncertain, is floating in the mid-air, until it is secured for all of us and incorporated into our common life."[2]

Second, Addams (like David Hume) believed that an innate sense of humanity generates altruistic desires. She thus found it entirely natural to help others.

Third, Addams asserted, community service connects us with people in ways that evoke our talents and lead to self-fulfillment:

> Nothing so deadens the sympathies and shrivels the power of enjoyment as the persistent keeping away from the great opportunities for helpfulness and a continual ignoring of the starvation struggle which makes up the life of at least half the race. To shut one's self away from that half of the [human] race['s] life is to shut one's self away from the most vital part of it; it is to live out but half the humanity to which we have been born heir and to use but half our faculties. We have all had longings for a fuller life which should include the use of these faculties.[3]

Individualism and Community

For Addams, community service was selfless, in the sense of unselfish; but it was not a matter of pure "selflessness" in the sense of a sacrifice of one's own interests and needs. Community involvement helped unfold her interests and capacities so as to create a richer self through relationships within a community. In this sense there are, and should be, mixed motives for volunteerism, and also for giving. Self-interest (concern for one's own good) and altruism (concern for the good of others) combine in ways that are mutually strengthening. The combination in no way lessens the virtue involved in the acts of altruism. Mixed motives are objectionable only when self-interest so dominates service that one's ability to help others is threatened.

Pursuit of individual self-interest and commitment to the good of the community have more often been seen as opposed rather than complementary in American traditions, according to the sociologist Robert Bellah and his co-authors in *Habits of the Heart*. The lone individualist, whether a cowboy or a corporate entrepreneur, is glorified. Social involvement is mistakenly equated with conformity, the passive acceptance of given social practices. The social rebel excites our imagination, while the community participant strikes us as a drudge. Jane Addams reminds us, however, that stunning individual expression is fully compatible with community service; indeed, community service can be an ideal forum for individual expression. Addams was an extraordinary individualist in precisely the sense honored in

American traditions: self-reliant, independent in thought, innovative, and tenacious in pursuit of her ideals.

In their studies of a wide cross-section of Americans, Bellah and his colleagues found many individuals who were engaged in community service of the sort Addams pursued. To mention just one, they discovered Cecilia Dougherty, an activist in the Campaign for Economic Democracy, which educates, advises, and organizes interracial tenement dwellers in Southern California. Her involvement in the group resulted from her sustained concern for the plight of the underprivileged, a concern that stemmed from her family's tradition of participating in worker reforms.

In reflecting on Dougherty and others like her, Bellah points out that individualism and commitment are creatively intertwined in their lives:

> It is characteristic of Cecilia Dougherty and the others . . . that they define themselves through their commitments to a variety of communities rather than through the pursuit of radical autonomy [i.e., separateness from community]. Yet Cecilia, like the others, exhibits a high degree of self-determination and efficacy. She exemplifies a form of individualism that is fulfilled in community rather than against it. Conformism, the nemesis of American individualism, does not seem to be a problem for Cecilia and the others. Their involvement in practices of commitment makes them able to resist pressures to conform.[4]

By *community* Bellah means a group of interdependent (mutually dependent) people with a shared history, who jointly participate in social practices, have a common forum for discussion and mutual decision making, and look to the future with a sense of shared hope. Understood in this way, a community is changing and responsive to individual initiative. In turn, it enables individuals to acquire extended and enriched identities through relationships with other people.

How Much Should We Give?

It might be objected, however, that individuality can be enriched and extended in many ways other than through community involvement. Rather than give our time and resources to the community, why should we not focus them entirely on our careers, our families, and our hobbies? After all, is it not the role of government to sustain community, and do we not satisfy our community duties by voting and paying taxes so that government can fulfill that role?

Moreover, the idea of a duty to give to the community (beyond the minimal requirements of citizenship) seems perplexing in that there seems to be no way such a duty can be structured and focused. To whom or to what are we obligated to give? Should our money go to the poor or to the fine arts? How much of our resources should we give? Does the amount (if anything) depend on our personal preferences, and, if so, how can something so personal or subjective have anything to do with morality?

One way to approach these questions is to apply Kant's distinction between perfect and imperfect duties. *Perfect duties* are those that hold for all situations: One ought to keep one's promises, be truthful, pay one's debts, not kill innocent people, and so on. Kant thought there were no exceptions to such duties; a more plausible view, however, as we saw in Chapter 2, is that these are prima facie duties that sometimes have legitimate exceptions when more pressing duties override them. *Imperfect duties,* by contrast, allow us discretion about when to act on them. In particular, the duty of beneficence or benevolence, which implies a specific duty of mutual aid—the duty to help other people who are in distress—allows us considerable discretion in deciding when and how much of our time and money we donate to philanthropic causes.

A difficulty with this view is that it provides no guidance for how our "moral discretion" should be exercised in helping other people. Apparently, we can give much or give little, depending on personal choice. In addition, because those who give much and those who give little both fulfill their "imperfect duty," they can be placed on an equal moral level.

If Kant seems to require too little from us in the way of community involvement, act-utilitarians seem to require an enormous amount. They state that we ought to give as much as we can in order to promote the most good for the most people, regarding each person as equal with ourselves. Complete impartiality should be our guide in dealing with others in need, and we should not give preference to ourselves or our families.

Peter Singer defends an extreme version of this doctrine. He argues that we should sacrifice luxuries in our lives in order to help save the thousands of people—at least thirty thousand people, most of them children—who die from starvation each day and the many others who live impoverished lives in countries such as Bangladesh, Ethiopia, and Somalia. All humans are part of a worldwide community, or "global village," and they make a legitimate claim on our wealth. We should respond to that claim by acting on the following utilitarian-inspired principle: "If it is in our power to prevent something bad from happening, without thereby sacrificing anything of comparable moral importance, we ought, morally, to do it."[5] The amount of giving required by this principle, as Singer insists, is considerable:

> I and everyone else in similar circumstances [of having great wealth compared to starving people] ought to give as much as possible, that is, at least up to the point at which by giving more one would begin to cause serious suffering for oneself and one's dependents—perhaps even beyond this point to the point of marginal utility, at which by giving more one would cause oneself and one's dependents as much suffering as one would prevent in Bengal [and other impoverished regions].[6]

Some utilitarians, especially rule-utilitarians, object that Singer's conclusion is too extreme. They allow that we can give some emphasis to our own needs and those of our families, and that to do so is compatible with the doctrine of impartiality. They believe that such conduct will actually lead to more overall good, because each of us is in the best position to promote her or his own good. Also, contributions in the extraordinary quantities recommended by Singer will erode one's long-term ability to help others. In adopting this position, however, utilitarians fail to resolve the same question that Kant faced: Just how much ought we to give to others?

Rights ethics offers two answers, depending on the kinds of rights recognized. If only negative rights are recognized—rights to be free from interference—then very little giving seems to be required of us. According to this libertarian theory of rights, we have a right to keep what we earn, and, apart from our families, no one has a right to share our resources unless we decide to share them.

A very different conclusion is reached if we recognize positive rights—rights to have the goods needed for a minimally decent standard of living. If each human has these rights, then impoverished people in this country and throughout the world have basic rights to shelter, clothing, and food. Those rights place on people who are advantaged obligations to provide assistance. This positive-rights view leaves open the question of whether giving should be accomplished through governments or by individuals, but it seems to require in any case that we give more than most of us do now, although precisely how much is again unclear.

Virtue ethics is often criticized as the theory least helpful in providing guidance for action in that it does not offer precise rules about how we ought to act or how much we ought to give. This criticism mistakenly assumes, however, that guidance must come in the form of rules. In fact, it can come in the form of ideals that inspire and focus our efforts. In particular, we can be guided by the virtue and the ideal of generosity in giving to the community more than is required by the minimal duties of morality, as we will see in the next section.

Generosity and Supererogation

Kant placed all actions into three categories: those required by duty (right), those forbidden by duty (wrong), and those morally neutral (permissible or "all right"; for example, the act of brushing one's teeth):

> A *duty* is an action to which we are obligated. . . . An action that is neither commanded nor forbidden is merely permissible, since there is . . . no duty with regard to the action. An action of this kind is called morally indifferent.[7]

This threefold classification, however, overlooks actions that are morally admirable—and hence not "morally indifferent"—but that are not required by duty. These acts are supererogatory, that is, morally good in ways that go beyond the requirements of duty.

David Heyd points out that *supererogation* refers to acts that exceed what is required by duties *to others* rather than to oneself. It is defined in terms of an altruistic aim or intention. To be sure, there may be mixed motives involved, such as a desire for fame coupled with a desire to help. If a person is to be generous, however, there must be an intention (aim, purpose) to promote the good of others. Accordingly, Heyd defines a supererogatory act as one that meets the following conditions:

1   It is neither obligatory nor forbidden.

2   Its omission is not wrong, and does not deserve sanction or criticism—either formal or informal.

3   It is morally good, both by virtue of its (intended) consequences and by virtue of its intrinsic value (being beyond duty).

4   It is done voluntarily for the sake of someone else's good and is thus meritorious.[8]

Generous actions meet these conditions, and generous persons have a disposition to perform generous acts. Generous actions go beyond what is morally required or obligatory, and they are done voluntarily with the intention to promote someone else's good. Admittedly, they may not be good in all respects: Generous acts sometimes fail to help others despite the best intentions; but they are intended to help and as such are admirable.

Generous giving of oneself—of one's time, talents, and money—to the community is one ideal worth pursuing. It represents an important virtue worthy of admiration precisely because, in sharing one's resources in benevolent and caring ways, one goes beyond the minimal moral requirements. This ideal also provides an answer to the question of how much to give: We should give generously—if we want to be generous persons! Although this answer shares the vagueness of the answers offered by duty ethics, utilitarianism, and rights ethics, the vagueness is, in a way, morally fruitful. As a positive ideal, generosity recognizes and praises higher degrees of benevolent giving, and, by allowing flexibility, it takes account of the personal aspect in giving.

"Degrees" of benevolent giving are frequently understood in terms of greater and lesser quantities: The more generous person seems to be the one who gives greater quantities. This view is reflected in James Wallace's definition of acts of what he calls *economic generosity* (which contrasts with generosity in judging other people):

1   The agent, because of his direct concern for the good of the recipient, gives something with the intention of benefiting the recipient.

2   The agent gives up something of his that has a market value and that he has some reason to value and, therefore, to keep.

3   The agent gives more than one is generally expected, because of moral requirements or custom, to give in such circumstances.[9]

The third condition places an emphasis on giving in quantities beyond what is obligatory or usual. This emphasis on quantities, however, overlooks an insight expressed in a well-known passage in the New Testament:

> And He sat down opposite the treasury, and began observing how the multitude were putting money into the treasury, and many rich people were putting in large sums. And a poor widow came and put in two small copper coins, which amount to a cent. And calling His disciples to Him, He said to them, "Truly I say to you, this poor widow put in more than all the contributors to the treasury; for they put in out of their surplus, but she, out of her poverty, put in all she owned, all she had to live on."[10]

In other words, the widow is more generous than are the rich donors, even though she gives a vastly smaller quantity. This suggests that degrees of generosity must be measured in relation to the resources of the giver rather than primarily in terms of custom or moral rules about what is required. It also suggests that Wallace's third condition needs to be modified:

3′ The agent gives more than is expected of someone having her or his resources and financial situation.

To Whom Should We Give?

Mere endorsement of generosity as an admirable ideal does not indicate to whom and to what we should give. Community has many dimensions. Should we give our resources to humanitarian efforts to feed and clothe the poor and to provide shelter for the homeless? Or should we give to the arts, to education, and to environmental causes? Should we give lots of small gifts or combine our resources into a few large gifts? (The same question could be asked about how we allocate the time we give in volunteering.)

Here we need to remind ourselves that generosity is fully voluntary and beyond the requirements of duty. Thus, it is up to each of us to whom and to what extent we give. We also need to remind ourselves that, wherever we draw the line between generous and required giving, there remains a large area of discretion in how we meet our imperfect duties to help others. Neither generous nor required giving is a matter of whim. On the one hand, we can give generously only when we are moved by benevolent concern for the good of others; that is, we should give thoughtfully in situations in which caring is evoked genuinely and in very personal ways. On the other hand, to meet our general duties to help others, we must exercise good judgment about how best to help—in which situations, in which ways, to which ends—so as to contribute to the world in meaningful ways.

To a significant degree, the occasions and objects of giving reflect, and should express, our personal interests. Some people are most deeply committed to humanitarian goals, some to educational goals, some to the arts, some to scouting and Little League baseball. Pursuit of these personal loyalties expresses the donor's concern about community better than impartial giving could. In fact, each of us participates in many communities of different sizes, ranging from a school, company, or church to a city, nation, or the world community. Most of us are able to give generously only to some of these overlapping communities. There seems to be no abstract duty to focus our energies on any one such community (say, the largest one), and hence, here again, much is left up to individual judgment and interests.

There is, in short, a large element of highly personal morality in decisions about where and how we display virtues like loyalty and generosity, and how best to meet our duties of mutual aid. However, *personal* does not mean *arbitrary:* Our judgment and interests are evoked and exercised thoughtfully, not whimsically, as we engage in intelligent and benevolent giving to help others.

SUMMARY

Philanthropy or voluntary service is voluntary giving for community or public purposes, whether gifts are large or small, in the form of money or time, or for purposes that are humanitarian, political, religious, environmental, educational, or cultural (among other possibilities). A community is a group of people related by shared history and hopes, location and interactions, interests and values. Loyalty to community is shown by actions that exceed such minimal participation as meeting one's responsibilities as a citizen. It is shown in voluntary contributions of one's time, talents, and resources to help others.

America's tradition of individualism is misconstrued when community involvement is equated with mere social conformism. As the life of Jane Addams exemplifies, service to community can express creative individual initiative and development of personality. Moreover, benevolent giving need not be "selfless" in the sense of actions done solely for the good of others. Mixed motives of self-interest and altruism do not negate or diminish the moral worth of giving to help others. The volunteer who, in helping others, also develops personal skills and expresses personal interests is often more vigorously motivated because of the mixed motives.

How much should we give, and to whom? Duty ethics, rights ethics, and utilitarianism do not provide clear-cut answers; neither does virtue ethics, but it does at least set forth generosity as an ideal that guides and focuses giving. Generosity is supererogatory in the sense that it exceeds what is required by moral duty and respect for others' rights. Generosity entails giving with the intention to benefit others, out of concern to promote their welfare. Degrees of generosity are measured by reference to one's resources and ability to help, as well as in terms of the quantities one gives beyond the customary or required amount. Basic duties to help others also take into account one's resources and ability to help.

DISCUSSION TOPICS

1 Present and defend your view (by appealing to an ethical theory) regarding how much one is obligated to give to help save starving people around the world. Should the homeless and starving people in one's local community or within one's country be given priority, or should they be considered equally with other disadvantaged people around the world? Is it obvious that the cause of world hunger should have priority over other worthy causes, such as education or the arts?

2 Consider the following observation by Brian O'Connell:

> There are some disturbing signs that giving and volunteering may not be held in high esteem by young adults. A recent study . . . has found that people between the ages of 18 and 34 do not place community service high on their lists of values.[11]

Is this observation supported by your own view of people in this age range, and do you agree with O'Connell that there is something disturbing about it? Does it suggest, for example, that people in this age group are more selfish than previous generations have been, or are there other forces at play, such as new economic pressures?

3 What, if anything, is wrong about a failure ever to make any philanthropic contribution or engage in any voluntary service to help others?

4 Ralph Waldo Emerson was a classic advocate for American individualism. Do you agree or disagree with what he says about philanthropy in the following passage?

> Do not tell me, as a good man did to-day, of my obligation to put all poor men in good situations. Are they *my* poor? I tell thee, thou foolish philanthropist, that I grudge the dollar, the dime, the cent I give to such men as do not belong to me and to whom I do not belong. There is a class of persons to whom by all spiritual affinity I am bought and sold; for them I will go to prison if need be; but your miscellaneous popular charities; the education at college of fools; the building of meeting-houses to the vain end to which many now stand; alms to sots, and the thousandfold Relief Societies;—though I confess with shame I sometimes succumb and give the dollar, it is a wicked dollar, which by and by I shall have the manhood to withhold.[12]

5 Is it better to give many small philanthropic gifts or one or two each year that are large? In answering this question, respond to the following claims:

> There are so many good causes that if we try to respond to them all, we dilute our ability to make a difference to any. But more important is the fact that we dilute ourselves. We run the risk of losing touch with what is really important to us.[13]

6 Assess the following argument: All the concern about motives and intentions in giving is entirely irrelevant. All that matters is the good done by acts of giving. Donations to relieve world hunger, for example, keep people alive no matter what motives or intentions lead people to make the donations.

7 One person regularly donates blood to the Red Cross without receiving any payment, while a second person gives blood only to commercial blood banks that pay for the blood. What moral good is exemplified by the first person that is absent in

the second? In general, what distinctive moral goods are made possible by voluntary service and giving?

8 Women have traditionally been encouraged (far more than men) to engage in voluntarism and philanthropy. Do you see any objections to this? In particular, does it or could it lead to exploitation of women who could be doing paid work that has greater economic benefits for them? In this connection, what does a feminist perspective suggest about the passage about the widow quoted earlier from the New Testament?

9 Sometimes philanthropy is immoral, other times it is foolish, and sometimes it combines good and bad. Evaluate the following examples: (a) donations of cash to a homeless person who uses the money to buy alcohol or drugs (as opposed to donations to a local organization that feeds the homeless); (b) donations to a world-hunger organization that has no plans for long-term solutions versus donations to an organization that does have such plans; (c) donation of a large gift to a private college in order to gain influence in how it is governed; (d) donations of money or time in support of the Ku Klux Klan. Comment especially on the role of respect for persons—in particular, respect for persons' autonomy—in promoting effective philanthropy.

SUGGESTED READINGS

Aiken, William, and Hugh La Follette (eds.). *World Hunger and Moral Obligation.* Englewood Cliffs, NJ: Prentice-Hall, 1977.

Bellah, Robert N., et al. *Habits of the Heart.* Berkeley University of California Press, 1985.

Bremner, Robert C. *American Philanthropy,* 2d ed. Chicago: University of Chicago Press, 1988.

Burlingame, Dwight F. *The Responsibilities of Wealth.* Bloomington: Indiana University Press, 1992.

Douglas, James. *Why Charity?: The Case for the Third Sector.* Beverly Hills, CA: Sage Publications, 1983.

Ellis, Susan J., and Katherine H. Noyes. *By the People: A History of Americans as Volunteers.* San Francisco, CA: Jossey-Bass, 1990.

Heyd, David. *Supererogation.* Cambridge, MA: Cambridge University Press, 1982.

Iichman, Warren F., Stanley Nider Katz, and Edward L. Queen (eds.). *Philanthropy in the World's Traditions.* Bloomington: Indiana University Press, 1998.

Jeavons, Thomas H. *When the Bottom Line is Faithfulness.* Bloomington: Indiana University Press, 1994

Kohn, Alfie. *The Brighter Side of Human Nature: Altruism and Empathy in Every Life.* New York: Basic Books, 1990.

Martin, Mike W. "Good Fortune Obligates: Gratitude, Philanthropy, and Colonialism," *The Southern Journal of Philosophy,* vol. 37 (1999): 57–75.

Martin, Mike W. *Virtuous Giving: Philanthropy, Voluntary Service, and Caring.* Bloomington: Indiana University Press, 1994.

Mellema, Gregory. *Beyond the Call of Duty: Supererogation, Obligation, and Offence.* Albany: State University of New York Press, 1991.

Monroe, Kristin Renwick. *The Heart of Altruism: Perceptions of a Common Humanity.* Princeton, NJ: Princeton University Press, 1996.

Odendahl, Teresa, and Michael O'Neill (eds.). *Women and Power in the Nonprofit Sector.* San Francisco: Jossey-Bass, 1994.

Oldenquist, Andrew. *The Non-Suicidal Society.* Bloomington: Indiana University Press, 1986.

Oliner, Pearl M. et al. (eds.). *Embracing the Other: Philosophical, Psychological, and Historical Perspectives on Altruism.* New York: New York University Press, 1992.

Paul, Ellen Frankel, Fred D. Miller, and Jeffrey Paul (eds.). *Altruism.* New York: Cambridge University Press, 1993.

Paul, Ellen Frankel, Fred D. Miller, Jr., Jeffrey Paul, and John Ahrens (eds.). *Beneficence, Philanthropy and the Public Good.* New York: Basil Blackwell, 1987.

Powell, Walter W., and Elisabeth S. Clemens (eds.). *Private Action and the Public Good.* New Haven, CT: Yale University Press, 1998.

Schneewind, J. B. (ed.). *Giving: Western Ideas of Philanthropy.* Bloomington: Indiana University Press, 1996.

Schrift, Alan D. (ed.). *The Logic of the Gift: Toward an Ethic of Generosity.* New York: Routledge, 1997.

Unger, Peter. *Living High and Letting Die.* New York: Oxford University Press, 1996.

Wuthnow, Robert. *Acts of Compassion.* Princeton, NJ: Princeton University Press, 1991.

Notes

PREFACE

1 William James, "The Moral Philosopher and the Moral Life," in *Essays on Faith and Morals,* ed. Ralph Barton Perry (New York: World Publishing 1962), p. 184. First published 1891.

2 Molière, *The School for Wives,* in *Tartuffe and Other Plays by Molière,* trans. Donald M. Frame (New York: New American Library, 1967), Scene 6.

PART ONE   *Character and Conduct*

1 Mary Midgley, *Can't We Make Moral Judgements?* (New York: St. Martin's Press, 1993), p. 26.

CHAPTER 1   *Moral Reasoning and Self-Interest*

1 Martin Gansberg, "38 Who Saw Murder Didn't Call Police," in Christina Sommers and Fred Sommers (eds.), *Vice and Virtue in Everyday Life,* 4th ed. (San Diego, CA: Harcourt Brace Jovanovich, 1997), pp. 46–49.

2 David Hume, *A Treatise of Human Nature* (Oxford: Clarendon Press, 1888), pp. 468–469.

3 Ayn Rand, *The Virtue of Selfishness* (New York: New American Library, 1961), p. ix.

4 Ibid., pp. 16–17.

5 Ibid., p. 17.

6 Owen Flanagan, *Varieties of Moral Experience: Ethics and Psychological Realism* (Cambridge, MA: Harvard University Press, 1991).

7 Ayn Rand, *The Virtue of Selfishness,* p. ix.

8 Ibid., p. 47.

9 Ibid.

10 Ibid., p. 92. Also see Eric Mack, "The Fundamental Moral Elements of Rand's Theory of Rights," in Douglas J. Den Uyl and Douglas B. Rasmussen (eds.), *The Philosophic Thought of Ayn Rand* (Urbana: University of Illinois Press, 1984), pp. 122–161; and Douglas B. Rasmussen and Douglas J. Den Uyl, *Liberty and Nature* (La Salle: Open Court, 1991), p. 111.

11 See Gregory S. Kavka, *Hobbesian Moral Philosophy* (Princeton, NJ: Princeton University Press, 1986), ch. 2; James Rachels, *The Elements of Moral Philosophy,* 3d ed. (New York: McGraw-Hill, 1999), ch. 5; and for psychological studies see Alfie Kohn, *The Brighter Side of Human Nature* (New York: BasicBooks, 1990).

12 See John Kekes, *The Examined Life* (Lewisburg, PA: Bucknell University Press, 1988); and Elizabeth Telfer, *Happiness* (New York: St. Martin's Press, 1980).

13 John Stuart Mill, *The Autobiography of John Stuart Mill* (Garden City, NY: Doubleday), p. 110.

14 See Charles Taylor, *The Ethics of Authenticity* (Cambridge, MA: Harvard University Press, 1991).

15 See Bernard Williams, *Moral Luck* (Cambridge, MA: Cambridge University Press, 1981).

16 Chris Matthew Sciabarra, *Ayn Rand: The Russian Radical* (University Park: Pennsylvania State University Press, 1995), pp. 267–270.

17 Jean-Paul Sartre, *Being and Nothingness,* trans. H. E. Barnes (New York: Washington Square Press, 1966), p. 76. The example of the student is also presented in "Existentialism Is a Humanism," trans. P. Mairet, in W. Kaufmann (ed.), *Existentialism from Dostoevsky to Sartre,* rev. ed. (New York: New American Library, 1975).

18 Joseph Butler, *The Works of Joseph Butler,* ed. J. H. Bernard. 2 vols. (London: Macmillan, 1900).

CHAPTER 2   *Theories of Right Action*

1 Much has been written about President Clinton, but one useful starting point for reflection is Gabriel Fackre (ed.), *Judgment Day at the White House* (Grand Rapids, MI: William B. Eerdmans, 1999).

2 Sir Walter Scott, *Marmion,* Stanza 17.

3 John Stuart Mill, *Utilitarianism* (Indianapolis, IN: Hackett, 1979), pp. 22–23, 25.

4 G. E. Moore, *Principia Ethica* (Cambridge, MA: Cambridge University Press, 1959). First published in 1903.

5 John Stuart Mill, *Utilitarianism,* pp. 8–9.

6 Ibid., p. 10.

7 A. I. Melden, "Are There Welfare Rights?" In Peter G. Brown, Conrad Johnson, and Paul Vernier (eds.), *Income Support: Conceptual Policy Issues* (Totowa, NY: Rowman & Littlefield, 1981).

8 Immanuel Kant, *Foundations of the Metaphysics of Morals,* trans. L. W. Beck (New York: Liberal Arts Press, 1959). Printed in A. I. Melden, *Ethical Theories: A Book of Readings,* 2d ed. (Englewood Cliffs, NJ: Prentice-Hall, 1967), p. 345.

9 Ibid., p. 339.

10 Ibid., p. 348.

11 Ibid., p. 328. Kant did often lecture on practical moral issues. See *Lectures on Ethics,* trans. Louis Infield (New York: Harper & Row, 1963).

12 David Ross, *The Right and the Good* (Oxford: Clarendon Press, 1930), p. 19.

13 Ibid., pp. 21–22.

14 Bernard Williams, *Ethics and the Limits of Philosophy* (Cambridge, MA: Harvard University Press, 1985), chap. 5.

15 John Dewey, *Human Nature and Conduct* (New York: The Modern Library, 1957), p. 183. First published in 1922.

16 John Dewey, *Theory of the Moral Life* (New York: Holt, Rinehart and Winston, 1960), p. 141. First published in 1908.

17 John Dewey, *Human Nature and Conduct*, pp. 37, 39.

18 Albert R. Jonsen and Stephen Toulmin, *The Abuse of Casuistry: A History of Moral Reasoning* (Berkeley: University of California Press, 1988), p. 18. For samples of recent pragmatic approaches in medical ethics see Glenn McGee (ed.), *Pragmatic Bioethics* (Nashville, TN: Vanderbilt University Press, 1999).

19 Immanuel Kant, "On a Supposed Right to Lie from Altruistic Motives," in L. W. Beck (trans. and ed.), *Critique of Practical Reason and Other Writings in Moral Philosophy* (Chicago: University of Chicago Press, 1949), pp. 346–350.

20 Jean-Paul Sartre, "The Wall," in Walter Kaufmann (ed.), *Existentialism from Dostoevsky to Sartre* (New York: New American Library, 1975).

21 Fyodor Dostoevsky, *Crime and Punishment*, trans. C. Garnett (New York: Bantam, 1981), pp. 58–59.

22 William K. Frankena, *Ethics*, 2d ed. (Englewood Cliffs, NJ: 1973), pp. 47–52.

C H A P T E R 3   *Theories of Virtue*

1 Aristotle, *Ethics*, trans. J. A. K. Thomson and H. Tredennick (New York: Penguin, 1976), p. 108.

2 Ibid., p. 104.

3 For further discussions, see John M. Cooper, *Reason and Human Good in Aristotle* (Indianapolis, IN: Hackett, 1986); and Nancy Sherman, *The Fabric of Character: Aristotle's Theory of Virtue* (Oxford: Clarendon Press, 1989).

4 Aristotle, *Ethics*, pp. 108–109.

5 Ibid., pp. 101–102.

6 Cf. Annette C. Baier, "Hume, the Women's Moral Theorist?" in E. F. Kittay and D. T. Meyers (eds.), *Women and Moral Theory* (Totowa, NJ: Rowman & Littlefield, 1987).

7 David Hume, *Hume's Ethical Writings*, Alasdair MacIntyre (ed.) (New York: Macmillan, 1965), p. 29.

8 Alasdair MacIntyre, *After Virtue* (Notre Dame, IN: University of Notre Dame Press, 1981), p. 204.

9 Ibid.

10 Ibid., p. 178. Italics deleted.

11 Ibid., p. 204.

12 Ibid.

13 Edmund L. Pincoffs, *Quandaries and Virtues* (Lawrence: University Press of Kansas, 1986), p. 78.

14 Ibid., p. 85.

15 Ibid., p. 89.

16 Plato, *The Republic*, trans. F. M. Cornford (New York: Oxford University Press, 1945), pp. 141–142.

PART TWO   *Multicultural Ethics*

1 Sissela Bok, *Common Values* (Columbia: University of Missouri Press, 1995), p. 24.

CHAPTER 4   *Diversity and Relativism*

1 Articles by Ray Rivera and Greg Burton under the general heading of "Family Secrets: When Incest Becomes a Religious Tenet," *The Salt Lake Tribune* (April 25, 1999), Section A.

2 Richard S. Van Wagoner, *Mormon Polygamy: A History,* 2d ed. (Salt Lake City, UT: Signature Books, 1989). For a wider study of polygamy in world cultures, see Peter Bredschneider, *Polygyny: A Cross-Cultural Study* (New York: Uppsala, 1995).

3 Ruth Benedict, "Anthropology and the Abnormal," *The Journal of General Psychology,* vol. 10 (1934): 59–82. Also see *Patterns of Culture* (Boston: Houghton Mifflin Co., 1934).

4 William Graham Sumner, *Folkways* (Boston: Ginn and Company, 1940), p. 29. First published in 1906.

5 See Carolyn Fluehr-Lobban, "Cultural Relativism and Universal Rights," reprinted in Christina Sommers and Fred Sommers (eds.), *Vice and Virtue in Everyday Life,* 4th ed. (Fort Worth, TX: Harcourt Brace, 1997), pp. 220–230.

6 Sissela Bok, *Common Values* (Columbia: University of Missouri Press, 1995); and Stuart Hampshire, *Morality and Conflict* (Cambridge, MA: Harvard University Press, 1983).

7 Colin M. Turnbull, *The Mountain People* (New York: Simon & Schuster, 1972).

8 Richard Borshay Lee, *The !Kung San: Men, Women, and Work in a Foraging Society* (Cambridge, MA: Cambridge University Press, 1979). The "!" in "!Kung" stands for a clicking sound. The !Kung were formerly called Bushmen or Hottentots by anthropologists.

9 Jeffrey Stout, *Ethics After Babel* (Boston: Beacon Press, 1988), p. 98.

10 Michael Walzer, *Thick and Thin: Moral Argument at Home and Abroad* (Notre Dame: University of Notre Dame, 1994).

11 Stuart Hampshire, *Morality and Conflict,* p. 163.

12 John Stuart Mill, *On Liberty* (Indianapolis, IN: Hackett, 1978), p. 54. First published in 1859.

13 Isaiah Berlin, "The Pursuit of the Ideal," in *The Crooked Timber of Humanity* (New York: Vintage, 1992), p. 11.

14 On the sciences, see Thomas Kuhn, *The Structure of Scientific Revolutions,* 2d ed. (Chicago: Chicago University Press, 1970); and Brian Fay, *Contemporary Philosophy of Social Science* (New York: Blackwell, 1996).

15 Friedrich Nietzsche, *Twilight of the Idols,* Section 1 of "The 'Improvers' of Mankind," in *Twilight of the Idols and the Anti-Christ,* trans. R. J. Hollingdale (New York: Harmondsworth, 1990), p. 66.

16 Friedrich Nietzsche, *Thus Spoke Zarathustra,* trans. R.J. Hollingdale (New York: Penguin, 1969), p. 85.

17 Friedrich Nietzsche, *Beyond Good and Evil,* trans. Walter Kaufmann (New York: Vintage, 1966), Section 227.

18 For some opposing interpretations see: Alexander Nehamas, *Nietzsche: Life as Literature* (Cambridge, MA: Harvard University Press, 1985); Charles Larmore, *The Morals of Modernity* (New York: Cambridge University Press, 1996); Peter Berkowitz, *Nietzsche: The Ethics of an Immoralist* (Cambridge, MA: Harvard University Press, 1995); Richard Schacht (ed.), *Nietzsche, Genealogy, Morality* (Berkeley: University of California Press, 1994); and Daniel R. Ahern, *Nietzsche as Cultural Physician* (University Park: Pennsylvania State University Press, 1995).

19 Arthur M. Melzer, Jerry Weinberger, and M. Richard Zinman in the Introduction to their anthology, *Multiculturalism and American Democracy* (Lawrence: University Press of Kansas, 1998), p. 4.

20 Stanley Fish, "Boutique Multiculturalism," in Arthur M. Melzer, Jerry Weinberger, and M. Richard Zinman (eds.), *Multiculturalism and American Democracy* (Lawrence: University Press of Kansas, 1998), pp. 69–88.

21 Lawrence Blum, "Antiracism, Multiculturalism, and Interracial Community: Three Educational Values for a Multicultural Society," in Rita C. Manning and Rene Trujillo (eds.), *Social Justice in a Diverse Society* (Mountain View, CA: Mayfield Publishing, 1996), p. 370.

22 Nathan Glazer, *We Are All Multiculturalists Now* (Cambridge, MA: Harvard University Press, 1997.

23 Anita Silvers, "Formal Justice," in Anita Silvers, David Wasserman, and Mary B. Mahowald (eds.), *Disability, Difference, Discrimination: Perspectives on Justice in Bioethics and Public Policy* (Lanham, MD: Rowman & Littlefield, 1998), p. 35.

24 Ibid., p. 127.

25 Ibid., p. 13. Quoted from *New York Times* (1 August 1996).

26 "Introduction," in Anita Silvers, David Wasserman, and Mary B. Mahowald (eds.), *Disability, Difference, Discrimination: Perspectives on Justice in Bioethics and Public Policy,* p. 1.

27 Max Scheler, *Ressentiment,* trans. William W. Woldheim (New York: Schocken Books, 1972), pp. 88–89.

28 Alasdair MacIntyre, *Dependent Rational Animals: Why Human Beings Need the Virtues* (Chicago: Open Court, 1999), p. 2.

CHAPTER 5   *Religious Ethics*

1 Cf. Mike W. Martin, *Meaningful Work: Rethinking Professional Ethics* (New York: Oxford University Press, 2000), ch. 10.

2 William James, *The Varieties of Religious Experience* (New York: Modern Library, 1902), p. 27. On Ludwig Wittgenstein, see *Philosophical Investigations,* trans. G.E.M. Anscombe (New York: Oxford, 1953).

3 William James, *The Varieties of Religious Experience,* p. 108.

4 Confucius, *The Analects,* trans. D.C. Lau (New York: Penguin, 1979), 15:24.

5 *Shabbath,* 31a.

6 Jeffrey Wattles, *The Golden Rule* (New York: Oxford University Press, 1996), p. 166.

7 Owen Flanagan, *Varieties of Moral Personality: Ethics and Psychological Realism* (Cambridge, MA: Harvard University Press, 1991), pp. 1–12.

8 Richard T. De George, *The Nature and Limits of Authority* (Lawrence: University Press of Kansas, 1985).

9 Plato, *Euthyphro,* trans. L. Cooper, in E. Hamilton and H. Cairns (eds.), *The Collected Dialogues of Plato* (Princeton, NJ: Princeton University Press, 1961), p. 178.

10 Larry May, *The Socially Responsive Self* (Chicago: University of Chicago Press, 1996), pp. 153–170.

11 Genesis 22:1–2, 9–10, King James version.

12 Jean-Paul Sartre, "Existentialism Is a Humanism," trans. P. Mairet, in W. Kaufmann (ed.), *Existentialism from Dostoevsky to Sartre,* rev. ed. (New York: New American Library, 1975), p. 351.

13 Søren Kierkegaard, *Fear and Trembling,* trans. A. Hannay (New York: Penguin, 1985).

14 James Davison Hunter, *Culture Wars: The Struggle to Define America* (New York: BasicBooks, 1991), p. 44.

CHAPTER 6 *Feminism*

1 Rosemarie Tong, "Feminist Philosophy," in Robert Audi (ed.), *The Cambridge Dictionary of Philosophy* (New York: Cambridge University Press, 1995), p. 262.

2 "Declaration of Sentiments and Resolutions, Seneca Falls," in Mariam Schneir, *Feminism: The Essential Historical Writings* (New York: Vintage, 1992), pp. 77–78.

3 Elizabeth Cady Stanton and The Revising Committee, *The Woman's Bible* (Seattle, WA: Coalition Task Force on Women and Religion, 1974), p. 131. First published in two parts in 1895 and 1898.

4 Sandra Lee Bartky, *Femininity and Comination: Studies in the Phenomenology of Oppression* (New York: Routledge, 1990).

5 Carol Gilligan, *In a Different Voice: Psychological Theory and Women's Development* (Cambridge, MA: Harvard University Press, 1993). First published 1982.

6 Lawrence Kohlberg, "Indoctrination Versus Relativity in Value Education," in G. Sher (ed.), *Moral Philosophy: Selected Readings* (New York: Harcourt Brace Jovanovich, 1987), pp. 102–112; and Lawrence Kohlberg, *The Philosophy of Moral Development* (San Francisco: Harper & Row, 1981).

7 Examples of these three directions, respectively, are: (1) Nel Noddings, *Caring: A Feminine Approach to Ethics and Moral Education* (Berkeley: University of California, 1984); (2) Claudia Card, *The Unnatural Lottery* (Philadelphia: Temple University, 1996); (3) Marilyn Friedman, *What Are Friends For?: Feminist Perspectives on Personal Relationships and Moral Theory* (Ithaca, NY: Cornell

University, 1993); and Daryl Koehn, *Rethinking Feminist Ethics: Care, Trust and Empathy* (New York: Routledge, 1998).

8 Ludwig Wittgenstein, *Philosophical Investigations,* 3d ed., trans. G. E. M. Anscombe (New York: Macmillan, 1953), p. 115.

9 Francis Bacon, *Novum Organum,* ed. T. Fowler (Oxford: Oxford University Press, 1889).

10 M. Vetterling-Braggin (ed.), *Sexist Language: A Modern Philosophical Analysis* (Totowa, NJ: Littlefield, Adams, 1981), p. 17; and see Virginia L. Warren, "Guidelines for the Nonsexist Use of Language, " *Proceedings and Addresses of the American Philosophical Association,* vol. 59 (1986).

11 Quoted from a study done by Sally Hacker and Joseph Schneider in 1972, in C. Miller and K. Swift, *Words and Women* (Garden City, NY: Anchor, 1976), p. 21.

12 Susan Griffin, *Rape: The Politics of Consciousness,* 3d ed. (New York: Harper & Row, 1986), pp. 23–24.

13 William B. Sanders, *Rape and Woman's Identity* (Beverly Hills, CA: Sage, 1980), pp. 50–51.

14 Susan Brownmiller, *Against Our Will: Men, Women, and Rape* (New York: Simon & Schuster, 1975), p. 354.

15 Robin Warshaw, *I Never Called It Rape: The Ms. Report on Recognizing, Fighting and Surviving Date and Acquaintance Rape* (New York: Harper & Row, 1988), pp. 29–30.

CHAPTER 7   *Race and Ethnic Identity*

1 Ralph Ellison, *Invisible Man* (New York: Vintage, 1972), p. 3.

2 Ibid., p. 4.

3 Naomi Zack, *Thinking About Race* (Belmont, CA: Wadsworth, 1998), p. 40.

4 W. E. B. Du Bois, "The Conservation of Races," in Howard Brotz (ed.), *Negro Social and Political Thought, 1850–1920* (New York: BasicBooks, 1966), p. 485.

5 Kwame Anthony Appiah, *In My Father's House: Africa in the Philosophy of Culture* (New York: Oxford University Press, 1992), p. 45.

6 Raphael S. Ezekiel, *The Racist Mind: Portraits of American Neo-Nazis and Klansmen* (New York: Penguin, 1996), p. xvii.

7 Jean-Paul Sartre, *Anti-Semite and Jew,* trans. George J. Becker (New York: Schocken Books, 1965), p. 53.

8 Gordon W. Allport, *The Nature of Prejudice* (Reading, MA: Addison-Wesley, 1979); Elliot Aronson, *The Social Animal* (New York: W. H. Freeman, 1992); and Paul L. Wachtel, *Race in the Mind of America: Breaking the Vicious Circle Between Blacks and Whites* (New York: Routledge, 1999).

9 Pierre L. van den Berghe, "Ethnicity as Kin Selection: The Biology of Nepotism," *The Ethnic Phenomenon* (New York: Elsevier Publishing Company, 1981).

10 Richard Wasserstrom, "On Racism and Sexism," in R. A. Wasserstrom (ed.), *Today's Moral Problems,* 3d ed. (New York: Macmillan, 1985), p. 7.

11 Iris Marion Young, *Justice and the Politics of Difference* (Princeton, NJ: Princeton University Press, 1990), p. 165.

12 Ibid., p. 174.

13 Ibid., p. 171.

14 Arthur M. Schlesinger, Jr., *The Disuniting of America: Reflections on a Multicultural Society,* Rev. ed. (New York: W. W. Norton, 1998), p. 20.

15 Ibid., p. 133.

16 Ibid., p. 147.

17 Martin Bernal, *Black Athena* (New Brunswick, N.J.: Rutgers University Press, 1987). For replies see Mary Lefkowitz, *Not Out of Africa: How Afrocentrism Became an Excuse to Teach Myth as History* (New York, 1996); and Mary Lefkowitz and G. M. Rogers (eds.), *Black Athena Revisited* (Chapel Hill: University of North Carolina, 1996).

18 Arthur Schopenhauer, *The World as Will and Representation,* trans. E. F. J. Payne (New York: Dover, 1969), vol. I, pp. 58–61, vol. II, pp. 91–101; and Mike W. Martin, "Humor and Aesthetic Enjoyment of Incongruities," in J. Morreall, *The Philosophy of Laughter and Humor,* pp. 172–186.

19 Cited in *Doe v. University of Michigan,* 721 F. Supp. 852 (E. D. Mich. 1989). Selections from this court ruling published in John Arthur and Amy Shapiro (eds.), *Campus Wars: Multiculturalism and the Politics of Difference* (Boulder, CO.: Westview Press, 1995), pp. 114–121.

20 Alan Dundes, *Cracking Jokes: Studies of Sick Humor Cycles and Stereotypes* (Berkeley, CA: Ten Speed Press, 1987), p. 53.

21 Ibid., p. 74.

22 Charles S. Farrell, "Black Students Seen Facing 'New Racism' on Many Campuses," *The Chronicle of Higher Education,* vol. 34, no. 20 (January 27, 1988): 1.

PART THREE   *Moral Standing*

1 Albert Schweitzer, *Out of My Life and Thought,* trans. A.B. Lemke (New York: Henry Holt and Company, 1990), p. 157.

2 Albert Schweitzer, "Religion in Modern Civilization," *The Christian Century* 51 (November 21 and 28, 1934), p. 1521.

3 Peter Singer, *The Expanding Circle* (New York: Farrar, Straus, and Giroux, 1981).

CHAPTER 8   *Abortion*

1 *Roe v. Wade, United States Reports,* vol. 410 (1973), pp. 113–178.

2 Nancy (Ann) Davis, "Abortion," in L. C. Becker (ed.), *Encyclopedia of Ethics* (New York: Garland, 1992), pp. 2–6.

3 See Paul Ramsey, "The Morality of Abortion," in D. H. Labby (ed.), *Life or Death: Ethics and Options* (Seattle: University of Washington Press, 1968); and John Noonan, "Abortion and the Catholic Church: A Summary History," *Natural Law Forum,* vol. 12 (1967): 125–131.

4 Don Marquis, "Why Abortion is Immoral," in S. J. Gold (ed.), *Moral Controversies: Race, Class, and Gender in Applied Ethics* (Belmont, CA: Wadsworth, 1993), p. 25. First published in *The Journal of Philosophy*, vol. 86 (1989): 183–202.

5 Ibid., p. 26.

6 Mary Anne Warren, "On the Moral and Legal Status of Abortion," in Hugh LaFollette (ed.), *Ethics in Practice* (Cambridge, MA: Blackwell Publishers, 1997), p. 84. This is a revised version of an essay widely anthologized—for example, in Joel Feinberg (ed.), *The Problem of Abortion*, 2d ed. (Belmont, CA: Wadsworth, 1984), pp. 111–112.

7 Michael Tooley, "In Defense of Abortion and Infanticide," in R. M. Baird and S. E. Rosenbaum (eds.), *The Ethics of Abortion* (Buffalo, NY: Prometheus, 1989), p. 49. First published in *Philosophy & Public Affairs*, vol. 2 (1972): 37–65.

8 See Baruch Brody, *Abortion and the Sanctity of Human Life: A Philosophical View* (Cambridge, MA: MIT Press, 1975).

9 Jane English, "Abortion and the Concept of a Person," in J. Feinberg (ed.), *The Problem of Abortion*, 2d ed. (Belmont, CA: Wadsworth, 1984), p. 153. First published in the *Canadian Journal of Philosophy*, vol. 5 (1975): 233–243.

10 Judith Jarvis Thomson, "A Defense of Abortion," in J. Feinberg (ed.), *The Problem of Abortion*, p. 174. First published in *Philosophy & Public Affairs*, vol. 1 (1971): 47–66.

11 Jane English, "Abortion and the Concept of a Person," in J. Feinberg (ed.), *The Problem of Abortion*, pp. 158–159.

12 Martin Benjamin, *Splitting the Difference: Compromise and Integrity in Ethics and Politics* (Lawrence: University Press of Kansas, 1990), pp. 151–171.

13 See Kristin Luker, *Abortion and the Politics of Motherhood* (Berkeley: University of California Press, 1984).

14 For an example, see Beth Maschinot, "Compromising Positions," *In These Times*, vol. 10 (November 20–26, 1985): 4.

15 See R. M. Hare, "Abortion and the Golden Rule," *Philosophy and Public Affairs*, vol. 4 (1975): 201–222; and Harry J. Gensler, "A Kantian Argument Against Abortion," *Philosophical Studies*, vol. 49 (1986): 83–98.

16 Sidney Callahan, "Abortion and the Sexual Agenda," in R. M. Baird and S. E. Rosenbaum (eds.), *The Ethics of Abortion* (Buffalo, NY: Prometheus, 1989), p. 137. First published in *Commonwealth* (25 April 1986): 232–238.

17 Anthony Weston, *Toward Better Problems: New Perspectives on Abortion, Animal Rights, the Environment and Justice* (Philadelphia: Temple University Press, 1992), p. 55.

CHAPTER 9   *Animals*

1 John Steinbeck, *Travels with Charley* (New York: Bantam, 1963), p. 8.

2 Ibid., p. 163.

3 Ibid., p. 33.

4 Ibid., p. 9.

5 Mary Midgley, *Animals and Why They Matter* (Athens: University of Georgia Press, 1984), p. 31.

6 René Descartes, *Discourse on Method,* excerpted in T. Regan and P. Singer (eds.), *Animal Rights and Human Obligations* (Englewood Cliffs, NJ: Prentice-Hall, 1976), p. 62.

7 Benedict de Spinoza, *The Ethics,* trans. R. H. M. Elwes (New York: Dover, 1955), Proposition 37, note 1.

8 Immanuel Kant, "Duties Towards Animals and Spirits," in *Lectures on Ethics,* trans. L. Infield (New York: Harper & Row, 1963), pp. 239–240.

9 Jeremy Bentham, *Introduction to the Principles of Morals and Legislation* (New York: Hafner, 1948), p. 311n. First published in 1789.

10 Peter Singer, *Animal Liberation,* rev. ed. (New York: Avon Books, 1990), p. 6.

11 Ibid., p. i.

12 Ibid., pp. 82–83.

13 II Sam. xii:3, King James version. Discussed in Mary Midgley, *Animals and Why They Matter,* p. 116.

14 Jeremy Bentham, *Introduction to the Principles of Morals and Legislation.* Quoted in Peter Singer, *Animal Liberation,* p. 210.

15 Peter Singer, *Animal Liberation,* pp. 121–128.

16 Ibid., pp. 47–48.

CHAPTER 10   *Environment*

1 William T. Blackstone, "Ethics and Ecology," in W. M. Hoffman and J. M. Moore (eds.), *Business Ethics,* 2d ed. (New York: McGraw-Hill, 1990), p. 473.

2 Cf. Gregory Kavka, "The Futurity Problem," in E. Partridge (ed.), *Responsibilities to Future Generations* (Buffalo, NY: Prometheus, 1980).

3 Thomas E. Hill, Jr., "Ideals of Human Excellence and Preserving Natural Environments," in *Autonomy and Self-Respect* (Cambridge, MA: Cambridge University Press, 1991), p. 104.

4 Ibid., p. 108.

5 Albert Schweitzer, *The Philosophy of Civilization* (Buffalo, NY: Prometheus Books, 1987), p. 309. First published 1949. For an explication and critique of Schweitzer's argument, see Mike W. Martin, "Rethinking Reverence for Life," *Between the Species,* 9 (1993): 204–213.

6 Ibid., p. 310.

7 Kenneth Goodpaster, "On Being Morally Considerable," in S. J. Armstrong and R. G. Botzler (eds.), *Environmental Ethics: Divergence and Convergence* (New York: McGraw-Hill, 1993), p. 352.

8 Aldo Leopold, *A Sand County Almanac* (New York: Ballantine, 1970), p. 239. First published 1949.

9 Ibid., p. 262.

10 J. Baird Callicott, "Environmental Ethics," in L. C. Becker (ed.), *Encyclopedia of Ethics,* vol. 1 (New York: Garland, 1992), pp. 313–314.

11 Paul W. Taylor, *Respect for Nature: A Theory of Environmental Ethics* (Princeton, NJ: Princeton University Press, 1986), p. 121.

12 Garrett Hardin, "Tragedy of the Commons," *Science,* vol. 162 (13 Dec 1968): 1243–1248.

13 R. Gordon Cummings, *Five Years of a Hunter's Life in the Far Interior of South Africa* (1850). Quoted in R. Carrington, *Elephants* (Chatto & Windus, 1958), p. 154; in M. Midgley, *Animals and Why They Matter* (Athens: University of Georgia Press, 1984), pp. 14–15.

14 Holmes Rolston III, "Challenges in Environmental Ethics," in D. E. Cooper and J. A. Palmer (eds.), *The Environment in Question: Ethics and Global Issues* (London: Routledge, 1992), p. 139.

15 Rosemary Ruether, *New Woman/New Earth: Sexist Ideologies and Human Liberation* (New York: Seabury Press, 1975), p. 204. Quoted by K. J. Warren, "Feminism and Ecology: Making Connections," *Environmental Ethics,* vol. 9 (1987): 3–20.

PART FOUR   *Sexual Morality*

1 Michel Foucault, *The History of Sexuality,* vol. I, trans. R. Hurley (New York: Vintage, 1980), pp. 155–156.

CHAPTER 11   *Sex and Love*

1 Marilyn French, *The Women's Room* (New York: Summit Books, 1977), pp. 361–362.

2 Ibid., p. 407.

3 Erich Fromm, *The Art of Loving* (New York: Harper & Row, 1956), pp. 38–39.

4 Shulamith Firestone, *The Dialectic of Sex: The Case for Feminist Revolution* (New York: Morrow, 1970), p. 145.

5 Ibid., p. 149.

6 Russell Vannoy, *Sex Without Love: A Philosophical Exploration* (Buffalo, NY: Prometheus, 1980), p. 26.

7 Roger Scruton, *Sexual Desire: A Moral Philosophy of the Erotic* (New York: Free Press, 1986), p. 30.

8 Ibid., p. 251.

9 Ibid., p. 337.

10 Ibid., p. 87.

11 Robert C. Solomon, "Love and Feminism," in R. Baker and F. Elliston (eds.), *Philosophy and Sex,* rev. ed. (Buffalo, NY: Prometheus, 1984), p. 66.

12 Stendhal (Marie Henri Beyle), *Love,* trans. G. Sale and S. Sale (New York: Penguin, 1975), p. 60.

13 David Henry Hwang, *M. Butterfly* (New York: Penguin, 1989).

14 Simone de Beauvoir, *The Second Sex* (New York: Vintage, 1952), p. 712.

15 Robert Nozick, *The Examined Life* (New York: Simon & Schuster, 1989), pp. 73–74.

CHAPTER 12   *Homosexuality and Homophobia*

1 Frederick Suppe, "Curing Homosexuality," in R. Baker and F. Elliston (eds.), *Philosophy and Sex,* rev. ed. (Buffalo, NY: Prometheus, 1984), pp. 394–395.

2 Malcolm Boyd, *Take Off the Masks* (Philadelphia, PA: New Society, 1984), p. 78.

3 Ibid., p. 5.

4 Martina Navratilova and George Vecsey, *Martina* (New York: Ballantine, 1985), p. 154.

5 Leviticus 18:22, King James version.

6 Romans 1:26–27, King James version.

7 Saint Thomas Aquinas, *On the Truth of the Catholic Faith,* Book 3: *Providence,* Part 1, trans. V. J. Bourke (New York: Doubleday, 1956). Quoted in R. Baker and F. Elliston (eds.), *Philosophy and Sex,* rev. ed. (Buffalo, NY: Prometheus, 1984), p. 15.

8 Roger Scruton, *Sexual Desire: A Moral Philosophy of the Erotic* (New York: Free Press, 1986), pp. 307–308.

9 Adrienne Rich, "Compulsory Heterosexuality and Lesbian Existence," *SIGNS: Journal of Women in Culture and Society,* vol. 5 (1980). Reprinted in C. R. Stimpson and E. Spector (eds.), *Women: Sex and Sexuality* (Chicago: University of Chicago Press, 1980), pp. 81–82.

CHAPTER 13   *Pornography and Fantasy*

1 Helen E. Longino, "Pornography, Oppression, and Freedom: A Closer Look," in L. Lederer (ed.), *Take Back the Night: Women on Pornography* (New York: Morrow, 1980), p. 42.

2 Robin Morgan, "Theory and Practice: Pornography and Rape," in L. Lederer (ed.), *Take Back the Night,* pp. 134–140.

3 Beverly LaBelle, "Snuff—The Ultimate Woman-Hating," in L. Lederer (ed.), *Take Back the Night,* p. 274.

4 Nancy Friday, *My Secret Garden: Women's Sexual Fantasies* (New York: Pocket Books, 1973), p. 109.

5 Matthew 5:28–29, King James version.

6 Herbert Fingarette, "Real Guilt and Neurotic Guilt," in *On Responsibility* (New York: BasicBooks, 1967), pp. 91–94.

7 "Excerpts from the Minneapolis Ordinance," in V. Burstyn (ed.), *Women Against Censorship* (Vancouver, British Columbia: Douglas & McIntyre, 1985), pp. 206–207.

PART FIVE   *Caring Relationships*

1 George Eliot, *Daniel Deronda* (New York: Penguin Books, 1967), p. 868. First published 1876.

CHAPTER 14   *Marriage and Adultery*

1 Shere Hite, *Women and Love: A Cultural Revolution in Progress* (New York: Knopf, 1987), p. 325.

2 Ibid.

3 John McMurtry, "Monogamy: A Critique," in R. Baker and F. Elliston (eds.), *Philosophy and Sex,* rev. ed. (Buffalo, NY: Prometheus, 1984), p. 111.

4 Ibid., p. 112.

5 Susan Moller Okin, *Justice, Gender and the Family* (New York: BasicBooks, 1989), pp. 135–136.

6 Francesca M. Cancian, *Love in America: Gender and Self-Development* (New York: Cambridge University Press, 1987), p. 3.

7 Ibid.

8 S. I. Benn, "Individuality, Autonomy and Community," in E. Kamenka (ed.), *Community as a Social Ideal* (London: Edward Arnold, 1982), p. 58.

9 John McMurtry, "Monogamy: A Critique," p. 111.

10 Ibid., p. 112. Italics deleted from original.

11 Ibid., p. 113.

12 Larry Martz, Vern E. Smith, Daniel Pedersen, Daniel Shapiro, Mark Miller, and Ginny Carroll, "God and Money," *Newsweek* (April 6, 1987), pp. 18–19.

13 Tom Morganthau, Margaret Garrard Warner, Howard Fineman, and Erik Calonius, "The Sudden Fall of Gary Hart," *Newsweek* (May 18, 1987), p. 23.

14 Richard Taylor, *Having Love Affairs* (Buffalo, NY: Prometheus, 1982), p. 12.

15 Ibid., p. 138.

16 Ibid., p. 158.

17 Ibid., p. 59.

18 Ibid., pp. 142–143.

19 Ibid., p. 146.

20 Jerome Neu, "Jealous Thoughts," in A. O. Rorty (ed.), *Explaining Emotions* (Berkeley: University of California Press, 1980), pp. 454–455.

CHAPTER 15   *Parents and Children*

1 Franz Kafka, *Letter to His Father* (New York: Schocken, 1966), p. 7. For an illuminating discussion, see Alice Miller, *Thou Shalt Not Be Aware: Society's Betrayal of the Child,* trans. H. and H. Hannum (New York: New American Library, 1986).

2 Ibid., p. 21.

3 Ibid., p. 89.

4 Kenneth Keniston and The Carnegie Council on Children, *All Our Children: The American Family Under Pressure* (New York: Harcourt Brace Jovanovich, 1977), pp. 17–18.

5 Maya Angelou, *I Know Why the Caged Bird Sings* (New York: Bantam, 1969).

6 Natalie Abrams, "Problems in Defining Child Abuse and Neglect," in O. O'Neill and W. Ruddick (eds.), *Having Children: Philosophical and Legal Reflections on Parenthood* (New York: Oxford University Press, 1979), p. 160.

7 Cf. Claudia Card, "Gratitude and Obligation," *American Philosophical Quarterly,* vol. 25 (1988): 115–127.

8 Jane English, "What Do Grown Children Owe Their Parents?" in O. O'Neill and W. Ruddick (eds.), *Having Children* (New York: Oxford University Press, 1979), p. 351.

CHAPTER 16   *Friendship*

1 Lillian Hellman, *Pentimento* (New York: New American Library, 1974), p. 93.

2 Ibid., p. 96.

3 Ibid., p. 95.

4 Ibid., p. 85.

5 Marilyn Friedman, "Friendship and Moral Growth," *The Journal of Value Inquiry,* vol. 23 (1989): 7.

6 Ibid., p. 8.

7 David B. Annis, "The Meaning, Value, and Duties of Friendship," *American Philosophical Quarterly,* vol. 24 (1987): 352.

8 Ibid., p. 354.

9 Montaigne, "Of Friendship," in *The Complete Essays of Montaigne,* trans. D. M. Frame (Stanford, CA: Stanford University Press, 1971), pp. 141–142.

10 E. M. Forster, "What I Believe," in *Two Cheers for Democracy* (New York: Harcourt, Brace & World, 1951), pp. 68–69. For an illuminating discussion of betrayal of friends, see A. I. Melden, *Rights in Moral Lives* (Berkeley: University of California Press, 1988), pp. 123–135.

11 E. M. Forster, *A Passage to India* (New York: Harcourt, Brace & World, 1924), p. 175.

12 James Rachels, *The Elements of Moral Philosophy,* 2d ed. (New York: McGraw-Hill, 1999), p. 19.

13 Lawrence A. Blum, *Friendship, Altruism and Morality* (Boston: Routledge & Kegan Paul, 1980), p. 76.

14 Aristotle, *Nicomachean Ethics,* trans. W. D. Ross, in R. McKeon (ed.), *The Basic Works of Aristotle* (New York: Random House, 1941), p. 1093.

15 Lillian B. Rubin, *Just Friends: The Role of Friendship in Our Lives* (New York: Harper & Row, 1985), pp. 60–61. (Italics removed.) Cf. Barry McCarthy, "Adult Friendships," in G. Graham and H. LaFollette (eds.), *Person to Person* (Philadelphia: Temple University Press, 1989), 32–45.

CHAPTER 17   *Interpersonal Conflicts*

1 John Rawls, *A Theory of Justice* (Cambridge, MA: Harvard University Press, 1971), p. 531.

2 Friedrich Nietzsche, *Thus Spoke Zarathustra,* trans. W. Kaufmann (New York: Penguin, 1978), p. 100.

3 Max Scheler, *Ressentiment,* trans. W. W. Holdheim (New York: Schocken, 1972), p. 48.

4 Jean Hampton, "Forgiveness, Resentment and Hatred," in J. G. Murphy and J. Hampton, *Forgiveness and Mercy* (New York: Cambridge University Press, 1988), pp. 73–74.

5 Gray Cox, *The Ways of Peace* (New York: Paulist Press, 1986), p. 129.

6 Martin Benjamin, *Splitting the Difference: Compromise and Integrity in Ethics and Politics* (Lawrence: University Press of Kansas, 1986), pp. 24–32.

7 John Sabini and Maury Silver, *Moralities of Everyday Life* (Oxford: Oxford University Press, 1982), p. 29.

8 Henry Fairlie, *The Seven Deadly Sins Today* (Notre Dame, IN: University of Notre Dame Press, 1979), pp. 67–68.

9 Immanuel Kant, *Lectures on Ethics,* trans. L. Infield (New York: Harper & Row, 1963), p. 218.

10 Eugene O'Neill, *The Iceman Cometh* (New York: Vintage, 1957), p. 239.

11 John F. Kennedy, *Profiles in Courage* (New York: Harper & Row, 1956), p. 17.

PART SIX   *Moral Autonomy and Integrity*

1 Alfred Tennyson, "Oenone," in Christopher Ricks (ed.), *The Poems of Tennyson* (London: Longmans, Green and Company, 1969), p. 392.

CHAPTER 18   *Self-Respect*

1 Immanuel Kant, *Lectures on Ethics,* trans. L. Infield (New York: Harper & Row, 1963), p. 126.

2 Immanuel Kant, *Foundations of the Metaphysics of Morals,* trans. L. W. Beck (Indianapolis, IN: Bobbs-Merrill, 1959), p. 47.

3 Immanuel Kant, *Lectures on Ethics,* trans. L. Infield (New York: Harper & Row, 1963), pp. 117–118.

4 John Rawls, *A Theory of Justice* (Cambridge, MA: Harvard University Press, 1971), p. 440.

5 Ibid.

6   Stephen L. Darwall, "Two Kinds of Respect," *Ethics,* vol. 88 (1977): 36–49.

7   Robin S. Dillon, "Toward a Feminist Conception of Self-Respect," *Hypatia,* vol. 7 (1992): 52–69.

8   Erich Fromm, *The Art of Loving* (New York: Harper & Row, 1956), pp. 48–53; and Joel Feinberg, "Absurd Self-Fulfillment," in P. van Inwagen (ed.), *Time and Cause* (Dordrecht, Holland: D. Reidel, 1980).

9   Fyodor Dostoevsky, *The Brothers Karamazov,* trans. A. H. MacAndrew (New York: Bantam, 1970), p. 697. The example of Lise is used by Irwin Goldstein in "Pain and Masochism," *Journal of Value Inquiry,* vol. 17 (1983): 219–223.

10   Fyodor Dostoevsky, *The Brothers Karamazov,* p. 703.

11   Theodore Isaac Rubin, *Through My Own Eyes* (New York: Macmillan, 1982), p. 171.

12   Virginia Woolf, "The New Dress," in *A Haunted House and Other Stories* (New York: Harcourt Brace Jovanovich, 1972), p. 47.

13   Nathaniel Hawthorne, *The Scarlet Letter* (New York: Norton, 1978), p. 107.

14   William M. Thackeray, *The Book of Snobs,* in W. P. Trent and J. B. Henneman (eds.), *The Complete Works of William M. Thackeray,* Vol. XIV (New York: Crowell, undated), p. 63.

15   Spiro T. Agnew, speech given on October 19, 1969, in New Orleans, Louisiana, printed in John R. Coyne, Jr., *The Impudent Snobs: Agnew vs. the Intellectual Establishment* (New Rochelle, NY: Arlington House, 1972), p. 248.

16   Quoted by John R. Coyne, Jr., ibid., p. 38.

17   Judith N. Shklar, "What Is Wrong with Snobbery?" in *Ordinary Vices* (Cambridge, MA: Harvard University Press, 1984), pp. 135–136.

18   Thomas E. Hill, *Autonomy and Self-Respect* (New York: Cambridge University Press, 1991), p. 171.

19   Robert C. Solomon, *The Passions* (Notre Dame, IN: University of Notre Dame Press, 1983), p. 295.

CHAPTER 19   *Self-Knowledge and Self-Deception*

1   Sigmund Freud, *The Complete Introductory Lectures on Psychoanalysis,* trans. J. Strachey (New York: W. W. Norton & Co., 1966). Also see Charles Brenner, *An Elementary Textbook on Psychoanalysis,* rev. ed. (Garden City, NY: Anchor, 1974). Roy Schafer translates Freud's language of defense into the more familiar talk about self-deception in *A New Language for Psychoanalysis* (New Haven, CT: Yale University Press, 1976).

2   Herbert Fingarette, *Self-Deception* (Atlantic Highlands, NJ: Humanities Press, 1969), p. 141.

3   Bishop Joseph Butler, "Upon Self-Deceit," in W. E. Gladstone (ed.), *The Works of Joseph Butler* (Oxford: Clarendon Press, 1896), pp. 177–178.

4   Samuel Johnson, *The Rambler,* in A. Murphy (ed.), *The Works of Samuel Johnson,* vol. 2 (London: S. and R. Bentley, 1823), pp. 181–187.

5 Ibid.

6 Fyodor Dostoevsky, *The Brothers Karamazov,* trans. C. Garnett (New York: New American Library, 1957), p. 49.

7 Sonia Johnson, *From Housewife to Heretic* (Garden City, NY: Anchor, 1983), p. 94.

8 Ibid., pp. 160–161.

9 Immanuel Kant, *The Doctrine of Virtue,* trans. M. J. Gregor (Philadelphia: University of Pennsylvania Press, 1964), pp. 92, 95.

10 Jack W. Meiland, "What Ought We to Believe? or the Ethics of Belief Revisited," *American Philosophical Quarterly* (1980): 15–16.

11 Reinhold Niebuhr, *The Nature and Destiny of Man,* vol. 1 (New York: Scribner, 1964), p. 203.

CHAPTER 20 *Self-Control and Courage*

1 See Thomas E. Hill, Jr., "Weakness of Will and Character," in *Autonomy and Self-Respect* (Cambridge: Cambridge University Press, 1991), pp. 120–122; and Gwynneth Matthews, "Moral Weakness," in G. W. Mortimore (ed.), *Weakness of Will* (London: Macmillan, 1971).

2 Plato, *Apology,* trans. G. M. A. Grube, in *The Trial and Death of Socrates* (Indianapolis, IN: Hackett, 1975).

3 Plato, *Protagoras,* trans. W. K. C. Guthrie, in E. Hamilton and H. Cairns (eds.), *The Collected Dialogues of Plato* (Princeton, NJ: Princeton University Press, 1963), p. 344.

4 Aristotle, *Nicomachean Ethics,* trans. W. D. Ross, in R. McKeon (ed.), *The Basic Works of Aristotle* (New York: Random House, 1941), p. 1041.

5 Alfred R. Mele, *Irrationality: An Essay on Akrasia, Self-Deception, and Self-Control* (New York: Oxford University Press, 1987), pp. 51–52.

6 Friedrich Nietzsche, *The Gay Science,* trans. W. Kaufmann (New York: Vintage, 1974), pp. 232–233.

7 Our discussion will rely on the important psychological study by C. R. Snyder, Raymond L. Higgins, and Rita J. Stucky, *Excuses* (New York: Wiley, 1983).

8 Elizabeth Glaser and Laura Palmer, *In the Absence of Angels* (New York: Berkley Books, 1991), p. 141.

9 Ibid., p. 157.

10 As reported in the local television news in Orange County, California.

11 Aristotle, *Ethics,* trans. J. A. K. Thomson and H. Tredennick (New York: Penguin, 1976), p. 103.

12 James D. Wallace, "Courage, Cowardice, and Self-Indulgence," in *Virtues and Vices* (Ithaca, NY: Cornell University Press, 1978), pp. 78–81.

13 Douglas N. Walton, *Courage: A Philosophical Investigation* (Berkeley: University of California Press, 1986), p. 191.

14 W. D. Falk, "Morality, Self, and Others," in H. Castaneda and G. Nakhnikian (eds.), *Morality and Language of Conduct* (Detroit, MI: Wayne State University Press, 1965), p. 103.

15 Mark Twain, *The Adventures of Huckleberry Finn* (New York: Dell, 1960), p. 122.

16 The term *dependent virtues* is used by Michael Slote in *Goods and Virtues* (Oxford: Clarendon Press, 1983), pp. 61–75.

PART SEVEN   *Moral Health*

1 Plato, *Republic*, trans. F. M. Cornford (New York: Oxford, 1945), 444e.

CHAPTER 21   *Responsibility and Therapy*

1 Jerome D. Levin, *The Clinton Syndrome: The President and the Self-Destructive Nature of Sexual Addiction* (Rocklin, CA: Prima Publishing, 1998), pp. 20–21.

2 Ibid., pp. 19–20.

3 Ibid., pp. 11–12.

4 Charles J. Sykes, *A Nation of Victims: The Decay of the American Character* (New York: St. Martin's Press, 1992), p. 13. Also see Wendy Kaminer, *I'm Dysfunctional, You're Dysfunctional* (New York: Vintage Books, 1993).

5 Friedrich Nietzsche, *On the Genealogy of Morality*, trans. Maudemarie Clark and Alan J. Swensen (Indianapolis, IN: Hackett Publishing, 1998), 2d Treatise, Section 16.

6 This is my interpretation, given that Nietzsche never carefully defines what he means by health, in light of the many passages where Nietzsche links health and self-love, together with: Friedrich Nietzsche, *The Gay Science*, trans. Walter Kaufmann (New York: Vintage, 1974); and Friedrich Nietzsche, *The Will to Power*, trans. Walter Kaurmann and R. J. Hollingdale (New York: Vintage, 1968), section 778. By contrast, Richard Norman thinks Nietzsche equates health with vitality (energy): *The Moral Philosophers*, 2d ed. (New York: Oxford University, 1998), p. 142. Daniel R. Ahern suggests Nietzsche equates health with self-mastery: *Nietzsche as Cultural Physician* (University Park: Pennsylvania State University Press, 1995), pp. 19–20.

7 *On the Genealogy of Morals*, 2d Treatise, Section 16.

8 Friedrich Nietzsche, *Thus Spoke Zarathustra*, trans W. Kaufmann (New York: Penguin, 1978), p. 100.

9 Sigmund Freud, *Civilization and Its Discontents*, trans. James Strachey (New York: W. W. Norton, 1961), p. 90.

10 Cf. Richard Norman, *The Moral Philosophers*, 2d ed. (New York: Oxford University Press, 1998), pp. 16–21; and Anthony Kenny, "Mental Health in Plato's Republic," in *The Anatomy of the Soul* (Oxford: Oxford University Press, 1973).

11 American Psychiatric Association, *Diagnostic and Statistical Manual of Mental Disorders: DSM-IV* (Washington, DC: American Psychiatric Association, 1994), p. xxi.

12 Erich Fromm, *Man For Himself: An Inquiry into the Psychology of Ethics* (New York: Fawcett, 1965), p. 17.

13 Erich Fromm, *The Sane Society* (New York: Fawcett, 1965), Chapter 3.

14 Plato, *Republic,* trans. F. M. Cornford (New York: Oxford, 1945), 444e.

15 Lawrence C. Becker, *A New Stoicism* (Princeton, NJ: Princeton University Press, 1998), p. 104.

16 Ibid.

17 For a helpful historically oriented discussion of the key issues see Ilham Dilman, *Free Will: An Historical and Philosophical Introduction* (New York: Routledge, 1999).

18 Neal O. Weiner, *The Harmony of the Soul: Mental Health and Moral Virtue Reconsidered* (Albany: State University of New York Press, 1993), p. 16.

19 Sigmund Freud, *Civilization and Its Discontents,* p. 91.

20 James Gilligan, "Beyond Morality: Psychoanalytic Reflections on Shame, Guilt, and Love," in Thomas Lickona (ed.), *Moral Development and Behavior* (New York: Holt, Rinehart, and Winston, 1976), pp. 144–145.

21 Ibid., p. 158.

22 Sigmund Freud, *Civilization and Its Discontents,* p. 90.

23 John P. Allegrante and Lawrence W. Green, "When Health Policy Becomes Victim Blaming," *New England Journal of Medicine,* vol. 305 (1981): 1528–1529.

24 Gary Watson, "Responsibility and the Limits of Evil: Variations on a Strawsonian Theme," in John Martin Fischer and Mark Ravizza (eds.), *Perspectives on Moral Responsibility* (New York: Cornell University Press, 1993), p. 138.

25 John Hospers, "Free Will and Psychoanalysis," in Wilfrid Sellars and John Hospers (eds.), *Readings in Ethical Theory,* 2d ed. (Englewood Cliffs, NJ: Prentice-Hall, 1970), p. 635.

CHAPTER 22 *Drug Abuse*

1 See Ken Liska, *Drugs and Human Body, With Implications for Society,* 3d ed. (New York: Macmillan, 1990); Erich Goode, *Drugs in American Society,* 3d ed. (New York: McGraw-Hill, 1989); and Robert E. Goodin, *No Smoking: The Ethical Issues* (Chicago: University of Chicago Press, 1989).

2 James B. Bakalar and Lester Grinspoon, *Drug Control in a Free Society* (Cambridge: Cambridge University Press, 1984), pp. 46–47.

3 Eugene O'Neill, *Long Day's Journey Into Night* (New Haven, CT: Yale University Press, 1956), p. 93.

4 James B. Bakalar and Lester Grinspoon, *Drug Control in a Free Society,* p. 33.

5 Herbert Fingarette, *Heavy Drinking: The Myth of Alcoholism as a Disease* (Berkeley: University of California Press, 1988), p. 104.

6 Ibid., p. 92.

7 Robert E. Goodin, *No Smoking: The Ethical Issues,* p. 95.

8 See David Boaz (ed.), *The Crisis in Drug Prohibition* (Washington DC: Cato Institute, 1990).

9 Erich Goode, *Drugs in American Society,* p. 236.

10 Ibid., p. 275.

11 Mathea Falco, *The Making of a Drug-Free America: Programs that Work* (New York: Times Books, 1992).

12 Immanuel Kant, *Lectures on Ethics,* trans. L. Infield (New York: Harper Torchbooks, 1963), p. 118.

13 Joseph R. DesJardins and Ronald Duska, "Drug Testing in Employment," in J. R. DesJardins and J. J. McCall (eds.), *Contemporary Issues in Business Ethics,* 3d ed. (Belmont, CA: Wadsworth, 1996), pp. 232–243.

14 David A. J. Richards, "Drug Use and the Rights of the Person," in S. Luper-Foy and C. Brown (eds.), *The Moral Life* (Fort Worth, TX: Harcourt Brace Jovanovich, 1992), p. 406.

CHAPTER 23 *Suicide and Euthanasia*

1 Albert Camus, *The Myth of Sisyphus* (New York: Vintage, 1955), p. 3.

2 Howard I. Kushner, *American Suicide: A Psychocultural Exploration* (New Brunswick, NJ: Rutgers University Press, 1991).

3 R. G. Frey, "Did Socrates Commit Suicide?" *Philosophy,* vol. 53 (1978): 106–108.

4 Howard I. Kushner, *American Suicide,* pp. 119–120.

5 St. Thomas Aquinas, *Summa Theologica,* vol. 2 (New York: Benziger Brothers, 1925), Part 2, Question 64, A5.

6 Thomas E. Hill, Jr., *Autonomy and Self-Respect* (Cambridge: Cambridge University Press, 1991), p. 95. Italics removed.

7 John Stuart Mill, *On Liberty* (Indianapolis, IN: Hackett, 1978), p. 9.

8 Glanville Williams, *The Sanctity of Life and the Criminal Law* (New York: Knopf, 1957), p. 27.

9 Quoted by Ronald Munson, *Intervention and Reflection: Basic Issues in Medical Ethics,* 4th ed. (Belmont, CA: Wadsworth, 1992), p. 148.

10 *Cruzan v. Director,* Missouri Department of Health, United States Supreme Court 110 S. Ct. 2841 (1990).

11 Marcia Angell, "Euthanasia," *The New England Journal of Medicine,* vol. 319 (November 17, 1988): 1348–1350.

12 James Rachels, "Active and Passive Euthanasia," in Ronald Munson, *Intervention and Reflection: Basic Issues in Medical Ethics,* p. 165.

13 See Bonnie Steinbock, "The Intentional Termination of Life," in B. Steinbock (ed.), *Killing and Letting Die* (Englewood Cliffs, NJ: Prentice-Hall, 1980), pp. 69–77.

14 Margaret Pabst Battin, "Euthanasia," in D. Van DeVeer and T. Regan (eds.), *Health Care Ethics* (Philadelphia: Temple University Press, 1987), pp. 62–63.

15 Ibid., p. 73.

16 These examples are from William E. Tolhurst, "Suicide, Self-Sacrifice, and Coercion," *The Southern Journal of Philosophy*, vol. 21 (1983): 109–121.

17 Stephen G. Potts, "Looking for the Exit Door: Killing and Caring in Modern Medicine," *Houston Law Review*, vol. 25 (1988): 504–511.

PART EIGHT   *Community and Wealth*

1 Josiah Royce, *The Problem of Christianity*, vol. II (New York: Macmillan, 1913), p. 52.

CHAPTER 24   *Money*

1 Woody Allen, *Without Feathers*. Quoted in Kevin Jackson (ed.), *The Oxford Book of Money* (New York: Oxford University, 1996), p. 17.

2 New Testament, I Timothy 6:10, King James version.

3 Christopher Lasch, *The Culture of Narcissism* (New York: Norton, 1979).

4 Adrian Furnham and Michael Argyle, *The Psychology of Money* (New York: Routledge, 1998), pp. 266–267.

5 Benjamin Franklin, "Advice to a Young Tradesman"; George Gissing, *The Private Papers of Henry Ryecroft*. Excerpts from both are in Kevin Jackson (ed.), *The Oxford Book of Money*, pp. 4–5.

6 John Kenneth Galbraith, *The Affluent Society*, 4th ed. (New York: Houghton Mifflin, 1984).

7 Theodore Levitt, "The Morality (?) of Advertising," *Harvard Business Review* (July/August 1970). Reprinted in W. Michael Hoffman and Jennifer Mills Moore (eds.), *Business Ethics*, 2d ed. (New York: McGraw-Hill, 1990), p. 449.

8 Adrian Furnham and Michael Argyle, *The Psychology of Money*, p. 136. Also see Philip Slater, *Wealth Addiction* (New York: E. P. Dutton, 1980); and Paul L. Wachtel, *The Poverty of Affluence: A Psychological Portrait of the American Way of Life* (New York: Free Press, 1983).

9 Thomas J. Stanley and William D. Danko, *The Millionaire Next Door* (New York: Pocket Books, 1996).

10 David E. Shi, *The Simple Life* (New York: Oxford University, 1985), p. 4. Also see David E. Shi, *In Search of the Simple Life* (Layton, UT: Peregrine Smith, 1986).

11 Robert Goodman, *The Luck Business* (New York: Simon & Schuster, 1995), p. 3.

12 Lisa Newton, "Gambling: A Preliminary Inquiry, *Business Ethics Quarterly*, vol. 3 (1993): 407.

13 These arguments are discussed by Robert Goodman, *The Luck Business*; and by Richard L. Lippke, "Should States Be in the Gambling Business?," *Public Affairs Quarterly*, vol. 11 (1997): 57–73.

14 Robert Goodman, *The Luck Business*, p. 42.

15 Ibid.

16 American Psychiatric Association, *Diagnostic and Statistical Manual of Mental Disorders,* 4th ed. (Washington, DC: American Psychiatric Association, 1994), p. 618.

17 Michael Scriven, "The Philosophical Foundations of Las Vegas," *Journal of Gambling Studies,* vol. 11 (1995):65.

18 The discussion here parallels that of William H. Shaw and Vincent Barry (eds.), *Moral Issues in Business,* 7th ed. (Belmont, CA: Wadsworth, 1998), Chapter 3.

19 Adam Smith, *An Inquiry Into the Nature and Causes of the Wealth of Nations* (New York: Oxford University Press, 1976), vol I., pp. 26–27.

20 Ibid., p. 456.

21 Richard B. Brandt, *A Theory of the Good and the Right* (New York: Oxford University, 1979), pp. 312–313.

22 Robert Nozick, *Anarchy, State, and Utopia* (New York: BasicBooks, 1974), p. 149.

23 Robert Nozick, *The Examined Life* (New York: Simon & Schuster, 1989), pp. 286–287.

24 John Rawls, *A Theory of Justice* (Cambridge, MA: Harvard University Press, 1971), p. 60.

25 Shlomo Avineri and Avner de-Shalit (eds.), *Communitarianism and Individualism* (New York: Oxford University Press, 1992); Markate Daly, (ed.), *Communitarianism: A New Public Ethics* (Belmont, CA: Wadsworth, 1994); and Amitai Etzioni (ed.), *The Essential Communitarian Reader* (New York: Rowman and Littlefield, 1998).

26 Fyodor Dostoevsky, *The Gambler,* trans. Andrew R. MacAndrew (New York: W. W. Norton & Company, 1964), p. 170.

27 Robert Goodman, *The Luck Business,* pp. 145–146.

CHAPTER 25 *Meaningful Work*

1 Studs Terkel, *Working* (New York: Avon Books, 1975), p. 1.

2 Ibid., pp. 1–2.

3 Ibid., p. 2.

4 Ibid.

5 Ibid., p. 390.

6 Ibid., p. 393.

7 Karl Marx, *Economic and Philosophical Manuscripts,* in E. Fromm, *Marx's Concept of Man,* trans. T. B. Bottomore (New York: Ungar, 1966), p. 98.

8 Quoted from the writings of the Reverend Richard Baxter by Max Weber, in *The Protestant Ethic and the Spirit of Capitalism,* trans. T. Parsons (New York: Scribner's, 1958), p. 162.

9 Gilbert C. Meilaender, "Friendship and Vocation," in *Friendship* (Notre Dame, IN: University of Notre Dame Press, 1981), p. 97.

10 Craig K. Ihara, "Collegiality as a Professional Virtue," in A. Flores (ed.), *Professional Ideals* (Belmont, CA: Wadsworth, 1988), p. 60.

11 Josiah Royce, *The Philosophy of Loyalty,* excerpted in J. K. Roth (ed.), *The Philosophy of Josiah Royce* (Indianapolis, IN: Hackett, 1982), p. 279.

12 Ibid., p. 281.

13 John Ladd, "Loyalty," in P. Edwards (ed.), *The Encyclopedia of Philosophy,* vol. 5 (New York: Macmillan, 1967), p. 98.

14 Cf. Ronald Duska, *Whistleblowing and Employee Loyalty,* excerpted in J. Halberstam (ed.), *Virtues and Values* (Englewood Cliffs, NJ: Prentice-Hall, 1988), pp. 246–251.

15 From Dan Applegate's memo, quoted by P. Eddy, E. Potter, and B. Page, *Destination Disaster* (New York: New York Times Book Co., 1976), p. 185.

16 Norman S. Care, "Career Choice," *Ethics,* vol. 94 (1984): 298.

17 Hastings Rashdall, "Vocation," in *The Theory of Good and Evil,* vol. 2 (Oxford: Clarendon Press, 1907), pp. 123–124.

18 David Hilfiker, *Not All of Us Are Saints* (New York: Ballantine Books, 1994), p. 19.

19 Cf. Peter A. French, *Ethics in Government* (Englewood Cliffs, NJ: Prentice-Hall, 1983), pp. 5–6.

20 Bernard Williams, "A Critique of Utilitarianism," in J. J. C. Smart and B. Williams, *Utilitarianism For and Against* (Cambridge: Cambridge University Press, 1973), pp. 97–98.

CHAPTER 26 *Community Service*

1 Brian O'Connell, "What Colleges Ought to Do to Instill a Voluntary Spirit in Young Adults," *The Chronicle of Higher Education* (April 15, 1987): 104. Robert L. Payton offers an overview of the importance of philanthropy, including a version of the definition of philanthropy adopted here, in *Philanthropy: Voluntary Action for the Public Good* (New York: Macmillan, 1988).

2 Jane Addams, *Twenty Years at Hull-House* (New York: New American Library, 1981), p. 92.

3 Ibid.

4 Robert N. Bellah, Richard Madsen, William M. Sullivan, Ann Swidler, and Steven M. Tipton, *Habits of the Heart: Individualism and Commitment in American Life* (Berkeley: University of California, 1985), p. 162.

5 Peter Singer, "Famine, Affluence, and Morality," in W. Aiken and H. La Follette (eds.), *World Hunger and Moral Obligation* (Englewood Cliffs, NJ: Prentice-Hall, 1977), p. 24.

6 Ibid., p. 26.

7 Immanuel Kant, *The Doctrine of Virtue,* trans. M. J. Gregor (Philadelphia: University of Pennsylvania Press, 1964), p. 21.

8 David Heyd, *Supererogation* (Cambridge: Cambridge University Press, 1982), p. 115.

9 James D. Wallace, *Virtues and Vices* (Ithaca, NY: Cornell University Press, 1978), p. 135.

10 Mark 12:41–44, New American Standard edition.

11 Brian O'Connell, "What Colleges Ought to Do . . . ", p. 104.

12 Ralph Waldo Emerson, "Self-Reliance," in R. Bellah et al. (eds.), *Individualism and Commitment in American Life* (New York: Harper & Row, 1987), p. 59.

13 John O'Connor, "Philanthropy and Selfishness," in E. F. Paul et al. (eds.), *Beneficence, Philanthropy, and the Public Good* (New York: Basil Blackwell, 1987), p. 114.

Index